Numbers

Numbers

An Exegetical Commentary

R. K. Harrison

BAKER BOOK HOUSE
Grand Rapids, Michigan 49516

Printed in the United States of America

First published in 1990 as part of the Wycliffe Exegetical Commentary

All Scripture quotations, unless otherwise noted, are the author's translation.

Library of Congress Cataloging in Publication Data

Harrison, R. K. (Roland Kenneth)
    Numbers / R. K. Harrison
      p. cm.—(The Wycliffe exegetical commentary)
    ISBN 0-8010-4380-8
    1. Bible. O.T. Numbers—Commentaries. I. Title. II. Series.
BS1265.3.H37   1990
222'.1407—dc20

89-27865

Table of Contents

Preface

The book of Numbers is of pivotal importance for all OT study because it covers the formative period of Israel's communal and religious life. During a four decade interlude, the fledgling nation was given its charter as a group of Hebrew tribes that had been unified by the covenant at Sinai. Subsequently, the Israelites were chastened for their lack of faith in the Lord's ability to provide for their needs, robbed of their warriors to a significant extent through rebellion and disobedience, and finally disciplined into a formidable military force that was to occupy the land of Canaan as their future homeland.

During this period, Israel's religious life was shaped by the promulgation of many laws from God that would establish the nature of her worship and prepare her for a settled community life beyond the confines of the wilderness. Through their separation from the perversions of contemporary pagan nations, the Israelites were to be dedicated to God as a holy people, witnessing to the lofty moral and spiritual ideals of the Sinai covenant.

The successes and failures of the wilderness wanderings are chronicled in Numbers by a divinely appointed group of annalists who assisted Moses and the priests in maintaining records of various kinds. All those persons furnished eyewitness accounts of life in the wilderness of Sinai, and these constituted the historical data of Numbers. Without such factually accurate sources it would have been impossible to formulate a coherent view of Israel's transition from captivity in Egypt to conquest in Canaan. The commentary discusses the way in which the various eyewitness sources and other materials were probably employed to produce the book in its canonical form.

I am greatly indebted to the officials of Baker Book House for their professional expertise in all stages of the book's production. My sincere thanks are due to Drs. K. L. Barker and R. F. Youngblood for valued comments on the manuscript, to Mrs. Adrienne Taylor, former librarian of Wycliffe College, Toronto, and the her assistants, Miss Gayle Ford and Mrs. Karen Wiseman, for their cheerful and immediate assistance whenever I needed it. This, unfortunately, was mostly at times when they were already busy. Finally, a special word of thanks must be extended to Miss Patricia Mason, library assistant, who cooperated willingly and decisively in solving a special problem in the narrative.

R. K. Harrison
July 1992

Abbreviations

The following abbreviations supplement the list adopted by the *Journal of Biblical Literature:*

Akk.   Akkadian
DNTT   C. Brown, ed., *New International Dictionary of New Testament Theology* (3 vols., E tr. 1975–1978)
E   English
EAEHL   M. Avi-Yonah and E. Stern, eds., *Encyclopedia of Archaeological Excavations in the Holy Land* (4 vols., E tr. 1975–1978)
EDT   W. A. Elwell, ed., *Evangelical Dictionary of Theology* (1984)
E tr.   English translation
GTTOT   J. Simons, *Geographical and Topographical Texts of the Old Testament* (1959)
HIOT   R. K. Harrison, *Introduction to the Old Testament* (1969)
IBD   J. D. Douglas et al., eds., *The Illustrated Bible Dictionary* (1980)
ISBE   G. W. Bromiley, general ed., *The International Standard Bible Encyclopedia,* rev. (4 vols., 1979–1988)
KD   C. F. Keil and F. Delitzsch, *Commentary on the Old Testament* (E tr. 1864–1901; reprinted 1973)
LBHG   Y. Aharoni, *Land of the Bible: A Historical Geography* (E tr. 1967; rev. ed. 1979)

lit. literally
MPB H. N. and A. L. Moldenke, *Plants of the Bible* (1952)
NASB *New American Standard Bible*
NIDBA E. M. Blaiklock and R. K. Harrison, eds., *The New International Dictionary of Biblical Archaeology* (1983)
par. parallels
pl. (s.) plate(s)
POTT D. J. Wiseman, ed., *Peoples of Old Testament Times* (1973)
rev. revised
THAT E. Jenni and C. Westermann, eds., *Theologisches Handwörterbuch zum Alten Testament* (2 vols., 1971–1976)
TOTC Tyndale Old Testament Commentaries
TWOT R. L. Harris et al., eds., *Theological Wordbook of the Old Testament* (2 vols., 1980)
Ugar. Ugaritic
ZPEB M. Tenney et al., eds., *The Zondervan Pictorial Encyclopedia of the Bible* (5 vols., 1975)

Introduction to the Commentary

PLACE IN THE CANON

The book of Numbers is a traditional and inseparable part of the five-volume collection known as the Torah or Pentateuch, the overall authorship of which has been attributed in orthodox Jewish and Christian thought to Moses. For this reason, Numbers must be examined against the background of inclusion in a literary corpus before it can be studied in its own right.

The first volume in the Pentateuch is Genesis, and, as its name implies, it is quite properly the book of beginnings. But as well as describing the world's origin, the creation of humanity, and the growth and distribution of early peoples, Genesis focuses more narrowly upon one specific area of humanity. The result is to bring those people's fortunes into increasing prominence and to describe how God the Creator covenanted with them—initially with Noah, and subsequently with Abraham.

To the latter God gave assurance of an incalculable number of descendants, and by the time of Abraham's grandson Jacob these promises were very much in evidence. Genesis narrates the way in which the sons of Jacob, who had become a sizable community, migrated to Egypt during a season of famine in Canaan and achieved great prosperity.

Exodus continues this theme but introduces a period of adversity

1

among the Israelites. Moses, later to become the preeminent Israelite leader, was born and after abandonment by his mother was found by an Egyptian princess and reared in the royal court. Exodus narrates his call by God to lead the Israelites to an independent life and describes graphically the processes by which this was achieved. The covenant at Sinai, whereby the twelve Hebrew tribes became one nation under God, proved to be the principal formative experience of Israelite religion. But its early, rather tentative stages of development received severe testing in subsequent wilderness experiences, due largely to the infidelity and disobedience of the Israelites.

Leviticus is a record contemporary with Exodus and has as its predominant concern the offices and functions of the newly-established priesthood. Although it contains certain historical narratives from the period of the wilderness wanderings, it was meant primarily as a compendium of ritual and other regulations by which the priests were intended to govern communal life. Central to the book are the two themes of (1) separation from what was unclean and (2) the individual and communal practice of holiness to the Lord.

Numbers describes graphically the experiences of the Israelites during the wilderness wanderings and shows the difficulties Moses encountered as he endeavored to guide God's people in times of hardship, apostasy, and open rebellion against God's will.

Lastly, Deuteronomy constitutes a covenant-renewal document in which the historical formulations of Ex. 20 are placed in a wider setting and described in terms of a formal, binding treaty between God and the Israelites. The grand conclusion of Deuteronomy, as indeed with Numbers, is that of the blessing of Israel's tribes by Moses immediately prior to his decease as they faced the challenging prospect of entering the Promised Land.

The book of Numbers cannot be understood properly in isolation from the remainder of the Pentateuch, and particularly from the first three books of that collection. It has to be studied against the general milieu of second-millennium B.C. life as depicted in the OT records and as it has been clarified and enhanced by modern archaeological and other studies. Although it is integral to the narrative and spiritual purposes of the Pentateuch, it exhibits its own values, which merit independent investigation in order to determine their contribution to the Pentateuch as a whole.

Thus Numbers contains information about this critical period of Israel's spiritual formation that was not of primary concern to Exodus, Leviticus, or Deuteronomy. Against the historical background of the wilderness wanderings it took special note of two censuses of the nation that were ordered by God for two different reasons. Of unusual character and significance is a group of prophetic utterances, delivered by a pagan soothsayer, which proved to have an important bearing upon both the immediate and more distant future of the Israelites.

Particular attention is paid to leadership as the narratives of Numbers unfold, including the appointment of community leaders from each of the tribes and the selection of family heads for special assignments. These represent the beginnings of organized community life at the civil rather than the specifically religious level and establish the principle that the Israelite theocracy was truly participatory, not just a sphere in which the hereditary priesthood could exercise its powers. The successors of both Aaron and Moses are named in Numbers, and the way in which they are introduced to their responsibilities is made clear. The activities and influence of scribes and annalists are evident in the detailed lists and statistics that have been preserved in Numbers, along with an outline itinerary of the wanderings in the wilderness. The book also alludes to certain matters described in Exodus and Leviticus, and by its concordant treatment of those issues it shows that it is firmly integrated with the two books both historically and spiritually as works that were given their characteristic literary form in the Mosaic era.

A wholistic study of the canonical record of the Torah shows it to be a unique assemblage of historically and theologically unified writings that follow the chronology introduced in the various component parts. The book of Numbers belongs integrally to the canonical context of the law and is of inestimable importance for its contemporary description of the formative period of Israelite society and its religious traditions under Moses. Numbers can therefore be considered properly as "eyewitness history" that, following the scribal traditions adopted by other ancient Near Eastern nations, was chronicled soon after the events occurred.

To think of Israelite traditions, as many liberal scholars have done, as having emerged gradually from the national consciousness over a prolonged period of time, with only the vaguest reference to a desert origin, would be false to Israel's own understanding of its national and religious beginnings. Those who were responsible for promulgating the Hebrew canon in its final form understood those matters, and by their activities they intended subsequent generations to follow the canonical order of events. It seems clear that Numbers was accorded canonical authority from the time it was written, and not least by those who passed through the events it described. It is thus evident that the book of Numbers is not merely a formal part of the Pentateuchal literary corpus but an organic one.

3

TITLE OF THE BOOK

The book of Numbers, as noted above, is the fourth book of the Pentateuch, a term that may have been derived from two Greek words, *pente* ("five") and *teuchos* ("tool," "implement," hence "scroll"). Regardless of its origin, it was first used in a commentary on the gospel of John by the patristic writer Origen (*c.* A.D. 185-254) to describe the Mosaic law.[1] Some scholars have suggested that the term *Pentateuch* could even have been applied to the first five books of the Hebrew canon of Scripture by Hellenistic Jews in Alexandria during the first century A.D. In any event, the title Numbers came from the LXX, a translation of the Hebrew Scriptures into Hellenistic Greek that was begun in Alexandria about 250 B.C. Greek *Arithmoi* was rendered *Numeri* in Jerome's Latin Vulgate (completed A.D. 405), and this title was adopted by all subsequent English versions.

When the law scrolls came to be designated by a Hebrew name, it was the custom to identify them in terms of the first word, or a very early word, of the scroll. Thus Numbers was either referred to as וַיְדַבֵּר, *wayĕdabbēr* ("and he spoke"), which is the first word of the book and was the title favored by some of the early Christian Fathers, or as בְּמִדְבַּר, *bĕmidbar* ("in the wilderness of"), the fourth word of the first verse. But among the Jewish religious authorities it also had an interesting name that may have dated from the exilic period. This designation was "The Fifth of the Musterings" and alludes to the fact that this particular segment of the law of Moses was concerned with the two occasions of census-taking to which the Israelites were subjected,[2] as recorded in chaps. 1 and 26. Some writers have expressed a preference for the MT designations over that of the LXX and other versions, alleging that the latter lay too much emphasis on the census lists. But while the traditional Hebrew title *bĕmidbar* places a somewhat different stress upon the book than is the case with the Greek title, there is no inherent incompatibility between the two, because both refer to the same general period in Israel's history.

Although Numbers is an important element in the Hebrew Torah or law, its legislative content constitutes only a small part of the narrative. But if the term *Torah* is understood in the sense of "teaching" or "instruction," one of the meanings of the Hebrew verb יָרָה, (*yārâ*, from which the noun *tôrâ* is derived), the book of Numbers will

---

1. PG 14, col. 444. In his controversy with the Marcionites, Tertullian (c. A.D. 155-220) used the Latin form of "Pentateuch" as a proper noun (PL 2, col. 282).
2. J. H. Hertz, ed., *The Pentateuch and Haftorahs* (London: Soncino, 1960), p. 567. In Talmudic times the Torah was also known as "The Five Fifths of the Law" (cf. *San.* 28a).

be seen to partake fully of the character of Torah as a manual of direction. More specifically, the historical and narrative sections of Numbers furnish the temporal and topographical settings that give the legislative content of the book proper validity within the Pentateuchal tradition.

LITERARY STUDIES OF NUMBERS

Among the Jews of the pre-Christian period, the book of Numbers was accepted without question as an integral part of the law of which Moses was deemed to be the author. Likewise the early Christian church, while it recognized that such religious institutions as the Tabernacle and the Passover had been superseded by the atoning work of Jesus Christ, nevertheless maintained the second-millennium B.C. authorship of the composition and regarded it as a genuine part of Moses' literary activity.

It was not long, however, before the traditional esteem of Numbers suffered a devastating rejection, along with the remainder of the OT, at the hands of Marcion. The wealthy son of a Christian bishop, Marcion studied Gnostic teachings in Rome about A.D. 139. By the time of his death, about A.D. 160, he had set forth in his *Antitheses* what he regarded as contradictions between the Old and New Testaments. Consequently he rejected the OT entirely and restricted his own canon of scriptural writings to a truncated form of Luke and ten of Paul's letters.[3]

Marcion's teachings were a prelude to other assaults upon the Christian faith, and especially upon the question as to the nature and validity of the OT canon. Prominent among these were the writings of Porphyry, a third-century A.D. opponent of Christianity, who was an avowed advocate of Neo-Platonism. More than was the case with the generally derogatory comments of Celsus, Porphyry's condemnations of Christianity laid emphasis upon the OT in general and the nature of prophecy in particular.[4] He was the first to deny any predictive element in OT prophecy,[5] and this led him to assign a Maccabean date to the book of Daniel. Although he seems to have accepted the

---

3. PL 2, cols. 263 ff. Another important attempt to undermine Christianity was made by Celsus in *The True Word*, about A.D. 180, and was refuted by Origen in *Contra Celsum*, about A.D. 250. Cf. PG 11, cols. 315 ff.
4. Cf. R. M. Grant, "Historical Criticism in the Ancient Church," *JR* 25 (1945): 183-90.
5. *Si quid autem ultra opinatus sit, quia futura nescient esse mentitum* ("But if there should be any supposition beyond this it is fraudulent, since the future cannot be known").

historicity of Moses, it is hard to ascertain if he regarded the Pentateuch as Mosaic.

During the Reformation period the Mosaic authorship of the Pentateuch came under scrutiny by Andreas Rudolf Bodenstein (1480-1541). Impressed by the fact that Moses could not possibly have written his own obituary (Deut. 34:5-9), he concluded that the authorship of the entire Pentateuch had been ascribed wrongly to Moses. His outlook may well have been a reaction to the work and teachings of his contemporary Martin Luther (1483-1546), with whom he found himself in constant conflict. The Mosaic authorship of the Pentateuch was also rejected by Benedict Spinoza (1632-1677), a Jewish philosopher who was influenced by the Jewish exegete Ibn Ezra (1092-1167). In these and similar speculations the book of Numbers was not singled out for special attention but tended to suffer the fate accorded to the Pentateuch as a whole.[6]

The seventeenth and eighteenth centuries witnessed a general departure from the kind of textual criticism that had characterized earlier writers and the adoption of what came to be known as "literary criticism." This process began in earnest with the work of the French Roman Catholic theologian Richard Simon (1638-1712), who denied the Mosaic authorship of the Pentateuch and attributed its compilation to a guild of scribes who assembled and edited sources of information over a prolonged period of time.[7]

A fresh departure was instituted by Jean Astruc (1684-1766), who employed a primitive form of source criticism to investigate the authorship of Genesis. In the process he suggested that all the passages in Genesis where God was described as Elohim could be placed in one column, which for him was the primary source of the book. This column, designated "A," was supposedly supplemented by a subordinate column ("B"), which Astruc formed by isolating all those verses in which God was referred to as Yahweh. The remainder of Genesis was regarded as interpolated material, which he divided among two other suggested columns ("C" and "D"). Astruc appeared satisfied with his arbitrary analysis of source material, and while his findings did not attract a great deal of scholarly attention at the time, they marked the beginning of a process by which the whole Pentateuch was to be fragmented into "documents."

After Astruc's death his approach was enlarged by J. G. Eichhorn (1752-1827), who expanded the Elohistic and Yahwistic sources that

---

6. For a more detailed treatment of this process see *HIOT*, pp. 6-11.
7. Simon's views were formulated in his book *Histoire Critique du Vieux Testament* (Paris, 1678; Rotterdam: Reenier Leers, 1685). It was so bitterly opposed by the Roman Catholic authorities that it was ordered destroyed.

Astruc had purported to discover. Otherwise Eichhorn held to a basically conservative approach to OT problems.[8] What came to be known as the "fragmentary hypothesis" of Pentateuchal composition occurred in the writings of A. Geddes, a Scottish Roman Catholic priest, who formulated his views in a book entitled *Critical Remarks* (1800).

In a commentary on the Pentateuch, German scholar J. S. Vater developed Geddes's views in 1805 and was supported in some degree by W. M. L. De Wette's *Introduction*.[9] The views of both scholars were repudiated by H. Ewald, who suggested that the Elohistic "source" that some scholars thought underlay the Pentateuch had actually been supplemented by older materials.[10] Subsequently Ewald asserted that some Pentateuchal materials did not belong to any of the proposed "documents" but instead may have had their origin in the Judges period.[11]

Documentary criticism of the Pentateuch was now proceeding apace, and by the middle of the nineteenth century no fewer than four principal sources had been isolated to the broad satisfaction of the literary critics. These were described as a Yahwistic document (J, the German equivalent of Y), an Elohistic source (E), a priestly compilation (P), and the book of Deuteronomy (D). These sources were held to have been assembled over a lengthy period of time by editors (redactors), who were not infrequently blamed for textual or other difficulties that seemed to present problems for the literary critics.

The question of the dating to be assigned to these supposed sources now became paramount. W. M. L. De Wette had argued that Genesis was based upon an E-type document, which he regarded as no earlier in origin than the time of King David. K. H. Graf,[12] however, maintained that the material was comparatively late in origin and assigned it to the time of Ezra, although he did not furnish any objective criteria for this assertion. Other scholars joined Graf in maintaining that the J-source was the basis of the Pentateuch and had been supplemented by E-type material thought to have come from the exilic period. This was completed by the addition of Deuteronomy, which, following De Wette's views, was assigned increasingly to the time of King Josiah (640-609 B.C.), and also by

8. J. G. Eichhorn, *Einleitung in das Alte Testament*, 3 vols. (Leipzig, 1780-1783).
9. W. M. L. De Wette, *Beiträge zur Einleitung in das Alte Testament* (Halle, 1807).
10. H. Ewald, *Die Komposition der Genesis kritisch untersucht* (Göttingen, 1823).
11. *HIOT*, p. 17.
12. K. H. Graf, *Die geschichtlichen Bücher des Alten Testaments* (Leipzig, 1865).

priestly material, some of which was dated as late as the period of Ezra (mid-fifth century B.C.).

This assigning of dates to the supposed literary components of the Pentateuch marked a move into the area of historical criticism. With it came a rearrangement of the relative antiquity of the sources from a PEJD pattern of compilation to a proposed JEDP order. This basic scheme was formalized by Julius Wellhausen (1844-1918), who had been one of Ewald's students, and his opinions quickly became the orthodox position of liberal scholarship. It followed the evolutionary theory of the age by supposing that Israel's traditions developed progressively from humble beginnings to a more advanced level of spiritual concepts. Thus the Pentateuch was no longer to be regarded as the foundation document of the nation of Israel but as its product over many centuries of Israelite existence.

Wellhausen accepted Graf's conclusions with an uncritical frame of mind and without thought of objective testing. On questions of dating he assigned the supposed Yahwistic material to the ninth century B.C., E-type sources to the eighth century B.C., and the priestly writings to about the fifth century B.C.[13] He also suggested that the so-called "Holiness Code" (Lev. 18-26) was added to the supposed P-type material after the time of Ezekiel and that further narrative sections had been compiled from the J and E sources. It seems clear that Wellhausen determined to rewrite Hebrew history according to the principles of Hegelian philosophy and the biological evolutionism that was gaining a firm foothold in the contemporary intellectual world.

Unfortunately for subsequent generations of scholars, Wellhausen did not employ the canons of objective criticism that were making important contributions to the descriptive sciences of his day. Instead he was influenced greatly by the type of speculation favored by the ancient Greeks, in which any explanation of phenomena that had the possibility of being likely was accepted without perceived need for objective demonstration.[14] The literary-critical hypothesis was all that mattered, and Wellhausen promulgated it forcefully, ignoring the opposition of conservative scholars and manipulating the data of Scripture where they did not accord with his opinions. The result was a theory of Pentateuchal origins that is still held as authentic by many liberal scholars, albeit with increasing misgivings.

---

13. J. Wellhausen, *Die Komposition des Hexateuchs* (Berlin: Reimer, 1877).
14. It would appear that the Greek physician was the only one governed by objective data. Cf. H. D. F. Kitto, *The Greeks* (Harmondsworth: Penguin, 1966), pp. 189-90.

Had Wellhausen paid attention to the admittedly scant findings of Near Eastern archaeology known in his day, it is doubtful that his hypothesis would ever have been promulgated—and certainly not in the form it assumed. Wellhausen based much of his objection to the Mosaic authorship of the Pentateuch on the assumption that writing was unknown until the time of the Hebrew monarchy, and therefore it was impossible for Moses to have committed anything to writing. Wellhausen ignored ancient examples of writing from Egypt and elsewhere,[15] and this proved to be a serious flaw in his scholarly method.

Many of Wellhausen's opinions are now perceived to be incorrect in the light of what is known about life in Bible times. To begin with, writing is recognized as having originated in Mesopotamia about 3300 B.C. and was in a sophisticated form long before the culture of Ebla, with its extremely complicated written language, was at its height (about 2400 B.C.). Contrary to Wellhausen's assertions, Pentateuchal materials were not restricted to a primary oral phase before being committed to writing. Literacy was at an advanced level in Mesopotamia, and the ancient scribes and court annalists habitually committed to writing anything that was of importance.

Oral knowledge of this material spread in contemporary society, since annals were stored in temple archives and thus were not normally available for casual perusal. The written form of the happenings was transmitted, where occasion required, in copies of the original that were made carefully by trained scribes. By no means have all the various records that were made in antiquity survived the ravages of time, but the OT furnishes a representative selection of ancient Hebrew scribal activity. Because the OT Scriptures were venerated as divine revelation, scrupulous care was taken to ensure that the copies made were as accurate as possible. In consequence, the ancient Hebrews, along with the Hittites and Greeks, have come to be regarded as preeminent recorders of history.[16]

Ancient Near Eastern studies have demonstrated the unsuitability of the various divine names as criteria for discerning underlying "documentary sources." This matter had already received attention from scholars such as J. Dahse,[17] H. M. Wiener,[18] and others. It is now known that no other literary composition in the ancient world was composed on a basis analogous to J, P, E, D, and the like. The occurrence of compound names such as *YHWH-Elohim* (cf. Gen. 2:4–3:24),

---

15. Cf. *HIOT*, pp. 59, 87.
16. C. H. Gordon, *Before the Bible* (London: Collins, 1962), p. 97.
17. J. Dahse, "Text-kritische Bedenken gegen den Ausgangspunkt der Pentateuchkritik," *ARW* 6 (1903), pp. 305-19.
18. H. M. Wiener, *Essays in Pentateuchal Criticism* (Oberlin: Bibliotheca Sacra, 1909); *Pentateuchal Studies* (Oberlin: Bibliotheca Sacra, 1912).

explained by Wellhausen as a conflation of "J" and "E" sources into "JE," can now be understood properly by reference to Egyptian and Ugaritic literary sources. In Egypt, Amun-Re was a familiar compound title in the Eighteenth Dynasty for the great universal deity, while in Canaan, gods such as Kothar-wa-Ḥasis and 'Ib-Nikkal (= Nikkal-wa-'Ib) were worshiped as individuals, despite their compound names.

This is not to deny, of course, that there were genuine written sources underlying the Pentateuch. Unfortunately the most obvious of these, in the book of Genesis, have either remained unnoticed by scholars or have been misunderstood for one reason or other. These materials make up the eleven sections from Gen. 1:1–37:2a, which can be isolated readily by locating the colophon phrase "these are the generations (or family histories) of," as described by P. J. Wiseman[19] and others.[20] There even appears to be a trace of such a literary source in Num. 3:1, which manifests elements of a Mesopotamian colophon.

Enough will have been said here[21] to alert the reader to the serious deficiencies of the Graf-Wellhausenian hypothesis and therefore its grave limitations for careful Pentateuchal study. In fact, it has been discovered to be so badly flawed that it misleads rather than directs aright, and therefore it must be considered an unreliable guide at best. Much liberal scholarship, which venerates the hypoth-

---

19. P. J. Wiseman, *New Discoveries in Babylonia About Genesis* (London: Marshall, Morgan & Scott, 1936); *Clues to Creation in Genesis* (London: Marshall, Morgan & Scott, 1977); American ed., *Ancient Records and the Structure of Genesis* (Nashville: Thomas Nelson, 1985).

20. *HIOT*, pp. 64, 545-46, 548-50. For other studies of the colophon see E. Leichty, "The Colophon," in *Studies Presented to A. Leo Oppenheim* (Chicago: Oriental Institute, 1964), pp. 147-54; H. Hunger, *Babylonische und assyrische Kolophone* (Neukirchen: Vluyn, 1968); W. G. Lambert and A. R. Millard, *Atrahasis: The Babylonian Story of the Flood* (Oxford: Clarendon, 1969), pp. 31-32; M. H. Woudstra, "The Toledot of the Book of Genesis and Their Redemptive-Historical Significance," *CTJ* 5 (1970): 187; H. M. L. Gevaryahu, "Biblical Colophons: A Source for the 'Biography' of Authors, Texts, and Books," VTSup 28 (1975): 42-59; D. S. DeWitt, "The Generations of Genesis," *EvQ* 48 (1976): 196-211; D. W. Baker, "Biblical Colophons: Gevaryahu and Beyond," *Ou-Testamentiese Werkgemeenskap van Suid-Afrika* 27 (1984): 29-61; D. T. Olsen, *The Death of the Old and the Birth of the New* (Chico, Calif.: Scholars Press, 1985): 98-110. For a contrary view see A. P. Ross, "Genesis," in *The Bible Knowledge Commentary*, ed. J. F. Walvoord and R. B. Zuck (Wheaton, Ill.: Victor, 1985), pp. 22-26.

21. For a more detailed analysis see *HIOT*, pp. 9 seq. See also V. P. Hamilton, *Handbook on the Pentateuch* (Grand Rapids: Baker, 1982); I. M. Kikawada and A. Quinn, *Before Abraham Was* (Nashville: Abingdon, 1985).

esis as an article of faith, has been perverted and led astray in consequence. The present study of Numbers repudiates the theorizing of Wellhausen and his followers and instead prefers to employ eclectic criticism, based upon the scribal traditions of antiquity, archaeological insights, firm linguistic evidence, and as accurate a Hebrew text as can be devised, in an attempt to comprehend the meaning of God's revealed Word.

THE MATERIALS OF NUMBERS

There are several different types of literature in the book, a fact that has been noticed by many commentators. Thus Numbers will be seen to contain such varied items as administrative directions for taking a census (1:1-44; 26:1-62), the resultant statistics (1:45-46; 26:51), summaries of Levitical laws and rituals (chaps. 8; 15; 18; etc.), a list of encampments during the wilderness wanderings (33:1-49), reports of spies (13:25-33), the steps taken to replace Aaron and Moses as leaders (20:25-28; 27:12-23), specimens of ancient Israelite poetry (10:35-36; 21:14-15, 17-18, 27-30), descriptions of miraculous occurrences (11:31-33), accounts of apostasy among the Israelites (16:1-35; 21:4-9; etc.), and prophetic utterances from a pagan source (chaps. 22-24). In summary it can be said that many divergent types of OT literature can be found in the book of Numbers.[22]

The miscellaneous nature of the collection, which led one author to describe the canonical Numbers as "almost a wilderness in the variety of its contents and the lack of any order in the arrangement of these contents,"[23] seemed ideally suited to the purposes of nineteenth-century literary criticism. Accordingly the liberal scholars envisaged the contents predominantly in terms of a "JE" combination along with admixtures of the supposed "P" document. S. R. Driver[24] cautiously summed up the general trend of scholarship by regarding "JE" and "P" as contiguous, though not generally interwoven, elements in the book of Numbers. "P" was thought to include 1:1–10:28; chaps. 18-19; 26-31; and 33, while a "JE" and "P" admixture included 13:1-17; chaps. 16-17; 20-22. "JE" was supposed to be represented mainly by chaps. 11-12; 22-24.

---

22. Cf. J. N. Oswalt, *ZPEB*, 4:462.
23. L. B. Longacre, *The Abingdon Bible Commentary* (Nashville: Abingdon-Cokesbury, 1929), p. 298.
24. S. R. Driver, *An Introduction to the Literature of the Old Testament* (Edinburgh: T & T Clark, 1906), pp. 60–69.

Insofar as the "D" source was thought to be represented in Numbers, it was generally imagined to be restricted to a small section comprising 21:33-35, which was recapitulated in Deut. 3:1-3.[25] Not surprisingly, European conservative scholars repudiated such an analysis based upon alleged underlying documents and regarded the book of Numbers as of Mosaic provenance. Driver's own function was to make "the most assured results of literary criticism," about which the proponents of the Graf-Wellhausenian hypothesis were inclined to boast, as acceptable as possible to the English-speaking world. In consequence, he cautiously included in his analysis some of the findings of A. Dillmann,[26] who had placed the Pentateuchal priestly material considerably earlier than Deuteronomy and had regarded the "Holiness Code" (Lev. 18-26) as being of even greater antiquity.

The simplistic notion that the underlying literary sources of a body of material can be adduced merely by ascertaining whether God is referred to as Yahweh or Elohim fails to consider varieties of provenance or to address itself to the possibility that genuine literary sources can be identified by other means. One such section, which stands outside the strict, classic formulation of Wellhausen and his followers, is the brief quotation from "The Book of the Wars of the Lord" (Num. 21:14-15). This fragment seems to have formed part of a collection of recorded miracles describing divine intervention in Israel's affairs. Although information about this material is scanty at best, it may have been part of a compilation of mighty divine acts intended to serve apologetic purposes for the nation, much as some of the historical psalms did at a later period.

Another extraneous source that was evidently of non-Israelite origin is the collection of prophetic oracles delivered by the Mesopotamian seer Balaam (Num. 22-24). The origin, nature, and transmission of these utterances have been the subject of inconclusive debate by scholars. In my view, to assign such materials arbitrarily to a "JE"

25. Following J. Wellhausen, *Komposition*, pp. 339-40. G. B. Gray, *A Critical and Exegetical Commentary on Numbers* (Edinburgh: T & T Clark, 1903), pp. xxix–xxxix, adopted similar conclusions.
26. Cf. A. Dillmann, *Numeri*, in *Kurzgefasstes exegetisches Handbuch zum Alten Testament* (Leipzig: Hirzel, 1886), pp. 89, 605, 644-47. Prominent European scholars who challenged the documentary hypothesis of Pentateuchal origins included E. W. Hengstenberg, *Beiträge zur Einleitung in das Alte Testament* (Berlin, 1831-1839); M. Drechsler, *Die Einheit und Echtheit der Genesis* (Leipzig: Hirzel, 1838); and C. F. Keil, who in conjunction with F. Delitzsch produced a commentary on OT books that was translated into English under the title *Biblical Commentary on the Old Testament* (Edinburgh: T & T Clark, 1872-1884). This series challenged the postulates of European literary critics so successfully that it has remained an important resource for conservative scholarship.

source is to fail to recognize their existence as a separate literary entity, extraneous to the Israelite narratives but incorporated into Numbers because of its importance for the historical and theological dimensions it exhibited.

Yet another literary source, the nature of which has seldom been understood properly by commentators, is the presence in Num. 3:1 of what appears to be a genuine colophon such as was characteristic of Babylonian literary texts in antiquity. Artifacts of this kind have been recovered in great quantity from various Near Eastern sites by archaeologists, and all exhibit, when undamaged, a typical format. A single tablet would commence with a title, after which the message the author intended to convey—whether personal, commercial, religious, or diplomatic—would be recorded. The conclusion of a tablet or a series of tablets was marked by a colophon, which would be basically equivalent to the title page of a modern book. Thus it would often contain the title of the tablet, along with a notation about the scribe who wrote it and who could also have been the owner of the tablet. A further annotation generally attempted to date the tablet by reference to known persons or events. If more than one tablet was used for the communication, as for example in the case of a religious epic, the individual tablets in the series were connected mechanically by means of "catch lines" that served to keep the material in proper order. This device, incidentally, is still used today in connection with legal documents, business contracts, and the like. Where a series of tablets was involved, the title of the collection was often recorded in the colophon of the final tablet. The colophon of the various Genesis "tablets" can be identified by the presence of the term תּוֹלְדוֹת, *tôlĕdôt*, which is used in a special technical sense to mean "histories," "records," or "family histories." It does not mean biological descendants, however, in the Genesis colophons, but in Num. 1:20-42 it bears this meaning because it occurs in a different literary and noncolophonic context.

To illustrate the nature and function of a colophon, reference can be made to the *Atrahasis Epic*, an ancient though not original account of the Flood. The colophons that appeared on each of the three tablets containing the Old Babylonian version of the Epic included the following information: date of composition, in terms of the month, the day, and the name of the king (Ammiṣaduqa); the title of the literary work; the number of lines; and the name of the scribe ("written by Ku-Aya, the junior scribe").[27] Num. 3:1 thus follows the general pattern of similar colophons in Gen. 2:4; 5:1; 6:9, and elsewhere. If Moses was in fact the compiler of the ancient source materials that make up

---

27. Lambert and Millard, *Atrahasis*, pp. 31-32.

Genesis, it would not have been surprising for him to have drawn up his personal records of the census along the classical lines of ancient Mesopotamia and to have included them in Numbers to validate his own authority and that of his brother, Aaron.

From the foregoing examples it will be apparent that attempts to delineate sources based upon other than ancient Near Eastern methods of compilation and transmission of literary materials are doomed to failure. Even with what is currently known about ancient scribal practices, there is still room for error and misinterpretation, which should urge caution upon the investigator. Despite this caveat, the basic approach is sound methodologically, inasmuch as it is based upon proper a posteriori (inductive) method, and not the groundless a priori (deductive) speculations of the Graf-Wellhausen school, which by their nature can never be amenable to objective demonstration.

STRUCTURE AND COMPILATION

In whatever written work Moses undertook personally during the wilderness wanderings, it is probable that he was responsible for substituting leather for the clay tablets that were used widely in the Amarna Age. (Amarna is a general designation for the mid-fourteenth century B.C., when Egypt ruled the Near East.) At the same time Moses undertook to engrave certain promulgations in stone (Ex. 34:28) to ensure permanence for the legislation, and this would indicate that at least two media of literary communication were available for his use. As an educated Egyptian (cf. Acts 7:22) he would probably have been able to communicate in Babylonian cuneiform, the language in which some of the tablets from el-Amarna were written,[28] although the materials for making tablets would be less accessible in the Sinai wilderness than papyrus. The latter is a durable material in dry climates but would not have survived readily beyond the confines of an arid environment. In a desert milieu it would be more difficult to obtain than supplies of tanned leather, which were readily available from the herds of the Israelites.

The diverse nature of the materials that compose the book of Numbers is reflected not only in the sources but also in opinions about the pattern according to which the book has been thought to have been assembled. Thus some scholars such as R. C. Dentan suggested that Numbers did not possess unity and was not composed

---

28. Published by J. A. Knudtzon and O. Weber, *Die El-Amarna Tafeln*, 2 vols. (Leipzig: Hinrichs, 1915). See also F. Thureau-Dangin, "Nouvelles Lettres D'El-Amarna," *RA* 19 (1922): 91-108; S. A. B. Mercer, *ANET* (1955): 482-90; C. F. Pfeiffer, *Tell el Amarna and the Bible* (Grand Rapids: Baker, 1963); A. Bowling, *ZPEB* 5:614-21; F. F. Bruce, *NIDBA*, pp. 23-24.

with a predetermined plan.[29] But he appears to have contradicted himself by disclosing not one pattern of composition but two. The first follows the traditional historical lines set out in the book itself— namely, the threefold division of the journey from Sinai to Canaan and the defeat by Amalek (chaps. 1-14); the traditional forty-year period of wilderness wanderings (chaps. 15-19?); and the concluding material describing the Israelite advance to the Jordan opposite Jericho (chaps. 20?-36). His second structural analysis was framed in geographic terms representing three locations, namely (1) the events at Sinai (1:1–10:10), (2) the events in the desert area south of Canaan (10:11–20:13), and (3) the events in Edom and Moab (20:14–36:13). For Dentan the time framework of the geographical analysis involved a period of twenty days (comparing 1:1 with 10:11), an interval of approximately thirty-eight years (comparing 10:11 with 33:38), and a final period somewhat greater than five months (comparing 33:38 with Deut. 1:3). Clearly the structure and composition of Numbers is more sophisticated than might be imagined at first sight.

In words reminiscent of the "fragmentary hypothesis," M. Noth maintained that Numbers was "an unsystematic collection of innumerable pieces of tradition of very varied content, age, and character."[30] In the main, however, the "P" document formed for him the bulk of the work, with some "J" material, some "E" sources, and elements of "D" toward the end of the book. Although some of the sources could conceivably be regarded as ancient (e.g., the Balaam narratives, chaps. 22-24), the preponderance of the material was for him late and basically unhistorical. The constituent elements were assembled to reflect the theological undertaking and practices of the postexilic Jerusalem community.[31]

In contrast to the delineation and manipulation of hypothetical literary sources as practiced by liberal scholars, it is now possible to entertain a properly-accredited process of compilation by recognizing the intrinsic historical worth of the various records emerging from the wilderness period. It is no longer necessary to regard these materials as folklore, passed on orally through many generations with the usual embellishments, because there is evidence in Numbers of the existence of literate administrators among the Israelite tribes.

These were the שֹׁטְרִים, *šōṭĕrîm* (to use their later name), a term first applied to the Egyptian organizers of the Israelite workers just prior to the Exodus.[32] As indicated in Numbers, they were of executive or

---

29. R. C. Dentan, *IDB*, 3:567.
30. M. Noth, *Numbers* (London: SCM, 1968), p. 4.
31. Ibid., p. 10.
32. Cf. Ex. 5:16-19, translated generally as "officers" or "foremen."

supervisory status, being first appointed to this position by Moses (Num. 1:16-18). Within a generation they had become recognized as a guild (Josh. 1:10) and were important to the nation because they were a literate group. The basic meaning of the verb שָׁטַר, *šāṭar*, is "to write" and is paralleled in Akkadian by *šaṭāru*, which has the same meaning. Their function, under the supervision of Moses, was to assist in recording and administering judicial decisions (cf. Deut. 16:18, etc.).

These persons were for the Israelites what the guilds of scribes or annalists were to pagan nations. Thus, following ancient Near Eastern scribal traditions as instructed by Moses, they would commit to writing whatever judicial decisions were made and would also be responsible for recording the occurrence of important events during the wilderness period. This group was also assisted in the task of record-keeping by Israelite priests, who themselves maintained cultic records (Num. 5:23; 17:3), and also by the literary activities of Moses himself (cf. Ex. 17:14; 24:4, 12; 34:27; Deut. 29:27; etc.). There can therefore be no doubt that, whatever their immediate titles, there was a group of literate persons present at all times to record, in whatever detail was thought necessary, the events of Israelite life throughout the entire period of the wilderness wanderings, thereby making it unnecessary to rely solely upon the memory of those occasions.

This early group, dignified subsequently by the title of scribes or annalists, made a fundamental contribution to Hebrew culture by helping to establish their successors as among the best historiographers in the ancient Near East, as contrasted with the propagandist activities of their counterparts in such countries as Egypt and Assyria. On the basis of this evidence, I agree with J. A. Thompson that "the present literary shape of Numbers is not secondary or artificial, but results from the simple fact that the original events took place in the same sequence, or approximately so."[33]

The general tenor of the book of Numbers implies that there were many *šōṭĕrîm* available to check and recheck such data as census lists and other so-called priestly materials, which, as E. E. Carpenter has remarked, reflect more than a priestly ambience.[34] With so many

---

33. J. A. Thompson, *The New Bible Commentary Revised* (London: Inter-Varsity, 1970), p. 169.
34. E. E. Carpenter and E. B. Smick, *ISBE*, 3:562. The authors illustrate such activity by reference to ancient Near Eastern parallels, e.g., E. A. Speiser, "Census and Ritual Expiation in Mari and Israel," *BASOR* 149 (1958): 17-25; C. H. Gordon, *Ugaritic Literature* (Rome: Pontificium Institutum Biblicum, 1949), pp. 124-25; Y. Aharoni, *LBHG* (1967), pp. 62, 69; G. E. Mendenhall, "The Census Lists of Numbers 1 and 26," *JBL* 77 (1958): 52-66.

carefully selected administrators on hand at all times who were dedicated to the service of God, the possibility of deliberate falsification
of data or participation in fraudulent behavior was minimal. It is
significant that, of those persons punished by God for serious offenses
(Num. 3:4; 12:10; 16:31-33), none was named as an elder or an admin-
istrator, which in itself attests to the integrity of the group subsequently known formally as *šōṭĕrîm*. The legislation that they were
responsible for recording frequently follows recognizable Near Eastern scribal traditions in such matters as employing an *inclusio*, a
repetitive device whereby the content of a legal passage is presented
in summary form at the end of the section of legislation. This scribal
practice occurs commonly in legal enactments written in cuneiform.

The presence of such diverse sources has had an obvious influence
upon the compilation of the book. Despite its present position in the
canon of Scripture, the narrative of Numbers 1:1 links the book historically with the end of Exodus (40:38) rather than with the conclusion of
the adjacent book of Leviticus (27:34). The order in which the early
materials of Numbers was compiled is subjected more to theological
considerations than chronological ones. Although the events in Num.
7:1–9:23 actually occurred before those recorded in 1:1–6:27, the
purpose of the final arrangement of materials reflected the desire of
Moses to complete the Exodus account of God's possession of the
Tabernacle (Ex. 40:34) with a description of the way in which it was
located in the midst of the twelve tribes, who had been organized for
that purpose following a census. The theological objective of emphasizing the holiness of the sanctuary took precedence over the actual
sequence of events, which had included donations for sanctuary service from the twelve tribes (Num. 7:1-89), the formal commissioning of
the Levites (8:1-26), and the second Passover celebration (9:2-14).

The chronological displacement is a comparatively minor matter,
since the dating of the various sections enables the alert reader to
make an appropriate reconstruction. What it does point out, however,
is the theological emphasis that proves dominant throughout the
book and to which all other considerations are to be subordinated.
The Tabernacle was the tangible indication not merely of God's presence with His people but of His essential holiness, which was to be
the standard for all community life in the nation. This factor explains
the position of the ritual regulations promoting holiness and separation from uncleanness (5:1-31) as well as the institution of the
Nazirites as a special demonstration of ritual holiness as a way of life.

With these preliminary conditions established, the way was
opened for Moses to introduce into the narrative several accounts of
incidents in the progress of the Israelites toward the Promised Land.
Here again the theological interest of the compiler is evident in the

way in which he adduces a stern religious message from the various acts of apostasy and rebellion against God's will (e.g., 11:1–12:16; 16:1-50; etc.). Since many of the ritual and social laws were fashioned to meet situations arising from a seminomadic experience, the migrations of the Israelites brings drama and crisis to the narrative. The legislation resulting from these episodes was devised on a seemingly ad hoc basis, but much of it found a permanent place in the legislative framework of the Israelite community. As Carpenter has indicated,[35] the legal and ritual materials have hortatory as well as punitive value, indicated by the placement of the second census list as a sign that national punishment for unbelief had ended.

Several OT books were written in a way that ignored chronological order and arranged the materials according to scribal or editorial principles that defy clear understanding. The prophecy of Jeremiah furnishes an outstanding example of this tendency. With the availability of such a diversity of sources for Numbers, it should not be surprising if the reader encounters in the book an arrangement of materials that is unconventional by modern Western standards. In any event, it must be remembered that the order in which the contents of Numbers were arranged was meant to suit the purposes of the compiler, and doubtless the ancient readers, to the fullest extent. Because of this, any attempt at understanding the finished product must be undertaken from the standpoint of ancient Near Eastern methods of compiling information, reporting of events, and utilizing the editorial process to emphasize concerns that were not always governed by strict chronological considerations.

In view of the availability of tanned leather in the wilderness period, it was without doubt the preferred material for recording and transmitting information. Its choice would be governed by its durable qualities compared with tablets of clay or stone, which even when available could fracture readily. Although papyrus rolls were used widely in Egypt, it would have been difficult for the Israelites to have secured them in the wilderness, unless they had access to them through caravan traders. In any event, papyrus lacked the resilience of leather, and it is doubtful that papyrus rolls would have survived years of usage under wilderness conditions.

Even Num. 2:1–3:1, a record written in the form of a Babylonian tablet complete with what resembles a colophon (3:1), would have been transmitted at this time on leather rather than stone, if only for practical reasons. Because the bulk of the records in Numbers were most probably annalistic and therefore written down at the time they were promulgated orally, or shortly thereafter, it is easier to explain

---

35. Carpenter and Smick, *ISBE*, 3:564.

what appear to modern readers as dislocations in terms of short scrolls being juxtaposed according to the theological purposes of the compiler. These, as has been observed above, were to demonstrate the need for making God's holiness central to the life of the covenant community (Num. 1:1–10:10) and thereafter to describe the outworking of this purpose in the day-to-day experience of wilderness existence.

In terms of structure, it is possible that the formal statement about God speaking to Moses in Numbers 1:1 and 2:1 indicates the commencement of two separate scrolls, which may well have been written by Moses himself, the second of which ends with a colophon (3:1). The remainder of chap. 3, along with chap. 4, which deal with cultic and census matters, could originally have formed two short scrolls. Further cultic regulations in chaps. 5 and 6 could have been appended to the contents of the preceding scroll shortly after it was written. Num. 7:1–8:4 constitutes priestly records that listed the offerings for the Tabernacle, but the stereotyped introductory formula, "Then the Lord spoke to Moses, saying" (8:5), might indicate the commencement of a new section of priestly material relating to the Levites (8:5-26) and continuing to 9:15, where another scroll section was perhaps appended, terminating at 12:16.

Two subsequent chapters containing historical and priestly records end by narrating Israel's failure to enter Canaan (14:45). Small sections dealing with cultic regulations (15:1-41) may have prefaced a lengthy priestly collection comprising Numbers 16-19, after which a scroll of historical narratives, some of them in fragmentary form, ended at 21:35. Num. 22-24 represents material from a pagan source that was acquired in some unknown manner by the Israelites. These chapters constituted a separate literary unit that was inserted into the narrative at the appropriate chronological stage. There is no doubt, however, that the aftermath (25:1-18) is specifically Israelite in origin.

Perhaps a new priestly scroll is marked by 26:1, which begins with an account of the second census and deals with other administrative and priestly concerns subsequently. A further scroll section may begin at chap. 31, which deals with historical matters and such issues as the division of the Transjordanian territory. The remainder of the book consists of an admixture of historical, priestly, and administrative matters that anticipate the settled occupation of Canaan (35:1–36:13). Most of the suggested scroll components were probably compilations of much smaller sections of scroll material, assembled by the *šōṭĕrîm* or the priests.

The rather general nature of the chronological framework undergirding Numbers made it possible for Moses and the *šōṭĕrîm* to insert legislative and cultic materials during the compilatory processes at places that best suited the theological interests of the narrative. Many miscellaneous social and cultic items for which laws were enacted could have arisen in any given year of the wilderness migrations, but the intent of the finished scroll was to ensure that the appropriate legislation had in fact been enacted, regardless of strict chronological or topographical considerations.

These suggestions as to the method of compilation of Numbers are conjectural, of course, but they are based upon known methods of recording and transmitting data in antiquity. Such considerations as the length of the components that were assembled to form the finished canonical book of Numbers are incapable of demonstration, although the text of the book provides valuable suggestions at certain points, especially where units appear to be self-contained. Although some writers may regard Numbers as an example of a rather haphazard literary pastiche, it is important to remember that the scribes of antiquity did not always make clear distinctions between religious, social, judicial, and moral legislation, since all of life was subsumed under religion. In such circumstances the recipients would be less aware of, or threatened by, discontinuity than the modern person, who is governed by more rigorous categorization.

Out of the literary activities of Moses and the *šōṭĕrîm* emerged a dynamic description of life at an important stage of Israel's existence. The resultant book was unified by a general chronological form, as has been observed previously, which was supported by the two "pillars" of the census-takings in chaps. 1 and 26. The insertion of materials such as historical narratives, divine commands, topographical information, statistics, and the like, in what the compiler deemed to be the appropriate places for his theological purposes, brings both variety and vitality to the chronology, resulting in a readable and absorbing composition. But the reader is always reminded that the diversity of the materials that came to make up the book was at all times subordinated to the Sinaitic covenant faith of the uniqueness of God and His lordship over His own people and the nations of the earth alike. It is this unity of belief and sense of destiny for Israel that enabled such different types of source material to be shaped into a single work of lasting historical and theological significance. In addition to establishing its own identity as a valid element of the Pentateuchal corpus, Numbers helps to integrate the materials of other books of that collection, notably Exodus and Leviticus, into the contemporary record by working certain incidents and divine commands into the narrative in order to record and expand the basic principles enshrined in it.

Whatever the conditions under which the basic literary units of

20

differing sizes were assembled to produce the finished work, the one constant factor was the supervision furnished by competent literary personnel under the direction and active participation of Moses. These individuals held the fate of the Israelite occupation of the Promised Land in their hands, and the emphasis they laid upon the quality of community life under the covenant in difficult circumstances indicates that they discharged their responsibilities with great success.

AUTHORSHIP AND DATE

In an age when scholars believed that writing originated only about the beginning of the Israelite monarchy period, despite abundant evidence to the contrary, it was obviously impossible to suggest that Moses might have written any literary compositions. But now that writing is known to have originated about 3300 B.C. in Mesopotamia and to have become a sophisticated medium of communication within a very few centuries, the question of the possible Mosaic authorship of works attributed to him has to be evaluated on a different basis. Intrinsic probability now becomes an important factor and has to be disproved first of all before any other considerations can be entertained. The probability that Moses wrote a significant amount of Numbers and supervised the editorial processes by which the bulk of the composition took shape within his lifetime has to be given careful consideration.

The materials that constitute the book come from a comparatively short but highly significant historical period that witnessed Moses' work as the civil leader of the emerging Israelite nation. The events described in Numbers occurred within an equally circumscribed area of the ancient Near East under conditions that were surprisingly uniform in physical character. The non-Israelites with whom Moses and the Hebrews had contact were all familiar peoples who lived in the Sinai wilderness, Canaan, or Transjordan. There is no event recorded in the book of Numbers that could not have been known to Moses in the second millennium B.C. The ancient Near Eastern evidence now available supports the claim of the book to authenticity and origin in the Mosaic era.[36]

Although some liberal scholars have been prepared to see some ancient materials in Numbers that could possibly have been Mosaic in provenance,[37] they have generally minimized the place of Moses in

---

36. G. J. Wenham, *Numbers*, TOTC (Leicester: Inter-Varsity, 1981), p. 24.
37. E.g., F. M. Cross, "The Tabernacle," *BA* 10 (1947): 52-68; J. Marsh, *IB*, 2:138; G. H. Davies, *IDB*, 4:503.

the authorship of the work. But by contrast the canonical form of the book is true to life in the Bronze Age, depicting a bustling, sometimes threatening, wilderness milieu in which a frequently harassed Israelite leader struggled to cope with the growing pains of a self-willed nation. If the narrative has any validity at all, it is because the figure of the Israelite leader dominated the human scene. As a result of his special relationship with God and his unique position as the human mediator of the Sinai covenant, he was enabled to bring order into the civil and religious life of the nation in a way that gave it a sense of destiny as God's people in human society. Without his leadership as leader and legislator at this crucial period of their growth, the Israelites would have degenerated into yet another seminomadic people, exhibiting little or no difference from their neighbors and having minimal significance for either the history or the spirituality of the human race.

The evidence that Numbers presents concerning its compilation conflicts dramatically with the manner in which liberal scholarship has accounted for its growth. The "skilled writers" to whom they frequently appeal as compilers or editors of the canonical book in the postexilic period were already present hundreds of years earlier in the persons of the *šōṭĕrîm*. As has been made clear earlier, these persons were the best equipped of any to record events as eyewitnesses and to assist in the assembling of the sources underlying the extant composition. Before these men were chosen for their responsible tasks it would have been natural for the overworked Moses to have written down and compiled things himself. But once the *šōṭĕrîm* were available in their special capacities as servants of the community, such tasks could be delegated to them as well as to the priests. In all ages, when a leader is described as having "written" some form of composition, it is both normal and proper to assume that he had enjoyed the benefit of assistance in carrying out his original creative idea. Consequently it is legitimate to recognize that the final appearance of the work was due in part to persons who attended to such mechanical details as the assembling of sources or the copying, the writing, and even the manual preparation of scroll materials.

Given the resources at hand in the Sinai wilderness, it was possible for the bulk of Numbers to have been written in small sections by Moses and the *šōṭĕrîm* and to have been assembled over a period of time into a lengthy scroll or scrolls, which, with one or two small exceptions, constituted the book in approximately its extant form. Under these conditions of literary activity over a comparatively short historical period, it is not improper to regard Numbers as a product of the great Hebrew leader, containing accurately recorded historical, legal, religious, and other matters that came from credible eye-witnesses.

As in other biblical books, allowances must be made for such additions as explanatory glosses by later scribes who wished to clarify the text for subsequent generations. But it is important to understand that, in the Near East, scribes functioned as copyists and not as editors in the modern sense. Hebrew scribes would be especially concerned with the preservation of the text they had received, a text they venerated as the revelation of their God. They did not indulge in attempts at propaganda, nor did they interfere with the artistry of the original compositions. Their prime concern was to preserve those sacred writings to which they had become heir and to make their significance clear by updating phraseology, topography, names, and any other archaic or obscure matters.

The kind of "editing" envisaged by modern scholars would already have taken place when the book was being compiled at the hands of Moses and his assistants and would require only the kind of changes mentioned above. During the wilderness period, therefore, Numbers took substantially the form with which the modern reader is familiar. Moses can be regarded as the supervising author, giving oversight to the assembling of relevant sources by the various literate officials and priests, adding his own written contributions, and probably acting as the final drafting editor.

A further degree of literary artistry in the structuring of Numbers appears in the fact that the events narrated involve the first two years and the last two years of Israelite life in the wilderness. Between these periods was a long interval of time about which very little is known. But if, following the literary device known as *merismus*, the beginning and the final years are linked together in the narrative, they can be taken as describing representatively the whole period of wandering in the Sinai wilderness as well as demonstrating the essential historical unity of the narrative.

Some scholars have urged the non-Mosaic authorship of Numbers on the ground that the narrative references to him are in the third person singular instead of the first person singular as might be expected. This argument can be refuted on two grounds: (1) The book of Numbers is not an autobiography of Moses but a collection of religious, secular, topographic, and other materials that often involve the Israelite leader in only an indirect manner. Where he is the center of attention, it is because of his function as the mediator of divine revelation and the individual who was commissioned principally to implement it. (2) In the literature of the ancient world, writing in the third person singular was a common practice. This literary tradition gradually spread across Europe westward and can be illustrated by the compositions of Julius Caesar, where the same usage is followed.

According to those who still adhere to the seriously-flawed Graf-Wellhausen hypothesis of Pentateuchal origins, the book of Numbers came into being through lengthy processes of oral transmission and thus is dated variously from the sixth to the third century B.C., insofar as the various writers venture to express a date.[38] I repudiate the Graf-Wellhausenian hypothesis and its attendant conclusions; but while affirming the overall Mosaic authorship of the book, I am aware that this affirmation raises certain problems connected with the book's dating.

Before John Garstang commenced his excavations at Jericho in 1929, the majority of scholars dated the Israelite exodus from Egypt in the thirteenth century B.C. Garstang's discoveries,[39] which were modified subsequently by Kathleen Kenyon, encouraged the acceptance of a fifteenth-century B.C. date for the exodus. Since Garstang's work, both dates have been argued, though somewhat inconclusively.[40] Until further and more decisive archaeological evidence is forthcoming, it is probably best to adopt a position that embraces both eventualities by placing the life and work of Moses within the Late Bronze Age (1550-1200 B.C.). The dating of the initial compilation is thus placed within a definite chronological span, and if allowance is made for the possibility of post-Mosaic additions of a minor nature by subsequent scribes, it is not too much to entertain a finished form of the book by the time of Samuel at the latest.

THE HEBREW TEXT

In process of transmission the Hebrew text of Numbers has suffered more than that of its contemporary, Leviticus. In one sense this is to be expected to a certain degree, since Leviticus, as a purely priestly handbook, would be tended more carefully than a composition that was not so specifically priestly in nature. Despite this disadvantage, Numbers has fared well when it is compared with some of the other OT books from a later period, as for example the prophecy

---

38. See G. E. Moore in *Encyclopaedia Biblica*, ed. T. K. Cheyne and J. S. Black (London: A & C Black, 1902), 3:3448; Gray, *Numbers*, p. ci; Marsh, *IB*, 2:138; P. J. Budd, *Numbers* (Waco, Tex.: Word, 1984), pp. xxii–xxiv.
39. J. Garstang, *Joshua-Judges* (London: Constable, 1931); cf. J. Sturdy, *Numbers* (Cambridge: Cambridge U., 1976), pp. 3-4.
40. For discussion and references see *HIOT*, pp. 174–77; G. L. Archer, *A Survey of Old Testament Introduction* (Chicago: Moody, 1974), pp. 223-34; J. Bimson, *Redating the Exodus and Conquest* (Sheffield: U. of Sheffield, 1978); W. H. Shea, *ISBE*, 2:230-38.

of Hosea, dated about 740 B.C., where a number of apparently accidental errors crept into the text in the process of transmission. Most of the textual problems of Numbers occur in the later chapters of the book, including 21:14, 18, 30; 23:10. It is interesting to note that the principal difficulties are found in the non-Israelite sources, especially in the Balaam narratives, and this may have been due to differences of dialect. The issues raised by these textual problems will be discussed in the appropriate sections of the Commentary.

THE THEOLOGY OF NUMBERS

The book of Numbers is a study in the contrast between God's faithfulness and human disobedience.[41] The subject of divine fidelity naturally involves a consideration of His attributes, which were revealed to Moses in a consummate example of propositional revelation (Ex. 34:6-7). The historical occasion was the giving of the Decalogue on Mount Sinai and its subsequent ratification by the assembled tribes. God's great love for His people was grounded in a legal agreement with them of a kind that was well understood in the Middle and Late Bronze Ages. It was of a reciprocal nature, demanding observance by both contracting parties and prescribing punishments for infidelity.

The covenant that was promulgated showed that divine love for Israel was not an unchecked outpouring of sentimental affection for the Hebrew tribes but an expression of God's essential being that was governed by justice and a desire to maintain His own rights under the agreement. What is commonly called the "Law of Moses" actually constituted a divinely ordained rule of existence, committed to Moses as a means of regulating the national, social, and spiritual life of the covenant people. Its core consisted of three parts: (1) The *Ten Commandments* (MT דְּבָרִים, *dĕbārîm*); or *Decalogue* (Ex. 20:1-17), which were of a timeless nature; (2) the *Judgments*, or *Ordinances* (MT מִשְׁפָּטִים *mišpāṭîm*), constituting decisive acts of God in dispensing justice, recorded so as to serve in the nature of precedents for later judges (21:1–23:33); and (3) the *Statutes* (MT חֻקִּים *ḥuqqîm*), the permanent rules of behavior prescribed by God at various times and recorded for human guidance.

Characteristic of God was His holiness, a concept that enshrined everything pure, ethical, moral, and just. Holiness belonged to God alone, who was known as the "Holy One of Israel" in later times (cf. 2 Kings 19:22; Ps. 71:22; and especially Isaiah), and consequently there

---

41. W. H. Griffith Thomas, *Through the Pentateuch Chapter by Chapter* (Grand Rapids: Kregel, 1985), p. 136.

was nothing in His creation that was intrinsically holy. Titles such as the one referring to God's holiness actually described His essence rather than some particular attribute, or some form of relationship such as that with the Israelites in the context of cultic worship.

Whereas God is and remains holy, the normal condition of humanity as a result of the Fall (Gen. 3:1-24) is one of sin, not grace. Although God's holiness is immutable, it can be applied in mercy or judgment in His relationships with His people, according to whether they are in a condition of ceremonial holiness or rebellion against His laws. God insisted upon holiness, with its concomitant righteousness, as the foundation for a proper relationship between Himself and Israel. In the sacrificial system He provided a means whereby accidental transgressions of His laws could be pardoned, or occasions where fellowship between Him and His people could be strengthened.

God's self-revelation makes it evident that His nature cannot be diminished in any way by the sin of His covenant people but shows equally that under the covenant legislation He could be provoked into retributive activity that was appropriate because it was provided for in the legal stipulations of the covenant. God did not exist on the basis of ethical separation from His people. Indeed, the opposite was the case, for He desired to draw them into the same kind of spiritual living that was separated from every consideration of the pagan world around them and dedicated solely to Him. This kind of holiness (Lev. 11:44) demanded commitment to His nature as a perfect spiritual Being and to His cause for mankind as mediated through His people. Those who wished to attain to this level of morality and spirituality could do so only by demonstrating complete loyalty to His commands and reinforcing this with an enthusiasm that translated the ethical ideal into practical activity. A purely subjective form of holy living, exercised as far as possible in isolation from society, as is frequently done today by "holy persons," would not be sufficient to satisfy God's requirements.

But if individual holiness was practiced and applied on a communal basis, the result would be the holy nation that God demanded of His people in community (Ex. 19:6). The "holiness" ascribed to Israel in Scripture was predominantly of the ritual or ceremonial variety, which permitted an individual to approach the Tabernacle for worship but for the most part did not penetrate very deeply into the wellsprings of human motivation. Nevertheless these "separated ones" were expected to lead moral, upright lives and to manifest their dedication to the covenant ethos by means of obedience to God's laws. In the end, however, only the most robust spiritually, among whom Moses himself was included, realized a need for a progressive movement in holiness toward the goal of perfection (Lev. 19:2; Deut. 18:13), a theme emphasized for His own followers by Jesus (Matt. 5:48, where the Greek *teleios* is the equivalent of the MT תָּם, *tām*, "a personality well developed in all areas").

Despite all the evidence of God's presence with them and of His power working on their behalf, the Hebrews found it very difficult to obey simple instructions that, if followed, guaranteed safety, material possessions, and spiritual blessing. Like many of their ancient Near Eastern contemporaries they were seminomads, going whenever and wherever the needs of the moment prompted. Previously they had made their own decisions, since they were not operating under any central law and were therefore free to do so. But now, with the implementing of the covenant, a cultural change of vast significance had overtaken them. Henceforth they were required to obey God's will implicitly, regardless of their personal feelings, because that will represented God's side of the covenantal agreement.

The egocentric character of fallen humanity is, by definition, one that follows the pursuit of its own interests in terms of survival and growth to the exclusion of those of others. Unfortunately, the wanton actions of the Israelites in the wilderness period illustrated their essential humanity, and all the more so since God required a spiritual ideal of them—namely, that they should live as a kingdom of priests and a holy nation. It is sometimes pleaded that the wilderness period witnessed only the formative experiences of the Israelites and that the claim for holiness was, after all, only a distant ideal. But that is not the sense of the text. When God demanded holiness from His people, He made possible at that very time a ceremonial form of it that would satisfy all normal ritual requirements when followed. This holiness, however, was only to serve as a preliminary phase of the deeper moral and spiritual growth that was to result in a person's being recognized as *tām* through exemplifying in a practical manner the high moral and ethical qualities of God.

The same is true, of course, in the spiritual life of the Christian. To commit one's life to Jesus Christ and receive the forgiveness of sin by His grace is but the beginning of a lifelong journey through this world's wilderness that is characterized by a progressive growth in grace and in the knowledge of Christ's saving work as revealed by the Holy Spirit (cf. Eph. 4:15; 1 Pet. 2:2; 2 Pet. 3:18; etc.). When this journey of faith is being undertaken in submission to the Lord's will, the believer will be occupied to a decreasing extent with selfish concerns and filled increasingly instead with the knowledge and glory of the Lord. In a word, the result will be less of self and more of Himself.

The ancient Israelites clearly did not understand the all-consuming nature of commitment, which might perhaps have been easier for them to grasp had they taken more seriously the reciprocal nature of the covenant. But at various times throughout their history they exhibited a blatant antinomianism that proceeded from the notion that, because they were God's chosen people, they were above the provisions of the law to which their ancestors subscribed, as though God's grace and love toward them absolved them from the rigors of a committed spiritual life and even permitted moral excesses in the name of "love." Unfortunately this wanton approach to spirituality did not pass away with the destruction of the Temple in Jerusalem (A.D. 70) but is still alive and well among supposedly "committed Christians," who use the widely-misunderstood "law of love" as an excuse for indulging in illegal and immoral activities, contrary to the strict prohibitions of the Decalogue and the teachings of Christ.

A Christian hymn-writer caught the spirit of the book of Numbers by interpreting the tenor of wilderness wanderings in terms of the Christian's journey through life under the Lord's guidance.[42] The writer's expectation was that of God—namely, that His ancient people would traverse the short extent of terrain from Mount Sinai to southern Canaan in obedience to His laws. As the commentary will show, this was not to be the case, and consequently the book is a record of wandering because of disobedience. Just as the Israelites were not intended to pass thirty-eight years in journeying from one place to another in the wilderness, so the Christian is not expected to have prolonged wilderness experiences through disobedience but to pass straight from redemption (Egypt) through instruction (Exodus) and worship (Leviticus) to the full Christian life.[43] The book of Numbers is therefore of fundamental importance, not merely for Hebrew history and religion but as an example of Christian living under the power of the Holy Spirit and also as a warning against indulging in the kind of sin that brought death to a whole generation of Israelites so long ago (1 Cor. 10:1-11; Heb. 3:7–4:11).

---

42. W. Williams, *Guide Me, O Thou Great Jehovah* (1745).
43. Griffith Thomas, *Through the Pentateuch*, p. 135.

1
Organizing the Census of Israel (1:1–4:49)

The chronology of the wilderness wanderings after the miracle of the Exodus is narrated by Numbers, which begins at the stage where the book of Exodus terminates. It constitutes the principal source of information for the occurrences between the last twenty days at Mount Sinai (Num. 1:1; 10:11) and the ultimate arrival of the twelve tribes at the lowlands of Moab in the fortieth year (22:1; 26:3; 33:50). The period of wilderness sojourn described is thus approximately thirty-nine years.

By contrast, the interval of time spanned by the events of Leviticus was a scant month. The legislative elements of that book were revealed to Moses after the Tabernacle had been completed (Ex. 40:17), while the Israelites were still encamped at Mount Sinai. But this short interval must not be understood to impugn the authenticity of Numbers, which was evidently assembled over a much longer period of time. During the interval covered by Numbers, the Israelite community was undergoing initial religious and social organization that would establish the community ideally as a kingdom of priests and a holy nation (Ex. 19:6).

A. MUSTERING OF ISRAEL'S WARRIORS (1:1-54)

This chapter is structured in three main sections: (a) selection of officials (vv. 1-16), (b) census (vv. 17-46), (c) exemption of Levites (vv. 47-54).

1. SELECTION OF OFFICIALS (vv. 1-16)

Translation

Now the LORD spoke to Moses in the tent of meeting in the Sinai wilderness on the first day of the second month in the second year after the Israelites came out of the land of Egypt, saying: (1:1)

Exegesis and Exposition

The scene is set at the foot of Mount Sinai, and the narrative is connected chronologically with the termination of construction work on the Tabernacle. The book of Numbers is linked to the last verse of Leviticus (27:34) by the Hebrew conjunction "and," indicating the basic continuity of the narrative. The complete Hebrew word וַיְדַבֵּר (*wayĕdabbēr*, "and he spoke") was one of the titles of Numbers in the pre-Christian period. To begin a sentence with "And" is often considered poor English literary style, and consequently it has been avoided in the present work, as in most modern translations.

The phrase "the Lord spoke to Moses" is normally described by scholars as an annunciation formula or the like, intended to introduce revelatory material of various kinds and marking the beginning of a section that would have been contained on a separate piece of writing material initially. Where instructions are involved, a closing formula normally concludes the body of material, as in Numbers 1:54, and is expressed by the assurance that the Israelites did precisely all that the Lord had commanded them.

But to dismiss the phrase in such a casual fashion without further consideration of its import is to miss the wonder of God's communicating with humanity. Speech is the first specific form of divine action in the process of creation, as Scripture depicts it to us in Gen. 1:3, and it characterizes the appearance of all subsequent created phenomena. From the standpoint of humanity, divine revelation depends upon speech being uttered and received intelligibly. Speech is a peculiar characteristic of the God of creation and was used frequently in Hebrew history to demonstrate His superiority over the false gods of the pagan Near East, who were mute and thus unable to communicate with their votaries. But Israel's supreme Deity summed up within Himself the essence of life and was able to verbalize His own moral and spiritual qualities to His people, and beyond them to any others who would hear and obey His voice. In these last days God has spoken to us by His Son, Jesus Christ, who is the brightness of His glory and the express image of His person (Heb. 1:2-3, KJV). Furthermore, God speaks to the Christian through the Holy Spirit, who searches out for the believer the depths of God's revelation as communicated through the OT prophets and supremely through His Son (cf. 1 Cor. 2:10-16).

In His address to Moses, God is described by His revealed name of YHWH (Ex. 6:3). In the *ASV* and *NEB* this was rendered by "Jehovah," which is a hybrid combination of the consonants YHWH and the vowels of אֲדֹנָי (*'ădônāy*, "lord"). This device had been adopted by the Hebrews at an early period because they regarded the word YHWH as being too sacred to pronounce, and traditional renderings have perpetuated this concept. Most modern scholars, however, have adopted the practice of using YHWH as though it were the personal name of God and generally transcribe it as "Yahweh," although this is conjectural because the original pronunciation is unknown. This procedure is a mistake on two counts: (1) YHWH is not a personal name as such but is a descriptive title denoting essential, purposive being; (2) although "Yahweh" may be regarded as one possible pronunciation, it cannot be shown to be correct and is quite possibly wrong.[1] For historical and philological reasons I respect Jewish sensitivities in the matter and avoid the use of the tetragrammaton altogether. Indeed, in most modern English translations the word YHWH is rendered by "Lord," and this tradition will be observed in this commentary.

Although the subject of the address is God, the object of divine attention is Moses in his capacity as civil leader of the Israelites, and he is addressed as he stands before God in the tent of meeting (MT אֹהֶל מוֹעֵד, *'ōhel mô'ēd*). This was one of several names by which the Tabernacle was known, others being אֹהֶל הָעֵדֻת (*'ōhel hā'ēdût*), מִשְׁכַּן הָעֵדֻת (*miškan hā'ēdût*), and simply הַמִּשְׁכָּן (*hammiškān*). All these terms described in one way or other the Tabernacle that was constructed in the wilderness. While it was being built, God met with Moses in a "tent of meeting" that was some distance away from where the Tabernacle was being fashioned (Ex. 33:7). This term was evidently applied subsequently to the finished Tabernacle. The variation of Hebrew terminology led to confusion in the different English versions.[2] Some scholars have restricted the term "tent of meeting" to the inner area of the Tabernacle, where God revealed Himself to Moses and Aaron, and have understood the word *tabernacle* as a comprehensive noun describing the whole curtained structure and its

---

1. For a contrary position see K. L. Barker, ed., *The NIV: The Making of a Contemporary Translation* (Grand Rapids: Zondervan, 1986), pp. 106-9.
2. Cf. R. K. Harrison, *Leviticus*, TOTC (Leicester: Inter-Varsity, 1980), p. 41; D. W. Gooding, *The Account of the Tabernacle* (Cambridge/New York, 1959); C. L. Feinberg, *ZPEB* 5:572-73.

contents. This interpretation of the phraseology will be followed in this commentary. The idea of a *mô'ēd* was familiar to the Egyptians, having been discovered in a literary source from that ancient land; it referred to the assembly of the inhabitants of Byblos and was dated about 1100 B.C. Once the Tabernacle had been constructed, God addressed Moses from between the cherubim in the Most Holy Place.[3]

The Tabernacle was a portable shrine familiar to the ancient Near Eastern scene. The same techniques employed to build the Tabernacle were well known to the Egyptians long before the time of Moses.[4] Portable tents of purification made of a framework of vertical pillars linked by horizontal bars and surrounded with curtains were depicted on the walls of Egyptian Old Kingdom (c. 2700-2200 B.C.) tombs.[5] At Karnak, Thutmose III built a large stone structure dated about 1470 B.C. that was a replica of the traditional wooden-pillared tent shrine.[6] In Near Eastern antiquity portable shrines accompanied kings and their armies to battle and were pitched in the center of the camp, where they would be safe from marauders. The purpose of these structures was to serve as a palladium, or place under divine protection, where kings and priests could consult freely with their gods. In the Amarna Age (fourteenth century B.C.) it had become common for the Egyptians to deploy their troops around such shrines when military campaigns were being conducted, a practice that the Israelites were to employ in their wilderness wanderings.

It is clear from this verse that the Tabernacle was beginning to function as the symbol of God's presence in the midst of His people and as a place for worship, now that the ritual revelations had been supplied to Moses. The first location was at the foot of Mount Sinai, in what the text describes as a "wilderness" (מִדְבָּר, *midbār*).[7] This term is rendered "desert" in most translations, but to the geographer the area is technically a "wilderness." The difference is that a desert is normally arid and devoid of vegetation except for occasional oases, and thus cannot support life to any significant extent. By contrast, while a wilderness may contain areas of barrenness, it is able to

---

3. Cf. R. A. Cole, *Exodus*, TOTC (Leicester: Inter-Varsity, 1973), p. 191.
4. Cf. K. A. Kitchen, "Some Egyptian Background to the Old Testament," *TynBul* 5–6 (1960): 7-13; B. S. Childs, *The Book of Exodus* (Philadelphia: Westminster, 1974), pp. 529-52.
5. A. M. Blackman, *The Rock Tombs of Meir* (Oxford: Oxford U., 1977), V, pls. 42, 43.
6. K. Lange and M. Hirmer, *Egypt: Architecture, Sculpture, Painting in Three Thousand Years* (London: Phaedon, 1956), pls. 137-39.
7. This term occurred in Ugaritic tablets dated about 1400 B.C. as *mdbr* (C. H. Gordon, *Ugaritic Manual* 3 [Rome: Pontificium Institutum Biblicum, 1955], p. 254, no. 458). There is no doubt that the word antedates the Amarna Age.

support human and animal life to a considerable degree. For the biblical student this is particularly the case when *midbār* is used in the OT of steppe land. This latter is found where the desert tapers off gradually to more fertile land, the intermediary phase consisting of shrubs and impoverished grassland but able to support grazing to some extent. It is possible to cultivate areas of steppe land or wilderness with modest success, especially when the proximity of an oasis or a natural spring affords a supply of water. Small wild animals that have adapted to arid conditions are often in evidence in a wilderness, along with much larger ones such as the camel that exhibit water-storing capabilities. Where the wilderness contains mountains with grassy plateaus, animals can graze comfortably.

Some of the biblical wilderness lands included upland pastures (Ex. 3:1; Ps. 65:12; Joel 2:22), the boundaries of which expanded or receded periodically, contingent upon the amount of rainfall. Such areas were the "wilderness pastures" mentioned in prophecy (Jer. 9:10; Joel 1:9-10). Despite the availability of food to a greater or lesser degree, the narratives of Numbers make it plain that the wilderness was no place for the serene contemplation of life, any more than it was in the time of Christ (cf. Mark 1:12-13).

In all periods the wilderness was the habitat of wild animals and even of demonic activity, according to some traditions (cf. Luke 11:24). In view of this it is hardly surprising that the Scriptures generally regarded the period of wilderness wanderings in negative terms (Num. 14:33; Deut. 1:19; 8:15; 32:10; Ps. 78:40; etc.). Later the wilderness motif came to have important religious significance, not merely for the testing of the infant Israelite nation but also for Elijah (1 Kings 19:4-8), John the Baptist (Matt. 3:1-6 and parallel passages), and Jesus Himself (4:1-11). Throughout Scripture, testing, self-denial, divine provision, and obedience to God's will were consistent features of the wilderness experience. Because the wandering Israelites managed to survive with their herds and flocks in these areas, the present commentary will translate *midbār* by "wilderness" rather than "desert."

The location of Mount Sinai, which gave its name to the wilderness area surrounding it, has been a matter of considerable debate among scholars. It has been identified variously with Jebel Mûsa, with Jebel Serbāl, with Ras eṣ-Ṣafṣafeh, and also with a volcanic mountainous peak near al-Hrob. Of these suggested locations, Jebel Mûsa and Ras eṣ-Ṣafṣafeh are the most likely choices. They constitute two peaks situated at opposite ends of a granite ridge of approximately three miles in length, stretching from northwest to southeast. Jebel Mûsa, about 7,363 feet high, is located at the southern extremity, while Ras eṣ-Ṣafṣafeh, about 6,540 feet high, is situated at the opposite end where the Monastery of Santa Katerina now stands. A plain of considerable size, which would probably have accommodated the Israelites (Ex. 20:18), spreads out at the foot of Raseṣ Ṣafṣafeh, a fact that has commended itself to many scholars as indicating the true "mountain of God."

But a strong tradition, nearly a millennium and a half old, has preferred to identify Mount Sinai with the imposing granite formation of Jebel Mûsa ("Mountain of Moses"), and in the absence of conclusive identification to the contrary it is generally regarded by scholars as the correct site. Mount Sinai is also known as Horeb in Scripture (cf. Ex. 3:1; 17:6; Deut. 1:2,6,19; 1 Kings 8:9; etc.), but the term could also refer to the entire mountain range, of which Mount Sinai is one great eminence. Some scholars have also suggested that it refers to a specific peak a little below Jebel Mûsa.[8]

The date of the divine revelation to Moses is given as the first day of the second month in the second year following the Exodus from Egypt. Because the Israelites had arrived in the wilderness in the third month following the Exodus (Ex. 19:1), they had thus spent nine months in the general vicinity of Mount Sinai. When this information is compared with Num. 9:1, which was dated at the beginning of the first month of the second year after the Exodus, it is evident that a strict chronology has not been followed. The difference of one month is a minor consideration, however, and the arrangement of the materials in the extant order indicates the relative importance attached to the two bodies of material. The census of men suitable for military service (Num. 1:2-46) provided not merely for a standing army in Israel but helped subsequently in the allotment of the promised land of Canaan (26:52-56). It thus focused attention on the future, whereas the circumstances of 7:1–9:23 looked back to events that had already happened as the Tabernacle was being set in operation, including the second celebration of the Passover (9:1-14). By this time the holiness of the Tabernacle had been established firmly in the minds of the Israelites.

The dating of this promulgation is related specifically to the Israelite departure from Egypt. Unfortunately this does not assist the modern reader very much, since there are two possible dates for that event: the fifteenth century B.C. or the thirteenth century B.C. (see

---

8. For studies on this subject see A. P. Stanley, *Sinai and Palestine* (New York: A. C. Armstrong, 1905 ed.), pp. 16-27; W. M. F. Petrie and C. T. Currelly, *Researches in Sinai* (London: John Murray, 1906), pp. 247-50; A. E. Lucas, *The Route of the Exodus of the Israelites from Egypt* (London: Arnold, 1938), pp. 44-45, 68; G. E. Wright, *IDB*, 4:376-78; G. I. Davis, *The Way of the Wilderness* (Cambridge: Cambridge U., 1979), pp. x-xii; F. C. Fensham, *IBD*, 3:1460-61; C. E. Armerding, *NIDBA*, p. 416, and bibliographies.

Introduction). In antiquity events were frequently dated in relationship to a great personage or notable happening (e.g., Isa. 6:1;
Amos 1:1). The Exodus provided for the Hebrews an unforgettable
event against which other succeeding time-spans could be reckoned.

Translation

**Take a census of the entire Israelite community by their family
groups and families, registering every male individually by name.**
(1:2)

Exegesis and Exposition

The command "take" is in the plural, thus indicating that Aaron
was expected to participate in the work along with Moses (v. 3). The
complete phrase means literally "lift up the head" (MT שְׂאוּ אֶת־רֹאשׁ, *sĕ'*
û'et-rō'š) and occurs elsewhere (Ex. 30:12; Lev. 5:24; Num. 1:49; 4:2;
Ps. 119:160; etc.). "Counting heads" is a simple way of arriving at a
total where stable groups are concerned. The purpose of the census
was to establish a base for a standing army in Israel and was not
intended for economic or sociological reference, as with the majority
of modern census-takings. Thus it was different from that counting
undertaken by Moses prior to the construction of the Tabernacle (Ex.
30:11-16), which not merely enumerated the people but enabled a tax
to be levied. The use of a census for administrative and military
purposes long antedated Moses in the ancient Near East.

Many scholars have assumed that the census commanded in Ex.
30:11-16 was not carried out immediately and that the Numbers
record (1:20-46) preserved the details of the registration. But the
chronologies of Exodus and Numbers make it clear that two distinct
events are involved. Exodus gives no information about the census
procedure but records the total of 603,550 people who were enrolled
and who paid a tax of one hundred talents of silver and 1,775 shekels.
If one talent equaled 3,000 shekels, the total amount collected was
301,775 shekels, which was used to make metal parts for the sanctuary. By the time the census of Num. 1:20-46 had been taken, the
Tabernacle was already fully operative, so from this fact alone it is
clear that a different event was involved. Furthermore, a tax levy did
not form a part of the Numbers enumeration.

Family groups (MT מִשְׁפָּחוֹת, *mišpĕḥôt*) and families (MT בֵּית אָבֹת,
bêt'ăbôt) were subdivisions of the tribe (MT מַטֶּה, *maṭṭeh*, or שֵׁבֶט, *šēbeṭ*)
in diminishing order. Most modern versions translate *mišpĕḥôt* by
"clans," which is more expansive than the family but can and does
include blood relatives. I will employ "family groups" instead of
"clans," since the latter is a Gaelic term describing a patriarchally
controlled group descended from a common ancestor and carries

with it a non-Semitic nuance, even though it describes the so-ciological situation quite accurately.

Except for the Levites, no Israelite male was to be exempt from the census. The instructions to Moses and Aaron were specific: Every male was to be registered individually (MT לְגֻלְגְּלֹתָם, lĕgulgĕlōtām, "with respect to their skulls") and by name to ensure a complete count.

Translation

You and Aaron are to list by their divisions all the men aged twenty years or older who can serve in Israel's army. (1:3)

Exegesis and Exposition

The purpose of the census is stated clearly so that those who were registered would understand the implications of what they were doing. Men above the age of twenty years qualified for military service. The expression "serve in the army" (MT יֹצֵא צָבָא, yōṣē' ṣābā') occurs throughout this chapter and is found again in 26:2.

Exemptions for disabled persons are not mentioned, but they may well have been taken for granted. In the ancient Near East all war was fought on behalf of a national god and was therefore a religious duty that demanded certain conditions of ceremonial holiness (cf. 2 Sam. 11:11).[9] The chief god of a state was normally a war-deity, and Israel's God was no exception to this rule (Ex. 15:3; Ps. 24:8; etc.), the expression "LORD of armies" (MT יהוה צְבָאוֹת, YHWH ṣĕbā'ôt) occurring nearly 280 times in the MT.[10] To be a soldier in a nation's army, therefore, offered an individual the privilege of serving his god in a most practical manner, as well as securing divine blessing when victory occurred. Although the MT term צָבָא, ṣābā', is generally used of military groups, it is also employed for other purposes, as with the Levites who ministered in the Tabernacle (Num. 4:3, 23, 30, etc.). No upward age limit was placed on a man's military service in the Lord's directions to Moses and Aaron, and there were notable Hebrews who engaged in war when they were at an advanced age. In Lev. 27:3, the period in a man's life between 20 and 50 years was regarded as his most valuable and productive one, according to the scale of monetary valuation designated by the law.

---

9. On ancient Near Eastern warfare see Y. Yadin, *The Art of Warfare in Biblical Lands* (New York: McGraw-Hill, 1963); P. C. Craigie, *The Problem of War in the Old Testament* (Grand Rapids: Eerdmans, 1978). Josephus (*Ant.* 3.12.4) held that military service for the Israelites ceased in a soldier's fiftieth year.
10. See, however, Barker, ed., *The NIV: The Making of a Contemporary Translation*, pp. 109-10.

Translation

To help you there will be one man from each tribe who is the head of his family. (1:4)

Exegesis and Exposition

For such a formidable task Moses and Aaron clearly needed assistance. Consequently a small group of literate family heads, one from each tribe, would help in the task of counting and recording. These men would thus provide written records that Moses could employ later as source materials when compiling the book of Numbers. These persons were senior members of the community and therefore responsible individuals. To them can be traced the beginnings of the *šōṭĕrîm* tradition in Israel.

Translation

These are the names of the men who will assist you: from Reuben, Elizur son of Shedeur; from Simeon, Shelumiel son of Zurishaddai; from Judah, Nahshon son of Amminadab; from Issachar, Nethanel son of Zuar; from Zebulun, Eliab son of Helon; (1:5-9)

Exegesis and Exposition

The senior representatives of the tribes had been selected to help (MT עָמַד, *'āmad*, "stand") in the registration. They would also serve as leaders when the tribes moved from place to place in the wilderness (Num. 2:3-31; 10:15-38). The names of these leaders appear again in 2:3-31; 7:12-83; 10:14-27, but in a different sequence. Commentators have sometimes pointed out that the tribes are arranged on the basis of chronological descent from Jacob. Reuben was the firstborn son of Jacob and Leah in Paddan Aram (Gen. 29:31-32; 35:23), and was so named ("See, a son!") because by having a son Leah hoped to win Jacob's affection to some extent from her more attractive sister, Rachel. While the latter continued childless, Leah bore Simeon, Levi, Judah, Issachar, Zebulun, and a daughter named Dinah (Gen. 30:21). Dinah, being female, was ineligible for leadership, as were Levi and his descendants. In any event, God had made special provision for the Levites, as will appear subsequently.

Of those who were selected leaders, few are mentioned in the OT apart from their duties as described in Numbers. Elizur the Reubenite, like his father, Shedeur, is otherwise unknown, as are also Shelumiel of Simeon and his father, Zurishaddai. Amminadab the Judahite was more renowned, being the father of Elisheba, wife of Aaron (Ex. 6:23), and father of Nahshon. The latter was an ancestor of Boaz and David (Ruth 4:20-22), and thus of Jesus Christ (Luke 3:32-33). The leader of Issachar, Nethanel (KJV Nethaneel), was otherwise unknown, as was his father, Zuar. Helon of Zebulun and his son Eliab are unmentioned in the OT apart from the reference to them in Numbers. This group constituted the offspring of Jacob by his wife Leah.

Translation

from the sons of Joseph: from Ephraim, Elishama son of Ammihud; from Manasseh, Gamaliel son of Pedahzur; from Benjamin, Abidan son of Gideoni; (1:10-11)

Exegesis and Exposition

This next grouping represents the offspring of Jacob by Rachel, with Joseph as her firstborn after years of frustration and infertility (Gen. 30:22-24). The leaders of the tribe of Joseph were chosen from the two branches procreated by Joseph's two sons: Ephraim his second-born son, and Manasseh his firstborn (Gen. 41:50-52). Although neither was of pure Semitic stock, having as their mother an Egyptian named Asenath, they were adopted by a grateful Jacob in Egypt and given the standing of such direct offspring as Reuben and Simeon (Gen. 48:5).

Ephraim, whose name means "doubly fruitful," had thousands of descendants, and the tribe became one of the most numerous in Israel (Gen. 48:19; Num. 1:32). Elishama son of Ammihud represented Ephraim, and both men achieved distinction by being ancestors of Joshua (1 Chron. 7:26-27). Manasseh furnished leadership in the personage of Gamaliel son of Pedahzur, but both men are unknown otherwise, although the name Gamaliel persisted into NT times (Acts 5:34-39; 22:3).

Rachel died after a difficult labor as she gave birth to her second son, whom in her dying moments she named Ben-Oni ("son of my sorrow"). Subsequently Jacob renamed him Benjamin ("son of the right hand"). Despite Jacob's obvious preference for Rachel, it is significant that the messianic line descended through Leah and her son Judah. Instead, Rachel became subsequently the symbol of the hardship and tragedy that the Israelites encountered (Jer. 31:15). Matthew saw in the slaughter by Herod the Great of the male infants of Bethlehem the fulfillment of Jeremiah's doleful prophecy (Matt. 2:16-18). Abidan, the leader of Benjamin, was the son of Gideoni, but both are unmentioned outside Numbers.

Translation

from Dan, Ahiezer son of Ammishaddai; from Asher, Pagiel son of Ocran; from Gad, Eliasaph son of* Deuel; from Naphtali, Ahira son of Enan. (1:12-15)

38

Exegesis and Exposition

Continuing the genealogical succession were the sons of Leah's handmaid Zilpah, who acted as a concubine for Jacob and produced Gad and Asher (Gen. 30:9-13; 35:26). In accordance with ancient Near Eastern tradition these babies would have been delivered onto the knees of the legal wife to make them legitimate family members and consequent heirs. The same would have been the case for the sons of Bilhah, Rachel's maid, who was also given to Jacob as a concubine (Gen. 35:25) and bore him sons named Dan and Naphtali.

The tribe of Dan was led by Ahiezer son of Ammishaddai, but the record of their activities was restricted to one or two references in Numbers. The Asherites were under the leadership of Pagiel son of Ocran (KJV, Ochran), but apart from their relationship and Pagiel's leadership nothing further is known about them. The leader of the Gadites was Eliasaph son of Deuel, but there is little information about these two men. Ahira son of Enan was the one appointed to represent the tribe of Naphtali, but outside the Numbers references nothing further is known about them.

The order in which the tribes of Dan, Asher, Gad, and Naphtali appear in the first chapter of Numbers varies from the sort of genealogical pattern that was being followed with the other sons of Jacob. Had the order of their births followed the chronology of the Genesis narratives, the four eponymous ancestors would have been listed after the birth of Judah and before that of Issachar and would have followed the order Dan, Naphtali, Gad, Asher. While it is evident that the children of concubines were placed at the end of the list of tribes in this chapter, any other reason for the divergence from the chronological order is unknown.

Some of the names in the list contain theophoric elements, syllables that reflect divinity. Thus Ammishaddai contains the form שַׁדָּי (*šadday*, "Almighty"), and hence his name has been taken to mean "the Almighty is (my) kinsman." Ancient names for God that appear in some titles are אָב (*'āb*, "father"), as in Eliab, which possibly means "(My) God is Father"; אֵל (*'ēl*), the common Semitic name for deity, found in Eliasaph, which may mean "(My) God has added"; צוּר (*ṣûr*, "Rock"), as in Zurishaddai, "the Almighty is (my) Rock"; and the common word אָח (*'āḥ*, "brother"), found in Ahiezer, which perhaps means "(My) brother is help."

All these theophoric elements antedate the second millennium B.C. and indicate something of the antiquity of these names. It is also noteworthy that some of the names in the list came to an end in the second millennium B.C., because they do not occur again after the period of the wilderness wanderings.

39

Although meanings have been suggested above for some names, caution must be urged in any attempts to derive the understanding of ancient names based upon supposed theophoric elements. For example, the tablets from Ebla, dated about 2400 B.C., contain names that end in *-ya*, which can be understood as a shortened form of the Hebrew tetragrammaton YHWH. From this evidence it could be concluded that the Eblaites were early believers in the God who revealed His name YHWH formally to Moses (Ex. 6:3). But further study of the complex language of Ebla seems to indicate that *-ya* was more probably a diminutive element, so that a name such as Abijah, for example, which is traditionally interpreted to mean "the Lord is my father," could well have been merely a traditional way of saying "my daddy."[11]

The way in which the Hebrew tribes were consistently reckoned as totaling twelve, representing the number of the sons of Jacob, is apt to be perplexing to the modern reader because of the variation of names, due to Jacob's adoption of Ephraim and Manasseh, the sons of Joseph, as his own sons. Consequently if the tribe of Levi is mentioned, only one tribe of Joseph is listed. But if Levi is not listed in the record, Joseph is divided into Ephraim and Manasseh. In the ordering of the tribes, Levi's place is assigned to Gad (Num. 1:26). To make the situation even more complex, it should also be remembered that tribal lines were not always drawn sharply in antiquity and could easily be blurred as the result of migrations or intermarriage.

Each tribe was treated on a basis of complete equality with all the others. Every one of them, of course, claimed a common ancestor, whether they were the offspring of Jacob's union with his legitimate wives Leah and Rachel or with the concubines that they provided for him. While the listing follows only general chronological order, no attempt was made to establish the superiority of one genealogy in relation to another or to formulate some kind of hierarchy. Instead, the covenant ethic of Sinai prevailed in requiring the Israelites to live and act as though each individual was a priest who was required to live with all the others as members of a holy nation. The same concept is applied in the NT to the Christian church by Peter, who urges holiness of life upon the believers (1 Pet. 1:15-16) and reminds them that they indeed constitute a royal priesthood and a holy nation (2:9).

Translation

These persons were chosen from the community of Israel, being leaders of their ancestral tribes and heads of their family groups. (1:16)

---

11. Cf. C. Bermant and M. Weitzman, *Ebla: A Revelation in Archaeology* (New York: Times Books, 1979), pp. 178-82.

Exegesis and Exposition

The individuals so appointed were God's choice, and not that of Moses, who merely carried out God's orders. Thus they were different from the advisers whom Moses selected on the advice of Jethro, his father-in-law (Ex. 18:15-26). Those persons, of unknown number, were of high character and were appointed to serve as judges and administrators in Israel. The ones now selected to assist Moses came from a somewhat later period of the initial wilderness wanderings and made up a group of literate officers to whom the origins of the *šōṭĕrîm* can be traced. There is a little uncertainty in the reading of the MT, but the meaning is clearly that they were called by God as competent leaders of Israelite community groups (MT אַלְפֵי, *'alpê*, lit. "thousands of"). No assessment is made of the full size of these community groups.

2. CENSUS (1:17-46)

Translation

So Moses and Aaron took these men who had been mentioned by name, and they assembled the entire community on the first day of the second month. The people recorded their ancestry by their families and family groups, and the men who were twenty years of age or older were listed by name individually, as the LORD had commanded Moses. Thus he compiled the register in the Sinai wilderness. (1:17-19)

Exegesis and Exposition

With the selection of officials who would conduct the census, Moses and Aaron were now able to commence the process of enrollment. They could be confident that the integrity of the officials, and the respect in which they were held by their families and the community as a whole, would furnish an adequate safeguard against carelessness, corruption, or indifference in the Lord's work. The narrative can be divided into two separate subsections: (1) the assembly of the community (vv. 17-19) and (2) the census statistics (vv. 20-46).

The nominating of leaders and the actual census took place immediately upon the Lord's command, and the people complied with the instructions to furnish their family ancestry. Because they constituted the only history that most individuals were likely to encounter, such records of ancestry (תֹּלְדוֹת, *tōlĕdôt*) were of great importance to the Hebrews, as they were to other ancient Near Eastern peoples. Needless to say, they were to prove extremely valuable where such matters as tribal membership and inheritance claims were involved.

41

The use of *tōlĕdôt* in Num. 1:20-42 is different from that in the eleven suggested colophons of Genesis, where it occurs in a technical scribal context as a consistent description of "narratives" or "(family) histories" in written form. In Numbers the term refers to biological descent from an ancestor and thus occurs in an entirely different context.

The registration statistics that were collected by the leaders would most probably have been assembled almost immediately in the form of a register.[12] Again, the main purpose of the procedure was noted, which was to have available the names of all able-bodied men for military conscription. Conscientious objection would have been regarded as rebellion against the Lord's leadership of the nation in a holy war against His enemies. Prompt and implicit obedience marked this particular phase of the wilderness journeyings.

Translation

From the descendants of Reuben, Israel's oldest son: According to the records of their family groups and families, all the men aged twenty years or older who were fit for military service were listed individually by name. The number from the tribe of Reuben was 46,500.

From the descendants of Simeon: According to the records of their family groups and families, all the men aged twenty years or older who were fit for military service were counted and listed individually by name. The number from the tribe of Simeon was 59,300.

*From the descendants of Gad: According to the records of their family groups and families, all the men aged twenty years or older who were fit for military service were listed individually by name. The number from the tribe of Gad was 45,650. (1:20-25)

Exegesis and Exposition

The census lists of the various tribes were reported according to a stereotyped pattern, which suited the character of the materials and made for easy memorization. The use of standard phraseology is marked by slight variations that probably reflected the individuality of the recording officials. Stereotyped expressions in Hebrew laws, cultic rituals, genealogies, and the like are common in the OT. The compilation of the register by tribes involved: (1) the name of the tribe, (2) the conditions required by the terms of the enrollment, (3) the repetition of the tribe's name, and (4) the total number of those registered. This was an administrative procedure that provided for only the barest minimum of error. The numbers will be seen to be

---

12. Cf. M. Noth, *Numbers*, p. 20.

approximate to one hundred, except for the tribe of Gad, which is rounded off to fifty (v. 25).

The order of the census records varies slightly from that of the list of recording officials, with the records of Gad being inserted before those of Judah in the MT. There appears to have been some difference of opinion about the propriety of this in antiquity, since the Pentateuchal text from which the LXX was prepared apparently placed Num. 1:24-25 after v. 37. This change, of course, could well have been made by the translator in the interests of consistency.

Translation

From the descendants of Judah: According to the records of their family groups and families, all the men aged twenty years or older who were fit for military service were listed by name. The number from the tribe of Judah was 74,600.

From the descendants of Issachar: According to the records of their family groups and families, all the men aged twenty years or older who were fit for military service were listed by name. The number from the tribe of Issachar was 54,400.

From the descendants of Zebulun: According to the records of their family groups and families, all the men aged twenty years or older who were fit for military service were listed by name. The number from the tribe of Zebulun was 57,400. (1:26-31)

Exegesis and Exposition

With this section of the enrollment the offspring of Leah are complete. The tribe of Judah, from which the Messiah descended, was considerably more populous than the others.

The offspring of the sons of Jacob born to Rachel came next.

Translation

From the sons of Joseph: From the descendants of Ephraim according to the records of their family groups and families, all the men aged twenty years or older who were fit for military service were listed by name. The number from the tribe of Ephraim was 40,500.

From the descendants of Manasseh according to the records of their family groups and families, all the men aged twenty years or older who were fit for military service were listed by name. The number from the tribe of Manasseh was 32,200.

From the descendants of Benjamin: According to the records of their family groups and families, all the men aged twenty years or older who were fit for military service were listed by name. The number from the tribe of Benjamin was 35,400. (1:32-37)

Exegesis and Exposition

The Ephraimites, who were among the most numerous of the twelve tribes, took precedence over Manasseh, according to the blessing and promise of the aged Jacob (Gen. 48:13-20). In this instance the patriarch, in adopting Joseph's sons as his own children, ignored other considerations and instead exercised an ancient patriarchal right reflected in the code of Hammurapi, section 170. Whatever the feelings of Joseph's brothers about the procedure may have been, they were in no position to contest the decision, since it was an integral part of Jacob's last will and testament. Jacob's action established the tradition that thereafter the order of precedence should be Ephraim, followed by Manasseh, and so it continued throughout the biblical tradition.

The offspring of Rachel are fully accounted for by this section of the register. Because the tribe of Levi was exempt from military duty so that it could fulfill other important functions, the tribe of Joseph was registered under two sections as represented by his sons in order to maintain the traditional number of twelve.

Translation

From the descendants of Dan: According to the records of their family groups and families, all the men aged twenty years or older who were fit for military service were registered by name. The number from the tribe of Dan was 62,700.

From the descendants of Asher: According to the records of their family groups and families, all the men aged twenty years or older who were suitable for military service were registered by name. The number from the tribe of Asher was 41,500.

***From the descendants of Naphtali: According to the records of their family groups and families, all the men aged twenty years or older who were fit for military service were registered by name. The number from the tribe of Naphtali was 53,400.** (1:38-43)

Exegesis and Exposition

The descendants of Dan, the firstborn son of Bilhah, Rachel's maid, were second in number to the tribe of Judah in being able to provide 62,700.

Translation

These were the numbers recorded by Moses and Aaron and the twelve leaders of Israel, *each one of whom represented his family. According to the records of their families, all the Israelites who were

fit for military service were enumerated. The total number was 603,550. (1:44-46)

Exegesis and Exposition

The size of these numbers has provoked discussion for many years, and various investigators have attempted to make them conform to modern ideas of reality. Some writers have suggested that the MT אֶלֶף (*'elep*, "thousand"), be rendered by "family" or "tent group,"[13] and this, with modifications, has commended itself to others,[14] even though the MT already contains its own term for "family."

Another suggestion, based upon a related Ugaritic term (*'lp*), was to revocalize the MT word to read אַלּוּף (*'allûp*, "chief," "captain," "leader"), as in Gen. 36:15; Ex. 15:15, and elsewhere.[15] On such a basis the total Israelite army could be computed at approximately 18,000 soldiers coming from a total population of about 72,000 people, as compared with 603,550 fighting men and a population of over two million Israelites if the MT figures are to be taken as they stand. It should be noted, however, that the figures given in the Numbers narrative are consistent with those contained in Ex. 12:37; 38:26.

A different approach has taken the figures as the calculations based upon the numerical value of the letters of a word or series of words.[16] But *gematria*, as this type of artificial calculation is known, is open to objections,[17] such as the fact that this system of numerical equivalents only came into use during the Maccabean period (second century B.C.). On such a reckoning the Hebrew letters for בני ישראל ("Israelites") would total 603, whereas Num. 1:46 gives the first census reckoning as 603,550. Discrepancies of this kind are much too large and unrealistic to give credibility to the system. Yet another proposal regards the numbers as having been evaluated on a basis of reckoning that used epic proportions in a manner that is no longer

---

13. So W. M. F. Petrie and C. T. Currelly, *Researches in Sinai*, pp. 207-10; A. H. McNeile, *The Book of Numbers* (Cambridge: Cambridge U., 1911), p. 7; J. Garstang, *Joshua-Judges*, p. 120.
14. E.g., G. E. Mendenhall, "The Census Lists of Numbers 1 and 26," *JBL* 77 (1958): 52-66; J. Bright, *A History of Israel* (London: SCM, 1959 ed.), p. 144.
15. So R. E. D. Clarke, "The Large Numbers of the Old Testament," *Journal of the Transactions of the Victoria Institute* 87 (1955): 82-92, and followed with some modifications by J. W. Wenham, "Large Numbers in the Old Testament," *TynBul* 18 (1967): 19-53.
16. H. Holzinger, *Numeri* (Tübingen/Leipzig: Mohr, 1903); G. Fohrer, *Introduction to the Old Testament* (London: SPCK; E tr. 1970), p. 184.
17. Cf. A. Noordtzij, *Numbers* (Grand Rapids: Zondervan, E tr. 1983), p. 24.

familiar to modern scholars. This view comes into conflict with the instructions in Num. 1:2, however, where God insists upon a literal head count.

Another objection to the large numbers is the statement of Moses (Deut. 7:7) that the Israelites were by comparison with contemporary nations the smallest numerically. This statement, of course, could have referred to the political and social importance of a group that, at the time, was virtually unknown as a national entity and entirely untried in battle.

On the assumption that the census records actually reflected the armed forces of the united monarchy period, some scholars, including Albright, suggested that the figures of Num. 1 constituted a retrojection to the Exodus period. There are two major objections to this view, however. First, the Numbers records depict Simeon as a strong (59,300) and independent tribe, whereas by the time of the monarchy it was in decline and merging with the tribe of Judah. Second, the figures of Numbers 1 are still large for the period of David and Solomon, thus calling the suggestion into serious question. If, as some scholars have indicated, there is the possibility of textual corruption, it has to be posited also of the numbers listed in Ex. 12:37; 38:26, where such a contingency is hard to demonstrate. Another attempt to account for the meaning of the term 'elep has been to interpret it as a "unit" or a "division" composed of a certain number of combatants. Thus to take the tribe of Reuben as an example, the total number of soldiers recorded as 46,500 could have meant "46 units totaling 500 men." Depending upon the size of the tribe, the "units" would have varied in size from 200 to 700 warriors. Although this approach has the advantage of bringing the numbers into greater consonance with those found in ancient Near Eastern texts that described the size of marauding groups, it encounters the formidable obstacle of the literal head count prescribed in Num. 1:2. Furthermore, the grand total of 603,550 cannot possibly mean "603 units totaling 550 men."

That the Israelites were clearly becoming a numerical threat to the Egyptians is indicated in Ex. 1:7. Pharaoh attempted to counter the population growth by instructing the Hebrew midwives to institute a policy of infanticide in the case of newborn Hebrew males. The fact that the names of the midwives were preserved indicates that they occupied an important position in the community, although scholars have wondered why only two such women were sufficient to serve so large a population. Most probably, however, these women were in administrative positions, supervising the activities of the Hebrew midwives and not performing the actual deliveries themselves. Although the LXX and the Vulgate seem to imply that they were non-Hebrew midwives who attended the Hebrew women, an attitude disproved by the discovery that Shiphrah and Puah were in fact genuine northwest Semitic women's names in the second millennium B.C., the problem still remains. Little is actually known about midwifery techniques in ancient Egypt, but the use of "birth stools" (MT אָבְנָיִם, 'obnayim, rendered "potter's wheel" in Jer. 18:3) implies that the women gave birth in a semi-upright position, which would necessitate both a supervisor and the presence of assistants.[18]

From these brief comments it will be apparent that there are difficulties with the large numbers both here and elsewhere in the OT that cannot be resolved without further information. Some believe that two million people could not have survived long in the wilderness, while others object to the large size of Israel's army on various grounds. A military force of 10,000 men was apparently common in the time of Hammurapi (c. 1790-1750 B.C.),[19] while an ordinary raiding party of 318 soldiers was mentioned in the Amarna letters (cf. Gen. 14:14), along with units of fifties and hundreds.[20] An elaborate explanation based on astronomical calculations has been adduced by Barnouin,[21] but its chief problem is that it presupposes a cultural background far more advanced in the areas of mathematics than was the case with the wandering Israelites. The conclusion at which Gispen arrived will probably be shared by many—namely, that the numbers in the MT are correct, whatever the accompanying difficulties.[22] A final sobering fact is that, regardless of whether the numbers are to be taken as they stand, all the members of that generation except Joshua and Caleb died before the Promised Land was finally occupied.

The modern reader could perhaps be forgiven for wondering, as many scholars have done, what possible reasons there could be in a wilderness environment for the mustering of such a large defensive force, when any opposition that might arise would be comparatively small. The answer seems to be that, at the time of the registration, the Israelites were expecting to march across the wilderness to the borders of Canaan as a prelude to invading and occupying the land that God had promised to them.

To be successful in this endeavor, an impressive military group

---

18. Cf. B. S. Childs, *Exodus*, pp. 16-17, 22-24.
19. D. Kellermann, "Die Priesterschrift von Numeri 1,1 bis 10,10," *BZAW* 120 (1970): 161; G. E. Mendenhall, *JBL* 77 (1958): 64-65.
20. W. F. Albright and G. E. Mendenhall, *ANET*, pp. 485-89.
21. M. Barnouin, "Les recensements du Livre des Nombres et l'astronomie babylonienne," *VT* 27 (1977): 280-303. Cf. G. J. Wenham, *Numbers*, pp. 62-66.
22. W. H. Gispen, *Het boek Numeri* (Commentar op het Oude Testament, 1959–1964; Kampen: J. H. Kok), 1:33.

was necessary as a visible demonstration of strength, so that if word of the magnitude of Israel's army preceded the arrival of the forces, the psychological effect would make the occupation of Canaan much easier. In fact, this kind of information did reach Israel's opponents in Transjordan with devastating effect (Num. 22:3), though the means of communication remains unknown. Unfortunately the plans for a speedy occupation of the promised homeland had to be abandoned by the Israelites after a reconnaissance expedition brought back a largely negative report (13:16-33). For their complaints and lack of faith in God's already-demonstrated power to provide, the people were sentenced to death in the wilderness, and a new mustering of smaller proportions, intended for a different purpose, was necessary before Transjordan and Canaan could be conquered (26:1-51).

The registration for military service followed the general traditions of the Middle Bronze Age, in which members of family groups and tribes were under obligation to fight defensive or offensive actions when summoned by their leaders. Some kings had substantial military forces at their command, and these included units that were especially trained in specific forms of warfare. But other armed groups, of which the Israelites were one, consisted predominantly of agricultural workers, pastoralists, and skilled craftsmen, none of whom could be expected to display significant military expertise. What the Israelites lacked in direct experience of war, however, they hoped to make up in sheer weight of numbers. In the end their expectations were rewarded, but not before they had succumbed to severe chastening from their God.

3. EXEMPTION OF LEVITES (1:47-54)

Translation

The families of the Levites, however, were not counted when the others were included in the compilation, because the LORD had instructed Moses: The only tribe that you must not enumerate is that of Levi. Do not include them in the lists of the other Israelites.

You shall appoint the Levites to be in charge of the Tabernacle of the Testimony and responsible for all its furnishings and equipment.

They shall carry the Tabernacle and all its furnishings, and they shall attend to it and camp around it. (1:47-50)

Exegesis and Exposition

The reason for segregating the Levites during the enumeration was to stress their future functions as appointed (i.e., set apart) ministers of the Tabernacle. They were required to maintain a condition of ceremonial holiness as part of their office, and therefore they could not prejudice their separation by indulging in certain activities such as fighting, which could incur ritual defilement under some conditions, such as contact with the dead. From this period onward the priesthood was the prerogative of the descendants of Levi, third son of Leah (Gen. 35:23), although there were other individuals outside that tribe who served as priests at various times (e.g., Judg. 17:5), following ancient patriarchal traditions (cf. Gen. 14:18; Ex. 18:1).

The Levites were the guardians of the Tabernacle, spoken of in v. 50 as the "Tabernacle of the Testimony" (MT מִשְׁכַּן הָעֵדֻת, *miškan hāʿēdut*). The tribe was chosen for this task instead of the firstborn sons of the tribal configuration of Israel, but in any event the numbers of both groups were very close (cf. Num. 3:39, 43). The Tabernacle was given this name because the tablets containing the Decalogue were put for safekeeping in the Ark of the Covenant by Moses. But the tent that made up the Holy Place and the Most Holy Place was also a covenant reminder (MT עֵדֻת, *ʿēdut*, "warning sign," "testimony") as were the curtains and the other cultic appurtenances of Israel's most sacred shrine. The rendering "testimony" reflects a cognate relationship between the Hebrew *ʿēdut* and the Akkadian *adê*, "covenant," "treaty."

In second-millennium B.C. Near Eastern traditions, one copy of the agreement made between a great overlord and a nation that had entered into a vassal relationship with him was kept by him, and a second copy was kept in the most sacred place honored by the vassal, so that it would be readily accessible for use in covenant-renewal ceremonies (cf. Josh. 24:25). In the case of the Israelites, both tablets of the law (one of which was a copy of the other) were kept in the Ark of the Covenant, as the sacred Ark was sometimes called.[23]

The duties attached to the Ark were thus of the highest ceremonial and religious importance. The Ark itself was a small, rectangular, box-like structure of acacia wood, plated inside and out with hammered gold and capped with a tightly fitting, solid gold lid surmounted by two gold cherubim. It was the chief cultic object of the Israelites and measured two and one-half cubits long, one and one-half cubits wide, and one and one-half cubits high (Ex. 25:10-15), or about forty-five by twenty-seven by twenty-seven inches. The por-

---

23. Cf. M. Kline, *Treaty of the Great King* (Grand Rapids: Eerdmans, 1963), pp. 14-19; *The Structure of Biblical Authority* (Grand Rapids: Eerdmans, 1972), pp. 35-36. The Ark was also the repository for a golden pot of manna (Ex. 16:32-34) and Aaron's rod that produced shoots (Num. 17:1-11). This tradition was being maintained even in NT times (Heb. 9:4). But at the dedication of Solomon's Temple only the tablets of the law remained in the Ark (1 Kings 8:9). The fate of the two other items is unknown.

table nature of the Ark was emphasized by the presence of carrying poles, which fitted into rings fastened to the side of the Ark (Ex. 37:1-9). Great care had to be exercised when moving it, lest accidental contact should result in death (cf. 1 Chron. 13:10).

In modern electronic terminology the Ark would be regarded as a giant capacitor, a simplified form of a condenser that stored an electrostatic charge. Most probably this charge would have been built up when God descended in power upon the finished Tabernacle (Ex. 40:34) and maintained thereafter by the dry wilderness atmosphere. The prohibitions against touching the Ark were intended to prevent a fatal discharge (cf. Uzzah in 2 Sam. 6:6-7). To ensure the safety of the community the Levites were grouped around the Tabernacle. They were committed to the ideal of holiness and were subservient to the civil leadership of Moses and subsequently Joshua, as well as to the high priest Aaron and his successors.

Translation

Whenever the tent is to move, the Levites shall dismantle it; and when the tent is to be reassembled, the Levites shall erect it. Any unauthorized person who approaches it shall be killed. The Israelites shall pitch their tents according to their divisions, with every man in his proper camp under his own standard.

But the Levites are to erect their tents around the Tabernacle of the Testimony so that divine anger will not beset the Israelites. The Levites are to be responsible for the Tabernacle of the Testimony. The Israelites did all this exactly as the LORD had commanded Moses. (1:51-54)

Exegesis and Exposition

The Lord's instructions were clear: The Levites alone were to attend to the dismantling and erecting of the Tabernacle when the tribes were on the march. They were to camp around it when stationary so as to prevent accidental defilement by curious strangers or wandering animals, or unauthorized entry by a group such as a desert raiding party. The kind of person referred to in v. 51 (MT זָר, *zār*, "stranger" KJV) was primarily an outsider who did not belong to the families of Israel by birth but had attached himself to the nation in some manner. The Israelites tended to regard such persons with caution, while at the same time offering hospitality to them. They seem to have been dispossessed persons belonging originally to other nations, and hence the Israelites were warned in later times (cf. Joel 3:17 [MT 4:17]) about the dangers of Israelite religion being defiled by the worship and cultic traditions of the "outsiders" (MT זָרִים, *zārîm*). Under the conditions laid down by the Lord, death was to be the penalty inflicted upon anyone who approached the sacred shrine without proper authorization. This regulation draws attention to the fundamental theme with which the first ten chapters of Numbers are concerned—namely, the importance of holiness in every aspect of community life.[24]

As a result, it was mandatory for the people to be dedicated to the spiritual ideals of the covenant God of Sinai and to resolve never to permit any defilement or pagan intrusion to destroy their relationship with Him. They were to be a holy people—socially, morally, and religiously—and the formal motto of the nation could well be taken from the engraving on the front of Aaron's ceremonial turban: "Holiness to the LORD." At this stage of the wanderings, still in the full flush of enthusiasm for the covenant following the dramatic events on Mount Sinai, the people obeyed the Lord's commands through Moses implicitly, as indicated in the assent formula with which the first chapter concludes.

God's ancient covenant with His people was based upon love (MT חֶסֶד, *ḥesed*), and the continuation of that same love in the New Covenant wrought by the shed blood of Christ (John 3:16) has led to the common assumption that love is the key to all the deep mysteries of the spiritual life. A closer reading of Scripture, however, reveals that in all ages God requires of His people the twin attributes of obedience and holiness. The latter is impossible without the former, so that, in the end, the most important attitude of the believer is obedience. At the covenant ratification ceremony on Mount Sinai the Israelites had made a solemn pledge to be obedient to all the Lord's stipulations (Ex. 24:7). In any event, their destiny was to turn upon their fidelity or infidelity to this solemn undertaking. For the Christian, the model of obedience to the Father's will is Jesus Christ, who was continually submissive up to the very point of dying on the cross (Phil. 2:8).

Additional Notes

1:1 מֹשֶׁה: For the etymology of this name see J. K. Hoffmeier, *ISBE*, 3:416-17.

1:2 שְׂאוּ: Although Moses was addressed in 1:1, this plural verb form indicates that Aaron, the religious leader of Israel, was also included. The command to Moses came in his capacity as civil leader of the Israelites, because the census was meant primarily for military purposes.

עֵדָה, "community," is normally rendered συναγωγή in the LXX, conveying the idea of "congregation" or "assembly." In the light of

---

24. Cf. B. S. Childs, *Introduction to the Old Testament as Scripture* (Philadelphia: Fortress, 1979), p. 196.

the instructions that the census was to be taken on an individual basis (לְגֻלְגְּלֹתָם), it is interesting to observe that some rounding off of totals seems to have been done.

1:3 אַהֲרֹן: For the etymology of this name see E. Mack, *ISBE*, 1:1.

צָבָא can mean a "host" or an "army," and by implication "war" or "battle." Commentators such as Noth, Snaith, and Wenham, *in loco*, have frequently interpreted the term as the equivalent of "military host." This should not be pressed too closely, however, since in 4:3, 23, etc., it is used of the religious service of the Levites in the Tent of Meeting.

The Samaritan Pentateuch renders תִּפְקְדוּ by the singular person, presumably to accord with 1:1.

1:4 אִישׁ אִישׁ לַמַּטֶּה expresses a distributive function, "a man for each tribe," as also אִישׁ רֹאשׁ לְבֵית אֲבֹתָיו, "each man the head of his father's house."

1:5 לְ occurs here as a prefix to tribal nominal sentences and serves as a preposition of specification, "with regard to Reuben," etc.

1:8 לְיִשָּׂשכָר: A *qere perpetuum* form. LXX reads Ἰσσαχάρ.

1:14 The father of the Gadite leader was known as רְעוּאֵל (LXX Ῥαγουήλ) in Num. 2:14, but דְּעוּאֵל in 7:42, 47; 10:20. There is considerable variation of MS tradition, with several favoring דְּעוּאֵל over רְעוּאֵל. BHS preferred דְּעוּאֵל, but the LXX read Ῥαγουήλ consistently. ד and ר are often confused in scribal transmission.

1:16 The *qere*, קְרוּאֵי, "those that had been chosen," is preferred to the *kethib*, קְרִיאֵי, which is probably the result of a copying error.

1:19 The LXX includes the MT כַּאֲשֶׁר צִוָּה יהוה אֶת-מֹשֶׁה as part of 1:18, which would furnish the section with a concluding assent formula. The resultant gain, however, is of minimal value, as is the BHS option to repoint וַיִּפְקְדֵם to a plural form in order to include Aaron and the chosen leaders.

1:22 Some scholars, with BHS, have suggested omitting פְּקֻדָיו, KJV, "those that were numbered of them," to preserve the character of the literary formula throughout, following the LXX and some MT MSS. Most modern commentators follow this practice in the interests of stylistic uniformity.

1:25 The enrollment data for Gad do not appear in this order in the LXX but are placed following 1:37. The dislocation may well have been deliberate to reflect Gad's position with Reuben and Simeon in the encampment and on the march.

1:42 The preposition has been omitted from בְּנֵי, being most probably dropped accidentally in transmission. Most modern translations restore it to maintain uniformity of style, following some MT MSS, the LXX, Vulgate, and Samaritan Pentateuch.

1:44 Scholars have found the phrase אִישׁ-אֶחָד לְבֵית-אֲבֹתָיו unusual.

BHS proposed emending it by removing אִישׁ־אֶחָד and following the
pattern of 1:4 by substituting לְמַטֶּה אֶחָד אִישׁ רֹאשׁ, influenced by the LXX
and other versions. Such an emendation is unnecessary, however, if
the disputed phrase is regarded as a summary statement occurring at
the end of the tabulations.

1:48 The MT אַךְ is rendered vigorously in the LXX by ὅρα, "see to
it that," "take care that." This Hebrew adverbial particle means
"but," "only," "surely." See R. J. Williams, *Hebrew Syntax* (Toronto: U.
of Toronto, 1967), p. 67, secs. 388-89.

1:50 וְאַתָּה serves to differentiate between the enumeration of the
Israelites and the appointment of the Levites to their special tasks in
the Tabernacle. On the use of פָּקַד in connection with Levitical service
see M. Gertner, "The Masorah and the Levites," *VT* 10 (1960): 252.

1:53 For קֶצֶף, "anger," "wrath," the LXX has ἁμάρτημα, "sin,"
"failure," which shifts the narrative's perspective from divine retribution to human error.

1:54 Following אֶת־מֹשֶׁה, the LXX inserts καὶ 'Ααρών, without any
textual justification in the Hebrew, but perhaps as a recognition of
the role that Aaron would play as the head of the Levitical priesthood.

B. ARRANGEMENT OF THE CAMP (2:1–3:1)

An analysis of this chapter reveals that it is made up of six main
components: (1) eastern tribes (vv. 1-9); (2) southern tribes (vv. 10-16);
(3) central group (v. 17); (4) western tribes (vv. 18-24); (5) northern
tribes (vv. 25-31); (6) summary (vv. 32-34).

1. EASTERN TRIBES (2:1-9)

Translation

The LORD spoke to Moses and Aaron, saying: Every one of the
Israelites shall encamp beneath the standard of his own division,
near the emblems of his family. They shall pitch their tents at some
distance from the Tent of Meeting. Toward the sunrise, on the east,
the divisions of Judah shall encamp beneath their standard. Nahshon
the son of Amminadab will lead the people of Judah. *His division
numbers 74,600. (2:1-4)

Exegesis and Exposition

In the ancient Near East, in order to gain a proper geographical
orientation the peoples faced in the direction of the rising sun—that is,
eastward. Once in this position they recognized that north lay to the
left hand, south to the right, and behind them was the west. For later
Israel the western border of her land was the Mediterranean Sea.

53

The concern of this chapter is to institute the arrangements resulting in the permanent deployment of the Israelites around the Tabernacle in the form of a rectangle. Nineteenth-century critics considered this type of formation as evidence of a late date for Numbers. Since then, however, further studies have shown that such a pattern was familiar in the Amarna Age. Kitchen has pointed out that the same format of deployment occurred under Rameses II (c. 1290-1224 B.C.), who would have been a contemporary of Moses if the Exodus occurred in the thirteenth century B.C. At that time Rameses was campaigning in Syria, and as was customary he took with him for divinatory purposes the large portable war tent of the divine king. This sacred shrine was guarded by Egyptian soldiers, whose divisions were encamped around it in a rectangular pattern.[25] A striking attestation to the historical accuracy of the rectangle formation of Numbers as a second-millennium B.C. phenomenon is that, in the following millennium, such military encampments were deployed in the round, as evidenced from Assyrian reliefs.

Thus the twelve tribes were also functioning defensively as a military guard, set to ward off attacks upon their shrine. They were encamped as a mobilized force, beside their standards (MT דְּגָלִים, děgālîm) and family emblems (MT אֹתֹת, 'ōtōt). In the ancient Near East a standard was a symbol fastened to the end of a pole and carried in the air in a manner similar to a flag. Its purpose was to signal for war trumpets to be sounded (cf. Isa. 5:26); to rally a company of soldiers, or even a tribe, so as to continue a battle; to point the direction to be followed at the start of a journey; or to rally the community for religious purposes. The design of these standards is nowhere described in Scripture, but on the analogy of the serpent emblem mentioned in Num. 21:8-9, it is possible that some standards displayed representations of animals or birds.[26] This is uncertain at best, however, in the light of the prohibitions of Ex. 20:4, and it may be that the poles merely displayed streamers of colored cloth. Jewish interpreters have understood the emblems traditionally as a type of flag bearing individual symbols.[27] Since the emblems were associated with a

25. K. A. Kitchen, "Some Egyptian Background to the Old Testament," p. 11; *HIOT*, p. 623.
26. Standards normally exhibited sacred cult animals, some of them of an imaginary form. Lions, wolves, unicorns, and horses were popular as ensigns or badges for standards, while the Assyrians favored a representation of the moon to honor Ashur, their principal deity. Ancient Near Eastern armies were normally preceded on the march by national cultic symbols. See T. W. Mann, *Divine Presence and Guidance in Israelite Tradition* (Baltimore: Johns Hopkins, 1969), pp. 169-73.
27. J. H. Hertz, ed., *The Pentateuch and Haftorahs*, p. 572.

group that was just one minor element of a tribe, it is possible that the special indicators of a family were small banners that, because of their size, could not be confused with the larger standards borne by the tribes. Having regard to the various symbols with which the family banner might have been decorated, the small flags would have made for easier identification.

The process of organizing large numbers of people according to a predetermined pattern was itself an imposing task, particularly for those for whom the departure from Egypt meant an end to discipline and regimentation. But this procedure served at least two important purposes: (1) each tribe knew its exact station in relation to those of the other tribes, and this form of segregation helped to preserve tribal and family unity while reducing the risk of jealousy or rivalry to a minimum; (2) the fact that the entire Israelite community was following the same instructions helped to weld the separate tribes together in obedience to the Lord and in loyalty to one another. Concomitant with this was the insistence that the Israelite encampment was to be kept clean at all times because it was God's habitation (Num. 5:3; Deut. 23:14), and this inculcated both a personal and communal sense of responsibility among the Israelites. Thus whatever was likely to interfere with this state of ceremonial cleanness was to be removed to an area well beyond the encampment.

In the prescribed arrangement, Judah was placed on the east side of the Tabernacle, where the entrance to the shrine was located. The fighting men were under the leadership of Nahshon. A disproportionate amount of time has been spent in speculating as to why Judah's division had been moved from the position that had been occupied in the census list (Num. 1:20-46). The common conclusion among those who upheld the theory of multiple composition for the Pentateuch over many centuries was that the "P" editors moved Judah to first place because of theological considerations. After all, it was becoming clear in the postexilic period that Judah, in retrospect, had been the preeminent tribe from the beginning. Indeed, it proved to be the principal survivor of the exile and the tribe to which the people looked for the coming Messiah. This resolved all doubts as to why postexilic editors rearranged the sources of Numbers and put them in their extant position. Such a speculative view still persists as an explanation among modern liberal writers.[28]

Fortunately the real reason is disarmingly simple. With 74,600 men mustered, Judah was by far the largest of the military divisions.

---

28. E.g., G. B. Gray, *Numbers*, pp. 14, 18; M. Noth, *Numbers*, p. 24; G. Fohrer, *Introduction to the Old Testament*, p. 185; P. J. Budd, *Numbers*, pp. 22-23; etc.

When Issachar and Zebulun, Judah's neighbors, were added, the total presented a formidable spearhead when on the march. The same was true when the Israelites were encamped, since the deployment of such a large force near the entrance to the Tabernacle would be more than sufficient to deter any would-be violator. With such a powerful advance guard, the psychological impression upon a potential adversary would be one of great might, and, when supplemented by the rest of the military units from the tribes, the wandering Israelites would convey the idea of overwhelming superiority of numbers, as befitted the grandeur of the Lord of armies, whose shrine was in their very midst. It must be concluded, therefore, that potential military muscle furnished the real reason for the priority of Judah as narrated in Num. 2:3 (cf. Gen. 49:8-12).

This chapter commenced with the annunciatory formula that seems to have introduced new sections of source material in Numbers.[29] Once the superiority of Judah's strength had been established, two other units were added to form the eastern guard of the Tabernacle.

Translation

The tribe of Issachar shall be stationed next to them, with Nethanel son of Zuar as the leader of the people of Issachar. His division numbers 54,400.

Next will be the tribe of Zebulun. Eliab son of Helon shall lead the people of Zebulun. His division numbers 57,400.

All those listed in the camp of Judah, according to their divisions, total 186,400. They shall march out at the head. (2:5-9)

Exegesis and Exposition

Issachar and Zebulun, two of the later sons of Leah, were chosen to be stationed along the east wall of the Tabernacle. Together the tribes of the last three sons of Leah, Jacob's first wife, provided the formidable total of 186,400 men, who would lead the company whenever a march was being undertaken. Their united strength was greater than that of any of the three remaining tribal groups.

2. SOUTHERN TRIBES (2:10-16)

Translation

The divisions of the camp of Reuben will be stationed to the south, beneath their own standard. The leader of the people of Reuben is Elizur son of Shedeur. His division numbers 46,500.

---

29. The phrase occurs in connection with Moses some thirty times, in conjunction with Aaron six times, but only once with Aaron alone.

Next to them the tribe of Simeon will be stationed. The leader of the people of Simeon is Shelumiel son of Zurishaddai. His division numbers 59,300.
Next will be the tribe of Gad. Eliasaph son of Deuel is leader of the people of Gad. His division numbers 45,650. All those listed in the camp of Reuben, according to their divisions, total 151,450. They shall march out second in line. (2:10-16)

Exegesis and Exposition

The descendants of Reuben, firstborn son of Leah and Jacob, and the offspring of Simeon, Reuben's younger brother (Gen. 35:23), were supplemented by the Gadites, whose eponymous ancestor was the first son of Leah's maid Zilpah.

3. CENTRAL GROUP (2:17)

Translation

When the Tent of Meeting is moved, the Levites will remain in the center of the camps. They will depart in the same order as they camped, each in his own place beneath his standard. (2:17)

Exegesis and Exposition

No statistics are recorded for the Levites here because their registration was to take place subsequently (Num. 3:1–4:49). For the moment the principal concern was for the place the Levites would occupy when the camp was on the move. At an early stage in the wilderness migrations (10:33) the Ark led the procession in search of a camping ground, carried presumably by a group of Kohathite Levites. This order evidently set the precedent for later marches, which would thus consist of the Ark and its bearers at the forefront of the long column followed by the triad of Judah. Between that body and the triad of Reuben would be Gershonite and Merarite Levites carrying the Tabernacle, while between the Reubenite triad and that of the Ephraimites would be the Kohathite Levites carrying the furnishings of the Tabernacle. The rear of the column was then brought up by the triad of Dan. Deployed in this manner, the Levites would be taking precautions to ensure that there was no possibility of damage to or interference with the contents of the sacred shrine.

4. WESTERN TRIBES (2:18-24)

Translation

The division of the camp of Ephraim will be located on the west, beneath their standards. Elishama son of Ammihud leads the people of Ephraim. His division numbers 40,500.

Next to them will be the tribe of Manasseh. Gamaliel son of Pedahzur leads the people of Manasseh. His division numbers 32,200.

Then the tribe of Benjamin will come. The leader of the people of Benjamin is Abidan son of Gideoni. His division numbers 35,400.

All those listed in the camp of Ephraim, according to their divisions, total 108,100. They shall be the third to march out. (2:18-24)

Exegesis and Exposition

Deployed on the west side of the Tabernacle were three tribes descended from Rachel, Jacob's favorite wife. Joseph was represented by his two sons, Manasseh and Ephraim, and as with the census the younger brother Ephraim was accorded precedence in conformity with his grandfather Jacob's farewell blessing (Gen. 48:5-20). Adjacent to the tribe of Ephraim were the descendants of Manasseh. This group of three guardian tribes was completed by the descendants of Benjamin, the second and last son borne by Rachel to Jacob. In the order of march the Rachel tribes were assigned to a position immediately behind the Levites.

5. NORTHERN TRIBES (2:25-31)

Translation

The division of the camp of Dan will be to the north beneath their standard. Ahiezer son of Ammishaddai is the leader of the people of Dan. His division numbers 62,700.

Next to them will camp the tribe of Asher. The leader of the people of Asher is Pagiel son of Ocran. His division numbers 41,500.

Then will come the tribe of Naphtali. Ahira son of Enan is the leader of the people of Naphtali. His division numbers 53,400.

All those listed in the camp of Dan total 157,600. They shall march out last beneath their standards. (2:25-31)

Exegesis and Exposition

The rectangle of the encampment on the north, and the final segment of the rear troops on the march, was filled by the descendants of the two sons of Rachel's maidservant Bilhah and by the second son of Leah's maidservant Zilpah.

This group represented a formidable rearguard that was almost as strong as the advance division. They were obviously intended to serve as a deterrent to any hostile attack from the rear because their very size would present a potential aggressor with pause for reflection. In the natural movements of flocks and herds, the strongest tend to lead whereas the weaker members lag behind in the rear. But for

58

Encampment of the Tribes of Israel

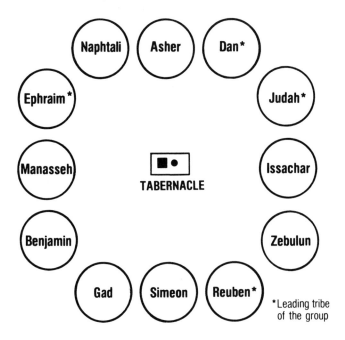

*Leading tribe
of the group

His people God provided an arrangement whereby such a situation would be forestalled, thus enabling the long caravan of Israelites to move through the wilderness in security.

The Christian needs to be reminded constantly that in the Lord's army the ideal is for every warrior to be strong (cf. Eph. 6:13-18). When the reality falls short of the ideal, the community of holy people must employ its fullest resources to help weaker brothers and sisters (cf. Acts 20:35; Rom. 15:1) and not allow the devil to ensnare and destroy them.

6. SUMMARY (2:32-34)

Translation

These are the Israelites, listed according to their families. The total number in the camps, according to the divisions, was 603,550.

The Levites, however, were not included in the detailed records with the other Israelites, in accordance with the LORD's command to Moses.

The Israelites followed carefully the commandments of the LORD to Moses. They pitched their tents and broke camp under their standards, each one with his family and family group. (2:32-34)

Exegesis and Exposition

In the organization of the tribes the four groups, composed of three tribes each, were named according to the one selected as the leader. The divisions numbered 603,550 potential fighting men[30] but did not include the Levites, who were later assigned noncombatant tasks. The detailed totals of the census correspond exactly with those arrived at when the men were mustered, and the entire operation proceeded quickly and smoothly because the Israelites followed to the letter the instructions that God had issued. The assent formula of verse 34 is obviously a reminiscence by the compiler. Had the covenant nation continued in this spirit of obedience, the subsequent history of the nation would have been very different from what transpired ultimately.

This section of source material in its completed form concluded with a statement that is very similar to the one terminating the account of the census (Num. 1:54), except that it occurs in a more expanded form and refers to details of camping and marching that were not appropriate to the concerns of the census. The abiding lesson of all this organizational detail is reflected in a plea by Paul to a disorderly and disobedient Christian fellowship to ensure that, in the Lord's service, everything should be done decently and in an orderly manner (1 Cor. 14:40).

Additional Notes

2:2 The tribes were to be located around (סָבִיב) the Tabernacle so that it would be protected on every side, although there would be a certain distance between the sacred shrine and its guardians. The term מִנֶּגֶד, LXX ἐναντίον, "opposite," "facing," means "away from the front of" (BDB 617b).

2:3 The phrase קֵדְמָה מִזְרָחָה, comprising two nouns augmented by *he locale*, exhibits tautology, but this is not unusual in Hebrew prose tradition (cf. Ex. 26:18; 38:13; etc.). One LXX manuscript erroneously read κατὰ νόσον, "on the south," but the codices Alexandrinus and Ambrosianus read πρῶτοι. These dealt with the problem by noting the priority of Judah (cf. Gen. 49:8-12) and ignoring the mistaken topography.

---

30. For Y. Yadin, *The Art of Warfare in Biblical Lands*, pp. 292-93, 396-97, the arrangement of the tribes resembled that of a military camp.

2:4 וּצְבָא֖וֹ וּפְקֻדֵיהֶ֑ם has been seen as another tautological phrase, but more properly it represents synonyms used technically by the *šōṭĕrîm* and elders for statistical purposes. Nothing would appear to be gained by eliding one or the other. The plural suffixal form וּפְקֻדֵיהֶם is replaced in 2:6, 8, 11 by the singular וּפְקֻדָיו. This has been viewed by some (e.g., G. B. Gray, *Numbers*, p. 20) as an indication of the editing of separate literary traditions. P. J. Budd, *Numbers*, p. 21 n. 6a, however, thinks that it could simply have been a scribal variation.

2:17 עַל־יָד֑וֹ, "upon his hand," designates a specifically assigned position that must be occupied to maintain proper order. The proposal of BHS to relocate the second half of this verse to the end of 2:2 is unsatisfactory because it introduces instructions that have nothing to do with the organizing of tribal groups around the Tabernacle. Instead, the section deals with the placement of the Levites in relationship to the Tabernacle and the way in which they are to be integrated into the larger encampment. Furthermore, the suggested relocation involves an unwarranted dislocation of the text that is not supported by any of the MT MSS or versions.

2:32 לְצִבְאֹתָם, "by their hosts," which occurs in 2:9, 16, 24, is omitted here, and instead the enumeration of warriors and the order of march is concluded by the mention of the tribal standards of the Danite camp. This variation was evidently intended to round off the narrative and thus should not be considered as scribal error or neglect of stereotyped literary forms.

2:34 This material is comparable to the assent formula of 1:54 but appears in a considerably more enlarged way subsequent to the adverb כֵּן by recording חָנ֣וּ לְדִגְלֵיהֶ֗ם וְכֵ֤ן נָסָ֙עוּ֙ אִ֣ישׁ לְמִשְׁפְּחֹתָ֔יו עַל־בֵּ֖ית אֲבֹתָֽיו.

COLOPHON (3:1)

Translation

These are the family records in the possession of Aaron and Moses at the time when the LORD addressed Moses on Mount Sinai. (3:1)

Those responsible for dividing the Hebrew Scriptures into chapters made the same unfortunate mistake here as in Gen. 1:31, when the true break in the narrative actually occurs after 2:4. They were unaware of the nature and occurrence of ancient Babylonian colophons, which are present in form in both Gen. 2:4 and Num. 3:1. As observed previously, the colophons of Mesopotamian tablets always occurred at the end of the material and looked back to its origin at the point where a title marked the beginning of a tablet or series of tablets.

When cuneiform studies were in their infancy, many OT scholars who were not professional cuneiformists commonly made such sweeping statements as that by Skinner,[31] who regarded the colophon as always looking forward (i.e., as a title or heading for subsequent material) and not backward (as a subscription). This erroneous interpretation is still widespread and was accepted uncritically by Olsen in a survey of literature on the origin and structure of Numbers.[32]

An imposing array of Babylonian sources indicates that the colophon normally repeated the title of the tablet, especially when an entire series was involved. It usually mentioned the name of the scribe, who may also have been the owner of the material, and attempted some form of dating. By application of form-critical analysis to Num. 3:1, the text gives indication of a colophon formulation according to typical Babylonian literary practice and identified, as in Genesis, by the formula "These are the *tôlĕdôt* (MT תּוֹלְדֹת) of. . . ."

Some of the alleged confusion in the understanding of the use of *tôlĕdôt* in the MT arises from a failure to understand that the word is used in two distinct senses. In the eleven occurrences of *tôlĕdôt* at the conclusion of sections of narrative material in Genesis, it is found as a technical term that describes "narratives" or "(family) histories" and is integral to the colophon structure. But in Num. 1:26-42 it is used in an entirely different context from its incidence in Genesis, and instead describes biological descendants. It is important to observe that the expression "these are the *tôlĕdôt* of" does not occur in connection with individual family genealogies mentioned in the census, because a different situation is being described that demands a different meaning of the term. But in Numbers 3:1 the usage reverts to the typical colophon of ancient Mesopotamia, where a larger body of material is being described as a unit. Unfortunately, modern Hebrew lexicons fail to observe that the word *tôlĕdôt*, which always appears in the plural, can be employed quite differently depending upon the occasion. But by using form-critical analysis it is easy to see which meaning is intended on a given occasion.

The colophon of Num. 3:1 can be analyzed as follows: *tôlĕdôt* at the termination of the statistics indicates the end of a body of material that had been recorded in Babylonian scribal fashion and looks back to 2:1. The probable scribes were Aaron and Moses, who compiled the data, probably with the assistance of the *šōṭĕrîm*, as God instructed them. The date of this activity was associated with the

---

31. J. Skinner, *A Critical and Exegetical Commentary on Genesis* (Edinburgh: T & T Clark, 1910), pp. 40-41.
32. D. T. Olsen, *The Death of the Old and the Birth of the New*, p. 112.

Lord's revelation to Moses at Mount Sinai, since this was the most obvious reference point, and the title of the material ("the LORD spoke to Moses and Aaron") was also recapitulated briefly at the end of the composition ("when the LORD addressed Moses").³³ Thus the narrative from Num. 2:1 to 3:1 represents a genuine record of historical events that was in the possession of Aaron and Moses, having been compiled in the manner of the ancient Babylonian scribes.

C. THE LEVITES AND THEIR CENSUS (3:2-51)

This chapter can be analyzed structurally as follows: (1) Aaron's sons (vv. 2-4); (2) numbering of Levites (vv. 5-13); (3) census of Levites ordered (vv. 14-16); (4) summary of family groups (vv. 17-20); (5) Gershonite census (vv. 21-26); (6) census of Kohath (vv. 27-32); (7) census of Merari (vv. 33-37); (8) summary (vv. 38-39); (9) substitution for firstborn (vv. 40-51).

1. AARON'S SONS (3:2-4)

Translation

The names of the sons of Aaron were Nadab, the eldest, along with Abihu, Eleazar, and Ithamar. These were the names of Aaron's sons, the anointed priests ordained to serve in the office of priest. *But Nadab and Abihu died suddenly in the LORD's presence because they had offered fire improperly before Him in the Sinai wilderness. They had no surviving sons, so Eleazar and Ithamar were left to perform priestly functions under their father's supervision. (3:2-4)

Exegesis and Exposition

This chapter demonstrates that, although Abraham's offspring were dedicated in a particular way to the worship of God in view of the covenant relationship established at Sinai, the Levites and the family of Aaron were consecrated specifically to His service (Ex. 28:2; Num. 3:12; cf. 1 Pet. 2:9). Though the introductory formula "these are the names of" (MT אֵלֶּה שְׁמוֹת, *'ēlleh šĕmôt*) appears elsewhere in the Torah as a formal genealogical or statistical indicator,³⁴ its purpose

---

33. For the use of the colophon in Canaanite literature cf. C. H. Gordon, *Ugarit and Minoan Crete* (New York: W. W. Norton, 1965), pp. 74, 87, 120. A Hurrian text from Ugarit proved to be a hymn with a musical score and a colophon containing the type of information found in Psalm titles. D. A. Foxvog and A. D. Kilmer, *ISBE*, 3:447.
34. E.g., Gen. 25:13; 36:10; Ex. 1:1; 6:16; Num. 27:1; 34:17; etc.

here is to introduce an abbreviated reference to Aaron's offspring so as to prepare the reader for the activities of Eleazar and Ithamar.

Aaron, the first high priest of Israel, was the first son of Amram, grandson of Levi (Num. 3:17-19). He had acted as Moses' spokesman (Ex. 4:16; 7:1) when Pharaoh refused to liberate the Hebrews from captivity. He supported Moses as he prayed during a battle with the Amalekites (Ex. 17:10, 12) and subsequently was included among those appointed to approach Mount Sinai closely (24:1, 9-10) to behold God's glory. This auspicious beginning was replaced quickly by shameful behavior in the fashioning of a bull idol (32:4), which almost provoked God to slaughter the Israelites. Aaron and his sons were inducted into the priestly office in an elaborate ceremony (Lev. 8:1-30), as commanded by God in Ex. 29:1-43, and charged with the responsibility of conducting the sacrificial worship of the Tabernacle.

Aaron's sons were described specifically as "the anointed priests" (MT הַמְּשֻׁחִים, hammĕšuḥîm) in accordance with God's command in Ex. 30:30. Anointing with oil was a special part of the ritual involving the commissioning of kings (1 Sam. 16:13) as well as religious persons such as prophets (1 Kings 19:16; Isa. 61:1). The Hebrew term מָשִׁיחַ, māšîaḥ ("anointed one"), came to be used of the Messiah (Gk. Χριστός, Christós) and was employed in early Christianity to identify Jesus as God's Messiah. By this means they acknowledged Him as God's chosen Servant, who would not merely be anointed with oil (Isa. 11:2; 42:1) but also with the Holy Spirit (Matt. 3:16; Luke 4:1, 18, 21; John 1:32-33) as He became our great High Priest through the work of Calvary. "Ordained to serve" is the translation of a technical phrase (MT מִלֵּא יָדָם, millē' yādām), meaning basically "to fill the hand." This term was also current in Mesopotamia, and in some Mari texts of about 1700 b.c.; it seemed to describe the distribution of booty among victorious armies. In Ex. 29:9 and Num. 3:3 it probably referred to offerings placed in the priests' hands during the consecration ceremony, which conferred upon them the authority to discharge priestly functions in the Tabernacle.

Despite Aaron's prominent position in the community, he was not a man of strong personality. Already his career was beginning to decline, and tragedy struck when his two oldest sons were destroyed dramatically by fire, perhaps in the form of a lightning bolt. This terrible incident was described in Lev. 10:1-7 and is recounted here both for the sake of the record and also to integrate both the period and the narrative of Leviticus into its proper place in the chronology of the wanderings.

The reason for the punishment of the offending priests was summarized by the statement that fire had been offered improperly in the Lord's presence. In the corresponding Leviticus account it is evident that several violations of cultic protocol had occurred: (1) there is no statement to the effect that the coals in their censers had actually been removed from the altar of burnt offering (cf. Lev. 16:12), which in the first instance had been ignited by God Himself; (2) the two men usurped the functions of the high priest, who alone was privileged to place incense upon a censer on the Day of Atonement and enter the Most Holy Place to atone for the sins of accident and inadvertence on the part of Israel; (3) the offending priests had broken a fundamental rule of Israelite cultic worship by introducing innovation into the sacrificial procedures.

By offering something that was not holy—that is, something that had not been consecrated properly to divine service—they had profaned God's holiness in an unwarranted manner. The swift retribution that followed was a stern reminder to all others that the covenant God was to be worshiped only according to the strict procedures set out fully in Leviticus. Moses and Aaron ought to have been consulted by these more junior members of the priestly hierarchy before any innovations were introduced, but this procedure was apparently thought unnecessary. To that extent, therefore, Nadab and Abihu were defying not only God but also their earthly leaders. Since God could brook no opposition to His lordship, the punishment of the offenders was as inevitable as it was speedy.

The fuller account in Lev. 10 contains instructions from God forbidding family mourning, which might well have evoked sympathy for the deceased brothers as they perished through disobeying God. The account does, however, allow the Israelites to bewail the event as a solemn warning to the community. Immediately after the event, God issued instructions to a shocked father that drunken priests were not to officiate at the sanctuary (Lev. 10:8-11) on penalty of death. This situation has led commentators to the conclusion that Nadab and Abihu were in fact intoxicated before they began their ritual duties and in this way were guilty of sacrilege. It was perhaps fitting that the transgressing priests were punished by a consuming fire, an expression that is used elsewhere to depict God's essential nature (Heb. 12:29).[35]

This incident made it evident that God's consecrated priests, as representatives of the larger "holy nation," must set an example of dedication, holiness, and strict obedience to the Lord's words at all times. For those living under the New Covenant the great High Priest, Jesus Christ, set an example of unqualified submission to the will of God in His life and death, leaving us an example to follow (1 Pet. 2:21). A life of commitment to Christ does not preclude the possibility

---

35. See R. K. Harrison, *Leviticus*, pp. 108-14.

of behavior that will disrupt the relationship between the individual and his Lord. But by the discipline of obedience, faith grows and is strengthened, so that the believer's life is enriched by the presence and power of the Holy Spirit.

The two men whose lives had been cut off so suddenly left no children, and thus their deaths reduced the ranks of the priesthood significantly. Now Aaron had only two sons remaining, namely Eleazar and Ithamar. Numbed by shock, these men participated in what was probably an accidental breach of the ritual involving the goat of the sin offering (Lev. 10:16-20). Aaron appeared confused by the situation, particularly because the rules for sacrificial procedure seemed to have been observed. He pleaded the impropriety of eating the offering under the tragic circumstances that had occurred, and this was evidently satisfactory to Moses. Nevertheless, future sacrificial procedures were to take place under Aaron's personal supervision. From the foregoing, therefore, it is clear that this brief insertion is not a formal genealogy, which in any event was already well known to all the Israelites of the wilderness period, but a summary statement designed to furnish consistency and continuity to the narrative, as well as to keep before the minds of the people the penalties attached to disobedience of God's revealed laws.

2. NUMBERING OF LEVITES (3:5-13)

Translation

Now the LORD spoke to Moses, saying: Bring out the tribe of Levi and present them as assistants to Aaron the priest.

They shall perform functions for him and the entire community at the Tent of Meeting by attending to the duties of the Tabernacle.

They are to be responsible for all the furnishings in the Tent of Meeting and minister to the religious needs of the Israelites as they serve in the Tabernacle.

You shall assign the Levites to Aaron and his sons; they alone of the Israelites are to be dedicated specifically to him.

*Appoint Aaron and his sons to function in the priesthood. Any unauthorized intruder shall be killed. (3:5-10)

Exegesis and Exposition

The interpolation relating to Aaron and his sons was followed by the announcement formula, which introduced the special ministry of the descendants of Levi. This formula is repeated in vv. 11, 14, suggesting three distinct phases in the organizing of the Levites for their ministry. Since the activities connected with their commissioning were doubtless conducted in full view of the Israelite congregation, the successive stages would make clear the rationale of their ministry and enhance their stature as guardians of the Tabernacle.

By divine command the Levites were presented ceremonially (lit. "made to stand," MT וְהַעֲמַדְתָּ אֹתוֹ, *wĕhaʿămadtā ʾōtô*) to Aaron to serve him[36] and the priesthood by their participation in Tabernacle duties. They also ministered to the entire community of Israel because of their special dedication to Aaron. An important Levitical task was to safeguard the furnishings of the Tabernacle in a way that would assist the priests in their duties and would preserve the ceremonial and spiritual integrity of the sacred shrine. As with the priests, the Levites did not take any oath of office, since their hereditary right made such a procedure unnecessary.

The Levites were responsible for dismantling the Tabernacle structure when the tribes were about to move their camp, for protecting its components during the march, and for reassembling the shrine when the tribes settled at a new site. Their commitment was to protect the structure to the point where any alien who violated its sanctity was to be executed (Num. 1:51). Milgrom[37] has interpreted their duties in terms of acting as a sacred guard, which indeed conveys the overall sense but is perhaps too military in character to describe an unarmed group of men.

The Levites served as a cultic cordon, forming a protective barrier around the outside of the Tabernacle and preventing unauthorized access to it. Although the Levites were unarmed, they were belligerent by nature (Gen. 45:5-7) and therefore capable of the same kind of military service as the other tribes (cf. Ex. 32:28). Their energies were directed deliberately by God to purposes in which militancy became an expression of zeal for the holiness of His shrine. One concomitant of their Tabernacle duties was that the Levites also protected the congregation from the possibility of incurring divine wrath. Equally important for community life was the status of the Levites as substitutes for all the firstborn males of Israel. Their principal character, therefore, was that of serving as human insulators in the course of discharging their religious duties. The Levites were to serve always as subordinates to the Aaronic priesthood, although both groups belonged to the same tribe.

The Levites were the spiritual forebears of the "keepers of the threshold" (*RSV* 2 Kings 22:4; 1 Chron. 9:19; *NASB*, *NIV* "doorkeepers"; *NEB* "those on duty at the entrance"), who were prominent

---

36. While most MT MSS read לֹא, (*lō'*), here, a few read לִי, (*lî* "to me"), along with the LXX and Samaritan Pentateuch.
37. J. Milgrom, *Studies in Levitical Terminology* (Berkeley, Calif.: U. of California, 1970), 1:8-10.

officials of the Solomonic Temple. Their duties in the kingdom period included prevention of defilement of the Temple precincts by the accidental incursion of animals, ceremonially unclean persons, or pagan intruders. This function has been paralleled by some scholars[38] with the ancient Near Eastern *sadin*, who guarded the pagan temples, attended to the ceremonies of the sanctuary, and assisted the priests in the sacrificial rituals. After a time their office apparently became hereditary (cf. Judg. 17:5; 1 Sam. 1:3) and seems to have embraced sacrificial functions that, in the Hebrew tradition, were more appropriate to the position of the Hebrew *kōhēn* (MT כֹּהֵן) than to that of the Levites.[39] According to Deuteronomy 10:8, the Levites were also authorized to pronounce blessings in the name of the Lord.

Translation

Then the Lord spoke to Moses again, saying: Look, I have selected the Levites from among the Israelites to take the place of the first male child born to every Israelite woman. The Levites belong to Me, because every firstborn child is Mine. When I destroyed all the firstborn in Egypt, I set apart for Myself all the firstborn in Israel, whether human or animal. They belong to Me. I am the Lord. (3:11-13)

Exegesis and Exposition

The second stage in the appointment of the Levites to ministry in Israel emphasized their distinctiveness as the Lord's special possession. They were to serve as substitutes for all the oldest children in Israel, and by this means the firstborn was sanctified instead of being sacrificed. This tradition of sanctifying the firstborn was initiated at the time of the Exodus (Ex. 13:2) and reiterated in recapitulations of Hebrew legislation (22:29-30; 34:19-20).[40] By this means the principle was established that God had adopted Israel as His firstborn (Ex. 4:22), and the nation was reminded that no such favors were accorded the Egyptians during the tenth, terrible plague (12:29). God had dealt a grievous blow to the Egyptians because their ruler had set his mind obstinately against freedom for the captive Hebrews. The chosen people of God had yet to learn that hardening their own hearts against their Redeemer's revealed will would bring about their own

---

38. E.g., R. de Vaux, *Ancient Israel: Its Life and Institutions* (London: Darton, Longman and Todd, E tr. 1961), p. 348.
39. W. O. McCready, *ISBE*, 3:965-66.
40. In accordance with this regulation Jesus, the firstborn son of Mary, was consecrated to God by being presented in the Temple (Luke 2:22-23).

destruction. Where necessary, God can and does chasten even His elect (cf. Heb. 12:6).

The idea of substitution in order to preserve and enhance human life is a distinctive feature of the Hebrew sacrificial system. God ordained that the lifeblood of a ceremonially clean animal could provide forgiveness for the sinner under the appropriate ritual circumstances. The blood, symbolic of life laid down as it was offered up to God for human sin (Lev. 17:11), furnished an atonement vicariously. OT sacrificial rituals made a blood offering mandatory if the sinner was to be cleansed from iniquity and his fellowship with God restored.[41] Life had to be exchanged for life, and this concept of substitutionary atonement was taken to its apogee by Jesus Christ on Calvary, who shed His blood for the forgiveness of human sin, thereby enabling us now to receive atonement (Rom. 5:11).

3. CENSUS OF LEVITES ORDERED (3:14-16)

Translation

Then the LORD spoke to Moses in the Sinai wilderness, saying: Compile a detailed register of the Levites by their families and family groups. You shall include every male a month old or older.

So *Moses listed all of them as he had been commanded by the LORD's word. (3:14-16)

Exegesis and Exposition

The third summons of the Lord concerning the ministry of the Levites required Moses to institute a census of the tribe on the same basis as that imposed upon the other Israelite tribes. This would negate the suggestion of some scholars that the firstborn of a family group, and not just the first male offspring of constituent parents, were to be registered. Clearly an actual head count was envisaged in the text by whatever techniques had been adopted earlier. The principal difference between this census and that of the tribes was that the age requirement for enrollment was lowered to one month. This fact emphasized the difference between this listing, which was for young Levites, and the one in chap. 4, which enrolled older Levites. Two distinct though correlative registrations are thus being contemplated. Inserted between them is an account of the registering of Israel's firstborn males and their redemption by the Levites (Num. 3:40-51).

The Lord commanded Moses to furnish a detailed list, which was

---

41. D. Kidner, *Sacrifice in the Old Testament* (London: Inter-Varsity, 1951), p. 14.

to be supplied according to the specifications laid down. Moses himself was the obvious person to accomplish this task, and God's instructions to him are followed by a note to the effect that they were carried out. The first two sections dealing with the Levites' appointment to ministry gave no formal indication that the people concerned had obeyed God's instructions. Because the Levites were consistently loyal to Moses and Aaron during the wilderness wanderings, it was probably felt both unnecessary and unduly repetitious for the short sections to be concluded with a stereotyped response formula. Hence it is important to accept Moses' stated affirmation of obedience to God's command as indicative of his actions in the two preceding stages.

4. SUMMARY OF FAMILY GROUPS (3:17-20)

Translation

These were the names of Levi's sons: Gershon, Kohath, and Merari.

Libni and Shimei were the names of the Gershonite family groups.

The Kohathite family groups were Amram, Izhar, Hebron, and Uzziel.

The Merarite family groups were Mahli and Mushi. These were the family groups belonging to the Levites. (3:17-20)

Exegesis and Exposition

The Levites about to be enrolled in this particular section of the census were not being registered for military service, as has been remarked above. It was their lot to minister in and around the Tabernacle as custodians and as assistants of Aaron and his sons. The descendants of Levi were listed in the normal order (cf. Ex. 6:16-19), but only the principal family groups were mentioned. The narratives of the enrollment follow the same general order, commencing with an introduction, continuing with an enrollment formula, recording the allocation of the particular group's camp, and ending with the name of each group's leader.

5. GERSHONITE CENSUS (3:21-26)

Translation

From Gershon arose the family groups of the Libnites and Shimeites. These were all Gershonite families, and the number of males a month old or older who were registered was 7,500.

The Gershonite family groups were to pitch their tents on the west, behind the Tabernacle. The leader of the Gershonite families was Eliasaph son of Lael.

The duties of the Gershonites in the Tent of Meeting included the Tabernacle proper, the tent itself with its covering, the curtain at the entrance to the Tent of Meeting, the hangings of the courtyard, the curtains at the entrance to the courtyard that surrounded the Tabernacle and the altar, and the ropes and everything else required to maintain it. (3:21-26)

Exegesis and Exposition

The descendants of Gershon (known as Gershom in 1 Chron. 6:17, 20, etc.) were to exercise a long and noble tradition of service to the Tabernacle and the subsequent Temple. In David's time the Gershonites included the family of Asaph, who were prominent musicians (6:32; 25:1-2), along with others who controlled the Temple treasuries (26:21-22) and exercised other executive positions (23:7-11). During the wilderness period the Gershonites were ordered to locate their tents to the west of the Tabernacle walls, under the leadership of Eliasaph, and were accorded oversight of the compound. In particular they were responsible for the tent-structure, which comprised the Holy Place and the Most Holy Place. Subsidiary duties involved maintaining the fine linen courtyard hangings and also the curtains at the entrance to the Tabernacle compound. Repairs, renovations, and the maintaining of supplies for the efficient operation of the sanctuary rounded out their responsibilities.

6. CENSUS OF KOHATH (3:27-32)

Translation

From Kohath descended the family groups of Amram, Izhar, Hebron, and Uzziel. They were all Kohathites.

The number of males one month old or older was *8,600. The Kohathites were responsible for caring for the sanctuary.

The Kohathite family groups were to encamp on the south side of the Tabernacle.

The chief over the Kohathite family groups was Elizaphan son of Uzziel.

Their responsibilities included the Ark, the table, the lampstand, the altars, the vessels of the sanctuary used in ministering, the curtain, and everything required for their maintenance.

The head of all the *Levitical leaders was Eleazar son of Aaron the priest. He was appointed to supervise those who were in charge of the sanctuary. (3:27-32)

71

Exegesis and Exposition

The second of the three divisions of the Levitical priesthood was composed of the offspring of Kohath, the second son of Levi (Ex. 6:16). Both Moses and Aaron came from this stock (6:16-20). In the wilderness period the larger group was subdivided into four families. The faults for which Jacob condemned their ancestor Levi (Gen. 49:5-7) were not in evidence among them in the wilderness era, and during the Hebrew monarchy they rendered exemplary service as musicians (1 Chron. 6:33-48). In a time of crisis they were loyal to Jehoshaphat (2 Chron. 20:19-21) and also assisted Hezekiah in cleansing the Temple of idolatry (29:12-14). The Kohathite families were responsible for the general care of the sacred tent and its contents and for transporting it when the Israelites struck camp. They discharged their duties under the supervision of Eleazar the priest, who became chief of the Levites after Nadab and Abihu perished (Lev. 10:1-6).

7. CENSUS OF MERARI (3:33-37)

Translation

From Merari came the family groups of the Mahlites and the Mushites. Both groups were Merarites, and the number of males one month old or older who were registered was 6,200. The leader of the Merarite family groups was Zuriel son of Abihail. They were to be stationed on the north side of the Tabernacle. The Merarites were responsible for caring for the Tabernacle's frames, its crossbars, posts, sockets, and all the work connected with their maintenance, in addition to the posts of the surrounding courtyard, their sockets, tent pegs, and ropes. (3:33-37)

Exegesis and Exposition

Two small family groups, the Mahlites and Mushites, made up the third division of the Levitical priesthood. Like the others they were musicians, and in the Davidic period they made up a fourth of the roster for sanctuary music. Their participation in Israel's religious life subsequently extended to support for the work of Hezekiah (2 Chron. 29:12) and Josiah (34:12) in connection with the Temple. The census indicates that they were the smallest of the three Levitical groups. It was their duty to care for the framework of the Tabernacle courtyard and the other related components. This was painstaking work in view of all the intricate and elaborate materials involved (Ex. 38:9-20).

72

8. SUMMARY (3:38-39)

Translation

In front of the Tabernacle on the east, Moses was to camp with Aaron and his sons beside the entrance to the Tent. Theirs was the responsibility of safeguarding the sanctuary on behalf of the Israelites. Any unauthorized person who approached the sanctuary was to be killed.

The total number of the Levites whom Moses *and Aaron registered at the command of the LORD, according to their family groups and including every male one month old or older, was 22,000. (3:38-39)

Exegesis and Exposition

Moses, Aaron, and Aaron's sons occupied the place of honor at the entrance to the sanctuary. The MT term מִשְׁמֶרֶת, (*mišmeret*), used of the guarding duties of the Levites, also occurs here. As the chief community leaders, Moses and Aaron bore the supreme responsibility for protecting the sacred shrine, especially at night. In this way they were functioning representatively for the whole Israelite community. In v. 38 the MT word וְאַהֲרֹן (*wĕ'ahărōn*, "and Aaron") does not occur in some Hebrew MSS and is also absent from the Samaritan Pentateuch. Textual problems of this kind also occur in the Hebrew of Num. 9:10; 21:30; 29:15 and most probably arose either as a result of scribal transmission or because of slightly variant MS traditions. The account of the enrollment was completed by noting the total of 22,000 Levites registered. This does not accord with the actual total of the three groups, which is 22,300. Although the registration process seems to have employed rounded numbers, it is curious that it should have occurred here, where it could have been corrected so easily. The explanation modern scholars generally adopt is to regard the word שֵׁשׁ (*šēš*, "six") in the Kohathite total (v. 28) as a wrong scribal transcription for שָׁלֹשׁ (*šālōš*, "three"). The addition of the letter *l* to the text thus brings the figures of vv. 22, 28, 34 into agreement with the total in v. 39 and still preserves the integrity of the grammatical construction.

9. SUBSTITUTION FOR FIRSTBORN (3:40-51)

This passage can be divided into two distinct sections, vv. 40-43 and vv. 44-51, in which the annunciation formula contains God's instructions to Moses and the concluding statement narrates his obedience to the divine command. The enumeration of the firstborn males and the substitution of the Levites in vv. 40-43 is paralleled inversely in vv. 44-51 by the substitution of the Levites and the enumeration of the excess Israelites. This section indicates something of the conscious historical, theological, and literary harmony that is characteristic of the Torah. Here certain commands of the Lord in Exodus (13:2,12) and Leviticus (11:44) are coordinated and given objective and specific expression in the religious life of the community.

Translation

Now the LORD said to Moses: Make a count of all the firstborn Israelite males who are one month old or older, and register their names.

Reserve the Levites for Me in substitution for all the eldest Israelite sons, and the livestock of the Levites instead of the firstborn of Israelite cattle. I am the LORD.

So Moses tabulated all the firstborn of the Israelites as the LORD had commanded him. The total number of firstborn males one month old or older who were registered by name was 22,273. (3:40-43)

Exegesis and Exposition

Having counted this particular group of Levites and registered them by name (cf. Num. 1:2), Moses was commanded by God to use them as substitutes for the Israelite firstborn, and their cattle for the Israelite livestock. The Levites and their animals both belonged to God and could be disposed of according to His will. Thus the Levites replaced the Israelite firstborn, whom the Lord had claimed as His own (Ex. 13:2) when He inflicted the tenth plague upon the Egyptians.

A count of those Israelite males to be redeemed indicated an excess of 273 firstborn over the registered Levites. If the census figures of chap. 1 are to be taken as a literal head count, which the narrative implies, the number of 22,273 males a month old or more has been alleged by some scholars to be disproportionately small, given a population of more than two million persons.

One solution considers this number as comprising those males born after the Exodus, since all other firstborn had been redeemed on the occasion of the first Passover (Ex. 12:22-23) when the Egyptian firstborn perished in the tenth plague. With the redemption of those born subsequent to the Exodus, God's claim to the firstborn would thus be complete. Not all scholars are satisfied with this explanation, however, since it is largely inferential. Noordtzij[42] thought that the

42. A. Noordtzij, *Numbers*, p. 41.

"firstborn" alluded to the first male offspring of a specific union between a man and his first wife, regardless of how many other "firstborn" males might be produced by subsequent wives. This proposal, however, would be difficult to demonstrate, particularly since such a distinct unit is not identified elsewhere or mentioned in terms of particular tasks in divine service.

Translation

The LORD also said to Moses: Take the Levites in substitution for all the firstborn of the Israelites, and the cattle of the Levites in place of their livestock. The Levites shall be Mine. I am the LORD.

In order to redeem the 273 firstborn Israelites who exceed the number of the Levites, collect 5 shekels for each of them, using as a standard the sanctuary shekel, which weighs 20 gerahs.

You shall donate to Aaron and his sons the money with which the excess Israelites have been redeemed.

So Moses collected *the redemption money for the people that the Levites could not replace.

From the Israelite firstborn he collected silver weighing 1,365 shekels by the standard of the sanctuary shekel.

In accordance with the LORD's instructions Moses then donated the redemption money to Aaron and his sons, following the LORD's command. (3:44-51)

Exegesis and Exposition

The redemption of the surplus 273 firstborn Israelites and their livestock was settled by a collection of money. The amount specified for each was five shekels, and the proceeds were to be donated to the Aaronides. The shekel (from שָׁקַל, *šāqal*, "to weigh") was a basic unit of weight familiar throughout the ancient Near East, although it varied in size, and therefore in value, from place to place. A "heavy" shekel such as those in use at Ugarit (Ras Shamra) weighed nearly half an ounce, as did similar ones from Megiddo, Gezer, and elsewhere.

The "sanctuary shekel" was first mentioned in Ex. 30:13, where a scribal annotation in the MT stated that it was composed of 20 gerahs (cf. Ezek. 45:12). The *beqaʿ* (MT בֶּקַע) or half-shekel of Exodus 38:26 would therefore have been equivalent in weight to 10 gerahs. On the basis of this reckoning, five shekels would have amounted to somewhat over two ounces of silver for each person, making for a total redemption weight of about thirty-five pounds. Quite possibly the weight of the "sanctuary shekel" was slightly heavier than that of other shekels, because it was usually thought proper to contribute more generously for religious purposes. The collected money was a weighed amount and was not in the form of coinage, which only came into being in Lydia a little before 700 B.C.[43]

The redemption money once obtained was transferred to the custody of Aaron and his sons, but with no indication as to how it was to be used. The chapter concludes in the manner of the two previous ones with an assertion of the obedience of Moses to the Lord's commands. While the literary structure of this section of the chapter gives independence to the two units involved, it also unifies them in theme and content.

Excursus on "Redemption"

In v. 46 the MT has a precision that cannot be rendered readily in English. It consists of the placing of אֵת (*ʾēt*, "the") in front of the three numbers that follow it. Clearly 273 distinct persons were being referred to as the surplus for which monetary payment was required. The root for "redeem" is פָּדָה (*pādâ*) and occurs in this section in both noun and participial forms. In v. 49 the phrase כֶּסֶף הַפִּדְיוֹם (*kesep happidyôm*) is probably a technical priestly expression meaning "ransom money." This is the only occurrence of פִּדְיוֹם (*pidyôm*) in the Hebrew Bible, but there is a close textual variant of it (הַפְּדוּיִם, *happĕduy[y]im*) in v. 51.

The term *pādâ* is one of three Hebrew verbs used to describe redemption in the OT, the others being גָּאַל (*gāʾal*) and כָּפַר (*kāpar*). It was the counterpart of the Akkadian *padû* ("ransom"), and was used in commercial law in ancient Babylonia (cf. J. J. Stamm, *Erlösen und Vergeben im Alte Testament*, 1940, pp. 6-11). It described the act of paying money in order to free things or persons that had come into the possession of someone else or another group. In Ugaritic the term was used in the sense of "to ransom" (*UT*, 19, no. 2013).

Pādâ is the most general of the MT terms employed to convey the concept of redemption and is used only of persons or other living beings. The purely commercial sense of a specified payment (redemption-money, or ransom) to obtain transfer of ownership (cf. Lev. 25:23-31) on behalf of someone in difficulty or bondage was given new and distinctive meaning at the Exodus, when God delivered His enslaved people at the cost of the death of the Egyptian firstborn human

43. Cf. A. Segré, "A Documentary Analysis of Ancient Palestinian Units of Measure," *JBL* 64 (1945): 357-75; R. B. Y. Scott, "Weights and Measures of the Bible," *BA* 22 (1951): 22-40; Scott, "The Scale-Weights from Ophel, 1963-64," *PEQ* 97 (1965): 128-39; O. R. Sellers, *IDB*, 4:830-33; Y. Aharoni, "The Use of Hieratic Numerals in Hebrew Ostraca and the Shekel Weights," *BASOR* 184 (1966): 13–19; F. B. Huey Jr., *ZPEB*, 5:918-21; D. J. Wiseman, *IBD*, 3:1634-35; H. W. Perkin, *ISBE*, 3:402-4.

beings and animals. The effect of such an action was to make the Israelites the Lord's firstborn (Ex. 4:22). This redemptive act was commanded by God to be observed by His people when they were in sedentary occupation of Canaan by dedicating the firstborn of human beings and animals to the Lord (Ex. 13:12-16).

As has been noted above, special provision was made for the Levites in this respect (cf. Num. 1:47-54). But anything that had been placed under the divine חֵרֶם (*ḥērem*, or "ban") could not be redeemed because it was already dedicated to the Lord (Lev. 27:28-29), as with the spoils of war (Josh. 6:17-19; 7:10-25). Redemption was always described in terms of some kind of cost factor. God was obviously not discharging a debt to someone by redeeming His elect at the time of the Exodus. But at that period, and on all subsequent occasions when the firstborn were redeemed, God made it clear that the price of a life was another life. The original cost factor subsisted in the effort that a loving, provident God made to redeem His chosen people by "passing over" the firstborn of Israel when He instituted the final plague upon Egypt.

The redemption of the firstborn from that time onward signified that God was claiming and sealing them as His own. Once this principle has been established, the Scriptures make it clear that the Lord of creation sheds His mercy over all His works. While His justice requires Him to punish the wicked, as defined by His revealed laws, He does not take pleasure in the death of a sinner (whether pharaoh or peasant) but rather desires that such a person will turn from the ways of wickedness and live (cf. Ezek. 33:11). Given this understanding, there is no further need to indicate ransom or redemption prices elsewhere in the OT.

Because the words *redemption* and *ransom* are frequently confused, which is not difficult to appreciate since the Hebrew words are cognates, it is best to consider *redemption* as the process and *ransom* as the price paid. (Cf. R. C. Dentan, *IDB*, 4:21-22; R. D. Knudsen, *ZPEB*, 5:49-51; W. B. Coker, *TWOT*, 2:716-17; E. F. Harrison, *EDT*, pp. 918-19; L. Morris, *The Apostolic Preaching of the Cross* [Grand Rapids: Eerdmans, 1965], pp. 18-27, 160-78; and bibliographies.)

Excursus on "Five Shekels"

Five shekels, which in the second millennium b.c. represented almost six months' wages for an ordinary laborer, was the amount fixed for the redemption price of the excess Israelite firstborn males (v. 46). The sum presumably also included the redemption of their livestock, because no mention was made of any extra provision. The MT emphasizes the distributive concept by repeating the number,

חֲמֵשֶׁת חֲמֵשֶׁת שְׁקָלִים (ḥămēšet ḥămēšet šĕqālîm), to imply "five shekels each." (For this use cf. R. J. Williams, *Hebrew Syntax* [1967], p. 8, sect. 15; p. 23, sect. 100.)

How this particular price was arrived at has been debated at some length. It has been assumed that the valuation reflected the average market price of a slave (cf. G. J. Wenham, "Leviticus 27:2-8 and the Price of Slaves," *ZAW* 90 [1978]: 264-65), but this seems a dubious reflection upon a segment of a nation that had so recently been freed from bondage. The book of Leviticus concludes with a passage dealing with the monetary value of persons offered under a vow to the Lord (Lev. 27:1-13), and it is possible that the principles enunciated there were being followed to some extent in Numbers.

But certain difficulties arise in that event. (1) The 273 Israelites were ordinary members of the community and were not described as votaries in any sense. (2) If the evaluation of Leviticus was being followed, there would have to be a sliding scale of value, since the surplus firstborn Israelites would be of different ages. The five-shekel scale in Lev. 27:6-8 was for a male child, whereas a mature Hebrew male was valued at 50 shekels of silver (27:3). In the case of such vows it was the responsibility of the attending priest to determine any individual's place on the monetary scale. Because the dedication of these Israelites was different qualitatively from that of their fellows who were represented by Levites, it seems probable that the sum of five shekels was intended to indicate a nominal payment that would be equal for young and old alike. (See also R. K. Harrison, *Leviticus*, pp. 235-36.)

Additional Notes

3:4 וַיָּמָת . . . לִפְנֵי יהוה was omitted by one Hebrew MS along with the Samaritan Pentateuch and Vulgate.

וּבָנִים לֹא-הָיוּ לָהֶם: Because of this contingency the various lines of descent of the priesthood traced their origins either to Eleazar or Ithamar.

עַל-פְּנֵי אַהֲרֹן can also mean "during the lifetime of," as in Genesis 11:28 (cf. BDB 818b; *RSV*).

3:7 לַעֲבֹד: The construct infinitive is used here as a verbal noun (gerund) and means "by (or in) performing." R. J. Williams, *Hebrew Syntax*, p. 39, sect. 195.

3:9 נְתוּנִם: The qal passive participle is repeated here for emphasis (GKC sect. 123e; R. J. Williams, *Hebrew Syntax*, p. 8, sect. 16); some Hebrew MSS have לִי, perhaps by attraction from Num. 8:16, and are followed by the LXX and the Samaritan Pentateuch.

3:10 The LXX adds ἐπὶ τῆς σκηνῆς τοῦ μαρτυρίου after וְאֶת-בָּנָיו אַהֲרֹן and appears to be glossing וְשָׁמְרוּ אֶת-כְּהֻנָּתָם by adding καὶ πάντα τὰ κατὰ τὸν βωμόν καὶ ἔσω τοῦ καταπετάσματος, which gives further details of their ministerial responsibilities.

3:16 The LXX inserts καὶ 'Ααρων after מֹשֶׁה and modifies the verb accordingly (ἐπεσκέψαντο), but with no apparent warrant. BHS proposed that צִוָּה be altered to צִוָּה and that the following word, with which v. 17 commences, be changed to יהוה, thus reading "as YHWH ordered him." This, however, involves several consonantal changes and does not appear necessary for the sense of the passage. The divine name would occur twice within the space of four words were BHS to be followed, a situation not required by the passage and that would also appear distorted when compared with other assent formulas.

3:21 הֵם as a demonstrative pronoun substitutes here for the verb "to be," as also in vv. 27, 33. See GKC sect. 136d; R. J. Williams, *Hebrew Syntax*, p. 25, sect. 115.

3:26 Two clauses, אֶת-מָסַךְ and וְאֵת מֵיתָרָיו, would appear to be direct objects of a nonexistent verb, and accordingly BHS suggests the elision of the accusative particles. Reasons for retaining them are given by A. B. Davidson, *Hebrew Syntax* (Edinburgh: T & T Clark, 1902), pp. 104-5, sect. 72 Rem. 4; P. P. Saydon, "Meanings and Uses of the Particle את," *VT* 14 (1964): 192-210; J. Macdonald, "The Particle את in Classical Hebrew," *VT* 14 (1964): 263-75.

3:28 One or two LXX Lucianic MSS make the change from ἑξακόσιοι, "six hundred," to τριακόσιοι, thereby emending שֵׁשׁ to שָׁלֹשׁ, as described in the commentary. The reading שֵׁשׁ, if a transcriptional error as seems probable, must have been very early in incidence, because LXX MSS in general seldom question the MT reading.

The phrase שֹׁמְרֵי מִשְׁמֶרֶת הַקֹּדֶשׁ is incorrectly considered by J. A. Paterson (*Numbers*, Leipzig: Hinrichs, 1900), p. 42, as a gloss. The phrase, which does not occur in vv. 22, 34, emphasizes the special responsibilities the Kohathites alone had in handling the most holy furnishings of the shrine.

3:30 אֱלִיצָפָן: The son of Uzziel and leader of the Kohathites has his distinctive name spelled as אֶלְצָפָן in Ex. 6:22; Lev. 10:4.

3:32 One would expect a plural form, הַלְוִיִּם, instead of a singular, הַלֵּוִי, to describe the company of Levites, and the Samaritan Pentateuch and one or two versions adopted such a change (cf. Num. 1:50). But the MT reading can be taken as a collective singular.

3:36 It is possible to understand וְכָל-כֵּלָיו וְכֹל עֲבֹדָתוֹ as a hendiadys construction, "and all their working tools," and the same may be true also for the plural form in 4:32.

3:39 וְאַהֲרֹן is omitted by some MT MSS, the Samaritan Pentateuch, and the Syriac Version. The name in the MT is marked by the *punctus extraordinarius*, indicating that the Masoretic scribes suspected some textual irregularity. This is one of ten such instances in the Torah. See E. Würthwein, *The Text of the Old Testament* (Grand Rapids: Eerdmans, 1979), p. 172.

3:47 See R. J. Williams, *Hebrew Syntax*, p. 8, sect. 15 and p. 23, sect. 100, for the repetition of numbers as distributives.

3:49 There was apparently some variation in the spelling of the term for "redemption" (money). In this verse it appears as הַפְּדְיוֹם, which is its only MT occurrence in this form. In 3:51, הַפְּדֻיִם was regarded by the *qere* as needing correction. If BHS is followed, the spelling הַפְּדוּיִם would only involve transposing two of the consonants occurring in the 3:49 form and would seem unobjectionable. See also GKC sect. 124a, d–f; R. J. Williams, *Hebrew Syntax*, p. 7, sect. 7; p. 9, sect. 19.

D. THE MINISTRY OF THE LEVITES (4:1-49)

Chapter 4 has four main components: (1) Kohathite service (vv. 1-20); (2) Gershonite service (vv. 21-28); (3) Merarite service (vv. 29-33); (4) census of Levites (vv. 34-49).

1. KOHATHITE SERVICE (4:1-20)

Translation

Then the LORD spoke to Moses *and Aaron, saying: Take a census of the Kohathites among the Levites, counting them by family groups and families, from the age of *thirty years up to fifty, comprising all who come to serve as workers in the Tent of Meeting.

The work of the Kohathites in the Tent of Meeting involves caring for the most sacred furnishings. (4:1-4)

Exegesis and Exposition

Once more the Lord instructs Moses and Aaron in the matter of a Levitical numbering. But this second census is no mere repetition of the one in the previous chapter. The historiography of Numbers is characterized by the revelation of God's being translated from oral pronouncements into immediate activity, which was recorded and incorporated into the social and spiritual fabric of the nation. The incidence of periodic assent formulas, indicating that Moses and Aaron did precisely what was commanded them, shows that punctilious attention was paid to the carrying out of God's orders. It becomes possible to see something of the process by which the religious faith and experiences of the infant nation were molded into a theocratic system that was to influence the Hebrews profoundly throughout their subsequent history.

The census described in chap. 4 is complementary to the one

contained in 3:1-39, which had as its purpose the registration of all male Levites one month old or older. Integral to the purpose of the first census was the general organizing of duties connected with the Tabernacle and the emphasis upon the special services the Levites were to render. The second census provided a register of all males of the tribe of Levi who were between thirty and fifty years of age. Such a procedure was undertaken to identify this group as "working Levites" and to specify the different kinds of duties of the various families. This census differs from the order in chap. 3, the family groups being listed according to the importance of their duties. But it observes the same basic pattern and describes the responsibilities of each unit. This is followed by a notation concerning the identity of the person who was supervising the group (4:16, 28, 33).

To the Kohathites was assigned the important task of looking after and maintaining the most holy furnishings of the Tabernacle. Although the Kohathites were to be available for service in the "cultic cordon" (MT מִשְׁמֶרֶת, *mišmeret*) along with other Levites (4:27-32), the MT makes it clear that they were actually an elite group of men in the prime of life who possessed particular skills. Milgrom[44] has identified three general descriptions of their activity: (1) מְלָאכָה, *mĕlā'kâ* (4:3), which he interpreted as "skilled labor"; (2) עֲבֹדָה or עָבַד (4:4, 23, etc.), signifying unspecified "physical work," and (3) שֵׁרֵת, *šôrêt* (4:12, 14), which appears to have described their functions as assistants to the priests.

This group was noted for its versatility, and it is possible that its more junior members would have served as apprentices, since Num. 8:24 indicates that Levites of the age of twenty-five years or more could participate in Tabernacle duties. The period between thirty and fifty years of age was undoubtedly the one in which the best service could be given in the care of the Tabernacle's sacred furnishings.

Translation

When it is time for the camp to move, Aaron and his sons shall come and take down the screening curtain and cover the Ark of the Testimony with it.

They shall then place over this a covering made from fine leather, spread a cloth of solid blue color over that, and put the Ark's poles into position.

They shall spread a violet cloth over the Table of the Presence and place on it the dishes, plates, and bowls, along with the flagons

---

44. J. Milgrom, *Studies in Levitical Terminology*, 1:60-70.

for drink offerings. The bread that is there continually is to remain on it.

Over these they shall drape a scarlet cloth, and on top of that a covering of fine leather, and place its poles in position. (4:5-8)

Exegesis and Exposition

When the people were about to break camp, the Kohathites began their duties associated with the task of transporting the sacred objects. They could not commence their work, however, until Aaron and his sons had screened the Ark from public view by covering it with the blue and scarlet curtain (Ex. 26:31) that separated the Holy Place from the Most Holy Place, where the Ark was located. The MT אֲרוֹן הָעֵדֻת, 'ārōn hā'ēdut, "ark of testimony," KJV) should be understood as the "ark of (i.e., containing) the covenant stipulations." On top of the curtain was placed a leather covering. MT עוֹר תַּחַשׁ ('ôr tahaš) is variously translated as "badgers' skins" (KJV, *NKJV*), "goatskin" (*RSV*), "porpoise skin" (*NASB, NEB*), "hides of sea-cows" (*NIV*). Those scholars who support the rendering of "porpoises" or "sea cows" in vv. 8, 10, 11, 12, 14, and 25 have supposed them to be the dugong (*Halicore Lemprichii*), a variety of dolphin occurring in the Gulf of Aqaba and the Red Sea. The *NIV* equates the "hide of a sea-cow" with the skin of a porpoise, following the Arabic cognate *tūḥas*, "dolphin," "porpoise."[45]

Although the skin of a marine mammal would provide a waterproof covering for the Ark, such a device would hardly be necessary in an area where there was minimal rainfall. A further problem with this interpretation is that, when the Tabernacle was being constructed, the Israelites were at a considerable distance from available dugongs. In addition, there is no evidence anywhere in the OT that the Hebrews knew how to catch the mammals or to prepare their skins, nor is there any indication in Numbers of any trading with Bedouin tribes who might have had such a commodity for sale.

The most conclusive evidence against the use of dugong or other similar dolphin skin is that, although the species possesses fins, its skin is smooth, not scaly, and therefore it would be ceremonially unclean and consequently prohibited under the provisions of Levitical law (Lev. 11:10). It is hard to imagine the Hebrews defiling their most holy shrine with such a covering, particularly since the legislation relating to such matters as clean and unclean species had but recently been promulgated. The Arabic cognate is thus seen to be both misleading and inappropriate.

---

45. Cf. R. F. Youngblood, *TWOT*, 2:967; *Fauna and Flora of the Bible*, United Bible Societies, Helps for Translators, 11 (1972), pp. 22-23.

Consequently it seems most consistent with the contextual situation to render *taḥaš*, by "goatskin" or "badger skin." It is highly probable that the term simply meant "leather"[46] and may have been borrowed straight from Egyptian *ths*.

Some doubt seems to exist about the locus of the poles by which the Ark was carried. According to Ex. 37:5, Bezalel inserted the gold-plated acacia poles into their rings when he had completed the Ark. When God was instructing Moses about the dimensions of the Ark, He commanded that the carrying-poles were to remain *in situ* (Ex. 25:15). This was evidently intended to make it clear that the Ark was a portable sanctuary.[47] This tradition was still being observed when the Ark was finally reposing in Solomon's Temple (1 Kings 8:8). At that time the carrying-poles were in their rings and were visible to contemporaries standing outside the inner sanctuary (2 Chron. 5:9).

But in Num. 4:6 the priestly supervisors of the sacred shrine, under the leadership of Aaron himself, were ordered to place the poles in position for transporting the Ark on its journey, implying that when the Ark was stationary the poles had been removed. Perhaps all that is meant is that the high priest was to ensure that the ends of the poles were unimpeded by coverings so that they could be grasped easily by the Kohathites. A similar procedure was required for the table containing the Bread of the Presence (v. 8), the golden altar (v. 11), and the bronze altar. The Table of the Presence was laid in the usual sedentary manner even when the Ark was being transported, but it was covered with cloth and leather to prevent exposure to the elements.

Of small dimensions, the Table was 2 cubits long, a cubit wide, and 1½ cubits high, or about 36 inches by 18 inches by 27 inches. Overlaid with pure gold and enhanced by a golden molding on the rim, it was also transported by gold-plated poles that fitted through rings fastened on the four corners made by the legs (Ex. 25:23-29). The structure served as a stand for the dishes (MT קְעָרֹת, *qĕʿārōt*) on which the Bread of the Presence ("continual bread," KJV) was placed, along with the plates (MT הַכַּפֹּת, *hakkappōt*; "spoons," KJV; "dishes for incense," RSV; "dishes," NIV), the bowls (MT הַמְּנַקִּית, *hammĕnaq-qiyyōt*; "flagons," NEB), and the flagons for drink offerings (MT קְשׂוֹת הַנֶּסֶךְ, *qĕśôt hannāsek*; "covers to cover withal," KJV). Apart from the flagons for offering libations and the plates for the Bread of the Pres-

---

46. Cf. J. C. Trever, *ISBE*, 3:97.
47. Nelson's *Illustrated Bible Dictionary*, Herbert Lockyer, Sr., gen. ed. (Nashville: Thomas Nelson, 1986), p. 98. The Tabernacle and its furnishings are reproduced conjecturally in P. F. Kiene, *The Tabernacle of God in the Wilderness of Sinai* (Grand Rapids: Zondervan, E tr. 1977).

ence, the precise use of the other utensils is not clear. The ceremonial bread (KJV "shewbread") was to be set out continually in the Lord's presence (Ex. 25:30) and consisted of two rows of six loaves each, symbolizing the twelve tribes. The loaves were replaced every Sabbath day, and the old bread was eaten by the priests.[48]

The table itself was a display stand, situated on the north side of the Holy Place. In appearance it was probably not unlike the low tables used in Mesopotamia and illustrated by discoveries in a Middle Bronze Age tomb at Jericho. Commentators sometimes liken it to the representation of a Jewish Temple table that appeared on the Arch of Titus (which can be seen today in the ancient forum in Rome), but this is conjecture. When being transported the table was covered with scarlet cloth, on top of which was a sheet of leather. No other cultic article was wrapped in scarlet. Since it was an open structure, the table would not carry an electrostatic charge, unlike the Ark, and therefore it would be safe to remove the carrying poles for storage purposes between journeyings.

Translation

They shall take a violet cloth and cover the lampstand, its lamps, wick trimmers, and trays, as well as all the jars of oil used to supply it.

Then they shall wrap it and all its equipment in a covering of fine leather and put it on a carrying-pole.

They shall spread a blue cloth over the gold altar, cover that with hides of fine leather, and put its poles in position.

They shall then take all the pieces of equipment used for serving in the sanctuary, wrap them in a blue cloth, cover them with a fine leather overlay, and put them on a carrying-pole. (4:9-12)

Exegesis and Exposition

The golden lampstand (MT מְנֹרַת הַמָּאוֹר, *mĕnōrat hammā'ōr*), commissioned in Ex. 25:31-40, was wrapped in a violet[49] cloth similar to the one on the Table of the Presence. The specifications for its manufacture were given in great detail, resulting in a magnificent arrangement of branches, calyxes, and petals hammered out from a single piece of pure gold. Seven lamps (MT נֵרֹת, *nērōt*) adorned it in such a manner as to shed their light over the area in front of it. It was located on the south side of the Holy Place, across from the Table of

---

48. H. F. Beck, *IDB*, 1:464; G. H. Davies, ibid., 4:506.
49. For the colors of Near Eastern antiquity see P. L. Garber, *ISBE*, 1:729-32 and bibliography.

the Presence. The *menorah* came to symbolize God's presence within the later Temple, and according to Jewish tradition it was never extinguished until the time when the *shekinah* (the divine presence) left the Temple prior to its destruction by the Babylonians. Splendid imitations of the *menorah* commonly adorn Jewish synagogues and are not unknown in Gentile religious circles.

Along with the lampstand were golden implements consisting of מֶלְקָחַיִם (*melqāḥayim*; "tongs," KJV, NIV; "snuffers," RSV), a word found only in the dual form and rendered in this commentary by "wick trimmers"; מַחְתֹּת (*maḥtōt*; "snuffdishes," KJV; "tongs," RSV, NIV; "firepans," NEB), apparently a general-purpose tray; and כְּלֵי שֶׁמֶן (*kĕlê šemen*), containers for the oil that supplied the lampstand. All the items associated with it were to be placed, when covered, on a מוֹט (*môṭ*), a term used to describe a pole but evidently one of a different style from the בַּדִּים (*baddîm*) used in transporting the Ark. It would appear that the pole was borne on the shoulders of two people walking in single file, much in the manner in which the spies carried back a huge bunch of grapes after reconnoitering Canaan (Num. 13:23). The NEB conveys the impression that the golden lampstand and its appurtenances were placed in a leather bag and slung on the pole, but the MT is not specific about this matter.

The golden altar of incense, commissioned in Ex. 30:1-10, was located outside the curtained entrance to the Holy Place, and it, too, had to be wrapped by Aaron and his sons in a sheet of leather, with its poles placed in position. Made of acacia wood plated with gold, it was small in size, being a cubit long by a cubit broad and 2 cubits high, or about 18 inches by 18 inches by 36 inches. The sides seem to have been solid, but beneath the horned projections at the upper corners were gold rings, two on both sides, into which the carrying-poles would fit. The accessories involved in burning incense morning and evening were to be placed in a blue cloth protected by a leather covering and transported on a pole.

Translation

They shall remove the ashes from the bronze altar and spread a purple cloth over it. Then they shall place upon it all the equipment used for ministering there—the trays, meat forks, shovels, and basins. Over it they shall spread a *covering of fine leather hides and insert its poles. (4:13-14)

Exegesis and Exposition

The bronze altar of sacrifice, the specifications for which occur in Exodus 27:1-8, was an acacia-wood structure plated with sheets of bronze, an alloy of copper and tin,[50] and measured 5 cubits long, 5 cubits broad, and 3 cubits high, or about 7½ feet square by 4½ feet high. As with the altar of incense, it was adorned with four horned projections that were integrated with the bronzed surface. This altar had bronze rings on both sides into which bronze-plated poles could be inserted. The altar, located in the courtyard of the Tabernacle, was a hollow box-like structure with a bronze grating fitted halfway up the altar (Ex. 27:5). Before the altar could be wrapped for its journey it was necessary for the ashes to be removed and carried away for disposal.

The utensils associated with this altar comprised pots (MT סִירֹת, sîrôt) for removing fat and ashes, shovels (MT יָעִים, yāʿîm, found only in the plural), basins (MT מִזְרָקוֹת, mizrāqôt; "tossing bowls," NEB; "sprinkling bowls," NIV), used for dashing blood against the altar (Ex. 29:16), pronged forks (MT מִזְלָגוֹת, mizlāgôt; cf. 1 Sam. 2:13), and trays (מַחְתּוֹת, maḥtôt; KJV, NASB, NEB "firepans"). Because the sacrificial altar was not an enclosed box containing an electrostatic charge, no danger was encountered when the poles were inserted for the journey.

The horned projections on the incense altar and the bronze sacrificial altar were smeared with blood during certain sacrificial rituals (Ex. 29:12; Lev. 4:7, 18, 25, 30, 34; 16:18). In a later period fugitives seeking refuge from pursuers could cling to the horns for divine protection (1 Kings 1:50-53; 2:28) from crimes except murder. The horns have been understood to symbolize the sacredness of the Lord's altar, but other explanations have also been advanced.[51] Horned altars have been unearthed at Megiddo, Gezer, and Dan, dating from the Early Bronze Age to the Iron Age (about 3000 B.C. to 1200 B.C. or later). From this latter period two terra-cotta altars were unearthed at Taanach.[52] Another similar limestone altar found at Palmyra in northern Syria bore the inscription חַמָּן (ḥammān, "altar of incense)."

Translation

When Aaron and his sons have finished covering the sanctuary and all the sacred vessels, and when the camp is due to move, then the Kohathites shall come to undertake the carrying. But they are not to touch any holy thing, lest they die. All these articles in the Tent of Meeting are what the Kohathites will carry.

Eleazar, son of Aaron the priest, will be in charge of the lamp oil, the fragrant incense, the daily grain offering, and the anointing oil.

---

50. See F. W. Richardson, NIDBA, pp. 107-8.
51. E. Ball, ISBE, 2:758.
52. H. M. Wiener, W. S. Caldecott, C. E. Armerding, ISBE, 1:100-104.

He will be responsible for the entire Tabernacle and its contents, the sanctuary and its equipment. (4:15-16)

Exegesis and Exposition

   The packing of the various articles in the sacred shrine was restricted to the most highly-placed cultic officials—namely, Aaron and his remaining sons. Such a limitation indicates the importance of this work, which involved the presence and power of God Himself. From recent experience the chosen priests were well aware of the punishment that would overtake those who disobeyed God's laws, and in particular they had been warned not to touch the sacred vessels and to avoid all contact with the Ark. This most revered object was sanctified in a special way because it was here that God appeared to Moses. If we are correct in describing the Ark in modern terminology as the equivalent of a vast capacitor containing a powerful electrical charge, the danger of instant death on contact with it was no idle threat.

   The technical details of the situation would have been lost on the Israelites, even if it had been possible for them to have learned of them. Unlike the Sumerians and Egyptians, the Hebrews had no rudimentary knowledge of electricity. The legislation in the Torah that prohibited the wearing of garments of mixed fibers (Lev. 19:19)[53] was aimed at forestalling the discomforts of static electricity, but the rationale was not explained to the Hebrews for the same reason. All of this is consistent with God's dealings with humanity, however. He does not explain to us mysteries that are beyond our understanding, nor does He always justify His ways to His children. Instead, He requires that all those who are committed to Him by covenant relationship shall obey His injunctions and reflect His holiness (Lev. 11:44). The same conditions are mandatory for all those who live under the New Covenant (1 Pet. 1:13-16).

   Once everything was ready for the journey, the Kohathites were to pick up the articles to be carried from the dismantled Tent of Meeting. The Levites acted at all times under the jurisdiction and supervision of the priests, an entirely proper relationship because God had appointed them to assist the priests in their duties. Eleazar was singled out to be in charge of four commodities: (1) שֶׁמֶן הַמָּאוֹר (*šemen hammā'ôr*), the lamp oil derived from pressed olives (Ex. 25:6; 27:20-21), which kept the lamps alight in the sanctuary from evening until morning; (2) קְטֹרֶת הַסַּמִּים (*qĕṭōret hassammîm*), the spiced incense (25:6; 30:34-38), the compounding of which for private purposes was

---

53. Cf. R. K. Harrison, *Leviticus*, p. 200.

87

prohibited on pain of death (34:38);[54] (3) מִנְחַת הַתָּמִיד (*minḥat hattāmîd*) or daily offering of grain, presumably a reference to the mixture of finely ground flour and oil that accompanied the sacrifice of two year-old lambs each day (29:38-41); (4) שֶׁמֶן מִשְׁחַת–קֹדֶשׁ (*šemen mišhat-qōdeš*), or sacred anointing oil (30:22-33).

It has sometimes been assumed that Eleazar himself was to carry the items mentioned in v. 16, but this does not seem to be the sense of the MT. It was his duty, however, to oversee the packing of all the items in the Tent of Meeting in such a manner that nobody except the priests saw the cultic objects. Once the equipment had been wrapped, it was the responsibility of the Kohathites to transport it carefully, whether the contents of the bundles were volatile or not.

Translation

The LORD said to Moses and Aaron: Do not allow the Kohathite family groups to be cut off from the Levites, but in order that they may live and not die when they come close to the most holy equipment, do this for them: Allow Aaron and his sons to enter the sanctuary and assign to each man his work and his appropriate load. But the Kohathites must not go in for even a momentary glance at the holy equipment, on pain of death. (4:17-20)

Exegesis and Exposition

The purpose of this short section is clear. God gave instructions to Moses and Aaron to warn them of potential physical danger to the Kohathites as they discharged their duties. Even the most accidental contact with the sacred objects of the sanctuary would result in sudden death. This penalty is expressed euphemistically by the phrase "cut off." Even the high priest, who alone of all other priests was required by his duties to enter the innermost room of the sanctuary once each year on the Day of Atonement (Lev. 16:34), stood in peril of his life if he was ceremonially unclean, or if he conducted the ritual improperly. Even a momentary glance (MT כְּבַלַּע, *kĕballaʿ*, "like a swallowing") at the exposed sacred objects was sufficient to bring immediate death to an unwary Kohathite.

As in other areas of the cultic regulations, the Creator of the universe must be approached with seriousness and sincerity, and the officiant must not deviate from the prescribed pattern. The ritual procedures must be followed to the last detail, and no innovation was to be countenanced, lest pagan practices creep into the veneration of the Most Holy One of Israel. Whatever individual idiosyncrasies

---

54. I know of no modern attempts to reproduce the sacred incense according to the recipe in Ex. 30:34-38.

Aaron and his sons may have had, they were required to be submitted totally to the will of God. In this attitude is crystallized the two ingredients for a rich, spiritual walk with the Lord—namely, complete trust and implicit obedience. Under the New Covenant the same is true for the Christian also, for whom, as the hymn writer has pointed out, there is "no other way."[55]

2. GERSHONITE SERVICE (4:21-28)

Translation

The LORD spoke to Moses, saying: Take a census of the Gershonites by their families and family groups.
Count all the men from thirty to fifty years of age who come to serve in the duties of the Tent of Meeting. (4:21-23)

Exegesis and Exposition

The annunciatory formula introduces a pericope relating to the registration and work of a senior group of Gershonites. Like the Kohathites, those enrolled were between the ages of thirty and fifty. The census procedures were identical in both cases, as was the designation of the place where they were to serve. What was different about the two groups, however, was the duties each performed. The "service" (MT צָבָא, ṣābāʾ) was a term used in Num. 1:3 to describe military service, but elsewhere it alluded to toil or trouble. The language suggests that the Kohathites, Gershonites, and Merarites were as well organized for serving God in the Tabernacle as the rest of the tribes were for battle.

Translation

These are the duties to be carried out by the Gershonite family groups in their service and general work.
They shall carry the curtains of the Tabernacle and the Tent of Meeting, its covering, and the outer covering of fine leather, the curtains at the entrance to the Tent of Meeting, the curtains for the entrance to the courtyard surrounding the Tabernacle and the altar, their ropes, and all the equipment employed in its service. The Gershonites must do everything connected with them. (4:24-26)

Exegesis and Exposition

The term עֲבֹדָה, ʿăbōdâ, implied physical labor for the Gershonites, as it did for the Kohathites, with the difference that the Gershonites handled the various fabrics that covered the sacred shrine, as well as the ropes and hangings of the Tabernacle itself, rather than the sacred

---

55. Daniel B. Towner, "When We Walk with the Lord" (1887).

objects within it. Their task was to dismantle, pack, transport, and reassemble the various fabrics and ropes as the occasion demanded. This was a less strenuous and exacting task than the work of the Kohathites, who were dealing with more volatile and potentially lethal objects.

A new term (MT מַשָּׂא, maśśāʾ), which was not applied to the Kohathites, described the burdens the Gershonites had to transport. For this, according to Num. 7:7, Moses had assigned two carts and four oxen that the leaders of Israel had given at the dedication of the Tabernacle and the altar. A final term (MT מִשְׁמֶרֶת, mišmeret), applicable also to the Kohathites, recognized that the Gershonites were also to be part of the cultic cordon of unarmed security guards, with particular responsibility for protecting the cloth and leather furnishings of the Tabernacle. These items are described in Ex. 26-27 and are summarized here in 4:25.

The curtains of the Tent of Meeting (Ex. 26:1-6) formed an inner lining of embroidered linen (MT יְרִיעֹת שֵׁשׁ מָשְׁזָר, yĕrîʿōt šēš mošzār) over which were draped matching goats' hair curtains. On top of these were placed rams' skins dyed red (MT עֹרֹת אֵילִם מְאָדָּמִים, ʿōrōt ʾêlim mĕʾoddāmîm), and surmounting that a further covering of fine leather (MT עֹרֹת תְּחָשִׁים, ʿōrōt tĕḥāšîm) for protection (26:7-14). The curtain (מָסָךְ, māsāk) separating the Holy Place and the Most Holy Place (26:36) was also woven to match the other draperies, except that it was not adorned with embroidered cherubim. Those curtains (MT קַלְעֵי הֶחָצֵר, qalʿê heḥāṣēr) that enclosed the total Tabernacle structure (27:9-18) were also of finely woven linen, a substance much favored in ancient Near Eastern religions. They were bulky in character, since they had to cover a length of 100 cubits (about 150 feet) on the north and south sides and 50 cubits (about 75 feet) on the west side. The entrance to the Tabernacle compound (MT שַׁעַר הֶחָצֵר, šaʿar heḥāṣēr; KJV "gate of the court") was located on the east side and was 20 cubits (about 30 feet) in width. The intervening space on either side was covered with separate curtains, each of which was 15 cubits (about 22½ feet) long. An elaborately woven screen (מָסָךְ, māsāk) was devised to form a covering for the entrance to the Tabernacle enclosure. The handling of all these materials was the responsibility of the Gershonites.

Translation

Aaron and his sons shall direct all the activities of the Gershonites, whether in carrying or in the performance of other duties. You shall assign to them the tasks for which they will be responsible.

This is the service allotted to the Gershonite family groups at the

Tent of Meeting. The activities will be under the direction of Ithamar, son of Aaron the priest. (4:27-28)

Exegesis and Exposition

As with the Kohathite Levites, the work of the Gershonites was intimately associated with that of Aaron and the priests. The Gershonites were under the supervision of Ithamar, who was a Kohathite Levite (Ex. 6:16-23). As Thompson has pointed out,[56] this genealogy indicates that Eleazar son of Aaron had heavier responsibilities than Ithamar, Aaron's fourth and youngest son. It would also suggest that the Zadokite Levites, as the house of Eleazar became known subsequently (cf. 1 Chron. 24:3, 6), took precedence over the Ithamarite Levites.

3. MERARITE SERVICE (4:29-33)

Translation

Make a compilation of the Merarites by their family groups and families.

Enumerate all the men from thirty to fifty years of age who come to serve in the duties of the Tent of Meeting.

This is what they have to carry in their work at the Tent of Meeting: the boards of the Tabernacle, its crossbars, posts, and sockets, the posts of the surrounding courtyard with their sockets, tent pegs, and ropes, along with everything else required to maintain it. You must assign to each man by name the load he must carry. (4:29-32)

Exegesis and Exposition

The instructions given by God to Moses in Num. 4:21 are also to be applied to the Merarites. They were to be security officers for the work of packing, carrying, and reassembling the physical framework of the Tabernacle. The framework's structural components were as follows. The boards (קַרְשֵׁי הַמִּשְׁכָּן, *qaršê hammiškān*), made of gold-plated acacia wood, were 100 cubits long (about 150 feet) and 1½ cubits wide (about 2¼ feet). There were 48 of these units, 20 on the north and south sides and 8 on the west. The boards were linked together by gold-plated acacia crossbars (MT בְּרִיחַ, *bĕrîaḥ*), which fitted into golden rings attached to the boards. According to Exodus 26:28, the center crossbar stretched from end to end along the length of the frame in the middle, while the 5 bars on the north, south, and west went only part of the way. A. R. S. Kennedy[57] argued plausibly

56. J. A. Thompson, *The New Bible Commentary Revised*, p. 175.
57. A. R. S. Kennedy, *Hastings' Dictionary of the Bible* (1898-1904), 4:659-67.

that the "boards" (KJV, *RSV*) or "planks" (*NEB*) consisted of two long *uprights* (MT יָדוֹת, *yādôt*) joined by cross-members after the fashion of a ladder. This design would make the framework lighter to carry and would also enable the beautiful curtains to be seen easily. The lower ends of the uprights fitted into silver sockets (MT אֲדָנִים, *'ădānîm*), of which there were 96.[58] The directions in Ex. 26:32-33 prescribed four gold-plated acacia posts (MT עַמּוּדִים, *'ammûdîm*) from which the curtain (MT פָּרֹכֶת, *pārōket*) that divided the Holy Place from the Most Holy Place was to be suspended.

As far as the courtyard area was concerned there were sixty of these posts, each fitting into a bronze base (Ex. 27:9-17) or socket (MT אֶדֶן, *'eden*) and secured by bronze pegs (MT יְתֵדוֹת, *yētēdôt*) and guy ropes (MT מֵיתָרִים, *mêtārîm*). Exodus mentions other articles of a general nature (כֵּלִים, *kēlîm*) that would be involved in the service of the Tabernacle, and these are alluded to in Num. 4:32. In v. 32 it is possible to construe the MT to mean either that each man is named for a specific task of carrying (so *NEB* and this commentary), or that the articles to be transported were given specific names (KJV, *NIV*). If the intention of the MT was to stress the names of the men, it is an unusual feature of the designation of Levitical duties and could be interpreted as emphasizing individual responsibility in the service of the Tabernacle in a manner not apparent to this degree previously.

Translation

These are the duties of the Merarite family groups as they work at the Tent of Meeting. Ithamar, son of Aaron the priest, shall supervise them. (4:33)

Exegesis and Exposition

As with the Gershonites, Ithamar was to oversee the work of the Merarites at all times, and in the same way they were supplied with wagons for transporting the wooden frames and their accessories (Num. 7:8) from the offerings made at the formal dedication of the Tabernacle's altar of sacrifice. Commentators have often affirmed that the tasks the Merarites were called upon to perform were of a low order, requiring no special skill. While it is true that their duties had nothing about them as unusual, responsible, and even dangerous as those of the Kohathites, the Merarites played an important part in ensuring the physical stability of the Tabernacle structure.

Had the Merarites been negligent in erecting the Tabernacle to

---

58. See D. W. Gooding, *IBD*, 3:1506-11; C. L. Feinberg, *ZPEB*, 5:572-83.

the point where it collapsed and exposed the Ark to public view, the effect would have been devastating for the entire congregation. In a community of priests and a holy nation, there is no fundamental difference of value in the kinds of service offered to the Lord. The hand does not take precedence over the eye in the body of believers, nor does the ear over the foot. All forms of service are legitimate and equal when they are done as unto the Lord. As Paul had to point out to the Corinthian Christians, bodily organs that seem delicate are important to human functioning. If the body as a whole is to function effectively, it can do so only when its members are united in pursuit of the common spiritual ideal (cf. 1 Cor. 12:12-26).

4. CENSUS OF LEVITES (4:34-49)

Translation

Moses, Aaron, and the community leaders enumerated the Kohathites by their family groups and families.

All men from thirty to fifty years of age who came to serve in the duties at the Tent of Meeting when counted by their family groups totaled 2,750.

This was the total of all the recorded Kohathite family groups who served in the Tent of Meeting. Moses and Aaron enumerated them according to the LORD's command through Moses. (4:34,37)

Exegesis and Exposition

Four elements characterized the census: (1) registering of eligible males, (2) statement of age-groups enrolled, (3) total number of males counted, and (4) closing formula for each of the three groups stressing the divine source of the census instructions and the human vehicle by which they were implemented (Num. 4:37, 41, 45, 49). The summary deals with the three Levitical groups in the order in which they occurred earlier in the chapter (4:1-34) but differs from that in chap. 3, which takes the three sons of Levi in order of seniority.

Translation

The Gershonites were counted by their family groups and families.

All men from thirty to fifty years of age who came to serve in the duties at the Tent of Meeting when counted by their family groups and families totaled 2,630.

This was the total of all the recorded Gershonite family groups who served in the Tent of Meeting. Moses and Aaron enumerated them according to the LORD's command. (4:38-41)

Exegesis and Exposition

The narrative follows the same literary pattern as that describing the Kohathite registration. This is an appropriate procedure for a statistical compilation inasmuch as it enabled numbers to be compared readily, made for easy memorization, established a standard scribal form for recording the proceedings, and made no differentiation in status between the various Levitical groups.

Translation

The Merarites were counted by their family groups and families.

All men from thirty to fifty years of age who came to serve in the duties at the Tent of Meeting when counted by their family groups totaled 3,200.

This was the total of all the recorded Merarite family groups who served in the Tent of Meeting. Moses and Aaron enumerated them according to the LORD's command through Moses. (4:42-45)

Exegesis and Exposition

The final group, the Merarites, was larger than the two preceding ones, but despite this no distinction was made in the process of registration or the status of the group.

Translation

Thus Moses, Aaron, and the Israelite leaders registered all the Levites by their family groups and families.

All the men from thirty to fifty years of age who came to perform the work of serving and carrying the Tent of Meeting numbered 8,580. (4:46-48)

Exegesis and Exposition

As noted earlier, there was probably some "rounding off" as far as the actual head count was concerned, but the differences in any event would have been minimal.

Translation

As the LORD had commanded them they were enumerated by Moses, each one being assigned his duties and instructed as to what to carry. In this manner they were registered, as the LORD had commanded Moses. (4:49)

Exegesis and Exposition

This chapter makes explicit the differences of status and function that existed between the priests (the sons of Aaron) and the Levites (the sons of Levi). By divine appointment it was the responsibility of the Levitical groups to act as aides to the priesthood and to operate strictly within the prescribed parameters. But in differing ways the duties and service of the Levites were of fundamental importance to the entire worshiping community of Israel. Therefore, as the Levites ministered to the priests they were also ministering to the whole people of God.

Excursus on Incense and Anointing Oil (4:16)

The resin (נָטָף, *nāṭāp*) is commonly identified with the exudate of the stacte shrub (*Commiphora opobalsamum*), but some writers have suggested species of the acacia, perhaps *A. senegal,* from which gum arabic is made. Others have proposed the *Astragalus gummifer,* producing tragacanth, which is still employed in pharmacy and industry, or possibly the shrub *Styrax officinalis,* which produces a liquid balsam that was formerly used medicinally. The onycha (MT שְׁחֵלֶת, *šĕḥēlet*) has been described in KB, p. 961, as comprising the closing flaps of the *Strombus* mollusk, which emit a pungent odor when burned. The word occurs once only in the Hebrew Bible, and thus its meaning is not certain. Some translators render it "onycha," following the LXX *(ὄνυχα, onycha),* meaning a nail or a claw (*NEB* "aromatic shell"), or some marine organism such as a mollusk that would convey a claw like appearance. Such marine organisms, however, were pronounced unclean under Levitical law (Lev. 11:10) and therefore would not be employed in the sacred incense. It does not appear appropriate for the mineral onyx to be included in a compound of vegetable materials, and therefore it is possible that onycha was actually a species of rock-rose, perhaps *Cistus salvifolius,* which secretes an aromatic gum known as ladanum (cf. *Fauna and Flora of the Bible,* United Bible Societies, 11, p. 149). Galbanum (MT חֶלְבְּנָה, *ḥelbĕnâ*) is another aromatic resin native to Persia and is secreted by the *Ferula galbaniflua* in a milky form that becomes amber in color when solidified. The plant is related to dill or fennel. The final principal ingredient, pure frankincense (MT לְבֹנָה, *lĕbōnâ*), is the aromatic exudate of different species of the genus Boswellia (cf. F. N. Hepper, *JEA* 55 [1969]: 66-72). Whereas galbanum would be imported from Persia, frankincense would be obtained most readily from the Sheba (Saba) area. It is uncertain if the Boswellia shrubs ever grew in ancient Canaan. When the compounded ingredients were heated, a strong balsamic odor would ensue that would fumigate the area of the altar. As befitted the majesty of the Lord, the sacred incense was only compounded at some expense, making the supervision of the priests necessary in its formulation and administration, both for ritual propriety and for controlling costs.

95

The compounder of the holy anointing oil was to follow carefully the directions given in Ex. 30:22-33. Moses was instructed to take 500 shekels (about 12½ pounds) of liquid myrrh (MT מָר-דְּרוֹר, *mor-děrôr*), coming most probably from the thorny tree *Commiphora myrrha* Nees, native to Arabia and Ethiopia and thus readily accessible; 250 shekels (about 6¼ pounds) of fragrant cinnamon (MT קִנְמָן-בֶּשֶׂם, *qinněmon-beśem*), the low shrub *Cinnamomum zeylanicum* Nees, the ripe fruit of which yields a fragrant oil, although in modern times cinnamon is obtained from the inner bark of young branches; the same amount of fragrant cane (MT קְנֵה-בֹשֶׂם, *qěnēh-bōśem*), probably the highly-scented ginger grass, *Andropogon aromaticus* Roxb., originating in northern India (cf. *MPB*, pp. 39-41); and 500 shekels weight of cassia (MT קִדָּה, *qiddâ*), the fragrant inner bark of the shrub *Cinnamomum cassia* Blume, which in modern times is often used to adulterate the more costly cinnamon. All these ingredients were compounded with a hin (about a gallon) of olive oil to make the holy anointing oil.

The completed batch would weigh about 37½ pounds, according to the standard of the sanctuary shekel, along with an extra 10 pounds of olive oil. As with the sacred incense, the anointing oil stressed the essential holiness and uniqueness of Israel's God. It was peculiarly His, and He would tolerate no imitations. Once more the emphasis is on obedience to His will as revealed through His servants. The Hebrews are warned that the penalty for disobeying God in this matter is death.

Additional Notes

4:1 While a few MT MSS not surprisingly omit וְאֶל-אַהֲרֹן, this seems unwarranted by the way in which the preposition is used for Aaron as specifically as for Moses.

4:2 נָשֹׂא אֶת-רֹאשׁ: An infinitive absolute form is used as an emphatic term here. The phrase occurs commonly in the records.

4:3 The LXX Codex Vaticanus reads εἴκοσι καὶ πέντε ἐτῶν here and πεντεκάιεἰκοσαετοὺς in vv. 23, 30, 35, 39, 43, 47, whereas the Codex Alexandrinus reads εἴκοσι, following 1 Chron. 23:24, 27.

4:13 The LXX is apparently following an independent MS tradition in reading καὶ τὸν καλυπτῆρα ἐπιθήσει ἐπὶ τὸ θυσιαστήριον instead of the MT וְדִשְּׁנוּ אֶת-הַמִּזְבֵּחַ.

4:14 The LXX and the Samaritan Pentateuch deal at greater length than the MT with cloths and coverings, and many scholars regard the material as midrashic in nature. The possibility that an independent MS tradition was being followed should not be discounted, however.

4:16 At the end of the verse the LXX reads ἐν πᾶσι τοῖς ἔργοις.

4:26 The LXX omits the MT וְאֵת-מָסַךְ פֶּתַח שַׁעַר הֶחָצֵר, perhaps as the result of a scribal error known as homoeoteleuton, provoked by the double occurrence of הֶחָצֵר.

4:31 The LXX supplies more details about the coverings and in v. 32 gives more information about the customs of the courtyard and other Tabernacle equipment.

4:49 The MT is difficult here. The singular verb פָּקַד makes for rather awkward reading: "According to the instructions (lit. "mouth") of the LORD he numbered them by the hand of Moses." While a plural verb might make the sentence smoother, the singular verb could well be viewed as exercising collective force and indicating that all the services of the *šōṭĕrîm* and tribal leaders (cf. v. 34) were concentrated administratively in Moses, who was held solely responsible, as civil leader, for communicating God's will to the Israelites.

2
Commands for Holiness in Israel (5:1–10:10)

Chapter 5 can be analyzed structurally into four main units: (1) separation of the unclean (vv. 1-4); (2) restitution for sin (vv. 5-10); (3) jealousy ordeal (vv. 11-28); (4) summary (vv. 29-31).

A. PURITY, RESTITUTION, AND THE JEALOUSY RITUAL (5:1-31)

1. SEPARATION OF THE UNCLEAN (5:1-4)

Translation

The LORD said to Moses: Order the Israelites to drive out of the camp every leper, everyone who has a discharge, and anyone who becomes ritually unclean through contact with a dead body.

You shall expel both male and female, putting them outside the camp so that they will not defile the camp where I dwell among you.

So the Israelites did this and expelled them from the camp. The Israelites did just as the LORD had instructed Moses. (5:1-4)

Exegesis and Exposition

This second section of Numbers opens with miscellaneous rules and regulations involving the immediate community life and setting out the traditions and procedures to be observed when the nation was settled in Canaan. In a kingdom of priests (Ex. 19:6), an emphasis upon holiness was bound to be given pride of place. One characteristic feature—separation from all forms of evil—was emphasized by God's command. The content follows the familiar form of the announcing of authority, the specific rules and procedures to be observed, and a note to the effect that the Israelites had obeyed the injunctions meticulously. In this instance the offenses that characterized impurity and pollution were leprosy (Lev. 13-14), bodily discharges (Lev. 15:2-25), and contact with a dead person or animal (Lev. 11:39; 21:1-4), all of which produced immediate ritual defilement.

Uncleanness was regarded as the opposite of holiness and therefore was contrary to God's intrinsic nature (Lev. 11:44, etc.) and to the character that He prescribed for His people. The rationale underlying "clean" (MT טָהוֹר, *ṭāhôr*) and "unclean" (MT טָמֵא, *ṭāmē'*) species or objects was not stated in Leviticus, but the enactments concerning the two conditions carried the same authority as the sacrificial regulations.[1] Social anthropologist Mary T. Douglas has suggested that, since holiness required individuals to conform to the class to which they belonged, uncleanness was indicated by conditions of nonconformity,[2] a position with which Wenham[3] is in general agreement.

Although Douglas is correct in stating that the Levitical legislation was designed to convey God's concept of the ideal to mankind, she appears to give less emphasis to the purely ethical and spiritual values characteristic of separation than the legislation demands. Holiness as an ethical value has no relevance for the animal creation, so that for nonhuman species, concepts of cleanness and uncleanness must be based upon other criteria. The differentiating factors are given in Leviticus as far as food is concerned, but without further explanation save that the unclean defiles the one in contact with it. There is nothing in Scripture to indicate that certain animal species are "nonconformist" because they may have fallen from a pristine state of animal grace. Though the whole of terrestrial creation has come under the curse of mankind's rebellion against God (Rom. 8:22), the chief concern of Leviticus seems to have been hygienic, since the prohibited animals carried the potentiality or actuality of infection through contact or ingestion. At all events, no expositor disagrees about the penalty for the infraction of regulations concerning cleanness and uncleanness, which were physical separation of the offender from the holy community for a period of time, or the ultimate fate of being "cut off" (MT כָּרַת, *kārat*), i.e., killed.

The leper (MT צָרוּעַ, *ṣārûa'*) was unclean because of being af-

---

1. R. K. Harrison, *Leviticus*, TOTC (Leicester: Inter-Varsity, 1980), p. 120.
2. Mary T. Douglas, *Purity and Danger* (London: Routledge and Kegan Paul, 1966), p. 53.
3. G. J. Wenham, *Leviticus*, pp. 19-20.

flicted with צָרַעַת, ṣāraʿat (Lev. 13:2, etc.), an ailment that struck abject
terror into the inhabitants of the ancient Near East. The term was
translated as "leprosy" in the KJV, following the LXX λέπρα (*lepra,*)
which was also adopted by the Vulgate. The *NASB* and *RSV* continued the KJV tradition, but subsequent translations, influenced by
studies denying that the term צָרַעַת (*ṣāraʿat*) meant the same as modern clinical leprosy (Hansen's disease), cast around for alternative
renderings. These came to include "infectious disease," "infectious
skin disease" (*NIV*), and "malignant skin disease" (*NEB*).[4] The
Hebrew term must be understood to be generic, as is indicated by the
general nature of the root צרע (*ṣrʿ*), meaning "to become diseased in
the skin."[5]

As will be clear from a perusal of Lev. 13, the suspected victim of
ṣāraʿat had to submit to examination by the priest, who as diagnosti-
cian was acting as a medical health officer for the community. Although the Hebrew of the chapter is both technical and obscure, it is
apparent that, by employing diagnostic tests that included quarantine (the earliest recorded use of this preventive procedure), the
priest-physician was ultimately able to differentiate between benign
and malignant forms of *ṣāraʿat.*

According to epidemiological and other studies, there is little
doubt that Hansen's disease, caused by the tiny organism *Mycobacte-
rium leprae,* was known and feared in Palestine by at least the time of
Amos (c. 760 B.C.). The dread disease may be the one referred to in a
cuneiform tablet from the Old Babylonian period (c. 2250-1175 B.C.),
but this cannot be demonstrated with certainty. If the *ukhedu* disease
of the Ebers medical papyrus from ancient Egypt (c. 2300 B.C.) was a
form of clinical leprosy, which is certainly possible, then the disease
would be well known in Egypt by 1500 B.C.

Despite claims by some modern doctors and theological writers
that the *ṣāraʿat* of Lev. 13 in its malignant form could not possibly
have been Hansen's disease, there are in fact striking correspon-
dences between it and the malignant form of *ṣāraʿat* described in
Leviticus.[6] Those who deny such an identification have failed to suggest a plausible clinical alternative.

The male or female who had a bodily discharge (MT זָב, *zāb*)

4. For a criticism of the NEB rendering see R. K. Harrison, *Leviticus,* pp.
137-38.
5. Cf. J. F. A. Sawyer, "A Note on the Etymology of ṢARAʿAT," *VT* 26 (1976):
241-45, who interprets *ṣāraʿat* in terms of cutaneous symptoms of the
disease.
6. On this see the table in R. K. Harrison, *ISBE,* 3:103-6, with bibliography.
See also ibid., *IDB,* 3:111-13; *Leviticus,* pp. 136-48; *DNTT,* 2:463-66; G. J.
Wenham, *Leviticus,* p. 192.

seems to have been afflicted predominantly with a discharge from the sexual organs. Legislation to deal with this situation occurred in Lev. 15:1-33, a passage that balanced two kinds of discharge, chronic and intermittent, against both sexes, making for four specific cases (vv. 2-12; 16-18; 19-24; 25-27) in a chiastic or introverted pattern. The most obvious discharge for a male would result from gonorrhea, a sexually-transmitted disease acquired from a partner infected with the organism *Neisseria gonorrhoeae*. A discharge from the rectum, such as would occur in cases of diverticulosis or other intestinal ailments, is a doubtful assessment of Num. 5:2, as with Lev. 15, since the presence of blood would almost certainly have drawn comment. As Wyper has pointed out, the temporary female discharge of v. 2 was menstruation,[7] whereas a chronic hemorrhagic discharge could result from a uterine fibroid, diverticulosis, or some other form of abdominal pathology, such as gonorrhea.

Contact with a dead body (MT לָנֶפֶשׁ, *lānāpeš*) seems to refer primarily to a deceased human being (cf. Num. 19:13), although נֶפֶשׁ (*nepeš*) is sometimes applied to animals as well (e.g., Lev. 24:18).[8] Dead persons were defiling to the touch and therefore conveyed ceremonial uncleanness to those who handled them. Once again, the prospect of acquiring some form of infection from such a contact seems to have been one of the concerns of the Levitical legislation.

For the foregoing varieties of ritual defilement the priest was authorized to expel the offenders from the camp in order to prevent the spread of uncleanness in the community. Though the concept of maintaining divine holiness was at the forefront of the Levitical legislation, there seems also to have been a hygienic concern for the welfare of the holy nation, symbolized by the priest acting as a medical health officer. This is evident in the Levitical stipulations regarding unclean foods, which could transmit various kinds of lethal bacteria, and the enactment governing the disposition of human feces (Deut. 23:12-14), which, if left exposed, could lead, among other infections, to anterior poliomyelitis through the activities of flies as vectors.

God's holiness involved separation from all forms of physical, moral, and spiritual defilement. Those who were unclean could have no doubt as to their condition if they were segregated in the general area of the camp latrines. While divine holiness separates from all that is unclean, it also has an integrating force in the personality (*nepeš*) of the one who obeys God's commandments by reinforcing a

7. G. Wyper, *ISBE*, 1:947. On this general topic see R. K. Harrison, *Leviticus*, pp. 158-66; G. J. Wenham, *Leviticus*, pp. 217-25.
8. B. K. Waltke, *TWOT*, 2:587-91, and bibliography.

positive response to discipline in terms of moral, mental, and physical health. As long as the Israelites were prepared to obey God's injunctions to the letter, they would be vigorous and prosperous witnesses to the wisdom and power of the one true God.

2. RESTITUTION FOR SIN (5:5-10)

Translation

Then the LORD spoke to Moses, saying: Speak to the Israelites: When any man or woman sins against another and thus is unfaithful to the LORD, that person is guilty.

He must confess the sin that he has committed, make full restitution for his wrongdoing, add one fifth to it, and give it to the person whom he has wronged. (5:5-7)

Exegesis and Exposition

In this passage, the second of three introduced by an annunciation formula, the members of the holy nation are introduced to the concept of personal sin (חַטָּאת, ḥaṭṭā't). This word is derived from a root חטא (ḥṭ'), which occurs nearly six hundred times in the OT. Its basic meaning is that of "missing" something, whether a specific objective, or a more general sense of losing one's way or failing to live up to a requirement or standard. In the causative form the verb means "to lead someone into sin."[9]

Commentators have pointed out the general relationship of this material to the legislation found in Ex. 22:7-15; Lev. 6:1-7 (MT 5:20-26), although there are certain differences in the Numbers text. The genre of this legislation is known by scholars as casuistic or case law,[10] in which the situation is introduced by the Hebrew particle כִּי (kî, "when"), followed by the procedure to be adopted. Where subsidiary contingencies arise, the particle אִם ('im, "if"), is used to deal with such situations, as in Num. 5:8. Case law was predominant in ancient Near Eastern legislation, the most familiar being the group of laws attributed to Hammurapi (18th century B.C.).[11]

Num. 5:5-10 can be analyzed structurally as follows: vv. 5-6, the protasis of the conditional situation, involving a breach of God's law; v. 7, the apodosis, in which the procedure leading to forgiveness is described; v. 8, a special contingency and the provision for it; vv. 9-10,

---

9. See G. H. Livingston, *TWOT*, 1:277-79, and bibliography.
10. See the early bibliography in W. J. Harrelson, *IDB*, 3:89, and later studies in R. K. Harrison, *ISBE*, 3:85.
11. On the problems involved in dating Hammurapi see *HIOT*, pp. 159-66.

the priest's portion. In the outline of the case, males and females are treated as equally open to acts of iniquity (Heb. "all the sins of mortals"),[12] and as potentially unfaithful to the Lord's commandments. Because of lack of obedience they would bring damage to the social and spiritual fabric of the kingdom. Conviction of sin brings with it a sense of guilt, which can be assuaged only by confession and reparation.

The basic theological assumption of the narrative is that the individual is in a sinful condition, the norm for humanity. Only as the chosen people elect to commit themselves to obey God's will can they expect the blessings of the covenant to apply to them. Where sin has been committed, there can be no forgiveness until confession and recompense have been made. The close relationship between God and Israel makes an offense against any individual a sin against the Lord (cf. Lev. 6:2; MT 5:21). God's people were commanded to love their neighbors as themselves (Lev. 19:18), a concept that was also prominent in the teachings of Jesus (Matt. 5:43-44; 19:19; etc.). To feel guilt (MT אָשָׁם, 'āšām) is to experience remorse because of wrongdoing and thus constitutes an acknowledgment of responsibility. Where אָשַׁם ('āšam) occurs as a verb in the Pentateuch (e.g., Lev. 4:13-27; 5:2-5, 17-23; Num. 5:6-7), it is normally accompanied by procedures for removing the guilt.[13]

In Levitical tradition reparation was generally based upon cash values, presumably in weighed amounts of silver, with a twenty percent increment as a penalty. Then as now, those lessons are learned most quickly that have an impact upon one's personal finances. As a result of presenting the restitution directly to the offended party and not by means of a substitute, the transgressor would be less likely to commit such an offense in the future, because his behavior would become public knowledge. The sacrificial rituals were not intended to cleanse from guilt as such, since this would be incorrect both scripturally and psychologically. The fact that sin has been committed is responsible for feelings of guilt, and once the offender has been cleansed from sin and assured of divine pardon, the feelings of guilt will be assuaged.

---

12. This appears to be a subjective genitive form, as with the KJV and *RSV*.
13. G. H. Livingston, *TWOT*, 1:78-80. For an extensive bibliography see also J. C. Moyer, *ISBE*, 2:580-81; C. A. Beckwith, "'Asham," *The New Schaff-Herzog Encyclopedia of Religious Knowledge* (1950): 5:95-96; L. L. Morris, *EvQ* 30 (1958): 196-210; J. Hempel, *IDB*, 2:156-61; S. J. De Vries, *IDB*, 4:361-76; L. R. Keylock, *ZPEB*, 2:852-53; J. Milgrom, *Cult and Conscience* (Leiden: Brill, 1976), pp. 1-14; *Studies in Cultic Theology and Terminology* (Leiden: Brill, 1983), pp. 53-54; D. Kellermann, *TDOT*, 1:429-37; R. Knierim, *THAT*, 1:251-56; W. G. Justice, *EDT*, pp. 489-90.

Translation

But if that person has no close relation to whom recompense can be made for the wrong, the restitution then belongs to the LORD and must be given to the priests, along with the ram of atonement with which the priest will make expiation.

All the offerings of holy gifts that the Israelites bring to the priest shall become his property.

Each man's holy gifts become his; whatever is given to the priest becomes his property. (5:8-10)

Exegesis and Exposition

In this case-law statement, notice is taken of a contingency in which the injured party has apparently died, perhaps as a result of the offense. What is worse, the person may have departed this life without having a close relative (MT גֹּאֵל, *gōʾēl*), such as a brother or uncle, to whom the compensation might be paid.[14] Under these circumstances the reparation, including the twenty percent surcharge, belonged to the Lord and became the perquisite of the priest. The "ram of atonement" (MT אֵיל הַכִּפֻּרִים, *ʾēl hakkippurîm*) prescribed in Lev. 6:6 (MT 5:25) was to be an unblemished animal that had been valued properly (Lev. 5:15, 18) and was thus acceptable as a guilt offering. Once this animal had been presented ritually to the priest after appropriate restitution had been made, the transgressor would receive atonement through confession of sin and the performance of the sacrificial procedures.

Pardon for the penitent sinner is an expression of God's love that occurs repeatedly in the Levitical sacrificial legislation, as it does also in the New Covenant teachings (1 John 1:9; etc.). The ostensible purpose of this procedure was to impress upon the chosen people the necessity for absolute honesty in social relationships. Many religious people live in a way that divorces their faith from ethics. Therefore, for the practicing Christian, the ethical teachings of the NT must be taken seriously as an integral part of the Christian faith.[15] The act of confession of sin must express the intention of the offender never to commit that transgression of the Lord's will again. Both the Old and New Covenant are emphatic that there can be no such circumstance as "easy forgiveness." The free pardon comes at the expense of life. In the Old Covenant, the life of a select animal is given to God instead of

---

14. For studies relating to the function of the kinsman-redeemer in Israel see A. R. Johnson, "The Primary Meaning of גאל," VTSup 1 (1953): 67-77; R. C. Dentan, *IDB*, 4:21-22; R. L. Harris, *TWOT*, 1:144-45; J. J. Stamm, *THAT*, 1:383-94; H. Ringgren, *TDOT*, 2:350-55.
15. R. K. Harrison, *Leviticus*, p. 73.

the life of the sinner. In the New Covenant, Christ's life was offered up to God on Calvary for the sin of the whole world.

The "holy gifts" received this designation because of their "separated" (MT קֳדָשָׁיו, *qŏdāšāyw*) character. They had been removed from the normal activities of life and devoted to God in the form of a contribution, which in turn became a priestly perquisite. The sacrificial rituals ensured that proper provision was made for both the Tabernacle and the welfare of the officiating priests and their families (cf. Lev. 7:14, 20; Num. 18:4, 26; 31:29; etc.). Under the principles of the New Covenant, Paul instructed the Gentile Christians of Corinth in the ancient Levitical tradition that those who ministered holy things at the sacrificial altar were also to be partakers of the altar (1 Cor. 9:13).

3. JEALOUSY ORDEAL (5:11-28)

This is the third section of the present chapter to be opened by an annunciation formula. The matters common to all three involve the holiness of the physical and spiritual body of Israel.

The wilderness period was formative for Hebrew religion, and the legislation given to Moses at Mount Sinai represents a concentration of cultic and spiritual instruction that was to be normative for the era of the wanderings and beyond. As is obvious from the announcement formulas, God speaks directly to Moses and also conjointly to Aaron. Even the celebrated prophets in a later age of Hebrew history were never accorded the privilege of such prolonged personal attention from God.

As with the preceding section, 5:11-28 introduces the concept of case law in relation to suspected marital infidelity by a woman. The legislation prescribed a specific form for dealing with such contingencies and imposed upon the priesthood the obligations of ensuring the discharge of justice. The passage can be analyzed as follows: vv. 11-14, a statement concerning actual or suspected infidelity by a wife; vv. 15-17, the woman is presented to the priest, who prepares to administer the test; vv. 18-23, the woman swears an oath at the priest's behest; vv. 24-26, the water is consumed and the ritual offering made; vv. 27-28, provision for the outcome of the test is stated.

Translation

The LORD spoke to Moses, saying: Address the Israelites and say to them: When a married woman strays morally and is unfaithful to her husband, and a man has sexual relations with her; if this is concealed from her husband, and her impurity is not disclosed, since there was no witness against her, and she was not caught in the act; if in such circumstances jealous feelings arise in her husband, and he

becomes suspicious of his wife when she is actually impure; or if he becomes jealous and suspects her even though she is not impure, (5:11-14)

Exegesis and Exposition

The seriousness of the legislation governing this matter is indicated by the fact that it is preceded by the standard annunciation formula. There is no indication in the MT as to whether the woman who goes astray morally (MT שָׂטָה, *śāṭâ*) does so by choice or is the unwilling victim of a man's concupiscence. But that adultery is being described is made explicit by the MT (וְשָׁכַב אִישׁ אֹתָהּ שִׁכְבַת־זֶרַע, *wĕšākab 'îš 'ōtāh šikbat-zera'*, "and a man lie with her with the emission of semen"). In either event, if the woman failed to disclose this violation of marital integrity and was not intercepted in the act, as happened to one woman in NT times (John 8:4, ἐπαυτοφώρῳ *epautophōrō*, a rare Greek term normally used of theft), her misdemeanor might never be known unless she behaved suspiciously or was harassed further by the offending male. Suspicion preceded factual evidence as the husband experienced feelings of jealousy (MT רוּחַ קִנְאָה, *rûaḥ qin'â*).

The Hebrew קָנָא (*qānā'*) occurs frequently to express strong emotional possessiveness such as covetousness or envy, but also in a more positive sense to signify "zeal." In terms of the marriage relationship, however, it denoted "jealousy," and under the circumstances described was a serious matter, because the law prescribed death as the punishment for adultery (Lev. 20:10; Deut. 22:22).[16] It has been noted frequently that there was no reciprocal provision whereby a woman might bring her husband before the priest on a charge of actual or suspected adultery. But this situation is not as chauvinistic as might appear at first sight. Because Eve dominated and compromised Adam in the Garden of Eden, contrary to the intention of the Creator, she was punished by being made subject to him (Gen. 3:16) and thereby exposed herself to evil as well as good circumstances. Consequently the law provided for a woman to be arraigned on a charge such as adultery without recourse to reciprocal action. But this procedure is governed by the provisions of covenant law, which a God who is also described as "jealous" or "zealous" (Ex. 20:5) will maintain scrupulously. An innocent woman, unjustly accused, had therefore nothing to fear.

Translation

then he is to take his wife to the priest, bringing an offering of one-tenth of an ephah of barley flour. He shall not pour any oil on it

---

16. L. J. Coppes, *TWOT*, 2:802-3.

or place frankincense upon it because it is a grain offering for jealousy, a grain offering to stimulate memory and bring about recall of wickedness. (5:15)

Exegesis and Exposition

With the formal presentation of the accused wife to the priest, the psychological implications of the procedure begin to come into focus. The woman was taken, perhaps under coercion, to the sacred shrine to confront God, and her husband brought along a grain offering prescribed for the ritual. This was a sacrificial gift on her behalf and consisted of barley flour, which was coarser and less costly than fine wheat flour (MT סֹלֶת, *sōlet;* Lev. 2:1; etc.). The amount prescribed, however, was the same as that required for the grain offerings (Lev. 6:20), but unlike them it was not to be accompanied by either oil or frankincense.

The absence of these two ingredients suggests that the flour was more in the nature of a sin offering (cf. Lev. 5:11), but this should not be understood as a presumption of guilt. The MT described it technically as קָרְבָּן (*qorbān*) to signify an offering that could be either sacrificed or merely employed in sanctuary worship (e.g., Num. 7:13, 17, etc.). In this instance the offering was presented to God as a sacrificial oblation, and a portion of it was burned on the altar before the woman was instructed to drink the potion mixed for her by the priest (vv. 25-26). The MT phrase מִנְחַת זִכָּרוֹן (*minḥat zikkārôn*) describes something designed to stimulate mental recall, while מַזְכֶּרֶת עָוֹן (*mazkeret ʿāwôn,*) employing a causative participle of the root זכר (*zkr,* "to remember"), focuses the mind on alleged or specific evil. In 1 Kings 17:18 the phrase could be rendered in terms of accusation of sin.[17]

The jealousy offering, rendered in the MT by the intensive plural קְנָאֹת (*qĕnāʾōt*),[18] gives some indication of the emotional factors governing the occasion and the degree to which God demanded that His laws of purity and holiness be obeyed. The woman, who had been brought into the divine presence under accusation of violating covenant law, could well be expected to experience emotions of resentment and apprehension, particularly if she was innocent, and degrees of fear ranging to stark terror if guilty. In short, the stresses were all that could be expected to be encountered by a woman on trial for her life.

---

17. Cf. BDB, p. 271a.
18. KD, 3:31.

108

Translation

The priest shall then bring her forward and station her before the LORD. He will take some holy water in a pottery jar, and picking up some dust from the Tabernacle floor he will put it into the water. (5:16-17)

Exegesis and Exposition

The procedure is not an idle performance in the presence of an unheeding pagan deity but a confrontation between a person suspected of immorality on the one hand and the Judge of all the earth on the other. As the woman stands in God's presence, the priest prepares the potion to be consumed by her. In this ritual she participates more actively than is normally the case in the Levitical sacrificial procedures. The "holy water" (*NEB* "clean water") would probably be taken from the laver near the shrine for the use of the priests (cf. Ex. 30:18) and was placed in a small earthenware jar.[19] To the jar was added the only other material component: dust (MT עָפָר, *ʾāpār*) from the sanctuary floor. Although the dust came from a ceremonially clean location, it still retained the character of dust with all its potential contaminants.

No stimulants such as alcohol or mind-disorienting vegetable substances such as cannabis oil or resin formed a part of this simple concoction. The ritual relied for its efficacy upon psychological suggestion interacting with a revived memory, as the person stood in Israel's sacred place before God. Some commentators have taken the combination of an earthen vessel and dust as an illustration of human frailty, whereas others have seen in the dust the food that God promised to the serpent (Gen. 3:14) as a curse of sin, thus symbolizing for the woman a state worthy of the deepest disgrace. While all of this may well be true, it is uncertain as to how far the accused woman would be able to accommodate such profound concepts in her moments of distress.

Translation

The priest shall then position the woman before the LORD, uncover her head, and put in her hands the offering to stimulate memory, which is the grain offering for jealousy. The priest shall also hold in his hand the bitter water that brings a curse upon her. (5:18)

---

19. On this "water of judgment" see J. Sasson, "Nu. 5 and the Waters of Judgment," *BZ* 16 (1972): 249-51.

Exegesis and Exposition

Having stationed the woman before the Lord, the priest then loosened her hair, which in general was a sign of mourning (cf. Lev. 10:6). Because loosened hair also was required of those who had leprosy (Lev. 13:45), the implications of uncleanness were present, if not the fact of it. The reason for the procedure in Numbers is not stated, although at the very least it indicated a presumption of shame and guilt. Prejudicial to the woman's case as this procedure might appear to be, it would actually work advantageously for an innocent person, who would be able to bring appropriate counter suggestions to the ritual with the proper degree of conviction.

The offering brought for the woman was made personal by being placed in her hands, while the priest stood before her, holding the water that was now described as "bitter" (MT מֵי הַמָּרִים, *mê hammārîm*).[20] The woman was now deemed to be responsible before God as a witness to her conduct as she held in her hands a prescribed stimulant to memory. In the most literal sense she was holding her life in her hands. The water that she would drink was "bitter" in terms of the awful potential consequences that would become actual if she were in fact guilty. Under those circumstances, whatever negative abdominal conditions were involved as a consequence of the ritual would be terminated by her execution if the provisions of the law for adultery (Lev. 20:10) were followed.

Translation

The priest shall then put her under oath and say to the woman: If no other man has had carnal relations with you, and you have not strayed morally and become impure while still married to your husband, may this bitter water that brings a curse keep you free from harm. (5:19)

Exegesis and Exposition

The preliminaries having been completed, the accused woman was now ready for the imposition of the oath (MT שְׁבֻעַת הָאָלָה, *šĕbuʿat hāʾālâ*, "oath of cursing"; cf. Gen. 27:28). Although this would undoubtedly impose great stress upon her, it also contained a presumption of her innocence, in which event the potion that was destined to produce physical changes would actually keep her from harm. In the preamble to the oath, the priest was emphasizing the covenantal

---

20. "Bitter" has been contested as the meaning of *hammārîm*, which comes from the root *mrr*, "to be bitter." The *NEB* followed G. R. Driver in the rendering "water of contention," but this is not a significant improvement upon the traditional KJV translation.

teaching of the sanctity of marriage and the Lord's abhorrence of adultery (whether physical or spiritual) in the cause of maintaining the holiness of the individual and the community alike. If the woman fulfilled the qualifications expressed negatively by the priest, she would emerge unscathed from the trial by ordeal.

Translation

But if, while married to your husband, you have strayed morally and have defiled yourself by having carnal relations with a man other than your husband (5:20)

Exegesis and Exposition

The seriousness of adultery was (and is) that the marriage relationship, which is covenantal in form, had been breached, contrary to divine law (Ex. 20:14). The husband had been denied the exclusive use of his wife's body, and his relationship with her had become prejudiced both by her disobedience and by her defilement (MT נִטְמֵאת, *niṭmēʾt*), a technical term describing both ritual and moral defilement. Even more precarious for the continuance of community holiness was that such behavior, if it were to go unchallenged, could reduce the people to the level of the surrounding pagan nations and destroy the ethos of moral and spiritual purity that was to characterize a chosen community.

Translation

(at this point the priest is to put the woman under this cursing oath and say to her), May the LORD make your people curse and denounce you as He brings upon you a miscarriage and makes your abdomen enlarge. (5:21)

Exegesis and Exposition

Having finished the preliminary declaration, the priest then pronounced the cursing oath over the woman. This procedure was different from the one in which oaths were accompanied by curses to ensure that the oath was kept (Gen. 24:41; 1 Sam. 14:24), or the kind associated with God's covenant with Israel at Mount Sinai (Deut. 27:11–26; 28:15–68), which provided for punishment consequent to the disobeying of the covenant stipulations.[21] The woman would be

---

21. On oaths and their consequences see F. C. Fensham, "Malediction and Benediction in Ancient Near Eastern Vassal Treaties and the Old Testament," *ZAW* 74 (1962): 1-9; D. R. Hillers, *Treaty-Curses and the Old Testament Prophets* (Rome: Pontificium Institutum Biblicum, 1964); M. R. Lehmann, "Biblical Oaths," *ZAW* 81 (1969): 74-92; A. C. Thiselton, "The Supposed Power of Words in the Biblical Writings," *JTS* 25 (1974): 283-99; F. C. Fensham, *ISBE*, 3:572-74, and bibliography.

punished only if she were already guilty, and if she were innocent the oath would work to her benefit.

To forestall the notion that magic might be involved, the text makes it clear that it was the Lord who would curse the woman by bringing about deleterious physical changes in her. The ingredients of the earthenware pot had no *ex opere operato* efficacy associated with them, and therefore the woman's acquittal or punishment would be of the Lord. If the former verdict, she had been reinforced in her righteous conduct. If the latter, she received the just rewards of transgression consequent upon proper legal procedure. Although the ingestion of the potion would no doubt produce stress, it was not intended as a means of determining guilt, as with the modern lie detector, since at best it would be only ancillary to that end.

The nature of the punishment that would occur consequent to guilt has been the subject of considerable debate among scholars ancient and modern. In dealing with the passage as a whole, the Mishnah noted the sequences that the thigh and abdomen would have followed in carnal relations, but beyond that it was not very specific.[22] The English versions generally interpret the MT to mean "body swell and thigh fall away," but the *NEB* diverges from this rendering and translates the Hebrew by "miscarriage or untimely birth." Perhaps the idea of the woman's ingesting water gave rise to the notion that the swollen abdomen resulted from dropsy, whether of the kidneys or ovaries, or, as Josephus suggested,[23] the accumulation of serous fluid in the abdominal cavity known medically as ascites.

If the terminus of the curse was physical death, the swelling would perhaps indicate preagonal ascites, in which a sudden, intense congestion of the large abdominal organs (viscera) occurs as a result of a serum discharge in the abdominal cavity. This contingency was often followed by the death of the woman involved. A less dramatic condition could have been pelvic peritonitis, a form of inflammation normally restricted to the peritoneum surrounding the uterus and Fallopian tubes. If a woman had experienced sexual congress with a man suffering from gonorrhea, such a peritonitis could have been the result and perhaps have led to the husband's suspicions in the first place.

The same effect, though of a less serious nature pathologically, could have been caused by pseudocyesis. This is a condition that exhibits some signs of pregnancy such as an enlarged abdomen, al-

---

22. *Tractate Ṣotah*, 1. 7.
23. *Ant.* 3.11.6.

though actual conception has not taken place. It is sometimes seen in highly neurotic women and would be susceptible to powerful psychological suggestion. The *NEB* seems to afford the most plausible explanation in suggesting miscarriage or spontaneous abortion, but it does not take account of the possibility of death. This would have occurred if an abortion was followed by uterine gangrene, a ruptured *placenta praevia*, or some other condition producing severe hemorrhage. Similarly, death would have been the end result of the process if the woman, having been adjudged guilty, was executed according to law (Lev. 20:10).[24] It is probably safest to conclude that, whatever the true nature of the punishment, it was deemed appropriate to the crime and fell upon the bodily organs that had engendered the woman's sin.[25]

Translation

May this water that carries a curse with it enter your body so that your abdomen enlarges and you suffer a miscarriage. Then the woman shall respond: Amen, so let it be. (5:22)

Exegesis and Exposition

The solemn words of the priest committed the woman to participation in the ceremony that could honor or disgrace her. She understood both the priestly authority that reinforced the actual words and the significance of the oath she was taking. This verse marks a shift from the responsible agent (i.e., God) to the effective instrument (i.e., the potion) that would implement the intent of the legislation.

The woman's response of "amen" (MT אָמֵן, *'āmēn*) was a familiar token of assent used by Jews and Gentiles alike. The word comes from a root אמן (*'mn*, "to be firm, reliable"), and was used in legal (Num. 5:22; Deut. 27:15-26) as well as religious ceremonies.[26] The meaning of "amen" was extended in the sayings of Jesus to signify "very truth" (Matt. 5:18; etc.). The occurrence of "amen" in Num. 5:22 is the first instance of its use, and that in a legal rather than a religious or devotional setting.

Translation

The priest shall then record these curses on the scroll and forthwith wipe them off into the bitter water. (5:23)

24. Cf. H. C. Brichto, "The Case of the *Sota* and a Reconsideration of Biblical Law," *HUCA* 46 (1975): 55-70.
25. *KD*, 3:32.
26. J. B. Scott, *TWOT*, 1:51-53; H. Wildberger, *THAT*, 1:177-209.

Exegesis and Exposition

As if the spoken word were insufficient for the accused woman, the curses were inscribed in ink on a scroll (MT סֵפֶר, *sēper*), implying the use of a small piece of leather for that purpose. The ink used for writing was made of soot or lampblack dissolved in a little water, to which gum arabic or gum acacia was normally added to bind the letters to the scroll. All of these ingredients were readily accessible in the Sinai wilderness. The resultant mixture was nontoxic and non-metallic and could be washed off the surface of leather very readily. The act of transferring the words of the curses from the scroll to the water, probably by rinsing, meant that the effective instrument would incorporate the very words the woman had accepted by assenting to them and would thus become a physical part of her being.

Translation

He shall make the woman drink the bitter water that carries a curse, and this water will enter her body to produce great suffering.

The priest shall take the grain offering, for jealousy from the woman's hand, wave the offering before the LORD, and bring it to the altar. (5:24-25)

Exegesis and Exposition

The water was now ready for the woman to imbibe. It was probably placed in her hands at this juncture, with all that such an act implied. The tension would be heightened, however, by the fact that, before the woman could drink the mixture, the priest had to take the jealousy offering of grain from her and perform the ritual of presentation at the altar. This mention of this ceremonial act helps to unify the narratives describing the preparation of the potion and its administration, which on casual reading seem disjointed and lacking in narrative smoothness because different perspectives have been recorded. The sacrificial offering of grain was "waved" (MT הֵנִיף, *hēnîp*, a causative form of נוּף, *nûp*, "to move to and fro, swing")[27] before God and then taken to the altar for burning.

Translation

The priest shall then take a handful from the grain offering as a memorial gift and burn it on the altar. After that he shall make the woman drink the water. (5:26)

---

27. For a discussion of the word see G. R. Driver, "Three Technical Terms in the Pentateuch," *JSS* 1 (1956): 97-105; W. Brueggemann, *IDB*, 4:817; J. Milgrom, *Studies in Cultic Theology and Terminology*, pp. 139-58, et al.

114

Exegesis and Exposition

This portion of meal constituted a memorial (MT אַזְכָּרָה, *'azkārâ*), which was a normal part of the sacrificial ritual involving grain offerings (Lev. 2:2, 9, etc.). This again would remind the woman that what was being done was according to divine law. The significance of the memorial portion has been debated by scholars.[28] It may have been a token offered to remind the worshiper of his or her God, although it is uncertain as to why this should have been thought necessary under the circumstances of sacrifice. It may have signified that an appeased deity was now ready to consider the worshiper before Him so that the remainder of the sacrifice could be offered, but that consideration does not apply to the situation narrated in Numbers 5. Probably the intent was to show openly the good faith of the worshiper, who by presenting a token of the offering to God demonstrated that he or she had not come with empty hands to worship the One who was the giver of all good things. Once the offering had been made (MT וְאַחַר, *wĕ'ahar*, "at that juncture"), the woman consumed the potion under the priest's supervision.

Translation

If she has become defiled and has been unfaithful to her husband,* when the priest has made her drink the water that carries a curse with it, the water will enter her body and produce severe suffering. Her abdomen will become enlarged, she will miscarry, and she will be cursed by her people. (5:27)

Exegesis and Exposition

The climax of the trial was now reached, and the woman's guilt or innocence would be demonstrated. In the normal course of events the effects of the liquid upon a guilty woman would be apparent within hours or perhaps days, during which time, unless secluded, she would be subjected to scrutiny. An innocent woman would know within a few hours that she had been vindicated by the trial and, by implication, that her husband had been rebuked in public for his suspicions. But even for an innocent woman, the prospect of physical affliction and spiritual condemnation would have been far from pleasant to endure, reflecting as it did upon her moral integrity.

Translation

But if the woman has not defiled herself and is free from impurity, she shall be judged innocent and will be able to bear children. (5:28)

---

28. Cf. H. Eising, *TDOT*, 4:79-80.

Exegesis and Exposition

Once the woman has been shown to be innocent, no further suspicion must rest upon her. She is ceremonially clean by decree and can resume her normal life, including childbearing. To be childless in a society where the chief end of marriage was procreation constituted a matter of great embarrassment, emotional turmoil, and ultimate reproach for the woman involved, as the experiences of barren women from the time of Sarah onward illustrate graphically. From the comment about childbearing capacity, some scholars have supposed that such would be part of the punishment of the adulterous wife who was convicted by the trial, provided she lived sufficiently long to experience that aspect of the penalty. In all of these matters God is shown to be the judge, and His will for His holy people must prevail.

4. SUMMARY (5:29-31)

Translation

This is the law for instances of jealousy, where a woman strays morally and defiles herself while still married to her husband, or when jealous feelings arise in a man because he suspects his wife. Then he shall station her before the LORD, and the priest shall bring all this law to bear upon her.

Then the husband will be free from guilt, but the woman will bear the consequences of her wrongdoing. (5:29-31)

Exegesis and Exposition

This brief summary of the legislation[29] regarding suspected or actual marital infidelity on the part of a woman emphasizes the main points of the procedure. It applied not only to an adulterous wife (who may not have been apprehended while committing the offense, and therefore with her paramour would not have been executed according to the provisions of Deut. 22:22), but also to a woman who was merely suspected by her husband.

Because a married woman could be the innocent victim of spite, hatred, or a paranoid reaction on the part of an emotionally unstable husband, it was important for her to have proper recourse to law so that, if necessary, she might be vindicated in public. But where the woman was guilty of an illicit liaison, the law would also take its proper course, and once the woman was convicted, the husband was

---

29. Styled a "Torah-subscript" in M. Fishbane, "Accusations of Adultery: A Study of Law and Scribal Practice in Numbers 5:11-31," *HUCA* 45 (1974): 31-36.

absolved from any sense of guilt in the matter of her fate. The legislation assumed that the accused woman would cooperate at all stages of the proceedings. Indeed, it would have been in her interests to do so, because any repudiation of the trial process would have been regarded as tantamount to a confession of guilt.

Excursus on 5:11-31

Numbers 5:11-31 has been the object of study in both ancient and modern times for a variety of reasons. As already noted, it was in essence a trial by ordeal, a procedure familiar in the ancient world (cf. G. B. Gray, *Numbers*, p. 44). It constituted a form of torture imposed to secure a confession in cases of suspected crime, especially marital infidelity. It could be brutal in character, but, as Thompson has pointed out, the ritual procedures in Numbers were lenient compared with the ordeals known in pagan circles. Even more significant is that it was more likely to result in a verdict of innocence, whereas the ordeals of paganism were weighted in favor of guilt (J. A. Thompson, *The New Bible Commentary Revised*, p. 176). Even though the procedure in Numbers may have been more humanitarian, it constituted something approaching the ancient equivalent of the modern lie detector test, with all the associated emotional stresses. Because it was a divinely enacted procedure, its provisions carried all the weight associated with covenant enactments.

The literary structure of the passage has puzzled readers for many centuries. Unless one is aware that repetition characterized ancient Semitic writings, it is possible to imagine that the accused woman was made to stand before God twice (vv. 16, 18) and was given the water to consume twice (vv. 24, 26), or possibly three times if the intent of v. 27 was misunderstood. The woman would also have the oath administered to her on two occasions (vv. 19, 21). In addition, the ritual appears quite complex at first reading, entailing three apparently distinct procedures that the narrative combines into one—namely, the meal offering, the "drink" offering, and the administration of the oath.

These and other theological problems were examined in the Mishnah. The treatise *Tractate Ṣotah* dealt with the passage in some detail and reflected unhistorical accretions that had grown around the biblical tradition, such as the notion that the woman could elect to withdraw from the ritual at certain points. The tractate also furnished information about the leather scroll containing the curses and the way in which they were written, all of which is conjectural.

But conjecture was not restricted to ancient authors, for when the atomizing tendencies of modern critical scholarship were brought to bear upon Numbers, various scholars fractured the MT into several hypothetical underlying "sources." D. B. Stade ("Die Eiferopfer-thora," *ZAW* 15 [1895]: 166-78), for example, alleged the presence of two sources. M. Noth (*Numbers*, p. 49) thought the narrative was composed of several distinct units that had been assembled by an editor. By contrast, a more unified perspective was reflected by D. Kellermann (*Die Priesterschrift von Numeri 1:1 bis 10:10* [Berlin: Töplemann, 1970], pp. 4-17), who thought the narrative constituted one basic source supplemented by two additions. Subsequent contributions to the discussion have tended to minimize or avoid textual fragmentation in the interests of examining philological, scribal, and cultural considerations. These include erudite and stimulating treatments by M. Fishbane ("Accusations of Adultery: A Study of Law and Scribal Practice in Numbers 5:11-31," *HUCA* 45 [1974]: 25-45); H. C. Brichto ("The Case of the *Sota* and a Reconsideration of Biblical Law," *HUCA* 46 [1975]: 55-70); J. Milgrom in R. Friedman, ed., *The Creation of Sacred Literature* (1981), pp. 69-75; T. Frymer-Kensky ("The Strange Case of the Suspected Ṣotah [Numbers V 11-13]," *VT* 34 [1984]: 11-26).

These authors generally attribute the repetitions to scribal practices common in antiquity and point out that the summary repetition of vv. 29-30 parallels subscripts commonly found in cuneiform law as well as that contained in the OT. Although the text at first reading may seem complex and possibly fragmentary in nature, it is in fact integrated by a device known as repetitive summarizing, which at various points in the narrative helps to identify and separate materials that are descriptive or prescriptive.

Thus vv. 24, 26, 27 do not describe three separate instances of drinking. The first one (v. 24) depicts the priest as the agent of administration who, having made a cereal offering to the Lord (vv. 25-26), dispensed the potion to the woman (v. 27). In the scribal mind the comprehensiveness of the legislation is matched by the complexity of Hebrew, which employs surprisingly few words for so important a subject. The fact that the legislation is ancient is guaranteed by the primitive character of the procedure imposed upon the accused woman (R. C. Dentan, *IDB*, 3:569).

Although this legislation was important for maintaining the sanctity of marriage in Israel, as well as for prohibiting the immoral kind of dalliance so common in the ancient Near East, the frequency with which it was applied in Israel is unknown. There are no recorded instances in the OT where trial by ordeal as prescribed in this passage was entertained, even though prohibitions against adultery were still being followed as late as the time of Jesus (Matt. 19:3-9; etc.). The legislation may have been designed for temporary use only, because there is no concluding stipulation to the narrative imposing it as an enactment or statute binding upon all future generations.

Perhaps the situation was comparable to that of older occidental cultures, which in modern times still have laws that have not been utilized for many centuries. The final word on this ancient legislation must be left to Thompson: "Strange as the whole circumstance and ritual may seem to us, it compares so favourably with non-Israelite practice that it may be taken as evidence of that generally considerate attitude of the law of Moses towards women."[30]

Additional Notes

5:2 מִן־הַמַּחֲנֶה: Excluding the unclean from the camp removed defilement from the Lord's presence. Elsewhere only lepers were to be banished. There does not seem to have been a special place outside the community where the unclean resided, and thus such persons could live in any location that did not compromise the holiness of the encampment. Cf. J. Milgrom, "Two Kinds of *ḥaṭṭā't*," *VT* 26 (1976): 333-37.

5:3 מִזָּכָר עַד־נְקֵבָה: I.e., everybody. Prepositions in this and the preceding verse are used liberally to provide added emphasis to the stipulations, as with אֶל־מִחוּץ. No person afflicted was to be exempted from this rule under any circumstances.

אֲנִי שֹׁכֵן בְּתוֹכָם: This expression recurs in Numbers 35:34 in a warning to the Israelites against defiling the Promised Land with blood.

5:8 גֹּאֵל: No specific mention of a redeemer is made in Leviticus 6:1-7.

לַיהוה לַכֹּהֵן: BHS, following the LXX, proposed changing לַיהוה to יְהָיֶה (LXX ἔσται), "shall be." This change, however, denies both the linguistic force and the theology inherent in הַמּוּשָׁב. Where no close relative existed to receive the reparation, it had to be paid to the Lord "for the benefit of" the priest (לַכֹּהֵן; the preposition is a לְ of advantage).

5:9 In attempting to reconcile the change in the preceding verse, the LXX reads τῷ κυρίῳ τῷ ἱερεῖ, and this is supported by one Hebrew MS.

תְּרוּמָה: This sacrificial term comes from the root רוּם, "to lift up," "elevate." In Numbers it describes such varied offerings as produce (15:19-21), tithes (18:24, 26-29), and plunder acquired in battle (31:29, 41, 52). In Exodus it is used of the shoulder of the peace offering (29:27), materials for the Tabernacle (35:5, 21, 24), and the half-shekel

---

30. J. A. Thompson, *The New Bible Commentary Revised*, p. 176.

offering (30:13-16). The term thus applies generally to any gift offered for the support of the priests. Cf. J. Milgrom, *Studies in Cultic Theology and Terminology* (Leiden: Brill, 1983), pp. 159-72.

It is possible to construe לְכָל־קָדְשֵׁי to mean "that is, all the holy things of" (so G. B. Gray, *Numbers*, pp. 42-43; cf. BDB, p. 514b), or to mean "of all the holy things of," where the possessed object would be indefinite (cf. R. J. Williams, *Hebrew Syntax*, p. 51, sect. 270).

5:17 מַיִם קְדֹשִׁים: The LXX reads ὕδωρ καθαρὸν ζῶν, "clean (or pure) running water." It is not necessary to invoke the presence of a holy stream or spring in the camp (cf. A. Dillmann, *Numeri, Deuteronomium, und Josua* [Leipzig: Hirzel, 1886], p. 28). Any uncontaminated water placed in a consecrated vessel would be ritually clean (cf. Ex. 30:28-29) and when poured out would be regarded as "running." For הַמִּשְׁכָּן the LXX reads τῆς σκηνῆς τοῦ μαρτυρίου, perhaps following an independent MS tradition.

5:18 וּפָרַע אֶת־רֹאשׁ: This indication of shame or mourning was forbidden to the priests (Lev. 10:6; 21:10).

מֵי הַמָּרִים: This is usually rendered "water of bitterness," i.e., bitter water, from the root מרר, "be bitter." The LXX reads here ὕδωρ τοῦ ἐλεγμοῦ, "water of testing" (cf. *NEB*), and this described the potion in a manner not inherent in the Hebrew root. Snaith went even further in arguing from Arabic terminology to the conclusion that the liquid was intended to procure an abortion (N. H. Snaith, *Numbers*, p. 202). The Hebrews could well have considered any water unfit for drinking as "bitter."

5:21 בִּשְׁבֻעַת הָאָלָה: The LXX renders this simply by ὁρκιεῖ. This act initiated the process of testing, commonly described as "trial by ordeal." The term needs to be understood properly and distinguished from similar ancient Near Eastern practices. In the latter, the ordeals involved an agent that was already dangerous in itself, such as fire, or water flowing in a river. If the accused died as a result of the agent, as for example in the case of a nonswimmer drowning, the person was deemed guilty. Ancient Near Eastern ritual procedures were quite separate from the ultimate sentence, which was pronounced judicially. Basically the accused was deemed guilty until proved innocent, a position still in evidence in some modern Near Eastern countries. In the biblical legislation the agent would have no effect if the accused person was innocent. There was no prior presumption of guilt, although it may have been suspected. If punishment was imposed, it issued from God, not from a human court. It was intimately associated with the ritual's outcome, and no interval of time was specified for the adverse working of the potion. Even though the emotional stresses could correctly be construed as an ordeal, the woman was deemed innocent until proved guilty, and an innocent person could be confident as to the final outcome.

5:27 וְהִשְׁקָה אֶת־הַמַּיִם: This clause is omitted in the LXX, the repetition of הַמַּיִם later in the verse perhaps having caused homoeoteleuton.

B. PURITY AND THE NAZIRITE VOW (6:1-27)

Chapter 6 can be analyzed structurally into five parts: (1) vow described (vv. 1-8); (2) contingencies for defilement (vv. 9-12); (3) discharging of vows (vv. 13-20); (4) summary (v. 21); (5) priestly blessing (vv. 22-27).

The ideal of purity is addressed from yet another perspective. In this instance the concept of holiness through separation and consecration was the object of legislation, which considered the behavior of individuals rather than the community as a whole. Although such "separated" persons were allowed to participate in community life, they were required to exhibit a particular type of sanctification, governed by specific rules and regulations as the result of a vow. This constituted a solemn undertaking that bound the individual concerned to live according to a prescribed pattern or to discharge specific acts or functions. The Nazirite legislation was meant to regulate the office procedurally and not to institute it. Some facets of the Nazirite's function may have antedated the Mosaic period.

Vows were a common feature of ancient Near Eastern religions, and those who undertook them in connection with temple or ritual functions such as the service of a god were known as votaries. Stob has distinguished between two kinds of vows in the Hebrew tradition: (1) those of voluntarily imposed self-discipline for the development of character, or of self-dedication for the achieving of specific goals, and (2) those consisting of promises made to God in response to an expected divine favor.[31]

Vows could also be part of daily worship (Ps. 61:8) or of the annual festival celebrations (1 Sam. 1:21), as well as constituting an act of thanksgiving for divine blessing (Ps. 116:12-14). A vow of abstinence connected with the dedication of cities to destruction (חֵרֶם, *ḥērem*) was undertaken periodically in time of war (Num. 21:1-3).[32] In the realm of personal discipline and sanctification for the achieving of certain goals, the vow of the Nazirite was by far the most important. The OT does not command anyone to take a vow at any particular time, because those acts were voluntary in nature. Nor was any-

31. G. Stob, *ZPEB*, 5:890.
32. G. H. Davies, *IDB*, 4:793.

one who abstained from making a vow necessarily regarded as sinful. But such vows as were made came under strict regulation so as to make clear to all that they were not to be undertaken lightly (cf. Prov. 20:25; Eccles. 5:4-6). Thus minors, or female children still residing at home, needed parental sanction, predominantly from the father, for their proposed action (Num. 30:3-5), and the vows made by a married woman required her husband's approval (30:6-8, 10-13). By contrast, vows undertaken by divorced or widowed women were held to be binding upon them.

1. VOW DESCRIBED (6:1-8)

Translation

The Lord spoke to Moses and said: Speak to the Israelites and tell them: When a man or woman takes a special vow, a vow of separation as a Nazirite to the LORD, (6:1-2)

Exegesis and Exposition

The legislation opens with the familiar annunciation formula. The vow could be undertaken equally by men or women on a voluntary basis, but it is deemed special by the causative use of the verb פָּלָא (*pālā'*, "to be extraordinary, wonderful"). The nature of the vow was characterized by the title נָזִיר (*nāzîr*), from the verb נָזַר (*nāzar*, "to separate or consecrate oneself").[33]

Under some conditions this separation could be for a specific period of time or for the duration of a special task, after which the vow could be discharged. The Nazirites were established by God as an example of commitment to Him and to the disciplines of their order. The consistent emphasis upon the vow to God was characterized by the seriousness of the undertaking, which made both the participants and their vows sacred.

In the Nazirite votary tradition it was possible for a person to be dedicated to that role without his or her knowledge or approval. Thus Hannah, who herself may have been a Nazirite, made a "bargain" with God to dedicate her son to the Lord's work were He inclined to give her one (1 Sam. 1:11). The vow that was thus imposed upon her firstborn son, Samuel, was intended to be lifelong in nature, but he was never mentioned in this way by the MT.

A fragment of the book of Samuel recovered from the fourth Qumran cave, however, made it apparent that the phrase "he shall be a *nāzîr* forever" had been omitted from the MT of 1 Sam. 1:22, appar-

---

33. For the different readings of the noun see T. E. McComiskey, *TWOT*, 2:568; J. Kühlewein, *THAT*, 2:50-53.

ently as the result of scribal error.[34] Despite this, the tradition of Samuel as a Nazirite persisted in the Hebrew teachings, being reflected in the Hebrew recension of Ecclus. 46:13.

In any event, the length of time that the individual Nazirite attached to his or her vow was incidental to the principal aim of the vow, which was to engender total devotion to the Lord.

Translation

he must abstain from wine and strong drink. He must not drink vinegar made from wine nor from other similar drink. He must not drink any grape juice, nor eat fresh or dried grapes. (6:3)

Exegesis and Exposition

Whereas priests on duty at the Tabernacle were prohibited from consuming intoxicating beverages as they exercised their ritual functions (Lev. 10:9), the Nazirite was forbidden to indulge in wine or strong drink at any time while his vow was in force. Wine (MT יַיִן, *yayin*) made from the expressed and fermented juice of grapes, and strong drink (MT שֵׁכָר, *šēkār*) manufactured by a distillation process that may well have been discovered by the Sumerians, were the principal adult beverages of Near Eastern antiquity.[35] Scholars frequently interpret the MT שֵׁכָר in terms of the Akkadian *šikaru*, "beer," a fermented rather than a distilled beverage. The correctness of this equation is questionable, however, since שֵׁכָר occurs in most Semitic languages as a general designation covering every kind of intoxicating drink, and thus is not restricted to beer.

Although wine was described by the psalmist as making glad the human heart (Ps. 104:15), the dangers accompanying the abuse of intoxicants were noted elsewhere (Prov. 21:20; 23:30-31). Although the Hebrew priests could drink alcoholic beverages as part of a meal, they were forbidden to imitate the conduct of certain religious functionaries of Mesopotamia and Canaan, who employed alcohol as a stimulant intended to produce inspiration. The Christian is urged to follow the Nazirite example by not being intoxicated with alcohol, but instead to be filled with the Spirit of God (Eph. 5:18; cf. 1 Cor. 6:10), because the mind and will of the Lord's servant must be under His control continually.

Even by-products of viticulture were to be avoided by the Nazirite, and these included sour wine and sour strong drink, fresh

---

34. F. M. Cross, "A New Qumran Biblical Fragment Related to the Original Hebrew Underlying the Septuagint," *BASOR* 132 (1953): 15-20.
35. R. K. Harrison, *Leviticus*, pp. 114-15. Cf. D. M. Edwards, *ISBE*, 3:993, and bibliography.

grapes, raisins, or fresh grape juice (MT מִשְׁרַת עֲנָבִים, *mišrat ʿănābîm*, "solution of grapes"). This prohibition must have imposed considerable dietary restrictions upon a votary in a land where clean fresh water was often a scarce commodity and the availability of milk was uncertain. Nevertheless the human body can survive, and even thrive, without ethyl alcohol, and the Nazirites lived to protest by their abstinence the rampant alcoholism that was a serious social problem in the ancient Near East.

Translation

During the period of his special vow he must not eat any product of the grapevine, from seed to skin. (6:4)

Exegesis and Exposition

The Nazirite vow bound the adherent to abstain from every form of evil (cf. 1 Thess. 5:22) as far as alcoholic beverages were concerned. To avoid temptation, no part of the grape, from seeds (MT חַרְצַנִּים, *ḥarṣannîm*) to skin (MT זָג, *zāg*), was to be consumed. The meaning of these two terms is uncertain. By such abstention the Nazirite was not merely following the priestly practices in the Tabernacle worship but was demonstrating his or her sanctification to the Lord by abstaining from even those common elements of food that could impair the committed relationship of the Nazirite to the Lord.

Innocent though raisin cakes might appear, they were denounced in Hos. 3:1 (KJV "flagons of wine") as constituting offerings to pagan gods. Were the Nazirite to eat them, this act could be interpreted as a tacit form of self-offering to a pagan deity and would constitute a violation of the oath. The life of the Nazirite was to be strict and disciplined, avoiding the allurements of sensuality. Many centuries later, the One who described Himself as the "true vine" (Gk. ἡ ἄμπελος ἡ ἀληθινή, *hē ampelos hē alēthinē*) would give new dignity to the fruit of that plant by employing it as a symbol of His blood outpoured for human salvation (Matt. 26:28 and par.).

Translation

As long as he is under a vow of separation, no razor may be used on his head. He must remain holy until the term of his separation to the LORD is completed, and he must allow the hair of his head to grow long. (6:5)

Exegesis and Exposition

The prohibition against shaving the head or cutting the hair during the period of the vow has an interesting parallel in the instructions regarding the planting of trees when Canaan is finally occupied.

All fruiting plants, including the vine, were to be allowed to grow freely for the first three years, and only after that time could the fruit be eaten to God's glory (Lev. 20:23). A similar prohibition in the jubilee year mentioned the unpruned vine (MT נָזִיר, *nāzîr*) specifically (Lev. 25:11). The Nazirite's life was to be analogous to that of the unpruned plants, which were left undisturbed so that in due course the fruit would be sufficiently mature to be of benefit to people.

The Nazirite's whole being, including hair and beard, had been committed to God, and the uncut hair, as his crowning glory, would indicate the nature of his allegiance.[36] Not even the sanctuary priests could claim this distinction. By contrast, those persons who shaved and trimmed the head and beard in various ways identified themselves as being devotees of pagan gods.[37] The term "hair" (MT פֶּרַע, *pera'*, KJV "locks") is from the same root as the term in Num. 5:18 (MT פָּרַע, *pāra'*), describing the loosened hair of the suspected adulteress.

The razor (MT תַּעַר, *ta'ar*) also served as a knife, as in the phrase תַּעַר הַסֹּפֵר (*ta'ar hassōpēr*, "knife of the writer"), or penknife (Jer. 36:23). As such it would be a simple knife of flint, as found at many archaeological sites in Canaan dating back to 3500 B.C. Flint was the preferred medium for a razor because it retained its cutting edge well and was easily sharpened when it became dull. Razors recovered from Bronze Age levels in Egypt and Palestine were frequently more elaborate in design[38] but did not hold a sharp edge for very long. Hence a flint knife continued to be the instrument of choice for circumcision long after the Iron Age began.

Translation

During the period of his dedication to the LORD he shall not have any contact with a corpse.

Not even when his father or mother, brother or sister dies shall he make himself ritually unclean on their account, because his vow of separation is on his head.

Throughout the term of his dedication he is consecrated to the LORD. (6:6-8)

Exegesis and Exposition

In addition to being prohibited from drinking alcoholic beverages, the Nazirite was not allowed to be polluted by any contact

---

36. For the place of hair in idol worship see W. R. Smith, *The Religion of the Semites* (London: A & C Black, 1901 ed.), pp. 327-35, 481-85; H. L. E. Leuring and R. W. Vunderink, *ISBE*, 2:597.
37. R. K. Harrison, *ISBE*, 3:502.
38. Pictured in R. W. Funk, *IDB*, 4:14.

with a dead person, no matter how close the relationship between them had been. The vow was not to be broken because of bereavement, since ritual purity and dedication were of paramount importance. Because the King's business demanded both haste and total commitment, Jesus once admonished a would-be follower who desired to attend his father's funeral to "let the dead bury their dead" (Gk. ἄφες τοὺς νεκροὺς θάψαι τοὺς ἑαυτῶν νεκρούς, *aphes tous nekrous thapsai tous heautōn nekrous*, Matt. 8:22), a "hard saying" that becomes intelligible in the light of the Nazirite tradition.

God had shown in the instance of Nadab and Abihu (Lev. 10:6) that those who bore the anointing oil were forbidden to grieve and had to delegate to other persons their responsibilities with regard to death. The Nazirite was set apart for a special duty or ministry, and his anointing must therefore take precedence over all other circumstances. Only if and when the term of the vow ended could the person begin to resume the former way of life.

2. CONTINGENCIES FOR DEFILEMENT (6:9-12)

Translation

If someone collapses and dies beside him and he consequently defiles his consecrated head, he shall shave his head seven days later, on the day of his ritual cleansing. (6:9)

Exegesis and Exposition

As with all other human beings, certain eventualities were beyond the Nazirite's control. One of these was ritual defilement because of inadvertent contact with the dead. Although the Nazirite could choose to obey his or her vow by refraining from visiting dead family members in order to tender respects, he or she could have no possible control over a situation in which a close companion or fellow Nazirite died suddenly in his or her presence.

The ensuing ceremonial defilement nullified the vow and necessitated ritual cleansing procedures. A week was to elapse between the accidental defilement and the priestly cleansing rites, and on the day that these were appointed to take place the Nazirite was to terminate his vow by shaving the hair of the head. But the Nazirite was still holy to the Lord, and hence the act of shaving should not be interpreted in the light of pagan practices, which were forbidden in Lev. 19:27; Deut. 14:1.

Translation

On the eighth day he must bring either two turtledoves or two young pigeons to the priest at the entrance to the Tent of Meeting.

The priest shall offer one as a sin offering and the other as a burnt offering to make atonement for sin because of his transgression by being in contact with a corpse. That same day he shall reconsecrate his head. (6:10-11)

Exegesis and Exposition

The formal cleansing ceremonies had points of contact with what was prescribed for the healed leper (Lev. 14:1-32) with regard to both the shaving and the offering, the latter being the least expensive of its kind. The turtledoves (MT תֹּרִים, *tōrîm*) and young pigeons (MT בְּנֵי יוֹנָה, *běnê yônâ*) were common items in the Levitical rituals (1:14; 5:7, 11; etc.). One bird was sacrificed as a sin offering (MT חַטָּאת, *ḥaṭṭā't*, 5:8) to atone for the defilement that the Nazirite's contact with death had produced, and the other formed the basis of a whole burnt offering (MT עֹלָה, *'ōlâ*).

The ancients maintained that the dove (*Turtur communis*) had no bile duct and thus was deemed clean and inoffensive.[39] Since it never retaliated when attacked, the dove came to symbolize Christian virtues such as peace. The pigeon (*Columba livia*) or "rock-dove" is considered to be the parent of the domestic species.[40] Both kinds of birds were available for purchase in NT times and were kept in one of the Temple courts (cf. Matt. 21:12; Mark 11:15; John 2:14-16). When the infant Jesus was presented in the Temple (Luke 2:22-24) after His circumcision, Mary and Joseph took advantage of the prescription in Lev. 12:8, where two turtledoves or two young pigeons were regarded as satisfactory offerings for the impoverished.[41] As far as the Nazirite was concerned, once the offerings had been presented, he or she was free to renew the vows that had been nullified by accidental circumstances or ritual contamination. This then involved the ceremonial reconsecration of the head as a public token of complete dedication to the Lord.

The MT does not describe the mechanics governing subscription to the Nazirite vow. There is no priestly formula of administration recorded such as that which formed part of the ritual procedures in the "law of jealousy" (Num. 5:19-26). Thus it appears at least possible that the Nazirite vow could have been a private, individual commitment to God. But whether or not it began with priestly assistance and blessing, it terminated in the sanctuary.

---

39. *Fauna and Flora of the Bible*, p. 23.
40. G. F. Hasel, *ISBE*, 1:987-89.
41. In Lev. 14:22 the same provision was extended to a poor leper.

Translation

He must rededicate himself to the LORD for the term of his vow and must bring a year-old male lamb as a guilt offering. The previous period does not count because he became defiled while he was dedicated. (6:12)

Exegesis and Exposition

A ritual of recompense was prescribed as part of the renewal process. The term of his vow (MT יְמֵי נִזְרוֹ, *yĕmê nizrô*, KJV "the days of his separation") must be begun afresh, as though he had never entered into a vow. The ritual also involved the presentation of a year-old male lamb, an unusual provision since Leviticus 5:16, on which the ceremony was based, prescribed a female lamb. The requirements for a guilt offering (MT אָשָׁם, *'āšām*, Lev. 5:14-19) specified an unblemished ram from the flock, which was to be assessed by the priest for its monetary worth instead of being sacrificed.[42] Though the law referred to accidental handling of sanctuary property or ignorance of what was required in sacrificial procedure, the concept of unwitting transgression applied equally to the Nazirite. The אָשָׁם (*'āšām*) was thus a recompense for being reinstated into the former condition of consecration to the Lord.

3. DISCHARGING OF VOWS (6:13-20)

Translation

When the period of his dedication is completed, the law of the Nazirite shall be as follows: He shall be brought to the entrance to the Tent of Meeting where he will present his offering to the LORD: a year-old male lamb without defect for a burnt offering, a year-old ewe lamb without defect as a sin offering, a ram without defect as a peace offering, along with their grain and drink offerings and a basket of unleavened bread composed of cakes and finely-ground flour mixed with oil and wafers smeared with oil. (6:13-15)

Exegesis and Exposition

When the appropriate time had been reached, the act of discharging the Nazirite vow had to be marked by the ceremonial dignity appropriate to a person who had lived in a special state of consecration to God. Proper cultic procedures are laid down in this section. Just as the taking of the vow was voluntary for adults, so its termination in cases where it was not lifelong is recognized as a conscious decision. The ceremony began with the Nazirite's being escorted to

---

42. Cf. M. Noth, *Leviticus* (1965), p. 47; R. K. Harrison, *Leviticus*, p. 71.

the sacred shrine, along with the prescribed offering. As with the recompense offering, a year-old male lamb was required for a burnt offering (MT עֹלָה, *ʿōlâ*), and for the sin offering (MT חַטָּאת, *ḥaṭṭāʾt*) a year-old unblemished ewe lamb.

For the peace offering (MT שְׁלָמִים *šĕlāmîm*, *NEB* "shared offering"; *NIV* "fellowship offering"; the Hebrew form is always plural) an unblemished ram of unspecified age was prescribed, and this sacrifice expressed the joy that attended the discharging of the Nazirite vow. Some scholars have associated the peace offering with Ugaritic *šlm* and its Akkadian cognate *šulmānu* to imply a "gift."[43] This appears to be a strained interpretation, however, because the root *šlm* carries the basic meaning of "peace" in Akkadian, Ugaritic, Aramaic, Phoenician, Syriac, Arabic, and Ethiopic.[44] Certainly in the Levitical sacrificial tariff the verb form meant "be intact," "be complete," and the peace offering was intended to assure the offerer that whatever was incomplete in him or her would be remedied as the worshiper came in penitence and faith to God, who hears and restores the sinner (cf. Ex. 15:26; Ps. 103:3).[45]

The grain offering (KJV "meat offering," "meat" being the medieval English term for *food*) follows closely the prescription in Lev. 2:4, although the amounts were not stated until Num. 15:4-7, and this included the required quantities for the drink offerings. The amount of the meal offering in Lev. 14:10 was three times that of Num. 15:4, which would indicate that the quantity varied with the kind of ritual. The prescriptions of Num. 15 followed the amounts recorded in Ex. 29:40, and these, being already known to the priests, were not noted here. The cakes had to be prepared from finely-ground wheat or barley flour, as opposed to the coarsely-ground variety offered by a poor person. The termination of the Nazirite vow involved a great deal of expense, which may suggest that the short-term Nazirite came from a wealthier family. For the lifetime votary, of course, cost was an unimportant feature of the vow.

Translation

The priest shall present all these before the Lord and make his sin offering and burnt offering.

He shall present the basket of unleavened bread and sacrifice the ram as a peace offering to the Lord, along with its grain and drink offerings. (6:16-17)

---

43. E.g., B. Levine, *In the Presence of the Lord* (Leiden: Brill, 1974), pp. 3-52.
44. M. F. Unger and W. White, Jr., *Nelson's Expository Dictionary of the Old Testament* (Nashville: Thomas Nelson, 1980), p. 283.
45. R. K. Harrison, *Leviticus*, p. 56.

Exegesis and Exposition

The officiating priest conducted the ritual in the normal manner, with the aim of strengthening the bond of peace and wholeness between God and the votary. In the MT the suffixes of the offerings of v. 15 (מִנְחָתָם וְנִסְכֵּיהֶם, *minḥātām wĕniskêhem*) are plural, whereas in v. 17 they are singular (מִנְחָתוֹ וְאֶת־נִסְכּוֹ, *minḥātô wĕ'et-niskô*), but this only means that the form in v. 17 is collective and that the difference is one of literary style.

Translation

Then the Nazirite shall shave off his dedicated hair at the entrance to the Tent of Meeting. He shall take his consecrated hair and place it in the flames where the sacrifice of the peace offering is burning.

After the Nazirite has shaved off his consecrated hair, the priest shall take the boiled shoulder of the ram, one unleavened cake, and one unleavened wafer from the basket, and place them in the palms of his hands. (6:18-19)

Exegesis and Exposition

The climax of the ceremony occurred in dramatic form when the Nazirite shaved off his consecrated hair, walked from the Tabernacle entrance to the altar where the peace offering was burning, and consigned the hair to the flames. This action has been seen variously as constituting an offering to God[46] or as a means of disposing of something potentially dangerous because of its sacred character.[47] In the latter connection it must be remembered that in the ancient Near East human hair possessed more than ordinary importance, and not least in Israel, where it formed an important component of the Nazirite vow. Thompson has suggested that this may have been because its rapid growth symbolized divine strength given to men (cf. Samson, Judg. 13-16).[48] Hair is actually a waste product of the body, as are fingernails and toenails, and although all of these can appear attractive with proper grooming, it is not easy for the modern reader to understand the attitude of the ancient Near Eastern peoples generally regarding the veneration of hair. The ceremony continued with the priest's placing of the boiled shoulder of the ram (MT הַזְּרֹעַ בְּשֵׁלָה, *hazzĕrōaʿ bĕšēlâ*) along with one unleavened cake and a wafer on the outstretched palms (MT כַּף, *kap*) of the Nazirite's hands.

---

46. So *KD*, 3:39; G. B. Gray, *Numbers*, p. 68.
47. So R. de Vaux, *Ancient Israel: Its Life and Institutions* (London: Darton, Longman and Todd, E tr. 1961), p. 436; M. Noth, *Numbers*, p. 57.
48. J. A. Thompson, *The New Bible Commentary Revised*, p. 177.

Translation

The priest shall then present them before the LORD as a waved offering. They are consecrated and belong to the priest, along with the breast of the waved offering and the hip of the raised offering. After this the Nazirite may drink wine. (6:20)

Exegesis and Exposition

Because these elements were still the property of the Nazirite, the ritual could only be concluded properly when they were transferred ceremonially to God by being presented as a waved offering. These portions then became the priest's perquisite, along with the hip and breast, once the memorial portion had been offered (Lev. 2:2-3). The peace (or "well-being") offering (Lev. 7:11-21) was the only sacrifice in which the donor was permitted to share (hence "shared" or "fellowship" offering) and was also unusual in that it alone of all the other offerings of animals did not provide atonement for sin.[49] Such an offering would furnish a fitting conclusion to the Nazirite's vow and would afford family members and friends the opportunity of celebrating the occasion by means of a sacrificial meal, including wine, which the Nazirite could now consume with impunity.

4. SUMMARY (6:21)

Translation

This is the law for the Nazirite who has vowed to the LORD his offerings in connection with his dedication, as well as anything else that he can provide. He must fulfill the vow that he has made according to the law governing his separation. (6:21)

Exegesis and Exposition

This brief summary statement of the legislation is comparable to that in Num. 5:29-31 relating to the jealousy ordeal. The discharging of the Nazirite vow was complete only when all its regulations had been met. Expensive though the process would be, the Nazirite was nevertheless encouraged to offer whatever he or she could afford beyond the prescribed minimum. This, however, being optional, would be governed by the circumstances and generosity of the individual. At a later time in Hebrew history richer persons defrayed the expenses involved in the ritual discharge when the Nazirite was a poor person.[50]

---

49. R. K. Harrison, *Leviticus*, p. 80.
50. Acts 21:24; *Mishnah Nazir*, ii, 5 seq.; *Ant.* 19.6.1.

5. PRIESTLY BLESSING (6:22-27)

Translation

The LORD said to Moses: Instruct Aaron and his sons, saying, This is the manner in which you shall bless the Israelites. Say to them: The LORD bless you and protect you; the LORD make His face shine upon you and be gracious to you; the LORD turn His presence toward you and give you peace. So they will pronounce My name over the Israelites, and I will bring them blessing. (6:22-27)

Exegesis and Exposition

This benediction, presented in the form of a wish for the future, is one of the most beautiful in the entire literature of spirituality. Happily it is not restricted in its usage or efficacy to God's ancient people or their modern offspring but brings great joy and peace to the Christian as well. Despite its disarming appearance, it is surprisingly intricate. It identifies the divine Author of all that is good as a Being who is able to bring prosperity and peace to His faithful people, in contrast to pagan deities, who were powerless in this respect. God used His servant Moses to mediate to Aaron the high priest and to his descendants the benediction that was to be the peculiar prerogative of the priesthood. It was never to be the privilege of Moses to use this form of benediction, as will be seen from the fact that, when he bequeathed a blessing (Deut. 33:1-29), it was much more in accord with the patriarchal last wills and testaments.

The MT form consists of three separate lines, in which the divine name YHWH is repeated in each for emphasis. Each line contains two invocations addressed to the God of the covenant, but the lines become progressively longer. Verse 24 contains three Hebrew words; v. 25 has five; and v. 26 has seven, the number signifying perfection or completeness. In addition, the second member of each pair applied the first in a particular way to the nation of Israel. Thus in v. 24 the Lord was not merely requested to bless His people in a general way but to afford them specific oversight and protection (MT שָׁמַר, *šāmar*, "watch," "keep," "guard"). In v. 25 not only would He be asked to bring His radiance to bear upon them but also to make His grace and compassion (MT חַנָּה, *ḥannâ*) an integral part of their experience. In v. 26 the Lord is invited to turn His face toward Israel but to do so in a manner that would result in the blessings of "peace" (שָׁלוֹם, *šālôm*).

The theology of the blessing is thoroughly consistent with that of the Sinai covenant. The chosen people can expect blessing only if they trust God and are obedient to His revealed will. God will then follow what they do with His blessing. Similarly, under the New Covenant, the Lord honored the faith and works of the earliest Christian disci-

132

ples with signs that followed, according to an ancient tradition (Mark 16:20). But God's blessing is no abstract conception, for in the Aaronic benediction it also watches over the Lord's people and keeps them safe from harm and danger. The basic meaning of the common verb *šāmar* is "to exercise great care over," "to perform carefully," "to give great attention to," "to guard."[51] If Israel is under God's watchful care, she will be kept safe from her adversaries and will pursue her life under the direct management of the Lord.

The expression "to make one's face shine" has been the subject of considerable discussion. The "face" of God is another way of speaking about His personality. In human beings a wide range of emotional responses is reflected by means of facial expressions. On this analogy, if the Lord's presence is radiating divine favor in the midst of His people, they can confidently expect Him to pour out His covenant mercies upon them.[52] The phrase is used of God alone except in Ecclesiastes 8:1, where it refers to the wisdom of human beings. Gordis has suggested that it means "be gracious toward," as though a court official was being advised to treat his other associates graciously.[53] Miller regards the shining countenance of God as a positive presence for help and favor and as a sign of the friendly and beneficent nearness of God who is gracious in His assistance as He turns to help human beings.[54]

The third line of the priestly benediction develops the thought of the second in that, by lifting up the face (MT נָשָׂא פָּנִים, *nāśā' pānîm*), God is in fact looking directly at His people so that they may receive the benefit of His full attention. The result is *šālôm*, which means peace, prosperity, completeness, health, safety, general well-being, and so on. Peace in the context of the Aaronic benediction does not mean the absence of war but rather the product of a spiritually mature, healthy, and integrated personality that serves God and man to the full. Most of the occurrences of the word describe the state of fulfillment that results from God's presence.[55]

The peace of God was made incarnate in Jesus the Messiah, who is described as the "peaceful prince" (Isa. 9:6) and fulfilled this role as He entered Jerusalem shortly before He was tried and crucified

51. J. E. Hartley, *TWOT*, 2:939.
52. R. K. Harrison, *ISBE*, 2:267.
53. R. Gordis, *Koheleth—The Man and His World* (New York: Jewish Theological Seminary, 1968 ed.), p. 286.
54. P. Miller, "The Blessing of God," *Int* 29 (1975): 245; cf. E. Yamauchi, *TWOT*, 1:302-4, and bibliography; D. N. Freedman, "The Aaronic Blessing," in J. L. Flanagan and A. W. Robinson, eds., *No Famine in the Land* (Missoula, Mont.: Scholars Press, 1975), pp. 35-48.
55. G. L. Carr, *TWOT*, 2:931; E. M. Good, *IDB*, 3:705-6.

(Matt. 21:1-9 and par.; cf. Zech. 9:9). In a continuation of the Old Covenant's spiritual ethos, Jesus also promised to give His followers the security of the peace of God, which transcends all human understanding.[56] By the use of the Aaronic benediction the priests will put the sacred name of the Lord into the hearts and minds of His people, and this will result in a blessing upon the nation.

The fact that the Aaronic benediction is found in the MT in its present place should not be taken as indicating that it formed a blessing at the termination of the Nazirite ritual. A blessing that concluded the sacrifices of Lev. 9:22 was pronounced by Aaron, but the actual words have not been preserved. They may have constituted the Aaronic benediction, but of this there is no evidence. The form of the blessings of Joshua (Josh. 22:6) and David (2 Sam. 6:18) is not recorded, nor is the blessing given by the priests and Levites to the people (2 Chron. 30:27), although in the latter case the Aaronic benediction may have been employed.

Excursus on the Nazirite Law

Whereas the traditional view of the origin of this material ascribed it to the wilderness period and Mosaic authorship, modern literary criticism assigned the section to the so-called "P" document, alleged to be no earlier than about 500 B.C. in its written form. Although some scholars recognized the possible pre-Mosaic origin of certain Nazirite practices, few have been willing to concede an early date for the Nazirite legislation. (For studies from this standpoint see the bibliography in J. C. Rylaarsdam, *IDB*, 3:527; P. J. Budd, *Numbers*, pp. xviii-xxvi.)

The position adopted by liberal scholarship is that the original Nazirites took lifelong vows, and of these persons Samson and Samuel were representative. By contrast, the Nazirites of Amos's day (Amos 2:11-12) undertook the vow for a specific task or for a clearly defined period. Many thus assumed at least two strands of tradition dealing with Nazirite law, which were combined by an anonymous editor late in Israel's history to produce the extant narrative. (See the references to Eichrodt and de Vaux in R. K. Harrison, *ISBE*, 3:502.)

The MT gives no indication that there were large numbers of charismatic Nazirites in the early monarchy period, as some have supposed, and Amos says nothing about the size of the movement in his day. Nor does the prophet speak of the Nazirites as of recent origin, unlike Jeremiah with regard to his contemporaries the Recabites (Jer. 35:1-9). It would appear that the Nazirites had experi-

---

56. The Pauline epistles frequently invoke "grace and peace" upon Christians as a form of greeting. Cf. Rom. 1:7; Gal. 1:3; Phil. 1:2; 1 Tim. 1:2; etc.

enced a prolonged history in Israel and that they could be either lifelong or temporary votaries at any given period. In view of the similarity of some Nazirite practices to those of second-millennium B.C. pagan nations, there seems no reason for denying the antiquity and Mosaic formulation of the Nazirite legislation.

New light was thrown upon the authenticity and antiquity of the Aaronic blessing when two small, corroded silver scrolls that had been used as amulets were recovered from an excavation at Ketef Hinnom, west of the Old City of Jerusalem, in 1979. The fragile nature of the artifacts made unrolling them a difficult and precarious task, and when it was accomplished finally in 1982 the tiny scrolls appeared to be blank.

Under magnification, faint writing appeared on the larger of the two scrolls, but it was only in 1986, when they were being prepared for exhibition, that the contents of these amulets became apparent. The discovery of the threefold repetition of the Divine Name—the first time the name YHWH has been found on an inscription in Jerusalem—led to the decipherment of the Aaronic priestly benediction on the amulets. It was in almost identical form to the MT of Numbers 6:24-26, and the script, which had been etched on the silver, was typical of that in use in the late seventh century B.C. This makes the scrolls from Ketef Hinnom the oldest biblical MSS yet discovered, predating the earliest Dead Sea scrolls by almost four centuries. The fact that the material was in amulet form testifies to a lengthy tradition of usage as a personal blessing. The scrolls also witness coincidentally to the fact that the Aaronic benediction was in written as well as oral form long before the supposed "P" document was compiled.[57]

Additional Notes

6:2 יַפְלִא: The hiphil form of the verb פָּלָא, "be special," "marvelous." The LXX adverb μεγάλως conveys the exceptional nature of the vow.

6:5 גַּדֵּל: The piel infinitive absolute of גָּדַל, "become great," and here "grow lengthy." The LXX reads τρέφων κόμην τρίχα κεφαλῆς. Maintaining the hair in this state was mandatory to the keeping of the vow.

6:13 יָבִיא אֹתוֹ: The MT hiphil imperfect of בּוֹא, "go," "come," with the third singular suffixal form of the accusative particle (LXX προσοίσει αὐτὸς) seems rough to BHS, which prefers either the third plural imperfect hiphil form (יָבִיאוּ) or the third singular qal imper-

---

57. Claire Safran, "Mystery of the Buried Amulet," *Reader's Digest* (June 1987), pp. 95-99.

fect (יָבוֹא). The subject of the MT "he shall cause him to come" is not indicated, but it is not difficult to imagine that the Nazirite would be accompanied by a friend, if only to assist with the sacrificial animals. Alternatively, the causative agent may have been a sanctuary priest who was to officiate at the ceremonies marking the end of the vow. On this basis it seems unnecessary to emend the MT. See also G. B. Gray, *Numbers*, p. 70.

6:23 תְבָרְכוּ: Benedictions occur in various forms, depending upon circumstances. Blessings may be proclaimed at the same time as they are being enjoyed, or predicted as future occurrences. God Himself may be the agent of blessings, or the object of human blessing because of His beneficence. See further A. Murtonen, "The Use of the Words LEBAREK and BERAKAH in the Old Testament," *VT* 9 (1959): 158-77.

אָמוֹר: P. J. Budd, *Numbers*, p. 75, has pointed out the uniqueness of this word as an infinitive absolute standing independently. Various suggestions, including haplography, have been made to account for the phenomenon, e.g., J. A. Paterson, *Numbers*, p. 45; G. B. Gray, *Numbers*, p. 74. The MT reads יִשְׂרָאֵל אָמוֹר לָהֶם, and, had אָמוֹר been prefaced by לְ, the consonant would have occurred three times within the space of seven letters. Whether or not the *šōṭĕrîm* objected to such a concourse on stylistic grounds, the MT is still satisfactory as it stands.

C. TRIBAL OFFERINGS AT THE DEDICATION OF THE ALTAR (7:1-89)

This lengthy chapter can be analyzed into sixteen components: (1) preliminaries to ceremony (vv. 1-3); (2) assigning of gifts (vv. 4-9); (3) time of presentation (vv. 10-11); (4) Judah (vv. 12-17); (5) Issachar (vv. 18-23); (6) Zebulun (vv. 24-29); (7) Reuben (vv. 30-35); (8) Simeon (vv. 36-41); (9) Gad (vv. 42-47); (10) Ephraim (vv. 48-53); (11) Manasseh (vv. 54-59); (12) Benjamin (vv. 60-65); (13) Dan (vv. 66-71); (14) Asher (vv. 72-77); (15) Naphtali (vv. 78-83); (16) summary (vv. 84-89).

1. PRELIMINARIES TO CEREMONY (7:1-3)

Translation

When the time came that Moses had completed the construction of the Tabernacle, he anointed and consecrated it and all its equipment. He anointed the altar and all its vessels and consecrated them.

Then the Israelite leaders, the heads of families that were tribal chiefs who had supervised the enumeration, presented offerings.

They brought as their gifts in the LORD's presence six covered

wagons and twelve oxen—one wagon from every two leaders and one ox each. These they presented in front of the Tabernacle. (7:1-3)

Exegesis and Exposition

The time (MT יוֹם, *yôm*) being addressed here is that of the occasion when Moses sanctified and dedicated the completed Tabernacle (Ex. 40:1-33), an event summarized in the account of the consecration ceremonies for Aaron and his sons (Lev. 8:10–11). According to the Exodus narrative, these events began on the first day of the first month of the second year following the departure from Egypt.

Had a strict chronology been the concern of the author, this material would have been placed after Lev. 8:11, because Aaron and his sons are nowhere mentioned in the narratives as officiants or celebrants, these functions being the prerogative of Moses. But if Num. 7 had been inserted in Leviticus at the suggested place, it would have disrupted the intent of the chapter and its immediate successors by diverting attention from the priestly consecration ceremonies of Leviticus and their aftermath.

The fact that Num. 7-9 is chronologically earlier than chaps. 1-6 is apt to puzzle modern readers, but the simple answer is that they supplement the earlier chapters by furnishing information not found either in Exodus or Leviticus. The Tabernacle was erected on the first day of the first month in the second year following the Exodus (Ex. 40:2, 17), followed by the consecration of Aaron and his sons, described more fully in Lev. 8:1-30. During the first month God also commanded Moses to ensure that the Passover was observed on the fourteenth day (Num. 9:2-5) and instructed him to receive the offerings from the various tribes (Num. 7:1-89), certain parts of which were needed to move the camp from site to site.

On the first day of the second month the census was commissioned (Num. 1:1), and on the twentieth day the Israelites began their journey from Sinai (Num. 10:11). Around this sequence of events the narratives are correlated so that they accommodate the overall interest of the compiler in major events such as the consecration of the Aaronides and the first census of Israel. Although the chronology was well known to the contemporary Israelites, the composition of Exodus, Leviticus, and Numbers gave prominence to spiritual and social matters that resulted in a correct, coherent whole, whether or not there was chronological discontinuity.

The first verse of this section recapitulates the events surrounding the consecrating of the sacred shrine. Moses anointed it (MT מָשַׁח, *māšaḥ*) by applying the holy oil, compounded according to the prescription in Ex. 30:23-31, and then consecrated (MT קִדַּשׁ, *qādaš*) it and all its equipment. The altar of burnt offering and its vessels were also

137

anointed and consecrated in a similar fashion. The anointing oil that was smeared on the Tabernacle and the altar was not intended for use in anointing human beings other than Aaron and the priests because it was dedicated for use in the sanctuary and therefore was holy. Its manufacture was prohibited by persons other than sanctuary personnel on pain of death (Ex. 30:33)

The leaders (MT נְשִׂיאִים, *nĕśî'îm*) of Israel are the individuals mentioned in Numbers 1:16 in connection with the first census of Israel, although the order in which the tribal representatives presented their offerings differs from the order of names in chap. 1. In God's provision these men brought gifts of wagons and draft animals to transport the Tabernacle and its equipment. The carts (MT עֲגָלוֹת, *'ăgālôt*) were probably based upon familiar Egyptian designs, consisting of a floor of two or three wooden planks fixed between two wheels of solid wood, after the Sumerian fashion. The wagon had vertical sides attached to the floor and was constructed in such a way that the contents could be protected by a canopy.[58] The oxen (MT בְּקָרִים, *bĕqārîm*) that pulled them were probably castrated bulls and therefore unsuitable for sacrificial purposes. Such castrates were renowned in the ancient Near East for their patience and strength, usually working in pairs when pulling carts. The MT term צָב (*ṣāb*) is a rare word describing a wagon covered by a canopy, whereas the noun שׁוֹר (*šôr*) is normally interchangeable in the MT with בָּקָר (*bāqār*, "ox").

2. ASSIGNING OF GIFTS (7:4-9)

Translation

Then the Lord spoke to Moses, saying, Receive these gifts from them. They shall be used in the duties at the Tent of Meeting. Offer them to the Levites as their particular duties require.

So Moses accepted the carts and oxen and donated them to the Levites. (7:4-6)

Exegesis and Exposition

Moses was instructed to accept the carts and the draft animals and to give them to the Levites for use in connection with general Tabernacle service—namely, the task of transporting the dismantled Tabernacle in the days of the wilderness wanderings. Although Aaron

---

58. Ancient Mesopotamian and Egyptian carts are depicted in the article by W. S. McCullough, *IDB*, 1:540. The spoked varieties of Egyptian and Assyrian carts are of a later design. D. J. Wiseman, *IBD*, 1:254, appears to favor the Assyrian pattern for the Israelite cart wheels rather than the earlier solid form.

was now high priest, he is not mentioned in connection with the receiving and distribution of the gifts, this evidently being an administrative function rather than one that belonged to the sanctuary and its staff.

Translation

He gave two carts and four oxen to the Gershonites, as their work required, and four carts and eight oxen he gave to the Merarites, as their work required.

They were all under the direction of Ithamar, son of Aaron the priest.

But he gave none to the Kohathites, because their work involved the holy furnishings, which they had to carry themselves on their shoulders. (7:7-9)

Exegesis and Exposition

The carts and oxen were divided among the three Levitical groups in the most practical manner. The Gershonites were allotted two wagons and four draft animals, and this was deemed adequate for their work of handling the coverings, curtains, hangings, and cords of the Tabernacle (Num. 3:25). The remaining four wagons and eight oxen were assigned to the Merarites, whose responsibility it was to handle the planks, bars, pillars, and sockets of the sacred shrine the pillars of the courtyard with their accompanying sockets, cords, and fasteners, along with the tools for dismantling and reassembling the structure (Num. 3:36-37; 4:31-32). Because of the heavy nature of the materials they were handling, they needed the remainder of the carts and oxen, leaving the Kohathites without any means of transport.

The duties of this latter group involved responsibility for the Ark of the Covenant, the Table of the Presence, the altars of incense and burnt offering, the sanctuary implements, and the Tabernacle veil (Num. 3:31; 4:4-15). All of these were especially sacred objects, and even the Kohathites were not permitted to see them uncovered, lest they die (Num. 4:20). Accordingly these objects were wrapped under the supervision of Aaron and the priests, after which they were placed in bags and delivered to the Kohathites, who carried them on their shoulders (v. 9).

3. TIME OF PRESENTATION (7:10-11)

Translation

At the time when the altar was anointed, the leaders brought their offerings for its dedication and presented them in front of the

altar, because the LORD had said to Moses: On consecutive days the leaders shall bring their offerings for the dedication of the altar. (7:10-11)

Exegesis and Exposition

The leaders of Israel began to bring their gifts immediately after the consecration of the Tabernacle. These were presented by the leaders *seriatim* on consecutive days. Doubtless the entire congregation would witness the sequence of events, which would be especially meaningful for the specific tribes on the days when their offerings were presented. Whatever demonstrations of tribal enthusiasm may have been manifested under such circumstances are not mentioned. The Israelites would assemble at an appropriate distance from the Tabernacle, and only the tribal leaders and their assistants would appear within the Tabernacle courtyard, due to restrictions of space.

Whatever the size of the individual tribes, each participated in the ceremonies on a basis of complete equality with the others. It would have been impossible for the twelve tribes to have presented their offerings simultaneously, since the courtyard could not have accommodated all the sacrificial animals at the same time.

The importance and dignity of the occasion demanded that the offerings of each tribe should be listed fully. For the modern student this chapter, the longest in Numbers and one of the longest in the entire OT, makes for monotonous reading, a fact that unfortunately clouds the significance of the material. The records are the work of the *šōṭĕrîm*, who enumerated the materials in a fashion as meticulous as that which was to be employed in conducting the first census the following month.

Because the administrative records begin and end in an identical manner, they have been understood as formulaic and descriptive.[59] It seems more appropriate, however, to regard them as prescriptive in nature—i.e., stating how the ceremony was to be conducted and furnishing the order in which the offerings were to be presented. The passages comprise statistics, collected in summary form and classified as administrative documents. But because of the importance of the occasion for the ongoing religious life of Israel, the statistics were included in their full form in what the compiler deemed the most appropriate position in Numbers.

In order to avoid undue repetition in the commentary, the offerings as a whole will be considered here. The record of each tribe commenced and terminated with the name of the leader, so that there

---

59. So B. A. Levine, "The Descriptive Tabernacle Texts of the Pentateuch," *JAOS* 85 (1965): 307-18.

could be no confusion, no neglect of any tribe, and no form of discrimination, however inadvertent. The names, as noted earlier, match those of Num. 1:5-15, although the tribes did not present their gifts in that order. In fact, only the tribe of Naphtali, the last tribe to be listed (1:15), kept the same position in the procession of tribal offerings (7:78).

No significance was attached to this change of order, but possibly the unrecorded feelings of some tribal leaders might have expressed the matter differently. Thus the descendants of Reuben, Jacob's first-born, might have experienced displeasure at having their family position usurped by Judah, the fourth son of Jacob and Leah, even though Judah, as the largest tribe, exceeded Reuben by 28,100 men. In any event, physical size was no longer the deciding factor, since Reuben forfeited his rights of primogeniture when Jacob discovered that he had engaged in a premature sexual liaison with his concubine Bilhah (Gen. 35:22). The reason for the order of presentation given here is that the tribes came forward according to their assigned order around the Tabernacle (Num. 2:1-31) and the order they were to follow when marching.

This material indicates that each tribe's offering included a deep silver dish (קְעָרָה, qĕʿārâ) weighing 130 shekels and a shallow silver bowl (מִזְרָק, mizrāq) weighing 70 shekels, both filled with fine flour mixed with oil as a grain offering. The sanctuary shekel was the standard by which all weights were reckoned.[60] In addition a gold dish (כַּף, kap, rendered "spoon" in some translations, following the KJV) of 10 shekels filled with incense made up the final offering of an object wrought in precious metal. The grain offerings were placed with the presentation of the vessels that contained them, following the procedures adopted in administrative texts.[61]

The sacrificial animals consisted of one young bull, one mature and one yearling ram for the burnt offering, a male goat as a sin offering, and two bulls, five mature rams, five male goats, and five yearling rams for the peace offering. Bulls, not oxen, were prescribed for sacrificial purposes, since the latter, as castrates, would not be acceptable. The order of sacrifices would thus be the עֹלָה (ʿōlâ) or whole burnt offering (Lev. 1:3-17; 6:9-13, MT 6:2-6), the sin offering (חַטָּאת, ḥaṭṭāʾt) for purification (4:1–5:13; 6:17-23), and the peace offering (זֶבַח הַשְּׁלָמִים, zebaḥ haššĕlāmîm; cf. 3:1-17; 7:11-36). In the MT the numbers are written immediately following the particular items, which indicates an early scribal recording procedure.

---

60. For this see Num. 3:47.
61. A. F. Rainey, "The Order of Sacrifices in Old Testament Ritual Texts," *Bib* 51 (1970): 487-96.

4. JUDAH (7:12-17)

Translation

The one who brought his offering on the first day was Nahshon son of Amminadab, *of the tribe of Judah.

His offering was composed of one silver platter weighing 130 shekels and one silver sprinkling bowl weighing 70 shekels, both according to the sanctuary shekel standard; each was filled with finely ground flour mixed with oil as a grain offering; one gold dish weighing 10 shekels, full of incense; one young bull, one mature and one yearling ram for a burnt offering; one male goat for a sin offering; and two bulls, five mature rams, five male goats, and five yearling rams, to be sacrificed as a peace offering. This was the contribution of Nahshon son of Amminadab. (7:12-17)

Exegesis and Exposition

The tribe of Judah, the largest in all Israel, which at the first census numbered 74,600 fighting men (Num. 1:27), had already become the one others would praise, as promised in Jacob's benediction (Gen. 49:8-12). The reference to Shiloh (if that is the correct reading of Gen. 49:10), frequently understood as messianic,[62] gave a dimension to Judah's future, as contrasted with the blessing of Moses (Deut. 33:7), which focused on the conquest of national enemies. Nahshon, who led the procession of daily presentations, was placed third in the list of Numbers 1:5-15 but first in that of 2:3-31.

5. ISSACHAR (7:18-23)

Translation

On the second day Nethanel son of Zuar, leader* of Issachar, presented his offering.

He brought one silver platter weighing 130 shekels and one silver sprinkling bowl weighing 70 shekels, both according to the sanctuary shekel standard; each was filled with finely ground flour mixed with oil as a grain offering; one gold dish weighing 10 shekels, full of incense; one young bull, one mature and one yearling ram for a burnt offering; one male goat for a sin offering; and two bulls, five mature rams, five male goats, and five yearling rams, to be sacrificed as a peace offering. This was the contribution of Nethanel son of Zuar. (7:18-23)

---

62. On this subject see N. K. Gottwald, *IDB*, 4:330; H. G. Andersen, *ZPEB*, 5:404; V. P. Hamilton, *TWOT*, 2:919, and bibliographies.

Exegesis and Exposition

The tribe of Issachar was fifth in size, numbering 54,400 at the first census of Israel (Num. 1:28-29). Nethanel was placed fourth on the list of leaders in 1:5-15 but second in that of 2:3-31. Apart from his activities in Numbers nothing further is known about him, although his name was common.

6. ZEBULUN (7:24-29)

Translation

On the third day Eliab son of Helon, leader of the Zebulunites, approached. He presented one silver platter weighing 130 shekels and one silver sprinkling bowl weighing 70 shekels, both according to the sanctuary shekel standard; each was filled with finely ground flour mixed with oil as a grain offering; one gold dish weighing 10 shekels, full of incense; one young bull, one mature and one yearling ram for a burnt offering; one male goat for a sin offering; and two bulls, five mature rams, five male goats, and five yearling rams, to be sacrificed as a peace offering. This was the contribution of Eliab son of Helon. (7:24-29)

Exegesis and Exposition

The tribe of Zebulun numbered 57,400 at the first census (Num. 1:29), making it the fourth largest tribe. Eliab occurred fifth in the catalog of leaders in 1:5-15 but third in 2:3-31. Outside of Numbers nothing further is known about him.

7. REUBEN (7:30-35)

Translation

On the fourth day Elizur son of Shedeur, leader of the Reubenites, approached.
He presented one silver platter weighing 130 shekels and one silver sprinkling bowl weighing 70 shekels, both according to the sanctuary shekel standard; each was filled with finely ground flour mixed with oil as a grain offering; one gold dish weighing 10 shekels, full of incense; one young bull, one mature and one yearling ram for a burnt offering; one male goat for a sin offering; and two bulls, five mature rams, five male goats, and five yearling rams, to be sacrificed as a peace offering. This was the contribution of Elizur son of Shedeur. (7:30-35)

Exegesis and Exposition

The tribe of Reuben numbered 46,500 males at the first census (Num. 1:21) and was thus seventh in military strength among the tribes. Outside of Numbers nothing is known further about Elizur, who was listed first in the table of leaders in 1:5-15 but fourth in 2:3-31.

8. SIMEON (7:36-41)

Translation

On the fifth day Shelumiel son of Zurishaddai, leader of the Simeonites, approached. He presented one silver platter weighing 130 shekels and one silver sprinkling bowl weighing 70 shekels, both according to the sanctuary shekel standard; each was filled with finely ground flour mixed with oil as a grain offering; one gold dish weighing 10 shekels, full of incense; one young bull, one mature and one yearling ram for a burnt offering, one male goat for a sin offering; and two bulls, five mature rams, five male goats, and five yearling rams, to be sacrificed as a peace offering. This was the contribution of Shelumiel son of Zurishaddai. (7:36-41)

Exegesis and Exposition

The descendants of Simeon numbered 59,300 warriors when the census was conducted (Num. 1:33) and were thus third in numerical strength. Of Shelumiel nothing further is known. He ranked second in the list of leaders in 1:5-15 but fifth in the catalog of 2:3-31.

9. GAD (7:42-47)

Translation

On the sixth day Eliasaph son of Deuel, leader of the Gadites, approached. He presented one silver platter weighing 130 shekels and one silver sprinkling bowl weighing 70 shekels, both according to the sanctuary shekel standard; each was filled with finely ground flour mixed with oil as a grain offering; one gold dish weighing 10 shekels, full of incense; one young bull, one mature and one yearling ram for a burnt offering; one male goat for a sin offering; and two bulls, five mature rams, five male goats, and five yearling rams, to be sacrificed as a peace offering. This was the contribution of Eliasaph son of Deuel. (7:42-47)

Exegesis and Exposition

The offspring of Gad numbered 45,650 at the first census (Num. 1:25) and thus ranked eighth among the tribes. No further information is forthcoming about Eliasaph other than what Numbers contains. He appeared eleventh in the list of leaders in 1:5-15 but sixth in 2:3-31. His father was known as Deuel in 1:14; 7:42, 47; 10:20. The same person, however, is mentioned in 2:14 as Reuel. This resulted from a scribal confusion of the letters *d* and *r*, which are similar in some Semitic scripts.

10. EPHRAIM (7:48-53)

Translation

On the seventh day Elishama son of Ammihud, leader of the Ephraimites, approached. He presented one silver platter weighing 130 shekels and one silver sprinkling bowl weighing 70 shekels, both according to the sanctuary shekel standard; each was filled with finely ground flour mixed with oil as a grain offering; one gold dish weighing 10 shekels, full of incense; one young bull, one mature and one yearling ram for a burnt offering; one male goat for a sin offering; and two bulls, five mature rams, five male goats, and five yearling rams, to be sacrificed as a peace offering. This was the contribution of Elishama son of Ammihud. (7:48-53)

Exegesis and Exposition

At the first census at Sinai, Ephraim's progeny included 40,500 men, making the tribe tenth in size (Num. 1:33). From the genealogy in 1 Chron. 7:26 it appears that Elishama son of Ammihud was the grandfather of Joshua. Elishama's activities were confined to the narratives of Numbers, and he was listed sixth in the catalog of leaders in 1:5-15 but seventh in 2:3-31.

11. MANASSEH (7:54-59)

Translation

On the eighth day Gamaliel son of Pedahzur, leader of the Manassites, approached. He presented one silver platter weighing 130 shekels and one silver sprinkling bowl weighing 70 shekels, both according to the sanctuary shekel standard; each was filled with finely ground flour mixed with oil as a grain offering; one gold dish weighing 10 shekels, full of incense; one young bull, one mature and one yearling ram for a burnt offering; one male goat for a sin offering; and two bulls, five mature rams, five male goats, and five yearling rams, to be sacrificed as a peace offering. This was the contribution of Gamaliel son of Pedahzur. (7:54-59)

Exegesis and Exposition

At the first census Manasseh had 32,200 fighting men enrolled and thus ranked twelfth among the Israelites (Num. 1:34-35). Gamaliel was placed seventh in the list of 1:5-15 but eighth in 2:3-31. Nothing further is known about him, although his name was to persist into NT times (Acts 5:34; 22:3).

12. BENJAMIN (7:60-65)

Translation

On the ninth day Abidan son of Gideoni, leader of the Benjamites, approached.

He presented one silver platter weighing 130 shekels and one silver sprinkling bowl weighing 70 shekels, both according to the sanctuary shekel standard; each was filled with finely ground flour mixed with oil as a grain offering; one gold dish weighing 10 shekels, full of incense; one young bull, one mature and one yearling ram for a burnt offering; one male goat for a sin offering; and two bulls, five mature rams, five male goats, and five yearling rams, to be sacrificed as a peace offering. This was the contribution of Abidan son of Gideoni. (7:60-65)

Exegesis and Exposition

Benjamin's descendants numbered 35,400 fighting men at the Sinai census (Num. 1:23), making the tribe eleventh in rank. Abidan was listed eighth in 1:5-15 but ninth in 2:3-31. Nothing further is known about him.

13. DAN (7:66-71)

Translation

On the tenth day Ahiezer son of Ammishaddai, leader of the Danites, approached. He presented one silver platter weighing 130 shekels and one silver sprinkling bowl weighing 70 shekels, both according to the sanctuary shekel standard; each was filled with finely ground flour mixed with oil as a grain offering; one gold dish weighing 10 shekels, full of incense; one young bull, one mature and one yearling ram for a burnt offering; one male goat for a sin offering; and two bulls, five mature rams, five male goats, and five yearling rams, to be sacrificed as a peace offering. This was the contribution of Ahiezer son of Ammishaddai. (7:66-71)

Exegesis and Exposition

In the first census at Sinai the Danites numbered 62,700 fighting men (Num. 1:39), thus ranking as second among the tribes. Ahiezer was placed ninth in the list of 1:5-15 and tenth in 2:3-31. He is otherwise unmentioned in the OT.

14. ASHER (7:72-77)

Translation

On the eleventh day Pagiel son of Ochran, leader of the Asherites, approached. He presented one silver platter weighing 130 shekels and one silver sprinkling bowl weighing 70 shekels, both according to the sanctuary shekel standard; each was filled with finely ground flour mixed with oil as a grain offering; one gold dish weighing 10 shekels, full of incense; one young bull, one mature and one yearling ram for a burnt offering; one male goat for a sin offering; and two bulls, five mature rams, five male goats, and five yearling rams, to be sacrificed as a peace offering. This was the contribution of Pagiel son of Ochran. (7:72-77)

Exegesis and Exposition

At the first census Asher numbered 41,500 fighting men (Num. 1:41), making them ninth among the tribes. Pagiel was mentioned in tenth place in the register of leaders in 1:5-15 but eleventh in 2:3-31. Beyond his activities in Numbers nothing is known of him.

15. NAPHTALI (7:78-83)

Translation

On the twelfth day Ahira son of Enan, leader of the Naphtalites, approached. He presented one silver platter weighing 130 shekels and one silver sprinkling bowl weighing 70 shekels, both according to the sanctuary shekel standard; each was filled with finely ground flour mixed with oil as a grain offering; one gold dish weighing 10 shekels, full of incense; one young bull, one mature and one yearling ram for a burnt offering; one male goat for a sin offering; and two bulls, five mature rams, five male goats, and five yearling rams, to be sacrificed as a peace offering. This was the contribution of Ahira son of Enan. (7:78-83)

Exegesis and Exposition

The final day's activity in the procession of offerings witnessed the presentation of gifts from the tribe of Naphtali. The listing at the first census of the nation (Num. 1:43) showed that the tribe had 53,400 men, making them sixth in size among the Israelites. Ahira ranked last in the list in 1:5-15 and occupied the same position in 2:3-31. He is unmentioned in the OT apart from his activities in Numbers.

16. SUMMARY (7:84-89)

Translation

This was the dedication offering for the altar from the leaders of Israel at its anointing: 12 silver platters, 12 silver sprinkling bowls, and 12 gold dishes.

Each silver platter weighed 130 shekels and each sprinkling bowl 70 shekels. Together the silver dishes weighed 2,400 shekels, according to the standard of the sanctuary shekel.

The 12 gold dishes full of incense weighed 10 shekels each, according to the sanctuary shekel. Together the gold dishes weighed 120 shekels.

The total number of animals for the burnt offering was 12 young bulls, 12 mature rams, 12 yearling rams, together with their grain offerings, and 12 male goats as the sin offering.

The total number of animals for the sacrifice of the peace offering was 24 bulls, 60 mature rams, 60 male goats, and 60 yearling rams. This was the offering for the dedication of the altar when it was anointed. (7:84-88)

Exegesis and Exposition

A summary statement following the tables of statistics has long been a common feature of such compilations. The weights of the vessels were based upon that of the sanctuary shekel, but for the benefit of modern readers the large silver platter would weigh about three and one-fourth pounds, whereas the small silver bowl would be about one and three-fourths pounds, and the gold sprinkling bowl would be a mere four ounces. By any standards, however, these gifts were costly, and thus the expenses would naturally fall more heavily upon a smaller tribe than a larger one. The precise repetition of detail ensured that each tribe shared equally in the offerings for the Lord's Tabernacle.

A. F. Rainey[63] followed B. A. Levine in showing that the narrative dealing with donations for the Tabernacle had been modeled along the lines of an ordinary ancient Near Eastern ledger from a sanctu-

---

63. A. F. Rainey, *ZPEB*, 5:202.

ary. The summary (vv. 87-88) is an inventory of the animals provided for the various offerings in accordance with the order in which they were presented by each tribe. The *šōṭěrîm* who were responsible for compiling the records made formal summary recognition of each tribe's contribution.

The exactness of the account and the repetition of the ritual procedures may appear tiresome, and even pointless, to the modern outlook, which would tend to condense the entire proceedings by means of a concise statement. But the importance of the ritual cannot be overestimated, because it showed that each tribe, regardless of its size, was on an equal footing with all the other tribes, and that each one approached the sacred national shrine with its offerings in precisely the same manner on an occasion that would never be forgotten.

For the ancient Hebrews, implicit obedience of the prescribed rites had the positive effect of bringing divine pardon and blessing upon the worshipers in various ways, and the negative effect of avoiding the use of pagan cultic innovations in Yahwistic worship. For the Christian, only those ritual procedures of prayer and adoration that are in full accord with the teachings of Scripture are acceptable to God. All others come from what, in an earlier age of worship in the Church of England, was described as proceeding from "the corrupt following of the Apostles."[64]

Translation

Now when Moses entered the Tent of Meeting to speak *with God, he heard the voice speaking to him from between the two cherubim above the cover on the Ark of the Testimony. So God spoke to him. (7:89)

Exegesis and Exposition

Because this passage is in the nature of an appendix, it has been the custom among liberal scholars to regard it as extraneous or independent material added from another source.[65] On closer observation, however, the verse proves to be an essential link between what has just happened and what is to take place in the sanctuary. Before Moses could know the latter he had to enter the Tent of Meeting so as to receive his instructions. The section is therefore contemporary with the termination of the offerings and introduces those who witnessed the stirring event to the further spectacle of their civil leader entering the sacred shrine and communing directly with God.

Whether or not the sound of the communication was heard by the

---

64. *The Book of Common Prayer,* Art. 25.
65. So G. B. Gray, *Numbers,* p. 77; M. Noth, *Numbers,* p. 65; et al.

Israelites is not stated. It emerged from between the two cherubim that surmounted the lid of the Ark. Once the Tabernacle had been completed, it was the place where God communed regularly with Moses (Ex. 25:22). So far, therefore, from this verse being a separate entity, it actually serves as a climax to the ceremonies. The Lord is communicating through Moses to the people and by implication making Himself available to the Israelites when they need an intermediary through whom they can present petitions to Him.

Additional Notes

7:12 נַחְשׁוֹן בֶּן־עַמִּינָדָב: The term "leader" (נָשִׂיא) has apparently dropped out of, or been accidentally omitted from, the MT here, because it occurs elsewhere in the chapter at the beginning of each tribal record. The LXX restored the omission by reading ἄρχων. The textual lapse is rather unfortunate in that Judah was already attaining preeminence at this stage of Israelite history.

7:13 וְקָרְבָּנוֹ: After this word the LXX adds the phrase τό δῶρον αὐτοῦ, and also in v. 19. Such slight stylistic divergences match the occasional modest departure in the MT from the normal statistical pattern and thus are not significant.

7:17 בָּקָר שְׁנַיִם: For this offering the LXX substitutes δαμάλεις δύο and continues in this way throughout the chapter.

7:18 Whereas in v. 12 נָשִׂיא had apparently been omitted accidentally, here the term for "tribe" (מַטֶּה) was neglected similarly, but was restored in the LXX, which reads τῆς φυλῆς.

7:87 מִנְחָתָם: Following this term the LXX added καὶ αἱ σπονδαὶ αὐτῶν. Information about drink offerings was probably inserted after the literary pattern of 6:15, where the MT reads נִסְכֵּיהֶם.

7:88 הֲנֻכַּת הַמִּזְבֵּחַ: After this phrase the LXX added μετὰ τὸ πληρῶσαι τὰς χεῖρας αὐτοῦ. This may have resulted from following an independent MS tradition, but it should not be taken as pointing to a deficit in the MT.

7:89 The MT is obscure here. אִתּוֹ evidently refers to God, but the succeeding clause וַיִּשְׁמַע אֶת־הַקּוֹל מִדַּבֵּר אֵלָיו introduces a reflexive sense by using the hithpael participle of דבר (the contracted form of מִתְדַּבֵּר) to convey the sense of hearing the voice speaking within himself. The LXX clarified the sense by inserting κυρίου after הַקּוֹל, and followed this by the participle λαλοῦντος. The hithpael form of דבר is not unique here, however, being found also in Ezek. 2:2; 43:6, but since the piel form (וַיְדַבֵּר) occurs at the end of the verse, BHS emended the hithpael form to the piel to read מְדַבֵּר, and this clarifies the obscurity acceptably. G. B. Gray, *Numbers*, p. 77, saw traditional rabbinic exegesis underlying the MT text, but a mistaken pointing by the Masoretes seems more probable.

On the cherubim see T. H. Gaster, *IDB*, 1:131-32; D. E. Acomb, *ZPEB*, 1:788-90; R. K. Harrison, *ISBE*, 1:642-43, and bibliographies.

D. CONSECRATION OF THE LEVITES (8:1-26)

Chapter 8 can be analyzed into three structural units as follows: (1) lighting the lamps (vv. 1-4); (2) separation of Levites (vv. 5-22); (3) work of Levites (vv. 23-26).

1. LIGHTING THE LAMPS (8:1-4)

Translation

The LORD said to Moses: Speak to Aaron and tell him: When you arrange the seven lamps, they are to illuminate the area in front of the lampstand. Aaron did so. He arranged the lamps so that they faced toward the front of the lampstand, as the LORD had instructed Moses.

This is how the lampstand was fashioned: It was made of beaten gold, from its base to its petals. Moses made the lampstand according to the pattern that the LORD had shown him. (8:1-4)

Exegesis and Exposition

A preliminary instructional section of a liturgical nature concerned the positioning of the golden lampstand that had been fashioned according to God's instructions (Ex. 25:31-40). The responsibility for arranging the lamps, stated in Lev. 24:3, is now seen to have been assumed by Aaron. The light was to shine on the area immediately in front of the lampstand so that it would illuminate the Tent of Meeting continually and light up the gold Table of the Presence.

The elaborate nature of the lampstand's construction was probably intended to resemble flowers and to look as different as possible from the stylized graven images of pagan antiquity. In constructing it as prescribed by God, Moses was continuing to obey God's commands implicitly.

2. SEPARATION OF LEVITES (8:5-22)

Translation

Then the LORD spoke to Moses, saying: Separate the Levites from the rest of the Israelites, and make them ritually clean.

Do this in order to purify them. Sprinkle the water of purification on them; then have them shave their entire bodies, wash their clothes, and in this way make themselves clean. (8:5-7)

Exegesis and Exposition

Now that the Tabernacle and its equipment had been dedicated, it was the turn of the Levites to be separated from the other Israelites ceremonially and be presented to the Lord. They had been commissioned in 3:5-8 as officiants to Aaron and his sons to assist them in worship at the Tabernacle.

Ritual cleansing involved Moses' sprinkling them with water (MT מֵי חַטָּאת, *mê ḥaṭṭā't*, "water of sin," KJV "water of purifying"), probably taken from the laver in the Tabernacle courtyard, as contrasted with the complete washing of the priests (Lev. 8:6), after which they were to shave their entire bodies (MT תַעַר עַל־כָּל־בְּשָׂרָם, *ta'ar 'al-kol-běśārām*) and wash their clothing. The shaving seems to have been for this special occasion only, unlike the traditions of the Egyptian priests, who were said to shave their whole bodies every three days. The ritual was similar to that required for the ceremonial cleansing of the leper (Lev. 14:7-9). In contrast to the priests, who were given new clothes (Lev. 8:13), the Levites retained their own garments. The Hebrew verb טָהֵר (*ṭāhēr*, "to be clean," "be pure") illustrates the difference between their cleansing, which made them ritually pure, and that of the priests, where the use of קָדַשׁ (*qādaš*, "to consecrate," "make holy") sanctified them (Lev. 8:12).

Translation

Then let them take a young bull with its grain offering of fine flour mixed with oil, and you shall take another young bull as a sin offering. (8:8)

Exegesis and Exposition

The ritual cleansing having been completed, the Levites were to present as a sacrifice for sin a young bull with its prescribed grain offering. Another sacrifice, consisting of a young bull as a sin offering, was intended to purify the Tabernacle from all pollution, such as would have been brought upon it by the presence of the Levites before their ceremonial cleansing. Now that the preliminaries were finished, the consecration ceremonies could commence.

Translation

Bring the Levites before the Tent of Meeting, and gather together the entire community of Israelites.

You shall bring the Levites before the LORD, and the Israelites shall lay their hands on the Levites.

Aaron shall present the Levites before the LORD as a waved offering from the Israelites, so that they may be ready to do the LORD's work.

152

After the Levites have laid their hands upon the heads of the young bulls, you shall offer one as a sin offering and the other as a burnt offering to the LORD, to make atonement for the Levites.

Station the Levites in front of Aaron and his sons, and then present them as a waved offering to the LORD.

In this way you will set the Levites apart from the rest of the Israelites, and the Levites will be mine. (8:9-14)

Exegesis and Exposition

The consecration ceremony was to occur in full view of the Israelite nation. The candidates were presented formally to the Lord, and then the people laid their hands upon them, signifying that they were participating in the consecration of the Levites. No doubt this would be done representatively, so that only the chosen leaders of the tribe would participate. The imposition of hands is an ancient ritual of uncertain origin that purported to convey authority or blessing. In the OT it occurred when Jacob blessed Joseph's children (Gen. 48:14) and was part of the consecration of Joshua by Moses (Num. 27:18-20). In later periods it also occurred in connection with healing (2 Kings 4:34). The tradition was prominent in the NT (Mark 5:23; Acts 8:15-18; 1 Tim. 4:14; etc.) and became a feature of Christian ordination.

At this juncture the Levites were engaged in a liturgical procedure, and until they were instituted into their sacred office they were also worshiping before the Lord. All the appropriate elements of the sacrificial system were observed as the spiritual requirements of the offerings were met. It is important to differentiate between *rite*—that is, the prescribed order of a cultic formulary—and *recte*, the penitent condition of the worshiper's heart and mind. The sinner could be assured of forgiveness only through the sacrificial ritual when the offering had been presented according to the latter consideration. Honoring God with the lips and not the heart (Isa. 29:13) is false worship and was criticized by Jesus (Matt. 15:8-9), who employed the concepts of *rite* and *recte* in denouncing the hypocrisy of Pharisaic worship.

The Levites were presented to the Lord as a waved offering (MT תְּנוּפָה, *tĕnûpâ*) from the Israelites. The waved offering was part of the ritual of the peace offering (Lev. 3:1-17; 7:11-36) and consisted of the priest's portion being presented to God in a waving motion[66] before it became the property of the officiating priest. He then consumed the food as God's representative, thus indicating to anyone who might have been observing the ceremony that the offering was in fact being

---

66. Cf. R. K. Harrison, *Leviticus*, pp. 82-83.

shared by God.[67] The sin offering (MT חַטָּאת, *ḥaṭṭā't*) cleansed the Tabernacle from impurity, whereas the burnt offering (MT עֹלָה, *'ōlâ*), the oldest form of sacrifice in Israel, atoned by nullifying and removing the effects of sin.

When the Levites had been presented ceremonially to God by the high priest, they were offered by him to serve the Lord as living sacrifices. This form of consecration was urged upon believers at Rome by Paul (Rom. 12:1). Precisely how the "waving" was accomplished is not stated, but it could have occurred as parallel ranks of Levites moved forward and then stepped back in unison in the Tabernacle court near the altar.

Translation

After this, the Levites shall enter the Tent of Meeting to perform their duties, since you have cleansed them and offered them as a waved offering.

These are the Israelites who have been dedicated entirely to Me. I have taken them as my own as a substitute for the firstborn, *the first male child born to an Israelite woman. (8:15-16)

Exegesis and Exposition

Having been made a תְּרוּמָה (*tĕrûmâ*) or consecrated offering to God, the Levites were ready to begin their work. The special nature of their relationship to God is now made clear. They were accredited substitutes for the firstborn males of Israel (cf. Num. 3:11-13) and assumed special obligations of service to God.

Translation

Every Israelite firstborn male is mine, whether human or animal. On the day that I killed all the firstborn in Egypt I set them apart for Myself, and I have accepted the Levites as a substitute for all the firstborn Israelites.

Of all the Israelites, I have given the Levites as a gift to Aaron and his sons, to perform the duties of the Tent of Meeting on behalf of the Israelites and to make atonement for the people of Israel, so that no tragedy will strike the Israelites when they approach the sanctuary. (8:17-19)

Exegesis and Exposition

With didactic purposes in mind, the prescriptions of Ex. 13:2, 12 are repeated. God's claim to the firstborn was linked with His great

---

67. A. F. Rainey, *ZPEB*, 5:208.

deliverance of Israel from Egypt and His demand that the firstborn of animals and persons be sanctified ("set apart") to Him. The firstborn was representative of the successive offspring, and the term (MT בְּכוֹר, *bĕkôr*) was applied by God to His people while they were still in bondage (Ex. 4:22-23) in anticipation of the covenant relationship. Because the firstborn son enjoyed special favors (Gen. 27:1-4; 37:22; 43:33; Deut. 21:17), Israel was accorded privileged standing among the nations as the Lord's firstborn.

In consequence of his sexual sin, Reuben forfeited the rights and privileges of the firstborn (Gen. 35:22; 49:3-4), and instead the special favor of representing the nation before God devolved upon the Levites (Num. 3:12-13), who are here characterized as a protective agency or shield that would forestall accidental defilement of the sanctuary and the consequences that would follow. The repetitions in the text (vv. 16*b*, 18) ensured that the rationale of the choice of the Levites as ministers would be familiar to everyone. Such a procedure is of some significance, because there were many occasions when God did not make clear to His people the reasons for His actions. The Levites are depicted as a gift to God from Israel, which He returned to His chosen people as assistants to Aaron and his sons.[68]

Translation

Moses, Aaron, and the entire Israelite community did with the Levites precisely as the LORD had commanded Moses.

The Levites purified themselves and washed their clothing. Then Aaron presented them as a waved offering before the LORD and made atonement for them to purify them.

After that, the Levites entered the Tent of Meeting to perform their duties under the jurisdiction of Aaron and his sons. As the LORD had commanded Moses regarding the Levites, so they did to them. (8:20-22)

Exegesis and Exposition

In this assent formula, it is made evident that the Lord's instructions regarding the consecration of the Levites were followed to the letter. The Levites were duly purified, presented, and sanctified, after which they were able to commence their duties. At this stage the entire community of Israel was obedient to the will of God, and the literary formula is consonant with other similar situations (Num. 1:54; 2:34; etc.).

---

68. For the palistrophic (chiastic) structure of vv. 12-19 see G. J. Wenham, *Numbers*, pp. 95-96.

3. WORK OF LEVITES (8:23-26)

Translation

The LORD spoke to Moses and said: With regard to the Levites, men who are *twenty-five years of age or older may come to participate in the work at the Tent of Meeting, but at the age of fifty they must retire from their regular duties and discontinue working. They may offer their associates assistance in performing their duties at the Tent of Meeting, but they themselves shall not undertake regular service. This is the way in which you are to assign the duties of the Levites. (8:23-26)

Exegesis and Exposition

This section contains instructions from God regarding the age qualifications of the Levites and the kind of work they could undertake at different stages of their lives. Males aged twenty-five years or older were eligible for either the laborious dismantling and erecting of the Tabernacle during the wilderness wanderings or the less onerous task of protecting the structure from any kind of defilement when it was erected (Num. 4:24-27). Because this legislation was enacted slightly earlier than that of Num. 4, the difference in age for commencing Tabernacle duty is probably to be accounted for on future circumstantial grounds.[69]

Young, energetic men would be needed, particularly when the community was on the march. But when the Tabernacle was stationary for a lengthy period, as at Kadesh-barnea, the duties would be well within the abilities of older men. Retirement from physical labor at the Tabernacle was mandatory when the Levites attained fifty years of age (cf. also 4:23). Thereafter the more senior Levites were to assist their younger associates as the need arose. In the early monarchy, when the sacred shrine was located permanently on Mount Zion, King David commissioned Levites from the age of twenty years and upward for Tabernacle service on the ground that the heavy physical labor (MT עֲבֹדָה, 'ăbōdâ) mentioned in Numbers was no longer necessary (1 Chron. 23:24-25).

This regulation was followed in subsequent periods (2 Chron. 31:17; Ezra 3:8), indicating that the overall age limit had changed somewhat. The change, slight though it was, could hardly have been implemented without divine sanction (cf. 1 Chron. 23:25). The various compilers of priestly statistics were merely noting the practices of their own immediate situation. It is possible that 22,000 Levites proved too numerous for efficient Tabernacle service, so that their

---

69. So A. Noordtzij, *Numbers*, p. 81.

numbers were reduced somewhat in later times by raising the age of entrance,[70] but whether this eventuality had been perceived within the scant space of one month is difficult to say. Nor is it possible to demonstrate the rabbinic contention that the Levites first served a five-year apprenticeship,[71] since all Levites seem to have commenced their Tabernacle service on an equal footing.

Those scholars who assume that Num. 8:23-26 is a postexilic appendix[72] added when the supposed "priestly" editors were assembling the material seem unaware that chap. 8 is chronologically prior to chap. 4 (cf. 7:1; 9:15). The *šōṭĕrîm* who were responsible for compiling those ancient lists would be well aware of the differences in 4:23 and 8:24, but since both enactments claimed divine warrant they were recorded and preserved as they were received. There is no convincing reason to challenge the state of the MT as it stands.

Additional Notes

8:4 יְרֵכָה ... פִּרְחָה: Two collective nouns, the first of which (יְרֵכָה) is often interpreted as "stem" but is rendered in the present work by "base." The root ירך admits of a variety of translations, but RSV supports "base." If the above readings are acceptable there is no need to supply plural suffixes, as the Samaritan Pentateuch did. The LXX reads ὁ καυλὸς αὐτῆς, "its stem." On the lampstand see C. L. Myers, *The Tabernacle Menorah*, AASOR 2 (Missoula, Mont.: Scholars Press, 1976).

8:8 בֶּן־בָּקָר normally refers to a calf or heifer (a calf that has not yet produced offspring). In this instance the calf would be male. The LXX reads μόσχον.

8:13 לִפְנֵי אַהֲרֹן: The LXX includes God in the ritual, reading ἔναντι κυρίου, ἔναντι 'Ααρών.

8:15 תְּנוּפָה: After this word the LXX adds ἔναντι κυρίου.

8:16 כָּל־רֶחֶם בְּכוֹר כֹּל: The MT is rather difficult here. To express the concept of a firstborn breaking out of the womb the Samaritan Pentateuch reads כָּל בְּכוֹר פֶּטֶר רֶחֶם, which modifies the MT order significantly. Probably the best approach would be to understand תַּחַת as being repeated before בְּכוֹר, and not to place כָּל before בְּכוֹר, as BHS suggests. The LXX reads ἀντὶ τῶν διανοιγόντων πᾶσαν μήτραν πρωτοτόκων πάντων.

8:21 וַיִּתְחַטְּאוּ: In seven out of the eight occurrences of the hithpael of חָטָא in the MT, the meaning is that of "cleansing oneself from un-

---

70. So G. J. Wenham, *Numbers*, pp. 97-98.
71. J. H. Hertz, ed., *The Pentateuch and Haftorahs*, p. 607.
72. E.g., S. R. Driver, *Introduction to the Literature of the Old Testament* (1912 ed.), p. 61; M. Noth, *Numbers*, pp. 69-70.

cleanness." The remaining instance is Job 41:25 (MT 17) and should probably be rendered "to withdraw." Cf. BDB, 307b; KB 1:289b.

8:24 חָמֵשׁ וְעֶשְׂרִים שָׁנָה: The LXX resolved the difference in ages by reading twenty-five instead of thirty in 4:22, 30, and the present verse. More than one MS. tradition evidently influenced the translation of the Pentateuch into Greek, or else the LXX translators were harmonizing intentionally. For a discussion, see G. J. Wenham, *Numbers*, pp. 97-98 n. 2.

E. OBSERVING THE PASSOVER: THE GUIDING CLOUD (9:1-23)

The materials of chap. 9 fall into two sections: (1) Passover regulations (vv. 1-14) and (2) the guiding cloud (vv. 15-23).

1. PASSOVER REGULATIONS (9:1-14)

Translation

In the first month of the second year after the people had left Egypt, the LORD spoke to Moses in the Sinai wilderness, saying: Let the Israelites observe the Passover at the appointed time.

Celebrate it on the proper date, the fourteenth day of this month, at twilight, in accordance with its rituals and ceremonies.

So Moses instructed the Israelites to keep the Passover.

*They observed the Passover at twilight on the fourteenth day of the first month in the Sinai wilderness, doing everything precisely as the LORD had commanded Moses. (9:1-5)

Exegesis and Exposition

As has been maintained previously, the materials in chaps. 7-9 are chronologically earlier than the first six chapters. This fact is made plain once more by the statement that the Lord uttered a proclamation regarding the Passover at the beginning of the second year after the exodus from Egypt. This event occurred immediately after the consecration of the Tabernacle, in the month prior to the census at Sinai.

The materials of this first section of chap. 9 can be analyzed more minutely as follows: (1) instructions regarding the Passover observance (vv. 1-5); (2) an emergency situation (vv. 6-8); (3) appropriate divine legislation (vv. 9-13); (4) an alien's rights (v. 14). The passage begins with a reminder from God concerning the obligation of the community to observe the Passover (Ex. 12:14) on the appointed day of the first month. This latter was known as Abib in the Pentateuch, but in the postexilic period it came to be called Nisan, from the

158

Akkadian *nisannu,* "first produce of the season" (cf. Neh. 2:1; Esther 3:7). With due ceremony the Passover lamb was slain on the fourteenth evening (MT בֵּין הָעַרְבַּיִם, *bên hā‛arbayim,* "between the evenings," i.e., probably at twilight).[73] Since darkness descends quickly in the Near East, the meal would have to be prepared and eaten in haste in order to comply with the divine legislation (Ex. 12:11). Again, Moses and the Israelites obeyed God's commands specifically and celebrated the second Passover,[74] as stated in the formula of obedience in v. 5. For the majority of those who participated, however, it was to be their last. Because the Israelites rebelled against God and longed to return to Egypt (Num. 14:1-4), they were not to experience another Passover celebration until they had entered the Promised Land (Josh. 5:10).

Translation

It so happened that some of them were unable to observe the Passover on that day because they had become ritually unclean through contact with a dead man, so they approached Moses and Aaron that day.

They said to Moses: We have become unclean because of a man's corpse. Are we to be prohibited from presenting the Lord's offering with the other Israelites at its appointed time?

So Moses replied to them: Wait here until I find out what the Lord's instructions are concerning you. (9:6-8)

Exegesis and Exposition

Even with the greatest of care, accidents still take place in a fallen human environment. An emergency presented itself because of ritual defilement (טָמֵא, *ṭāmē’*) through contact with a dead person. According to Num. 5:2, such individuals were to be expelled from the camp in order to maintain its ceremonial purity, since death was regarded as a defiling condition. But the men involved did not want to miss celebrating the Passover and desired to know what they might do in order to avoid such an unfortunate contingency. The situation was not merely an emergency, however, but one that presented a new problem for which Moses needed divine guidance. Accordingly, he presented his petition to the Lord, probably in the Tent of Meeting.

---

73. KB, 3:732, has "in the dusk." See also R. B. Allen, *TWOT,* 2:694.
74. For literature on the Passover see bibliographies in J. C. Rylaarsdam, *IDB,* 3:668; J. B. Segal, *The Hebrew Passover* (London: SPCK, 1963); J. Jocz, *ZPEB,* 4:611; V. P. Hamilton, *TDOT,* 2:1791; M. R. Wilson, *ISBE,* 3:678-79.

Translation

Then the LORD spoke to Moses, saying: Address the Israelites and say: If any of you or your descendants become ritually unclean through contact with a corpse, or are away on a lengthy journey, they may still celebrate the LORD's Passover. At twilight on the fourteenth day of the second month they may observe it. They shall eat the lamb with unleavened bread and bitter herbs. They shall not leave any of it overnight or break any of its bones. They shall celebrate the Passover in accordance with all its ordinances. (9:9-12)

Exegesis and Exposition

The response from God resulted in an addition to the extant ordinances (MT מִשְׁפָּטִים, *mišpāṭîm*) and statutes (MT חֻקֹּת, *ḥuqqôt*) regarding the Passover. Hereafter, anyone who became ceremonially defiled through contact with a dead person, or was away on a lengthy journey,[75] could still participate in Passover celebrations, but on the fourteenth day of the second month (Ziv) instead of the regular time in the first month (Abib).[76] The four-week interval would have provided ample opportunity for the defiled to recover his ceremonial purity and for the journeying Israelite to return home. Aside from this period of delay, the Passover ritual was to be observed precisely as legislated (Ex. 12:3-11, 46).

Translation

But if a person who is ritually pure and is not on a journey neglects to observe the Passover, that individual shall be cut off from his people, because he did not present the LORD's offering at its appointed time. Such a man will bear the consequences of his sin.

If an alien has settled among you and wishes to keep the LORD's Passover, he must do so according to the Passover ritual and its ceremonies. You shall have one law that is binding on alien and native alike. (9:13-14)

Exegesis and Exposition

This generous provision was meant to cover two kinds of emergency only and was not intended to accommodate the lazy, forgetful,

---

75. In the MT the word "lengthy" (רְחֹקָה, "remote," "distant") was marked by *puncta extraordinaria*, a series of dots that perhaps indicated that the literal sense of the term was too severe for the overall meaning of the verse. See *KD*, 3:51.
76. These names are two of only four Canaanite months mentioned in the OT that the preexilic Israelites used, the others being Ethanim (the seventh month) and Bul (the eighth month). Otherwise, where months were not designated numerically, Babylonian names were employed.

or indifferent. If such negligent individuals did not observe the Passover at the appointed time, their disobedience would be penalized. Some scholars have supposed that execution by the community was meant,[77] others have seen it as the direct act of God,[78] and a few have thought of it as meaning exclusion from the community,[79] which in a wilderness environment was tantamount to a death sentence. Whatever the precise nature of the penalty, it carried the full weight of divine assurance and thus was a matter of the gravest consequence.

The provision for the resident alien (MT גֵּר, *gēr*) summarizes the legislation in Ex. 12:43-49. In Num. 9:14, however, the resident alien is the only kind of non-Israelite mentioned, the omitted groups being the foreigner (MT בֶּן–נֵכָר, *ben-nēkār*), the temporary resident (תּוֹשָׁב, *tôšāb*), and the hired laborer (שָׂכִיר, *śākîr*). The *gēr* and the native Israelite were to be treated equally, since the Israelites were once in the same condition themselves (Deut. 23:8 [MT 23:7]).

2. THE GUIDING CLOUD (9:15-23)

Translation

On the day that the Tabernacle, that is to say, the Tent of Meeting, was set up, a cloud covered it. From evening until morning the cloud above the Tabernacle had a fiery glow.

It continued in this manner. The cloud covered it, and at night it was bright like fire.

Whenever the cloud lifted over the Tabernacle, the Israelites would begin marching. Wherever the cloud settled, there the Israelites pitched their tents.

At the LORD's command the Israelites moved their camp, and at the LORD's command they pitched their tents. As long as the cloud stayed above the Tabernacle they remained in their camp. (9:15-18)

Exegesis and Exposition

This section recapitulates the events of Ex. 40:34 and describes in greater detail the significance of the cloud (MT עָנָן, *'ānān*) that had settled on the Tabernacle. To that extent the material helps to integrate the narratives of Exodus and Numbers into the same chronological sequence. The explanatory gloss "Tent of Meeting" probably means that the cloud was centered over the Holy Place and the Most

---

77. E.g., G. B. Gray, *Numbers*, pp. 84-85.
78. E.g., J. Milgrom, "A Prolegomenon to Lev. 17:11," *JBL* 90 (1971): 154-55.
79. E.g., R. A. Cole, *Exodus* (1973), p. 109; P. J. Budd, *Numbers*, p. 98. On this matter see G. J. Wenham, *Leviticus*, pp. 241-42; E. Kutsch, *THAT*, 1:859; E. Smick, *TWOT*, 1:456-57.

Holy Place and thereafter overshadowed the entire Tabernacle court. The Israelites had first experienced God's leadership by means of a cloudy pillar immediately prior to the Exodus (Ex. 13:21-22), and the fiery glow of the overshadowing cloud at night would have reminded them vividly of God's mighty deliverance at the Re(e)d Sea and of His continued presence with them. Some commentators have thought that the cloudy pillar of the Exodus and the cloud that descended on the Tabernacle were identical. Although this is possible, Thompson is probably correct in supposing that there were two different phenomena involved: (1) the guiding cloud, and (2) the cloud of God's presence.[80] In any event, the very fact that a cloud was in existence in the wilderness in such close proximity to the ground is an amazing occurrence in itself, since clouds are unusual features of the wilderness environment.

Rationalistic explanations of the phenomenon vary from retrojections of the fire-pillar imagery from the Solomonic Temple[81] to the activity of volcanoes in the Sinai area[82] or even farther away on the European mainland. Attempts to relate 'ānān to a supposed cognate word in Ugaritic ('nn)[83] have been shown to be unsatisfactory by the work of R. Good.[84] The burning glow (MT מַרְאֵה-אֵשׁ, mar'ēh-'ēš) of the cloud might well have suggested a latent fire that could flare out and devour delinquent Israelites at the slightest provocation.

Its brightness by night proclaimed God's sovereignty, while its darkness during the day concealed His majesty. The lifting of the cloud would constitute the signal for the tribes of Israel to move their camp, and conversely, when the cloud halted at a particular place, the tribes pitched their tents and remained in that location until the cloud rose once more. When it descended upon the Tabernacle, it signified to the Israelites that God was present in their midst.

Translation

When the cloud remained over the Tabernacle for a lengthy period, the Israelites obeyed the LORD's instructions and did not resume

---

80. J. A. Thompson, *ZPEB*, 4:796.
81. G. H. Davies, *IDB*, 3:817.
82. M. Noth, *Exodus* (1962), p. 109.
83. Cf. T. W. Mann, "The Pillar of Cloud in the Reed Sea Narrative," *JBL* 90 (1971): 15-30; G. E. Mendenhall, *The Tenth Generation* (Baltimore: Johns Hopkins, 1973), pp. 32-66, 209-13.
84. R. Good, "Cloud Messengers?" *UF* 10 (1978): 436-37. For other discussions see J. Pedersen, *Israel, Its Life and Culture* III-IV (London: Oxford U., 1940), pp. 728-37; G. A. Lee, *ISBE*, 3:871. J. H. Hertz, ed., *The Pentateuch and Haftorahs*, p. 609, maintained that the cloud covered only that part of the Tabernacle in which the Ark of the Covenant was located.

The Tabernacle in the Wilderness

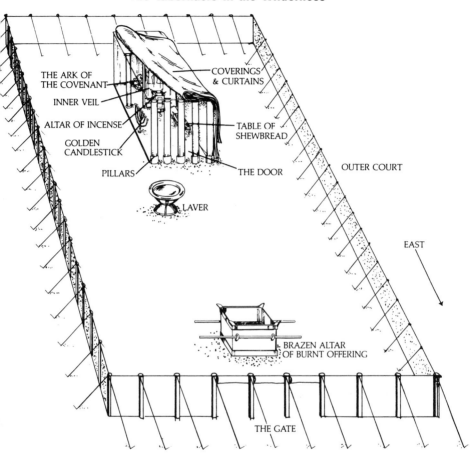

marching. Thus it was that, when the cloud rested upon the Tabernacle for a few days, they remained encamped according to the LORD's instructions; and when the LORD gave the command they would move out in ranks.

Thus even if the cloud stayed above the Tabernacle only from evening until morning, they would begin their journey when it lifted in the morning. Whether it was day* or night, they would march out when the cloud lifted.

Whether the cloud stayed above the Tabernacle for two days, a month, or longer, the Israelites would remain encamped and did not move on; but when it lifted they would set out.

They remained encamped at the LORD's command, and at the

LORD's command they took up their journey. They obeyed the LORD's orders in accordance with His command given through Moses. (9:19-23)

Exegesis and Exposition

However long or short the interval of encampment was to be, the Israelites followed the Lord's instructions implicitly, no matter what inconveniences might have been experienced. The repetitions from v. 17 onward in this chapter, while superfluous and even tedious to the modern reader, were of great importance to the ancient *šōṭĕrîm* and those for whom they compiled their records. This was one of the comparatively few occasions when God's people obeyed Him without questioning. The miracle of the Exodus was still fresh in their minds, and the presence of the fiery cloud was a welcome and continuing assurance that the Lord was still governing their destiny.

The repetitions in the text, a feature of both Hebrew and Ugaritic literature, give coherence both to the narratives themselves and to the spiritual attitude of the Hebrews that the sources reflected. The people were one in faith, obedience, and action, in a recapitulation of the covenant ratification events at Sinai (Ex. 24:6-7) that was to become increasingly less frequent as the months passed. The repetitions, then, should be viewed as organic rather than purely mechanical functions of style.

At this stage of the desert sojourn the tribes would remain in close order, and the Levites would be occupied in following their duties according to the Lord's instruction (MT מִשְׁמֶרֶת, *mišmeret*). It is misleading to imagine the marching Israelites strung out across the wilderness in long columns. Nor would all of them be huddled together around one oasis when they were encamped. Most probably they would move along in order according to family and tribal groups, as the regulations for the march prescribed. When they encamped, they would be living in the areas where there were one or two springs that would supply their needs. On rare occasions when there was no local water available, miraculous provision was made (e.g., Num. 21:16-18).

In all probability the Levites kept the cloud under close observation, and thus they would have been the ones to alert the priests and the various tribal leaders when the cloud moved. However long or short the sojourn, the signal for departure was unmistakable. Just how far the cloud rose above the Tabernacle is not stated, but there can be no doubt that it was visible in its characteristic form, as it was at the period of the Exodus. Its presence was God's assurance that He was leading His people into the land of promise, having already freed them from bondage.

The mention of possible intervals of time for encampment is deliberately imprecise so as to leave room for variables, the nature of which is not specified. Some scholars have questioned the translation of יָמִים, *yāmîm* ("days"), by "year," the rendering of most modern English versions, following the KJV. In view of the lack of decisive evidence, it is probably best to translate the word in terms of an undefined interval, as with the RSV ("a longer time"). The formula of obedience in vv. 18-19 is repeated in v. 23 in abbreviated form. Again it is made clear that the specific cloud movements were God's work, whether for marching or for remaining in camp, and that they were being obeyed implicitly. Since the MT does not mention specific night marches, it is possible that the intent of the instructions was to engender preparedness to obey God's will at any given moment as a function of spiritual discipline. The chapter ends as it began by showing the role of Moses as the mediator of God's commands. Some scholars have purported to see a palistrophe (chiasm) in vv. 18-23, but the attempts appear to be contrived.

Additional Notes

9:2 בְּמוֹעֲדוֹ: The LXX reads the plural, κατὰ καιροὺς, here, but the singular, καιρὸν, in vv. 7, 13. The Samaritan Pentateuch reads the plural on all three occasions.

9:3 בַּחֹדֶשׁ הַזֶּה: The meaning looks back to v. 1, following the ordinance of Ex. 12:14. The LXX makes the month specific by describing it as τοῦ μηνὸς τοῦ πρώτου.

9:5 וַיַּעֲשׂוּ אֶת־הַפֶּסַח: The LXX omits this phrase and begins the verse with ἐναρχομένον τῇ τεσσαρεσκαιδεκάτῃ ἡμέρᾳ. It also omits בֵּין הָעַרְבַּיִם, concluding the verse with the mention of the Sinai desert. These omissions probably reflect a variant MS tradition from the MT.

9:13 וּבְדֶרֶךְ: The LXX adds μακρᾷ to ὁδῷ, apparently to show that the prescribed penalty of being "cut off" would be eminently fair.

9:16 הֶעָנָן יְכַסֶּנּוּ: The LXX adds ἡμέρας, which the MT evidently understands.

9:20 וְיֵשׁ אֲשֶׁר יִהְיֶה: The existential particle יֵשׁ with a noun clause is here expressing an existing situation, as in the following verse.

יָמִים מִסְפָּר: These terms are nouns in apposition to express measure or number (R. J. Williams, *Hebrew Syntax*, p. 17, sect. 69), making the proposed BHS emendation unnecessary.

9:21 וְלַיְלָה: Following this word the LXX omits the phrase וְנַעֲלָה הֶעָנָן וְנָסָעוּ. The LXX translators seem to have experienced textual difficulties here. One MS, Codex Ambrosianus, omitted the phrase πρωί καὶ ἀναβῇ ἡ νεφέλη, whereas the same MS and Codex Alexandrinus read ἡ νεφέλη ἀπαρούσιν.

9:22 יָמִים: The time span expressed here presents some difficulties because of its indeterminate nature. Most modern English trans-lators render the term by "one year" on the basis of passages such as Judg. 17:10; 1 Sam. 1:3; 27:7, and others. Certain passages, including Gen. 40:4; 1 Kings 17:15; Neh. 1:4; etc., suggest an indefinite period of time. The *RSV* avoids supporting the concept of a specific interval. For the view that יָמִים is actually a technical term signifying an interval of four months, see F. S. North, "Four Month Season of the Hebrew Bible," *VT* 11 (1961): 446-48.

הֶעָנָן עַל־הַמִּשְׁכָּן: Further textual problems in the LXX are evident here. Codices Alexandrinus and Ambrosianus omitted τῆς νεφέλης σκιαζούσης, while the Tabernacle was merely referred to as αὐτῆς.

וּבְהֵעָלֹתוֹ יִסָּעוּ was omitted by the LXX, being probably thought of as an unnecessary addition to the MT.

F. THE TRUMPETS (10:1-10)

This short section deals exclusively with the regulations govern-ing the use of the silver trumpets for peace or war.

Translation

The LORD spoke to Moses, saying: Make two trumpets of ham-mered silver. Use them for assembling the community and directing the moving of the encampment. (10:1-2)

Exegesis and Exposition

To implement the Lord's guidance and to assist in organizing the movement of a large body of Israelites in their appointed order, a specific means of communication was established. By divine com-mand to Moses, two silver trumpets were to be fashioned. The in-structions for their manufacture are by no means as detailed as those for the furnishings of the Tabernacle, but like the cherubim (Ex. 25:18) they were to be hammered (MT מִקְשָׁה, *miqšâ*) out of a silver ingot in the form of two sheets of metal that would then be bent into the form of a trumpet (MT חֲצוֹצְרָה, *ḥăṣôṣĕrâ*).

Smelting furnaces for reducing silver ore must have been known in the ancient Near East prior to 3000 B.C. because of the presence of corroded silver artifacts in the tomb of Pu-Abi at Ur (c. 2700 B.C.). They thus antedate by half a millennium the furnaces discovered about 1972 by Russian archaeologists in the vicinity of Mount Ararat. Tablets from Ebla dated c. 2500 B.C. show that silver constituted an early form of money; they describe cattle received from Mari as trib-ute being valued in silver. With such a metallurgical prehistory, cou-pled with a knowledge of Egyptian manufacturing techniques, the making of silver trumpets would have presented no problems to the skilled Hebrew workmen.

Scholars have sought the origin of the Hebrew term for "trumpet" in a root חצר (*ḥṣr*), meaning either "to stretch" or alternatively, a "stalk," "tube." The silver trumpet would thus differ from the convoluted ram's horn (שׁוֹפָר, *šôpār*) in being straight and having a tapered shape much like that of the Egyptian trumpets. The *ḥǎṣôṣěrâ* was preeminently a priestly instrument, and from the very beginning in Israel the trumpets were used in pairs (Num. 10:1-10). At a much later period they increased in numbers significantly when used on occasions of celebration.[85]

The silver trumpets could be expected to produce a sharper, clearer note than the muffled rumblings of the ram's horn, but neither of those instruments would be able to play more than four notes of a musical scale. Long silver trumpets were in common use for military, religious, and purely social functions in Egypt during the Amarna Age (14th century B.C.),[86] and at the end of that period some silver trumpets were placed in the storage chamber of King Tutankhamun's tomb. I have heard two of these trumpets played, and because they had been fitted with modern mouthpieces for the occasion, their range of musical notes exceeded considerably what would have been the case in antiquity. The sound emitted was clear and piercing, which would be ideal for summoning people for an important function or rallying them in times of emergency.

The dimensions of the trumpets are not recorded in the narrative, but they were probably modeled on the style found in Tutankhamun's tomb, and if this was the case they would have been approximately two feet long and tapered from about one-half inch at the mouthpiece to about three and one-half inches at the bell end. In all, they would constitute elegant additions to the various implements used by the priests in their duties.[87]

Translation

When both trumpets are sounded, the entire community must gather before you at the entrance to the Tent of Meeting.

---

85. As, for example, at the feast of drawing water. Cf. *Mishnah Sukkah*, 5. 1.
86. H. Hickmann, *La Trompette dans l'Egypte ancienne* (Cairo: Institut francaise d'archaéologie orientale, 1946), p. 46; "Die Kultische Verwendung der altägyptischen Trompete," *WO* 1 (1950): 351-55.
87. For further studies see C. Sachs, *The History of Musical Instruments* (New York: W. W. Norton, 1940); E. Werner, *IDB*, 3:472-73; H. M. Best and D. Huttar, *ZPEB*, 4:320-24; D. A. Foxvog and A. D. Kilmer, *ISBE*, 3:438-40 and bibliography.

If only one is sounded, the leaders who are heads of Israelite family groups shall assemble before you.

When you sound the advance, the camps located on the east side shall begin their march. When you sound the advance the second time, then those camps that are located* on the south side shall begin their march. The trumpet blast will be the signal for moving off.

When you want to assemble the community, you shall blow the trumpets, but not in the same manner as when you sound the advance. (10:3-7)

Exegesis and Exposition

The whole congregation was required to assemble before the entrance to the Tent of Meeting when members heard both trumpets blown. Whether they were blown in unison, concurrently, or with different pitches is not stated. If only one trumpet was sounded, it was the signal for the leaders to assemble in the presence of Moses. The MT for "sound" (תָּקַע, tāqaʿ) is a word that means to "strike," "drive," or "blow on a trumpet." The signal for breaking camp (תְּרוּעָה, tĕrûʿâ) was evidently different in tone and might possibly have had the staccato quality of an alarm.[88]

The NEB gives the impression that sounding the advance was in fact the signal for a shout, as Judah, Issachar, and Zebulun prepared to move. Although shouting no doubt accompanied the ordering of the various groups, it is not indicated specifically in the MT. The basic meaning of the root רוע (rwʿ) is "to give a blast on a trumpet" and only secondarily to shout in battle (Josh. 6:10; etc.). In this section of Numbers the reference is clearly to the sounding of a trumpet.

When the summons to advance was sounded a second time, it was the turn of the tribes located on the south of the Tabernacle—namely, Reuben, Simeon, and Gad—to commence marching out. The tribes on the west and north would then assemble and join the march in the same manner, although this is not stated specifically in the MT. The LXX, however, remedied this deficiency by mentioning the two remaining groups in their own order (LXX Num. 10:6).

Translation

The sons of Aaron, the priests, are to blow the trumpets. This is to be a permanent injunction for you and is binding upon all future generations.

When you engage in battle in your own land against an enemy who is oppressing you, you shall sound an alarm on the trumpets.

---

88. As opposed to *KD*, 3:55, who associated such tones with the *tāqaʿ*. See *Mishnah Rosh Hashanah*, 4.9.

You will then be remembered before the LORD your God and will be saved from your enemies. (10:8-9)

Exegesis and Exposition

The use of the silver trumpets was restricted to the Aaronides, to be employed for the sacred purposes of the community. They were given in perpetuity (MT לְחֻקַּת עוֹלָם, *lĕḥuqqat ʿôlām*), a term used of ordinances relating to such priestly matters as cultic attire (Ex. 28:43), sanctuary rituals (27:21; Lev. 24:3), sacrifices (Lev. 3:17; Num. 15:15), and others. Its binding nature for the future (MT לְדֹרֹתֵיכֶם, *lĕdōrōtêkem*) ties the scope of ʿôlām, to the continuity of the nation and the priesthood. "Perpetuity" thus terminated after A.D. 70, when Jerusalem was destroyed and the nation was dispersed. Two additional uses of the trumpets looked forward to the occupation of Palestine by the Israelites. When an enemy attack threatened, the trumpets were to be sounded so that God would remember the needs of His covenant people and give them victory over their opponents. The MT phrase בֹּא מִלְחָמָה (*bôʾ milḥāmâ*, "come/go to war") implies defensive measures against an aggressor, as opposed to the deliberate mobilizing of forces for an attack (בֹּא לַמִּלְחָמָה, *bôʾ lammilḥāmâ*), as in Numbers 31:21; 32:6. The MT niphal perfect נוֹשַׁעְתֶּם (*nôšaʿtem*, "be helped," "be saved") has a simple passive force here rather than a reflexive one.

Translation

Also at times when you are rejoicing, such as at your stated festivals and on the first day of every month, you shall blow the trumpets over your burnt offerings and your peace offerings. The trumpets shall be a memorial for you before your God. I am the LORD your God. (10:10)

Exegesis and Exposition

The second use involved peaceful activities of a religious nature, where their blasts would again bring to God's attention the spiritual and communal needs of the Israelites. The appointed festivals that were marked by special sacrifices were Passover, Harvest, Weeks (Pentecost), Day of Remembrance, Day of Atonement, and Tabernacles (Booths). The offerings are prescribed in Lev. 23:1-44 and Num. 28-29, the latter reference including the Sabbath offering.

The celebration of the commencement of the months (MT בְּרָאשֵׁי חָדְשֵׁכֶם, *bĕrāʾšê ḥodšēkem*) by a trumpet blast was more of a calendrical reminder than the celebration of a major festival and was perhaps instituted to focus attention upon the Lord of Sinai, thereby forestalling the pagan-style veneration of the new moon. On the first day of the seventh month, the festival of the new moon, or feast of trumpets, marked the beginning of the civil year and also commemorated the start of the sabbatical (seventh) month (Num. 29:1). Every festival in the Torah, regardless of its purpose, was associated in some manner with the number "seven," often thought of as signifying perfection or completeness. Thus every seventh day, every seventh month, every seventh year, and every year that occurred after forty-nine years, was marked by a festive celebration. On those occasions the silver trumpets were blown over the offerings to call the nation to remembrance before God and to prepare her for worship and fellowship with Him.

This first major section of Numbers closes with the asseveration by God that He is the supreme Lord and ruler of His people Israel. The nation is the visible expression of His existence, personality, and saving power. Without Him they are meaningless, but they have been chosen specifically out of His abundant love to be a witness to the surrounding nations because of their constitution as a kingdom of priests and a holy nation (Ex. 19:6).

Such a lofty spiritual ideal could only be accomplished in the spirit of the ratification of the covenant at Mount Sinai (Ex. 27:7) by hearing the revealed commands of God and obeying them in faith. As long as the Israelites realized that they owed their continuance as well as their origin to Him, they would prosper in their ways. As they began their journey from Sinai through the wilderness to Moab, they carried with them this living, powerful watchword: I am the Lord your God.

Additional Notes

10:2 מִקְשָׁה: The root is unfamiliar, but the translation appears to be "beaten" or "hammered." Cf. BDB, p. 904b; KB, 2:562a.

10:3 וְתָקְעוּ: The LXX reads σαλπίσεις here, which is peculiar in view of the plural usage in v. 4 and elsewhere.

10:6 תֵּימָנָה: The departures of the northerly and westerly military units is unmentioned in the MT. The LXX remedies the deficiency, thus presenting a full account of the procedures involved when an alarm had been sounded. There is no reason to think that the LXX material was original and had been dropped somehow from the MT. The Hebrew merely uses two sections of the camp as representative of the procedure, since this had already been formulated in Numbers 2:3-31.

3
From Sinai to Kadesh (10:11–12:16)

A. COMMENCEMENT OF THE JOURNEY (10:11-36)

This section can be analyzed structurally into seven units: (1) the departure begins (vv. 11-12); (2) Judah leads the march (vv. 13-17); (3) the tribes led by Reuben follow (vv. 18-21); (4) the tribes led by Ephraim follow them (vv. 22-24); (5) the tribes led by Dan bring up the rear (vv. 25-27); (6) summary (v. 28); (7) proposed departure of Hobab (vv. 29-36).

1. THE DEPARTURE BEGINS (10:11-12)

Translation

Now it happened on the twentieth day of the second month in the second year that the cloud lifted from the Tent of the Agreement. So the Israelites set out from the Sinai wilderness on their journeyings until the cloud settled in the wilderness of Paran. (10:11-12)

Exegesis and Exposition

The historic journey commenced with the cloud of the divine presence signaling the time of departure from Sinai by rising above the sacred shrine that housed the commandments ("tabernacle of the testimony," KJV, *NIV*; "Tabernacle of the Tokens," *NEB*; "Dwelling of the commandments," *NAB*). The Israelites had spent eleven months in the area of Mount Sinai (cf. Ex. 19:1), and it was now time for them to begin the great adventure of marching out to possess the Promised Land under God's leadership.

The wilderness of Paran was the traditional home of Ishmael (Gen. 21:21), where he married an Egyptian woman and reared a family of twelve sons (25:13-15). The area of Paran is ill-defined but is thought to have constituted a large portion of land located southwest of Palestine in the east-central region of the Sinai peninsula. It constituted the southern limit of Chedorlaomer's attack (14:16) and evidently formed a border with the Arabah and the Gulf of Aqaba to the east, but it was actually east of the wilderness of Shur, which adjoined Egypt. Most allusions to Paran place it between Mount Sinai and the district northward from Elath to Kadesh-barnea.[1] Some scholars have been more specific in identifying it with the desert of et-Tîh in the north-central area of the Sinai peninsula, but this is uncertain.

2. JUDAH LEADS THE MARCH (10:13-17)

Translation

So they started out on this first occasion at the LORD's command through Moses.
The standard of the camp of the Judahites went out first with their divisions, with Nahshon son of Amminadab as leader. (10:13-14)

Exegesis and Exposition

Although God was the supreme commander of the expedition, Moses was the general officer who received the divine commands and relayed them to the Israelites. As the cloud ascended from the sacred shrine, the tribes would assemble expectantly in their predetermined order, the Tabernacle would be dismantled and packed for the journey, and the whole procession would move off.

The tribe of Judah led the way, as had been arranged previously (Num. 2:3), under the command of Nahshon son of Amminadab. In succeeding verses the names of the leaders are given for the fourth time, the other occasions being 1:5-15; 2:3-31; 7:12-83. This repetition in chap. 10 was deemed important because of some variations in detail from earlier narratives dealing with the order to be followed when marching. The "first occasion" relates to the initial movement from the camp at Mount Sinai. The statement of 10:12 is a summary of the journey, the details of which occupy 10:13–12:16. From this

1. Cf. B. Rothenberg, *God's Wilderness* (London: Thames & Hudson, 1961), pp. 165-69; Y. Aharoni, *LBHG* (1979 ed.), p. 199; J. L. Mihelic, *IDB*, 3:657; J. M. Houston, *ZPEB*, 4:599-600; T. V. Brisco, *ISBE*, 3:662.

material it will appear that Paran was actually the third camping ground, the first being Kibroth-hattaavah (11:34) and the second Hazeroth (11:35).

The Judahites followed their tribal standard (דֶּגֶל, *degel*), which was evidently a symbol set on a pole and by which the tribe was identified. Such standards were familiar to ancient Near Eastern peoples and were often adorned with banners. R. de Vaux, however, thought that the *degel* was nothing more than a pole or mast that was raised to send signals to an armed body,[2] but this view neglects the variation of design that would be needed to establish the distinction between the tribes.

The OT has little to say about the standards apart from their use in rallying the Israelites and thereby helping to identify the various tribes. It has been suggested that אֹת (*'ōt*) in Num. 2:2 represents the ensign of a particular family group and *degel* the standard of one of the four units making up three tribes each, but this is conjectural.[3] What have been identified as metal standards have been recovered from Palestinian sites. Two from the Late Bronze Age were unearthed at Hazor and Beth-shan, while an additional one was found at the Iron Age II level at Tell esh-Shari'ah.[4] In later Hebrew history the Talmudic authorities assigned a specific pictorial emblem to each of the tribal standards, apparently reflecting in some way the blessing of Jacob (Gen. 49:3-27), but these are also conjectural.

Translation

In charge of the divisions of the tribe of Issachar was Nethanel son of Zuar, while in charge of the divisions of the Zebulunites was Eliab son of Helon.

Then the Tabernacle was dismantled, and the Gershonites and the Merarites set out, transporting it. (10:15-17)

Exegesis and Exposition

Issachar, the second tribe of the Judahite triad, followed under the leadership of Nethanel son of Zuar, while Zebulun, led by Eliab son of Helon, brought up the rear of the triad. So far the order given in earlier chap. has been preserved, but at this juncture additional information is supplied. The Gershonites, who were camped on the west behind the Tabernacle (Num. 3:3), and the Merarites, who were

---

2. R. de Vaux, *Ancient Israel*, pp. 226-27.
3. E.g., by J. H. Hertz, ed., *The Pentateuch and Haftorahs*, p. 572; M. F. Unger, *Unger's Bible Dictionary* (Chicago: Moody, 1966), p. 315.
4. This latter site was identified with Gath in 1966 by G. E. Wright. For differing views and bibliography see J. E. Jennings, *NIDBA*, pp. 205-7.

stationed on the north side of the Tabernacle, dismantled the structure and carried it behind the Judahites on the march. Their position on the journey had not been mentioned in chap. 2 because the Levites had not been enumerated and assigned their duties at that point.

2. THE TRIBES LED BY REUBEN FOLLOW (10:18-21)

Translation

The standard of the camp of Reuben set out with its accompanying divisions, with Elizur son of Shedeur as leader.

In charge of the divisions of the tribe of Simeon was Shelumiel son of Zurishaddai, while in charge of the divisions of the Gadites was Eliasaph son of Deuel. (10:18-20)

Exegesis and Exposition

The second triad of Hebrew tribes was led by Reuben, followed by the tribe of Simeon and the Gadites. So far the order prescribed in chap. 2 has been maintained, but then there comes a further procedural modification having to do with the Kohathite Levites.

Translation

Then the Kohathites set out, carrying the sacred vessels. The Tabernacle was to be assembled prior to their arrival. (10:21)

Exegesis and Exposition

The Kohathites took up their position behind the Reubenite group, bearing the sacred Ark, the table, and other sanctuary furnishings (Num. 3:31). When the Israelites were on the march, the Ark and other sacred items that belonged in the sanctuary remained in the center of the tribes, just as they did when the company was encamped. Only in the settlement period (cf. Josh. 3:3) did the Ark precede the Israelite forces. The MT מִקְדָּשׁ (*miqdāš*, "sacred vessels") is a term that also means "temple" or "sanctuary," but is understood by the LXX and most modern versions to be metonymy for the sanctuary's vessels.[5]

The text then explains the rationale of the additional information regarding the Kohathites. They were positioned in such a way that by the time they had arrived at the camping ground the Tabernacle's structural units would already have been reassembled, ready for the Kohathites to exercise their task of replacing the sacred vessels in

---

5. *KD*, 3:559.

the Holy Place and the Most Holy Place. This seems to be the sense of the terse MT expression עַד־בֹּאָם (*'ad-bō'ām*) rather than the *NEB* rendering "on their arrival found the Tabernacle set up," which takes as an accomplished fact what was actually only being anticipated.

4. THE TRIBES LED BY EPHRAIM FOLLOW THEM (10:22-24)

Translation

The standard of the camp of the Ephraimites set out with their divisions, with Elishama son of Ammihud as leader.

In charge of the divisions of the tribe of Manasseh was Gamaliel son of Pedahzur, while in charge of the divisions of the tribe of Benjamin was Abidan son of Gideoni. (10:22-24)

Exegesis and Exposition

The third group of three tribes was led by the Ephraimites, followed by Manasseh and Benjamin.

5. THE TRIBES LED BY DAN BRING UP THE REAR (10:25-27)

Translation

Then the standard of the camp of Dan, the rear guard of all the camps, went out with the divisions, with Ahiezer son of Ammishaddai as leader. In charge of the divisions of the Asherites was Pagiel son of Ocran, while in charge of the Naphtalite divisions was Ahira son of Enan. (10:25-27)

Exegesis and Exposition

The final group of three tribes proceeded under the Danite standard, followed by the Asherites and the tribe of Naphtali. These three tribes made up a strong rear force, described in the MT as מְאַסֵּף לְכָל־הַמַּחֲנֹת (*mĕ'assēp lĕkol-hammaḥănōt*, the "assembler of all the camps").

6. SUMMARY (10:28)

Translation

This was the order of march of the Israelite divisions as they commenced their journeyings. (10:28)

Exegesis and Exposition

Finally the arrangements to be followed after the Israelites have broken camp are now stated in full, but summarized here in a concluding statement. The procession was characterized by strong ad-

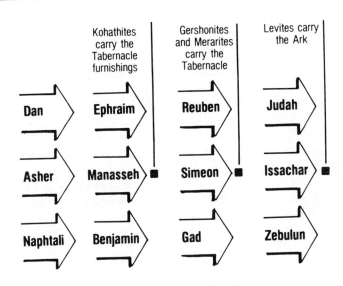

Marching Order of the Tribes

vance guard and rear guard units. The same scribal attention to detail that marked the census recording and the list of offerings at the dedication of the sacrificial altar is evident here in the care with which the arrangements for the march were recorded. By imposing strict instructions with regard to life in the community, God was endeavoring to inculcate in His people a disciplined way of life that would reflect His own high moral and spiritual character.

7. PROPOSED DEPARTURE OF HOBAB (10:29-36)

Translation

Now Moses said to Hobab son of Reuel the Midianite, the father-in-law of Moses: We are now starting out for the place about which the LORD said: I will give it to you. Come along with us and we will treat you generously, for the LORD has promised great benefits for Israel. (10:29)

Exegesis and Exposition

There is some question as to the identity of Hobab, who is mentioned again in Judg. 4:11. The MT's statement that he was the son of Reuel (KJV "Raguel") would make him Moses' brother-in-law, whereas in Judg. 4:11 he is described as the father-in-law of Moses. Furthermore, in Judg. 1:16; 4:11 Hobab is traced to Kenite ancestry, whereas in Ex. 3:1; 18:1 Jethro (Reuel) is described as "the priest of Midian." The solution to this problem is made more difficult by a lack of adequate information.

Jethro is frequently identified with Reuel on the basis of Ex. 2:18, 21; 3:1, and thus Hobab becomes Moses' חֹתֵן (*ḥōtēn*), a relative by marriage and probably a brother-in-law (Judg. 4:11, *NAB, NIV, NEB*). Some writers even entertain the idea that Jethro, Hobab, and Reuel were one and the same person.[6] The ambiguity of the MT of Judg. 4:11 is reflected in translations that read "father-in-law" (e.g., *RSV, NASB, NKJV*), thereby making an uncertain tradition more confusing.

In an attempt to solve the impasse, some commentators have identified Hobab with Jethro (Reuel),[7] following Islamic tradition, which itself unfortunately cannot be verified. Others have suggested that the name Hobab may have been formerly included in Ex. 2:18, thus implying that Reuel was the title of a family group.[8] In order to clarify the text of Judg. 4:11, it has been argued that the phrase "the son of Reuel the Midianite" in Num. 10:29 had dropped out of the genealogy by the time of the Judges, thus tending inadvertently to identify Hobab with Reuel (Jethro), which was not supported by earlier traditions.[9]

Any identification of Hobab with Jethro in Num. 10:29 would make nonsense of the narrative in Ex. 18:27, where Moses allowed his father-in-law to return to Midian after receiving his counsel concerning judicial procedures. Thompson is undoubtedly correct in saying that the purpose of Judg. 4:11 was to state the exact Kenite group to which Heber belonged. It was (1) Hobab's branch of the family group (as in Judg. 1:16), and (2) relatives of Moses by marriage, making Hobab the brother-in-law of Moses.[10]

The question of the names "Reuel" and "Jethro" has also been discussed by commentators, and accordingly it has been suggested that Reuel may be a tribal rather than a personal name, or that both belong to different documentary "sources." Alternative names were comparatively common in the ancient Near East, as can be illustrated from Ugaritic and Egyptian sources,[11] so on this analogy it would not be unusual for a Reuel-Jethro combination to exist along with others such as Jacob-Israel. The choice of one or other of the

---

6. C. P. Gray, *ZPEB*, 3:584.
7. A. E. Cundall, *Judges*, TOTC (Leicester: Inter-Varsity, 1968), p. 56.
8. Cf. R. F. Johnson, *IDB*, 2:615.
9. J. Crichton, *ISBE*, 2:1055.
10. J. A. Thompson, *The New Bible Commentary Revised*, p. 180.
11. Cf. C. H. Gordon, *Before the Bible*, pp. 236-38, for pairs of names.

names for use in speech or literature would be entirely at the discretion of the person concerned. It is also possible that Reuel is a proper name whereas Jethro, meaning perhaps "His Excellency," is Reuel's priestly title. The different tribal designations of Kenite and Midianite associated with Jethro, although unexplained in the MT, need indicate nothing more than evidence of the admixture of the Hebrew peoples at that particular period.

After Jethro returned home (Ex. 18:27), Moses explained to Hobab, his brother-in-law, that the Israelites were starting out on their journey to the land that God had promised them. Knowing that Hobab was thoroughly familiar with the Sinai terrain, Moses invited him to stay with the Israelite community, evidently on a consultative basis. How and when Hobab had joined the Hebrews in the wilderness is not stated in the MT, but he may have attached himself to the tribes when Reuel visited Moses at Mount Sinai (Ex. 18:5).

Translation

But he said to him, No, I will not go. I am returning to my own land and my own people.

Then Moses said, Please don't forsake us. You know the best places for us to encamp in the wilderness, and you will be our guide. If you come with us, you can be certain that whatever good things the LORD will do to us, we will do the same to you.

So they moved away from the mountain of the LORD and traveled for three days. The Ark of the LORD's covenant went ahead of them for the three days' journey to find them a place to rest. (10:30-33)

Exegesis and Exposition

Hobab was evidently unimpressed with Moses' proposal, even though it contained the assurance of divine blessing. The attraction of his homeland was uppermost in his feelings, probably more so because his father had departed earlier, and in any event Hobab did not appear anxious to commit himself to Moses for even the few weeks that would have been required for a journey directly from Mount Sinai to the southern border of Canaan.

It is possible that Hobab was concerned about his father's health, but this is not stated in the MT. Moses, however, renewed his entreaty and amplified the content of his earlier statement, stressing Hobab's role as topographical guide (MT עֵינָיִם, 'ênayim, "eyes," as in several English versions), subservient to the Lord's overall bidding. This would be an extremely valuable service, for, as Keil and Delitzsch point out, in the areas where the sign for encampment was given, the oases and small pastures are often concealed in the valleys and mountains that are spread out in the wilderness.[12] Hobab's response is not recorded, but the presence of Kenites in Canaan as allies of the Judahites (Judg. 1:16) would indicate that Hobab, whose activities are not mentioned in Numbers, had decided to stay with the Israelites and fulfill the role Moses had indicated. On this basis the Israelites broke camp under the Lord's guidance, with the Ark of the Covenant being carried ahead of the company.

This arrangement differs from that understood from Num. 2:11; 10:13-28 but does not conflict with the predominant wilderness tradition of enclosing the Ark in the moving column of Israelites. The present occasion appears to have been a special one, and the presence of the Ark at the head of the nation in fact enhanced the position of the Lord as the absolute leader of His people, enthroned by the presence of the cloud upon His Ark.

The procession marched for three days before a suitable area for the encampment was revealed. This journey would test the organization of the tribes for such marches. The place where the cloud paused is unnamed.

Translation

*The cloud of the LORD overshadowed them by day when they moved their camp.

Whenever the Ark started out, Moses would say: Rise up, LORD. May your enemies be scattered and those who hate you flee before you.

Whenever it halted, he would say: Return, LORD, to the countless thousands of Israel. (10:34-36)

Exegesis and Exposition

Commentators have sometimes been divided over the extent to which the cloud overshadowed the Israelites. Some have imagined that it was restricted to the front of the procession, thus depicting God shrouded in cloud as He occupied His throne. Others have supposed that the cloud covered the entire company, either at the beginning when they were organizing the move or while they were journeying. It would have been necessary for the cloud to have remained at a certain height above the ground, otherwise it would have made the Israelites' vision of the terrain rather hazy.

Two pronouncement formulas conclude this section. They reflect the concept of God as the Lord of armies, and His people as ritually

---

12. *KD*, 3:60–61.

pure warriors, fighting His battles. In the ancient Near East, wars were deemed to be conflicts between opposing gods, whose peoples did the actual fighting. Thus all war was "holy," with the warriors acting as representatives of their deities.[13] The formulas were spoken by Moses alone, imploring help for the journey and its eventualities, and for God to protect the Israelite forces against marauders when encamped. The theme of the first invocation recurs in Ps. 68:1 (MT 2), using the same words for hatred (שָׂנֵא, *śānē'*) and flight (נוּס, *nûs*) in the context of a holy war as it recapitulated the wilderness experience of Israel. The expression "countless thousands of Israel" (so *NEB*) looks back to the organization of Num. 1:5-16. The formulas have also been seen as an early variety of Hebrew war hymn.

Additional Notes

10:11 The Samaritan Pentateuch includes a section that instructs the Israelites to journey toward Amorite territory and possess the land the Lord had promised to the patriarchs. The addition reflects the text of Deut. 1:6-8.

10:17 וְהוּרַד: Whereas the MT has the hophal perfect of יָרַד, the LXX reads καθελοῦσιν, reflecting the הוֹרִדוּ of 4:5 and the יוֹרִידוּ of 1:51.

10:29 N. H. Snaith, *Numbers*, p. 224, prefers the pointing חָתָן instead of חֹתֵן, but this term in the absolute means "son-in-law" or "brother-in-law." The MT qal participle חֹתֵן stands in apposition to מֹשֶׁה and thus does not require a change in pointing.

10:33 דֶּרֶךְ שְׁלֹשֶׁת: This phrase occurs twice in the verse, and accordingly some commentators have seen the second occurrence as an accidental repetition (e.g., N. H. Snaith, *Numbers*, p. 225). But the LXX has the same reading as the MT, so it is probable that the duplication was stylistic rather than transcriptional. In the LXX v. 34 follows v. 36, which to the translators seemed to make a better ending to the chapter.

10:34-36 The state of the MT has aroused considerable discussion. The LXX, apparently following a different manuscript tradition, placed v. 34 after v. 36, perhaps to emphasize the Lord's continuing care of His nation. The ancient scribes used inverted *nuns* (letter "n"), possibly as a form of parentheses or brackets, as though they sensed a textual dislocation.

The same symbols occur also in Ps. 107:23-28, 40, where they do not seem to point to any textual difficulties, and thus their signifi-

---

13. On the concept of "holy war" see L. E. Toombs, *IDB* 4:797; E. Stern, *ZPEB*, 5:895, and bibliographies; P. C. Craigie, *The Problem of War in the Old Testament* (1978); K. L. Barker, gen. ed., *The NIV Study Bible*, p. 290.

cance is uncertain. It seems preferable therefore to retain the order of
the MT. Some scholars have interpreted the tetragrammaton in v. 36
as a construct form, "LORD of," possibly because something had apparently fallen out of the MT. This is the reading of the *NEB*, and of
commentators such as J. Sturdy (*Numbers*, p. 78), and others. W. G.
Plaut (*Numbers*, p. 103) reads, "Return, O LORD, you who are Israel's
myriads of thousands." This interpretation of the uncommon form
רְבֹבוֹת fails to preserve adequately the distinction between God and
His people. BHS has similarly unhelpful marginal suggestions for
dealing with the term. Although the MT is somewhat unusual, it is
still acceptable.

In 10:36 the qal imperative שׁוּבָה is the counterpart of the command in v. 35 (קוּמָה). Budd (*Numbers*, p. 112) suggests reading שֶׁבָה
("rest"), with the result that the Ark could be made to "rest" or to
"return," depending on the pointing. But as Noth (*Numbers*, pp. 79f.)
indicates, such a procedure is entirely conjectural and unsupported
by manuscript tradition.

The two statements constitute cultic formulaic pronouncements
rather than excerpts from secular battle songs. In the Ugaritic epics,
Baal was regarded as the one who would emerge supreme over everyone else: "I alone am he who will rule over the gods, yea, command
gods and men, even dominate the multitudes of the earth" (Baal and
Anat, text 51: VIII, lines 50-52). Moses confidently expected the Lord to
return to the Israelite nation (Deut. 30:3), whereas at a later period
Isaiah (24:23; 59:20) and Ezekiel (37:26-28) were fully persuaded that
the Lord would return to Zion. The ancient liturgical nature of the two
utterances in this passage has been preserved in the traditional synagogue Torah service, in which the first saying commences, and the
second terminates, the worship.

B. MOSES' LEADERSHIP TESTED (11:1-35)

There are six structural components in chap. 11: (1) general complaints (vv. 1-3); (2) complaints about food (vv. 4-9); (3) Moses' own
complaints (vv. 10-15); (4) God's response (vv. 16-25); (5) Eldad and
Medad (vv. 26-29); (6) quail provided (vv. 30-35).

1. GENERAL COMPLAINTS (11:1-3)

Translation

**It so happened that the people began *to complain, and this dis-
pleased the LORD. When He heard it His anger flared up; fire from
the LORD broke out among them and burned on the edge of the
encampment.**

Thereupon the people cried out to Moses, and when Moses prayed to the LORD, the fire died out.

So he named that place Taberah, because the fire of the LORD had burned among them. (11:1-3)

Exegesis and Exposition

Quite probably the people were fatigued after their experience of marching for three days. The euphoria of the Sinai experience was now being put to practical test, and the Israelites discovered, like many saints since that time, that the "mountain-top" experience is not infrequently followed by a sojourn in an emotional and spiritual "valley." Their complaints are not specified in the MT, but the fact that they even indulged in such ungrateful behavior shows how superficial was their thankfulness to God for His mighty deliverance from Egypt, and how little was their faith in Him as provider and in Moses as His appointed leader.

The Israelites were experiencing a crisis of serious proportions and were complaining because of resentment and frustration. The verb אָנַן (*'ānan*, "complain") is a rare word that occurs elsewhere in Lamentations 3:39 and is found only in the hithpo'el. The assent of obedience formula, so noticeable in earlier chapters, is now conspicuous by its absence. The crisis would therefore appear to be first and foremost one of faith.

As an expression of His displeasure[14] God sent His people a stern warning in the form of a fire that broke out at one end of the encampment, doubtless causing an already emotionally disturbed company to experience shock and abject terror. The source of the fire is not stated other than that it proceeded from the Lord rather than from an extraneous natural occurrence, and as such it was reminiscent of the situation that involved Nadab and Abihu (Lev. 10:2). In a panic the Israelites sought Moses to act as an intercessor on their behalf, and his pleadings to God were answered as the fire died out. The event was commemorated by naming the location of the incident Taberah, from בָּעַר (*bā'ar*, "to burn"). The place is mentioned again in Deut. 9:22 but is not listed in the sites recorded in Num. 33, and the location cannot be identified.[15]

---

14. MT אַפּוֹ (*'appô*), a term used of a bodily organ, normally the nose, which flares in human anger and is thus appropriate for expressing God's wrath. Cf. G. Van Groningen, *TWOT*, 1:58 and bibliography; G. Sauer, *THAT*, 1:220-24.

15. In KB, 3:65, the omission is explained by supposing that Taberah was one part of the encampment subsequently named Kibroth-hattaavah. Both designations are onomastic etiologies.

2. COMPLAINTS ABOUT FOOD (11:4-9)

Translation

There were among the Israelites a mixed group who craved different food. Again the Israelites *began wailing, and they cried: Will nobody give us meat to eat? (11:4)

Exegesis and Exposition

Dissatisfaction with the local food is one of the commonest complaints among people who travel any distance from home. On this occasion the grumbling originated not with the Israelites but with foreign elements who had fled from Egypt with them. Nevertheless the Hebrews were evidently in sympathy with the protest, because the dissatisfaction quickly became contagious. The "complaining motif" of Exodus and Numbers constitutes a serious spiritual offense, because it describes open rebellion against God and not simply a monotonous diet.[16]

What the wilderness Hebrews were doing in effect was testing the goodness of God and His ability to provide for all their needs by demanding food. This was in itself a sinful act, because people in both the old and new dispensations are forbidden to tempt the Lord their God (cf. Deut. 6:16; Matt. 4:7; Luke 4:12).

Translation

We recall the fish in Egypt that we devoured in great quantities, as well as cucumbers, watermelons, leeks, onions, and garlic. But now we feel completely parched, and we can see nothing at all except this manna. Now the manna was similar to coriander seed and was colored like resin. The people went up and down collecting it and ground it in handmills or pounded it in mortars. They cooked it in pots and made it into cakes. It tasted like pastry made with olive oil. When the dew settled on the camp at night, the manna fell with it. (11:5-9)

Exegesis and Exposition

Fresh vegetables are not easy to obtain in desert areas unless they have been grown at an oasis. Even sophisticated modern technology encounters considerable difficulty in making the desert bloom like a rose. For the wandering Israelites the luscious vegetables irrigated by water from the Nile would have been remembered with longing, and

---

16. See G. W. Coats, *Rebellion in the Wilderness* (Nashville: Abingdon, 1968).

even the supplies of meat from the flocks and herds would not have been adequate compensation. So the travelers looked back wistfully on the varied diet of the Egyptians, forgetting the conditions of slavery they had experienced in Egypt.

Leeks (MT חָצִיר, *ḥāṣîr, Allium porrum* L.),[17] onions (MT בְּצָלִים, *běṣālîm, Allium cepa* L.),[18] and garlic (MT שׁוּמִים, *šûmîm, Allium sativum* L.)[19] were staple, delicious items of Egyptian diet, along with the mouth-watering melons (MT אֲבַטִּחִים, *'ăbaṭṭiḥîm;* cf. the Arabic *baṭîḥ,* a generic term for such species as *Cucumis melo* L. and *Citrullus vulgaris* Schrad.),[20] as well as cucumbers (MT קִשֻּׁאִים, *qiššū'îm),* evidently a species of the genus Cucumis, although there are no Egyptian references to it.[21] The fish of Egypt would probably have included edible crustaceans, which were forbidden by later Levitical law, as well as fish normally cured in brine. These latter would have included carp, perch, and Cichlidae from the lower Nile, but these would not have violated the strict Levitical dietary laws since in fact the latter had not been promulgated at that particular period.

The Hebrews were complaining not only about dehydration (MT נַפְשֵׁנוּ יְבֵשָׁה, *napšēnû yĕbēšâ,* "our souls are dried up"), which is one of the grave perils of traveling through large arid areas (cf. Gen. 21:15-16), but also about the bland taste of the manna that the Lord had provided (Ex. 16:15). This substance (מָן, *mān)* came with the night dew and was composed of small white or pale yellow flakes similar to frost or coriander seed, about one-eighth of an inch in diameter. It could probably have been eaten raw, but it was normally ground or cooked in wafers or thin cakes.

Attempts to identify it with an edible substance from the Sinai peninsula have encountered considerable difficulties. A fungus or lichen has been sought without success, but a more likely prospect is seen in the sweet yellowish balls that are secreted by the tamarisk tree (*Tamarix gallica).* Bodenheimer[22] favored this because, among other things, it melted in the heat of the sun, as the biblical manna did. Unfortunately the tamarisk only exudes this substance for a few weeks commencing in June, whereas in the OT the manna fell regularly for six days out of seven over a period of approximately forty years, until the Israelites entered Canaan at Gilgal (Josh. 5:12). In any

---

17. *MPB,* pp. 34-35.
18. *MPB,* p. 33.
19. *MPB,* p. 32.
20. *MPB,* pp. 80-81.
21. *MPB,* pp. 80-81, 88; cf. M. Zohary, *IDB,* 2:289.
22. F. S. Bodenheimer, "The Manna of Sinai," *BA* 10 (1947): 2-6.

event shrub secretions must be disallowed as possible explanations, since manna is described as atmospheric in origin.[23]

3. MOSES' OWN COMPLAINTS (11:10-15)

Translation

Now Moses heard all the families of the people wailing at their tent doors, and the LORD's anger was aroused greatly. Moses also was very disturbed. So Moses said to the LORD: Why have You brought this trouble on Your servant? Why is it that I have not found blessing from You, and why have You made me responsible for all these people? Did I conceive these people? Did I bring them into the world? Are You telling me that I have to carry them in my arms, as a nurse carries a baby, *to the land You promised by oath to their ancestors? Where am I to obtain meat to give to all these people? They are wailing all over me, saying: Give us meat to eat. (11:10-13)

Exegesis and Exposition

Moses was already feeling the pressures of leadership over a people whose faith was melting away at the first sign of difficulty. The complaining and wailing of the people brought him into the Lord's presence in the Tent of Meeting. In his overwrought state, Moses seems to have justified the criticisms that were later raised against his leadership by Korah, Dathan, and Abiram (Num. 16:3).

Nevertheless, Moses had obeyed God's commands and felt that the response of the Israelites to their initial adversity would set a precedent for the future. Now he was being asked to provide food and was not able to do so, for this, after all, was the Lord's function. This passage, with its note of desperation, introduces the concept of the vicarious or substitutionary suffering of the nation's leaders as they bear their burdens of office. It is further demonstrated by the prophet Hosea (eighth century B.C.) in a dramatic personal parable of God's relationship with apostate Israel (Hos. 1-3). The theme is continued by the descriptions of Jeremiah's burdensome vocation as a prophet (Jer. 15:18; 20:7-12) and the work of the Suffering Servant (Isa. 52:13–53:12). Cf. also Ex. 32:31-32; Rom. 9:2-3.

Translation

I cannot carry all these people by myself. The burden is too heavy for me. If this is how You intend to treat me, kindly kill me immedi-

---

23. For discussions of manna see J. L. Mihelic, *IDB*, 3:259-60; W. E. Shewell-Cooper, *ZPEB*, 4:68; B. S. Childs, *Exodus* (1974), pp. 270-304; G. L. Carr, *ISBE*, 3:239-40; Carr, *TWOT*, 1:511-12.

ately. But if I have found favor with You, do not let me face any more trouble. (11:14-15)

Exegesis and Exposition

Exhausted by all the responsibilities that had been placed upon him since the departure from Egypt, Moses felt that he could no longer lead the Israelites if they had lost their faith in God and needed to be nursed as helpless children or cajoled as recalcitrant adolescents. He is here pleading for help from the great bearer of burdens, and he does so on the basis of his own past fidelity to the Lord's commands. But in his desperate condition he would prefer death to continuing under the current circumstances, as other servants of the Lord were also to affirm in later days (Elijah, 1 Kings 19:4; Jeremiah, Jer. 20:14-18). The MT emphasizes Moses' urgent plea for instant death by following the imperative of the verb הָרַג (hārag, "kill") with an infinitive absolute, i.e., הָרְגֵנִי נָא הָרֹג (horgēnî nāʾ hārōg).

4. GOD'S RESPONSE (11:16-25)

Translation

The LORD replied to Moses: Assemble seventy of Israel's elders who are known as leaders and officials among the people. Bring them to the Tent of Meeting and let them stand there with you. Then I will come down and converse with you there. I will take part of the Spirit that has been conferred upon you, and I will put it upon them. They will assist you in bearing the burden of care for the people, so that you will not have to carry it alone. (11:16-17)

Exegesis and Exposition

God responded graciously to Moses in his predicament by proposing a delegation of his authority. Seventy elders, including the šōṭĕrîm ("officials"), were to assemble with Moses before the sacred shrine, and God would then bestow upon them a part of the gifts of grace that Moses had received originally. Thus they would share in his understanding, and all could work in harmony to fulfill God's plan for His people. The MT seems to imply that, at his commissioning, Moses had been given by God all the abilities that would be necessary for successful leadership. It is therefore unfortunate that Moses was unable to discharge his responsibilities to the level of God's expectation, especially since God does not require His servants to perform beyond their capabilities. But however willing even the greatest might be, there are occasions when the weakness of the flesh betrays their higher vocation (cf. Matt. 26:41; Mark 14:38). Moses, however, was still the accredited civil leader of Israel, but now he was supplied with informed and competent help. God's graciousness to His obedient servants was shortly to be contrasted with the severity of His judgments upon the disobedient and rebellious. Whether the seventy elders mentioned here were identical with the seventy who accompanied Moses and saw God on Mount Sinai (Ex. 24:9-11) is not stated.

Translation

Then announce to the people: Consecrate yourselves in readiness for tomorrow, and you shall eat meat. The LORD heard you when you were wailing, Who will give us meat to eat? For we were well off in Egypt. Now the LORD will provide meat for you, and you shall eat it. Not just for one day, two days, five days, ten days, or twenty days shall you eat it, but for an entire month, until it comes out of your noses and makes you sick. This is because you have rejected the LORD who is in your midst and have wailed before Him, saying, Why did we ever leave Egypt?

Moses replied: Here I am, surrounded by 600,000 people on the march, and you are promising them meat for a whole month. Are the flocks and herds going to be slaughtered for them to make sufficient provision for them? Would they have enough if all the fish in the sea could be caught for them? (11:18-22)

Exegesis and Exposition

The assistants to Moses having been appointed, the Israelites were then to assemble before God in a state of ceremonial purity. God's message to them was that He had indeed heard their wailing and would certainly provide them with meat, which they would be compelled to eat. The message, rising to a dramatic climax as expressed by the steady progression of numbers in v. 19, is in effect proclaiming the punishment accorded by a righteous God to His disobedient followers. Even Moses was caught unawares by its intensity and, like his fellow Israelites, began to fall into the grave error of questioning the Lord's ability to provide. His reaction was centered upon the material concomitants of the situation and not upon the power of God.

Translation

The LORD replied to Moses: Has the LORD's power suddenly been limited? You will see today whether or not My words will come true.

So Moses went out and proclaimed the LORD's words to the people. He assembled seventy of their elders and stationed them around the Tent. (11:23-24)

187

Exegesis and Exposition

In a magnificent affirmation that has been the comfort of countless believers through the ages, God assured Moses that His power was still mighty to save. Though many thousands needed to be fed (cf. Matt. 14:21; 15:38, and par.), nothing was beyond the Lord's reach (MT הֲיַד יהוה תִּקְצָר, *hăyad YHWH tiqṣār*, "Is the Lord's hand shortened?"). With this assurance, Moses relayed God's orders to the people and assembled his future co-leaders and administrators around the Tent of Meeting.

Translation

Then the LORD descended in the cloud and spoke to him. He took part of the Spirit that was upon him and bestowed it upon the seventy elders. When the Spirit rested upon them they uttered prophecies, but they never did so again. (11:25)

Exegesis and Exposition

God did for Moses as He had promised, coming down in a cloud with power as He had done on Mount Sinai (cf. Ex. 19:9, 18). The divine Spirit (MT רוּחַ, *rûaḥ*) by which Moses had been guided and inspired was conferred upon the assembled elders, with the startling result that on this one occasion they uttered prophecies. Commentators have generally been quick to warn against the notion that Moses' portion of God's Spirit had been depleted quantitatively, as though it were a material thing. Rather, the men who now shared his spiritual vision to a wider degree than they had done previously would be all the more enabled to support him in the task of leadership to which he had been called. By the divine act of delegating the spiritual gifts, the community would become stronger as all the leaders cooperated with Moses.

The kind of prophesying in which the leaders engaged is a matter of some conjecture, due largely to wide disagreement about the origin and nature of the verb נָבָא (*nābā'*) and its derivatives.[24] It is now known, however, that the noun נָבִיא (*nābî'*) in cognate form was in use in the third millennium B.C., its antiquity having been demonstrated by its appearance at Ebla in the form *na-ba-um*, occurring in a Sumerian-Eblaite bilingual vocabulary dated about 2400 B.C.

The situation narrated in the present passage does not describe the concept of "authorized spokesman" favored by some scholars, nor is there any evidence of ecstatic activity on the part of the recip-

---

24. For discussion and bibliographies see G. V. Smith, *ISBE*, 3:986-1004; J. Jeremias, *THAT*, 2:7-26; R. D. Culver, *TWOT*, 2:544-45.

ients.[25] God's Spirit evidently bestowed upon them the qualities of power and wisdom, which Paul, in writing to Timothy under the New Covenant, recognized as gifts of the Spirit (2 Tim. 1:7).

5. ELDAD AND MEDAD (11:26-29)

Translation

Now two men, named Eldad and *Medad, had stayed behind in the camp, and the Spirit came to rest upon them also. They had been included in the registration but had not actually gone to the Tent. Nevertheless, they prophesied in the encampment. (11:26)

Exegesis and Exposition

Two men who had not been present when God's spiritual gifts were bestowed upon the seventy proved to be recipients of the Lord's beneficence also. Eldad and Medad had not assembled with the other elders before the sacred shrine, for reasons not explained in the MT, even though they were required to do so. The Hebrew narrative did not supply pedigrees for these men, and like their colleagues they were not mentioned elsewhere. It is evident that the gift of the Spirit was independent of their presence with the others. The activity of God's Spirit cannot be restricted to human configurations or cultic rituals. Instead, it is as unstructured as the wind (cf. John 3:8) and thus can be expected to function independently anywhere and at any time in trusting and obedient persons.

Translation

A young man ran and said to Moses: Eldad and Medad are prophesying in the camp.

Joshua son of Nun, who had been Moses' servant from his youth, interrupted and said: My lord Moses, stop them!

But Moses said to him: Are you jealous on my account? I could wish that all the LORD's people were prophets and that the LORD would place His Spirit upon them. (11:27-29)

Exegesis and Exposition

Whatever activity was produced in the two men by the Spirit's bestowal, it was sufficient to attract the attention of Joshua, the assistant and ultimate successor to Moses as Israel's leader. His plea to Moses to halt the prophesying of Eldad and Medad was evidently an

---

25. See K. L. Barker, "Zechariah," in *The Expositor's Bible Commentary* (Grand Rapids: Zondervan, 1985), 7:605-6 and notes.

attempt to protect the prerogatives of Moses as leader from being usurped by the elders. In that event he did not understand the significance of the Lord's action in giving spiritual gifts to the elders so that they could support, and not usurp, the leadership of Moses.

Although Moses detected and doubtless sympathized with Joshua's zealous attitude, he assured him that the occurrence was not merely to be tolerated but to be commended and by implication given proper support. The memorable response of Moses to his assistant has struck a resounding note in the hearts of believers over many centuries. To be filled with the Spirit and to proclaim the Lord's message of love and forgiveness forthrightly is surely the highest aspiration of all those who are in fellowship with the Lord. The MT קָנָא (qānāʾ) is usually understood to mean "zeal" or "envy,"[26] and in this passage Moses employed it to describe the second of these emotional responses, suggesting that Joshua was becoming jealous of the two men.

This may not have been entirely the case, however, if the occurrence of the term in the Decalogue (Ex. 20:5) is actually describing God as one who "maintains His rights." This rendering seems preferable in the Ten Commandments to the traditional translation of "jealous," because it emphasizes the reciprocal nature of the covenant. The Israelites who acquiesced to the agreement did not acquire all the rights that it embodied at the ceremony of ratification on Mount Sinai (Ex. 24:3-8), although they frequently behaved as though they had. But if God is also recognized as having important rights under the covenant, it will be seen that His punitive acts consequent upon rebellion and apostasy are justified. In the case of Joshua, therefore, it may well be that his concern was to safeguard the divinely-given rights of Moses as civil leader, rather than simply becoming jealous of two subordinate Israelites who, in any event, never reappeared in the historical narrative.[27]

6. QUAIL PROVIDED (11:30-35)

Translation

Then Moses returned to the camp with the elders of Israel. Now a wind from the LORD arose and drove quail in from the sea. It left them fluttering near the encampment, a distance of about a day's walk on either side. They were all around the camp, and about three feet above the ground. (11:30-31)

---

26. For discussion and bibliographies see G. Sauer, *THAT*, 2:647-50; L. J. Coppes, *TWOT*, 2:802-3.
27. See K. L. Barker, "Zechariah," *The Expositor's Bible Commentary*, 7:612.

Exegesis and Exposition

God was as good as His word in providing food for His rebellious and discontented people in the form of quail (MT שְׂלָוִים, *śalwîm*).[28] These birds belonged to the genus *Coturnix*, which also includes pheasants and partridges.

The phenomenon of quail migration is still observable today as the birds leave their winter habitat in Africa and fly northward by stages in the spring, usually in March and April. If they followed the coast of the Red Sea into the Sinai peninsula, they would have been diverted easily into the Israelite camp by a strong wind. The quail were most probably either the species *Coturnix communis* or *C. dactylisonans* and would have come over in vast quantities, flying with the wind just above the surface of the ground. Because of the length of their journey and the force of the unusual wind, they would fall exhausted as they came inland.[29]

Translation

The people stayed up all that day and night, and all the next day, to gather the quail. Nobody gathered less than ten homers, and they spread them out all around the camp. But while the meat was still between their teeth, and before they had even chewed it, the LORD's anger flared out against the people, striking them with a severe plague. Therefore Moses called the name of that location Kibroth-hattaavah, because it was there that they buried those who had craved other food. From Kibroth-hattaavah the people marched to Hazeroth and encamped there. (11:32-35)

Exegesis and Exposition

The abundant provision promised for the hungry Israelites' needs was indicated by the fact that the birds were distributed (MT שָׁטוֹחַ, *śāṭôaḥ*) all across the campsite. The *homer* was the largest measure that the Hebrews possessed and was equivalent to about sixty bushels. Some idea of the quantity can be understood from the remarks of Pliny, who told of a boat crossing the Mediterranean Sea that promptly sank when a large number of quail alighted on it.[30] While some birds were devoured immediately, others appear to have been

---

28. The LXX, apparently following Aristotle's terminology, reads ὀρτυγόμητρα, "a bird which migrates with quail," perhaps the *Rallus crex* or land-rail, rather than the common *Ortux*.
29. For observations on the behavior of quail, see Aristotle, *History of Animals* 8. 597b; H. B. Tristram, *The Natural History of the Bible*, pp. 229-33.
30. Cited by A. Parmelee, *All the Birds of the Bible* (New York: Harper, 1969), p. 76.

gutted and spread out to dry on the hot sand, in the Egyptian manner.[31]

What appears to have been an epidemic of food poisoning was the punishment the Israelites suffered as a result of their disobedience and wanton craving. The numbers of those who died are not given in the MT, but the name that Moses bestowed upon the area—"graves of craving"—would suggest a significant mortality. Kibroth-hattaavah has not been identified with certainty, but according to W. S. LaSor it must be approximately halfway between Mount Sinai (Jebel Musa) and Hazeroth,[32] the latter probably being identified with 'Ain Hadra,[33] some fifty miles northeast of the mountain. Kibroth-hattaavah could also be identified plausibly with Rueis el-Ebeirij,[34] a location about ten hours' march from Jebel Musa.

Additional Notes

11:1 בְּאָזְנֵי: Some MT MSS have בֵּינֵי here, emphasizing presence rather than auditory receptivity. But the latter theme is mentioned again in v. 18, thus making the MT preferable.

11:4 וַיָּשֻׁבוּ: The LXX and Vulgate emend the MT to וַיֵּשְׁבוּ, "and they sat down," but this does not necessarily represent a textual improvement. In Judg. 20:26 the MT has וַיִּבְכּוּ וַיֵּשְׁבוּ, "and wept and sat," so that the idea of weeping as conveyed by this verse is by no means strange.

11:5 זָכַרְנוּ: The perfect form expresses the experience of a state of mind.

11:6 בִּלְתִּי אֵין כֹּל בִּלְתִּי, here without אִם, introduces an exceptive clause.

11:10 אֶת–הָעָם: The particle introduces an accusative of specification (R. J. Williams, *Hebrew Syntax*, p. 14, sect. 57).

11:11 לָשׂוּם: The qal infinitive construct with לְ here expresses consequence or result. For the palistrophic structure of Num. 11:11-14 see G. J. Wenham, *Numbers*, p. 108 n. 2.

11:12 עַל appears to be a mistake for אֶל, as corrected by the Samaritan Pentateuch and the LXX, though BDB indicates that the two prepositions can be used interchangeably (p. 41 n.2).

11:13 עָלָי: Here עַל is employed in an adversative sense to express disadvantage.

11:14 מִמֶּנִּי: The particle מִן with suffix is used in an absolute

---

31. Cf. Herodotus, *History* 2.77, where fish is mentioned.
32. W. S. LaSor, *ISBE*, 3:12.
33. Cf. F. M. Abel, *Géographie de la Palestine*, 2 (Paris: Le Coffre, 1938), p. 214.
34. J. Simons, *GTTOT*, sect. 431, p. 255.

comparative manner to describe a quality of excessive degree (R. J. Williams, *Hebrew Syntax*, p. 58, sect. 318).

11:15 הָרֹג . . . הָרְגֵנִי: The qal imperative singular with the qal absolute infinitive of הָרַג indicates emphasis. In Hebrew the infinitive normally follows the imperative.

11:17 אִתְּךָ בְּמַשָּׂא: The inseparable preposition –בְּ is used here in a partitive sense.

11:20 יַעַן: This preposition occurs here with a noun clause introduced by כִּי.

11:22 –אֶת: This demonstrative term here introduces an emphatic accusative of specification.

11:26 מֵידָד: For this name the Samaritan Pentateuch and the LXX read "Modad," which P. J. Budd, *Numbers*, p. 124, thinks may have been the original form. If Eldad and Medad had not been among the seventy elders registered, it is doubtful that they would have received the gift of the Spirit.

11:29 מִי־יִתֵּן: This phrase, normally accompanied by a construct infinitive, introduces an optative clause. It can, however, occur in nonverbal clauses, as here.

11:32 שָׁטוֹחַ . . . וַיִּשְׁטְחוּ: When the absolute infinitive follows a finite verb of the same root, it expresses repetitive activity. Thus the Israelites were engaged continuously in spreading the quail around the camp to dry. Some LXX manuscripts confused the spelling of the verb and understood שָׁחַט, "to slaughter," instead of שָׁטַח, "to spread out." This may have resulted from a transcriptional error in the Hebrew text from which the translators were working.

C. MOSES OPPOSED BY MIRIAM AND AARON (12:1-16)

The material in chap. 12 can be subdivided into five sections: (1) accusation and God's response (vv. 1-5); (2) God's defense of Moses (vv. 6-9); (3) punishment upon Miriam (vv. 10-12); (4) seven-day quarantine (vv. 13-15); (5) departure from Hazeroth (v. 16).

1. ACCUSATION AND GOD'S RESPONSE (12:1-5)

Translation

While at Hazeroth, Miriam and Aaron began to talk in opposition to Moses because of his Cushite wife (for he had married a Cushite woman), and they said: Has the LORD only spoken through Moses? Has he not spoken through us as well? The LORD heard this.

Now Moses was a very meek man, the most humble of everyone in the world. Immediately the LORD said to Moses, Aaron, and

193

Miriam: The three of you go out to the Tent of Meeting. So the three
of them went out. Then the LORD descended in the cloudy pillar and
stood at the entrance to the Tent of Meeting, where He called for
Aaron and Miriam. Both of them stepped forward. (12:1-5)

Exegesis and Exposition

At ʿAin Hadra, if the site of Hazeroth has been identified correctly,
there occurred the first rebellion against Moses himself rather than
against God. Surprisingly enough, the offenders were family members—namely, Miriam, the sister of Moses, and Aaron, his brother,
both of whom were older than Moses. The issue appeared to be connected with Moses' role as a leader but was subsumed under objections to the woman that Moses had married.

Why Miriam and Aaron were so disgruntled is not easy to understand, since Aaron was the high priest who alone stood yearly in the
presence of the sacred Ark, while Miriam, described as a "prophetess"
(Ex. 15:20), played a leading part in the rejoicing that followed the
crossing of the Re(e)d Sea. Nevertheless, the Cushite woman was
made the principal excuse, if not the real cause, for the protest. .

Opinion is divided on the identity of both the woman concerned
and the country from which she came.[35] Taking the latter first, MT
כּוּשׁ (kûš) has been identified with a region of continental Africa,
either Ethiopia (KJV) or Nubia by some authorities, but alternatively
with the territory of the Kassites (Akk. *kaššû*) in Mesopotamia by
others. According to Isa. 18:1 Cush was on the Nile, while in Esther
1:1 Cush represented the southern boundary of Egypt.[36] If the "land
of Cush" (Gen. 2:13) did indeed refer to Kassite holdings,[37] it is rather
curious that the Kassites are not mentioned elsewhere in the OT,
whereas the peoples to the south of Egypt were. If the woman whom
Moses had married was indeed a descendant of Cush, she could trace
her line back to Ham, son of Noah (Gen. 10:1). The Hamites lived
principally in Nubia or Ethiopia.

The scornful appellation "Cushite" might suggest racial discrimination on the part of Miriam, but if the woman came from ancient
Ethiopia or Nubia her physiognomy would be little different from
that of Miriam herself, since the people living on the southern border
of Egypt were not distinctively Negroid. Some commentators have

---

35. G. B. Gray, *Numbers*, pp. 122-23; M. Noth, *Numbers*, p. 94; W. F. Albright,
    Archaeology and the Religion of Israel (Baltimore: Johns Hopkins, 3d ed.,
    1953), p. 205.
36. W. S. LaSor, *ISBE*, 1:839.
37. Cf. E. A. Speiser, *Oriental and Biblical Studies* (Philadelphia: U. of Pennsyl-
    vania, 1967), pp. 25-28.

suggested that she was Zipporah, but others have seen her as a woman whom Moses took to wife either during Zipporah's absence (Ex. 18:2) or subsequent to her death. A further opinion has maintained that she was a second wife to Moses, whether contemporaneous with or subsequent to Zipporah.

Favoring the woman's identification with Zipporah is the use in Hab. 3:7 of Cushan and Midian in synonymous parallelism. If the color of skin and shape of facial features was a factor, the term "Cushite" could also have been applied equally well to the Midianites, who were tanned nomads from northwest Arabia. The explanatory gloss of v. 1, while meaningful at the time it was inserted, has proved more of a hindrance than a help to modern scholars because of their lack of knowledge of the original circumstances. Because we are now so far removed in time from that period, it is doubtful if this particular problem will ever be resolved. Regardless of other considerations, however, the woman was obviously being used as a means of launching an attack upon the Israelite leader, evidently by jealous siblings.

Verse 3 has long been employed as an argument against the Mosaic authorship of Numbers and/or of the Pentateuch as a whole. It has been seen as an expression of vain self-display or a glorification of Moses' own gifts and excellences that he prided himself on possessing.[38] Other writers have interpreted the verse as an explanatory gloss inserted by a later copyist to show how inappropriate the charge of arrogance was for a man of such patience and humility. In deference to this opinion some translations have placed this verse in parentheses.

Although it may well be correct to see this as an explanatory gloss, there can be no doubt that, observed over a lifetime, humility was uniquely characteristic of Moses. As such it has been suggested that עָנָו (*'ānāw*) should really be translated by "more humble than," and while this is probably true as an overall retrospective estimation of his life's difficulties, it is not certain that the word can bear such an interpretation. Perhaps "more tolerant" or "more long-suffering" would express the sense of the MT better.[39]

On hearing the charge, the Lord summoned Moses, Miriam, and Aaron to the Tent of Meeting and appeared to them in a cloud. The dramatic suddenness of the Lord's response must have shocked

---

38. Cf. *KD*, 3:77.
39. The spelling of the masculine singular adjective varies between עָנָו (*'ānāw; kethib*) and עָנָיו (*'ānāyw; qere*), involving only a slight consonantal change. For the possibility that the word here means "miserable" see C. Rogers, "Moses: Meek or Miserable?" *JETS* 29 (1986): 257-63.

Miriam and Aaron, but this drastic action was necessary in order to confirm the unique qualities of their brother and to vindicate him. It was also a warning that the Lord attends to the welfare of His obedient servants and does not forsake the cause of the righteous (cf. Ps. 37:25). The Lord's order to Aaron and Miriam to stand in His presence at the entrance to the Tabernacle showed that He considered both of them to be subject to Moses as the leader of the people.

2. GOD'S DEFENSE OF MOSES (12:6-9)

Translation

Then He said: Listen now to My words. When there is a prophet among you, I the LORD reveal Myself to him in a vision and speak to him in a dream. Not so with my servant Moses. He alone of My entire household is trustworthy. With him I commune face to face, openly, and not in riddles, and he sees the form of the LORD. Why, then, were you not afraid to speak against My servant Moses? Thus the anger of the LORD flared against them, and He left them. (12:6-9)

Exegesis and Exposition

God stated His case forcefully and uncompromisingly and challenged Miriam and Aaron for daring to speak against Moses. This section is in poetry and employs the 3:3 pattern of word stresses, which is the normal way of writing Hebrew epic verse. There are a few textual problems, which, however, actually serve to enhance the force of the message.

The reasons for Moses' uniqueness are made clear to the complainants. Whereas God would reveal Himself indirectly in dealing with a prophet, with Moses He spoke face to face. This distinction was maintained, with the possible exception of Isaiah (6:1), throughout the entire history of Hebrew prophetism. But even Isaiah's experience of "seeing" was essentially visionary, whereas Moses met periodically face to face—i.e., "openly"—with God. Although God had in fact spoken through others, such as the elders who prophesied when part of the gifts of Moses were bestowed upon them, it was the great Israelite leader himself who was commissioned to convey the Lord's will to the covenant community (cf. Heb. 3:2-6).

3. PUNISHMENT UPON MIRIAM (12:10-12)

Translation

When the cloud lifted from the Tent, Miriam suddenly became leprous, like snow. Then Aaron turned toward Miriam, and there she was, a leper. Then Aaron said to Moses: Please, my lord, do not hold

us responsible for this sin, which we have committed so foolishly and wickedly. Do not let her be like a stillborn child, coming out of the womb with its flesh half-decayed. (12:10-12)

Exegesis and Exposition

The angry rebuke meted out by God to Miriam and Aaron had frightening consequences for Moses' sister. As the Lord left them, Miriam became covered with a white skin affliction that was one of the dreaded cutaneous conditions known as צָרַעַת (*ṣāra'at*). The legislation for this particular class of disease occurs in Lev. 13-14 and makes clear the intense seriousness with which it was taken. *Ṣāra'at* is a generic term for a group of pathological conditions and serves the same sort of function as the term *cancer*, which covers a wide range of degenerative tissue states.

The "leprosy" of the OT included skin ailments of varying severity as well as such occurrences as mildew or rot in clothing and mineral efflorescence in stone buildings. In all instances the priest, acting as a public health official, was given careful directions, couched in specific language no longer clear to modern scholars, as to differential diagnosis. Miriam's "leprosy" was not the chronic *ṣāra'at*, which I regard as being identical with modern clinical leprosy (Hansen's disease), but instead was probably psoriasis, a disfiguring and embarrassing skin disease in which erupted red patches are covered with white scales. It is sometimes the consequence of emotional stress based upon deep guilt. An alternative affliction might have been leucoderma, which results from a partial or total absence of pigment in the skin. The acquired variety of leucoderma is known as *vitiligo*, as distinct from the congenital form, which is described as *albinism*. Moses himself had once experienced Miriam's form of "leprosy" (Ex. 4:6-7), but that was clearly not the chronic variety of *ṣāra'at*, partially because it disappeared as quickly as it came and also because of the description "white as snow" (MT כַּשָּׁלֶג, *kaššāleg*), which was not a clinical sign of chronic *ṣāra'at*.[40]

Aaron's punishment was shock at seeing his sister's condition with its attendant uncleanness, a situation that required her to appear before the priest for a diagnosis (Lev. 13:13). Aaron apologized to Moses immediately and begged him to pity his misguided sister, who could be suspected of chronic leprosy if any raw flesh appeared subsequently in her skin (Lev. 13:14). In his words Aaron acknowledged Moses as his superior, confessed the denunciation of the Israelite leader as sinful and foolish, and pleaded to be absolved of responsi-

---

40. On leprosy see G. J. Wenham, *Leviticus*, pp. 194-97; R. K. Harrison, *Leviticus*, pp. 136-39; Harrison, *ISBE* 3:103-6 and bibliography.

bility for such a terrible and misguided act. He addressed his request to Moses quite properly as the one against whom the offense had been committed, evidently in the conviction that he would appeal to God for Miriam's punishment to be removed. Were she to be afflicted for the rest of her life with her ailment, it would be as bad as if she had emerged into the world as a stillborn fetus that had already begun to putrefy *in utero*.

4. SEVEN-DAY QUARANTINE (12:13-15)

Translation

So Moses cried out to the LORD, saying: God, please heal her, I beg! Then the LORD replied to Moses: If her father had even spat in her face, would she not have remained disgraced for seven days? Let her be excluded from the camp for seven days, and after that she can be brought back. So Miriam was excluded from the camp for seven days, and the people did not move on until she was brought back. (12:13-15)

Exegesis and Exposition

Despite the earnest plea of Moses, God was unwilling to pardon Miriam's behavior lightly, because by rebelling against Moses she had committed the serious offense of questioning God's judgment and authority. So that she would understand completely the implications of what she had done, she was forced to bear the shame of a public rebuke. In practical terms this involved living as an outcast beyond the encampment for seven days, just as she would have done if, in a family argument, her father had given her a sign of rejection by spitting on her.

According to the law (Lev. 15:8) such an action defiled the recipient of the sputum, who had to wash his or her body and clothing before being regarded as ceremonially clean.[41] Leviticus is the oldest document to associate sputum with uncleanness, and it is interesting to note that the ritual of levirate law (Deut. 25:9) contained this element of rejection and defilement.[42] Modern public health officials are very much aware of sputum as a means of conveying infection of various kinds.

---

41. At Qumran, spitting in the assembly was punished by thirty days of segregation (1QS vii, 13; cf. W. J. 2.8.9).
42. By NT times spittle had healing qualities attributed to it, and Jesus followed Jewish customs in this respect (Mark 7:33; 8:23; John 9:6). In the story of Lazarus (Luke 16:19-31) it has been suggested that the dogs, in licking the diseased beggar's sores, were exemplars of a ministry of compassion that was not shown by human beings.

5. DEPARTURE FROM HAZEROTH (12:16)

Translation

After that, the people set out from Hazeroth and encamped in the wilderness of Paran. (12:16)

Exegesis and Exposition

By the end of a week Miriam was permitted to return to the camp and resume a state of ceremonial purity. It is possible that she kept her skin affliction to the end of her life, since the MT does not say that she was cured by the time she returned to the community. According to Levitical law, Miriam would have been considered ritually clean as long as the whiteness was not replaced by raw flesh, which would be symptomatic of chronic ṣāraʿat. The march resumed with the departure from Hazeroth, and the Israelites encamped subsequently at an unspecified site somewhere in the large expanse of the Paran wilderness.

Additional Notes

12:1 וַתְּדַבֵּר: Miriam seems to be the spokesperson because this verb is in the third person feminine singular, indicating that she might have been envious of the Cushite woman. Syntactically a singular verb usually precedes compound subjects but has a plural form when it follows them. For the questions arising about the translation see A. R. Hulst, *Old Testament Translation Problems*, United Bible Societies (Leiden: Brill, 1960), p. 10.

כֻּשִׁית: LXX reads Αἰθιόπισσαν.

12:2 הֲרַק אַךְ־רַק: רַק ("only") is technically redundant here in view of the presence of אַךְ. It was probably added for emphasis in view of the nature of the complaint.

12:6 נְבִיאֲכֶם: The MT form, "a prophet among you," is rare, the singular noun נָבִיא being augmented by a second person plural masculine suffix. The MT here appears as a condensed form of נָבִיא ("prophet") and לָכֶם ("to you").

The next word, יהוה, is distanced from the verb "reveal" (יָדַע), which has an unusual reflexive form (אֶתְוַדַּע) with the preposition אֶל ("with"), which occurs again in Genesis 45:1.

The participle נֶאֱמָן, from אָמַן, "to be steady," "be faithful," in v. 7 is probably better translated "trustworthy."

12:8 וּתְמֻנַת: The feminine construct singular of תְּמוּנָה means "shape," "form," or "image." The LXX, interpreting the word as a metaphysical attribute, reads τὴν δόξαν κυρίου εἶδεν.

12:11 The MT expression בִּי אֲדֹנִי אַל־נָא, "please, my lord, I beg

199

you," is unusual in linking אַל with נָא, but emphasizes the urgency of the situation adequately.

12:12 כַּמֵּת: The LXX here has ὡσεὶ ἔκτρωμα, which emphasizes the sense of an aborted fetus.

12:15 מִרְיָם: Perhaps to show that the regulations of Lev. 14:9 were being followed, the LXX added ἐκαθαρίσθη.

4
Israel at Kadesh (13:1–20:13)

A. REPORTS ON THE PROMISED LAND (13:1-33)

Chapter 13 exhibits four structural units: (1) names of spies (vv. 1-16); (2) their instructions (vv. 17-20); (3) their activities (vv. 21-25); (4) their reports (vv. 26-33). As with the previous chapter it describes consecutive events issuing from a single initial activity.

1. NAMES OF SPIES (13:1-16)

Translation

The LORD spoke to Moses, saying: Send men to investigate the territory of Canaan, which I am giving to the Israelites. Send one man from each of the ancestral tribes, and let him be a leader. So Moses sent them from the wilderness of Paran according to the LORD's command. All of them were leaders in the Israelite community. (13:1-3)

Exegesis and Exposition

The third major division of Numbers deals with events in the region of Kadesh. The narrative locates this place in the wilderness of Paran (Num. 12:16; 13:26), a poorly-defined area in the east-central portion of the Sinai peninsula, bordered on the northwest by the wilderness of Shur, on the northeast by the wilderness of Zin, and by the Sinai desert to the south. The Israelites journeyed across the "great and terrible wilderness"—the central highlands now known as et-Tih—and settled for nearly forty years (14:34) at Kadesh-barnea (Deut. 1:19–20). Topographically the site was regarded as part of the wilderness of Paran and was glossed accordingly by the LXX.[1] From the data of Gen. 14:5-7, El-paran was located south of Kadesh, so the latter could properly be described as on the border of the Paran wilderness.[2]

Kadesh-barnea lay south of the Canaanite border and was situated close to the Wadi el-Arish, the "river of Egypt." The appellation *barnea* was used to distinguish it from other places named Kadesh or Kedesh, but its meaning is otherwise unknown. It was an ideal location for what proved to be a lengthy Israelite sojourn, because there were three oases in the area: 'Ain el-Qudeirat, 'Ain Qedeis, and 'Ain Qoseimeh. The first of these was supported by the investigations of Woolley and Lawrence[3] and has remained the major oasis of choice by other scholars.[4]

The distance from Horeb (Sinai) to Kadesh-barnea is given in Deut. 1:2 as an eleven-day journey, which has been confirmed by Aharoni[5] and again suits the general topography. The Israelites would have been able to pasture their flocks without difficulty for an indefinite period, although this is not to affirm that all the surviving Israelites remained in that locality for the entire period of nearly forty years without some external movement.

From this strategic location God ordered, by means of an annunciation formula, that men be dispatched to explore the Promised Land. To preserve impartiality, one person of prominence was to be chosen as a representative from each tribe.

Translation

These were their names: from the tribe of Reuben, Shammua son of Zaccur; from the tribe of Simeon, Shaphat son of Hori; from the tribe of Judah, Caleb son of Jephunneh; from the tribe of Issachar, Igal son of Joseph; from the tribe of Ephraim, Hoshea son of Nun; from the tribe of Benjamin, Palti son of Raphu; from the tribe of Zebulun,

---

1. LXX Num. 33:36 reads: εἰς τὴν ἔρημον Φαράν, αὕτη ἐστὶν Καδής.
2. S. Cohen, *IDB*, 3:1-2; R. K. Harrison, *ISBE*, 3:1.
3. C. L. Woolley and T. E. Lawrence, *The Wilderness of Zin* (Palestine Exploration Fund Annual; London: 1914-1915), pp. 53-57.
4. E.g., D. Baly, *The Geography of the Bible* (London: Lutterworth, 1974), p. 252.
5. Y. Aharoni, *The Holy Land: Antiquity and Survival*, 2, 2/3 (1957), pp. 289-96; cf. E. K. Vogel, *Bibliography of Holy Land Sites* (Cincinnati: Hebrew Union College-Jewish Institute of Religion, 1982), p. 6.

Gaddiel son of Sodi; from the tribe of Manasseh (a tribe of Joseph), Gaddi son of Susi; from the tribe of Dan, Ammiel son of Gemalli; from the tribe of Ashur, Sethur son of Michael; from the tribe of Naphtali, Nahbi son of Vophsi; from the tribe of Gad, Geuel son of Maki.

These are the names of the men whom Moses sent to explore the land. But Moses named the son of Nun "Joshua" instead of Hoshea. (13:4-16)

Exegesis and Exposition

Even a cursory glance will show that these persons were not the elders listed in Num. 1:5-15. The order of the tribes is somewhat different also, being uniform up to the listing of Issachar in both compilations but diverging with the recording of Ephraim and Benjamin as taking precedence over Zebulun in 1:5-15. After Manasseh, the positions of Dan and Asher correspond in both lists, but the positions of Gad and Naphtali are reversed. These variations make it clear that the šōṭĕrîm were not bound by stereotyped forms, and the lists serve as an indication of their contemporaneous nature, since apart from Joshua of Ephraim and Caleb of Judah the men are not named again in the wilderness narratives.

Their appointed task was to reconnoiter the territory of Canaan and to bring back a report on their findings. An addition by the šōṭĕrîm, or perhaps by an even later scribe, noted the change of name from Hoshea (MT הוֹשֵׁעַ, *hôšēaʿ*, "salvation") to Joshua (MT יְהוֹשֻׁעַ, *yĕhôšuaʿ*, "the LORD saves"; LXX Num. 13:16 Ἰησοῦν, *Iēsoun*), later pronounced יֵשׁוּעַ (*yēšû(a)ʿ*), probably under Aramaic influence, as in Neh. 8:17, LXX Ἰησοῦς, *Iēsous* (cf. Matt. 1:21). Precisely how these men were chosen is not stated. They may have been elected by tribal elders, or they may even have volunteered for the task. Moses probably did not select them, because his responsibility was simply to send them out on their mission (vv. 1-3).

2. THEIR INSTRUCTIONS (13:17-20)

Translation

When Moses sent them to investigate the land of Canaan, he said to them: Go up through the Negev, and onward into the hill country. Find out what the land is like: whether the people who inhabit it are strong or weak, few or many; whether the land they live in is good or bad; whether the cities they inhabit are like camps or fortified towns; whether the land is rich or poor; and whether or not there are forests there. Enter bravely, and bring back some of the fruit of the land. (It was the time of year for the first ripe grapes.) (13:17-20)

Exegesis and Exposition

Their instructions were simple but comprehensive. Moses required information about the topography of the Negev and the hilly central area of Canaan, the distribution and strength of the population, the quality of the land, whether the people were semi-sedentary or sedentary, and the degree of forestation.

Since the reconnaissance party was undertaking its exploits toward the end of July, Moses requested it to bring back samples of the local produce. The question about the relative strength or weakness of the people in v. 18 is phrased disjunctively using the interrogative particles -הֲ . . . -הֲ, *hă-* . . . *hă-* (MT הֶחָזָק הוּא הֲרָפֶה, *heḥāzāq hûʾ hărāpeh*).

3. THEIR ACTIVITIES (13:21-25)

Translation

So they went up and investigated the land from the wilderness of Zin as far as Rehob, near Lebo Hamath. They went up through the Negev *and came to Hebron, where Ahiman, Sheshai, and Talmai, descendants of Anak, were living (Hebron had been built seven years before Zoan in Egypt). When they reached the Valley of Eshcol, they cut down a branch bearing a single cluster of grapes, two of them carrying it between them on a pole. They also took some pomegranates and figs. The place received its name, Valley of Eshcol, because of the grape cluster that the Israelites cut there. After forty days they returned from their reconnaissance of the territory. (13:21-25)

Exegesis and Exposition

The men who had been selected for this responsible task traversed the wilderness of Zin, which was north and adjacent to the wilderness of Paran,[6] and slipped into Canaan unobserved.

They explored the terrain as far as Rehob, near Lebo Hamath. Rehob, subsequently named Beth-rehob (2 Sam. 10:6), was located at the northern end of the Jordan valley (*beqaʿ*) and was mentioned in the topographical list of Thutmose III. Its exact location is unknown, but it was in the vicinity of Laish (Dan).[7] The name Lebo Hamath has sometimes been rendered "entrance" or "pass" of Hamath (e.g., *NKJV*; cf. KJV "as men come to Hamath"), but the place in question is a Canaanite, not a Syrian site, and is therefore best identified with

---

6. So J. L. Mihelic, *IDB*, 4:959; J. M. Houston, *IBD*, 3:1684.
7. G. W. Van Beek, *IDB*, 1:396; cf. J. Simons, *GTTOT*, p. 7.

the modern Lebweh, about fourteen miles north-northeast of Baalbek.[8]

In the Negev they scouted Hebron, where the Anakim were living. These inhabitants included Ahiman, Sheshai, and Talmai, who were to be driven out ultimately by Caleb (Josh. 15:14) and killed by Judahite forces (Judg. 1:10). These references seem to imply two separate accounts of their defeat. Woudstra has suggested that Joshua's destruction of Hebron (Kiriath-arba) and Debir (Kiriath-sepher) was followed by reconstruction of a kind that necessitated later conquest by Caleb. Alternatively, Caleb's exploits, being achieved under Joshua's command, may have been credited to him and not to Caleb.[9] The three names mentioned in the present passage may have been designations of family groups and not necessarily of individuals who were alive at the time. Anak was a pre-Israelite inhabitant of Canaan whose descendants may have occupied territory in the Hebron area (cf. Josh. 11:21-22). In Num. 13:22, 28, 33; Deut. 1:28; Josh. 11:21 and elsewhere, the MT consistently names Hebron as the home of the Anakim, who may have been mentioned in the Egyptian execration texts (19th to 18th centuries B.C.) under the name *Iy-ʿanaq*, whose three leaders or chiefs bore Semitic names. The Anakim were a warlike and tall people, the latter feature most probably indicating a genetic deterioration in the family stock and pointing also to their great antiquity. They became proverbial in Israel for their formidable military strength (Deut. 9:2).

An explanatory gloss demonstrates the equal antiquity of the Anakim's hometown of Hebron by relating it chronologically to the Egyptian city of Zoan. This latter, originally named Djaʿnet (Tanis), used to be identified with Rameses and the Hyksos city of Avaris, but excavations have established that this is incorrect.[10] The beginnings of Tanis are unknown apart from the reference in Num. 13:22, but by the Egyptian New Kingdom period (*c.* 1570-1150 B.C.) it was known as Sekhet Djaʿnet, or "fields of Tanis," which finds its counterpart in the Hebrew "fields of Zoan" (Ps. 78:12, 43).[11] From obscure beginnings it became an important Egyptian political center (cf. Isa. 19:11, 13; 30:4; Ezek. 30:14).

Hebron was also an influential Canaanite city, located about nineteen miles south of Jerusalem in hilly but fertile terrain. Excava-

8. Cf. H. F. Vos, *ISBE*, 2:603.
9. M. H. Woudstra, *Joshua* (NICOT; Grand Rapids: Eerdmans, 1981), p. 197.
10. K. A. Kitchen, *NIDBA*, p. 384 and bibliography; B. Beitzel, *The Moody Atlas of Bible Lands* (Chicago: Moody, 1985), pp. 85-87.
11. K. A. Kitchen, *NIDBA*, p. 435.

tions at Jebel er-Rumeida, site of the ancient tell, have revealed an occupational history beginning about 3300 B.C., and in the Middle Bronze Age it was protected by a stout wall. The construction work mentioned in Numbers was evidently reconstruction or extension of earlier buildings. If the founding of Tanis is dated correctly in the Hyksos period, the rebuilding or extension of Hebron would have taken place about 1728 B.C. When Abraham lived in the area (Gen. 12-25), Hebron was known as Kiriath-arba.[12]

The Valley of Eshcol (MT נַחַל אֶשְׁכֹּל, *naḥal 'eškōl*, "valley of a cluster") may possibly be identified with the wadi north of Ramet el-'Amleh, in an area that still produces delicious grapes. The name "Eshcol" has probably survived in Burj Haskeh, a site about two miles north of Hebron, overlooking the wadi. The Canaanite name of the valley, however, has not been preserved. The size of the grape cluster, probably an entire vine, which the spies brought back to Kadesh attested to the productivity of the soil, which also supported pomegranate and fig orchards. The reconnaissance party would be returning about the time the vintage harvest (September to October) was just beginning.

4. THEIR REPORTS (13:26-33)

Translation

They left it and came back to Moses, Aaron, and the entire Israelite community in the wilderness of Paran at Kadesh. There they reported to them and to the whole assembly and showed them the fruit of the country. They addressed Moses and said: We went to the land where you sent us. It is indeed flowing with milk and honey, and here is its fruit. But the inhabitants are strong, and the cities are fortified and very large. Moreover, we saw the descendants of Anak there. The Amalekites live in the Negeb; the Hittites, Jebusites, and Amorites live in the hill country; and the Canaanites reside by the Sea and along the banks of the Jordan. (13:26-29)

Exegesis and Exposition

Their mission accomplished after a month of exploring, the men presented their report to Moses and the community. The people were impressed by the fruits of the land, which agreed with God's promises concerning its productivity (Ex. 3:8). They were reminded, however,

---

12. See V. R. Gold, *IDB*, 2:575-77; H. G. Stigers, *ZPEB*, 3:107-10; S. J. Schultz, *ISBE*, 2:670-71; J. J. Davis, *NIDBA*, pp. 232-33.

that God had also spoken of the indigenous inhabitants of Canaan (3:17), and it was this part of the report, presented soberly, that gave the situation a different perspective.

Archaeological discoveries at Canaanite sites of that period have confirmed the presence of strong fortifications surrounding cities such as Hebron. But what really produced apprehension in the minds of the Israelites was the strength of the population, which contained Anakim elements of fearsome reputation.[13]

The spies furnished an accurate report of the distribution of the various races occupying the territory, locating the Amalekite nomads in the Negev, which was their normal habitat. Other Amalekites who had descended from Esau no doubt flourished among the tribal groups in Transjordan.[14] The hill country was occupied by Hittites, Jebusites, and Amorites. The Hittites of Canaan appear as indigenous people of the central uplands (Gen. 23:3-20), with whom Abraham dealt. Yet it is hardly accurate to regard them as "native Canaanites";[15] instead, they should be considered as one of the ethnic groups of the second millennium B.C. (cf. Ezek. 16:3, 45). They could have constituted an early Hittite colony in Canaan, which the Assyrian annals frequently described as *Ḫattu*, but had become indigenized over the generations. They may perhaps have been Hurrians, and this could account for second-millennium B.C. references to Canaan as the "land of the Hurrians."[16] It is to be hoped that further archaeological discoveries will help to resolve the problem of Hittite presence in Canaan.

The Jebusites were another ethnic group living in the hill country of Canaan. They were few in number but lived among the Amorites, Canaanites, and Girgashites (Gen. 15:21), while still maintaining their identity as descendants of Canaan's third son (10:16). Their chief stronghold was Jebus, the Jerusalem of later times (Josh. 18:28; Judg. 19:10). The earliest occupational levels of the city date from about 3300 B.C.,[17] but the Jebusites occupied the site in the Middle Bronze Age (c. 1950-1550 B.C.) and during that period brought the spring of Gihon within the city by means of underground tunnels. Jerusalem

---

13. In Deuteronomy 1:28 the LXX translated עֲנָקִים by γίγαντες, "giants."
14. Cf. J. A. Thompson, *ISBE*, 1:104.
15. So C. H. Gordon, *Introduction to Old Testament Times* (New Jersey: Ventnor Publishers, 1953), pp. 111, 113.
16. H. Hoffner, *POTT*, pp. 197-228; F. F. Bruce, *ISBE*, 2:720-23; K. A. Kitchen, *Ancient Orient and Old Testament* (London: Tyndale, 1966), p. 52 n. 91; F. W. Bush, *ISBE*, 2:756-57 and bibliography.
17. W. S. LaSor, *ISBE*, 2:1004 and bibliography.

was bypassed by the conquering Israelites under Joshua and was only captured in the time of David.[18]

The Amorites (Akk. *Amurrû*) were sometimes regarded in a general sense as the inhabitants of Canaan during the Bronze Age (cf. Gen. 14:7; 48:22; Deut. 3:8; etc.), and in the Amarna Age (14th century B.C.) the name Amurru described a Syrian kingdom, the southern border of which reached eastward from Sidon to Damascus and the desert. In the annals of Sennacherib[19] the kings of Amurru were those of Phoenicia, Philistia, Ammon, Edom, and Moab. The background of the Amorites is thus a complicated affair, which is hardly surprising in view of their nomadic heritage.[20]

The Canaanites, the final group mentioned here, occupied areas along the Mediterranean coast and the river Jordan. Their origins are also obscure and perhaps not very reputable if a text from Mari describing "thieves and Canaanites" is any indication.[21] Early Egyptian references to Canaan seem to allude to a mercantile class,[22] but the Canaanites were a diverse group at best. By the end of the Bronze Age (c. 1200 B.C.) the Phoenicians and Canaanites were virtually identical in matters of culture.[23]

Translation

Then Caleb silenced the people before Moses, saying: Let us go up and occupy the land, for we are well able to conquer it. But the men who had gone up with him said, No, we cannot attack these people. They are stronger than we. They then presented the Israelites with a discouraging report of the land they had reconnoitered, saying: The land we traversed as spies is a country that will swallow up its inhabitants. All the people we saw there are of great stature. We even saw the Nephilim *(the descendants of Anak came from the Nephilim), and we seemed like grasshoppers both to ourselves and to them. (13:30-33)

Exegesis and Exposition

Caleb halted the reports, obviously feeling that they were becoming too discouraging by magnifying the nature of the opposition. His

18. J. Simons, *Jerusalem in the Old Testament* (Leiden: Brill, 1952), pp. 60-61, 246-47.
19. A. L. Oppenheim, *ANET*, p. 287.
20. A. H. Sayce and J. A. Soggin, *ISBE*, 1:113-14.
21. Cf. G. Dossin, "Une Mention de Cananéens dans une Lettre de Mari," *Syria* 50 (1973): 277-82.
22. Cf. *ANET*, pp. 245-47.
23. W. F. Albright, *The Bible and the Ancient Near East* (New York: Doubleday, 1961), p. 328; A. R. Millard, *POTT*, pp. 29-52; C. G. Libolt, *ISBE*, 1:585-91 and bibliography.

proposal to march into Canaan and occupy it immediately was rejected as too dangerous, and by that act of repudiating the opportunity for conquest the Israelites rejected God's will for them. It is
hardly surprising that the spies were overwhelmed by the vigor and
diversity of the sedentary Canaanite civilization as compared with
the quiet, undeveloped nature of nomadic life in the wilderness of
Sinai.

The final item of reminiscence, which seemed to settle the matter,
was the encounter of the spies with the renowned Nephilim (KJV
"giants"), who according to the scribal gloss in v. 33 were the reputed
ancestors of the Anakim. It is not certain if the Nephilim of Gen. 6:4
were the same as the "mighty men" or if they were a separate group.
The record is an extremely old portion of Semitic historiography,
occurring as part of Tablet Three (Gen. 5:3–6:9*a*) according to the
tablet hypothesis of the construction of Genesis. Needless to say, the
significance of that material has been far from exhausted by modern
scholarship.[24] At all events, the gigantic stature of these people as
compared with the much smaller Hebrews intimidated the spies.
Because of possible genetic factors that pointed to a deterioration of
the Nephilim stock, the Israelites might well have found them much
less formidable than previously imagined, once they had engaged
them in battle. Clearly they were not motivated at that stage by the
courage of a David (1 Sam. 17:4-50).

Additional Notes

13:1 The Samaritan Pentateuch adds material to commence the
chapter that reflects the MT of Deut. 1:20-23, perhaps as an explanatory gloss.

13:17 זֶ֫ה: An enclitic use of the demonstrative pronoun for emphasis: "go up indeed."

13:18 הֶחָזָק הוּא הֲרָפֶה: An interrogative clause in which the dis-
junctive question was expressed by הֲ . . . הֲ.

13:22 וַיָּבֹא: Some Hebrew MSS, the LXX, and versions substitute
the plural here (וַיָּבֹאוּ). Possibly the final ו dropped out of the text at
an early stage of transmission.

13:24 לַמָּקוֹם הַהוּא: The inseparable preposition with a substantive
expresses specification here: "with respect to this place."

קָרָא: Many versions have the plural here, but in a collective sense
the singular is acceptable.

13:28 וְהֶעָרִים בְּצֻרוֹת גְּדֹלֹת מְאֹד: In this verse the predicative adjectives follow the substantive and agree in gender and number. When

---

24. Cf. E. A. Speiser, *Genesis* (AB; New York: Doubleday, 1964), pp. 44-46; H.
Van Broekhoven and R. K. Harrison, *ISBE*, 3:518-19.

predicative adjectives precede the substantive, they need not exhibit agreement (e.g., Ps. 119:137).

13:33 הַנְּפִלִים . . . . בְּנֵי: The LXX omitted this clause and referred to the Nephilim as γίγαντες, but it seems unnecessary to emend the MT on this account.

בְּעֵינֵיהֶם: Following this word the Samaritan Pentateuch closes the chapter as it commenced it by adding a short section of Deuteronomy, namely 1:27-33.

B. REBELLION AGAINST GOD (14:1-45)

Chapter 14, which continues the narrative of chap. 13, contains three major sections: (1) dissatisfaction with the spies' report (vv. 1-10); (2) God threatens punishment (vv. 11-38); (3) Israelites experience defeat (vv. 39-45).

1. DISSATISFACTION WITH THE SPIES' REPORT (14:1-10)

Translation

Then the entire Israelite community cried out in alarm and wept all that night. The Israelites complained about Moses and Aaron, and the whole congregation said to them: If only we had died in the land of Egypt, or if only we had perished in this wilderness! Why has the LORD brought us to this land only to fall by the sword, that our wives and children should become as plunder? Would it not be better for us to go back to Egypt? So they said to one another, Let us choose a leader and return to Egypt. Then Moses and Aaron fell prostrate before the entire Israelite assembly that had gathered there. (14:1-5)

Exegesis and Exposition

The Israelites reacted to the reconnaissance report in panic, unmindful of God's delivering and sustaining power during the journey from Egypt to Kadesh. Even worse was the fact that they were rebelling against God and defying His purpose, which was that the Israelites were to occupy the land of Canaan. Although they were ceremonially holy, they were not possessed of strong individual faith. Instead, they were relying upon the community as a whole for personal blessings.

As with the majority of people who do not trust in the Lord's mighty power (cf. Gen. 18:14; Isa. 50:2; 59:1; 1 Cor. 1:25; etc.), the Israelites became consumed with fear and worry, which are the antitheses of faith. As an alternative to suffering death themselves in battle and having their wives and children experience the atrocities foisted upon captives in war, many of the men even contemplated a return to Egypt, even though that would entail almost certain slavery and possibly death. But if they were to take this desperate step they would need a different leader, and their apostasy issued in yet another public repudiation of the leadership of Moses.

Translation

Joshua son of Nun and Caleb son of Jephunneh, who were among those who had explored the land, tore their clothes and addressed the entire gathering, saying: The land we traversed and surveyed is exceedingly good. If the LORD is pleased with us He will bring us into that land, a land flowing with milk and honey, and will give it to us. But do not rebel against the LORD, and do not be afraid of the land's inhabitants, because we shall devour them. They have lost their former protection, and the LORD is with us. Do not be afraid of them. But the whole assembly threatened to stone them, and all at once the glory of the LORD appeared *in the Tent of Meeting to all the Israelites. (14:6-10)

Exegesis and Exposition

While Moses and Aaron lay prostrate before God, Joshua and Caleb tore their clothes in the traditional gesture of mourning and tried to quell the panic that the people were manifesting. The two men endeavored to plead the merits of Canaan, tokens of which the spies had brought back with them, describing it by the eloquent phrase "flowing with milk and honey" (MT זָבַת חָלָב וּדְבָשׁ, *zābat ḥālāb ûdĕbāš*). In the OT milk was used figuratively of abundance (Gen. 49:12; Isa. 7:21-22), and as a food it ranked second only to bread, being one of the first things to be set before the weary traveler (Gen. 18:8). Because of climatic conditions the milk thickened quickly after it was drawn from the animals, so that "milk" was actually milk curds, which could be eaten with bread or churned into butter (Prov. 30:33). The honey was the wild variety (Deut. 32:13; Judg. 14:8-9; etc.), although the offering of honey with the firstfruits might indicate that bees were domesticated to some degree (2 Chron. 31:5). Because honey was fermentable, the name may have been used on some occasions as a euphemism for a strong alcoholic beverage. In figurative usage honey signified sweetness (Song of Sol. 4:11; Ezek. 3:3; etc.) as well as sumptuous fare (Song of Sol. 5:1; etc.). When coupled with milk it depicted an abundance of good things, which included the pomegranates and figs brought back by the spies.

In addition to these assurances of abundant provision, Joshua and Caleb proclaimed confidently that the Israelites would conquer the native inhabitants (MT לַחְמֵנוּ הֵם, *laḥmēnû hēm*, "they are our food"). Under God's leadership the former "protection" (MT צִלָּם מֵעֲלֵיהֶם, *ṣillām mēʿālêhem*) that they had enjoyed would disappear, because it was now God's will for them to be destroyed by the Israelites. All that was needed for victory, therefore, was submission to God's will and trust in His mighty power. But the people ignored these pleadings, and just as Moses, Aaron, Joshua, and Caleb were about to be executed by a violent mob of Israelites, God Himself intervened by appearing in His glory in the Tabernacle. The term כָּבוֹד (*kābôd*) refers to the reality of His presence manifested in power, splendor, and holiness as the supreme ruler of His people, who, unlike the pagan gods, was a living Being, dwelling in the midst of His people. The presence of God's glory portended blessing for His obedient followers, but for those who were rebellious it pointed to the implementation of the covenant curses.

2. GOD THREATENS PUNISHMENT (14:11-38)

Translation

The LORD said to Moses: How much longer will these people scorn Me? How much longer will they disbelieve Me despite all the signs that I have performed among them? I will inflict pestilence upon them and take away their inheritance, but I will make of you a greater and more numerous nation than they.

But Moses replied to the LORD: Then the Egyptians will hear about it, for by Your power You brought these people out from their midst, and they will tell it to the inhabitants of this land. They have heard that You, LORD, are with this people; that You, LORD, are seen face to face; that Your cloud stands above them; and that You go before them in a cloudy pillar by day and a fiery pillar by night. (14:11-14)

Exegesis and Exposition

God was understandably angry with His covenant people because the nation was still rejecting Him after all that He had already done and was promising to do for them in the future. The Israelites seem to have gained the impression that the Sinai covenant was one of privilege for them without any responsibilities. This misguided notion was obtained despite the fact that the covenant was a legal undertaking that contained clearly defined reciprocal rights and responsibilities as essential elements in the agreement.

But like many other "ceremonially holy" adherents of religion, the Israelites repudiated their relationship with God when adversity appeared to threaten them. Their penalty for rejecting God would be extinction as well as replacement by a new nation founded upon God's four faithful servants.

212

Moses was not enthralled by such a prospect, and so he entered into discussion about it with God. He pleaded that God's reputation among the nations would be damaged seriously by such an action. The Lord of Sinai was already known and feared by those who had heard about the defeat of the Egyptians at the time of the Exodus. The MT שָׁמְעוּ (*šāmĕ'û*, "they will hear") in vv. 13-14 implies that the Egyptians would first learn about God's predicament and that they would then spread the news among others. Moses was well aware of the constant flow of intelligence among the ancient Near Eastern peoples and was anxious to protect the Lord from embarrassment because of default by His people.

Translation

Now if You kill this people at a single blow, the nations that have heard of your fame will then say: Because the Lord was not able to bring the people to the land that He swore to give them, He killed them in the wilderness. (14:15-16)

Exegesis and Exposition

If such a disaster as God was proposing were to fall upon the Israelites, He would then be accused of impotence by the surrounding nations. In short, the mighty God of Israel would be reduced to purely human stature, to His great shame.

Translation

Now, I beg, let my Lord's power be shown to be great, just as You have proclaimed it, saying: The Lord is longsuffering and full of love, forgiving sin and lawbreaking. But guilty people are not exonerated thereby, for He punishes the children for their fathers' sins to the third and fourth generation. Please forgive the wickedness of this people according to Your great mercy, just as You have pardoned them from the time that they left Egypt until now. (14:17-19)

Exegesis and Exposition

Instead of becoming involved in a most embarrassing situation if the nation was to be annihilated in the wilderness, Moses implored God to continue manifesting His power and greatness as revealed to His people in Ex. 34:6-8. That passage, which Moses quoted in summary form here, is a classic example of propositional revelation for those who deny the existence of such.[25] It lists some of God's at-

---

25. Cf. C. F. D. Moule, *IDB*, 4:55, and the majority of OT liberal scholars.

tributes, including His patience (MT אֶרֶךְ אַפַּיִם, *'erek 'appayim*, "forbearing," lit. "long of nose," an ancient literary image signifying "compassion"),[26] abundance of love (MT רַב־חֶסֶד, *rab-ḥesed*),[27] and His forgiveness of sin and the violation of His laws (MT נֹשֵׂא עָוֹן וָפָשַׁע, *nōśēʾ ʿāwōn wāpāšaʿ*). But for the unrepentant and those who hate God (Ex. 20:5), divine punishment follows them through their offspring "to the third and fourth generation."[28] All four generations could conceivably be living under the same roof. Out of fidelity to His nature and His covenant love, God must of necessity punish the apostate in a manner inversely comparable to the way in which He blesses the godly and the obedient.

On the basis of these revealed qualities of the divine nature, Moses appealed for God to forgive the rebellious Israelites, not only because of His love that inspired the covenant relationship in the first place but also because of the forgiveness that He extended to them on account of their complaints and bitterness even before He delivered them from the Egyptians.

Translation

Then the LORD replied: I have forgiven them as you have begged. But truly, as I live, the entire earth shall be filled with the LORD's glory. (14:20-21)

Exegesis and Exposition

God responded to the entreaty of Moses by declaring the Hebrews pardoned. In this gracious act to an undeserving people He demonstrates the essence of His nature, which, as revealed in Jesus, is to love mankind to the uttermost (John 3:16) in order to make eternal life available for believers in Christ. The forgiveness of apostate Israel reveals only one aspect of His glory, which ultimately will fill the whole earth. This theme is celebrated frequently in later prophetic literature.[29]

Translation

But not one of these men who have witnessed My glory and the signs that I did in Egypt and in the wilderness, yet have disregarded My instructions and have tempted Me ten times, shall see the land

---

26. V. P. Hamilton, *TWOT*, 1:72.
27. For the various interpretations of *ḥesed* see R. L. Harris, *TWOT*, 1:305-7, and bibliography; H. J. Stoebe, *THAT*, 1:600-621.
28. The MT merely reads שִׁלֵּשִׁים and רִבֵּעִים in Gen. 50:23; Ex. 20:5; 34:7, etc., leaving the word "generation" (דּוֹר) to be understood. A lengthy interval of time seems implied.
29. Cf. Isa. 6:3; 11:9; Ezek. 39:21; Hab. 2:14; etc.

which I gave on oath to their ancestors, nor shall any of those who treated Me with scorn see it. But because My servant Caleb manifested a different spirit within himself and has followed Me fully, I will bring him into the land which he explored, and his descendants shall inherit it. (14:22-24)

Exegesis and Exposition

Even though God had thus been faithful to His essential Being, He also needed, as a "jealous" God, to maintain His own rights under the covenant provisions. Accordingly a sentence of gradual extermination was passed upon the ungrateful rebels who had tempted Him time after time (MT זֶה עֶשֶׂר פְּעָמִים, *zeh ʿeśer pĕʿāmîm*, "these ten times"). This phrase seems to be idiomatic, expressing repetition, but *The NIV Study Bible* also allows for literal interpretation by isolating ten specific incidents as follows: (1) Ex. 14:10-12; (2) 15:22-24; (3) 16:1-3; (4) 16:19-20; (5) 16:27-30; (6) 17:1-4; (7) 32:1-35; (8) Num. 11:1-3; (9) 11:4-34; (10) 14:3. From these examples it will be seen that the Israelites never trusted consistently in God's promises, despite repeated demonstrations of supernatural power on their behalf. Such holiness as they observed seems seldom to have come close to the level of the spirituality manifested by Moses, Joshua, and other great leaders. One such person was Caleb son of Jephunneh, who gave evidence of being controlled by a different form of motivation (MT רוּחַ אַחֶרֶת, *rûaḥ ʾaḥeret*, KJV "another spirit"): total obedience to the Lord's will. Because of this fidelity he would enter the Promised Land, whereas those who had scorned God's promises would not.

Translation

The Amalekites and Canaanites are living in the valleys; so tomorrow you must turn back and move out toward the wilderness along the road to the Red Sea. (14:25)

Exegesis and Exposition

The sentence of punishment for Israel was concluded by a peremptory statement ordering them to avoid the inhabitants of the valleys in the Negev and the uplands farther north. Instead, the camp was to withdraw into the wilderness in a southwesterly direction, since the way to the north was blocked.

Translation

Then the LORD spoke to Moses and Aaron, saying: How long have I to tolerate this evil community that grumbles at Me? I have heard the complaints that the Israelites make against Me. Say to them: As I live, says the LORD, I will do to you those very things that you have

215

spoken in My hearing. In this wilderness the corpses of those of you who have grumbled at Me shall lie, every one of you twenty years of age or older who was enumerated in the census. With the exception of Caleb son of Jephunneh and Joshua son of Nun, you shall under no circumstances enter the land that I swore to make your dwelling. (14:26-30)

Exegesis and Exposition

Even though the fateful sentence had been passed, it seems that the people were still complaining. Perhaps they were even more incensed about their fate, especially if they had been expecting unquestioning forgiveness of their rebellious behavior. But there are limits to God's tolerance, if only because He expects the sinner to repent, abandon his or her sinful ways, and live a righteous life. The lack of obedience and faith, which was unfortunately typical of the Israelites at this time, was used many centuries later to caution Christians about repeating the same pattern of behavior and thereby experiencing the same drastic results (1 Cor. 10:10; Heb. 3:12-18). With a fine sense of appropriateness, God punished the rebels by allowing them to receive the very thing they had desired—namely, to die in the Sinai wilderness (cf. Num. 14:2). All those on the register who were over twenty years of age would die in the wilderness, except Caleb and Joshua. Under no conditions would the others inhabit the land promised by God to their ancestors, because God had sworn it (MT נָשָׂאתִי אֶת-יָדִי, *nāśā'tî 'et-yādî*, "I lifted My hand") as a solemn oath.

Translation

But your little ones, whom you said would be taken as spoils of war, I will bring into the land you have scorned, and they shall enjoy it. But as for you, your bodies shall be in this wilderness. Your sons shall be nomads in the wilderness forty years, paying the price of your infidelity until the last of your corpses lies in the desert. For each of the total number of days in which you explored the land—namely, forty—you shall suffer for your wickedness one year for each day—that is, forty years—and you shall know what it means for Me to reject you. (14:31-34)

Exegesis and Exposition

It was not God's purpose to eliminate the households of the rebels completely, however. Once again He showed that His mercy was over all His works by demonstrating concern for the younger offspring who would be bereaved. These were the very ones whom the rebels imagined would fall prey to the hostile peoples of Canaan. But God contrasted the coming deaths of their progenitors with a promise of

216

hope for their own future. He assured them that they would survive the wilderness experience and would ultimately enjoy the occupation of Canaan. In the meantime, however, the people would be wilderness "nomads" (MT רֹעִים, *rōʿîm*, "shepherds") who would feed their flocks on the available pastureland. God then explained the rationale behind the number "forty," and in so doing He drove home the dreadful nature of the punishment. The repeated emphasis on "corpses" (MT פֶּגֶר, *peger*) carried an ominous tone, not only because of the finality that death brought about but also because corpses would defile the ceremonial holiness of the community (cf. Num. 19:11). The forty-year sentence was also an appropriate symbol of rejection. The number is commonly held to characterize a generation and is thus a round number (cf. Ps. 95:10).

The symbolism should not necessarily be regarded as a reliable guide, however. If a generation was reckoned from a person's birth to that of his firstborn, it need only have involved a period of some twenty years. But if it was calculated from a person's birth to his death, it could involve sixty years or even more. The number forty can also be understood literally in some instances, as R. L. Harris[30] has pointed out in connection with the occurrence of the forty-year figure mentioned on the Moabite Stone.[31]

Translation

I the LORD have spoken. I will assuredly do so to all this iniquitous community that has united against Me. In this wilderness they shall be swallowed up, and there they shall die. These men whom Moses sent to explore the land, and who, on their return, made the whole community grumble at him by bringing back a bad report of the land, these very individuals who spread the evil report about the land died suddenly before the LORD. Of all the men who went to explore the land, Joshua son of Nun and Caleb son of Jephunneh alone remained alive. (14:35-38)

Exegesis and Exposition

In a final repetition of His death threat, God made clear that having sworn, He would not repent. Drastic action was needed if any further acts of repudiation of His will were to be avoided. But time itself would add further emphasis to the Lord's sentence. As the years of desert sojourn passed, each one would remind the survivors of

---

30. R. L. Harris, *ZPEB*, 2:678.
31. F. M. Cross and D. N. Freedman, *Early Hebrew Orthography* (AOS 36; New Haven, Conn., 1952), pp. 39-40. See also G. R. Driver in F. F. Bruce, ed., *Promise and Fulfillment* (Edinburgh: T & T Clark, 1963), pp. 62-90.

Israel's supreme act of rebellion against the Lord of the covenant. Thirty-eight years (cf. Deut. 2:14) had been added because of this repudiation of God's purposes to what should have been, at best, an eighteen-month stay in the Mount Sinai region. The incident and the sentence are both recapitulated in the narrative for purposes of emphasis.

On this occasion, however, the mention of the offenders' deaths is included. They were struck down by "plague (MT מַגֵּפָה, *maggēpâ*) before the LORD." Precisely what happened is uncertain, as is the interval of time during which the extermination of the rebels took place. The Hebrew term can mean "defeat" and "blow" as well as "plague" and "pestilence," but as used here it describes something accompanied by fatal consequences. Because the act of execution occurred in the Lord's presence, the transgressors were perhaps struck down by fire or lightning. An epidemic plague would have involved others than the guilty ones and would have defiled the camp and hence is unlikely, particularly since only a modest number of men were involved. These deaths were but a token of God's punishment, which was to be worked out fully in the years ahead.

3. ISRAELITES EXPERIENCE DEFEAT (14:39-45)

Translation

Then Moses reported all these words to the whole Israelite community, and they went into deep mourning. They arose early in the morning and went to the crest of the hill country, saying: We are journeying to the place that the LORD promised. We have sinned. But Moses responded: Why do you still disobey the LORD's command? You will not be successful in this plan. Do not go, in case you are defeated by your enemies, for the LORD is not in your midst. For the Amalekites and Canaanites are there to confront you, and you shall fall victim to the sword. Because you have turned away from the LORD, He will not be with you. (14:39-43)

Exegesis and Exposition

Deep sadness overtook the camp when the death sentence was carried out on the ten spies, and with remorse came the determination to attempt some form of redress. Rising early the next day, the Israelites marched to the foothills (so *NAB*) on their way to enter Canaan. Moses evidently intercepted them and was told that they acknowledged their sin and were now prepared to fulfill the Lord's plan. They had apparently marched out without either the guiding cloud or the Ark of the Covenant to accompany them.

218

Although the expedition may have been well meant, it was fraught with danger because it constituted a second act of disobedience, a situation the Israelites apparently had not recognized until Moses pointed it out to them. Even though they had a dedicated, obedient leader such as Moses, they still did not appreciate that a believer has to live by individual faith (Hab. 2:4) and in complete submission to God's will. Nor did they obey when Moses stated that the Lord had forsaken them. Clearly they had learned little or nothing from their previous experiences.

Translation

Nevertheless they still insisted stubbornly on going to the crest of the hill country, although neither Moses nor the Ark of the Lord's Covenant left the encampment. Then the Amalekites and Canaanites who occupied those hills came down and attacked them, driving them back as far as Hormah. (14:44-45)

Exegesis and Exposition

Stubborn behavior (the MT has the causative form of the verb עָפַל, *ʿāpal*, "be arrogant," and thus means "act presumptuously") characterized their departure. Had their foray been used creatively under the Lord's direction, it would have resulted in victory over the hill-country Amalekites and Canaanites. But the Lord was not only absent from their midst; He was also actively opposed to them (v. 41) for disobeying His orders. Consequently the Israelites suffered defeat and the ignominy of being chased by their opponents, as illustrated by Deut. 1:44, to a place named Hormah. The designation means "destruction" or "devotion" (i.e., to destruction) from the root חרם (*ḥrm*).

The precise location of the place has been disputed, with Albright putting it at Tell esh-Sheri'ah, about a dozen miles northwest of Beersheba,[32] whereas Mazar identified it with Tell el-Milḥ, some eight miles southwest of Tell Arad,[33] which itself is of uncertain location.[34] Yet another suggestion is a site nearly four miles west of Tell el-Milḥ, known as Tell Meshash.[35] The most that can be said is that Hormah was apparently a settlement in the north-central Negev area of Palestine. It was an ancient location, being mentioned in the Egyptian Execration Texts of the nineteenth to eighteenth centuries B.C.

---

32. W. F. Albright, "Researches of the School in Western Judaea," *BASOR* 15 (1924): 6-7.
33. B. Mazar, "The Sanctuary of Arad and the Family of Hobab the Kenite," *JNES* 24 (1965): 297-303.
34. See J. A. Thompson, *NIDBA*, pp. 36-37.
35. Y. Aharoni, *EAEHL* 1, pp. 88-89.

Additional Notes

14:1 וַיִּבְכּוּ: The LXX and other versions employ the collective singular.

14:2 לוּ־מַתְנוּ: The perfect is used with לוּ in an optative sense to express unfulfilled desire. The LXX reads ὄφελον ἀπεθάνομεν.

14:10 בְּאֹהֶל מוֹעֵד: After this clause the LXX adds the explanatory phrase ἐν νεφέλη ἐπὶ τῆς σκηνῆς, but it is unnecessary to emend the MT to accommodate this gloss.

14:11 בְּכֹל הָאֹתוֹת: Here the preposition ־בְ expresses disadvantage: "in spite of."

14:18 וְרַב־חֶסֶד: The LXX and Samaritan Pentateuch add "and truth."

וָפֶשַׁע: The LXX and Samaritan Pentateuch add "and sin."

14:23 לַאֲבֹתָם: The LXX here inserts a section regarding the off-spring of the rebels inheriting the land, reflecting Deut. 1:39. But see also 14:31.

14:24 עֵקֶב הָיְתָה רוּחַ אַחֶרֶת: The MT expresses a causal clause by means of a preposition (עֵקֶב) followed by a noun clause.

14:31 וְיָדְעוּ: LXX reads καὶ κληρονομήσουσιν, "and they shall possess," probably anticipating Deut. 1:39.

14:34 יוֹם לַשָּׁנָה יוֹם: The noun repetition is a distributive, "one day for each year."

תְּנוּאָתִי: The sense of hostility to Israel conveyed here has been interpreted as "to frustrate me" by R. Loewe, "Divine Frustration Exegetically Frustrated," in P. R. Ackroyd and B. Lindars, eds., *Words and Meanings* (Cambridge: Cambridge U., 1968), pp. 137-58.

14:40 חָטָאנוּ: Following this verb the Samaritan Pentateuch adds the material in Deut. 1:42.

14:45 הַהוּא: The Samaritan Pentateuch inserts here some clauses based upon Deut. 1:44.

עַד־הַחָרְמָה: Both the Samaritan Pentateuch and the LXX have in-sertions from Deut. 1:45. Both versions seem to have exhibited af-finity for the first chapter of Deuteronomy in the latter part of Num. 14, though this should not be taken as a reason for modifying the MT.

C. VARIOUS LAWS AND STATUTES (15:1-41)

Chapter 15 is divisible into three parts, each beginning with the declaratory formula "The LORD said to Moses": (1) sacrificial ordi-nances (vv. 1-16); (2) regulations concerning sins of omission (vv. 17-36); (3) rules concerning tassels (vv. 37-41).

1. SACRIFICIAL ORDINANCES (15:1-16)

Translation

The Lᴏʀᴅ spoke to Moses, saying: Address the Israelites and say to them: When you have entered the land where you are to live, which I am giving you, and you make an offering by fire to the Lᴏʀᴅ, to create a pleasing aroma to the Lᴏʀᴅ from the herd or flock, whether a burnt offering, or a sacrifice to discharge a vow, or as a freewill offering, or as part of a festival ritual, the one who presents his offering to the Lᴏʀᴅ shall bring a grain offering of one-tenth of an ephah of finely ground flour mixed with one-fourth of a hin of oil. (15:1-4)

Exegesis and Exposition

The thirty-eight years of wilderness wandering can be considered properly to have commenced at this juncture. A distinction must be drawn between the journey from Egypt at the Exodus to Mount Sinai, which was God's plan for Israel, and the long period of sojourn in the Sinai peninsula, which was not His will but constituted a punishment for the nation's disobedience.[36] The enactments contained in this chapter, revealed by God to Moses for the Israelites to observe when finally they occupied Canaan, were probably recorded by the *šōṭĕrîm*. This priestly material may have been inserted at this stage to furnish spiritual consolation to the Israelites as they lamented their wilderness trials. The mention of "the land" that God had promised them gave the nation some hope for the future. The various regulations also provide the reader with an interlude of relief from the rehearsing of Israel's apostasy, as well as furnishing important supplementary information about the sacrificial system, notably in terms of the theology of atonement.

When any kind of burnt sacrifice was offered to the Lord for whatever purpose, it was to be accompanied by a grain offering composed of one-tenth of an ephah (nearly two quarts) of finely ground flour, mixed with one-fourth of a hin (nearly one quart) of oil. The regulations for the whole burnt sacrifice (Lev. 1:3-17) are augmented here by an accompanying cereal offering that was different from the voluntary prescription of Lev. 2:1-16. This supplement was also required for the peace offerings (Lev. 3:3-17), the freewill offerings (7:16), and the sacrifice celebrating the beginning of the month (Num. 28:11-15). In the festival presentation (Lev. 23:1-44), provision had

---

36. W. H. Griffith Thomas, *Through the Pentateuch Chapter by Chapter*, pp. 146-47.

already been made for a cereal offering, but even this looked forward to occupation in the Promised Land. The enhancement of the offerings by the addition of wine libations represents a new and significant development.

The legislation looked forward to a time when the Israelites would be able to harvest grain in their own land (Lev. 23:10). It was not imposed as an accompaniment to wilderness burnt sacrifices because grain and oil, the products of a developed agricultural economy, were scarce in a desert milieu. Thus these enactments reflect a wilderness environment and confirm the genuine nature of the narrative's historical perspective.

Translation

You shall prepare with each lamb for the burnt offering or the sacrifice one-fourth of a hin of wine as a drink offering. In the case of a ram, prepare as a grain offering two-tenths of an ephah of finely ground flour mixed with one-third of a hin of oil. As a drink offering you shall present one-third of a hin of wine as a pleasing aroma to the LORD. When you prepare a young bull as a burnt offering or a sacrifice for discharging a vow, or as a peace offering to the LORD, (15: 5-8)

Exegesis and Exposition

The prescription for a ram was somewhat larger than for the younger sacrificial animals, presumably to reflect the greater maturity and physical bulk of the animal being offered. The accompanying drink offering of wine was also increased correspondingly. A young bull fell under the same principle, whatever the purpose of the sacrifice.

Translation

then you shall present with the young bull a grain offering of three-tenths of an ephah of finely ground flour mixed with half a hin of oil. You shall bring as the drink offering half a hin of wine as a pleasing aroma to the LORD. This is the procedure required for each young bull or ram, each lamb or young goat. Do this for each one, according to the number that you present. (15:9-12)

Exegesis and Exposition

The amount of cereal offering for a bullock was increased, and the amount of the drink offering was raised comparably. The purpose of these supplements was expressed figuratively in terms of God's deriving pleasure from the sacrifices. The offering of a sacrifice represented a considerable financial outlay for the worshipers, which in itself tested their seriousness and sincerity.

Translation

Every native-born person shall do these things according to this procedure when presenting an offering made by fire as a pleasing aroma to the LORD. If an alien is living with you, or whoever else is residing permanently among you in coming generations, and is desirous of presenting an offering made by fire, a pleasing aroma to the LORD, he must do precisely as you do. The statute shall apply both to members of the community and the alien living among you, as a permanent regulation for all future generations. You and the alien shall be alike in the LORD's sight. The same laws and rules will apply equally to both you and the alien living in your midst. (15:13-16)

Exegesis and Exposition

The expression "pleasing aroma" (MT רֵיחַ נִיחֹחַ, *rêaḥ nîḥōaḥ*) is not meant to be taken literally and is normally considered an archaic linguistic survival.[37] The sacrifice placated God and appeased His anger, which was constantly threatening to break out upon human beings. The rationale of sacrifice was to employ a prescribed procedure whereby peaceful coexistence between a holy God and sinful human beings became a possibility.[38] The prescriptions for the wine offering (MT יַיִן לְנֶסֶךְ, *yayin lĕnesek*) contained no instructions concerning its presentation or disposition. If the drink offering was intended to produce the same kind of sensory effect as the animal in process of being sacrificed, it would probably have been poured on the animal offering as it was burning, thereby becoming vaporized and ascending with the smoke of the sacrifice.

Provision was made for a resident alien (MT גֵּר, *gēr*) to participate in the Israelite rituals, but in each instance he or she had to conform to the procedures followed by native Israelites, so that there would be no possibility for the infiltration of pagan religious practices.

The MT חֻקָּה (*ḥuqqâ*, "statute") is a legal term used to describe a divine ordinance that was binding upon Israelite and resident alien alike. In certain places in the MT it parallels מִשְׁפָּט (*mišpāṭ*, "judgment") and מִצְוָה (*miṣwâ*, "commandment"), as in 2 Sam. 22:23; Ps. 18:22 (MT 23), and elsewhere. In v. 15 the *ḥuqqâ* is made permanent (MT עוֹלָם, *ʿôlām*) and further explained by the phrase בְּדֹרֹתֵיכֶם (*bĕdōrōtêkem*, "for future generations").[39] the root חקק (*ḥqq*) means "inscribe," "engrave," and by implication signifies the unchanging character of something that has been "written in stone." In v. 16 two other legal terms are

37. R. K. Harrison, *Leviticus*, p. 47.
38. G. J. Wenham, *Leviticus*, p. 56.
39. Cf. J. P. Lewis, *TWOT*, 1:317-18; G. Liedke, *THAT*, 1:626-33 and bibliographies.

employed: תּוֹרָה (*tôrâ*) and מִשְׁפָּט (*mišpāṭ*). The first means literally "teaching," "instruction," whether of human or divine origin, and refers to covenant enactments in general. Here it is a specific religious law enforcing cultic uniformity and banning discrimination.[40]

Mišpāṭ, "rule," "decision," "judgment," is a common OT term that describes a specific application of the larger concept of divine Torah. In this instance it legislated for the contingency in which persons other than native Israelites wished to participate independently in the ritual of the burnt offerings. While the ancient Israelites did not seem to have "evangelized" in the modern Christian sense, their faith was nevertheless deemed to be a legitimate sphere of participation for potential converts, since in the Abrahamic covenant God stated that through the patriarch all earthly families would bless themselves (Gen. 12:3, KJV "be blessed"; NAB "find blessing").

2. REGULATIONS CONCERNING SINS OF OMISSION (15:17-36)

This is the second section to be introduced by an annunciation formula, indicating direct revelatory communication from God to Moses. The section is thereby added to the corpus of covenant law, which is a dynamic rather than a static entity.

Translation

The LORD spoke to Moses again, saying: Address the Israelites and say to them: When you enter the land to which I am bringing you and you are eating the food of the land, you shall present a raised offering to the LORD. You shall present a cake from the first preparation of the finely ground flour as a raised offering. As an offering of the threshing floor you shall present it. Throughout future generations you must give to the LORD a raised offering from your first preparation of flour. (15:17-21)

Exegesis and Exposition

The Israelites were instructed to make a special offering to God when they finally occupied Canaan and were farming the land. It was to be a "lifted" or "raised" (KJV "heave") offering, removed as a "firstfruit" of the coarse meal (MT רֵאשִׁית עֲרִיסֹת, *rēʾšît ʿărîsōt*) and presented to God in the form of a cake (MT חַלָּה, *ḥallâ*). This duty was intended to remind the Israelites that the produce of the land, like the

---

40. On law in the OT see K. L. Barker, *ZPEB*, 4:543-44; W. J. Harrelson, *IDB*, 3:77-89; R. A. Cole, *ZPEB*, 3:883-94; R. K. Harrison, *ISBE*, 3:76-85; J. E. Hartley, *TWOT*, 1:403-5; G. Liedke and C. Petersen, *THAT*, 2:1032-43 and bibliographies.

territory itself, belonged properly to God and constituted His gracious gift to them.

The first reference to a raised offering (MT תְּרוּמָה, *tĕrûmâ*) is in Ex. 29:27 in connection with the consecration of the priests. In Lev. 7:14, a portion of the peace offering (NEB "shared offering"), when connected with thanksgiving, was presented for the priest's use in the form of a cake of unleavened or leavened flour. The Levitical instructions provide a more detailed picture of the proceedings than is found elsewhere. In general, a raised offering accompanied all voluntary sacrifices (Ex. 35:24; 36:3) as well as those in which it was prescribed by law (30:15; Lev. 7:14). The raised offerings were different from the waved offering (MT תְּנוּפָה, *tĕnûpâ*) in the manner they were presented, which was evidently of a more complex and symbolic nature.[41] This enactment was intended to be a permanent part of all future ritual life at the beginning of the harvest season, usually early in April.

Translation

If you sin unintentionally and do not observe all these commandments the LORD has given to Moses—namely, everything that the LORD commanded you through him, from the day that the LORD promulgated them and continuing throughout future generations— should this be done without intent and the community is unaware of it, then the entire congregation is to offer a bullock for a burnt offering as a pleasing aroma to the LORD, along with its prescribed grain and drink offerings, and also one male goat for a sin offering. (15:22-24)

Exegesis and Exposition

An important part of the casuistic legislation dealt with accidental sin, whether committed by the entire community or by an individual. These transgressions could include actions undertaken in ignorance of Levitical law, inadvertent neglect or violation of Tabernacle or priestly protocol, or some other social misdemeanor that, although unintentional in nature, had the effect of violating the sanctity of the whole community of priests. Because the transgression was not deliberate, no specific moral guilt was attached to it.

Nevertheless, the neglect or inadvertence was a serious offense because the enactments, of which it constituted a violation, had been promulgated for all time. We are thus introduced to the concept that ignorance of the law does not constitute an excuse for violating it. This principle has been incorporated into modern legal theory with devas-

---

41. Cf. G. J. Wenham, *Leviticus*, pp. 126-27; R. K. Harrison, *Leviticus*, pp. 82-83; A. Bowling, *TWOT*, 2:565.

225

tating effects for many an offender. Levitical law (Lev. 4:13-21) provided a more elaborate ritual for inadvertent community sin than is the case here. The reason seems to be that the present passage is dealing with an individual's accidental transgression, of which the community was unaware but which came to light subsequently.[42] Nevertheless, the congregation's spiritual solidarity was impaired, and atonement therefore had to become a community concern. The resultant offerings were intended to avert possible divine recriminations and to please the Lord.

Translation

The priest must make atonement for the entire Israelite community, and they shall be pardoned because the offense was not deliberate. They shall bring their offering—a burnt offering and a sin offering—before the LORD for their accidental sin. The entire Israelite community, including the resident aliens, will be forgiven because everyone was involved in the accidental wrongdoing. If an individual sins unintentionally, he shall bring a yearling female goat for a sin offering. (15:25-27)

Exegesis and Exposition

Once the burnt offerings had been presented in accordance with correct procedure, the community, including any resident aliens, was forgiven, and spiritual solidarity was restored. This passage teaches an invaluable lesson about the need for preserving the people of God as a separated, holy community, in which each individual's spiritual well-being is of fundamental importance to the vitality of the group as a whole. Paul expresses a similar concept in his attempt to stress the need for maintaining the spiritual integrity of the Body of Christ (1 Cor. 12:12-27). The Israelite community is described by the term עֵדָה, *ʿēdâ* (KJV "congregation"). This word occurs commonly in literature connected with priestly activities and, according to Hurvitz, dropped out of use after the exile.[43] Its presence in this section is thus an important attestation to the early date of the material.

Translation

The priest shall make atonement for the person who transgressed by sinning accidentally, to make atonement for him, and he shall be pardoned. The same law applies to everyone who commits sin unin-

---

42. Cf. R. K. Harrison, *Leviticus*, p. 64.
43. A. Hurvitz, "Linguistic Observations on the Biblical Usage of the Priestly Term *'Eda* (עֵדָה)," *Tarbiz* 40 (1971): 261-67.

tentionally, whether he is a native Israelite or a resident alien. (15:28-29)

Exegesis and Exposition

When an individual, as distinct from the community, committed an inadvertent transgression, the sacrifice of a young female goat (15:27) was required in order to effect atonement. Once again, the principle of impartiality applied where a resident alien had been involved.

Translation

But anyone who sins deliberately, whether a native Israelite or an alien, insults the LORD. Such a person must be cut off from his people, because he has brought contempt upon the LORD's word and has broken His commandments. Such a person shall be cut off entirely; his guilt shall be his very own. (15:30-31)

Exegesis and Exposition

This passage is important for an understanding of the OT system of sacrificial worship, for it describes the only kind of transgression for which the law provided no sacrifice. The sin was deliberate in the sense that it was committed in full knowledge of its being prohibited by covenant law. The translation "deliberately" is represented by the MT בְּיָד רָמָה (*běyād rāmâ*, "with uplifted hand"), as though the transgressor was about to attack God or rebel against Him wantonly. Such an attitude indicated scorn for God's covenant enactments. Blatant defiance of the revealed truths of the Sinaitic covenant constituted a direct, conscious repudiation of the God of that covenant, the penalty for which was to be "cut off," i.e., removed from membership in the community by being executed (Lev. 24:11-16). This penalty also applied to the resident alien as well as to the native Israelite.

Translation

While the Israelites were in the wilderness, they discovered a man gathering wood on the Sabbath day. Those who caught him gathering wood brought him to Moses, Aaron, and the entire community. They put him in custody, because there were no clear instructions about dealing with him. Then the LORD said to Moses: The man must undoubtedly be executed. The entire community must stone him outside the camp. So the whole community brought him outside the encampment and stoned him to death, as the LORD had instructed Moses. (15:32-36)

227

Exegesis and Exposition

Although this incident occurred at an unspecified time and place in the period of the wilderness wanderings, it was inserted here as an illustration of someone's acting in deliberate defiance of God's revealed law. The offense involved a conscious violation of the rules governing the Sabbath (Ex. 20:8-11), and the offender was apprehended and brought before Moses, Aaron, and the entire community to be tried. His case apparently set a precedent, and in the absence of specific instructions for dealing with such matters, the counsel of the Lord was sought.

The transgression was deemed a capital one, and the transgressor was ordered to be stoned (MT רָגוֹם אֹתוֹ בָּאֲבָנִים, *rāgôm ʾōtô bāʾăbānîm*, "to kill him with stones," using an infinitive for a finite verb form) by the whole community away from the camp. The sentence was consistent with existing instructions from God (Ex. 31:14-15; 35:2), which Moses and the Israelites had either forgotten or were reluctant to apply. The decision may have seemed severe to some observers for a comparatively minor offense, but a fundamentally important principle was at stake here.

The event illustrates the fact that unfortunately the normal human condition is not grace but sin. The act of gathering fuel was a calculated gesture of disregard or distaste for the law, which declared the Sabbath a holy day on which work was prohibited. To categorize the transgression as "minor" is to misunderstand the nature of sin. The so-called little white lie is just as much sin in the sight of God as is murder, for both are violations of Decalogue law.

If the arrogant rebel had not been punished, the Israelite community would have degenerated quickly into the kind of self-indulgent society that arose at a later period (Judg. 19:30; 21:25). The death sentence was carried out in a locality that would not bring defilement upon the camp. Community participation in the execution ensured that everybody shared in the responsibility for it.

Two lessons were thus imprinted on the minds of the Israelites: (1) they became aware that God would brook no high-handed behavior from His covenant people; (2) the holy nation must remain in that spiritual condition and avoid every contamination of sin and evil.

Many scholars have regarded this section as an interpolation of the *midrash* variety, which constituted a running commentary on the Hebrew text of a kind used increasingly in the postexilic period.[44]

---

44. So G. B. Gray, *Numbers*, p. 183; N. H. Snaith, *Numbers*, p. 253; P. J. Budd, *Numbers*, p. 177; M. Noth, *Numbers*, p. 117; etc.

The purpose of the passage is to drive home how important it was for Israel to obey the Sabbath laws and maintain ceremonial holiness by obeying God's commandments. In the light of Talmudic traditions Weingreen saw the narrative as corresponding to the rabbinic tradition of placing a fence around the law. Thus picking up pieces of wood was the first step in the process of making a fire on the Sabbath, which the law forbade (Ex. 35:3).[45] This approach was disputed by Phillips,[46] who suggested that the repudiation of covenant law even exceeded the rules of Sabbath observance by engaging in domestic labor. To correct the wrong a particular decision was required, as in other situations.

If, however, the plain purpose of the passage is kept in view, it hardly seems necessary to indulge in exotic interpretations. The man's activities were premeditated, and such defiance deserved the capital penalty prescribed by the law. God was not acting in a capricious or willful manner but was merely executing known judgments upon an obdurate transgressor. Had he repented and confessed, he would have been forgiven and restored.

3. RULES CONCERNING TASSELS (15:37-41)

The third and final section of this chapter is again introduced by a formula of announcement.

Translation

The LORD spoke to Moses, saying: Address the Israelites and say to them: For all generations to come you must make tassels on the corners of your garments and put a blue thread on every tassel. You will have these tassels to look at and be reminded of all the LORD's commandments, that you may obey them and not follow immoral behavior incited by your own hearts and eyes. Thus you will remember to obey all my commandments and be consecrated to your God. I am the LORD your God, who brought you from Egypt to be your God. I am the LORD your God. (15:37-41)

Exegesis and Exposition

The tassels (MT צִיצָת, *ṣîṣit*, KJV "fringes") were meant to hang from the corners of the upper garment (MT בֶּגֶד, *beged*, the כְּסוּת, *kesût* of Deut. 22:12; etc.), which was generally worn on top of other

---

45. J. Weingreen, "The Case of the Woodgatherer (Numbers XV 32-36)," *VT* 16 (1966): 361-64.
46. A. Phillips, "The Case of the Woodgatherer Reconsidered," *VT* 19 (1969): 125-28.

clothing, although the term has a wide usage in the OT.[47] The tassel was probably made by twisting the overhanging threads of the warp and woof of the completed garment into a knot that would hang down. By seeing the tassels as they walked, the Israelites would be reminded of their redemption and also of God's commandments, which they were pledged to obey.

Elaborately woven garments with fringes and tassels were common in ancient Egypt and Babylonia.[48] Traditionally the blue thread placed on each tassel symbolized the celestial origin of the law.[49] Since blue was also a royal color, it could also symbolize the majesty of Him who had given the law to mankind.

The popularity of tassels was still evident in NT times. Jesus wore garments adorned with tassels, and on occasions sick people touched them in order to be granted instant healing (Matt. 9:20; 14:36). The tasseled shawl has passed down through Judaism as a garment worn during prayer.[50] The use of such articles, however, does not convey sanctity upon the wearer. Holiness is not a condition acquired through contact with "holy" objects but is the result of a heartfelt determination to serve the One who announces Himself to His people by the authoritative declaration "I am the Lord your God."

Additional Notes

15:5 הָאֶחָד: LXX adds ὀσμὴν εὐωδίας τῷ κυρίῳ, correcting a supposed MT deficit in the light of vv. 7 and 10.

15:6 אוֹ לָאַיִל: After this phrase the LXX adds ὅταν ποιῆτε αὐτὸν ἢ εἰς ὁλοκαύτωμα ἢ εἰς θυσίαν, perhaps a modification of the instructions with which v. 8 commences.

15:20 עֲרֹסֹתֵכֶם: This word, found only in the plural, is written defectively here, the fuller form occurring in the following verse.

15:24 לִשְׁגָגָה: The inseparable preposition for this word is normally –בְּ, as in vv. 27, 29; Lev. 4:22.

15:30 מְגַדֵּף: This verb, "revile," "blaspheme," occurs only in the piel. The position of the word יהוה emphasizes the serious nature of a total and deliberate rejection of covenant mercies.

---

47. J. M. Myers, *IDB*, 1:869; W. G. Plaut and W. W. Hallo, *Numbers*, in *The Torah, A Modern Commentary* (New York: Union of American Hebrew Congregations, 1979), pp. 151-52.
48. Cf. S. Bertman, "Tasselled Garments in the Ancient East Mediterranean," *BA* 24 (1961): 119-28; B. Rothenberg, *Timna: Valley of the Biblical Copper Mines* (London: Thames and Hudson, 1972), pp. 123-24.
49. Cf. F. J. Stephens, "The Ancient Significance of Sisith," *JBL* 50 (1931): 59-70; J. E. Hartley, *TWOT*, 2:765 and bibliography.
50. See J. H. Hertz, ed., *The Pentateuch and Haftorahs*, pp. 633-34.

15:35 רָגוֹם אֹתוֹ: The qal infinitive absolute form here substitutes for the imperfect indicative. Cf. Num. 30:3; Deut. 15:2; etc.

D. FURTHER REBELLION AGAINST MOSES AND AARON (16:1-50)

Chapter 16 can be subdivided into three principal sections: (1) Korah and others rebel against Moses (vv. 1-30); (2) punishment of rebels (vv. 31-43); (3) Aaron atones for Israel (vv. 44-50). The entire chapter is a single, well-integrated narrative that describes a rebellion of major proportions and concludes with a dramatic redemption. There may have been other unrecorded attempts to repudiate the leadership of Moses and Aaron, but the present one preserved a tense incident in the wilderness wanderings.

1. KORAH AND OTHERS REBEL AGAINST MOSES (16:1-30)

Translation

Korah son of Izhar, son of Kohath, son of Levi, with Dathan and Abiram, sons of Eliab, and On, son of Peleth, who were Reubenites, assembled followers and rebelled against Moses along with some 250 Israelites, reputed community leaders, representatives of the assembly, people of good standing. (16:1-2)

Exegesis and Exposition

The pedigree of Korah is traced back to Levi. Izhar was the brother of Amram, the father of Aaron and Moses. He was thus an uncle of these two leaders. Aside from his activities here, nothing is known of the life of Korah. That he was of some standing is indicated by his pedigree, which was comparatively lengthy. As a Kohathite he was a descendant of the second son of Levi and a member of one of the three great priestly divisions (cf. Ex. 6:16-19).

Dathan and Abiram were the sons of Eliab, a Reubenite whose family was one of the most prominent in the tribe, but aside from this incident the two men are unknown. Just as unfamiliar is On, son of Peleth, one of the Reubenite chiefs. His name does not appear elsewhere in the narrative, and he is not even mentioned when disaster overtakes his fellow conspirators. A rabbinic tradition maintained that his wife prevailed upon him to part company with those who were opposing Moses.[51] If this actually occurred, it is reminiscent of a

---

51. Ibid., p. 639.

much later woman's attempt to intervene on behalf of Christ's life (Matt. 27:19).

These persons assembled[52] a company of 250 prominent Israelite leaders from the whole company of Israel and confronted Moses and Aaron. The status of this group is made clear by the repetitive explaining, indicating that this movement was a rebellion at the highest level of community life. Korah's motives may have been the product of jealousy because his cousins Moses and Aaron had been appointed to the highest positions in the covenant community. He may also have resented his exclusion from the priestly office, even though he was a Levite. Instead, he was restricted to less exalted duties in the service of the Tabernacle. The other Reubenites displayed the unsettled, impetuous temperament of their eponymous ancestor (Gen. 49:3-4). Their complaints were of a different nature, however, for they were challenging Moses' leadership and reviling him for unfulfilled promises (Num. 16:13-14). Nevertheless, behind this action must have lurked dissatisfaction because their progenitor Reuben had been deprived of his birthright, and with this the position of head over the nation.

Translation

They confronted Moses and Aaron and said to them: You have assumed far too much authority, for everyone in the entire community is holy, and the LORD is present with them. Why then do you exalt yourselves above the LORD's community? (16:3)

Exegesis and Exposition

Apparently all four dissenters joined in their complaints against the leaders. The nature of the charge was that of Aaron's priestly family usurping the privileges and functions that belonged properly to the people as a whole. This was thus not merely rebellion against Moses and Aaron as individuals but against God, who had appointed them to their high offices (cf. Ex 3:10; 28:1). Two words are used for "congregation" in the MT: עֵדָה (*'ēdâ*) and קָהָל (*qāhāl*). The difference has been explained in terms of the former describing the natural integration of the tribes, whereas the latter relates to the divine calling of the nation as a whole.[53]

Translation

When Moses heard this he prostrated himself and spoke to Korah and all his associates: Tomorrow morning the LORD will make clear

---

52. Cf. J. Liver, "Korah, Dathan and Abiram," in C. Rabin, ed., *Studies in the Bible* (ScrHier 8; Jerusalem: Magnes Press, 1961), pp. 189-217.
53. *KD*, 3:106.

who is His and who is holy, and He will cause that person, the individual of His choice, to be made to approach Him. (16:4-5)

Exegesis and Exposition

First, Moses adopted the traditional posture of surrender or supplication (cf. Num. 14:5) without indicating whether he was yielding to despair at the rebellion or, as some have thought, was supplicating God for help. He refused, however, to discuss any charge of monopoly or usurpation. Instead, he referred the matter to God for His adjudication. Moses replied to Korah, who was acting as spokesman, but his response was intended for all the others. On the following day, he assured them, God would reveal the identity of the individual who was His choice for high priest.

Translation

Do this: You and your companions, Korah, must take censers; place fire and incense in them before the LORD tomorrow. The man whom the LORD chooses shall be the holy one. You are assuming too much authority yourselves, you sons of Levi. (16:6-7)

Exegesis and Exposition

The test that God was to impose was not unlike a trial by ordeal, since it imposed upon Korah and his followers a procedure that would issue in a decision that could prove fatal. When they were informed that the procedure was to constitute a form of trial by fire offered before the Lord, they would remember immediately the fate of Aaron's two sons, Nadab and Abihu, who had perished through offering fire improperly (Lev. 10:1-2).

They would be under even greater emotional stress if they remembered God's pronouncements that He would be sanctified in those who approached Him at the shrine (10:3). Although the complainers may have been in a condition of ceremonial holiness, their thoughts were of rebellion against God and His chosen leaders. In declaring how God would once again choose His holy priest from among the community, Moses neatly turned the tables on Korah and his confederates by telling them that they were now taking too much authority upon themselves (MT רַב־לָכֶם, *rab-lākem*, "much to you").

Translation

Then Moses addressed Korah: Listen now, sons of Levi: Is it not sufficient for you that the God of Israel has separated you from the rest of the Israelite community, to bring you close to Himself, to perform the duties of the Tabernacle, and to stand before the community as their ministers? He has brought you near to Him, and your brothers the Levites with you. Are you trying to obtain the priesthood as well? You and all your companions have banded together against the LORD. What is Aaron that you should complain so much against him? (16:8-11)

Moses discerned correctly the real motive for Korah's rebellion. Korah wanted a popular election to be held for the office of high priest with himself as a candidate. In his view he was the only suitable person for that exalted function. To set Korah's position in Israel in proper perspective, Moses pointed out the great privilege of his having been called to serve God in the ministry of the sanctuary. Moses evidently perceived that this status did not satisfy Korah's ambitions, however, and for this reason he questioned him directly on the matter of his desire to be high priest in Israel, without receiving any apparent rebuttal.

The test in which Korah and his fellow conspirators would participate would involve them in priestly activities. To offer incense before the Lord brought the ministrant directly into God's presence. Moses ended his rebuke by accusing Korah and his associates of rebelling against God, since it was He, not the people, who had appointed Aaron to his office. Korah's kind of political intrigue was to be repeated many times through the centuries, as though the highest cultic office constituted a prize to grasp.

Translation

Moses also sent to summon Dathan and Abiram, sons of Eliab, but they said, We are not coming. Is it not enough that you have brought us away from a land flowing with milk and honey to kill us in the wilderness? Now you also want to behave like a prince over us. Furthermore, you have not brought us into a land flowing with milk and honey, nor have you given us an inheritance of fields and vineyards. Do you think that you can blind the eyes of these people? We are not coming. (16:12-14)

Exegesis and Exposition

Having begun with the ringleader, Moses now summoned the others, who were apparently lurking in the background while Korah addressed Moses. Although he sent for them to stand before him, they refused to obey his instructions, in keeping with their repudiation of his leadership. They did, however, present their own complaint from a respectable distance, stating their case in the fashion that Korah had employed. In essence, they were not only complaining about Moses as national leader but also objecting to the quality of his leadership. Unmindful of the harsh conditions of life in Egypt that the

Hebrews had experienced prior to the Exodus, Dathan, Abiram, and their supporters remembered it as a land of great prosperity. Under normal conditions Egypt was indeed a place of plenty, but it is wrong to imagine that slaves participated in such bounty to any significant extent. It appears that the diet of the working class consisted largely of onions, supplemented with bread made from rough grain, and this contrasts sharply with the picture being painted by Dathan and Abiram. What they were contesting was the claim that the wilderness march, with all its hazards and discomforts, was but an interlude prior to the Israelite occupation of their own land of milk and honey (MT חָלָב וּדְבַשׁ, *ḥālāb ûdĕbaš*),[54] a prospect that seemed very far from being realized.

From the standpoint of the rebels, it appeared that Moses had lured the Israelites from Egypt to let them perish in the Sinai wilderness, and thus his promises of future prosperity were false. Precisely what advantage that turn of events could possibly have had for Moses was not explained by the conspirators. A particularly annoying feature was their perception of Moses desiring to be a "prince" over them, evidently a sarcastic reference to his former status as prince of Egypt.[55] The rebels assured Moses that they had discerned his scheme, and he should not think that he could "blind their eyes," i.e., deceive (*NEB* "hoodwink") them. They were thus adamant in their refusal to approach him. Their address is voiced in chiastic structure.[56]

Translation

Then Moses became very angry and said to the LORD: Take no notice of their offerings. I have not taken so much as a donkey from them, nor have I done wrong to any of them. So Moses said to Korah: You and all your associates present yourselves before the LORD, you and they, along with Aaron.

Each of you take his censer and put incense in it, a total of 250 censers, and each shall present it before the LORD. You and Aaron shall each bring a censer. So everyone took his censer, placed fire in it, sprinkled incense upon it, and stood at the entrance to the Tent of Meeting, with Moses and Aaron. (16:15-18)

---

54. The term *dĕbaš* can also mean "syrup of dates" (KB, 1, p. 203), thus not necessarily referring predominantly to wild honey (so J. A. Patch, *ISBE*, 2:749-50).
55. Jealousy leading to insubordination seems to have motivated the rebels. Although all the covenanted Israelite males were technically priests, Moses was the divinely appointed civil leader of the community and thus deserved obedience and cooperation.
56. G. J. Wenham, *Numbers*, p. 136 n. 1.

Exegesis and Exposition

The insubordination of the rebels was intolerable, and Moses turned in anger to God, asking Him to ignore their offerings. If Moses was indeed behaving like a prince, as the insurgents were alleging, he wished it to be known for the record that he had not taken any of their property nor harmed them at all, unlike the princes of secular kingdoms who wielded the power of life and death over their subjects. At a later period the dictates of an autocrat were to be described in similar, though expanded, terms by Samuel in his account of the functions of a secular king (1 Sam. 8:11-17) as contrasted with his own life-style (12:3).

Having justified himself before God and the witnesses, Moses then gave final instructions for the next day's test, as indicated in v. 5. We see here a typical example of a proposition being introduced in summary form, only to be expanded later in the narrative. At the trial the censers were prepared as specified, and the 250 participants assembled on the east side of the Tabernacle at the entrance, confronting Moses and Aaron.

Translation

When Korah had assembled the entire community to oppose them at the entrance to the Tent of Meeting, the glory of the LORD appeared to the whole assembly. The LORD spoke to Moses and Aaron, saying: Stand clear of this assembly, that I may annihilate them instantly. (16:19-21)

Exegesis and Exposition

When the scene was fully set for the judgment of God to be issued on the matters of contention, the Lord appeared in glory (cf. Num. 14:10). But instead of vindication, the rebels were promised destruction, and Moses and Aaron were warned to distance themselves from the insurgents lest they, too, be engulfed by the disaster.

Translation

Then they prostrated themselves and cried out: O God, God of the spirits of humanity, will You be angry with the entire assembly when only one man has sinned? So the LORD spoke to Moses, saying, Address the community, and tell them to move away from the tents of Korah, Dathan, and Abiram. (16:22-24)

Exegesis and Exposition

The two leaders of Israel had the well-being of their people at heart, disobedient and rebellious though they were. In their intercession they adopted the posture of abject humility before a sovereign and pleaded that it was better for one man, i.e., Korah, to suffer death instead of the entire community of Israel incurring divine wrath. In the age of the New Covenant a Jewish high priest was to make the same claim in regarding the life of Jesus as expendable, compared to that of the whole nation (John 11:50). In evident assent God ordered Moses and Aaron to send the rest of the community some distance away from the tents of the ringleaders.

Translation

Then Moses stood up and went to Dathan and Abiram, the leaders of the Israelites following him. Then he spoke to the assembly, saying: Move away immediately from the tents of these wicked men. Do not touch any of their belongings, in case you are destroyed because of their sins. (16:25-26)

Exegesis and Exposition

Since Dathan and Abiram would not come to him when summoned, Moses approached them, in the company of Israel's leaders, while the community looked on. He signaled the fate of the rebels by warning members of the community to leave the area of their tents, and not to steal their belongings, lest they become involved in the destruction. It appears that God's communications to Moses were not heard by anyone else, hence the necessity for him to relay the information to the community.

Translation

So they moved from the vicinity of the tents of Korah, Dathan, and Abiram. Then Dathan and Abiram came out and stood at the entrance to their tents, along with their wives, sons, and young children. Then Moses said: This is how you will realize that the Lord has sent me to do all these things and that they are not of my own devising. If these men die a natural death like anyone else, if they experience the fate that is common to all, then the Lord has not sent me. But if the Lord does something entirely new, and the earth opens its mouth and swallows them and all their possessions, and they descend alive into the grave, then you will know that these men have scorned the Lord. (16:27-30)

Exegesis and Exposition

As the crowd moved hurriedly away, the offenders stood defiantly at their tent openings with their families, observing the situation. As with the general principles of trial by ordeal, if the rebels survived the test to die naturally, it would be an indication that Moses had not been commissioned by God as the nation's leader. But Moses envisaged a new and terrifying phenomenon, namely an earth movement producing a large fissure (MT וּפָצְתָה הָאֲדָמָה אֶת־פִּיהָ, *ûpāṣĕtâ hā 'ădāmâ 'et-pîhā*, "the ground opened her mouth"), which would bury them alive.

2. PUNISHMENT OF REBELS (16:31-43)

Translation

Then it happened that, as he finished speaking all these words, the ground split apart under them. The earth opened its mouth and devoured them along with their dwellings: all of Korah's people along with their possessions. So they and their accomplices descended alive into the grave. The earth closed over them, and they disappeared from the assembly. (16:31-33)

Exegesis and Exposition

The tension must have been overwhelming when the earth shook and split open beneath the rebels. Verse 32 emphasizes the scope of the calamity from the standpoint of an eyewitness, describing the demise of Korah and his confederates. Their descent alive into the grave (MT שְׁאוֹל, *šĕ'ôl*), and immediate entombment, was a fate that the Israelites had never witnessed before. The family of Korah is not mentioned as standing with him at the tent door, and it appears from the reference to his sons in Num. 26:11 that they survived the incident by dissociating themselves from him.

In an attempt to understand the purely physical mechanics of the engulfing of the confederates, Hort suggests that the camp was pitched on a *kewir*. This is an area of land with a fairly solid crust overlying marsh-like terrain and occurs in an area stretching from the Arabah to the Red Sea.[57] Although such an area might well have been a physical concomitant of the miraculous incident, it would in no way detract from the supernatural cause of death but would even enhance it, since this was specifically an act of divine judgment and not merely a seismic phenomenon.

"Sheol," or "the grave," was known to the Mesopotamians as the "netherworld," which for them was located just below ground level. In Hebrew thought it was the repository of both good and bad at death (cf. Gen. 37:35 with Num. 16:30). There has been much theological debate about the nature of the Sheol experience and the afterlife, as regards both salvation and punishment. There is no teaching about the immortality of human beings in the Torah (Pentateuch), a consideration that was important for Sadducean theology.

---

57. G. Hort, "The Death of Qorah," *AusBR* 2 (1959): 26.

Nevertheless, if the deceased was considered to be in the presence of the living God to some extent, he or she could be expected to experience some form of afterlife. In the present passage it is probably best to understand Sheol as equivalent to "the grave," without imposing upon the concept ideas that were apparently not current at the time in Israel.[58]

Translation

At their cries all the Israelites who were nearby fled, screaming: The earth is going to swallow us up also. Fire also came out from the LORD and burned up the 250 men who were offering incense. Then the LORD spoke to Moses, saying: Tell Eleazar son of Aaron the priest to retrieve the censers from the blaze, for they are holy, and to scatter the burning coals at a distance, for the censers are holy. Let the censers of these men who sinned at the cost of their lives be made into hammered sheets as a cover for the altar. Because they presented them before the LORD they are holy, and they shall serve as a sign to the Israelites. (16:34-38)

Exegesis and Exposition

Sensing their own imminent destruction, the Israelites near to them ran away, screaming in terror. At the same time fire flared out from the Lord and killed the remaining 250 rebels while they were still holding their burning censers. The mode of death was evidently like that of Nadab and Abihu,[59] but here, as also on that occasion, precisely how the fire caused their deaths is unknown or whether the term "fire" (MT אֵשׁ, *'ēš*) was a synonym for a lightning flash. It may well have been the same as that which consumed the burnt offering, which also alarmed the onlookers (Lev. 9:24).

The catastrophe presented a problem in the matter of retrieving the censers, which were ceremonially holy. To preserve the integrity of the fire and to prevent its unauthorized use, Eleazar son of Aaron was instructed to scatter it, presumably within the Tabernacle enclosure, while the bronze censers were to be collected and hammered out into sheets for covering the altar of sacrifice. This protected cover-

---

58. There is a large body of literature on this subject. See T. H. Gaster, *IDB*, 1:787-88; H. Buis, *ZPEB*, 5:395; A. C. Myers, *ISBE*, 1:898-901; G. Gerleman, *THAT*, 2:837-41; N. J. Tromp, *Primitive Conceptions of Death and the Nether World in the Old Testament* (BibOr 21; Rome: Pontifical Biblical Institute, 1969), pp. 21-23 et passim; R. L. Harris, *TWOT*, 2:892-93 and bibliographies. See also R. L. Harris in *The NIV: The Making of a Contemporary Translation*, pp. 58-71.
59. Cf. J. C. H. Laughlin, "The 'Strange Fire' of Nadab and Abihu," *JBL* 95 (1976): 559-65.

ing, however used, would serve as a memorial to the slain, and, even more important as a reminder to the community of the penalties for disobedience and apostasy. In this respect it exercised a function somewhat similar to that of the tassels (Num. 15:38-41).

Translation

So Eleazar the priest took the bronze censers presented by those who had been burned up, and they were hammered out as a covering for the altar, as the LORD had instructed him through Moses, to constitute a reminder to the Israelites that no outsider except a descendant of Aaron should come to burn incense before the LORD, that he might not become like Korah and his companions. (16:39-40)

Exegesis and Exposition

By stark contrast with the rebellious Israelites, Eleazar obeyed implicitly the Lord's command through Moses and had the bronze cover made. It may perhaps have served as a reinforcement or replacement for the original bronze cover (Ex. 38:2) made by Bezalel, and in any case it may have been intended to preserve the acacia-wood structure of the altar. To safeguard the future holiness of the sanctuary, a regulation was promulgated that prohibited anyone other than a priest in good standing from offering incense in the Lord's presence.

Translation

On the next day the entire Israelite community complained about Moses and Aaron, saying: Now you have killed the LORD's people. It so happened that when the community had assembled to oppose Moses and Aaron and had turned toward the Tent of Meeting, suddenly the cloud covered it, and the LORD's glory appeared. Then Moses and Aaron came in front of the Tent of Meeting, (16:41-43)

Exegesis and Exposition

Moses and Aaron had not yet recovered from the trauma of the rebels' sudden death when they were assailed again by the whole nation, which wished to project its guilt upon the two Israelite leaders. Israel's complaint was that Moses and Aaron had caused the deaths of some of the covenant people. The fact that the deceased had been ringleaders of a rebellion was overlooked in the Israelites' indignation. The Israelite community had assembled not to confess its sins and seek atonement but to scold and rebel further, indicating that the community had derived few if any spiritual insights from the tragedy. But in the midst of the people's activities as agitators the cloudy

240

pillar covered the Tabernacle, as the Lord of Sinai descended in further judgment.

3. AARON ATONES FOR ISRAEL (16:44-50)

and the LORD said to Moses: Get away from this gathering so that I can blot them out at once. At this they fell prostrate. Moses then said to Aaron: Take a censer and put fire in it from the altar, sprinkle incense upon it, and take it quickly to the assembly to make atonement for them. The LORD's anger has flared out, and the plague has begun. So Aaron followed the instructions of Moses and ran into the middle of the assembly. The plague had already begun in the community, so he offered the incense and made atonement for them. Aaron stood between the dead and living, and the plague stopped. (16:44-48)

Exegesis and Exposition

Once again God stated that He would destroy His entire community, a threat that caused Moses and Aaron once more to fall facedown in submission. A plague had already begun in the encampment, and emergency action was clearly needed. Fortunately Moses was equal to the situation, and apparently without prayer or consultation with God he instructed Aaron to make atonement for the sins of the people while there was still time. Even though God's power would undoubtedly have wiped out the covenant community had it remained unrestrained, He was obedient to His own regulations in honoring the act of priestly atonement for the Israelites.

Translation

Those who died in the plague were 14,700 in addition to those who had perished in the Korah incident. Then Aaron returned to Moses at the entrance to the Tent of Meeting, for the plague had ended. (16:49-50)

Exegesis and Exposition

As is to be expected in the records of the *šōṭĕrîm*, the statistical information about the casualty rate is included in a summary of the event. Once Aaron was satisfied that the plague had terminated, he returned to Moses at the Tabernacle entrance. Whether the plague was of the same variety as that recorded in Num. 14:37 is impossible to say.

Additional Notes

16:1 וַיִּקַּח does not have an explicit object, but the present translation understands "followers" as being implied. For emendations see

P. J. Budd, *Numbers*, p. 180. A favored reading, וַיָּקָם, involves consonantal changes. Cf. T. J. Meek, "Some Emendations in the Old Testament," *JBL* 48 (1929): 167-68.

וְאוֹן בֶּן־פֶּלֶת: Because of the obscurity of this person, some scholars have supposed that the term resulted from dittography. It is difficult, however, to see how ואון could be a dittography of יאב, as Graf proposed (L. Elliott Binns, *Numbers* [London: Methuen, 1927], p. 109). The LXX has φάλεθ, "Phaleth," which some commentators think should be read as "Pallu," as in Num. 26:8 (פַלּוּא). The foregoing suggestions are inadequate as reasons for removing from the MT a pedigreed Reubenite, however obscure.

16:4 וַיִּפֹּל עַל: BHS suggests emending this to וַיִּפְּלוּ, so that with פָּנָיו the phrase would read: "And his face fell." Unfortunately a singular verb would be required for this purpose, and consonants would also be lost. The MT is in accordance with the phraseology of 16:22 and thus needs no alteration.

16:11 כִּי תַלּוֹנוּ עָלָיו: This noun clause introduced by כִּי expresses result. The *qere* reads תלינו, which was probably the original.

16:13 The MT הִשְׂתָּרֵר . . . תִשְׂתָּרֵר uses the reflexive infinitive of the verb שָׂרַר, "to govern," "make oneself ruler," "play the king." This is the only occurrence of the reflexive of שָׂרַר in the MT.

16:14 אַף לֹא: אַף here has the sense of "in addition," followed by a word or a clause, and is not very common in Hebrew prose.

16:15 לֹא חֲמוֹר: In a later period Samuel was to make exactly the same claim (1 Sam. 12:3). The LXX reads ἐπιθύμημα, "desirable possessions," but this detracts from the emphasis of the MT.

16:30 וְאִם־בְּרִיאָה יִבְרָא: This feminine singular noun followed by a cognate verb construction seems to have been misunderstood by the LXX, which read ἐν φάσματι δείξει. The reading is peculiar, if only because cognate relationships were familiar linguistic constructions in Greek. An apparition or a portent is very different from an entirely new created thing.

וּבָלְעָה אֹתָם: After this phrase the LXX inserts a few words from v. 32, probably due to a copying error, since in v. 32 the LXX omits אֶת־פִּיהָ.

16:37 (MT 17:2) וְאֶת־הָאֵשׁ: The accusative particle here carries a determinative force that makes the apparent object the actual subject of the clause. See R. J. Williams, *Hebrew Syntax*, p. 15, sect. 59.

16:40 (MT 17:5) לְמַעַן אֲשֶׁר לֹא־יִקְרַב: לְמַעַן is often followed by אֲשֶׁר to indicate purpose. Here the noun clause appears in the negative, which is rare.

16:44 (MT 17:9) אֶל־מֹשֶׁה: Here the LXX adds καὶ Ἀαρών, as well as in 17:8 (MT 17:23) and 17:11 (MT 17:26).

16:49 (MT 17:14) הַמֵּתִים: From the records of males registered in

Num. 1:46 (603,550), the numbers killed here (14,700) constituted less than 3 percent of the fighting force.

E. A SIGN FOR THE REBELS (17:1-13)

This short chap. 17 does not match the MT verse for verse. The reason is that the MT 17:1-15 is the same as the English 16:36-50, with the result that the MT 17:16-28 corresponds to the English 17:1-13. The English numbering follows that of the LXX. The chapter divides into two connected units: (1) Aaron's rod alone buds (vv. 1-9); (2) Aaron's rod preserved as a memorial (vv. 10-13). Both sections commence with the annunciatory formula "The Lord spoke/said to Moses."

1. AARON'S ROD ALONE BUDS (17:1-9)

Translation

The LORD spoke to Moses, saying: Address the Israelites and obtain from them a rod from each tribe, one from every tribal leader, making twelve in all, and write each person's name on his rod. On the rod of Levi you shall write Aaron's name, for there must be one staff for the head of every tribe. Then place them in the Tent of Meeting before the Ark of the Testimony, where I will meet you. The rod belonging to the man of my choice will blossom. In this way I will rid myself of the Israelites' grumbling and their continual complaining. (17:1-5)

Exegesis and Exposition

God was becoming impatient with the Israelites' continual whining, bickering, and complaining. Yet another test was planned to establish Aaron's position as high priest authoritatively and finally. An object lesson, the results of which would be evident to all, contained an element of drama. Twelve rods, each inscribed with a tribe's name, with the Levites' rod bearing Aaron's name, were to be sequestered overnight before the Ark of God. The rod that blossomed would carry the name of God's choice as spiritual leader of the people. This particular trial followed hard on the heels of the one described in the preceding chapter in the expectation that the identity of Israel's high priest would be established once and for all.

Translation

So Moses issued directions to the Israelites, and their leaders gave him twelve rods, one for the leader of each of their tribes, and Aaron's rod was included. Then Moses placed the rods in the LORD's

presence in the Tent of Meeting. **The next day Moses entered the Tent of Meeting and discovered that the rod of Aaron of the house of Levi had sprouted, put out buds, produced blossoms, and borne ripe almonds. Then Moses brought out all the rods from the LORD's presence to all the Israelites. They examined them, and each man selected his own rod.** (17:6-9)

Exegesis and Exposition

For once the Israelites obeyed their leader, but perhaps with some misgivings as the events of the following day were awaited. It seems probable that the choice of wooden rods was a random affair. The MT מַטֶּה (*maṭṭeh*) can mean a "branch," "stalk," "staff," or "scepter," as well as "tribe." God's promise that one rod would sprout had already been fulfilled in the few hours before Moses approached the Ark. The rod of Levi—i.e., Aaron's rod—bore buds, flowers, and almond nuts, doubtless to the astonishment of all present. As with some of the miracles of Jesus, such as the changing of water into wine (John 2:1-10), what is involved is a foreshortening of the temporal sequences required to produce the result. Just as water gradually becomes wine through the normal processes of grape growth and harvesting, so the almond rod became a fruitful branch of the kind that would have been normal under ordinary conditions of development.

Why the Levites chose an almond branch is uncertain; it may have constituted an unofficial tribal emblem. The almond is one of the earliest trees to blossom after the winter, and its beautiful clusters of white flowers, which precede the growth of the leaves, is a welcome harbinger of spring. It blooms in Palestine about the beginning of February, and there as elsewhere it brings joy in the promise of new life. The almond's early appearance gave it the name of "watcher," "the awake one" (MT שָׁקֵד, *shāqēd*, from the verb שָׁקַד, *shāqad*, "to watch," "be awake"). In a play on words, the prophet Jeremiah related the rod of an "almond" tree to the idea of God "watching" over His word to fulfill it (Jer. 1:11-12). The almond's flower was so striking and luxurious that it was suited admirably for the patterns of the elegant bowls that graced the golden lampstand of the Tabernacle (Ex. 25:33; Num. 8:4).

2. AARON'S ROD PRESERVED AS A MEMORIAL (17:10-13)

Translation

The LORD said to Moses: Bring Aaron's rod back before the Ark of the testimony, to be preserved as a warning to the rebellious, that you may finally quell their complaints, lest they die. This is what Moses did. He acted precisely as the LORD had directed him. (17:10-11)

Exegesis and Exposition

Moses was instructed to bring the fruiting rod back to the Ark as a warning (MT אוֹת, 'ôt) for the guidance of future generations, rebellious or not. This is the second instance (the manna being the first) of an object provoked by an attitude of disobedience being employed after a miracle to serve as a reminder to the nation. God had now made clear His choice for the office of high priest, and as a consequence Aaron was vindicated in public. Further fomenting of trouble or rebellion in Israel would meet with swift retribution. This short chapter has all the marks of an eyewitness who saw and heard what had transpired and recorded the incident with such fidelity that it became a permanent part of Hebrew tradition, being referred to in NT times (Heb. 9:4). Moses' obedience to the Lord's commands stands in stark contrast to the repudiation of God's commands by the Israelites, who only a short time earlier had been pledging cooperation in the covenant relationship and obedience to God's will (Ex. 24:7).

Translation

The Israelites spoke to Moses and said: We are bound to die. We are finished, all of us. Anybody who even comes close to the Tent of the LORD will die. Shall we perish, one and all? (17:12-13)

Exegesis and Exposition

The Israelites had obviously been badly frightened by the events of the past few days, because they had witnessed the awesome power of God being turned, not against their national enemies as had been the case with the Egyptians at the time of the Exodus, but against themselves, chosen by God though they were. They were now in mortal fear of approaching the Tabernacle on pain of death, and this would probably be sufficient for a while to forestall further rebellion.

Additional Notes

17:4 (MT 17:19) לָכֶם: The Samaritan Pentateuch, some MT MSS, and two versions read the singular here.

17:13 (MT 17:28) הַקָּרֵב: The repetition of this word is most probably accidental dittography and may be omitted along with the LXX, Vulgate, and Syriac.

F. REGULATIONS FOR THE PRIESTS (18:1-32)

Chapter 18 and its successor have been inserted into the chronological sequence so as to make clear how the duties of the Tabernacle's ministers followed logically upon the selection of Aaron to fulfill the most exalted spiritual office in the nation. The chapter can be analyzed in terms of four units: (1) responsibilities of priests and Levites (vv. 1-7); (2) the priests' sacrificial portion (vv. 8-19); (3) responsibilities of Levites (vv. 20-24); (4) Moses' instructions to the Levites (vv. 25-32).

As with the preceding chapter, each of the sections commences with an annunciatory formula. The nature of their contents in the light of what transpired in chap. 17 reflects contemporaneity and presents a picture of conscious theological integration.

Now more than ever the Israelites had to acknowledge their high priest as God's chosen servant and recognize the responsibilities for ministry that he bore. They also had to understand that no further interference with his office would be tolerated by God. Finally they had to acknowledge that, while they were all technically priests in a holy nation (Ex. 19:6), the cultic structure demanded a priestly hierarchy so that life and worship might proceed under God with decency and order.

In the new dispensation, Paul laid down the roles that Spirit-filled Christians could exercise (Eph. 4:11-12), but at the same time he appointed elders (πρεσβύτεροι, _presbyteroi_), overseers (ἐπίσκοποι, _episkopoi_), and deacons (διάκονοι, _diakonoi_) to direct the worship of local congregations and to minister to Christ's Body, the church, on a wider basis as the need arose. In the new kingdom of priests (1 Pet. 2:5), such a hierarchy parallels that of the OT priests and Levites. Those elected to an office in the hierarchy are not necessarily superior spiritually or otherwise to the remainder of the fellowship, but by virtue of their office they are representative of it.

1. RESPONSIBILITIES OF PRIESTS AND LEVITES (18:1-7)

Translation

The LORD said to Aaron: You, your sons, and your tribe shall be responsible for the sanctuary. You and your sons shall together be answerable for any violation of your priestly functions. Bring with you your fellows from the tribe of Levi, your father's tribe, to be associated with you and serve you while you and your sons are ministering before the Tent of Meeting. They shall fulfill your needs and those of the Tent of Meeting, but they shall not approach the furnishings of the sanctuary and the altar, lest they die together with you. They shall be associated with you and attend to the requirements of the Tent of Meeting in every respect. No unauthorized person shall come near you. You shall attend to the duties of the sanctuary and the altar, so that anger may never again fall upon the Israelites. (18:1-5)

246

Exegesis and Exposition

It might appear strange at first sight to find God addressing Aaron personally, but God was in fact dealing with His high priest and, having vindicated him in his office publicly, was now formally commissioning him, the priests, and the Levites, and instructing them in the responsibilities and restrictions of their offices.

Responsibility for the sanctuary involved obligations relating to its violation. This is made clear so as to forestall any further approach to the Tabernacle by unauthorized individuals. The priests were under obligation to abide strictly by the ceremonial regulations or else suffer the fate of Nadab and Abihu. Any thought of deviation from, or innovative addition to, the prescribed rituals was prohibited. The Levites were also requested to take up their duties as prescribed. They were always subsidiary to the priests in status and were subject to continual supervision by them.

This section is the most comprehensive statement of legislation regarding the Levites in the entire Pentateuch, and it is one outstanding merit of the book of Numbers that it has been preserved in this manner. The Levites constituted that distinctive portion of the tribe of Levi that had been separated to God and given as His gift to Aaron and his descendants (Num. 3:9; 8:19), who were themselves set apart for the priestly office. A very important function the Levites exercised was that of acting as a protective shield for the covenant community so that, when they were discharging their duties as prescribed, they would be protecting the members of the various tribes from an outbreak of divine anger.[60]

Translation

See! I myself have taken your brother Levites from all the Israelites as a gift for you, provided by the LORD to perform the duties of the Tent of Meeting. But only you and your sons may perform priestly duties involving everything at the altar and inside the veil. That must be your duty. I bestow your priesthood service upon you as a gift. Any unauthorized person who infringes upon it shall be executed. (18:6-7)

Exegesis and Exposition

The separation of the Levites is emphasized again in this section. This is an important statement to the nation as a whole, since the

---

60. The notion of the Levites acting as "spiritual lightning conductors" (cf. J. Milgrom, *Studies in Levitical Terminology*, p. 31; G. J. Wenham, *Numbers*, p. 143) is incorrect. Their duties were meant to prevent divine wrath from striking, not to absorb and disperse its force. They were in fact insulators, who protected the Israelites from the force of God's wrath.

Levites, like the priests, acted as representatives of the people in their relationship with God. The separation of both groups symbolized the holiness and purity that God demanded of His covenant nation.[61]

2. THE PRIESTS' SACRIFICIAL PORTION (18:8-19)

Translation

The Lord then said to Aaron: See! I myself have made you responsible for my raised offerings. All these holy gifts from the Israelites I allot to you and your sons as your perquisite for all future generations. This part of the most holy offerings retained from the fire is to be yours. Every offering of theirs, whether cereal, sin, or guilt offerings that they bring to Me as a most holy gift, shall belong to you and your sons. You shall eat it as something particularly holy. Every male shall eat it. It must be treated as holy. (18:8-10)

Exegesis and Exposition

The priests were to derive their support from sacrificial offerings of various kinds. The cereal offering (Lev. 2:1-16), the sin offering (4:1–5:13), and the guilt offering (5:14-19) belonged to the priests, apart from a small portion that was offered to God on the altar. As such they were regarded as especially holy and were restricted to the officiating priest and his family. This enactment restated the provisions already made in Leviticus.

Translation

The raised offering that they present along with all the Israelite waved offerings shall also belong to you. I have given them to you and your offspring living with you as a perpetual ordinance. Everyone who is ritually pure in your household may partake of it. I have also given to you all the best of the oil, the new wine, and the grain that they have presented to the Lord as firstfruits. Whatever first ripe fruit of the land they present to the Lord shall become yours. Everyone in your household who is ritually pure may partake of it. (18:11-13)

Exegesis and Exposition

In addition, the raised (KJV "heave") offering and the waved offering[62] were deemed priestly perquisites as a perpetual ordinance. These offerings were not restricted to the priests, however, but could be eaten by ceremonially clean members of their households. Choice portions of the firstfruits offered by the Israelites were also the lawful

---

61. Cf. C. L. Feinberg, *ZPEB*, 4:854.
62. See on Num. 15:19-21.

property of the priests and their families. Because of the important position of the priests in the community as ministers of God's revelation, the people were made responsible for attending to their material needs.

Translation

Everything in Israel that has been devoted to the Lord shall be yours. The firstborn of every womb, whether human or animal, that is brought to the Lord shall be yours. You must, however, redeem the firstborn human beings, as well as every firstborn male of unclean animals. When they are one month old, you shall redeem them at the established price of five shekels of silver by the standard of the sanctuary shekel, which weighs twenty gerahs. But the firstborn of a cow, sheep, or goat shall not be redeemed, for they are holy. Sprinkle their blood on the altar and burn their fat as an offering made by fire for a pleasing aroma to the Lord. Their flesh shall be yours, just as with the raised breast and the right hip. (18:14-18)

Exegesis and Exposition

Provision is made in this passage for those things obtained as a result of the "ban" (MT חֵרֶם, *ḥērem*). In Lev. 27:28 the word appears in connection with an individual's freely dedicating something from his property to God's service. As such it was regarded as the Lord's exclusive possession and therefore could not be disposed of or redeemed in any way.[63] Persons were also sometimes put under the ban, as is evident from the time of the occupation of Canaan.[64] In those instances where people were involved, the ban carried with it the sense of utter destruction of persons or things that were accursed before God (Num. 21:2-3).

The rationale for exterminating entire cities in the period when Canaan was being occupied was that they were running rampant with Canaanite idolatry, which could contaminate the chosen people, as it did ultimately. Individuals who were placed under the ban for whatever reason were in effect being sentenced to death (Lev. 27:28-29).[65]

The firstborn of humans or animals belonged to the Lord, but whereas humans and unclean animals had to be redeemed (MT פָּדָה, *pādâ*), the clean animals, being ceremonially holy, served as food for the priests and their families, the portions being regulated according

---

63. R. K. Harrison, *Leviticus*, p. 237.
64. Cf. Josh. 6:17; 7:1, etc.; 1 Sam. 15:3.
65. See C. Brekelmans, *THAT*, 1:635-39; L. J. Wood, *TWOT*, 2:325 and bibliographies.

to the procedures of Lev. 7:29–34. The idea of redemption was that of transferring the ownership to another by paying a price of some kind. It appears to have originated in commercial circles in Mesopotamia, but in the OT it is used exclusively of redeeming persons or other living things. The verb is only used once in the MT, however, to describe redemption from sin (Ps. 130:7-8).[66]

The term derived its theological significance from God's powerful act in delivering His people from the Egyptians and reached its fullness in the New Covenant when God redeemed the world from sin by the substitutionary atonement of Jesus as the Lamb without blemish. In the above passage, the cost of redeeming firstborn children and animals was set at five silver shekels (cf. Lev. 27:6), estimated to weigh about two ounces. This amount was about five months' pay for the average laborer in biblical times.[67]

Translation

All the raised offerings from consecrated gifts that the Israelites offer to the LORD I am giving to you, your sons, and your daughters, as a perpetual ordinance. It is an everlasting covenant of salt in the presence of the LORD with you and your descendants. (18:19)

Exegesis and Exposition

The ordinance that allowed the priests to claim the raised offerings presented to the Lord by the Israelites was described as a permanent "covenant of salt" (MT בְּרִית מֶלַח, *bĕrît melaḥ*). The concept probably owed its origin to the nature of salt, which, in preserving food from decay, symbolized permanence.[68] This regulation furnished security for Aaron while he lived and also for the priesthood when occupation of Canaan was a reality. The OT does not give any indication of a special ritual attaching to such a covenant, unless the salt formed an ingredient of a covenantal meal or was otherwise received as a gift. The idea that sharing salt implied the formation of a bond between the two parties is found as late as Ezra 4:14, where the MT reads דִּי־מְלַח הֵיכְלָא מְלַחְנָא (*dî-mĕlaḥ hêkĕlā' mĕlaḥnā'*, "we have been salted with the salt of the palace"). Those who had been maintained by the royal palace felt under obligation to be loyal to the provider and to report to the Persian king what they considered to be treasonable activities being carried on by the returned Jews in Jeru-

---

66. R. C. Dentan, *IDB*, 4:21-22; J. J. Stamm, *THAT*, 2:389-405; W. B. Coker, *TWOT*, 2:716-17.
67. G. J. Wenham, *Leviticus*, p. 338.
68. J. H. Hertz, ed., *The Pentateuch and Haftorahs*, p. 647.

salem. But even this allusion does not indicate the presence of a
formal bond between the complainants and Artaxerxes; it merely
suggests that salt was one of the ingredients of diet with which they
had been supplied through the king's bounty (cf. Ezra 6:9).

3. RESPONSIBILITIES OF LEVITES (18:20-24)

Translation

Then the LORD said to Aaron: You will have no inheritance in the
land, nor any holding among them. I am your share and your inheritance among the Israelites. See, I have given to the Levites all the
tithes in Israel as their inheritance, as recompense for the work that
they perform—namely, the duties of the Tent of Meeting. From now
on the Israelites must not approach the Tent of Meeting, lest they
suffer the consequences of sin and die. But the Levites shall perform
the duties of the Tent of Meeting and be responsible for transgressions against it. This shall be a lasting ordinance for all future generations—namely, that they shall have no inheritance among the Israelites. I have given to the Levites as their inheritance the tithes of the
Israelites that are presented to the LORD as a raised offering. This is
why I have said to them that they are to have no inheritance among
the Israelites. (18:20-24)

Exegesis and Exposition

This passage is important for the understanding it furnishes
about the constitution of the priests and Levites. Aaron and his offspring were forbidden to hold a territorial allotment when Canaan
was occupied, unlike all the other tribes. Although Aaron died before
the nation entered the land, the ordinance still applied to his descendants. The priests and Levites were to be freed as far as possible from
normal social responsibilities so that they could devote themselves
wholeheartedly to the service of God. Their trust was to be placed in
Him completely as far as subsistence was concerned, so that they
could say properly, in the words of a later psalmist, "The LORD is the
portion of my inheritance and my cup; You maintain my lot" (Ps.
16:5).

Nevertheless, proper material compensation was forthcoming
from the people for the Levites. Those who officiated at the altar were
to subsist upon their assigned portion of the offerings and consecrated gifts brought to the Tabernacle. The Levites were assigned a
tithe (MT מַעֲשֵׂר, *maʿăśēr*), the giving of which was already an ancient
tradition that Abram had honored (Gen. 14:20). Normally the giving
of a tenth part involved agricultural produce and animals rather than

money,[69] as has become the modern custom.[70] There is nothing essentially wrong with such a substitution, however, and it is of interest to note that the term "pecuniary" (pertaining to money) is derived from the Latin *pecus* ("cattle").

Once more the Israelites were warned against coming near the Tabernacle, which pointed out the importance of the Levites, who were commissioned to safeguard the nation's sanctuary. As Thompson has pointed out, the Israelites were under obligation to the Levites for assuming the risk entailed in approaching holy things[71] and being responsible for transgressions against it. The rationale of the prohibition against the priests' and Levites' owning property is made clear, most probably for the benefit of the Israelite community, so that they would understand the part they played in maintaining the service of the sanctuary. In the occupation of Canaan they had no territory assigned to them apart from forty-eight villages[72] but were dependent upon the Lord for their sustenance. In a similar manner the Christian has no permanent city on this earth but lives in the hope of possessing a heavenly country (cf. Heb. 11:16).

4. MOSES' INSTRUCTIONS TO THE LEVITES (18:25-32)

Translation

Then the LORD spoke to Moses, saying: Address the Levites in this manner and tell them: When you accept from the Israelites the tithes that I have given you from them as your heritage, you shall present to the LORD one-tenth of the tithe as a raised offering. Your raised offering shall be regarded as though it were grain from the threshing floor or juice from the winepress. In this way you will also offer to the LORD a raised offering from all your tithes received from the Israelites, and you shall donate the LORD's raised offering from it to Aaron the priest and his descendants. (18:25-28)

Exegesis and Exposition

An interesting provision required the Levites to pay tithes to the priests as the Lord's representatives, even though they themselves received the tithe given to the Lord. The tithe for the Levites was an entirely new feature, as was a tithe of the tithe. This offering to God

---

69. Cf. J. Milgrom, *Cult and Conscience*, pp. 55-62.
70. On the tithe see H. H. Guthrie, *IDB*, 4:654-55; C. L. Feinberg, *ZPEB*, 5:756-58; R. B. Allen, *TWOT*, 2:704 and bibliographies.
71. J. A. Thompson, *The New Bible Commentary Revised*, p. 187.
72. These were distributed throughout the tribal territories (Num. 35:2-8; Josh. 21:8-41).

was to be of the best portion of the tithe given by the people and was to be regarded as though it had come from the threshing floor or the winepress—that is, as though they had produced it themselves as farmers. Once the offering had been made to Aaron, the Levites were free to enjoy the remainder.

Translation

From all the gifts you receive you must offer every raised offering due to the LORD from the best and holiest part. Thus you shall say to the Levites: When you offer the choicest part, it will be regarded as the product of the threshing floor and the winepress. You and your households may eat it anywhere, because it represents wages for your work in the Tent of Meeting, and you shall not incur any guilt when you present the choicest part of it. You will not be profaning the sacred gifts of the Israelites, and you will not die. (18:29-32)

Exegesis and Exposition

God's demands in worship are scrupulous and exacting. Only flawless animals were to be brought for sacrifice, and the best quality grains were to be provided for the cereal offerings. Failure to meet these high specifications would result in punishment (cf. Mal. 1:6-8, 12-14; 2:1-4). Here the Levites were required to donate the choicest and holiest parts (MT מִכָּל–חֶלְבּוֹ אֶת–מִקְדְּשׁוֹ, *mikkol-ḥelbô 'et-miqdĕšô*), which would then become the perquisite of the priests. Again the offerings were to be regarded as though they were the actual produce of the Levites. Once the prescribed tithe had been paid to the priests, the remainder was available to the Levites and their families to be eaten without restriction as to locale.

The reward given to the Levites in recognition of their important service to the Tabernacle was the privilege of being able to eat a portion of the sacrifices that belonged to the priests. The nature of the Levites' functions exempted them from any form of sin or guilt as long as they were discharged in accordance with the Lord's stipulations. These regulations constituted the final specific rules for the Levites.

This bountiful provision for the Levites ensured their survival through the ensuing centuries and served as the basis for certain Pauline admonitions about the church's responsibility to its ministrants.[73] As long as the Israelites continued to adhere to the laws governing sacrifice, the priests and Levites were assured of a substantial livelihood.

---

73. 1 Cor. 9:4-10, 13-14; cf. Matt. 10:9-10.

Additional Notes

18:6 לָכֶם: Omitted by the LXX and Vulgate, but this does not improve on the MT.

18:7 The juxtaposition of clauses seems a little awkward here, but the cognate form וַעֲבַדְתֶּם עֲבֹדַת emphasizes the important character of the priestly ministry and should therefore not be regarded as dittography, as BHS suggests.

מַתָּנָה אֶתֵּן: The KJV translates literally, "I have given your priest's office *unto you* as a service of gift," but LXX reads δόμα τῆς ἱερατίας ὑμῶν, "a gift of your priesthood."

18:9 מִן־הָאֵשׁ: Whereas the MT understood fire offerings, the LXX read τῶν καρπωμάτων, which would appear to refer to vegetable offerings or presentations of grain.

18:14 כָּל־פֶּטֶר: With this and the foregoing list of priestly perquisites, God ensures an adequate livelihood for those ministering at the altar as long as the Israelites engage consistently in worship at the Tabernacle.

18:23 הַלֵּוִי: The singular form is used collectively for the Levites as a group. It is thus unnecessary to follow those versions that adopt the plural form.

18:29 מִכָּל־חֶלְבּוֹ: The MT reads more smoothly if the verb תָּרִימוּ is understood.

G. TWO RITUALS FOR UNCLEANNESS (19:1-22)

Chapter 19 consists of two principal components, both dealing with ceremonial purity and therefore of great importance as priestly enactments: (1) the red heifer ritual (vv. 1-10); (2) purification from uncleanness (vv. 11-22).

1. THE RED HEIFER RITUAL (19:1-10)

Translation

Now the LORD addressed Moses and Aaron, saying: This is a regulation of the law that the LORD has ordained. Instruct the Israelites to bring you a red heifer without blemish or defect, one that has never borne a yoke. You shall give it to Eleazar the priest, so that he can take it outside the encampment and slaughter it personally. Eleazar the priest shall take some of the blood on his finger and sprinkle it seven times toward the front of the Tent of Meeting. (19:1-4)

Exegesis and Exposition

An annunciation formula begins this chapter. The interests of the priests and Levites had been met in various ways, and now it was the proper time for procedures to be enacted that would cleanse the ordinary members of the community from uncleanness or ritual defilement. This was a precaution to ensure that the purity of the Tabernacle was not violated, however unintentionally, by the pollutions of impurity or death.

The legislation exhibits concerns similar to those of Lev. 12-15, where laws for purification are set out in detail. Since much of that material had been revealed jointly to Moses and Aaron, it is possible that the present chapter had its origin at about the same time but was inserted into Numbers at the present place by the šōṭĕrîm or Moses himself because of its connection with the duties of the priests and Levites and, more specifically, to meet the anxieties of the community about accidental defilement. The enactment is classified as a חֻקָּה (ḥuqqâ), a term used normally to describe a divine revelation that is perpetually binding.[74] Here the MT חֻקַּת-הַתּוֹרָה (ḥuqqat-hattôrâ, KJV "ordinance of the law") gives the enactment special emphasis.[75]

The Israelites were to bring a young, unblemished, reddish-brown cow, presumably resembling the color of blood, that had never worked under a yoke and could therefore be committed entirely to ·the Lord's service. It was thus as close to virginal purity as one could expect in an animal, and accordingly it met the standards demanded by God in this unusual ritual. It was the responsibility of Eleazar to oversee the slaughtering of the animal outside the encampment and to conduct the sprinkling of blood in front of the Tabernacle.

Translation

While he watches, the heifer shall be burned entirely—skin, flesh, blood, and offal. The priest shall take cedar wood, hyssop, and scarlet wool and shall throw them upon the fire that is burning the heifer. Then the priest shall wash his clothes and bathe himself with water. Then the priest may enter the encampment, but he shall be ritually unclean until evening. The one who burns the heifer shall also wash his clothes, bathe in water, and be ritually unclean until the evening. (19:5-8)

Exegesis and Exposition

Eleazar was also to see to it that the young cow was burned completely and then to add to the sacrificial flames cedar wood, hyssop, and scarlet wool. These latter items were also prominent in

---

74. As associated with Passover (Ex. 12:14), Unleavened Bread (12:17), Day of Atonement (Lev. 16:29, 31, 34), Tabernacles (23:41), etc. See G. Liedke, *THAT*, 1:621-32; J. P. Lewis, *TWOT*, 1:317-18 and bibliographies.
75. This rare phrase occurs elsewhere only in Num. 31:21.

the cleansing ritual for leprosy (Lev. 14:4). Here, as there, it is not easy to understand the reason for using cedar wood and red wool, unless their aroma was a consideration. Cedar (probably *Juniper lycia* L. or *J. phoenicia* L.)[76] was renowned for its durability because its oil content made it resistant to rotting, and thus it might have symbolized resistance to future defilement. It would thus constitute an early example of the concept of acquired immunity, some aspects of which are still a mystery.

The red wool has been understood generally as a symbol of blood, though why that interpretation should be thought either necessary or desirable is not clear when one considers the abundance of sacrificial blood that was present. It might possibly have served a practical purpose as a cloth container in which the hyssop had been placed.[77] This latter herb was used in certain biblical rituals and occurred in several varieties in ancient Canaan. There is some doubt about the precise identification of hyssop, however, because it may have been a designation of several labiate plants such as thyme (*Thymus capitatus* L.), sage (*Salvia triloba* L.), or marjoram (*Origanum maru* L.).[78] The fact that sour vinegar was offered to the crucified Christ by means of a bunch of hyssop (Gk. ὕσσωπος, *hyssōpos*, John 19:29)[79] attests to the ability of the plant to retain fluid in its foliage.

After the priest had washed his body and his clothes he was allowed to reenter the encampment, although he was considered ceremonially impure until the evening. The same procedure was also binding upon the person who burned the young cow, whoever he might be. The passage seems to envisage the presence of at least one assistant, with Eleazar acting as the supervisor of the ritual.

Translation

Then a man who is ritually clean shall gather up the heifer's ashes and deposit them in a ceremonially clean location outside the encampment. They shall be stored for the assembly of the Israelites for use in the water of ritual cleansing. The man who gathers up the heifer's ashes must also wash his clothes and be ritually impure until the evening. This will be a permanent enactment both for the Israelites and the alien who lives among them. (19:9-10)

---

76. MT אֶרֶז, Ugar. *arz*. For the identification of this tree see *MPB*, pp. 66-70.
77. See R. K. Harrison, *Leviticus*, p. 150.
78. On the identification of hyssop see R. K. Harrison, "The Biblical Problem of Hyssop," *EvQ* 26 (1954): 218-24; Harrison, *ISBE*, 2:790; *MPB*, pp. 160-62, 222-23; W. E. Shewell-Cooper, *ZPEB*, 3:235.
79. Some scholars have read ὑσσῷ, "javelin," instead of ὑσσώπῳ and translated "they put a sponge filled with vinegar upon a javelin."

Exegesis and Exposition

The ashes of the sacrifice were to be collected by a ritually clean person, probably an ordinary Israelite, and stored in a ceremonially clean location beyond the encampment for use in connection with a water potion intended for ritual purification from sin. As with other legal enactments that involved the sanctity of community life, the statute applied to native Israelite and resident alien alike.

There are several points of contact with Lev. 14:10-32; 15:13, 27, where a sacrifice occurs and the use of water is prescribed. Where the latter was deemed insufficiently potent to effect a thorough cleansing, however, additives were employed to reinforce its efficacy, as with blood (14:6) and dust from the Tabernacle (Num. 5:17). But nowhere else in the OT are ashes used in a cleansing ritual, although pagan examples have been recorded.[80] Again the ritual is distinctive in that, alone in the OT, sacrificial blood was burned in the ceremony, with only a token amount being sprinkled at the entrance to the Tabernacle.

The blood was evidently burned to enhance the purifying properties of the ashes when used ritually. The sacrifice was different from those prescribed in Leviticus in that it occurred not at the altar in the Tabernacle enclosure but at some distance from the camp on an altar about which the MT says nothing. The general procedure accords with what anthropologists, sociologists, and others call rites of aggregation for restoring alienated persons to community life[81] as practiced in some primitive cultures.

2. PURIFICATION FROM UNCLEANNESS (19:11-22)

Translation

Anyone who touches the corpse of any individual shall be unclean for seven days. On the third and seventh days he shall purify himself with water, and then he shall be clean. But if he does not purify himself on the third and seventh days, he will not be clean. Whoever touches the body of a deceased person and does not purify himself defiles the LORD's Tabernacle. Such a person shall be cut off from Israel. He shall be deemed ritually unclean because the water of purification was not sprinkled upon him. Thus his uncleanness remains upon him. (19:11-13)

---

80. Cf. B. S. Easton and R. K. Harrison, *ISBE*, 2:672-73.
81. Cf. E. R. Leach, *Culture and Communication* (Cambridge: Cambridge U., 1976), pp. 78-79.

Exegesis and Exposition

The relationship between the preparation of heifer ashes and the cleansing of impure persons now becomes clear. This section accordingly gives detailed directions for purification in specific instances. One of these contingencies was death, which rendered ceremonially unclean anybody who had direct contact with the corpse (Lev. 21:1-3). There is no evidence that this regulation applied to dead animals, since the carcasses of unclean beasts were recognized as sources of pollution in any case (11:8-40).

During the seven-day duration of the defilement, the individual involved was expected to wash with water on the third day and then be ceremonially clean after further ablutions at the end of the period. If the person failed to observe both days of ablution, he or she merely prolonged the period of defilement. Failure to observe this ritual by community members would defile the Tabernacle, and the offender would be executed for not making use of the purifying water (MT מֵי נִדָּה, *mê niddâ*, "water of removal").[82]

Translation

This is the regulation that applies when a person dies in a tent. All who enter the tent and those who are already in it shall be ritually unclean for seven days, and every open container that has no covering upon it is ritually unclean. Anyone in the countryside who touches a person killed with a sword, or who has died naturally, or who touches a human bone, or a grave, shall be ritually unclean for seven days. (19:14-16)

Exegesis and Exposition

Death was considered to be so defiling that a person dying in a tent brought uncleanness upon the occupants and any visitors for a seven-day period. Even containers that were not sealed by a secure (MT אֵין־צָמִיד פָּתִיל עָלָיו, *'ên-ṣāmîd pātîl 'ālāyw*, "no covering, [no] string on it") lid to keep possible infection at bay (cf. Lev. 11:32) were also unclean. The same uncleanness attached to casual contacts in the open countryside (MT פְּנֵי הַשָּׂדֶה, *pĕnê haśśādeh*) with dead people and their remains, whether buried or not. For this reason the Hebrews avoided known graves wherever possible, and by NT times it had become customary to paint them with whitewash as a warning to strangers or the unwary (cf. Matt. 23:27; Acts 23:3).

---

82. On this expression see T. E. McComiskey, *TWOT*, 2:556.

Translation

For a ritually impure person you must take some of the ashes of the heifer burned for purification from sin, place them in a jar, and pour running water over them. Then a ritually clean man must take some hyssop, dip it into the water, sprinkle it on the tent, on all its furnishings, on the persons who were present, or on the individual who touched a human bone, one who had been killed, a man who had died naturally, or a grave. The ritually pure person is to sprinkle the unclean on the third and seventh days, and on the seventh day he shall purify himself by washing his clothes and bathing in water. At evening he shall be deemed clean. (19:17-19)

Exegesis and Exposition

The regulations governing the death of a person in a tent are more stringent for those who have had direct contact with the deceased than for an individual who might have had casual contact with a corpse under different circumstances. The legislation evidently deals with situations where people nursed a dying family member or friend until death supervened. Under such conditions they would have been in close contact with the deceased person and thus potential carriers of infection. Ritual uncleanness in such situations lasted for a week, and then a program of cleansing was undertaken, using a potion consisting of some of the red heifer's ashes that had been placed in a container and mixed with running (MT חַיִּים, *ḥayyîm*, "living") water. The services of a ritually clean individual were then enlisted to sprinkle the defiled people and articles with the liquid, using a bunch of hyssop as an aspergillum. This ritual was enacted twice during the week, and at the conclusion the sprinkler was required to wash himself and his clothing before being regarded as ritually clean (MT טָהֵר, *ṭāhēr*).[83]

Translation

But the individual who is ritually impure and does not purify himself shall be cut off from the community, because he has defiled the LORD's sanctuary. Because the water of purification has not been sprinkled upon him, he is ritually unclean. This shall be a perpetual ordinance for them. The one who sprinkles the water of purification must wash his clothes, and anyone who touches the water of cleansing

---

83. For the use of this term see E. M. Yamauchi, *TWOT*, 1:343-45 and bibliography; J. Milgrom, "The Paradox of the Red Cow (Num 19)," *VT* 31 (1981): 62-72.

will be impure until evening. Anything that an impure person touches shall become unclean, and anyone who is in contact with it also becomes unclean until the evening. (19:20-22)

Exegesis and Exposition

There are obvious hygienic reasons that death should be so defiling, but equally important ceremonial ones also. Death is the penalty imposed upon humanity for disobeying God's commands, and thus every person's death testifies to rebellious human nature. In the ancient world death was normally viewed as a great calamity, to be attended by loud mourning for prolonged periods. Climatic conditions often made it necessary for the deceased to be buried as quickly as possible, unless embalming was practiced (as in Egypt).

The legislation in this passage reminds the reader that it is alien to God's nature to countenance sin (Hab. 1:13), and therefore those who ignore His provisions for sins of accidental defilement will suffer the death that is God's penalty for disobedience. So important was this enactment that its permanent nature was stressed, along with its basic ritual procedures, in a concluding summary.

In the ancient world, such ceremonies as the foregoing expressed fundamental truths about holiness and the removal of ritual impurity in societies that depended closely upon a correct relationship with their gods. Earlier scholars tended to see the ritual in terms of pagan mythology and fertility-cult worship,[84] but such views misunderstood the spiritual significance of the ritual, which was intended to remove accidental defilement of ritual uncleanness and had nothing in common with pagan death-and-resurrection myths.

Hosea's comparison of Israel with a red heifer (Hos. 4:16; 10:11) led the author of Hebrews to refer to the ritual of Num. 19 in terms of the atoning work of Christ, who typified the ideal Israel. Hebrews demonstrates the inadequacy of the OT sacrificial system by comparing it with the atonement of Christ, the great High Priest. Jesus did not have recourse to Tabernacle or Temple rituals when He died on the cross, nor did He resort to the blood of bulls and goats or a heifer's ashes for ceremonial purification (Heb. 9:11-13). In either dispensation the shedding of blood ensured forgiveness of ceremonial defilement for the penitent sinner. One important category of sin for which no provision was made in the ancient Hebrew sacrificial system was known as "sin with a high hand" (Num. 15:30). The lack of any ceremonial procedures to deal with such a situation may have occurred

---

84. Cf. W. R. Smith, *The Religion of the Semites* (London: A. & C. Black, 1889), pp. 140-338; G. B. Gray, *Numbers*, pp. 241-56.

because the very thought of apostasy was inconceivable at the time the Sinaitic covenantal legislation was promulgated.

This chapter, with its predecessor, closes an important segment of legislation dealing with the relationships of priests, Levites, and ordinary members of the Israelite community. Certain features that had been presented previously in a general context now become specific, and new rituals such as that of the red heifer are introduced. The chapters also represent the last body of law to be promulgated before the death of Aaron occurred. It would thus appear that all important rituals had now been dealt with, and for the future the law as now proclaimed was to be applied.

Additional Notes

19:2 חֻקַּת הַתּוֹרָה: Although somewhat unusual, the MT expression should not be emended to חֻקַּת הַפָּרָה, as suggested by BHS. The phrase occurs in 31:21, while לְחֻקַּת מִשְׁפָּט is found in 27:11; 35:29.

אֵלֶיךָ: The singular here has been thought to support the omission by some MSS of וְאֶל־אַהֲרֹן from v. 1.

19:3 וּנְתַתֶּם: The singular is read here by the LXX and Vulgate, perhaps reflecting the MS tradition from which the translations were made. Eleazar the priest was to officiate because the ritual was to take place beyond the sanctuary, thus excluding Aaron from the ceremony (Lev. 21:12).

לְפָנָיו: This word has presented problems of interpretation. The LXX gives a third person plural sense to וְשָׁחַט and reads καὶ σφάξουσιν αὐτὴν ἐνώπιον αὐτοῦ. This reading is followed by the Vulgate. The phrase is obviously an attempt to accommodate an apparent difficulty in the MT. The present translation has retained the singular verbs and has rendered לְפָנָיו by "personally."

19:14 בָּאֹהֶל: The LXX reads ἐν τῇ οἰκίᾳ here and ἐπὶ τὸν οἶκον in v. 18.

19:19 וְטָהֵר בָּעֶרֶב: The LXX and Vulgate prefer to follow the MT textual form of verses 7-8, 10, 21-22 and read "he shall be unclean until evening." The period of time "until evening" was the shortest possible interval for ritual impurity to last.

H. WATER DISCOVERED IN THE WILDERNESS (20:1-13)

Chapter 20, which for the purposes of this commentary will be divided into two major sections (vv. 1-13; vv. 14-29), introduces a summary of the wanderings from Kadesh-barnea to Transjordan. Each major section has two subsections, and as a result the chapter can be analyzed as follows: (1) further Israelite complaints (vv. 1-7);

(2) Moses strikes the rock (vv. 8-13); (3) rejection of petition to Edomites (vv. 14-21); (4) death of Aaron (vv. 22-29). The chapter as a whole is a literary unit covering an unspecified period of time, but v. 14 introduces a new stage in the narrative.

1. FURTHER ISRAELITE COMPLAINTS (20:1-7)

Translation

Then the entire congregation of Israel entered the wilderness of Zin in the first month, and they halted at Kadesh. It was there that Miriam died and was buried. (20:1)

Exegesis and Exposition

The final stage of Israel's journey through the wilderness brings the description of events to the second major travel narrative of Numbers—i.e., 20:1–21:35. The first such narrative describes the journey from Mount Sinai to Kadesh (11:1–12:16). The present record recounts what happened in the "first month," but unfortunately the MT does not indicate the year. If one compares 20:22-29 with 33:38, however, it is apparent that the Israelites were in the Kadesh region for many years, because Aaron's death is narrated in chap. 20 and had occurred some forty years after the Exodus.

During the lengthy encampment in the general area of Kadesh, the adult members of the rebellious generation died and were succeeded by their offspring who knew only a wilderness environment as their home. Prior to the "first month" in what was probably the fortieth year after the Exodus, the people came through the wilderness of Zin and commenced preparations for a journey that terminated in the Moabite plains. According to Deut. 1:46 they remained at Kadesh-barnea for a period of time that may have been as long as three or four months. This pause was probably necessitated by the need for marshaling the fighting forces of the nation and acquainting the new generation of men with their duties when on the march.

Miriam's death occurred from unspecified causes, although she was doubtless well advanced in years. In accordance with Hebrew tradition, a period of mourning would have followed her burial. She had played a prominent part in Israel's fortunes from the time of the Exodus, but she was not consistently supportive of her younger brother, Moses. Some commentators have drawn parallels between her and another important NT Miriam—namely, Mary the mother of Jesus. Unfortunately for the senior Miriam the contrasts are more significant than the resemblances. Although both women sang praises to God for His mighty works in their lives, the OT Miriam was

262

self-willed and disobedient to God on occasion, whereas her NT counterpart was obedient to the Lord's commands, even when she did not fully understand them. Moses' sister died without recorded epitaph.

Translation

There was no water for the community, so they banded together against Moses and Aaron. The people quarreled with Moses and said: If only we had died when our brothers perished in the LORD's presence! Why have you brought the LORD's community into this wilderness, to let us and our livestock die here? Why have you brought us out of Egypt to this dreadful place? There is no grain here, no figs, or vines, or pomegranates, nor is there any water to drink. (20:2-5)

Exegesis and Exposition

Yet another crisis arose that led to complaints from the Israelites. The marshaling of the entire nation at Kadesh, prior to the advance toward Moabite territory, had contributed to a shortage of water. This might suggest that not all the tribes had lived at Kadesh-barnea for the past thirty-eight years. More important, it raises the question as to whether the Kadesh of 20:1 was Kadesh-barnea or another Kadesh in the wilderness of Zin. In favor of the former is the fact that two places of the same name would probably not have been close to one another. Both the neighboring 'Ain el-Qoseimeh and 'Ain Qedeis have been suggested as locations for Kadesh, but in either case the supply of water was too meager to sustain a large number of people and their flocks. It is possible that the events of Num. 20 describe the results of migration from one site to another in the area of Kadesh-barnea, where the three oases were located, until the water supplies were finally exhausted. The narrative specifically mentions the whole congregation, which would explain the great drain on the resources of water.

In a disturbing repetition of the past (Num. 11:4-5; 14:2) the Israelites again avowed that they would rather have died when their relatives were struck down by the Lord's anger (16:32-35). Following an earlier pattern of rebellion they rebuked Moses and questioned his leadership. The community had depleted the resources of the Kadesh area, because they complained about a shortage of grain and fruits such as they had professed to know when they were captives in Egypt. As has been observed previously, there is considerable doubt as to whether slaves would have enjoyed what was essentially a middle- and upper-class Egyptian diet, despite their protestations. Certainly the slave population would have eaten large quantities of Egyptian onions (*Allium cepa* L.), a staple food item that was also grown in

Canaan and Syria. Onions were fried, boiled, roasted, eaten raw, and made into soup.[85]

Translation

So Moses and Aaron went from the assembled group to the entrance to the Tent of Meeting. They prostrated themselves there, and the glory of the LORD appeared to them. Then the LORD spoke to Moses and said: (20:6-7)

Exegesis and Exposition

In desperation Moses and Aaron lay prone once more before the Lord, begging for His guidance. In retrospect, the occasion marked a crucial period in the history of the wilderness wanderings. Indeed, it bore a far greater significance than Moses realized, because it had a direct bearing upon his own future.

2. MOSES STRIKES THE ROCK (20:8-13)

Translation

Take the rod, and you and your brother, Aaron, gather the assembly together. Speak in front of all of them to that rock, and it will pour out its water. In this way you will produce water for them from the rock and give it to them and their animals to drink. So Moses took the staff from the LORD's presence, as He commanded him. (20:8-9)

Exegesis and Exposition

As before, Moses received instructions from God. Taking the rod, the symbol of his authority, which had been stored in the Tabernacle in the Lord's presence, he was merely required to speak to a nearby rock, which would then produce streams of water.

The rod in question has sometimes been interpreted as Moses' own staff (cf. Ex. 7:20; 14:16; etc.). Probably, however, it was Aaron's rod, which had been deposited in the inner sanctuary. If this was the case, it would presumably be meant to indicate that there was no dichotomy between the leadership functions of the two men. Moses was obedient to the Lord's instructions, and thus the scene was set for both blessing and tragedy.

Translation

Then Moses and Aaron gathered the community together in front of the rock, and Moses said to them: Listen, you rebels! Must we

---

85. W. E. Shewell-Cooper, *ZPEB*, 4:528.

bring water for you out of this rock? Then Moses raised his arm and struck the rock two blows with his rod. Water gushed out, and the community and their animals drank of it. (20:10-11)

Exegesis and Exposition

Unfortunately Moses did not carry out God's orders implicitly, as he had always done previously. Instead of speaking to the rock as God had commanded him, he addressed the Israelites in a hostile manner, describing them as "rebels" (MT הַמֹּרִים, *hammōrîm*, from מרה, *mrh*, "be rebellious").[86] To augment his disobedience he then hit the rock twice with the rod. While this action produced the desired amount of water, it violated God's instructions and therefore constituted an act of rebellion. The correct response would have been faith and obedience, which had always been characteristic of Moses' behavior. This unusual expression of anger and frustration, however, served to introduce a personal element that detracted from the glory of the Lord, and this proved to be Moses' undoing.

Translation

But the LORD said to Moses and Aaron: Because you did not trust me sufficiently to maintain my holiness in the sight of the Israelites, you shall not bring this assembly into the land which I have given them. This was commemorated as the Waters of Meribah, where the Israelites quarreled with the LORD and where His holiness was maintained among them. (20:12-13)

Exegesis and Exposition

God's response was immediate and forthright. Because Moses had not trusted Him fully and followed His instructions to the letter, both Moses and Aaron would die in the wilderness with the other rebels and would not enter Canaan with the victorious Israelites. Such a dramatic and tragic outcome necessitated a name by which the place might be remembered. The designation "Meribah" is derived from רִיב, *rîb* ("to strive," "to engage in a lawsuit").[87] There are thus two places named "Meribah" (Ex. 17:7; Num. 20:13), and the one in this

---

86. Later Jewish tradition associated the Hebrew with the Greek adjective μωρός, "foolish," and interpreted it to mean that the Israelites were presuming to teach their teachers. Cf. J. H. Hertz, ed., *The Pentateuch and Haftorahs*, p. 656. This meaning, while perceptive, is not easy to sustain from the MT.

87. This term is employed, among other usages, in connection with God's covenantal prerogative to "take His people to court" for breaking the stipulations of the agreement at Sinai. The KJV renders the term by "controversy." Cf. Jer. 25:31; Hos. 4:1; etc.

narrative was known as Meribah-kadesh in order to distinguish it from the one near Mount Horeb (cf. Deut. 32:51; Ezek. 47:19; 48:28). Neither site has been identified. The name "Meribah" ("contention") is an example of onomastic etiology, as is "Massah" ("test") in Ex. 17:7; Deut. 6:16; and so forth.

In Deut. 33:8 the blessing of Moses distinguishes carefully and perhaps painfully between the two incidents and localities.[88] The name exhibits tragically the spectacle of conflict between the disobedient Israelites, for whom submission to God's will was no longer a priority, and the holy God of the covenant, who was determined to maintain His rights (Ex. 20:5) and ensure that His holiness would continue to be the cornerstone of community life. The MT contains a wordplay on "holy" (קָדֵשׁ, *qādēš*) and Kadesh.

Questions concerning the presence of water in the wilderness areas of Sinai have been raised periodically, partly in an attempt to discredit the miraculous element when water resulted from the exercise of God's power. It is not widely known that the water table in the Near East has always been surprisingly high for reasons that geologists are not able to explain. The Sinai peninsula today receives less than four inches of rain annually, and there is no reason for thinking that this level has varied significantly over the millennia.

Rain occurs in the form of thunderstorms or cloudbursts in the winter months. Much of the water evaporates or runs off through seasonal wadis, while the remainder percolates through the surface of the ground to form an aquifer or reservoir. Very often this accumulation of water is located just beneath a thin layer of rock, which when placed under pressure will fracture readily and produce a supply of water. Oases are really the result of such a body of water emerging in the form of a spring. While water is thus a matter of perennial concern in wilderness areas, it is readily accessible if one is able to discover its presence.[89]

But even more pressing than locating water was the sin of Moses and Aaron. Evidently Aaron was deemed to be guilty by association, because he acquiesced in what Moses was doing and was included in the "we" of v. 10. Consequently the overall blame fell upon the great Israelite leader, who was reputed for his humility (or for being frequently humiliated, as was suggested in connection with the comments on Num. 12:3).

---

88. P. C. Craigie, *Deuteronomy*, (NICOT; Grand Rapids: Eerdmans, 1976), p. 396; J. L. Mihelic, *IDB*, 3:354; L. J. Wood, *ZPEB*, 4:190-91; N. J. Opperwall and G. A. Lee, *ISBE*, 3:324.
89. K. A. Kitchen, *IBD*, 3:1645. Cf. C. S. Jarvis, *Yesterday and Today in Sinai* (Edinburgh: W. Blackwood, 1931), pp. 174-75; N. Glueck, *Rivers in the Desert* (New York: W. W. Norton, 1968), p. 22.

The sin Moses and Aaron committed was twofold: (1) they disobeyed God's instructions and acted as though they possessed the power to produce water from the rock; (2) the substitution of human activity ("we") for that of God had the effect of compromising divine holiness, which was an unpardonable act of insubordination.[90]

In extenuation of Moses' behavior it could be urged that he was coming to the end of a long and active life, that he was in despair at the many frustrations that he had experienced during nearly forty years of wilderness wandering, and above all that he felt keenly the enormous burden of leading a nation that had been rebellious almost from the time of leaving Mount Sinai.

Even though summary punishment had been imposed by God upon the offenders, the Israelites had still not learned the lesson that the Lord must be served in implicit obedience. It was the task of a later Hebrew prophet to teach a nation chastised by exile that evil is by nature far more pervasive than good. Hence even a small amount of unbelief can weaken an activity of grace (Hag. 2:11-14).

Heb. 3:11–4:16 dwells at some length on the wilderness disobedience of the Israelites and shows that Jesus Christ, our great High Priest, is superior to Moses in both character and office. The Savior is indeed the true "living water" (John 7:37-38), who gives by His grace the gift of eternal life to those who submit to His lordship.

Excursus on Numbers 20:2-13

The general tenor of the story of events at Meribah is reminiscent of the Israelites' complaints immediately after their liberation from Egypt (cf. Ex. 16:2; 17:2). It is not necessary, however, to argue from the alleged similarity of the narratives to the conclusion that they are duplicates. The similarity is obvious because both situations occurred in a wilderness environment—namely, the areas of Sin/Rephidim and Zin respectively. In the wilderness of Sin the complaint involved a shortage of food (Ex. 16:3), whereas at Rephidim the problem was a lack of water (17:2). In the wilderness of Zin the Israelites were short of both food and water. In Ex. 17 the account mentions Moses and ignores Aaron, whereas in Num. 20 both Moses and Aaron are involved.

The statement in Num. 20:3 makes reference to the events of Num. 16:49 and is not connected chronologically with Ex. 17. But the most striking difference is that in the Exodus narrative, Moses used the rod that he held when the Re(e)d Sea parted at the time of the Exodus (Ex. 14:16) to produce the needed water, and he acted in

---

90. P. J. Budd, *Numbers*, pp. 218-19; L. J. Dubois, *Beacon Bible Commentary*, p. 458.

complete obedience to God's commands. By contrast, in Num. 20, Moses took the rod that had been deposited in the Lord's presence and deliberately disobeyed God by striking the rock instead of merely addressing it (Num. 20:10-11). Superficially the two narrative accounts appear reasonably close enough to be duplicates, but on closer analysis any ostensible similarity proves to be environmental and coincidental, not chronological.

Additional Notes

20:4 לָמוּת: The LXX reads, more aggressively, ἀποκτεῖναι ἡμᾶς.

20:8 וְהוֹצֵאתָ: The LXX reads a plural verb, ἐξοίσετε, here, and for וְהִשְׁקִיתָ reads ποτιεῖτε, apparently to ensure that Aaron's role was not neglected.

20:12 יַעַן always occurs in a causal sense and here is followed by a noun clause.

20:13 בָּם: The Samaritan Pentateuch augments the narrative with additions from Deut. 3:24-28.

5

From Kadesh to Moab (20:14–21:35)

A. DENIAL AND DEATH (20:14-29)

1. REJECTION OF PETITION TO EDOMITES (20:14-21)

Translation

From Kadesh, Moses sent messengers to the Edomite ruler, saying: This is a message from Israel, your brother. You are aware of all the hardships that have befallen us. Our ancestors went down into Egypt, where we lived for many years. The Egyptians treated us and our ancestors badly, but when we cried to the LORD for help He heard our cry, sent a messenger, and brought us out of Egypt. Now we are here at Kadesh, a town on the edge of your country. Please give us permission to pass through your territory. We will not trespass on fields or vineyards, nor will we drink water from any wells. We will stay on the King's Highway. We will not turn off to the right or left until we have traversed your country. (20:14-17)

Exegesis and Exposition

The reason for sending this announcement of intentions was that Moses desired to approach Canaan from the east, because an attempted foray from the south in earlier days had proved disastrous (Num. 14:45). The request is couched in polite, friendly, yet deferential language and shows that Moses, formerly a prince of Egypt, was acquainted with the niceties of diplomatic communication.

In the ancient Near East it was normal for rulers to address each other with formal salutations that mentioned rank and prowess and for vassals to be respectful and solicitous in writing letters to their overlords. Thus, in a letter recovered from el-Amarna containing a message from the governor of Jerusalem to the pharaoh appealing for help against the marauding ʿApiru and others, the writer greeted his overlord as follows: "To the king, my lord, my Sun-god, say: Thus says Abdiheba thy servant. At the feet of the king, my lord, seven times and seven times I fall. Behold, the king, my lord, has set his name at the rising of the sun and at the setting of the sun."[1] In the light of these considerations the letter can be analyzed as follows: (1) recipient (v. 14); (2) annunciation formula ["this is a message from . . ." (v. 14)]; (3) correspondent ("Israel") and his status ["your brother"] (v. 14); (4) circumstances prompting the communication (vv. 14-16); (5) petition (v. 17).

The letter reviewed the history of the Hebrews from their descent into Egypt (Gen. 46:5-6) to the time of their wanderings in the Sinai peninsula. Much of this information was probably already familiar, perhaps in greater detail, to the Edomites, since they were descendants of Esau, Jacob's twin brother (36:9; cf. Deut. 23:7 [MT 8]). Their territory, which was evidently occupied originally by the Horites (Deut. 2:22), was located south and east of the Dead Sea from the Wadi el-Ḥesa to the Gulf of Aqaba.

The request contained the assurance that the Israelites would not pillage the terrain if they were permitted to pass through Edomite territory and would not even drink the local water. Instead, they would follow the King's Highway (MT דֶּרֶךְ הַמֶּלֶךְ, *derek hammelek*), an ancient route linking southern Arabia with Rabbath-Ammon, Damascus, and the lands beyond. Bronze Age fortresses have been discovered at intervals along this general route, but there may have been other subsidiary roads through Transjordan. The anonymous "king" may have been the person originally responsible for developing the route, probably for trading purposes.[2]

The petition suggests that Edomite territory adjoined or included some parts of the wilderness of Zin. This is hard to determine, however, because the borders of Edom were never clearly defined. Nor should it be assumed from the tenor of the request that Edom was a formidable, unified nation at this period. The earliest archaeological reference to the people of Seir occurs in the fourteenth-century B.C.

---

1. C. J. Mullo Weir, *DOTT*, p. 43; cf. W. F. Albright and G. E. Mendenhall, *ANET*, pp. 488-89.
2. See S. Cohen, *IDB*, 3:35-36; D. E. Hiebert, *ZPEB*, 3:842; J. R. Kautz, III, *ISBE*, 3:39 and bibliographies.

texts from el-Amarna, which mentioned incursions of Bedouin tribes from the "lands of Seir" but did not name any Edomite cities or leaders. This suggests a typically nomadic Bronze Age group that was not organized along national lines.[3] The reference to the messenger (MT מַלְאָךְ, *mal'āk*, "angel" in many English versions) recalls the activity of the divinely appointed Being described in Ex. 23:20.

Translation

But the Edomites answered him: You shall not pass through. If you attempt it, we shall march out and attack you with the sword. So the Israelites replied: We will go along the highway, and if we or our livestock drink any of your water we will pay for it. We simply want to journey across your country. But they insisted: You shall not pass through. The Edomites then came out against them with a large and strong army. Thus the Edomites refused to allow the Israelites passage through their territory. Israel then turned away from them. (20:18-21)

Exegesis and Exposition

Without observing any of the niceties of diplomatic protocol, the Edomites replied with a brusque refusal. Although the Israelites promised to follow the highway (MT מְסִלָּה, *mĕsillâ*), offered to pay for any water consumed, and required no other favors (MT רַק אֵין-דָּבָר, *raq 'ên-dābār*, an emphatic affirmation) apart from passage (MT בְּרַגְלַי, *bĕraglay*, "on my feet"), the request was still denied flatly. In antiquity it was usual for some conditions to be imposed upon those who traveled through another's territory, whether it was a toll in goods or money or some other kind of stipulation. The persistence of Moses abated when the Edomites mustered a powerful show of force (MT בְּיָד חֲזָקָה, *bĕyād ḥăzāqâ*, "with a strong hand"), and the Israelites withdrew from a possibly devastating confrontation. It is significant that nowhere in this account is any direction from the Lord mentioned.

2. DEATH OF AARON (20:22-29)

Translation

Then the whole assembly of the Israelites set out from Kadesh and came to Mount Hor. The LORD addressed Moses and Aaron in Mount Hor by the border of Edomite territory, saying: Aaron will be taken to be with his ancestors. He shall not enter the land that I have

3. *ANET*, pp. 259-62; W. F. Albright and G. E. Mendenhall, *ANET*, pp. 486-88; E. MacDonald, *ISBE*, 2:18-21.

given to the Israelites because you rebelled against my command at the waters of Meribah. (20:22-24)

Exegesis and Exposition

The precise location of Mount Hor has been a matter of considerable dispute. It was located somewhere on the edge of the territory the Edomites considered their own (Num. 33:37). The name always appears in the MT with the definite article (הֹר הָהָר, *hōr hāhār*, "Hor the mountain"), suggesting that it was a prominent ridge or rocky outcrop. Deut. 10:6 states that Aaron died at Moserah. There is no conflict between the two accounts, however, since the name (MT מֹסֵרָה, *mōserâ*, "chastisement")[4] was applied to the event itself, not to the location of Aaron's death.

Josephus identified Mount Hor with Jebel Nebi Harim ("The prophet Aaron's mountain"),[5] a rugged, twin-crested sandstone elevation near Petra. This location is unlikely, however, because (1) it would have involved the Israelites in a journey across Edomite territory, and (2) the mountain was too inaccessible for the Hebrews to witness the transfer of the high priestly office from Aaron to his son Eleazar. A more suitable location would be a site to the north and east of Kadesh-barnea, and accordingly some have suggested Jebel Madurah about fifteen miles northeast of Kadesh. This mountain was on the northwest edge of territory claimed by Edom and as such constituted a suitable point of departure for approaching Canaan by a southerly route.[6]

Once the Israelites arrived at Mount Hor, Aaron was warned by God of his impending decease in the beautiful euphemism יֵאָסֵף אַהֲרֹן אֶל־עַמָּיו, *yēʾāsēp ʾahărōn ʾel-ʿammāyw*, "Aaron shall be gathered to his people," a phrase first used of Abraham (Gen. 15:15; 25:8) and interpreted by many as an early intimation of life after death. Whether this is actually the case or not, Aaron was accorded the status of his patriarchal ancestors.

Translation

Take Aaron and his son Eleazar, and ascend Mount Hor. Strip Aaron of his garments and put them on his son Eleazar, for Aaron will be taken to be with his ancestors. He will die there. So Moses did exactly as the LORD commanded. They ascended Mount Hor, while the entire community watched them.

---

4. The MT has the plural form מֹסֵרוֹת, *mōserôt*, in Num. 33:30-31.
5. *Ant.* 4.4.7.
6. See J. L. Mihelic, *IDB*, 2:644; S. Barabas, *ZPEB*, 3:201; R. K. Harrison, *ISBE*, 2:755-56; M. H. Heicksen, *NIDBA*, p. 1 and bibliographies.

Moses stripped Aaron of his garments and put them upon Eleazar his son, and Aaron died there on the summit of the mountain. Then Moses and Eleazar descended the mountain. When the entire community saw that Aaron was dead, all Israel lamented him for thirty days. (20:25-29)

Exegesis and Exposition

Although Moses must have been reluctant to officiate at the death of his brother, it was nevertheless important for the formal transfer of office to be witnessed publicly. Therefore Moses carried out the Lord's instructions precisely, and Eleazar assumed the chief spiritual office in Israel, doubtless with great emotion as he contemplated the imminence of his father's death. Aaron was probably buried under a cairn of stones. Once the obsequies had been observed, Moses and Eleazar descended the mountain, and a thirty-day period of mourning ensued. Since this was the same length of time as that which later commemorated the passing of Moses, it appears to have been the norm for Israelites of high rank.

Aaron's character exhibited conspicuous gifts, as with his eloquence (Ex. 4:16) before the pharaoh and his general support of his younger brother, Moses. His weaknesses were also evident, however, as with the idolatrous incident at the foot of Mount Sinai (32:4) while Moses was on the mountain communing with God, as well as with the offense that deprived him of the privilege of entering Canaan (Num. 20:12, 24). This first great spiritual mediator between God and the Israelite nation was commemorated in later Jewish thought as the ideal peacemaker.[7]

In the Christian tradition he has been seen to prefigure Christ, our High Priest, who fulfilled His atoning office after the Aaronic pattern (Heb. 9:7-15). This involved His mediatorial function, His anointing with the Spirit (John 3:34), and His entrance into heaven, now to appear in the divine presence (Heb. 9:24), as Aaron entered the Most Holy Place on the Day of Atonement (Lev. 16:12).[8] Human types are necessarily imperfect, however, and so the Christian can rejoice in the sinless perfection of Jesus, who obtained our redemption on Calvary, not by the blood of bulls and goats but by His own blood (Heb. 9:11-15).

Additional Notes

20:14 אֱדֹם: The Samaritan Pentateuch here adds to the text with material from Deut. 2:2-6.

---

7. J. H. Hertz, ed., *The Pentateuch and Haftorahs,* pp. 638-39; W. G. Plaut and W. W. Hallo, *Numbers,* pp. 198-99.
8. M. F. Unger, *Unger's Bible Dictionary* (Chicago: Moody, 1966), p. 2.

20:17 נַעְבְּרָה־נָּא: The Samaritan Pentateuch here has an indicative rather than a cohortative force. Cf. LXX παρελευσόμεθα.

20:19 בְּרַגְלַי: Here the LXX adds παρὰ τὸ ὄρος, perhaps for emphasis, or possibly by dittography from the beginning of the verse.

20:25 הֹר הָהָר: Here the LXX adds ἔναντι πάσης τῆς συναγωγῆς, perhaps included from v. 27.

B. VICTORIES ON THE WAY TO MOAB (21:1-35)

Chapter 21 is structured in terms of four units: (1) victory at Hormah (vv. 1-3); (2) plague of fiery serpents (vv. 4-9); (3) approach to Moab (vv. 10-20); (4) victory over Sihon and Og (vv. 21-35).

1. VICTORY AT HORMAH (21:1-3)

Translation

When the Canaanite ruler of Arad, who lived in the Negev, heard that the Israelites were coming along the road to Atharim, he attacked them and took some prisoners. The Israelites therefore made a vow to the Lord, saying: If You will indeed deliver these people into our power, we will obliterate their cities. The Lord listened to the Israelites speaking and handed the Canaanites over to them. So they obliterated them and their cities. They named that place Hormah. (21:1-3)

Exegesis and Exposition

Some scholars have regarded these three verses as a later insertion, since Num. 21:4 seems to come logically after 20:29. There is no need to adopt this view, however, since Arad in southern Canaan was only a short distance northwest of Mount Hor. The site, Tell Arad, was of great antiquity, being settled as early as the fourth millennium B.C., and was an important center in the Early Bronze Age.[9]

The Canaanite king, hearing of the approach of Israel, decided that attack was the best form of defense and met with initial success in the form of a few prisoners. But after Israel's vow (MT נֶדֶר, *neder*) of extermination, God gave them victory at Hormah, where in earlier days they had been defeated by the Edomites (Num. 14:45). This calamity was thus avenged, and the event signaled the beginning of victory for the chosen people. The vow or votive offering always took place between persons and God, not between human beings. In v. 2 it

---

9. See S. Cohen, *IDB*, 1:185; H. G. Andersen, *ZPEB*, 1:245; Y. Aharoni, *ISBE*, 1:227-29; J. A. Thompson, *NIDBA*, pp. 36-37; M. Avi-Yonah, *EAEHL*, 1:74-89 and bibliographies.

was the equivalent of the חֵרֶם, *ḥērem*, or devoted offering, in this case for total destruction by war.[10] The name "Hormah" means "destruction," or "devoted to destruction,"[11] and for the Israelites it symbolized the forcible removal of all that was alien to the faith and ethic of the Sinai covenant. This rebirth of fighting spirit and determination to keep pledges and obligations was not maintained unimpaired, however, for it was tarnished by further misfortune.

2. PLAGUE OF FIERY SERPENTS (21:4-9)

Translation

They then traveled along the road to the Red Sea from Mount Hor so as to go around Edomite territory. As the Israelites journeyed they became impatient. They criticized both God and Moses, saying: Why have you brought us from the land of Egypt to die in the wilderness? We have neither food nor water, and we detest this monotonous diet. So the LORD sent poisonous snakes among them, which bit the people so that many of the Israelites died. (21:4-6)

Exegesis and Exposition

Whatever the precise location of Mount Hor, the Israelites moved away from it westward into the wilderness of Zin in the direction of the Re(e)d Sea (MT יַם סוּף, *yam sûp*), so as to avoid entering land claimed by the Edomites. By following a southwest route they kept away from further military confrontations, but this involved them in a long journey south to approximately the north end of the Gulf of Aqaba. Having reached that area, they then turned east until they could see the wooded uplands of the Seir mountain range stretching to the north. This journey took them to the most southerly part of the Arabah, the vast expanse of upland and mountain extending from the Sea of Galilee southward on both sides of the Jordan to the Gulf of Aqaba.

Some scholars have suggested an alternative possibility for the journey, involving a march southward to a point midway between the Dead Sea and the Gulf of Aqaba, and thence northeast to Punon, supposedly located in Edomite territory. Thereafter they would travel to Oboth, a site presumed to be located in the north-central area of the Arabah, and then to the southern end of the Dead Sea, where by turning east they could move along the border between Moab and Edom.[12]

---

10. Cf. C. A. Keller, *THAT*, 2:39-43; L. J. Coppens, *TWOT*, 2:557-58.
11. See on 14:45.
12. L. J. Du Bois, *Beacon Bible Commentary*, p. 461.

The journey proved arduous, and again rebellion broke out due to discouragement as well as dissatisfaction with the diet. The Israelites had yet to learn that one victory does not necessarily win a war. Their opinion about the manna was expressive (MT קְלֹקֵל, qĕlōqēl, "good for nothing," "contemptible"; KJV "light"; NKJV "worthless"; NAB "wretched"; NEB "miserable fare"; NIV "miserable"). This protestation constituted blatant rebellion, the punishment for which was swift and dramatic. A plague of poisonous serpents broke out in the camp (MT נְחָשִׁים הַשְּׂרָפִים, nĕḥāšîm haśśĕrāpîm), and many Israelites succumbed to their bites.

For those who understand this incident to be historical and not mythological,[13] the reptiles and their effects have occasioned considerable discussion. Since their designation is almost identical linguistically to the Hebrew נְחֹשֶׁת (nĕḥōšet, "copper" or "bronze"), the description נְחָשִׁים (nĕḥāšîm) may well have referred to their color.[14] Others, influenced by such translations as "fiery," have supposed that the bite produced erythema, a severe inflammatory condition caused by the snake venom. The reptile in question may have been the אֶפְעֶה ('epʿeh) a species of adder usually identified with the *Echis carinatus* that lives in the sandy wastes of Sinai. Another sand viper, the *Cerastes cerastes*, has been proposed, but while its venom is used to kill small rodents, it is seldom powerful enough to cause death to human beings.

The *E. carinatus* or *E. coleratus*, sometimes known as "carpet viper," occurs in great numbers in Africa and elsewhere in the East. Both species are reputed to have a more powerful venom, on the basis of comparative body weight, than any other viper. These snakes can grow up to two feet in length and, according to observers, are provoked easily.[15] Since the incident was a natural event actuated by supernatural considerations, the most poisonous desert reptile would be eminently suitable for inflicting divine punishment upon the rebellious Israelites.

An alternative suggestion has been made by Wolff,[16] who regarded the "fiery serpents" not as reptiles but as a nematode infection. A nematode is an order of *Vermes*, or worms, and includes such parasitic organisms as pinworms, roundworms, and trichinae. Wolff thought that the Israelites sustained infection by a Guinea worm (*Dracunculus medinensis*) through drinking polluted water. When the

---

13. Representatives of the mythological interpretation include F. S. Bodenheimer, W. S. McCullough, and W. G. Williams, *IDB*, 4:289-91.
14. For a discussion see R. L. Alden, *TWOT*, 2:571-73.
15. G. S. Cansdale, *ZPEB*, 5:357-58.
16. R. J. Wolff, *ISBE*, 4:1209-10.

worm gains access to the body it emerges ultimately under the skin of the arms and legs, erupting into an infected sore that is inflamed and painful. Once the worm's head emerges the parasite can be removed by gentle traction. The traditional method is to roll it around a short stick and attempt to withdraw it carefully, a process that takes several days at the least.

Attractive though Wolff's view is, it presents certain difficulties: (1) it is not easy to see how the nematode in question would have been ingested, since the Israelites were complaining about a chronic shortage of the very medium in which the nematode lives; (2) wherever water was available, whether produced by natural or divine means, it would seem to have been pure, unlike the waters of the Nile, which to this day are polluted by parasites; (3) although nematode infection can be a painful and awkward experience, it is seldom lethal unless the parasitic worm is broken during removal and a generalized infection results.[17] By contrast, the bite of a deadly viper would have brought about death quickly, which seems to be the impression conveyed by the MT.

Translation

Then the people came to Moses and said: We have sinned in speaking against the LORD and against you. Plead with the LORD to take away the snakes from us. So Moses interceded for the people. The LORD said to Moses: Fashion a poisonous snake and set it on a pole. When anyone who has been bitten looks at it, he shall recover. So Moses fashioned a bronze snake and placed it on a pole, so that anyone who had been bitten by a snake would recover by looking at the bronze snake. (21:7-9)

Exegesis and Exposition

Stunned by the tragedy of their punishment, the people came in a contrite though desperate frame of mind. They confessed their sin to Moses and urged him to secure pardon for them from God. The Lord's response was somewhat homeopathic in nature, consisting of a bronze serpent erected upon a pole that mediated God's healing power to any sufferer who looked upward at it.[18] Thus by the Lord's decree the power of the serpent had been broken.[19]

Despite the conjectures exhibited by translations, the material composition of the serpent is unknown. Brass, copper, and bronze have all been suggested, but none is entirely persuasive. Brass, an

---

17. Cf. R. H. Pousma, *ZPEB*, 2:141.
18. Cf. Wisdom 16:10.
19. *KD*, 3:140-41.

alloy of copper and zinc, is not represented archaeologically in the biblical period, whereas bronze, a more complex alloy of copper, zinc, and tin, was very well known in the Near East. From this it will appear that copper was obviously the most widely-used metal of the period, whether pure or in alloy form, until the Iron Age, which began about 1200 B.C. Among many other uses, copper was employed widely for making snakes used in cult worship by the ancient Near Eastern peoples. Thus it is possible that Moses fashioned a serpent hurriedly from some copper implements and hoisted it on one of the tribal or family standards.

Archaeological discoveries in the area of Timna, a site about fifteen miles north of Ezion-geber at the northern end of the Gulf of Aqaba, have shed light on the Numbers narrative. When Rothenberg was excavating the ore-smelting site at Timna, he uncovered the ruins of a small temple that had been used by the Egyptians in the thirteenth century B.C. The site was apparently destroyed in the middle of the following century and was rebuilt by the Midianites, who converted it into a tent-shrine somewhat similar to the Israelite Tabernacle. From this shrine Rothenberg recovered the remains of various offerings and gifts, including a five-inch copper serpent with a gilded head.[20] If Wolff is correct in his conjectures, the Mosaic copper servant would have been impressive indeed, perhaps as much as three feet in length.

Although the intention of both God and Moses was to furnish an emblem of healing rather than an object of veneration, the copper serpent was preserved for centuries by the Israelites. But when Canaanite paganism overtook the nation, the serpent became something to be worshiped and accordingly was destroyed by King Hezekiah during a period of religious reformation (2 Kings 18:4).

Jesus used the metal serpent as an illustration of His own ministry on the cross. He did not specify the material composition of the object, the Greek text (John 3:14) rendering "serpent" by the common word ὄφις (ophis), as also in the allusion to this incident in 1 Corinthi-

20. B. Rothenberg, *Timna: Valley of the Biblical Copper Mines* (London: Thames & Hudson, 1972), pp. 129-32, 152, 183-84, and pls. XIX-XX. On the place of the serpent in the religious life of Israel see K. R. Joines, "The Bronze Serpent in the Israelite Cult," *JBL* 87 (1968): 245-56; *Serpent Symbolism in the Old Testament* (New Jersey: Haddonfield House, 1974), pp. 85-96; D. J. Wiseman, "Flying Serpents," *TynBul* 23 (1972): 108-10. A similar Late Bronze Age site at Tell Mevorakh yielded cylinder seals, beads, bronze weapons, and a coiled bronze snake eight inches long. See E. Stern, "A Late Bronze Age Temple at Tell Mevorakh," *BA* 40 (1977): 89-91; *Excavations at Tell Mevorakh, II: The Bronze Age* (Jerusalem: Institute of Archaeology, Hebrew University, 1984), pp. 28-39.

ans 10:9. As with Hezekiah, Jesus regarded the metal object as fact and not myth. The objective reality of the metal serpent is evident from the fact that King Hezekiah of Judah could have produced the artifact at any time on request.

Jesus compared His impending crucifixion to the saving event of the days of Moses. Just as the serpent brought deliverance when raised on a pole for all to see, so He, who was made sin for us (2 Cor. 5:21), would be raised on a cross to deliver mankind from the penalty of wickedness (John 12:32). In the same way that the ancient Israelite was required to look in faith at the bronze serpent to be saved from death, so the modern sinner must also look in faith at the crucified Christ to receive the healing of the new birth (John 3:14-16).

3. APPROACH TO MOAB (21:10-20)

Translation

The Israelites moved on and camped at Oboth. Subsequently they moved on from Oboth and encamped *at Iye Abarim, in the wilderness on the eastern edge of Moab. From there they moved on and camped in the valley of Zered. From there they moved on and camped on the farther side of the Arnon, in the wilderness that stretches into Amorite territory. The Arnon marked the frontier of Moab, lying between Moab and the Amorites. (21:10-13)

Exegesis and Exposition

These and the following verses describe incidents and stations on the way to Moabite territory. The material is selective rather than comprehensive in nature, with the full itinerary of the journey from Egypt to Canaan being given in Num. 33:1-49. The intent of this particular section is to move as quickly as possible from the Paran wilderness to the fertile territory of Moab.

From their place of punishment the Israelites moved to Oboth. The expectation for marching was heightened by the prospect of an invasion of enemy territory in Transjordan. Oboth, literally "water skins," is evidently the designation of an oasis that is difficult to identify, but it seems to have been east of Edom, lying somewhere between Punon (Feinan) and Zered (Wadi el-Hesa).[21]

After an undetermined interval of time, the camp moved on to Iye Abarim ("distant regions") on the southeastern border of Moab. It was mountainous territory, and from the principal peak, Mount Nebo, Moses was given the opportunity of viewing the Promised

---

21. W. S. LaSor, *ISBE*, 3:578 and bibliography.

Land. The name of the area had evidently been bestowed in the patriarchal age by the Hebrews as they gazed eastward across the Jordan to the imposing mountain ridges on the horizon.[22] Pursuing their
journey and still keeping east of Moabite territory, they camped in
the valley of Zered (perhaps "willows"). The wadi, when replenished
with rain, tributaries, and perennial springs, feeds an oasis,[23] which
would furnish a suitable though temporary campsite for the Israelites. The next stage of the march took them beyond the Arnon, the
modern Wadi el-Mujib, a deep gorge running across the plateau of
Moab and forming a natural frontier of an imposing nature between
Moabite and Amorite territory.

The Moabites were descendants of Lot by his elder daughter
through incestuous union (Gen. 19:33). They tended to stay in the
general area of their ancestral home and took over other lands occupied by the Emim (Deut. 2:10-11). While the Moabites regarded the
territory north of the wadi as their own, both the Amorites (Num.
21:26) and the Ammonites (Judg. 11:13) had laid claim to substantial
parts of the area.[24] By following the route stated above, the Israelites
avoided confrontation with the Moabites by keeping to the east of the
fertile uplands on the east shore of the Dead Sea and traveling in the
drier areas between Moab proper and the eastern desert.

Translation

**This is why the Book of the Wars of the LORD speaks of: *The
watershed in Suphah and the wadis; the Arnon and its sloping valleys; the steep clefts leading to the settlement of Ar and falling off
toward the frontier of Moab. (21:14-15)**

Exegesis and Exposition

The Arnon was not just a single wadi but was fed by tributaries,
as noted above, that cut into the plateau and formed other ravines
that could also have been styled "the Arnon." This configuration was
so impressive as to have been mentioned in an ancient record entitled
"Book of the Wars of the Lord," which confirmed the biblical statement that Arnon was on the frontier of Moab.

The "Book" is but one of the many Hebrew literary sources that
have perished over the millennia. It seems to have been made up of a
collection of early victory songs and poetic descriptions of military
exploits, but apart from this reference it is unmentioned in Scripture.
The antiquity of the brief citation is attested to by the difficulty of the

---

22. W. J. Beecher, *ISBE*, 1:3.
23. V. R. Gold, *IDB*, 4:954; G. R. Lewthwaite, *ZPEB*, 5:1056.
24. H. L. Ellison, *ISBE*, 1:297-98.

Hebrew text. The *RSV*, *NAB*, and *NIV* give a quite literal translation of the MT, treating Waheb and Suphah as place names. In that event a subject and verb need to be supplied, such as "The Israelites marched through. . . ." The KJV, following the Vulgate, emended the beginning to read "What he did in the Red Sea," supplying a needed verb and reading יַם-סוּף (*yam sûp*) for סוּפָה (*sûpâ*), but this is at best conjectural. The *NKJV*, however, follows the *RSV*, while the *NEB* speaks cautiously of "Vaheb in Suphah" with a marginal note on the first of these two words.

Christensen has proposed emending MT אֶת-וָהֵב (*'et-wāhēb*) to אָתָה יהוה (*'ātâ* YHWH, "the LORD came"), thus providing a needed verb and repointing the particle *'et* (indicating the direct object of a verb) to read *'ātâ*, "he (i.e., God) came."[25] These changes, though minor, are rather subjective, and although they glorify a victorious Deity they tend to shift the emphasis from a description of the rugged terrain, which seems to have been the original intention. If Suphah is in fact a place name, it was probably in an area near one of the tributary wadis of the Arnon. Ar may have been either a city or a region of Moab on the south bank of the Arnon (cf. Deut. 2:18, 36). Alternatively, it could have been a name used as a synonym for Moab.[26]

Translation

From there they journeyed to Beer, the well where the LORD said to Moses: Assemble all the people, and I will give them water. Then the Israelites sang this song: Spurt up, well-water! Sing its praises— the well sunk by the leaders, dug by the nation's notables, with their scepters and their staffs. From the wilderness they journeyed to Mattanah, from Mattanah to Nahaliel, from Nahaliel to Bamoth, and from Bamoth to the Moabite valley where the top of the elevation overlooks the wilderness. (21:16-20)

Exegesis and Exposition

The site of Beer (meaning "well") is unknown, but it was here that the Lord instructed the Israelites to dig for water. A site in the Wadi et-Themed has been suggested, since it would probably be the most suitable area north of the Arnon for such activity.[27] Success was commemorated in a work song. In a parched land the discovery of an

---

25. D. L. Christensen, "Num. 21:14-15 and the Book of the Wars of Yahweh," *CBQ* 36 (1974): 359-60. Cf. A. R. Hulst, *Old Testament Translation Problems*, p. 10.
26. J. W. Whedbee, *ISBE*, 1:217.
27. E. D. Grohman, *IDB*, 1:374. It is probably the Beer-elim of Isa. 15:8.

underground water source was a cause for celebration. It has been supposed by scholars that the various lines of the composition were sung antiphonally, with perhaps three groups chanting a line each. On the other hand it could have arisen spontaneously, with the first two lines hailing the presence of the water being sung in unison and, as the work came to a conclusion, being added to by references to the participation of the nation's leaders. This discovery would give the Israelites great encouragement as they faced the prospect of conquest in Transjordan.[28] The MT at the end of v. 18 (וּמִמִּדְבָּר מַתָּנָה, *ûmimmidbār mattānâ*) has been rendered by the NEB "a gift from the wilderness," understanding *mattānâ* as a common noun ("gift," "present") rather than a proper noun, "Mattanah." While the idea of water as a gift from the wilderness is attractive, it involves the NEB in substituting the name "Beer" for "Mattanah" in v. 19, which is not warranted by the text.

The subsequent stations on the way to the Moabite valley are difficult to locate. Mattanah has been identified tentatively with Khirbet el-Medeiyineh, about eleven miles northeast of Dibon,[29] where potsherds point to an occupational history beginning shortly before 1200 B.C. If Nahaliel was a town, it has not been discovered at the time of writing, and it may simply have constituted a temporary halting place in some such area as the Wadi Waleh, a major tributary north of the Arnon, or the Wadi Zerqa Maʿin, which flows into the Dead Sea.[30] Bamoth may be an abbreviated form of Bamoth-baal (Num. 22:41) but is of uncertain location. A site on the west edge of the Transjordanian plateau south of Mount Nebo and near modern Khirbet el-Quweiqiyeh seems to be a reasonable identification.[31]

The final station for this portion of the march was a valley sheltered by a towering crag. This elevation is sometimes named Pisgah in translations and commentaries, since the MT הַפִּסְגָּה always appears with the definite article *happisgâ*. Pisgah thus indicates a major peak in the mountain range, of which the highest was Mount Nebo.

4. VICTORY OVER SIHON AND OG (21:21-35)

Translation

Then the Israelites sent messengers to Sihon, the Amorite ruler, saying: Allow us to pass through your country. We will not trespass

28. Cf. D. N. Freedman, "Archaic Forms in Early Hebrew Poetry," *ZAW* 72 (1960): 105-6.
29. Cf. N. Glueck, "Explorations in Eastern Palestine," *AASOR* 14 (1934): 13-27.
30. W. S. LaSor, *ISBE*, 3:476.
31. Y. Aharoni, *The Land of the Bible* (London: Burnes & Oates, 1966), pp. 98, 308; W. C. Kaiser, Jr., *ZPEB*, 1:458.

on your fields or vineyards, and we will not drink water from your wells. We will keep to the King's Highway until we have passed through your territory. (21:21-22)

Exegesis and Exposition

The Israelites sent the same kind of polite diplomatic message to the Amorite ruler as had been sent to the Edomites (20:14-17), requesting the same privileges of transit and receiving the same negative response. Whereas the Edomite ruler was not named, the king of the Amorites was spoken of as Sihon, about whom nothing is known save for his exploits in Num. 21. His holdings stretched from the Arnon river in the south to the Jabbok, which was located about twenty miles north of the northern end of the Dead Sea.

Translation

But Sihon refused to allow the Israelites to pass through his territory. He mustered all his forces and marched toward the wilderness against the Israelites. When he came to Jahaz he attacked Israel. But the Israelites put him to the sword and occupied his country from the Arnon to the Jabbok, but only as far as Ammonite territory because the Ammonite border was strong. So the Israelites conquered all these Amorite cities and occupied them, including Heshbon and all its surrounding villages. (21:23-25)

Exegesis and Exposition

Sihon followed the course adopted by the Edomites and marched out with his full army against Israel. The confrontation occurred at Jahaz, a place of uncertain identification although important in the Middle Bronze and Iron Ages. It was mentioned on the Moabite Stone (lines 18-21) as occupied by the Israelite king Omri (885-873 B.C.) when he was engaged in war with Mesha, the Moabite ruler. When Ahab's son Jehoram (852-841 B.C.) was defeated by Mesha, the city reverted to Moabite control (2 Kings 3:4-27). Three sites in the neighborhood of Medeba have been suggested as possible locations for Jahaz,[32] with an additional one in Moab north of the Arnon River.[33]

The Israelites were faced with the choice of repelling the Amorites or being themselves pushed into the Arnon gorge. There is no record of God's miraculous intervention save in the resolute will of His people, who seem to have learned to a great extent the lesson of

---

32. These are: Khirbet et-Teim (one mile southwest), Umm el-Walid (seven miles southeast), and Jalul (three and a half miles east). See also *GTTOT*, p. 262.
33. The modern Khirbet Umm el-Idham, about five miles north of Dibon in Moabite Transjordan.

submission to Him. So great was the Amorite defeat that the vanquished were driven north to the Ammonite border. Because this was a strong defensive barrier, the Amorites were trapped and slaughtered, whereupon the Israelites occupied their towns and villages. The Israelites did not attack the Ammonites (for reasons given in Deut. 2:19) but chose instead to consolidate their hold upon Amorite territory.

Sihon's capital city, Heshbon, has commonly been identified with Tell Hesban, but this poses some problems if only because archaeological excavations at the site from 1969 to 1978 revealed no traces of a settlement there prior to 1200 B.C. This circumstance could be accounted for by supposing that the semi-sedentary nature of the Amorites has left no permanent trace of a settlement, or that Heshbon should be identified with another of the neighboring tells that have Middle and Late Bronze Age remains. Alternatively, Heshbon could have been the ancient Amorite name that was transferred to the town at Tell Hesban at a subsequent time. Further excavations in the area may go far toward solving this problem. Heshbon was an ancient city well known to the Israelite tribes, and on the basis of its conquest under Moses it was denied to the Ammonites, since it had been captured from the Amorites (Judg. 11:12-28).[34]

Translation

Heshbon was the capital city of Sihon, the Amorite ruler, who had made war on the former Moabite ruler and had taken over all his land as far as the Arnon. Consequently those who compose proverbs say: Come to Heshbon! Let it be rebuilt! Let Sihon's city be restored! Fire flared up from Heshbon; a blaze burned Sihon's city. It devoured Ar of Moab, the rulers of the lofty Arnon. Evil be upon you, Moab! You are dead, you people of Chemosh! He has made his sons fugitives, and his daughters the slaves of Sihon, the Amorite king! But we have overpowered them. Heshbon is devastated as far as Dibon. We have shattered them all the way to Nophah, which extends to Medeba. (21:26-30)

Exegesis and Exposition

Perhaps the *šōṭĕrîm* added an interesting historical note to augment the bare narrative about the conquest of the Amorites. As such it was joined to an ancient war ballad to the effect that the Moabites had once claimed the plain, or Mishor area, from the Arnon to north

---

34. On Heshbon see L. T. Geraty, *ISBE*, 2:699-702 and bibliography.

of Heshbon and the plain in the Jordan valley east of Jericho. An early (MT רִאשׁוֹן, *ri'šôn;* KJV, *NEB, NIV* "former"; *JB* "first") king of Moab had been defeated by Sihon and had lost all the fertile plain area as a consequence.

The proverbs of antiquity would include songs, riddles, poems, and the like composed by poets and bards to catch the dramatic flavor of an event or to perpetuate the significance of an important occasion. The present composition is basically an ancient poetic reminiscence formulated shortly after the event. It is of the character of Egyptian victory songs or paeans composed on an extemporaneous basis by soldiers as they marched home in triumph.

This early "Song of Heshbon" seems to have originated as an Amorite war-taunt, sung as the people commemorated their conquest of the Moabites. The event must have been widely known in the general area, because the Israelites were now adapting it to their own purposes and quoting it as they contemplated their own conquest of Heshbon. The song became enshrined in Hebrew historical tradition because it was cited again centuries later by Jeremiah (48:45-46) in an abbreviated and modified form as he, too, contemplated the devastation of Moab. In the taunt-song, the Amorite composer hastened to invite his victorious countrymen to restore Heshbon and make it a worthy capital for Sihon. Having celebrated the destruction of the Moabite capital, he turned to other Moabite towns including Ar, which may be a city or an area of territory including or even synonymous with Moab itself.[35] The concept of "holy war" is evident in the statement that the defeat of the Moabites resulted from their god's inability or unwillingness to save them.

Chemosh, the Moabite deity, is mentioned eight times on the Moabite Stone, an inscription by King Mesha of Moab about 850 B.C.[36] On this monument Chemosh is described directing military activities and employing the *ḥērem* or "ban" as a form of warfare (line 17). In the inscription his name is conjoined with that of Ashtar, which suggests that Chemosh may have been a star deity paired with the goddess Ishtar (Venus).[37] The fire that "flared out" from Heshbon evidently

35. P. D. Hanson, "The Song of Heshbon and David's Nir," *HTR* 61 (1968): 301, and D. K. Stuart, *Studies in Early Hebrew Meter* (Chico, Calif.: Scholars Press, 1976), p. 93, read עָרֵי, "cities of," instead of MT עָר, assuming that both words would have been spelled similarly in antiquity. This emendation, however, is conjectural at best.
36. W. F. Albright, *ANET,* pp. 320-21; E. Ullendorff, *DOTT,* pp. 195-98; W. F. Albright, "Is the Mesha Inscription a Forgery?" *JQR* 35 (1945): 247-50; P. D. Miller, Jr., *ISBE,* 3:396-98 and bibliography.
37. G. H. Livingston, *ZPEB,* 1:786; T. Nicol and W. S. LaSor, *ISBE,* 1:640-41.

reached into the Moabite kingdom as far as Nophah and beyond it to Medeba.

The location of Nophah is unknown, but there are textual difficulties in v. 30, as indicated by the LXX καὶ αἱ γυναῖκες ἔτι προσεξέκαυσαν πῦρ ἐπὶ Μωάβ (*kai hai gynaikes eti prosexekausan pyr epi Mōab*, "and the women again poured fire upon Moab"). This represents a significant textual variation from the MT, which is rendered literally by the KJV. The *RSV* and the *NEB*, following the LXX and the Samaritan Pentateuch reading, emended the text to נפח אש (*nph 'š*, "fire was blown up"). All proposed emendations and restorations of MT here are conjectural. It is curious that the remainder of the taunt-song has, by contrast, been preserved so well.[38] Medeba, however, presents no problems of identification, being situated about twenty miles south of Rabbath-Ammon (the modern Amman) on the King's Highway between Heshbon and Dibon.

From this victory paean, later generations would learn how Israel came to occupy Amorite territory. It is ironic that the Hebrews used an earlier Amorite composition celebrating Sihon's defeat of the Moabites to express their own victory over the Amorites.

Translation

Thus the Israelites settled in Amorite territory. Then Moses sent spies to Jazer, and the Israelites captured its surrounding villages and dispossessed the Amorites who were living there. (21:31-32)

Exegesis and Exposition

Using the newly conquered territory as a base of operations, Moses sent scouts to Jazer, a fortified Amorite city north of Heshbon and close to Amman. It can probably be identified with the ruined site known as Khirbet Jazzir near es-Salt. During its lengthy history it passed through Amorite, Israelite, Moabite, and Ammonite hands.[39] In order to ensure security while other attacks were being made, Moses expelled all the Amorites from the area.

Translation

Then they turned and advanced along the road to Bashan. Og the ruler of Bashan and all his forces marched out and met them in battle at Edrei. The LORD said to Moses: Do not be afraid of him, because I have delivered him, his entire nation, and his land into your power. Do

---

38. For a discussion of the text see A. R. Hulst, *Old Testament Translation Problems*, p. 11.
39. S. Cohen, *IDB*, 2:805-6; M. H. Heicksen, *ZPEB*, 3:409-10; F. E. Young, *ISBE*, 2:971 and bibliographies; *GTTOT*, p. 119.

to him what you did to Sihon, the Amorite king, who ruled in Heshbon. So they defeated him along with his sons and all his people, leaving no survivors. Then they occupied his country. (21:33-35)

Exegesis and Exposition

The next maneuver saw the Israelites advancing into northern Transjordan to the territory of Og, king of Bashan, probably following an ancient caravan route for the attack. The area was first occupied in the Early Bronze Age (c. 3000-2000 B.C.), and the inhabitants found the fertile tableland ideal for growing wheat and raising cattle. Its boundaries are indeterminate, but in general its northern extremity reached to Mount Hermon, its eastern flank was the Jebel Druze, and its western border was formed by the hills east of the Sea of Galilee. Og, its ruler, was the last survivor of the giant Rephaim, one of the pre-Israelite races occupying Canaan.[40] They were tall in stature, as were the Anakim (cf. Deut. 2:11), and even in the early monarchy their unusual height and large weapons were still remembered (2 Sam. 21:16-22; 1 Chron. 20:6-8).

Og was recorded in Hebrew history as the possessor of a large iron bedstead measuring nine cubits long and four cubits wide—i. e., about thirteen feet by six feet (Deut. 3:11). This artifact was on display in Rabbath-Ammon long after Og's death, lending historical credibility to him. Some question has been raised about the "bedstead" (MT עֶרֶשׂ בַּרְזֶל, *'ereś barzel*), and on the basis of discoveries of black basalt sarcophagi in the region it has been suggested that the bedstead was actually a sarcophagus made from the iron-like basalt rock.[41] A major obstacle to this view, however, is the fact that nowhere in the MT does *'ereś* mean sarcophagus.

The majority of liberal scholars have dismissed the traditions regarding Og's stature as legendary or mythological, but such an assessment fails to take into account certain biological possibilities. Whatever Og's size, he was much taller than the Israelites opposing him. He was the last surviving king of an ancient people who had already suffered heavy losses at the hands of the Ammonites (cf. Deut. 2:21), and his great stature seems to indicate hypertrophy of the long bones of the body. This genetic phenomenon is one indication of impending extinction of the stock, and thus the tradition about Og's stature should be viewed in the same light as that of Goliath and his companions.[42]

40. See R. F. Schnell, *IDB*, 4:35; B. K. Waltke, *ZPEB*, 5:64-66 and bibliographies.
41. Cf. P. C. Craigie, *Deuteronomy*, p. 120.
42. Cf. R. K. Harrison, *ISBE*, 1:956.

Og bravely followed the same tactical procedures as the ill-fated Amorite king, and with the same result, because God had delivered the ruler and his people into Israelite hands. Edrei, located at the southern end of Bashan, stood on the site of the modern city of Derʿa.

The morale of the invading Israelites was now high, and as a result they had secured a foothold in a productive area of Transjordan. The victories against Sihon and Og became yet another example of God's mighty acts on behalf of His people (cf. Josh. 2:10; 9:10; Pss. 135:11; 136:19-20). It was a token of what would follow if only the Israelites continued to be obedient to God's will.

When Glueck carried out surface explorations in Transjordan,[43] he concluded that no areas contained sedentary urban populations in the Bronze Age but that a sudden spurt of settled sites occurred in Edom and Moab during the thirteenth century b.c. This view cannot now be substantiated in the light of excavations at various sites in Transjordan.[44] In any event, this would have little bearing upon the authenticity of the wilderness narratives, which do not require heavily populated towns or cities.

Additional Notes

21:5 בֵאלֹהִים וּבְמֹשֶׁה: The use of בְּ- in these two words for quite different meanings is unusual. The LXX interpreted the first word to mean "to God" (πρὸς τὸν θεὸν), thus understanding the preposition בְּ- to mean "with." In the case of the second word the בְּ- is adversative, indicating disadvantage. See also GKC, sect. 59a. The majority of English translations render בְּ- as adversative in both instances.

21:11 בְּעִיֵּי הָעֲבָרִים: All the versions diverge from the MT significantly here. The LXX appears to have followed an independent tradition, whereas the Samaritan Pentateuch resorts, as before, to interpolating material from Deuteronomy, in this case from Deut. 2:17-19. On the wilderness itineraries generally see G. W. Coats, "The Wilderness Itinerary," *CBQ* 34 (1972): 135-52; G. I. Davies, "The Wilderness Itineraries," *TynBul* 25 (1974): 46-81.

21:14 וָהֵב בְּסוּפָה: For this designation the Samaritan Pentateuch reads "Waheb on the Reed Sea," while the LXX diverges completely by reading "he has set Zoob aflame" (τὴν Ζωὸβ ἐφλόγισεν). The LXX reading may have resulted from confusing a *waw* and a *zayin*, thus

---

43. N. Glueck, *The Other Side of the Jordan* (New Haven, Conn.: ASOR, 1970 ed.).
44. Cf. C. M. Bennett in P. R. S. Moorey and P. J. Parr, eds., *Archaeology in the Levant* (Warminster: Aris and Phillips, 1978), pp. 164-71; E. K. Vogel, *ISBE*, 2:1110-25 and bibliography.

taking the Hebrew to be זהב. The Vulgate seems to have emended והב
to יהב, again through confusion of consonants.

21:17 אָז: After this particle the preterite sense of the verb occurs
in prose and archaic Hebrew poetry, following Ugaritic and Moabite
constructions. See R. J. Williams, *Hebrew Syntax*, pp. 35-36, sects.
176-77. The syntax attests to the antiquity of the passage. For emendations see D. N. Freedman, "Archaic Forms in Early Hebrew Poetry,"
ZAW 72 (1960): 101-7.

21:18 הָעָם: The LXX has plural ἐθνῶν.

6
Consolidation in Transjordan
(22:1–33:56)

The fifth section of Numbers traces the history of the Israelite wanderings during their sojourn in Transjordan. How long they were encamped in Moab is unknown, but Moses would have spent a great deal of time and effort in organizing the military forces of Israel in case of a surprise attack. His southern flank was protected by the Arnon defile, and up to that time the Ammonites in the north and east had shown no aggressive intent toward Israel. This phase of the journey to Canaan finds the Israelites in the shadow of a towering mountain once more. But now they were within easy reach of their objective, with only the defenses of Jericho to impede their occupation of Canaan.

A. BALAAM HIRED TO CURSE ISRAEL (22:1-41)

Chapter 22 introduces the activities of Balak, king of Moab, and a Mesopotamian seer named Balaam. It can be analyzed into four sections: (1) Balak's invitation declined (vv. 1-14); (2) a second invitation extended (vv. 15-21); (3) God opposes Balaam (vv. 22-35); (4) Balaam meets Balak (vv. 36-41).

1. BALAK'S INVITATION DECLINED (22:1-14)

Translation

Then the Israelites moved on and camped in the plains of Moab on the side of the Jordan across from Jericho. Now Balak, son of Zippor, saw what the Israelites had done to the Amorites. The Moabites were greatly afraid of the people because they were so numerous. They were sick with apprehension about them. (22:1-3)

Exegesis and Exposition

When the forces of Israel encamped in Transjordan opposite Jericho, Balak, son of Zippor and ruler of Moab, became concerned about the proximity of the armies that had decimated the kingdoms of Sihon and Og. The Israelites had been careful not to provoke the Moabites to battle, journeying well to the east of their territory as they moved north to the Arnon gorge. Now Balak feared for the safety of his own kingdom, and his trepidation was shared by his subjects, who must have heard reports about the fate of Sihon and Og.

Translation

The Moabites therefore said to the Midianite elders: This horde is going to lick up everything around us, as a bull devours the grass in the field. So Balak, son of Zippor, who was ruler of Moab at that period, dispatched messengers to Balaam, son of Beor, who was at Pethor near the river in *his native land, saying:

> An entire nation has come from Egypt. They cover the whole landscape, and now they are settling next to me. Please come at once and put a curse on these people, because they are too powerful for me. Perhaps I shall be able to conquer them and expel them from the land. For I know that those whom you bless are indeed blessed, and those whom you curse are accursed. (22:4-6)

Exegesis and Exposition

Unaware that it was not God's plan for Moab to be attacked, since it was not a Canaanite nation, Balak outlined to the Midianite tribal chiefs the dangerous position of Moab. The remark about being consumed in the way that cattle ate grass was an apposite simile, because the territory of Bashan, which the Israelites had already conquered, was well known for its cattle (cf. Deut. 32:14; Ps. 22:12; Ezek. 39:18; Amos 4:1). Specialized assistance was clearly required, so the Moabite king sent a delegation to Balaam, the son of Beor.

This man's home was in Pethor, a town located on the west bank of the Euphrates about twelve miles south of Carchemish. Pethor is identified with the *Pedru* found in the topographical lists of Thutmose

III (fifteenth century B.c.) and also with *Pitru*, a city captured by Shalmaneser III in 857 B.c.[1] The MT describes Balaam as residing in "his native land" (MT עַמּוֹ בְּנֵי־אֶרֶץ, *'ereṣ běnê-'ammô*, "the land of the sons of his people"), but some translators have emended "his people" (עַמּוֹ, *'ammô*) to read "Amaw" (עֲמָיו, *'ammāyw*), the name of a city listed in a fifteenth-century B.c. inscription from Alalakh. This is an inoffensive identification suggesting that Amaw was in the general area of Carchemish[2] and augmenting the historical testimony to Balaam's existence.

Balak's reason for desiring to consult with Balaam was that Balaam was a typical Mesopotamian diviner,[3] whose activities have been illumined by discoveries from ancient Near Eastern sources.[4] That Balaam was a real person and not a legendary figure has been made evident additionally by the discovery at Deir 'Alla in modern Jordan of an Aramaic prophetic text. Its author is described as "Balaam son of Beor" and is spoken of as a seer of the gods whose specialty was that of a professional imprecator who imposed curses upon others. This material was recovered from what seemed to be a sanctuary or a shrine and testifies to the high esteem that Balaam claimed in antiquity,[5] a position now conceded by all but the most skeptical.[6]

1. A. L. Oppenheim, *ANET*, p. 278.
2. A. S. Yahuda, "The Name of Balaam's Homeland," *JBL* 64 (1945) 547-51; cf. W. F. Albright, "The Home of Balaam," *JAOS* 35 (1915): 386-90; "Some Important Recent Discoveries: Alphabetic Origins and the Idrimi Statue," *BASOR* 118 (1950): 16 n. 13.
3. S. Daiches, "Balaam—a Babylonian *bārū*," *Hilprecht Anniversary Volume* (Leipzig: 1909), pp. 67-70; *Bible Studies* (London: Edward Goldston, 1950), pp. 110-19; R. Largement, "Les Oracles de Bile'am et la mantique sumero-akkadienne," *Travaux de l'Institut catholique de Paris: Memorial du Cinquantenaire* 10 (1964), pp. 37-50.
4. Cf. R. Castellino, "Un 'giudizio divino' con rituale in Mesopotamia?" *JCS* 9 (1977): 3-6, 32-36.
5. So J. Hoftijzer and G. van der Kooij, *Aramaic Texts from Deir 'Alla* (Leiden: Brill, 1976), pp. 173-92, 268-82; A. Caquot and A. Lemaire, "Les Textes araméens de Deir 'Alla," *Syria* 54 (1977): 193-202; J. Hoftijzer, "Prophet Balaam in a Sixth Century Aramaic Inscription," *BA* 39 (1976): 11-17; H. P. Muller, "Einige alttestamentliche Probleme zur aramäischen Inschrift von Deir 'Alla," *ZDPV* 94 (1978): 56-67; R. W. Wilson, *Prophecy and Society in Ancient Israel* (Philadelphia: Fortress, 1980): pp. 132-33; P. R. McCarter, "The Balaam Texts from Deir 'Alla: The First Combination," *BASOR* 239 (1980): 49-60; J. A. Hackett, "The Balaam Text from Deir ' Alla" (HSM; 1984); D. T. Olsen, *The Death of the Old and the Birth of the New*, p. 154.
6. E.g., T. L. Thompson, *The Historicity of the Patriarchal Narratives* (New York/Berlin: W. de Gruyter, 1974); J. Van Seters, *Abraham in History and Tradition* (New Haven, Conn.: Yale U., 1975).

Archaeological discoveries at Mari, located about halfway between Babylon and Aleppo, have provided further information about
pagan Near Eastern prophetism. The remains of an ancient school for
scribes included archives containing more than twenty thousand
cuneiform tablets, which compare in importance with similar materials from el-Amarna, Ugarit, and Ebla.[7] These tablets reflect life in
the Early and Middle Bronze Age I periods, until the city was devastated by Hammurapi of Babylon (c. 1792-1750 B.C.).[8]

A small group of Mari letters dealt with brief ecstatic utterances of
a prophetic nature. The city was apparently a place where divinatory
priests and prophets were trained. The cultic prophets were divided
into two main groups, the first comprising the *āpilum* or oracle-priest,
the *assinnum* or male cultic prostitute, and the *muḫḫûm*, an ecstatic
prophet. The second, of a more advanced nature technically, comprised the *maḫḫum*, an ecstatic soothsayer, and the *bārûm*, a highly
qualified professional diviner.

The Mari material did not disclose the means by which those
persons were inspired. It is possible that Mesopotamian ecstatic
prognosticators used mind-altering substances such as alcohol,
hashish, or fungus-infested rye grain.[9] Balaam may have had some
connection with Mari and its divinatory priests and prophets and
may possibly have been trained there.[10] It is important to note, however, that even though Balaam prophesied, the MT describes him not
as a prophet but as "the soothsayer" (הַקֹּסֵם, *haqqôsēm*, Josh. 13:22).

The message sent to this highly qualified diviner was short and to
the point, much as divinations themselves often were in the ancient
Near East. Balak wished Balaam to exercise his training in cursing
and proclaim maledictions upon Moab's unexpected and unwelcome
neighbors so that, having this advantage over them, he could extermi-
nate them. Balak's invitation ended with an ingratiating comment
that reflected his knowledge of Balaam's expertise.

The curse as such was widely held to possess an inherent ability
to bring about its intended effect and seems often to have had much
in common with sympathetic magic. Thus the nineteenth-century
B.C. Egyptian Execration Texts, constituting the names of national
enemies inscribed upon pottery bowls ready for smashing, reflected

---

7. P. W. Gaebelein, Jr., *ISBE*, 3:245-48 and bibliography; B. J. Beitzel in R.
   K. Harrison, ed., *Major Cities of the Biblical World* (Nashville: Thomas
   Nelson, 1985), pp. 156-69.
8. On this date see *HIOT*, pp. 159-66; R. E. Hayden, *ISBE*, 2:604.
9. This fungus, *Claviceps purpurea*, contains medically useful substances,
   one of which is lysergic acid. But the diethymanine derivative (LSD) is a
   formidable mind-disorienting chemical.
10. See H. B. Huffmon, "Prophecy in the Mari Letters," *BA* 31 (1968):101-24;
    reprinted in *BAR* (1970), 3:199-224.

the firm belief that once the bowls had been cursed and destroyed, a like fate would ensue for those named under the curse.[11]

Curses (cf. 1 Sam. 17:43) were generally uttered in the name of a god, a feature that was evidently imagined to confer upon them the power of self-realization. If a curse could not be written down (cf. Zech. 5:3) for some reason, it was deemed sufficient for it to be uttered aloud. The MT אָרָה (*'ārâ*, "be under a curse") seems to convey the magical notion of being placed under a spell, and for this to happen the curse would need to be pronounced according to a specific formula devised by the priest-magicians.

Translation

Then the elders of Moab and Midian left, taking with them a fee for divination. They came to Balaam and gave him the message from Balak. He said to them: Stay here overnight, and I will bring back to you whatever reply the LORD gives me. So the Moabite leaders stayed with him. (22:7-8)

Exegesis and Exposition

The delegation of Moabite and Midianite chiefs were careful to take with them a fee for Balaam's services (קְסָמִים בְּיָדָם, *qěsāmîm běyādām*, KJV "rewards of divination") when they delivered the message. The fee could have consisted of gold or silver, ornaments, animals from flock or herd, or a combination of these. The pagan diviner indicated that he would consult the Lord (MT יהוה, *YHWH*), the God of Israel, about the matter and then would give them an answer.

The period of time after darkness had fallen was preferred for diviners and soothsayers to consult with their gods, according to ancient Near Eastern magical traditions. But for all his pagan associations, Balaam had some acquaintance with the mighty God of Israel, as was only appropriate for a man of his professional standing, whose success depended to a considerable extent upon his being familiar with the deities of all the surrounding nations. Balaam not only knew of the Lord but also testified to it in the presence of Balak's Moabite delegation (Num. 22:18), probably to increase their confidence in him.

Translation

God came to Balaam and asked: Who are these men with you? Balaam answered God: Balak, son of Zippor, king of Moab, has sent me a message:

A people that has come from Egypt is covering the entire landscape. Come, now, and put a curse on them for me. Perhaps I shall be able to defeat them and expel them. (22:9-11)

---

11. T. Lewis and R. K. Harrison, *ISBE*, 1:837-38.

Exegesis and Exposition

Just as under the influence of God's Spirit the pagan prophet was to speak what was factually correct and spiritually true, so here in this response to the Lord's question Balaam responded in a forthright, accurate manner. The *šōṭĕrîm* apparently disliked the idea of their national deity coming to the pagan seer and therefore used "God" (MT אֱלֹהִים, *ĕlōhîm*) instead of "the Lord" (MT יהוה, *YHWH*). This passage reminds the reader that it is a fault of believers to imagine that they alone can be used by the Lord in His service. The Scriptures make clear that the Lord of Sinai is also God of the whole earth, who can devastate (Isa. 24:1-6) as well as re-create (65:17). Although He has chosen Israel to witness to His existence and power in human society and has bound her to Himself in a covenant relationship, His overall sovereignty is not thereby restricted. If His people disobey His will, He can use foreigners to discipline them while glorifying His own name and exerting His rule over the world.

Translation

But God replied to Balaam: Do not go with them. Do not curse these people, because they are to be blessed. The next morning Balaam rose and said to Balak's leaders: Return to your homeland. The Lord has refused to allow me to accompany you. So the Moabite leaders assembled and returned to Balak, saying: Balaam refused to come with us. (22:12-14)

Exegesis and Exposition

God's reply to the pagan soothsayer was polite but unequivocal. Balaam was prohibited from going to assist Balak because the Israelites were to be blessed and not cursed. Whatever his inner feelings, Balaam bowed to God's will and allowed the matter to end there. Obediently he sent the delegation back home with the discouraging tidings that Israel's God had refused him permission to return with them.

2. A SECOND INVITATION EXTENDED (22:15-21)

Translation

Then Balak sent other messengers, comprising princes who were more numerous and prestigious than the others. They came to Balaam and said to him: This is a message from Balak, son of Zippor: Please do not let anything prevent you from coming to me, because I shall bestow great honor upon you, and I will do whatever you bid me. Come and put a curse on these people for me. (22:15-17)

Exegesis and Exposition

In the belief that Balaam might have felt slighted by the comparatively low social ranking of the original delegation, and perhaps even sensitive to the possibility that the consulting fee might have been too small for such a reputable soothsayer, Balak dispatched a more noble deputation with the promise that "great honor" would be bestowed upon Balaam in recompense—apparently leaving open the exact amount of his stipend. The proprieties of ancient Near Eastern diplomatic tradition were evidently being observed here.

Translation

Then Balaam replied, saying to Balak's servants: Even if Balak were to give me his house filled with silver and gold, I could not disobey the command of the LORD my God to any extent, whether small or large. Now therefore please stay the night here also, so that I can discover what else the LORD has to say to me. (22:18-19)

Exegesis and Exposition

In obedience to Israel's God, Balaam declined to visit Balak and curse the Israelites, no matter how greatly he was honored. He was adamant about obeying to the letter the word of the Lord (MT פִּי יהוה, *pî YHWH*, "the mouth of YHWH"). The fact that Balaam spoke of the Lord as "my God" (MT אֱלֹהָי, *'ĕlōhāy*) should not be taken, in the light of subsequent events, as an indication that he was a true believer in Israel's God. Rather, he seems to have been referring courteously to the deity for which he was acting as spokesman. He requested time to commune with God during the night hours in case further instructions from God were forthcoming. This is what the MT מַה־יֹּסֵף (*mah-yōsēp*, "what else") seems to imply, and not Balaam's expectation of a greater reward than had been offered by Balak up to that time, thereby concealing greed.

Translation

God appeared to Balaam during the night and said to him: Since these men have come to fetch you, get up and go with them. But be sure that you do only what I tell you. So Balaam got up in the morning, saddled his donkey, and went off with the Moabite princes. (22:20-21)

Exegesis and Exposition

All too many people are more than ready to decide policy and give orders, but when it comes to following simple instructions, whether of human or divine origin, they experience great difficulty.

297

Having become satisfied that Balaam was indeed a man of his word and that he could be relied upon to follow instructions, God gave him permission to go with the deputation to Balak on condition that he continued to obey when God spoke to him.

3. GOD OPPOSES BALAAM (22:22-35)

Translation

Then *God became very angry because he had gone, and the LORD's angel took up a position on the road to block his way. Now he was riding on his donkey, accompanied by two servants. When the donkey saw the angel of the LORD standing in the road with a drawn sword in his hand, she swerved off the road into a field, whereupon Balaam beat the donkey so as to get her back on the road. (22:22-23)

Exegesis and Exposition

God's reaction seems to contradict the permission He had granted in v. 20, but some interpreters have seen it as a response to Balaam's behavior in setting out (MT הֹלֵךְ הוּא, *hôlēk hû*'), the character of which is not mentioned other than that he had two servants with him. These commentators imply that God had observed greed and pleasure in Balaam's attitude as he savored the prospect of future riches[12] and suddenly was concerned that he might not, after all, keep his word to speak God's message. To correct this potentially dangerous situation a dramatic theophany was required.

Accordingly the Lord sent out His angel, a surrogate for the Lord Himself, to halt Balaam as he rode with his two servants, identified by Targumic tradition as Jannes and Jambres.[13] The donkey was the first to see this awesome appearance and understandably avoided it. For her pains she suffered a beating by Balaam. There is nothing unusual in the donkey's behavior on this occasion, since animals can often apprehend the onset of danger before human beings do and have not infrequently saved lives as a consequence.

But Balaam was oblivious to any form of danger, perhaps because he was preoccupied with the prospect of meeting the ruler of Moab. Balaam's contemplation of the rewards that Balak would bestow upon him could have blotted out any other considerations. The reference to the angel is significant because here God's surrogate becomes

---

12. So *KD*, 3:168-69.
13. Thus the Jerusalem Targum to Numbers 22:24 considered them as magician servants of Balaam instead of Egyptian magicians (Ex. 7:11, 22; 2 Tim. 3:8), whereas the Tractate *Yalkut Shimeoni* on Exodus 2:15 regarded them as Balaam's sons. Cf. C. E. Armerding, *ISBE*, 2:966 and bibliography.

an adversary (MT שָׂטָן, śāṭān) to Balaam, where elsewhere the angel of the Lord generally exercises a protective role (cf. Gen. 24:7, 40; Ex. 13:21; Josh. 5:13; etc.).

Translation

> Then the angel of the LORD stood on a narrow track between the vineyards, where there was a fence on either side. When the donkey saw the angel of the LORD she pressed herself against the fence and crushed Balaam's foot against it. So he beat her a second time. Then the angel of the LORD went farther ahead and stood in a narrow place where there was no room to turn, either to the right or the left. When the donkey saw the angel of the LORD, she lay down under Balaam. This made Balaam furious, and he beat the donkey with his rod. (22:24-27)

Exegesis and Exposition

The angel made a further attempt to block Balaam's progress through a fenced vineyard, and again the donkey endeavored to avoid him, crushing her master's foot and receiving a second beating. A third angelic manifestation in an impassable area so terrified the animal that she simply crouched down on the path, and for this she suffered a third, more severe beating.

Threefold repetition is a structural device in this section of Numbers. Thus the donkey tried to evade the angel three times (vv. 23, 25, 27), whereas Balaam had three meetings with God before finally arriving at Moab (vv. 12, 20, 22-35). In chap. 23 Balaam requested three sacrifices before speaking his oracles (vv. 1, 14, 29). Furthermore, the entire story of Balaam can be divided into two main sections (22:7-35; 22:36-24:25) consisting of three parts each (22:7-14, 15-20, 21-35, matched by 22:36-23:12, 23:13-26, 23:27-24:25). In each case God insists that Balaam should speak only what He commands. The whole narrative is presented in such a way as to cover three pairs of consecutive days with unrecorded intervals of time.[14] By any standards this non-Israelite material has been assembled in a sophisticated interconnecting pattern that bespeaks an advanced and sensitive literary culture.

Translation

> Then the LORD opened the mouth of the donkey, and she said to Balaam: What have I done to you to make you beat me three times? (22:28)

---

14. For a more detailed analysis of this configuration see G. J. Wenham, *Numbers*, p. 24.

Exegesis and Exposition

Balaam's insensitivity to the Lord's presence made it necessary for God to open the mouth of the donkey before Balaam's own eyes could be opened. This incident is one of the most celebrated in the entire scriptural corpus and has commonly been ridiculed, doubted, or treated with embarrassment because the phenomenon of a speaking animal does not occur in normal experience.

In order to place the incident upon a proper foundation of fact, it must be observed that in describing an event there is sometimes a difference between the narrating of the happening, whether oral or written, and the event itself. In the case of Balaam there were eyewitnesses including the soothsayer himself, his two servants, and the princes of Balak. The donkey was heard to be braying in protest at the same time that Balaam was chastising it verbally and administering what he regarded as a well-deserved beating. Only as the beatings stopped and the animal continued to bray in response to Balaam's remarks would the onlookers become surprised and perplexed.

As the donkey brayed, she conveyed a message of anger and resentment that the seer understood in his mind in a verbal form and to which he quite properly responded verbally. Through her opened mouth the braying animal retaliated against her undeserved treatment by uttering sounds that were unintelligible to the other onlookers but that Balaam was able to comprehend through processes of mental apperception that are not well understood. This situation may be paralleled to some extent in charismatic religious utterances, where an individual suddenly begins articulating in an apparently incoherent manner that becomes intelligible to the audience only when its meaning has been communicated by an interpreter.

Two illustrations from the NT may throw some light upon Balaam's situation. The first was an event in the life of Jesus after Palm Sunday (John 12:12-15). As He was expressing some distress concerning His impending death and asking that in all things His Father's name might be glorified, a heavenly voice said, "I have both glorified it and will glorify it again" (12:28 KJV). The account goes on to say that some of the bystanders thought it thundered (βροντὴν γεγονέναι, *brontēn gegonenai*). Other eyewitnesses were more perceptive spiritually and attributed the noise to the voice of an angel (ἄγγελος αὐτῷ λελάληκεν, *angelos autō lelalēken*), and Jesus affirmed that the voice (φωνή, *phōnē*) had occurred for their sakes. There were thus three different interpretations of the event, one of them—incorrect, as it happened—being completely naturalistic.

The second event, which may be considered to be analogous to that involving Jesus, occurred in the experience of Saul of Tarsus, who at the time was on a mission to capture any Christians he found in Damascus and bring them back to Jerusalem. Before he arrived at Damascus he encountered a blinding theophany. Accompanying the bright light was a voice: "Saul, Saul, why persecutest thou me?" (Acts 9:4 KJV). Saul responded by saying, "Who art thou, Lord?" In response, the speaker revealed that He was Jesus, whom Saul was persecuting. He then ordered him to enter Damascus, where he would be told what he must do. According to rabbinic tradition, any voice from heaven would have been understood to constitute the voice of God Himself. But what is especially significant about the occurrence on the road to Damascus is that those who were traveling with Saul "stood speechless, hearing a voice but seeing no man" (Acts 9:7, KJV).

In connection with the Balaam incident, God spoke through the normal braying of the donkey in a manner that was intended for only one recipient: the animal's owner. In the same way God spoke to both Jesus and Saul of Tarsus in a fashion intended for them only, and because the message was in the nature of a private communication on those occasions its content and meaning were hidden from the bystanders. As far as the theophany to Balaam was concerned, his traveling companions would learn the significance of the donkey's braying only by being informed about it on a first-hand basis by its recipient. In all the miracles discussed above, the real significance is in the content of the communication from God and not the form adopted to convey it.

Translation

Balaam said to the donkey: Because you have made me look stupid. If I had a sword in my hand, I would have killed you by now. So the donkey replied to Balaam: Am I not the donkey that you have ridden ever since you got me, even to this day? Have I ever been disposed to do this to you? No, he replied. (22:29-30)

Exegesis and Exposition

The encounter between the animal and its owner continued along conversational lines, until even Balaam conceded that the situation was unusual and that their relationship had never before deteriorated so seriously. Now was the opportunity for the theophany to be manifested to the pagan prognosticator.

Translation

Then the LORD opened Balaam's eyes. He saw the angel of the LORD standing on the road, a drawn sword in his hand. Balaam bowed his head and fell prostrate. The angel of the LORD said to him: Why did

you beat your donkey three times? Look, I came here as an adversary, because what you are doing is perverse. The donkey saw me and tried to avoid me three times. If she had not swerved, I would certainly have killed you by now but would have spared her life. (22:31-33)

Exegesis and Exposition

Balaam's eyes were already open in a physical sense, but hitherto he had been blind to the spiritual realities confronting him. To "open the eyes" (MT יְגַל ... אֶת-עֵינֵי, *yĕgal ... 'et-'ênê*) means to heighten the apperceptive powers of the mind.

The first result of this experience was a sense of sin as the Mesopotamian seer fell prostrate before the Lord's messenger, who was now understood to be in an adversarial relationship with Balaam. The angel asked the prostrate soothsayer the same question as that of the donkey. He then stated the nature of his mission in terms of an attempt to frustrate Balaam's perverted behavior. There is a certain irony at this point. As a practitioner of divination, Balaam was doubtless trained in such techniques as extispicy, whose practitioners examined bodily organs of slaughtered animals for omens predicting the future. Competent though he may have been in such areas, he was blind to the significance of his donkey's behavior, unable initially to see what his animal had already seen three times. The angel's pronouncement seems to indicate that the offense the divine messenger was condemning was the prospect of great reward rather than the commitment to speak only what God had commanded him to utter.

Translation

Balaam said to the Lord's messenger: I have sinned, because I did not know that you were standing there, blocking the road against me. But if you are displeased with me, I will go back home. Then the angel of the Lord said to Balaam: Go on with the men, but say only the things that I tell you. So Balaam went off with the princes of Balak. (22:34-35)

Exegesis and Exposition

Balaam suddenly became aware that he was confronted by a power of a kind that surpassed all his previous experience. The basic meaning of חָטָא (*ḥāṭā'*, "to sin") is "to miss the mark," so that probably what Balaam was admitting to was a procedural error or the taking of a wrong direction. Much as Balaam may well have wanted to do otherwise, he was now compelled to speak and act as the all-powerful God of Israel dictated. His offer to return home may simply have been the result of self-interest in wanting to avoid further punishment and perhaps even to secure the Lord's forgiveness by his complaisance.

But had this offer been implemented, it would have frustrated God's plan to use him as a spokesman for blessing upon Israel. He seems thus to have been forced against his will to speak only the words that God put into his mouth.

4. BALAAM MEETS BALAK (22:36-41)

Translation

Now when Balak heard that Balaam was arriving, he went out to meet him at a Moabite city located on the Arnon border at the boundary of his territory. Then Balak said to Balaam: Did I not send again and again, asking you to come? Why didn't you come to me immediately? Am I not able to reward you sufficiently? Balaam said to Balak: Look, I have arrived finally. But what power have I to say anything as of myself? The word that God places in my mouth is what I must speak. (22:36-38)

Exegesis and Exposition

The anxious Balak was now greatly relieved by the arrival of Balaam, and though still annoyed with him he met the seer and the Moabite delegation at a point on the northeast border of his kingdom.[15] Balak was irritated by his guest's reluctance to accept his first invitation and asked bluntly if the reward was inadequate. Balaam did not answer the questions directly, however, but instead concentrated upon his duties, telling Balak that he would hear only God's words.

Translation

Then Balaam went with Balak to Kiriath-huzoth. Balak sacrificed bulls and sheep, and he sent some to Balaam and the princes accompanying him. On the following day Balak took Balaam and brought him up to Bamoth-baal, that from there he might see the full extent of the Israelites. (22:39-41)

Exegesis and Exposition

Having met Balaam at the border of his territory, Balak escorted him by stages to a place where he would be able to see where the invading Israelites were encamped. The delegation journeyed to Kiriath-huzoth, a "city of streets," close to Kir in Moab. If this were

---

15. For KJV "a city"; *NEB* reads "Ar," presumably referring to the place mentioned in Num. 21:15. This involves changing the MT עִיר to עָר, but the variant has no support in the ancient versions. The "city" was probably Kir.

the capital of Moab, it might perhaps be identified with Kir-hareseth.[16] On the day after a sacrificial meal had been held in honor of the occasion, Balaam was given an opportunity of viewing Balak's dreaded foes.

During the festivities Balaam would doubtless have had the opportunity of examining the entrails of some of the animals offered in sacrifice, as was the common practice among Babylonian diviners. One particularly important organ was the liver, the condition of which enabled those skilled in hepatoscopy to formulate predictions according to what was observed.[17] Balaam would have been thoroughly familiar with such procedures and would have employed them on other occasions. But now, commissioned as he had been by God, any inspection of livers would have been merely a formal gesture to his worried host, since his utterances were to be governed by a quite different form of inspiration.

Balaam was enabled to survey the Israelites from an elevation called Bamoth-baal ("high places of Baal"). The location is unknown, but it was on the western side of the Transjordanian plateau, perhaps somewhat north of Mount Nebo.

Additional Notes

22:5 עַל־הַנָּהָר: The LXX reads נהר as a construct, "river of the land," and this is followed by the Vulgate and the KJV.

עַמּוֹ: The Samaritan Pentateuch, Vulgate, and Syriac versions emend to עַמּוֹן in an attempt to solve an apparent difficulty in the MT. But to locate Balaam's home in Ammonite territory is incorrect. The "River" is evidently the Euphrates, which did not flow through the land of Ammon.

22:6 אָרָה־לִי: Here לְ is a preposition of interest expressing advantage.

מְבֹרָךְ וַאֲשֶׁר: The relative particle here appears without a proper antecedent.

22:10 The MT omits לֵאמֹר, "saying," which is supplied by the LXX and Vulgate.

22:13 אַרְצְכֶם: LXX has πρὸς τὸν κύριον ὑμῶν, reading אֲדוֹן for אֶרֶץ. The change is difficult to substantiate.

22:18 גְדוֹלָה: After this word the LXX adds ἐν τῇ διανοίᾳ μου.

22:20 וַיָּבֹא אֱלֹהִים: The Samaritan Pentateuch reads "the angel of God," intending a surrogate to be understood.

16. Cf. W. S. LaSor, *ISBE*, 3:40-42.
17. I. Mendelsohn, *IDB*, 1:856-58; W. L. Liefeld, *ZPEB*, 2:146-49; D. E. Aune, *ISBE*, 1:971-74 and bibliographies.

22:22 אֱלֹהִים: The Samaritan Pentateuch and the LXX MS Codex Ambrosianus read יהוה here, perhaps because יהוה occurred elsewhere in vv. 22-25. The *šōṭĕrîm* were not bound by mechanical stylistic consistency, however, as has been noted elsewhere.

22:29 The MT here uses the particle לוּ to introduce an optative clause. Thus the meaning of לוּ יֶשׁ-חֶרֶב בְּיָדִי is: "Would that I had a sword in my hand!"

22:32-33 The *NEB* renders כִּי-יָרַט הַדֶּרֶךְ לְנֶגְדִּי as "but you made straight for me," emending יָרַט to יָרְטָה. The LXX follows the MT in reading ὅτι οὐκ ἀστεία ἡ ὁδός σου ἐναντίον μου. The *NEB* emendation is weak and has the added disadvantage of making the MT read more roughly. Accordingly it is preferable to retain the KJV rendering, which was adopted by the *RSV*. יָרַט is rare, being found again only in Job 16:11. Balaam is embarking upon a foolhardy enterprise with less than the highest motives in mind.

The MT אוּלַי in v. 33 is the usual Hebrew word for "perhaps," and thus it would be appropriate to consider it a misspelling or faulty transcription of the negative particle לוּלֵי, "if not," "unless," as many scholars do.

B. BALAAM BLESSES ISRAEL AND RETURNS HOME (23:1–24:25)

Chapter 23 can be assessed in terms of four units: (1) Balaam's first prophecy (vv. 1-10); (2) relocation and repetition of ritual (vv. 11-17); (3) Balaam's second prophecy (vv. 18-24); (4) further relocation (vv. 25-30).

Chapter 24 continues the narratives dealing with Balaam's prophetic oracles. His third, fourth, and final utterances are recorded, after which he returned home. The chapter is structured in terms of three principal sections: (1) Balaam's third prophecy (vv. 1-14); (2) Balaam's fourth prophecy (vv. 15-19); (3) Balaam's final prophecies and return home (vv. 20-25).

1. BALAAM'S FIRST PROPHECY (23:1-10)

Translation

Then Balaam said to Balak: Build seven altars for me here, and prepare seven bulls and seven rams also. So Balak did exactly as Balaam had specified. Balak and Balaam then sacrificed a bull and a ram on each altar. Then Balaam said to Balak: Stand here with your offering, and I will withdraw. Perhaps the Lord will come to meet with me. Whatever He reveals to me I will disclose to you. So he went off to a deserted height. (23:1-3)

305

Exegesis and Exposition

Before Balaam uttered his first prophetic oracle, appropriate preparations had to be made in accordance with accepted principles of ancient Near Eastern rituals. He therefore ordered Balak to prepare animals for sacrifice on seven different altars. Balak followed Balaam's instructions meticulously, since the success of the whole prophetic enterprise depended upon securing the approval of deity through correct ritual performance, as was also the case in the Hebrew sacrificial system. Once the animals had been sacrificed, Balaam withdrew to a quiet elevation so as to compose himself for further instructions from God.

The number seven has always carried a peculiar fascination for Semitic peoples, perhaps because it was connected with the Sabbath.[18] Whereas bulls were not as numerous in antiquity, sheep were raised in enormous quantities, and in Israel many male sheep were preferred for sacrificial offerings. Many scholars have regarded the number of sacrificial animals mentioned at this period as grossly exaggerated. It is therefore instructive to learn that the sacrificing of large numbers of sheep is still practiced in some areas of the Near East. Thus a traveler to the city of Van in eastern Turkey in 1987 arrived on the eve of Kurban Bayram, the second most important religious holiday in the Islamic calendar. He had difficulty in walking through the city market because he was overwhelmed by huge numbers of sheep that everyone seemed to be taking home. On inquiry he was informed that, during the four or five days of festival, more than two million sheep would be slaughtered to Allah.[19]

At ancient pagan sacrifices that were undertaken before the beginning of an important enterprise, the viscera of the sacrificial animals were inspected, as mentioned above, and there would have been no shortage of specimens on this occasion if Balaam had chosen to use them. What Balak was expected to do while waiting for Balaam to return must remain a matter of conjecture.

Balaam's choice of a quiet elevation reflects the tradition that the tops of mountains were the closest locations to the gods, who could be expected to descend and communicate with their votaries. The tradition may have originated with the Sumerians, whose ziggurats, or staged temple towers, were meant to represent artificial mountains. On the uppermost level the builders constructed a small shrine for their patron deity in the expectation that priests and worshipers might receive a divine visit on ceremonial occasions.

18. Cf. M. H. Pope, *IDB*, 4:294-95; W. White, Jr., *ZPEB*, 4:457; G. G. Cohen, *TWOT*, 2:898-99.
19. *Toronto Globe and Mail*, February 27, 1988, section F, p. 14.

Translation

God met with Balaam, who said to Him: I have prepared seven altars, and on each of them I have sacrificed a bull and a ram. Then the LORD put words into Balaam's mouth, saying: Go back to Balak and speak what I tell you. So Balaam returned to him, and he was still standing beside his sacrifice, along with all the Moabite princes. (23:4-6)

Exegesis and Exposition

God indeed met with the pagan prognosticator and heard a report about preparations for the prophecy. The Lord appears to be treating the seer just as He would have dealt with Moses under comparable circumstances. Indeed, God was about to perform another "mighty work," using a non-Israelite professional seer as a medium of prophetic blessing for the covenant people. Accordingly Balaam was dispatched to Balak with instructions to speak only as he was informed. He found Balak still standing at his post, along with his court retinue.

Translation

Then Balaam began his prophetic oracle, saying:

> Balak, king of Moab, brought me from Syria,
> from the eastern mountains, saying:
> Come, pronounce a curse upon Jacob for me.
> Come, denounce the Israelites.
> But how can I curse those whom God has not cursed,
> or denounce those whom the LORD has not denounced?
> I see them from the peaks;
> from the hills I watch them.
> There they are! A people that dwells apart,
> not considering itself one of the nations.
> Who can count the dust of Jacob,
> or number even *one quarter of the Israelites?
> May I die the death of the righteous!
> May my end be as theirs! (23:6-10)

Exegesis and Exposition

The "oracles of Balaam" have been the object of study for many decades, and this activity has produced a large body of literature. From an early period the material was recognized as non-Israelite in origin, and when linguistic studies determined the characteristic forms of Hebrew poetry, the oracles took their proper place in that body of OT literature. In the heyday of Pentateuchal literary criticism, various scholars argued over the amount of the oracles to be allocated to the supposed "J" and "E" material thought to be represented in the oracles.[20] Since that time literary critics have continued the discussion, using various kinds of analysis and discovering supposed narrative "layers," textual corruptions, and other literary phenomena.[21]

But no significant progress was made until 1944, when W. F. Albright published his landmark analysis of the material. He employed philological analysis and text-critical study to demonstrate that the Balaam oracles were ancient poems going back to the twelfth or thirteenth century B.C. These conclusions were supported by an imposing array of arguments based upon the grammar and lexicography of comparable Northwest Semitic texts from the same general period. Albright dated the MT form to the tenth century B.C.,[22] with the oracles antedating the narrative framework by a century or two, on the evident assumption that the material had experienced a long history of oral transmission.

Conjectures of this variety make the mistake of ignoring the traditions of scribal transmission as now known from various ancient Near Eastern sources. First, any event of significance was committed to writing at the time it happened or shortly thereafter. The written tradition would then be passed on to posterity as a permanent record. Coexistent with this was an oral form of the occurrence, coming first from eyewitnesses and used as a means of circulating the information in contemporary society. Only as it was handed down to subsequent generations did it acquire a degree of "transmission," but under ordinary circumstances there was always an official archival record against which the oral version could be checked. The written form might outlast the oral, or vice versa. In some situations both would undoubtedly perish together. Second, ancient scribes functioned according to strict professional rules. Their main task, after compiling or recording various events, was to take earlier materials, and update them in terms of grammar and style. The ancient Sumerians were especially meticulous in such matters, and the Hittite and Hebrew scribes followed in the same general tradition. In the case of the renowned Balaam, therefore, a written and an oral form of his doings would be in existence not long after his exploits, which would have

---

20. Cf. H. Gressmann, *Die Schriften des Alten Testaments* 3 (Göttingen: Vandenhoeck and Ruprecht, 1914), pp. 52-70; G. B. Gray, *Numbers*, pp. 309-11; M. Noth, *Numbers*, p. 171.
21. D. T. Olsen, *The Death of the Old and the Birth of the New*, p. 154.
22. W. F. Albright, "The Oracles of Balaam," *JBL* 63 (1944): 210, 226. For an extensive bibliography on this subject see D. T. Olsen, *The Death of the Old and the Birth of the New*, pp. 228-30.

been made especially memorable if only because of his encounter with the angelic messenger and the superstitious veneration in which such an exploit would have been held by his traveling companions.

Precisely how and when the Balaam oracles came into the hands of the Hebrews is unknown. But the fact that the Israelites were already familiar with an Amorite taunt-song indicates something of the extent to which information was exchanged freely among second-millennium B.C. peoples. The oracles are an ancient kind of Hebrew poetry, and thus it is possible that by the period of Samuel the Hebrew šōṭĕrîm had already updated some of the more primitive linguistic expressions.

But to regard this material as having been in oral form until the eighth or seventh century B.C. is an erroneous interpretation of scribal activity. Oral transmission may have been the sole way in which traditions were handed down in illiterate medieval Europe in areas such as Germany and Scandinavia, but such processes did not apply in the ancient Near East, where there were always two kinds of transmission, the literary and the oral.

The first oracle (23:1-10) exhibits a symmetrical pattern of lines written in synonymous parallelism. Smick[23] has analyzed the material in terms of three broad statements (vv. 7a, 9a, 10b), informing the reader of Balaam's mission, function, and final expectations. Coming after the first couplet are two quatrains about Israel (vv. 7b-8, 9b-10a) in which Balaam is angry about his inability to pronounce a curse upon Israel but at the same time notes the distinctive place Israel occupied among the nations.

The opening verse seems to have been a ritual statement in which the seer identified himself and addressed the deity to whom he was praying in order to acquaint Him with the nature of his request. In disclosing his identity Balaam stated that he had come from northeastern Syria (MT אֲרָם, 'ărām), from the eastern mountains (MT הַרְרֵי־קֶדֶם, harĕrê-qedem), the latter being a Canaanite term for the mountainous region of eastern Syria. The salutation was a summary of Balak's invitation to him, which God had given Balaam permission to repeat. The tension in the seer's mind arises from his knowledge that God had determined to bless Israel. Whether Balaam approved of the situation, he was being used by the all-powerful God of Israel for a specific prophetic purpose and was unable to mount any resistance. Therefore, any attempt that he might make to curse the Israelites in order to satisfy Balak, or for that matter his own inner greed, would prove futile.

---

23. E. B. Smick, *ISBE*, 3:566.

As Balaam gazed at the nation of Israel spread out beneath him, he affirmed its uniqueness in the world. His statement was accurate, because the Israelites were the only people to be linked with a living God by means of a covenant relationship. By contrast, all other contemporary nations worshiped idols, which were expressly prohibited in Israel. As Hertz has expressed it: "Israel has always been a people apart, a people isolated and distinguished from other peoples by its religious and moral laws, by the fact that it has been chosen as the instrument of a Divine purpose."[24] The "dust" of Jacob looks back to Gen. 13:16, which would be unknown to Balaam, and is a way of describing a countless multitude. The Mesopotamian seer, in his final sentence, claims the promise of Gen. 12:3, thereby sharing in the blessing that belongs to God's chosen.

2. RELOCATION AND REPETITION OF RITUAL (23:11-17)

Translation

Balak said to Balaam: Whatever have you done to me? I brought you here to put a curse upon my foes, but instead you have done nothing but bless them. But he replied: Must I not be careful to speak only what the LORD has put into my mouth? (23:11-12)

Exegesis and Exposition

Balak's anguish at the thought of the hired seer yearning for a share in Israel's future blessings is phrased politely, although the intent is unmistakable. Balaam, however, had acted as promised. Furthermore, he had already warned Balak that this would be the case, thereby giving him no recourse.

Translation

Then Balak said to him: Please come with me to another area from which you may observe them. There you will see only a part, not the whole of them. Curse them for me from there. So he took him to the field of Zophim on top of the elevated place, where he built seven altars, offering a bull and a ram on each altar. Balaam said to Balak: Stand here beside your sacrifice while I meet with the LORD over there. (23:13-15)

Exegesis and Exposition

Balak in his desperation apparently felt that a different topographical perspective on the situation would produce more satisfactory results. Accordingly he suggested that Balaam should move to

24. J. H. Hertz, ed., The *Pentateuch and Haftorahs*, p. 674.

an area where he had a less extensive view of the Israelite camp. This was agreed upon, and they ascended to the field of Zophim on the elevated area mentioned in Num. 21:20, which was close to Mount Nebo. The "field of Zophim" has not been identified, and it may not even be correct to regard Zophim as a proper name since the word simply means "watchers." Perhaps a better rendering would therefore be "the area for observers," "a lookout post," or a similar phrase. The sacrificial ritual was repeated with full ceremony, and once more Balak was stationed beside his offering while Balaam conferred with God some distance away.

Translation

Then the Lord met with Balaam and gave him an utterance to speak, saying: Go back to Balak and proclaim what I tell you. So he returned to him, and Balak was still standing beside his sacrifice, along with all the Moabite princes. Balak asked him: What has the Lord said to you? (23:16-17)

Exegesis and Exposition

God's instructions to Balaam were the same as before, as was the background of sacrificial ritual. But Balak was curious as to the nature of Balaam's communication with God. By way of response to Balak the Mesopotamian seer began to prophesy again.

3. BALAAM'S SECOND PROPHECY (23:18-24)

Translation

Then he commenced his prophetic oracle, saying:

>Stand up, Balak, and listen!
>Hear me, son of Zippor!
>God is not a human being, that He should lie,
>nor a mortal man, to change His mind.
>Has He spoken and then refrained from acting?
>Has He made promises and not fulfilled them?
>I have been commanded to bless.
>He has already bestowed blessing,
>and I cannot reverse it.
>He has not noticed any wickedness in Jacob,
>nor has He recognized evil in Israel.
>The Lord their God is with them.
>Theirs is the acclamation of a king!
>God brought them from Egypt;
>they are as strong as a wild bull.

311

> He has recognized no spell against Jacob
> nor countenanced any sorcery against Israel.
> Now it must be said of Jacob, and of Israel:
> See what God has done!
> The people arise like a lioness;
> they stand erect like a lion
> that will not relax until he has devoured his prey
> and drunk the blood of the slain. (23:18-24)

Exegesis and Exposition

The second pronouncement is considerably longer and more articulate than the first. It is therefore unusual for utterances attributed to ancient seers, which were usually brief and cryptic in meaning and mostly devoid of theological content. The oracle comprises an introductory section (v. 18), two following passages (19-21a; 21b-23), and a conclusion (v. 24). Balaam began by informing Balak that Israel's God is a morally consistent Being whose nature it is to fulfill His promises. Because Balaam had been instructed to bless Israel, he had no choice but to obey, if only because it was impossible for him to reverse God's decisions. The MT of vv. 21-23 is difficult to translate, and this seems to reflect the antiquity of the original, along with possible scribal updating. Consequently the various English translations exhibit a range of interpretation. In v. 21 the KJV reads, "He hath not beheld iniquity in Jacob, neither hath he seen perverseness in Israel," which is followed broadly by the *RSV*, *NEB*, and *NIV*. The latter, however, offers an alternative rendering in a footnote: "He has not looked on Jacob's offenses / or on the wrongs found in Israel," which places a different interpretation upon the MT. In the rendering adopted for this commentary, God was clearly regarding Israel, the sons of Jacob, as an ideal spiritual community that had no evident spot or blemish (cf. v. 10). As Wenham has pointed out, Balaam perceived this ideal in his vision,[25] so that in effect he was proclaiming the lofty spiritual standards of the Sinaitic covenant as the means by which Israel would live as a righteous nation. Loyalty to these ideals would continue to inhibit the presence of spots or blemishes. The MT עָמָל (*'āmāl*, "wrong," "misery," "trouble") also carries the more emphatic meaning of "disaster."

The KJV and *RSV* translation of the final colon of the verse, "the shout of a king is among them," is rendered as a clause in apposition to the preceding colon, so that the people are represented as acclaim-

---

25. G. J. Wenham, *Numbers*, p. 175.

ing the Lord as a king among them (cf. Deut. 33:5).[26] The sense of the
MT can also be interpreted as indicating that the victorious Israelites
were being given the kind of prestigious treatment normally accorded to royalty, which would include the sounds of trumpets (MT
תְּרוּעָה, *těrû'â*).

In v. 22 Balaam grounds Israel's existence firmly in history and
describes the nation in its victories as a "wild bull" (MT רְאֵם, *rě'ēm*,
Akkad. *rîmu*, Ugar. *rum*). Scholars generally agree that this animal
was the now-extinct Aurochs (*Bos primigenius*), rendered unfortunately in the KJV by the mythical name "unicorn." The Aurochs was
the ancestor of modern domesticated cattle. A large, powerful beast
with long horns, it was a preferred animal for hunting in the Middle
Bronze Age.[27] It is thus ironic that Balaam should have been proclaiming publicly the preeminent might of Bashan's conqueror to
Balak, who was so anxious to see his potential enemy attenuated. The
MT is amenable to various renderings here. The KJV speaks of God's
having "the strength of an unicorn," and the *NEB* likens His power to
the curving horns of the wild bull. The *NIV*, by contrast, regards the
Israelites as having the strength of a wild ox, whereas the *NAB* speaks
of God as "a wild bull of towering might."[28]

Verse 23 reiterates the theme of v. 21 in proclaiming the ideal of
an Israel enshrining the moral standards of the Sinai covenant. The
victories achieved so far made it possible for Israel to be admired by
her neighbors. The phrase לֹא-נַחַשׁ בְּיַעֲקֹב (*lō'-naḥaš běya'ăqōb*) can be
rendered "no spell *against* Jacob" or "no spell *in* Jacob." The same
construction is repeated in connection with Israel in the next colon.
Although the inseparable preposition *bě-* can mean "in," "on," "by,"
and "with," it can also mean "against" on occasion. Perhaps this was
a development from the use of *bě-* as "on," envisaging an adversarial
relationship. Meaning is determined by context, and in this verse
either sense is legitimate.

The message of the seer appears to be that no kind of magic has
any place, whether intrinsic or extrinsic, in the life of the Israelite
people. All other nations had recourse to spells, incantations, and
other forms of the magical arts. In the light of his own experiences as
a *qôsēm*, Balaam could make this assertion with confidence. He knew

26. An NEB footnote translates the MT less ambitiously as "royal care is
    bestowed upon them," following the tradition of the LXX, the Samaritan
    Pentateuch, and the Targum Onkelos. Cf. W. F. Albright, *JBL*, 63 (1944):
    215 n. 43; A. R. Hulst, *Old Testament Translation Problems*, pp. 11-12.
27. G. S. Cansdale, *ZPEB*, 5:930.
28. The textual problems are surveyed by W. F. Albright, *JBL* 63 (1944):
    215-16.

that, for the Israelites, the living God of Sinai was the nation's strength and that therefore sorcery and incantation were unnecessary. A renowned ancient Near Eastern prognosticator thus proclaimed in public his conviction that any form of divination is superfluous where God is in control.

Balaam's oracles contain several literary ironies. In v. 25 the seer likened Israel to a prowling lioness (MT לָבִיא, *lābî'*, which can also mean "lion") looking for food. The feminine is preferred here because the lioness does most of the tracking and killing when on the hunt, while the lion moves up and down, roaring to distract the prey. The lion was the traditional emblem of Judah, Dan, and Gad, and its attributes as "king of the beasts" made it also a symbol of Christ in Rev. 5:5.

4. FURTHER RELOCATION (23:25-30)

Translation

Then Balak said to Balaam: Do not put any curses on them, and do not bless them either. Balaam replied: Did I not tell you that I must do everything that the LORD tells me? Then Balak said to Balaam: Come with me, and I will take you to yet another place. Perhaps God will be content to let you curse them for me from there. So Balak guided Balaam to the top of Peor, overlooking Jeshimon. Then Balaam said to Balak: Build seven altars for me here, and prepare seven bulls and seven rams also. So Balak did exactly as Balaam had directed, sacrificing a bullock and a ram on each altar. (23:25-30)

Exegesis and Exposition

We see here a continuation of the conflict between two strong-willed men, neither of whom was prepared to modify his position. Optimistic even in his desperation, Balak attempted yet another change of locale in what would be a final attempt to secure curses upon his potential adversary. This strategy is interesting because Balaam had informed Balak in the presence of his retinue that further attempts to execrate the Israelites would be of no avail. The ravenous beast was lying in wait with God's blessing, ready to pounce upon any unsuspecting prey.

While Balaam still insisted that he must speak God's words, no matter what the consequences might be, Balak persuaded him nevertheless to accept yet another change of location in the expectation that God would finally allow Balaam to curse the Israelites. The same sacrificial rituals as before were followed meticulously, not merely because any deviation might have brought divine wrath upon both the seer and the person for whom he was working but also because this particular occasion was to represent Balak's last attempt to secure the destruction of the Israelites. The latter knew to their cost (Lev. 10:1-2) what the price was for any variation of ritual procedure that could have led to the introduction of pagan innovations. Although Balaam was not subordinate to the requisites of Israelite cultic worship, he was determined not to stray with respect to his promises to God. Yet a deviation in procedure did occur in the activities of Balaam just prior to the uttering of his third oracle, which was to preface a dramatic outpouring of God's power upon him.

5. BALAAM'S THIRD PROPHECY (24: 1-14)

Translation

Now when Balaam perceived that the LORD intended to bless Israel, he did not go and have recourse to divination, as on previous occasions, but instead he turned toward the wilderness. (24:1)

Exegesis and Exposition

By this time Balaam had had sufficient opportunity to reflect upon the significance of what had happened as a result of his prognostications. God was clearly determined to bless His people, no matter what the obstacles were. At this stage there occurred a deviation from Balaam's previous behavior. Instead of communing with the Lord in the hours of darkness, he abandoned any pretense of looking for auguries (MT נְחָשִׁים, *nĕḥāšîm*, "omens") as on previous occasions (MT כְּפַעַם בְּפַעַם, *kĕpaʿam bĕpaʿam*, "as time after time").

Looking for signs of God's approbation is an indication of shallow and immature faith. It is an evil and adulterous generation that keeps on looking for a sign (Matt. 12:39; 16:4) instead of trusting God implicitly. Seeking signs is equivalent to tempting God, an activity prohibited to ancient Israel (Deut. 6:16) as well as to members of the New Covenant in Christ (Matt. 4:7; Luke 4:12). The just person shall live by his or her faith (Hab. 2:4; Heb. 10:38); whatever is not of faith is sin (Rom. 14:23). Once the believer has appropriated God's revealed will by faith and has acted upon it, the message will often be confirmed by signs that will follow (cf. Mark 16:20), and these will assure the believer of the validity of both the act of faith and its outworking.

According to Smick's analysis,[29] the third oracle has an introductory strophe (vv. 3-4), followed by two stanzas (vv. 5-6) that introduce the body of the prophecy (vv. 7b-9a). A final benediction (v. 9b) picks

---

29. E. B. Smick, *ISBE*, 3:566; "A Study of the Structure of the Third Balaam Oracle," in J. H. Skilton, ed., *The Law and the Prophets* (Nutley, N.J.: Presbyterian and Reformed, 1974), pp. 242-52.

up the theme that opens the two stanzas beginning in v. 5. The prediction of a future Israelite monarchy (v. 7b) climaxes the oracle and is set off in the present translation. As with the second oracle, the third prophecy has a sophisticated literary form, which fortunately is amenable to less textual emendation.

Translation

As he looked, he saw the Israelites camped tribe by tribe, and the Spirit of God came upon him. Then he commenced his prophetic oracle, saying:

> This is the proclamation of Balaam, son of Beor,
> the oracle of the man with closed eyes,
> the pronouncement of him who hears the
> very words of God,
> who, falling prostrate with eyes wide open,
> beholds a vision from the Almighty.
> How beautiful your tents are, Jacob,
> your habitations, you Israelites!
> They are like valleys stretched out,
> like gardens along a river,
> like aloes planted by the LORD,
> like cedars beside the waters.
> Water shall pour out of their buckets;
> their offspring shall be like flowing waters.
> Their king shall be greater than Agag.
> Their kingdom shall be exalted.
> God has brought them from Egypt.
> They are as vigorous as a wild bull.
> They devour hostile peoples,
> breaking their bones in pieces
> and wounding them with arrows.
> They crouch and lie down like a
> lion or a lioness.
> Who will dare to disturb them?
> Blessed shall he be who blesses you,
> and accursed shall he be who curses you. (24:2-9)

Exegesis and Exposition

From his vantage point Balaam had looked westward across the desert and had seen the might of Israel's forces encamped around the Tabernacle. As he continued looking, God's Spirit came upon him, and he uttered a splendid prophecy that described in expressive language the marvelous future that God's covenant people would enjoy.

It is important to distinguish this form of ecstatic possession from both the anointing of God's Spirit (Isa. 61:1) and the bestowal of the Holy Spirit on the Day of Pentecost (Acts 2:1-4). Balaam's spiritual experience should instead be compared with periodic gifts of the Spirit that enabled individuals to perform a variety of services to God (cf. Judg. 3:10; 6:34; 11:29; 1 Sam. 16:13; etc.).

Empowered by this ecstatic experience, Balaam followed his normal procedure by announcing his identity and his intention to proclaim the words of God. He described his oracle as a נְאֻם (nĕʾum, "utterance"), a technical term for a divine oracle that occurs three times in vv. 3-4. It is normally understood as the most solemn asseveration of divine truth that a human being can utter in the Lord's name.[30]

These two verses are also of interest because they furnish a non-technical description of Balaam's apperceptive processes. Although he had been previously the "man with closed eyes" (MT הַגֶּבֶר שְׁתֻם הָעָיִן, haggeber šĕtum hāʿāyin), he now heard the very words of God through the Spirit. Although lying prone, he now had his eyes opened fully (MT גְּלוּי עֵינָיִם, gĕlûy ʿênāyim) to see the revelation of the Lord. Balaam's language is comparable to that found in later Hebrew prophets (Ezek. 13:7; Amos 1:1; Mic. 1:1) to describe his perception, the verb חָזָה (ḥāzâ) meaning "to receive in a vision."[31]

These spiritual experiences could occur whether the subject was awake or asleep, the difference being one of a state of awareness. Balaam was evidently in an ecstatic trance that prevented normal sensory stimulation from interfering with the divinely revealed vision. His comment about "open eyes" could perhaps suggest his surprise at finding himself in this condition if he had been in the habit of prognosticating with closed eyes.

Once Balaam had been blind to spiritual truths, but now he could see (cf. John 9:25) and acknowledge that his vision came from the Almighty (MT שַׁדַּי, šadday, an ancient title for God occurring nearly fifty times in the MT, predominantly in Job).[32] The NEB expression "with staring eyes" captures the attitude of the ecstatic visionary perfectly. What Balaam was now seeing transcended the immediate limitations of time and space as he gazed into the future. The source of his vision was contained in and proceeded from the Almighty.

---

30. D. Vetter, *THAT*, 2:1; L. J. Coppes, *TWOT*, 2:541-42.
31. See H. E. Freeman, *An Introduction to the Old Testament Prophets* (Chicago: Moody, 1968), pp. 37-41; D. Vetter, *THAT*, 1:533-37. For prognosticators speaking in poetic form see G. Fohrer, *History of Israelite Religion* (Nashville: Abingdon, 1972), pp. 224-25.
32. M. Weippert, *THAT*, 2:873-81; V. P. Hamilton, *TWOT*, 2:907 and bibliography.

Balaam's prophetic admiration for Israel attained new heights of poetic description. The nation would flourish and prosper, lacking nothing that was good. The valley bottoms usually contained fertile areas, and the wadis provided water in season. Israel would be highly productive and would reflect the luxury of flourishing aloe trees. The majority of OT references to the aloe (MT אֲהָלִים, 'ăhālîm) are to the lign aloes ("wood of aloes"), probably the eaglewood (*Aquilaria agallocha* Roxb.), a tall tree found in India and Malaysia. The decaying wood emits a distinctive fragrance and was employed as a perfume and fumigant. Some scholars have objected to the identification of the aloe tree seen by Balaam with the eaglewood, which is not native to Canaan. But the statement in the vision is figurative rather than literal. The point seems to be that the future homeland of the Israelites would be like the garden of a rich man, who can afford costly trees and exotic shrubs. As an alternative to the eaglewood, some commentators have suggested the terebinth (MT אֵלָה, 'ēlâ), a common Palestinian tree often confused by translators with the oak tree and comprising one or other species of the genus Pistacia.[33] The original form of the MT in this passage probably read אֵלִים ('ēlîm, "terebinths"), which may have been revised by later scribes to 'ăhālîm, "aloes."[34] The cedars (MT אֲרָזִים, 'ărāzîm), however, are native Palestinian trees, and the reference here is to the stately *Cedrus libani* Loud., the most massive tree found in Palestine, often attaining a height of one hundred twenty feet. Cedars are renowned for their fragrant, durable wood, used in later times for pillars, boards, ceilings, and a wide variety of carved work. The strength and versatility of the material, therefore, furnished a flattering and complimentary aspect to Israel's predicted future.

The reference to water implies an irrigation economy that would operate once the land was occupied, indicated by the figure of water pouring out of pairs of buckets. The MT here uses a dual form of דְּלִי (dŏlî, "bucket"), to describe a pair of containers carried by means of a yoke across the neck and shoulders. Israel's offspring (MT זֶרַע, zera‘, "seed") would resemble a flooding wadi in appearance, pointing to a vast future population.

The purpose of this oracle was to predict Israel's future state as a monarchy, and this expectation is embodied firmly in the center of this prophecy. God's promises to the Hebrew patriarchs would be fulfilled (cf. Gen. 17:6, 16; 35:11). Balaam predicted the demise of King Agag, an Amalekite ruler of a people that had been enemies of

---

33. *MPB*, pp. 118-20, 179-80.
34. R. K. Harrison, *ISBE*, 1:98.

Israel from the time of the attack on them in the wilderness (Ex. 17:8-12). The identity of Agag has provoked some discussion and among other things has led to the suggestion that it was a throne name held by at least two persons.[35] In any event the Israelites defeated the last king Agag, though because of King Saul's disobedience the task was left to Samuel to complete (1 Sam. 15:7-33).

In v. 8 Balaam recapitulates the thought expressed in his first utterance (Num. 23:22) and emphasizes that Israel owed its strength to its God. Israelite archers were beginning to gain a reputation for their skills, and because all their national enemies possessed expert companies of archers, it was important for the Israelites to be proficient in this area also. The *NEB* emends חִצָּיו (*ḥiṣṣāyw*, "his arrows") to read "limbs" (הֲלָצָיו, *ḥălāṣāyw*), but this change is unnecessary. Verse 9 repeats the image of the nation as a regal lion (Num. 23:24) stalking and capturing its prey, thus confirming the prediction regarding Judah as the "lion's cub" (Gen. 49:9, *NIV*). So ferocious would be the lion and his mate that people would disturb them at their dire peril. Again, God's ancient promise to Abraham that through him all the families of the earth would "bless themselves" (Gen. 12:3; KJV has "be blessed") is reinforced by a pagan prognosticator prophesying under the influence of the Spirit of God. A final, fundamental part of that divine assurance was the provision that those who cursed the Israelites would themselves be accursed.

Although the Jewish descendants of the ancient Israelites have been set aside partially and temporarily as a spiritual vehicle for the coming of God's kingdom and "replaced" by the Christian church, they are still the offspring of His ancient chosen people. As such they will exercise a renewed role in God's purposes when the times of the Gentiles have been fulfilled (Rom. 11:25). For the present they are enemies of the gospel because they have rejected Christ as their Messiah, but they are still regarded with affection by the Father because in His love He chose their ancestors as His people. Nevertheless, repentance and faith are mandatory for Jew and Gentile alike if the purposes of God are to be fulfilled in both groups. Anti-Semitism is therefore precluded, for those who persecute Jews will encounter God's punishment themselves.

Translation

At that, Balak became very angry with Balaam. He clapped his hands violently and said to Balaam: I sent for you to put a curse on

---

35. Cf. W. C. Kaiser, Jr., *ZPEB*, 1:68. M. Noth, *Numbers*, p. 191, identified Agag with the man killed by Samuel (1 Sam. 15:33) and used this conclusion to date the discourse in the time of Saul.

my enemies, and instead you have blessed them abundantly three consecutive times. (24:10)

Exegesis and Exposition

Balaam made clear that God was neither willing nor able to turn away from the people whom He had chosen as a vehicle of revelation in the world. Seeing that his prospects for bringing curses upon the Israelites were doomed to failure, Balak became angry with the Mesopotamian seer. He clapped his hands together furiously, which in some cultures was a sign of execution, and once again reviled Balaam for his prophetic stance.

Translation

Now then, get yourself home. I had promised to reward you handsomely, but the LORD has stood in the way of your being rewarded. So Balaam replied to Balak: Didn't I also say to the messengers whom you sent to me that though Balak were to give me his house full of silver and gold, I could not willingly disobey the command of the LORD my God to any extent, whether good or bad? I have to say whatever the LORD tells me. Now I am returning to my own people. Come now, and I will advise you as to what this people will do to your nation in the future. (24:11-14)

Exegesis and Exposition

Balak's resentment continued to express itself in the most practical way possible. Balaam was ordered to return home without receiving any professional fee for his services. The seer reminded Balak that he could not disobey God's command in any respect. He had been true to his promise, and therefore Balak must accept the consequences, however galling they might be. The king, however, was not to be appeased by the seer's claim of fidelity to his mission. He used the situation to Balaam's disadvantage by reminding him that God had intervened to the extent of preventing the seer from receiving his fees. This must have been a disconcerting turn of events for one who had been motivated by greed in accepting Balak's commission to curse Israel. But instead of calling down imprecations upon the angry Balak, the Mesopotamian seer ignored the loss of his professional fee, and, under the influence of God's Spirit, he began to predict, without any financial cost to Balak, what his future would be.

6. BALAAM'S FOURTH PROPHECY (24:15-19)

This utterance is shorter than the second and third, and like them it has a stereotyped introduction (vv. 15-16). Balaam was still hearing

320

the words of God, and consequently he described the splendor of Israel's king and his conquests of nations such as Moab and Edom (vv. 17-19).

Translation

Then he commenced his prophetic oracle, saying:

> **This is the proclamation of Balaam, son of Beor,**
> **the oracle of the man with closed eyes,**
> **the pronouncement of him who hears the**
> **very words of God,**
> **who has knowledge from the Most High,**
> **who, falling prostrate with eyes wide open,**
> **beholds a vision from the Almighty:**
> **I see him, but not just yet.**
> **I observe him, but not close at hand.**
> **A star shall come from Jacob,**
> **a scepter will rise from Israel.**
> **He shall crush the skulls of Moab,**
> **the heads of all the sons of Sheth.**
> **Edom shall be conquered;**
> **Seir, his enemies, shall be enslaved,**
> **but Israel shall perform mighty deeds.**
> **A ruler shall emerge from Jacob,**
> **who shall blot out the remains of**
> **the city. (24:15-19)**

Exegesis and Exposition

Balaam was either feeling the effects of his trance like condition, or else he reverted to it under the influence of the Spirit of God. At all events, the circumstances for prophesying were those of the third oracle, and the words he uttered were God's own. In it he spoke of Israel's future ruler, although like most prophets he alluded to the time ahead in general terms. His knowledge (MT דַּעַת, *da'at*) consisted of information given to him by God, which he proclaimed in visionary form as a seer (MT חֹזֶה, *ḥōzeh*). The events he envisioned were not on the immediate horizon, but they were approaching and would come into view gradually.

The emergence of the great ruler was described by Balaam in terms of an astral metaphor, "star" (MT כּוֹכָב, *kôkāb*), such as was employed by Isaiah to describe the king of Babylon (Isa. 14:12; MT הֵילֵל בֶּן־שָׁחַר, *hêlēl ben-šāḥar*, "brilliant star, offspring of the dawn," where some versions, following the KJV, render *hêlēl* by "Lucifer").

The same concept appears in the NT, where Jesus is described as the Root and Offspring of David, the Bright and Morning Star (Rev. 22:16, KJV). A royal personage was symbolized by the presence of a scepter (MT שֵׁבֶט, šēbeṭ), a rod of royal office. No description of a royal scepter has been preserved by the MT, but representations of them on Near Eastern monuments indicate that there were two kinds, one a long, slender ornamented rod, and the other shorter and weighted at one end like a mace.[36]

The macelike scepter may well have been intended here, since skulls were to be battered, for which purpose the Egyptian variety of mace would have been most satisfactory. Kings led their forces into battle and were armed with appropriate weaponry. Thus on the slate palette of Narmer, who founded the First Dynasty of Egypt about 3100 B.C., the tall figure of the king was depicted crushing the skull of an enemy with a heavy mace while he held the hapless victim by the beard.[37]

Similarly the battered skull of the mummified Sekenenre, an Egyptian ruler at Thebes who fell victim to the Hyksos king Apophis, shows the result of brutal beating by a mace and perhaps also by an axe.[38] Thus for such a weapon to be mentioned by Balaam portended ill for the intended recipients, among whom Balak's people would be numbered. The mention of "skulls" (MT פֵּאָה, pē'â, "side," "region," "corner") indicated that Moab was being regarded as a head, which would be assailed on both sides and crushed by the conqueror. The "sons of Sheth" (MT בְּנֵי־שֵׁת, bĕnê-Šēt) have sometimes been identified with the *Shutu*, an aggressive Canaanite group mentioned in the nineteenth-century B.C. Egyptian Execration Texts, but many commentators regard the name as descriptive of the Moabites. If the phrase actually means "sons of tumult," i.e., warriors, it would be paralleled by the oracle relating to the destruction of Moab in Jer. 48:45. Equally catastrophic would be the destiny of Edom, land of the offspring of Esau, which would become servile to the mighty sons of Jacob because of God's blessing.[39] When the fighting had been completed, Israel would have vanquished those nations that had rejected her requests to use the King's Highway into Transjordan. No weapon against God's elect people would prosper (Isa. 54:17) as long as they remained faithful to their covenant obligations.

---

36. See illustrations in L. E. Toombs, *IDB*, 4:234-35; W. J. Cameron, *ZPEB*, 5:292-93.
37. J. Finegan, *Light from the Ancient Past* (Princeton, N.J.: Princeton U., 1951 ed.), p. 73 and pl. 28.
38. G. Steindorff and K. C. Seele, *When Egypt Ruled the East* (Chicago: U. of Chicago, 1963 ed.), p. 28.
39. See Malachi 1:2-3.

Despite this promise of victory over Moab, the nation did not begin to decline until about 735 B.C. and was the object of periodic prophetic denunciation. In Jeremiah's oracle (Jer. 48:1-47) the prophet utilized some of the phraseology of Numbers, reflecting the language of Num. 21:27-30 as well as Balaam's utterance in 24:17. The Moabites were incorporated ultimately into the Nabateans after the fourth century B.C.

In the ancient Near East the appearance of a new star was normally interpreted by astronomers and astrologers (whose functions did not admit of sharp differentiation, unlike their modern counterparts) as a token of a special event. The word "star" (MT כּוֹכָב, *kôkāb*, LXX ἄστρον, *astron*) should not be taken in the narrow modern sense, since for the ancients it covered such celestial phenomena as constellations, meteors, and comets.

The literature from Ras Shamra (Ugarit) contains a fertility text in which the goddess Asherah undertakes a lengthy journey on a donkey, adorned with elaborate trappings as befitting a royal consort. The Holy One, whose name is Amrr and is described as *qdš*, goes ahead of her, lighting the way like a star (*kkbkb lpnm*).[40] The commencement of the reign of Augustus was marked by the appearance of a comet, which remained in sight for a whole week. Undoubtedly Augustus regarded the phenomenon as favorable to him and his empire[41] because of its brightness, general shape, and position in the heavens. According to Cicero,[42] astrologers observing a celestial configuration predicted the birth of a person who would devastate the Near East. This "star" marked the birth of Alexander the Great. A group of Magi made a journey to Bethlehem to see the infant Jesus because, according to Matthew, they had seen His star "in the east" (KJV; a better rendering of the Greek ἐν τῇ ἀνατολῇ, *en tē anatolē*, would be "in its ascendancy").[43] Magi also paid ceremonial visits to other rulers,[44] thus indicating a link in antiquity between a star's appearance and a significant potential or actual occurrence.

Because of the obvious eschatological tone of Balaam's prophecy, the identity of the "star" has been a matter of considerable debate. The reference seems to be primarily to David, the second king of Israel, who by any standards was a stellar person in his own right. It was in his day that Moab first lost its independence (2 Sam. 8:2; 1

---

40. C. H. Gordon, *Ugaritic Handbook: Baal and 'Anat*, Text 51:IV, lines 5-17; *Ugaritic Literature*, p. 31.
41. Pliny, *Natural History* 2. 23. 94.
42. Cicero, *De Divinatione* 1. 47.
43. See Matthew 2:2.
44. Pliny, *Natural History* 2. 30. 6.

Chron. 18:2). But the eschatological theme continued long after David had died, and with the growth of messianic expectation an ideal David in the form of the Messiah was awaited. Not until the sixth century B.C., however, was the term *messiah* (MT מָשִׁיחַ, *māšîaḥ*, "anointed one") used as the title of a king who would come to rule the Israelites in later days (Dan. 9:25-26). In the Maccabean period (167-137 B.C.) the expectation was for the rise of a military ruler who would defeat the nation's political enemies and bring freedom to the people. But a contemporary breakaway Jewish religious sect apparently related to the Essenes established a settlement at Qumran on the northwest shore of the Dead Sea.

The sectaries interpreted the Hebrew Scriptures in terms of their own conflict with the ruling Jewish authorities and looked earnestly for a time when a messiah would come. In particular, they interpreted the prediction of Balaam in specifically messianic terms (1QM 11:6-7). Toward the end of the Jewish nation's existence the leader of the final Jewish war of independence was a man named Bar Kosiba, but he had his name changed to Bar Kochba, "son of a star." If he was expecting to fulfill a prophetic messianic role, however, he was doomed to disappointment, being slain by the Romans in A.D. 135.

The early followers of Jesus expected Him to fulfill messianic expectations by performing signs (John 7:31) prior to delivering the nation from enslavement to Rome (12:34). So ardent was the desire for a messiah-king at the beginning of the first century A.D. that any person who appeared to have some form of charisma or anointing was thought to be a possible candidate for the office. Thus John the Baptist, who reminded people of Elijah and the prophecy connected with his reappearance in the end time (Mal. 4:5-6), was asked directly if he was indeed the Messiah (John 1:20). Jesus revealed Himself to the Samaritan woman as the long-promised Messiah (4:25-26), but apart from that incident He spoke in such terms only to His disciples. He finally made public testimony of the fact at His trial (Matt. 26:63-64; Mark 14:61-62; Luke 22:67-70), thereby revealing His "messianic secret" (cf. Mark 8:29-30). Only after Christ's ascension did the Christian church proclaim Jesus as the crucified and risen Messiah of God (Acts 5:42; 17:3; etc.). As such, Jesus fulfilled supremely the role predicted by Balaam of a divinely-appointed king who far exceeded the work of His earthly ancestor David by ushering in God's kingdom upon earth (Matt. 12:28; Luke 11:20).[45]

---

45. For studies on the concept of Messiah see E. Jenni, *IDB*, 3:360-65; J. Jocz, *ZPEB*, 4:198-207; O. A. Piper, *ISBE*, 3:330-38 and bibliographies.

7. BALAAM'S FINAL PROPHECIES AND RETURN HOME (24:20-25)

Translation

Then Balaam looked at Amalek and commenced his prophetic oracle, saying:

> Amalek held first place among the nations,
> but he shall come to destruction at the last.

Then he looked at the Kenites and commenced his prophetic oracle, saying:

> Your dwelling place seems secure,
> and your nest is set in a rock.
> Yet fire shall overtake you Kenites
> when Assyria takes you captive.

Then he commenced his prophetic oracle, saying:

> Oh, who shall live when God performs this?
> People are gathering from the north,
> ships from beside the sea.
> They will conquer Asshur
> and will devastate Eber.
> So shall it end in destruction.

Then Balaam arose and left, returning to his home. Balak also went his own way. (24:20-25)

Exegesis and Exposition

Still under the influence of the divine Spirit, the soothsayer uttered a few short prognostications relating to the Amalekites and the Kenites, with additional comments on the destinies of other peoples. These prophecies were brief in comparison with the second and third oracles especially. In character and content the sayings were more like the utterances of pagan prognosticators, which were apt to be brief and cryptic. Balaam's oracle promised the destruction of the Amalekites, a Sinaitic people of obscure origin who may have regarded themselves as the "first of the nations" because of their origin or status.[46] The Amalekites persisted in Canaan until the time of Hezekiah (c. 716-686 B.C.), when the Simeonites captured their stronghold in Mount Seir (1 Chron. 4:43).

Balaam's oracle regarding the Kenites presents certain textual difficulties, and as a result the English versions have different and

---

46. J. A. Thompson, *ISBE*, 1:104.

sometimes conflicting renderings.[47] The Kenites were among the nomadic tribes whose territory was promised to Abraham (Gen. 15:19). As Balaam prophesied he made a pun on their name (MT קֵינִי, *qênî*) by speaking of their nest-building (MT קֵן, *qānan*) in the rocky heights, probably at Sela, perhaps the modern Umm el-Bay-yarah overlooking Petra. The problem in translation occurs in v. 22, which reads literally: "Nevertheless Kain shall be wasted. How long shall Asshur take you captive?" The second line can also be construed to read: "How long? Asshur shall carry thee away captive."[48] The *NAB*, by contrast, translates v. 22 as "Yet destined for burning—even as I watch—are your inhabitants," whereas the *NJB* reads "But the nest belongs to Beor; how long will you be Asshur's captive?" The *NEB* follows a different direction by translating "Your refuge . . . is doomed to burning, O Cain. How long must you dwell there in my sight?"

The presence of Assyria (MT אַשּׁוּר, *'aššûr*) in the oracle is puzzling if Balaam's reference was in fact to this mighty Mesopotamian empire of later times. If that was the case, then the Israelites would be engulfed in the depredations that would swallow up the Kenites ("metal-workers"). But if *'aššûr* was a reference to the tribe of Asshurites mentioned in Gen. 25:3; 2 Sam. 2:9, Balaam was in fact speaking about an obscure north Arabian group of Abrahamic stock that inhabited southern Canaan and therefore is not to be confused with Assyria, as seems to have happened during the literary transmission of the oracle.

Balaam's final prophetic utterance contains problems of interpretation also. Albright proposed a redivision and emendation of verses 23b-24a by omitting the vowel sounds, so that instead of the Hebrew ים יחי משמאל וצים מיד כתים, *ym yḥy mśm'l wṣym myd ktym*, the emendation would read ים יחי משמאל וצים מירכת ים, *ym yḥy mśm'l wṣym myrkt ym*. The MT words *myd kt* were joined together and an *r* substituted for the letter *d*.[49] The resultant text would then read: "The islands will gather in the north, ships from the distant sea." Although it is impossible to be certain, this was quite probably the state of the text when it was transmitted without vowels or vowel letters and again seems to have been misunderstood by the scribes who had to deal with the archaic writing.

The conquering invaders would destroy Asshur, presumably the Asshurite tribes, and demolish Eber, the latter probably being the nomadic descendants of the patriarch Eber, who was of the line of

---

47. For a discussion of the textual problem see W. F. Albright, *JBL* 63 (1944): 222. His emendations are followed by many translators.
48. J. H. Hertz, ed., *The Pentateuch and Haftorahs*, p. 680.
49. W. F. Albright, *JBL* 63 (1944): 222-23.

Shem (Gen. 10:21, 24-25; 11:16-17). If Eber is linked with Ebrium, the third-millennium B.C. king of Ebla (Tell Mardikh), the reference could be to some of his family members who had migrated when Ebla came under Hittite rule in the seventeenth century B.C.[50] The general description fits maritime conditions and activities by the Sea Peoples in the Levant of the Late Bronze Age.

Having delivered himself of his final utterance, Balaam departed for his home, apparently unthanked and unremunerated by Balak. But despite this treatment there could be no thought on Balaam's part of trying to recall his prognostications or to do other than leave with Balak the apprehensions he himself felt about the coming days. The result of Balaam's visit to the Moabites constituted a legacy, the effect of which would be felt for many generations. He must have broken his homeward journey somewhere in Midian, perhaps to offer oracles to someone else in need of advice, but the MT does not record this eventuality. At all events, Balaam perished when the Israelites destroyed the Midianites (Num. 31:8).

Additional Notes

23:1 לִי . . . לְ: The preposition לְ is used here to express advantage.

23:3 עַל־עֹלָתֶךָ: A collective singular is used here, making the plural of the Samaritan Pentateuch and the Syriac unnecessary.

יהוה: The LXX and Samaritan Pentateuch preferred אֱלֹהִים.

מַה־יַּרְאֵנִי: This is an uncommon indefinite use, "whatever," of the interrogative particle מָה.

שְׁפִי: The LXX reads εὐθεῖαν, "straight (line)." The sense seems to be that Balaam went up a narrow track to an exposed, rocky elevation.

23:8 מָה אֶקֹּב: The interrogative מָה is here used adverbially: "How?"

23:10 אֶת־רֹבַע: "The quarter part" is in apposition to the noun מִסְפָּר, "number," and this has sometimes been made into a separate line ("who has numbered the fourth part of Israel?"). A variant reading for רֹבַע, namely תַּרְבַּעַת, "sands," attracted Albright because of its affinity with the Akkad. *turbu'tu*, "dust," as well as its parallelism with the preceding line. But the text is very difficult to construe and gives every indication of being second millennium B.C. in origin. See W. F. Albright, *JBL* 63 (1944): 213 n. 28. W. G. Plaut and W. W. Hallo, *Num-*

---

50. On Ebla see K. A. Kitchen, *The Bible in Its World* (Exeter: Paternoster, 1977), pp. 37-55; C. Bermant and M. Weitzman, *Ebla: A Revelation in Archaeology* (New York: Times Books, 1979); G. Pettinato, *The Archives of Ebla* (New York: Doubleday, 1981); P. Matthiae, *Ebla: An Empire Rediscovered* (London: Hodder & Stoughton, 1980); H. W. Perkin, *NIDBA*, pp. 440-42; W. S. LaSor, *ISBE*, 4:750-58 and bibliography.

bers, p. 229, who supported this reading, noted that dust was used in Mesopotamian magical rites. See also A. R. Hulst, *Old Testament Translation Problems,* p. 11.

יְשָׂרִים: The plural seems awkward here, since the last word in the verse, כָּמֹהוּ, "like him," is singular. Cf. D. N. Freedman, "Archaic Forms in Early Hebrew Poetry," *ZAW* 72 (1960): 101-7. The LXX reads ὡς τὸ σπέρμα τούτων, thus adopting a plural, כָּהֶם, as the versions generally did, and regarding the "end" in terms of abundant descendants.

23:15 The LXX and Samaritan Pentateuch read "and Balaam said" instead of the MT "he said." As in 23:3, 6, both versions adopt the plural form for the MT עָלָתֶךָ.

23:26 יהוה יְדַבֵּר: As in some other instances, the Samaritan Pentateuch, the LXX, and the Vulgate prefer to read "God" instead of the tetragrammaton.

24:3 שְׁתָם: The LXX reads ὁ ἀληθινῶς ὁρῶν, "the one who sees truly." The MT שְׁתָם has been interpreted in opposite ways to describe either "shut" or "open" eyes. The KJV and other English versions have preferred the latter meaning, apparently influenced by the LXX. The present translation renders שְׁתָם by "closed" to heighten the contrast with גְלוּי in v. 4.

24:4 שֹׁמֵעַ נְאֻם: The LXX MS Codex Ambrosianus omitted this clause, as did the Samaritan Pentateuch, for reasons that are difficult to justify. By removing this phrase the poetic balance of the verse is disturbed.

נֹפֵל: Here the LXX adds ἐν ὕπνῳ, presumably in an attempt to interpret the psychic processes.

24:5 מַה־טֹבוּ: The particle מַה is used in an exclamatory sense here: "How!" Cf. Genesis 28:17.

24:6 G. B. Gray, *Numbers,* p. 363, suggested that אֲהָלִים and אֲרָזִים should be transposed, on the ground that cedars did not grow beside water. This opinion was supported by W. F. Albright, *JBL* 63 (1944): 207-53; J. de Vaulx, *Les Nombres* (Paris: J. Gabalda, 1972), p. 284. There is no manuscript evidence to support this view, however, and since the passage is poetic it is doubtful if a factual reconstruction would enhance the description significantly.

24:8 מוֹצִיאוֹ: W. F. Albright, *JBL* 63 (1944): 207-53, preferred the verb נָחָה, as in the Samaritan Pentateuch and LXX. But since יָצָא is the verb normally used in connection with the Exodus, it seems unnecessary to modify the MT.

24:17 אֶרְאֶנּוּ: This qal future of ראה was given a causative force by the LXX, which read δείξω, "I will cause him to see"—i.e., "I will show him."

אֲשׁוּרֶנּוּ: The LXX reads μακαρίζω, "I bless (him)."

כּוֹכָב: By the rabbinic period this word had acquired here a specific regal connotation, as in the Targum Onkelos.

שֵׁבֶט: The LXX reads ἄνθρωπος here, whereas the Targum Onkelos has "an anointed one."

פַּאֲתֵי: The LXX reads ἀρχηγοὺς, "leaders," followed by the Vulgate and Targum Onkelos.

פֵּאָה means "region," "district," "corner," "border," and the translation "skulls" describes the "corners" of the head.

וְקַרְקַר: The Samaritan Pentateuch here reads קָדְקֹד, "crown of the head," rather than the MT that means to "shatter," "devastate." This emendation followed Jer. 48:45, which appears to reflect the phraseology of Num. 24:17. The construction occurs again in Ps. 68:21 (MT 68:22), where קָדְקֹד is also the direct object of מָחַץ.

שֵׁת: Here regarded as in apposition to מוֹאָב and perhaps describing an indigenous people whom the Moabites conquered.

24:22 לְבָעֵר: This phrase is difficult. The LXX translators apparently worked from a Hebrew text that read קֵן עָרְמָה, "a nest of rubbish," and translated it by γένηται τῷ βεωρ νεοσσιὰ πανουργίας, "there shall be to Beor a nest of corruption."

תִּשְׁבֶּךָ: The qal future singular of שָׁבָה, "carry off," "lead into captivity," is read by the MT here. The *NEB*, however, understood the word to be derived from the verb יָשַׁב, "to dwell," and rendered the phrase "How long must you dwell there in my sight?"

24:23 אוֹי מִי: Because there is no parallel clause, some scholars have thought that a line dropped out of the text (cf. W. F. Albright, *JBL* 63 [1944]: 207-53; J. de Vaulx, *Les Nombres*, p. 296). The *NEB* attempts a reconstruction and reads "Ah, who are these assembling in the north?" There is no manuscript evidence for inserting additional material, and because of the general difficulty and non-Israelite provenance of the material it seems inadvisable to alter the MT.

24:24 עֵבֶר: The LXX read Ἑβραίους here, along with the Syriac and Vulgate, in an apparent attempt to interpret the MT.

Excursus on Balaam

The nature, character, and mission of this ancient seer have been matters of discussion for centuries and have produced a variety of opinions. From what is now known about Mesopotamian divinatory traditions and practices, it seems clear that he was a mantic prophet of the *bārû* variety. As a קוֹסֵם (*qôsēm*), Balaam exercised his profession at a more advanced level than some other diviners and is presented in Numbers as the preferred seer for the purposes of destruction that Balak, son of Zippor, had in mind for his enemies the Israelites.

His religious tradition was that of a polytheist, and as a professional seer it was his responsibility to know the names of all the gods with which he would be dealing. He would thus have experienced no difficulty in declaring the existence of Israel's God and may well have heard of His exploits in Egypt and the wilderness in the same manner as the Transjordanian peoples received tidings of the Amorite defeat at the hands of Israel. This, and possibly other information about the deployment of the Israelite forces, could have been communicated to Balaam in any event by the deputations from Balak in the form of an official "briefing."

But although Balaam behaved in some respects like a Hebrew prophet in that he submitted to the guidance of God's Spirit, he did not stand theologically within the covenant tradition established between God and the Israelites on Mount Sinai. Some expositors have supposed that Balaam may have been seeking a knowledge of the true God, but this is not easy to sustain in the light of subsequent events. The narrative shows that although he followed the Lord's instructions meticulously, he was evidently behaving in this manner because God had compelled him and not because he felt free to obey in an *ex animo* manner.

At the time that he was first approached by the ambassadors of Balak, his services were being solicited on the basis of a standard procedure for securing an act of divination, in which the nature of the required duties would be stated and remuneration offered or at least discussed (Num. 22:6-7). At this stage Balaam gave no indication as to whether the fee was adequate but took steps to inquire of God concerning the assignment. When God refused Balaam permission to go, the seer sent the delegation of Moabites and Midianites back home. At this point personal ambition and greed do not appear to be part of the picture. A second delegation from Balak, promising great honor for Balaam, elicited only a commitment from the seer to say what the Lord had commanded him, no matter how great a professional fee Balak gave him.

It was then that Balaam was informed by God that the Israelites were to be blessed, not cursed, and this immediately provoked a conflict of interest in which Balaam was acting for both God and Balak to the detriment of the latter, who was his patron. Perhaps as Balaam was returning to Moab with the second deputation, having received permission from God to do so, he began to contemplate ways of resolving his dilemma to the extent that he would derive some fiscal benefit from it. If that was the case, it would account for the sudden change in the Lord's attitude toward him (22:22).

Whatever may have transpired in this connection, the Mesopotamian seer was caught in a situation in which he had to obey the commands of an all-powerful God on the one hand and try to appease an obstinate, belligerent king of Moab on the other. Some commentators have regarded his reference to "the Lord my God" (22:18) as evidence of his spiritual fidelity to the God of the Sinai covenant. In all probability, however, he was merely identifying the particular God for whom he would be serving as spokesman and adding the appellation אֲדֹנָי (*ădônāy*) as a title of respect ("Sir"), much as modern Israelis use the word אֲדוֹנִי (*'ădônî*). The fact that what he said does not appear to have reflected his innermost spiritual convictions is indicated by the way in which his statement turned out to be for his own destruction, because the words were basically false.

By nature, therefore, Balaam must be regarded as self-seeking and greedy. He could speak God's words only because, under the compulsion of the prophetic Spirit, he had no other choice. His true character as an instrument for evil rather than good, once divine constraints had been removed, is seen in his advice to the Midianites to seduce the Israelite men through the worship of Baal-peor (25:1-3; 31:15-16).

Balaam was thus not a genuine Hebrew prophet but was exercising the functions of a Mesopotamian *bārû* when he was used by the God of Israel for the revelation of His will. While Balaam stands outside the tradition of Hebrew prophecy, the oracles he proclaimed under the inspiration and control of the Spirit of God constitute an important medium for the revelation of the Lord of Sinai as the God of Israel. Throughout the oracles Balaam is not the one who is pursuing the leading role. Rather, it is the Lord who is supremely at work, giving promises of blessing through the mouth of a pagan prognosticator that were to be a lasting part of Israelite tradition.

As indicated in the commentary, some of the words of Balaam were referred to partially by the sectaries at Qumran, being mentioned, for example, in *CD* 7:9-20 (for the text see C. Rabin, *The Zadokite Documents*, I [Oxford: Clarendon, 1954], pp. 27-31; see also the comments of F. F. Bruce, *Biblical Exegesis in the Qumran Texts* [London: Tyndale, 1959], p. 37). The document *4QTestimonia* contained citations from Num. 24:15-17, but without any commentary, interspersed with prophetic material from Deuteronomy. In 1QM 11:6, the "Star" and "Scepter" of Num. 24:17-19 were mentioned specifically, while in *CD* 7:18-21 the "Scepter" was regarded as the Prince of all the Congregation, and the "Star" was identified with the Seeker of the Law who was coming to Damascus to fulfill the prophecies of Num. 24:17-19.

The historical influence of Balaam was not confined to the Qumran sectaries, however. At the time of the Second Jewish Revolt (A.D. 132-135), Rabbi Akiba proclaimed Simon Bar Kosiba, the commander of the Jewish forces in A.D. 132, as Messiah and applied to him the promise recorded in 24:17 (see R. K. Harrison, *The Dead Sea*

Scrolls [London: English Universities, 1961], pp. 46-47). Unfortunately the leader of the rebels did not fulfill the high responsibility envisaged in the Balaam utterance, being destroyed with his forces in A.D. 135 by Roman troops.

While continuing to cherish the promises inherent in the utterances concerning the "Star," Jewish tradition generally was critical of Balaam. Perhaps the most pointed comment to illustrate this position can be found in *Tractate Berakot*, 7a: "How could Balaam possibly know the mind of the Most High when he didn't even know the mind of his animal?" Cf. N. H. Snaith, *Leviticus and Numbers* (London: Thomas Nelson, 1967), p. 286.

In an outstanding treatment of the Balaam utterances by R. B. Allen (*The Theology of the Balaam Oracles: A Pagan Diviner and the Word of God*, Th.D. diss., Dallas Theological Seminary, 1973), the author traces the diversity of opinion over the centuries regarding the character of Balaam (pp. 163-72). Among the early Fathers, writers such as Philo, Augustine, Gregory of Nyssa, and others would have agreed with A. B. Davidson (*Old Testament Prophecy* [Edinburgh: T. & T. Clark, 1903]) in regarding him as a "monstrosity of prophecy." Other moderns who regarded Balaam as standing outside Israel's prophetic tradition were Samuel Cox (*Balaam: An Exposition and a Study* [London: Kegan, Paul, Trench, 1884], p. 38); Th. C. Vriezen (*The Religion of Ancient Israel* [Philadelphia: Westminster, 1967], pp. 208-10), who regarded Balaam as a "prophet of Baal"; W. Eichrodt (*Theology of the Old Testament* [Philadelphia: Westminster, 1961, 1967]), 1:296; C. von Orelli (*Old Testament Prophecy* [Edinburgh: T. & T. Clark, 1892], p. 17), who regarded him as a kind of clairvoyant. Y. Kaufmann (*The Religion of Israel: From Its Beginnings to the Babylonian Exile* [Chicago: U. of Chicago, 1960], pp. 84-85), however, described Balaam more cautiously as a pagan mantic transformed into a prophet of the Lord. The conservative position was expressed ably by E. J. Young, *My Servants the Prophets* (Grand Rapids, Eerdmans, 1961), pp. 26-27, 177.

Those writers who regarded Balaam as a true prophet of Israel included Tertullian, Jerome, and others, while in modern times this view was supported by Alexander Whyte (*Bible Characters: Adam to Achan* [London & Edinburgh: Oliphants, 10th ed., n.d.], pp. 264-65). A. R. Gordon (*The Prophecies of the Old Testament* [New York: G. H. Doran, 1916], p. 16) also spoke favorably of him as a "man of deep insight into the mysteries of life." J. Pedersen described him as a "typical man of God" (*Israel: Its Life and Culture* III-IV [London: Oxford U., 1940, pp. 124-27]). A. R. Johnson (*The Cultic Prophets in Ancient Israel* [Cardiff: U. of Wales, 1962], p. 32) also held a similar view of his character.

Whatever explanations of Balaam's behavior may be offered by scholars, ancient or modern, the OT references to him are consistently negative. In Num. 31:8 his death is recorded along with the slaughter of the five Midianite kings, while in 31:16 he is blamed for the seduction of the Israelite men at Baal-peor. Although Balaam had been unable to curse Israel because of God's control over his mind, he came perilously close to achieving spiritual catastrophe for Israel by endangering the nation's state of ceremonial holiness, a crisis that demanded and received immediate action (31:17). In Deut. 23:4-5, Balaam's exploits are mentioned in connection with the prohibition against Ammonites and Moabites entering the assembly of the Lord. This passage seems to differ in interpretation somewhat from the Numbers narrative, stating that "God would not listen" to Balaam, as though the seer had made a proposal that God rejected outright and "turned the curse into a blessing for you." Even though Balaam may have had, or thought that he had, the power to implement the curses that he pronounced, the Numbers narrative gives the impression that they had never been formulated and thus were not even potential, much less actual.

In Josh. 13:22, the death of Balaam is again mentioned in connection with the Midianite rulers' decease, and on this occasion his practice of divination is noted. In the speech on the occasion of the covenant renewal ceremony at Shechem (24:1-24), Joshua recapitulates briefly the period between the Exodus and the occupation of Canaan, and in vv. 9-10 he follows the tradition about Balaam as recorded in Deuteronomy.

The final reforms of Nehemiah, involving the exclusion from Israel of people of foreign descent (Neh. 13:1-3), were reinforced by an appeal to the legislation of Deut. 23:3-6. The only mention of Balaam in prophetic literature occurs in Micah 6:5, where the Lord lodges a formal legal complaint against His disobedient vassal Israel. In a brief recapitulation of His dealings with the nation from the time of the Exodus, God urges His covenant people to remember how Balak, king of Moab, desired to destroy them and how Balaam intervened for blessing upon His people. For a thorough treatment of the theology of Num. 23-24 see R. B. Allen, "The Theology of the Balaam Oracles," in *Tradition and Testament:* edited by J. S. Feinberg and P. D. Feinberg (Chicago: Moody, 1981), pp. 79-119.

The NT continues the OT tradition of condemning Balaam in terms of three specific passages. In 2 Peter 2:15-16, Balaam is castigated for yearning after the "wages of wickedness," the result of which was that he was made to look foolish by a talking donkey. Following in the perverse way of Balaam was therefore to be avoided by all teachers of the Christian faith. In Jude 11, perverted teachers with whom Jude had to contend are described as having rushed for profit into Balaam's error of consuming greed. The final Balaam illustration is in Rev. 2:14 in a letter sent by John to the Christian community in Pergamum. The false teachers in that part of Asia Minor had been emulating the wickedness of their spiritual ancestor Balaam by counseling sexual profligacy and the consumption of food offered to idols. Some expositors have seen a threefold emphasis upon Balaam in these three passages—namely, his way, his error, and his teaching—but these are merely different aspects of the man and his mission. Nowhere in the NT is Balaam commended for uttering the oracle in which, as expressed by Merrill, "he spoke one final word, one of the most glorious prophecies in the Old Testament" (E. H. Merrill, *An Historical Survey of the Old Testament* [New Jersey: Craig, 1966], p. 125).

The last word on Balaam should rest with Merrill F. Unger, who sees Balaam as at best a man with limited knowledge of the God of Israel. The Mesopotamian seer is for him a pagan magician who fell under the overwhelming influence of the Lord for a short period in his career but served Him from a basic standpoint of greed. Unger further allows that whatever knowledge Balaam may have had of Israel's God was necessarily distorted by the corruptions of paganism, which formed part of Balaam's religious tradition. "Such a combination of pagan magic, personal greed, and the professed service of the Lord could not be permanent, but was compatible only with a transitional state in his experience of the divine dealing" (M. F. Unger, *Biblical Demonology: A Study of the Spiritual Forces Behind the Present World Unrest* [Wheaton, Ill., 1952], p. 125).

C. ISRAEL'S SIN AND GOD'S PUNISHMENT (25:1-18)

Chapter 25 is structured in terms of three units: (1) adulterous Israel (vv. 1-3); (2) God's punishments (vv. 4-9); (3) aftermath (vv. 10-18). It continues the story of Israelite exploits that were interrupted by the Balaam narratives.

1. ADULTEROUS ISRAEL (25:1-3)

Translation

While Israel remained in Shittim, the men began to have sexual relations with the Moabite women who invited the people to sacrifices offered to their gods. The people banqueted and then prostrated themselves before the Moabite gods. So the Israelites joined in worshiping the Baal of Peor, and the Lord's anger was stirred up against Israel. (25:1-3)

Exegesis and Exposition

It is not easy to say why the Israelites submitted to the temptations instigated by Balaam (Num. 31:8, 16). Perhaps they were feeling flushed with victory, and even though they were conscious of their covenant obligations they perhaps felt superior to the moral laws that those commitments enshrined. During a period of inactivity the soldiers may have become somewhat restless and felt the need for adventure among the women of Moab. Tradition has approved of soldiers' taking sexual liberties with women of occupied lands.

The location of the encampment was Shittim (*NKJV* "Acacia Grove") or, in its fuller form, Abel-shittim (Deut. 33:49). This was a site in the plains of Moab and has been identified with Tell el-Kefrein, seven miles east of the Jordan and six miles north of the Dead Sea. Glueck, however, preferred a more imposing site just over a mile east of Tell el-Kefrein named Tell el-Hamman, where the remains of strong Iron Age I-II fortresses were discovered.[51]

Whatever the motivation, the Israelites made the mistake of fraternizing with enemies of the Sinai covenant. Great spiritual triumphs are often followed by periods of severe temptation, and the Hebrews were probably victims of such a cycle because they were not vigilant about matters of faith. The occasion might have appeared harmless when presented as a sacrificial meal to the Moabite deities to which the Israelites, predominantly the men, were invited.

What they experienced was a foretaste of the same kind of depraved cultic practices they would encounter in the Promised Land. Although the Moabites worshiped Chemosh instead of the Canaanite Baal, the essential nature of Moabite religion was that of fertility worship, if the female images found at Early Bronze II-III levels at Bab edh-Dhra' are any indication. Canaanite religion was doubtless the most depraved and morally corrupt of any cultic system the world has ever known. Canaanite religious practices were condemned by OT writers, but the full significance of their strictures was not apparent until the accidental discovery of the ancient Canaanite city-state of Ugarit (modern Ras Shamra).

Archives uncovered there yielded texts written mostly in the native language that show a close affinity to biblical Hebrew. The tablets include religious epics of various kinds written in poetic form. The head of the deities at Ugarit was a shadowy figure named El, a generic name for deity occurring throughout the ancient Near East.

---

51. N. Glueck, "Some Ancient Towns in the Plains of Moab," *BASOR* 91 (1943): 7-18; *Explorations in Eastern Palestine*, AASOR 25-28 (1945-1948): 221, 371-82.

His son (or nephew) and successor was Baal ("lord," "master," "husband"), the alleged offspring of a union between El and his consort Asherat, the Asherah of the OT writers. Baal (or Hadad) was a fertility deity and, with his bloodthirsty wife, Anat, variously identified with Asherah and Astarte/Ashtoreth, was venerated by means of the most sensuous, orgiastic practices known to humanity.

These sexual excesses were condoned—indeed, encouraged—by the traditions of the various Near Eastern gods and goddesses, where the latter were often regarded as sacred prostitutes whose behavior was to be emulated by their worshipers. It was this sort of activity in which the unsuspecting Israelites would be expected to participate once the sacrificial meal had been concluded.[52] The narrative gives some idea of the form the ritual would take. Having eaten a festive meal at which the wine would flow freely, the Israelites would follow the Moabite women as they prostrated themselves before the local Baal, their god Chemosh, and probably his consort Ashtar (mentioned on line 17 of the Moabite Stone), as a preliminary to indulging in carnal behavior. From the account in Numbers the Israelites evidently participated without inhibitions, thereby breaking the commandment that prohibited the worship of any god save the Lord of Sinai (Ex. 20:3–5) and ignoring completely the regulation that forbade adultery (20:14). It was small wonder that such blatant and flagrant apostasy aroused God's anger against the offenders. The "Baal of Peor" was the lord or god of the Moabite mountain area known as Peor. Some scholars have suggested that the shrine dedicated to this deity was the place where Balaam delivered his final oracle, but this cannot be maintained with any certainty.

2. GOD'S PUNISHMENTS (25:4-9)

Translation

Then the LORD said to Moses: Arrest all the leaders of the people and execute the transgressors in broad daylight before the LORD, that

---

52. The literature on Ugarit is enormous. Reports of the various archaeological campaigns were published by C. F. A. Schaeffer in *Syria* from 1929 onward. A comprehensive bibliographical guide is K. Burgerhof, M. Dietrich, and O. Loretz, *Ugaritische Bibliographie der Jahre* 1928-1966, in four volumes. These are supplemented by P. C. Craigie, *Ugaritic Studies I*, 1972-1976; *II*, 1976-1979. C. H. Gordon produced a major *Ugaritic Handbook* in 1947 that included texts in transliteration. His *Ugaritic Textbook* (AnOr 38) was published in 1965. A concise, untechnical introduction by P. C. Craigie, *Ugarit and the Old Testament* (Grand Rapids: Eerdmans, 1983), includes a guide for further study and reading. See also M. Liverani and W. S. LaSor, *ISBE*, 4:46-48, 937-41, and bibliographies.

the fury of the LORD's anger may turn away from Israel. So Moses said to the Israelite judges: Each of you must execute those of his men who joined in worshiping the Baal of Peor. One of the Israelites brought a Midianite woman to his family before the very eyes of Moses and in full view of the whole Israelite community who were weeping at the entrance to the Tent of Meeting. (25:4-6)

Exegesis and Exposition

The Midianite women who had, with the Moabites, prostrated themselves before the deities in worship were evidently cultic prostitutes indulging in the kind of imitative fertility rituals mentioned by Herodotus.[53] For such an appalling disregard of the covenant, capital punishment was the only appropriate fate. While God is a God of love, He is also jealous to maintain His rights under the covenantal agreement—namely, the worship of His chosen people, the observance of His enacted laws, and obedience to His revealed will. If the apostasy were not halted at this point, the situation would be out of control and complete chaos would result.

The tribal leaders, who should have been preventing the pagan worship and the accompanying sensual orgies, were commanded by God to be publicly exposed or impaled, once their limbs had been broken,[54] in the expectation that their swaying bodies would convince the survivors of the gravity of their crime. Moses seems to have modified God's orders by asking the judges (MT שֹׁפְטִים, *šōpĕṭîm*) of the nation to execute only those who participated actively in the offense, in accordance with Hebrew law (cf. Deut. 24:16). One blatant Israelite even brought with him a Midianite woman as his "companion," ignoring both the presence of Moses and the Israelite women who were weeping at the door of the Tabernacle court because of the severity of God's anger upon the community.

Translation

Now when Phinehas, son of Eleazar, the son of Aaron the priest, saw it he left the assembly, and taking a javelin in his hand he followed the Israelite man into the tent and drove the spear through both of them into the woman's body. At this the plague against the Israelites was halted. Those who died in the plague were 24,000. (25:7-9)

Exegesis and Exposition

At the sight of this travesty of covenantal observance, Phinehas, grandson of Aaron the deceased high priest, could no longer contem-

---

53. Herodotus, 1.199.

plate the thought of the camp's being polluted by the presence of a pagan prostitute. Some commentators have suggested that the man had taken his Midianite companion into the Tabernacle compound, a procedure forbidden by Levitical law, and had begun to have carnal relations with her. Others think that the rear area (MT קֻבָּה, qubbâ)—i.e., the innermost part of the family tent—was involved, and this seems to be a preferable explanation. Phinehas put a quick end to this disgraceful activity by driving his spear through the man's torso into that of his partner. The lower part of the woman's stomach (MT קֳבָתָה, qŏbātāh, a rare word found elsewhere only in Deut. 18:3) was penetrated by the blow, which may have ruptured the abdominal aortas of both offenders.

Phinehas saw the situation as a crass example of a pagan ritual sex act between a non-Israelite woman and a male member of a community that had ceremonial holiness as its ideal. Such behavior could be punished only by execution, the position that God Himself had already taken. A plague (MT מַגֵּפָה, maggēpâ) of unspecified nature had apparently broken out already, and this provoked the weeping of the Israelite women. With the action of Phinehas the plague came to an end. Whether Moses' orders to the judges were carried out is not recorded, but the casualties resulting from the episode numbered 24,000 (23,000 in 1 Cor. 10:8), a number the Israelites could ill afford to lose, especially if most of the offenders were fighting men. It has been suggested that the refusal of Moses to carry out God's orders for the execution of the leaders led to the onset of the plague, and this must be considered a distinct possibility.[55] In later Hebrew tradition Phinehas was commended for his resolute behavior in halting the plague (Ps. 106:30).

3. AFTERMATH (25:10-18)

Translation

Then the LORD addressed Moses, saying: Phinehas, the son of Eleazar and grandson of Aaron the priest, has averted My anger from the Israelites, because he was determined, as I was, to maintain My rights among them, so that I would not put an end to Israel as a result. For this you must tell him that I am establishing My covenant of peace with him, and it shall be to him and his descendants a

---

54. KD, 3:205; G. J. Wenham, Numbers, pp. 186-87. W. G. Plaut and W. W. Hallo, Numbers, p. 197, suggest an unspecified but cruel method of execution.
55. Cf. W. H. Gispen, Het Boek Numeri, 2 (Kampen: J. H. Kok, 1964), p. 147. For the difference between the MT and Paul's assessment see KD, 3:206.

covenant of a permanent priesthood, because he was concerned to maintain the rights of his God and thus made atonement for the Israelites. (25:10-13)

Exegesis and Exposition

By his prompt action Phinehas had interpreted the mind of God precisely, and his zeal for the holiness of the covenant had saved the nation from destruction.[56] As a priest he had given practical expression to the holiness and righteousness expected of God's priests. In them, ceremonial holiness must pass beyond the ritual and cultic to penetrate and purify their moral and spiritual natures.

The community at large is often favorably impressed by a godly, dedicated life of service by the Lord's priests. Since all believers in Christ are members of God's holy priesthood (1 Pet. 2:5), the obligations of a life consecrated to Christ involve persons other than those who have been ordained formally to public ministry.

Because of apostasy and sin, atonement was required before divine forgiveness could be bestowed. The atonement Phinehas had made was the sacrifice of two human offenders. The MT intensive form of the verb כָּפַר (*kāpar*) means "to atone by offering a substitute."[57] In the Levitical sacrificial regulations an animal served as a substitute for the penitent sinner. The life of the animal, symbolized by its blood (Lev. 17:11), was required in exchange for the life of the transgressor.

In the situation that confronted Phinehas, he was defending God's holiness by sacrificing the lives of the sinning couple, thereby dispensing with the ritual of animal substitution. Atonement having been made, God could then pardon His wayward people by halting the spread of the plague. The reward given to Phinehas and his descendants was an agreement entitling them to enjoy the eternal possession of the priesthood (MT בְּרִית כְּהֻנַּת עוֹלָם, *běrît kěhunnat ʿôlām*). His zeal and its practical application had restored the covenant relationship between God and Israel. The high priesthood thus promised continued among the Israelites, with the exception of an interval during the time of Eli (1 Sam. 1-3; 14:3), until the final dissolution of the Jewish state in NT times.[58]

Christian interpreters have seen Phinehas as a type of Christ. He was an ideal Hebrew priest who made an atoning sacrifice for his people and rebuked apostasy. Jesus transcended Phinehas, however,

---

56. On the actions of Phinehas see S. C. Reif, "What Enraged Phinehas?" *JBL* 90 (1971): 200-206.
57. R. L. Harris, *TWOT*, 1:452-53.
58. *KD*, 3:207.

in being the sinless Son of God, whose teachings prepared the way for a new covenant relationship through His blood, shed to redeem human beings from the curse of sin. Whereas Phinehas wielded the javelin, Jesus was the recipient of a spear-thrust at His death (John 19:34). Paul places a moral rather than a soteriological interpretation upon the incident (1 Cor. 10:6-8), urging believers to avoid sexual immorality.

Translation

Now the name of the Israelite who was stabbed to death with the Midianite woman was Zimri son of Salu, a family leader among the Simeonites. The name of the Midianite woman who was killed was Cozbi daughter of Zur. He was a family leader among the Midianites. Then the LORD spoke to Moses, saying: Harass the Midianites and kill them, because they harassed you with the treachery by which they seduced you in connection with Peor, and with their sister Cozbi, daughter of a Midianite leader. She was killed when the plague struck because of Peor. (25:14-18)

Exegesis and Exposition

A statistical note, evidently furnished by the šōṭĕrîm, supplied the pedigrees of the victims of Phinehas's atoning activity. The Israelite, named Zimri, came from a prominent Simeonite line, being the son of Salu and one of the great tribal leaders.[59] Apart from this information, nothing further is known about either father or son. When women are named by pedigree in the OT, they are recognized as being important for social or other reasons. The Midianite transgressor's name was recorded as Cozbi ("deceiver"), the daughter of Zur ("rock"), one of the five Midianite kings (Num. 31:8) who subsequently succumbed to the Israelites. It appears that Zur had been killed earlier by Moses (Josh. 13:21). Apart from this there is no further information about Cozbi and her father.

Reprisals against the Midianites were called for, and accordingly God instructed Moses to commence harassing attacks against Midian. The time was not yet opportune for a full-scale war, since Israel's military strength had been weakened by the most recent plague. But the nation had experienced a foretaste of the idolatry that she could expect to encounter in Canaan. From the disastrous outcome of the Moabite temptation the people also learned that the covenant ideal

---

59. M. Noth, *Die israelitischen Personennamen im Rahmen der Gemein-semitischen Namengebung* (BWANT 3/10; Stuttgart: Kohlhammer, 1928), pp. 174-75.

would demand of them rejection of such invitations to apostasy and evil in the future.

Additional Notes

25:4 כָּל־רָאשֵׁי: BHS would emend this to רִשְׁעֵי, "evil ones," but the MT makes clear that the tribal leaders were to be executed as representative of the immorality, while the other adulterers were destroyed by the plague. The proposed emendation is thus incorrect and unnecessary.

25:6 אֶל־אֶחָיו: The LXX reads προσήγαγεν τὸν ἀδελφὸν αὐτοῦ πρὸς τὴν Μαδιανεῖτιν, which is a misunderstanding of the MT.

25:8 אֶל־קֻבָּתָה: According to BHS this is an incorrect repetition of הַקֻּבָּה, so that the woman would have been killed "in her shrine" (cf. S. C. Reif, *JBL* 90 [1971]: 100-106). This view presupposed that the Midianite woman was acting in a divinatory capacity, whereas the MT understood her to have committed adultery with an Israelite, which was a prohibited act. The proposed emendation must therefore be considered implausible.

25:15 בֵּית־אָב: This explanatory gloss identifies Zur as a prominent Midianite and was most probably an original feature of the *šōṭĕrîm* record.

D. THE SECOND CENSUS (26:1-65)

Subsequent to (1) the proclamation of a census (vv. 1-4), the remainder of chap. 26 can be broken down in terms of tribal units: (2) the tribe of Reuben (vv. 5-11); (3) the tribe of Simeon (vv. 12-14); (4) the tribe of Gad (vv. 15-18); (5) the tribe of Judah (vv. 19-22); (6) the tribe of Issachar (vv. 23-25); (7) the tribe of Zebulun (vv. 26-27); (8) the tribe of Manasseh (vv. 28-34); (9) the tribe of Ephraim (vv. 35-37); (10) the tribe of Benjamin (vv. 38-41); (11) the tribe of Dan (vv. 42-43); (12) the tribe of Asher (vv. 44-47); (13) the tribe of Naphtali (vv. 48-50); (14) total persons registered and the division of the land (vv. 51-62); (15) summary (vv. 63-65).

1. PROCLAMATION OF A CENSUS (26:1-4)

Translation

It happened that, when the plague was over, the LORD addressed Moses and Eleazar son of Aaron the priest, saying: Take a census of the entire Israelite community by families, registering those twenty years of age or older, who are able to fight in Israel's army. So Moses and Eleazar the priest addressed them in the Moabite plains by the

Jordan, opposite Jericho, saying: Make an enumeration of men twenty years old or older, just as the LORD commanded Moses and the Israelites who came from the land of Egypt. (26:1-4)

Exegesis and Exposition

Chapter 26 follows its precursor chronologically. The rationale for the new census is not hard to discover. A generation had passed since the first mustering of people eligible to serve as warriors (Num. 1:2–4:49), during which time the older members of the community had died in the wilderness as a punishment for their rebellion against God's will (14:29-32).[60]

In the meantime their successors had journeyed to Transjordan, where they had won important victories. They were now encamped on the upland plains of Moab, ready to harass the Midianites before entering Canaan. Accordingly, a new estimate of Israel's military strength was necessary. It would account for population variations and furnish information necessary for the proper deployment of the soldiers.

But the census also served an additional purpose, which was of considerable sociological importance. When the land of Canaan was divided up among the Israelite tribes, it would be done proportionate to the relative size of the various tribes. An accurate count was therefore necessary so that there would be no perceived inequity of treatment. Whereas Aaron had helped Moses organize the first census, Eleazar now replaced his deceased father in this capacity. The summons was conveyed to the assembled Israelites, and the procedure followed four decades earlier was again employed. The recording officers (*šōṭĕrîm*) are not mentioned here, but successors would have been recruited where necessary. The same lower age limit of twenty years was again prescribed by God. As compared with the first registration, the second one includes the families or family groups of which the various tribes were composed.

2. THE TRIBE OF REUBEN (26:5-11)

Translation

Reuben was Israel's firstborn. His descendants were: through Hanoch, the Hanochites; through Pallu, the Palluites; through Hezron, the Hezronites; and through Carmi, the Carmites. These are the Reubenites, numbering 43,730. Pallu's son was Eliab. Eliab's sons

---

60. *KD*, 3:97.

were Nemuel, Dathan, and Abiram. These were the Dathan and Abiram who as community leaders rebelled against Moses and Aaron and joined with Korah in defying the LORD. Then the earth opened its mouth and swallowed them, together with Korah, whose followers died when the fire engulfed 250 men. They served as a warning. The Korahites, however, did not perish. (26:5-11)

Exegesis and Exposition

As Jacob's firstborn son, Reuben was accorded pride of place as a courtesy, although he had lost his right to become the leader of Jacob's sons because of an illicit liaison with his father's concubine (Gen. 35:22; 49:4). This crime would be forever associated in Hebrew history with the name of Reuben. In Egypt Reuben fathered four sons, Hanoch, Pallu, Hezron, and Carmi (46:9), from whom emerged the principal families of the tribe.

At this census the number of available fighting men had decreased to 43,730, whereas a generation earlier the registration stood at 46,500. Pallu was notable as the grandfather of Dathan and Abiram, two of Eliab's three sons. These were the men who joined with Korah in the disastrous rebellion against God in the wilderness (Num. 16:1-35) and were engulfed along with 250 other men. The narrative remarks here that members of the family of Korah did not lose their lives, a fact not made clear in Num. 16. It is typical of Scripture that certain names and associated events are not allowed to die but recur in the narratives from time to time. The present section seems to indicate the reason— namely, that the events were to serve as a warning that needed to be recalled periodically.

3. THE TRIBE OF SIMEON (26:12-14)

Translation

The descendants of Simeon by their family groups were: through Nemuel, the Nemuelites; through Jamin, the Jaminites; through Jakin, the Jakinites; through Zerah, the Zerahites; and through Shaul, the Shaulites. These are the Simeonites, numbering 22,200. (26:12-14)

Exegesis and Exposition

The offspring of Simeon, the second son of Jacob (Gen. 29:33), branched out into five principal divisions. In Gen. 46:10; Ex. 6:15, a son named Ohad was listed, but since he had no recorded offspring he apparently died in childhood. He is not mentioned in the lists of 1 Chron. 4:24-25. In the first census the Simeonite warriors numbered

59,300 and were the third largest unit among the tribes. Just before entering Canaan the tribe had shrunk to a little more than one-third of its original size.

4. THE TRIBE OF GAD (26:15-18)

Translation

The descendants of Gad by their family groups were: through Zephon, the Zephonites; through Haggi, the Haggites; through Shuni, the Shunites; through Ozni, the Oznites; through Eri, the Erites; through Arodi, the Arodites; and through Areli, the Arelites. These are the Gadites, numbering *40,500. (26:15-18)

Exegesis and Exposition

Gad was Jacob's seventh son (Gen. 30:10-11) and was blessed with no fewer than seven sons himself. These family groups made up the tribe of Gad, which at the second registration furnished 40,500 fighting men. Their numbers had decreased slightly from the first census, when they had 45,650 warriors.

5. THE TRIBE OF JUDAH (vv. 19-22)

Translation

The sons of Judah were Er and Onan, but they died in Canaan. The descendants of Judah by their family groups were: through Shelah, the Shelanites; through Perez, the Perezites; and through Zerah, the Zerahites. The descendants of Perez were: through Hezron, the Hezronites; through Hamul, the Hamulites. These are the Judahites, numbering 76,500. (26:19-22)

Exegesis and Exposition

Judah, the fourth son of Jacob (Gen. 29:35), was the father of Er by the daughter of a Canaanite man named Shua. She bore him a second son named Onan (38:2-4). Her third son, Shelah, was born at Chezib. God slew Er for an unspecified act of iniquity, and when his brother Onan refused to consummate properly a form of levirate marriage with Er's widow (38:8-9) the Lord slew him also. Because Onan died without children, that portion of the line was traced thereafter through Shelah, the youngest son. Judah then fathered twin sons, Perez and Zerah, by Tamar his daughter-in-law (38:27-30), and these formed the second main part of the line of Judah. Perez became Judah's "second" son after Er and Onan had died, with Shelah being recognized as the official "first." Perez, through whom the line of David and Jesus would be traced, had numerous offspring (cf. Ruth

4:12) from his two sons, and in the second census the military men numbered 76,500, being the largest of the tribes—as it had been at the first census, when 74,600 men were registered.

6. THE TRIBE OF ISSACHAR (26:23-25)

Translation

The descendants of Issachar by their family groups were: through Tola, the Tolahites; through Puah, the Puhites; through Jashub, the Jashubites; and through Shimron, the Shimronites. These are the descendants of Issachar, numbering 64,300. (26:23-25)

Jacob's ninth son was Issachar and was born at Paddan-aram (Gen. 30:18). He fathered four sons, each of whom produced family groups to make up the tribe. Puah, his second son, was also known as Puvah (46:13), and his descendants are described in the MT of v. 23 as "Punite." The present translation "Puhite" follows the Samaritan Pentateuch, the LXX, and the Vulgate. In Genesis 46:13 Jashub was named Iob (KJV "Job"), due apparently to a copyist's error. Together these families had 64,300 men at the second registration, which represented a significant increase in numbers when compared with 54,400 at the first.

7. THE TRIBE OF ZEBULUN (26:26-27)

Translation

The descendants of Zebulun by their family groups were: through Sered, the Sardites; through Elon, the Elonites; and through Jahleel, the Jahleelites. These are the Zebulunites, numbering 60,500. (26:26-27)

Exegesis and Exposition

Zebulun was Jacob's tenth son (Gen. 30:19-20). Little is known about his life except that he had three sons through whom the tribe flourished. At the first registration 57,400 warriors were enrolled, but the second showed a slight increase to 60,500 men. Sered's descendants are called Seredites in the Hertz translation[61] and also in the *NAB*, but in most other versions they are known as "Sardites."

8. THE TRIBE OF MANASSEH (26:28–34)

Translation

The descendants of Joseph by their family groups through Manasseh and Ephraim were: The descendants of Manasseh: through

---

61. J. H. Hertz, ed., *The Pentateuch and Haftorahs*, p. 688.

Machir, the Machirites, Machir being the father of Gilead, and through him came the Gileadites. These were the descendants of Gilead: through Iezer, the Iezerites; through Helek, the Helekites; through Asriel, the Asrielites; through Shechem, the Shechemites; through Shemida, the Shemidaites; and through Hepher, the Hepherites. Now Zelophehad son of Hepher had no sons but only daughters, whose names were Mahlah, Noah, Hoglah, Milcah, and Tirzah. These are the Manassites, numbering *52,700. (26:28-34)

Exegesis and Exposition

Because the descendants of Levi were not registered as a tribe in this narrative, the tribe of Joseph was divided into two sections allotted to his sons Ephraim and Manasseh, in order to maintain the total number of the tribes at twelve. Manasseh was Joseph's firstborn and with his brother Ephraim was adopted by Jacob on his deathbed (Gen. 48:5), who in the process bestowed the first place and the consequent birthright blessing on Ephraim (48:13-20). Thus while the usual MT order is "Ephraim and Manasseh," following the tradition established by Jacob, the reverse is the case here in recognition of the fact that Manasseh was Joseph's elder son (46:20).

So little is known about Manasseh that some scholars have suspected him of remaining unmarried but having an Aramean concubine whose son, Machir, founded the people of Gilead. They then settled in the land that had been captured from the Amorites. In 1 Chron. 7:14-16, Machir's wife was named Maachah, who bore him two sons, but the MT seems to have suffered disruption in the process of transmission. Iezer, also known as Abiezer and Jezer, and the other sons of Gilead were ultimately to settle west of the Jordan. Zelophehad, grandson of Gilead, had no sons but instead was favored with five daughters, who were the beneficiaries of a decision by God (Num. 36:1-12). The inclusion of women in tribal genealogies was rare, but in this instance it was a necessity because of the lack of male heirs. The number of Manasseh's warriors at the first registration was 32,200, but this had increased significantly during the interval, and at the second census the total stood at 52,700.

9. THE TRIBE OF EPHRAIM (26:35-37)

Translation

The descendants of Ephraim by their family groups were: through Shuthelah, the Shuthelahites; through Beker, the Bekerites; through Tahan, the Tahanites. The descendants of Shuthelah were:

through Eran, the Eranites. These are the Ephraimites, numbering 32,500. All these comprised the Josephites by their family groups. (26:35-37)

Exegesis and Exposition

Before his father Joseph died, Ephraim's family had reached the third generation (Gen. 50:23). It is possible that somewhat after Joseph's death the events recorded in 1 Chron. 7:21 occurred. There is considerable variation between the genealogy given here and the Ephraimite list of 1 Chron. 7:20-27.

The descendants of Shuthelah are spoken of as Shuthalites (*NEB, NKJV*) or Shuthelahites (*NAB, NIV, JB*). The Bekerites have been described as Bachrites (*NEB, NKJV*) or Bechrites (*NAB*). These were, with the Tahanites, the three principal family groups, but a second-generation family of Eranites received particular mention. At the second census the Ephraimite soldiers numbered 32,500, which constituted a significant reduction from the 40,500 fighting men of the earlier registration. This assessment, with the foregoing, completed the totals of the house of Joseph.

10. THE TRIBE OF BENJAMIN (26:38-41)

Translation

The descendants of Benjamin by their family groups were: through Bela, the Belaites; through Ashbel, the Ashbelites; through Ahiram, the Ahiramites; through Shupham, the Shuphamites; through Hupham, the Huphamites. The sons of Bela were Ard and Naaman: through Ard, the Ardites; through Naaman, the Naamites. These are the Benjaminites by their family groups, numbering *45,600. (26:38-41)

Exegesis and Exposition

Benjamin, Jacob's youngest son (Gen. 35:18), had ten sons according to Gen. 46:21, whereas here only five are mentioned. This difference is probably the result of some of Benjamin's sons dying at an early age or not having any offspring through marriage. Two second-generation Benjaminites, Ard and Naaman, are mentioned, but other than their tribal affiliation nothing more is known about them. The genealogy of Benjamin furnished here is different from the list in 1 Chron. 7:6-7; 8:1-5. In the first census the Benjaminites had 35,400 warriors registered, but by the second the number had increased significantly to 45,600.

11. THE TRIBE OF DAN (26:42-43)

Translation

The descendants of Dan by their family groups were: through Shuham, the Shuhamites. These constituted the Danites. All of them are Shuhamites, numbering 64,400. (26:42-43)

Exegesis and Exposition

Dan was the fifth son of Jacob (Gen. 30:6). His son was named Shuham, the Hushim of Gen. 46:23, and since this name appears to be a plural equivalent it designates the Shuhamites. From this single family group there grew a prolific tribe. At the first registration the Danites furnished 62,700 soldiers, whereas at the second census the number had increased slightly to 64,400, making the tribe of Dan the second largest in the nation.

12. THE TRIBE OF ASHER (26:44-47)

Translation

The descendants of Asher by their family groups were: through Imnah, the Imnites; through Ishvi, the Ishvites; through Beriah, the Beriites. Through the descendants of Beriah: through Heber, the Heberites; through Malchiel, the Malchielites. Asher also had a daughter named Serah. These are the Asherites, numbering 53,400. (26:44-47)

Exegesis and Exposition

Asher was the eighth son of Jacob (Gen. 30:13). Asher himself had four sons and one daughter (1 Chron. 7:30), but apparently one son, Ishvah, did not survive to produce children. A second generation through Beriah saw the rise of the Heberites and Malchielites. At the time of their departure from Egypt the Asherites numbered 41,500, occupying the ninth position among the tribes in terms of military strength. By the second census their numbers had increased to 53,400 warriors, advancing their position to fifth.

13. THE TRIBE OF NAPHTALI (26:48-50)

Translation

The descendants of Naphtali by their family groups were: through Jahzeel, the Jahzeelites; through Guni, the Gunites; through Jezer, the Jezerites; and through Shillem, the Shillemites. These are the Naphtalites, numbering *45,400. (26:48-50)

Exegesis and Exposition

Naphtali was the sixth son of Jacob (Gen. 35:25). When he went down to Egypt he had four sons (46:24), as listed here. The family groups were prolific and at the first census numbered 53,400 warriors, making them sixth in rank among the Israelite tribes. But during the wilderness wanderings their numbers decreased, and at the second registration they could muster only 45,400 warriors, reducing them to eighth place.

14. TOTAL PERSONS REGISTERED, AND THE DIVISION OF THE LAND (26:51-62)

Translation

The total of the Israelites enumerated was 601,730 men. (26:51)

Exegesis and Exposition

When compared with the results of the first registration at Mount Sinai, which reported a total of 603,550 men (Num. 1:46), the second census in Moab showed only a modest degree of attrition. The old generation had been replaced by its successor, which was now virtually at the same level of military strength. The result of the second enumeration must have provided encouragement to Moses as he entertained the prospect of further military maneuvers against his hostile neighbors.

Translation

Then the LORD spoke to Moses, saying: The land shall be divided as an inheritance, according to the numbers of names enrolled. You shall give a larger inheritance to a larger group, and a smaller one to a lesser group. An inheritance shall be allotted in proportion to its size in the enumeration. The land shall be distributed by lot. They shall gain their heritage according to the names of their ancestral tribes. Each inheritance is to be apportioned by lot among the larger and smaller groups. (26:52-56)

Exegesis and Exposition

The second primary purpose of the census in Moab was now becoming evident. On the basis of the statistics collected by Moses, Eleazar, and the šōṭĕrîm, the Promised Land would be apportioned proportionately among the tribes once it had been occupied. The principle of distribution was equitable inasmuch as it was based upon the comparative sizes of the tribal groups. The distribution was determined by casting lots.

The casting of lots (MT גּוֹרָל, *gôrāl*) was used for a variety of purposes and was widely believed to afford the deity concerned an opportunity for furnishing an authoritative and impartial decision. Thus the detecting of guilty persons (Josh. 7:14; 1 Sam. 14:42), the selection of the correct goat to be sacrificed on the Day of Atonement (Lev. 16:7-10), the choosing of Saul as king of Israel (1 Sam. 10:20-21), the arranging of priestly Temple duties (1 Chron. 24:5; 25:8)—all were decided by means of the lot. The nature and size of the *gôrāl* is not specified in the OT, but it would have been made of material comparable to other implements used by the priests. One kind of sacred lot was the Urim and Thummim, small enough to be stored in a pocket of the ephod worn by the high priest.[62]

The assigned areas were to be known by the ancestral names of the tribes who acquired them, and in the process of apportionment three concepts would become evident: (1) the land in its entirety as well as in its allotted portions belonged to God alone; (2) the manner of assigning it made clear the fact that the different areas constituted God's gift to His people; (3) the mechanics of lot-casting would be equitable and would thus forestall jealousy and dissension among the tribes.

Translation

These were the Levites who were enumerated according to their families: Through Gershon, the Gershonites; through Kohath, the Kohathites; through Merari, the Merarites. These were also Levite families: the Libnite family, the Hebronite family, the Mahlite family, the Mushite family, and the Korahite family. Kohath was the ancestor of Amram. The name of Amram's wife was Jochebed, daughter of Levi, who was born to him in Egypt. To Amram she bore Aaron, Moses, and their sister, Miriam. To Aaron were born Nadab and Abihu, Eleazar and Ithamar. But Nadab and Abihu died when they offered unauthorized fire before the LORD. All those male Levites a month old or older numbered 23,000. They were not included in the enumeration of the other Israelites because there was no property allocation for them among the Israelites. (26:57-62)

Exegesis and Exposition

The separate enumeration of the Levites parallels the practice in Num. 3:14-39, but only in the sense that they were segregated be-

---

62. Cf. I. Mendelsohn, *IDB*, 3:163-64; F. E. Hamilton, *ZPEB*, 3:988; D. E. Aune, *ISBE*, 3:172-73; C. Van Dam, ibid., 4:957-59 and bibliographies.

cause of their specifically holy functions. They were not liable for military service and had not been included in the second census because they were not to have any tribal lands allocated to them. Instead, they were to have forty-eight villages, distributed among the various tribes, in which to live, because the Lord Himself was their inheritance.

The three main divisions of the family of Levi—namely, Gershon, Kohath, and Merari—follow the pattern of 3:21-37, except that their duties are not recapitulated even in summary form. Five different families are then mentioned, but the list given in Num. 3 is in an incomplete form here because the Shimeites (3:21), Izharites, and Uzzielites (3:27) are omitted. Why this recording procedure was adopted is unknown. The Korahites are described in the KJV and *NKJV* as "Korathites."

Two of Aaron's four sons perished dramatically as the result of violating Tabernacle protocol. On both occasions the census procedures for the tribes involved males aged twenty years or more, and for the Levites all males above one month of age. The total of Levites for the second census was 23,000 as compared with 22,000 in the first registration. The Levites thus experienced the smallest variation of any of the groups registered. As with the first census, the figures of the second enrollment appear to have been rounded off.

15. SUMMARY (26:63-65)

Translation

These are the ones enumerated by Moses and Eleazar the priest, who counted the Israelites in the plains of Moab along the Jordan opposite Jericho. None of these was included among the ones numbered by Moses and Aaron the priest when they conducted a census in the Sinai wilderness. For the LORD had informed them that they would certainly die in the wilderness. So there was not one of them left except Caleb son of Jephunneh and Joshua son of Nun. (26:63-65)

Exegesis and Exposition

The summary indicates that Moses and Eleazar set an example of obedience to God's will in the performance of their duties. The passage also makes clear that God's promise of death in the wilderness for the rebellious generation had been fulfilled to the very last individual. But God's commitment to preserve Caleb and Joshua for their fidelity (Num. 14:36) is also recalled. Now that the death penalty had been imposed to God's satisfaction, a new generation could begin the task of entering and possessing the Promised Land.

Excursus on the Two Censuses in Numbers

There has been some discussion among scholars as to the archetypal form of a supposed census list, as though the two recorded in Numbers were not original and independent but were variations of one primary list from which both had been derived. Thus M. Noth (*Das System der Zwölf Stämme Israels* [BWANT 4/1; Stuttgart: Kohlhammer, 1930], pp. 7-28, 122-32) concluded that the list in Num. 26 was the more original. A generation later, in a thoroughgoing criticism of Noth's position, A. D. H. Mayes (*Israel in the Period of the Judges* [London: SCM, 1974], pp. 8-11, 16-31) concluded that the list in Num. 1 was the earlier of the two.

This kind of speculation is fruitless and loses its significance immediately if the *šōṭĕrîm*, acting under the supervision of Moses, are accepted as responsible recording officials who stood in the tradition of ancient Near Eastern annalists and scribes. As such they recorded all the most important events of the period as and when they happened, so that a written record was available for archival purposes in addition to the oral tradition of events. On such a basis the two census records would be independent listings that served different purposes, as indicated above. The constant presence and attention of the *šōṭĕrîm* would guarantee the accuracy of the data recorded over a period of four decades and would furnish a valid historical resource for future generations of scribes.

Additional Notes

26:1 בֶּן־אַהֲרֹן: Omitted by the LXX.

26:5 בְּנֵי־רְאוּבֵן: After this clause BHS suggests the addition of לְמִשְׁפְּחֹתָם, "by their families," to conform to the style of vv. 12, 15, 20, etc. It is not necessary, however, to impose a mechanical inflexibility upon the chapter.

26:12 נְמוּאֵל: The Syriac version changes this name slightly to read "Jemuel," perhaps influenced by MT Gen. 46:10; Ex. 6:15.

26:13 זֶרַח: In Gen. 46:10; Ex. 6:15 this individual was known as "Zohar."

26:15 The descendants of Gad (vv. 15-18) are placed by the LXX after the data for Zebulun (vv. 26-27), presumably influenced by the order in Gen. 46:14-16.

צְפוֹן: The MT of Gen. 46:16 spells the name צִפְיוֹן.

26:16 אָזְנִי: The MT of Gen. 46:16 reads the name as אֶצְבֹּן.

עֵרִי: The Samaritan Pentateuch and the LXX prefer "Ad(d)i," perhaps resulting from a confusion between *d* and *r*.

26:17 אֲרוֹד: The present translation reads "Arodi," with Gen. 46:16, the LXX, and Vulgate versions. The final letter seems to have dropped out in transmission.

אַרְאֵלִי: There is some variation in the spelling of this name in the versions. The Samaritan Pentateuch has "Aroli," but the LXX, followed by the Vulgate, reads "Ariel."

26:18 The LXX MSS are not unanimous about the total of 40,500, some adding an extra 4,000 men. One hand of Codex Vaticanus used the older Attic form τεσσαράκοντα, whereas Codex Alexandrinus and other codices preferred the Ionic τεσσεράκοντα.

26:21 חָמוּל: For this name the Samaritan Pentateuch and LXX read "Hamuel."

26:23 פֻּוָה: KJV "Pua." The Samaritan Pentateuch, LXX, and Vulgate read "Puah," following 1 Chron. 7:1.

26:28 The LXX follows a different order of the MT tribal statistics, placing Gad's descent (vv. 15-18) after that of Zebulun (vv. 26-27) and following it with data concerning Asher (vv. 44-47) before continuing with the descendants of Joseph.

26:34 There is further LXX MS confusion about the total of Manasseh's descendants, with Codex Alexandrinus reading 62,500.

26:35 תַחַן: The Samaritan Pentateuch reads a final *m* on this word instead of *n*, while the LXX has τάναχ.

26:36 עֵרָן: For this name the Samaritan Pentateuch and LXX have "Edan."

26:38 אַשְׁבֵּל: The Samaritan Pentateuch has the expanded form "Ashbeel," whereas the LXX has a different spelling, "As(h)uber."

26:41 The LXX has yet another variation from the MT statistics for the descendants of Benjamin. This one sees the total placed at 35,500.

26:42 שׁוּחָם: The fact that only one family is named here does not necessarily indicate a corrupt state of the Hebrew text. The MT states that only one family group was involved in the phenomenal growth of the tribe, and there is no MS evidence to the contrary.

26:43 The MT enumeration of the Danites was increased from 64,400 to 64,600 by the LXX codices Alexandrinus and Ambrosianus.

26:44 יִשְׁוִי: This name and its variant spelling, יִשְׁוָה, occur in Gen. 46:17, with the Samaritan Pentateuch and the LXX preferring the latter.

26:50 Some LXX MSS reduce the number of Naphtali's recorded descendants to 30,300, but one hand of Codex Vaticanus, as well as codices Alexandrinus and Ambrosianus, lend some support to the MT figure of 45,400 men.

26:57 לֵוִי: The Samaritan Pentateuch, LXX, and Syriac versions, together with the Targum Onkelos, have "sons of Levi," but the LXX and Samaritan Pentateuch read it in the following verse.

26:58 הוֹלִד: The MT is written defectively for הוֹלִיד, the hiphil of יָלַד, with the meaning "caused to bear," "procreated," and thus in a more general sense "ancestor" rather than the specific "father." The genealogy presents problems, doubtless because it was recorded in compressed form. There were ten generations between Joseph and Joshua, according to 1 Chron. 7:14-27, but only four are actually recorded from Levi to Moses for the corresponding period. Kohath was born before Jacob migrated to Egypt (Gen. 46:11), and since Moses was 80 years old at the time of the Exodus (Ex. 7:7), he must have been born some 350 years after Kohath. It thus seems best to regard Amram as a descendant of Kohath rather than a linear son, and his wife, Jochebed, as a "daughter of Levi" in a general sense of tribal descent. These two persons then became the parents of Aaron, Moses, and Miriam (Ex. 6:20; Num. 26:59). On OT genealogies generally see R. K. Harrison, *ISBE*, 2:424-28.

26:61 לִפְנֵי יהוה: After this phrase the LXX adds ἐν τῇ ἐρήμῳ Σινα.

E. INHERITANCE LAWS AND LEADERSHIP TRANSITION (27:1-23)

Chapter 27 continues the historical narrative of its precursor and can be divided into three units: (1) special inheritance laws (vv. 1-11); (2) Moses set aside (vv. 12-14); (3) appointment of Joshua (vv. 15-23).

1. SPECIAL INHERITANCE LAWS (27:1-11)

Translation

A deputation came, consisting of the daughters of Zelophehad son of Hepher, son of Gilead, son of Machir, son of Manasseh, from the family groups of Manasseh son of Joseph. The names of the daughters were Mahlah, Noah, Hoglah, Milcah, and Tirzah. They appeared before Moses, Eleazar the priest, the leaders, and the entire community at the entrance to the Tent of Meeting. Our father died in the wilderness, they said, but he was not associated with those companions of Korah who rebelled against the LORD, but he died for his own sins and left behind no male heirs. Why should our father's name disappear from his family group just because he had no son? Give to us property among our father's relations. So Moses presented their case to the LORD. (27:1-5)

Exegesis and Exposition

God's stated plans for the allocation of territory in Canaan to the various tribes on the basis of population ratios had aroused anxieties in the minds of Zelophehad's five daughters. In this section their father's pedigree is set out in full, and each of the women is named in order of seniority. The women presented a petition to Moses, Eleazar, the elders, and the whole community, following proper protocol, in which they expressed legitimate concerns about the future of their father's heritage. They pointed out that he had not been associated with Korah's rebellion but had died the kind of death that marks the normal sinful condition. Because he had left no son, he would not be given an inheritance in Canaan. Zelophehad's family name would thus have died out if his daughters married.

To forestall this unfortunate contingency, the daughters requested the same right of territorial possession as that which applied to the male tribal members. For Moses this situation involved decisions that were out of his jurisdiction, and accordingly he approached the Lord.

The women were not rejected out of hand as interfering females who had no right to infringe upon male prerogatives. Instead, they were listened to carefully and without recorded protest, as though the entire group sympathized with their plight. This spirit of unanimity was shared by Moses, who accorded the women the right of audience and promised to present their petition to the Lord for judgment.

Translation

The Lord addressed Moses, saying: Zelophehad's daughters have made a proper claim. You must indeed give *them an inheritance of property among their father's relatives, to enable their father's inheritance to pass to them. You shall address the Israelites, saying: If a man dies and does not leave a son, you shall turn his heritage over to his daughter. If he has no daughter, you shall allocate his inheritance to his brothers. (27:6-9)

Exegesis and Exposition

There is no indication in the MT as to how long Moses had to wait for a decision from God. The case would set a precedent, and the decision would have an important bearing upon the status of women in Israel for future generations. In a patriarchal society any attempt to undermine the basic authority of the man over the woman would be resented. The formulation of this new addition to the existing corpus of case law was given to Moses, who was told that the daughters' petition was legitimate. Accordingly, Moses was to proclaim a statute requiring all property to be handed over to daughters where there was no surviving son, or to the deceased man's brothers in the absence of a female heir. The rights (MT מִשְׁפָּט, *mišpāṭ*) of the daughters had thus been secured.

355

Translation

But if he has no brothers, you shall give his inheritance to his uncles. If his father had no brothers, you shall give his inheritance to the relative nearest him in his family, that he may inherit it. This shall constitute a legal requirement for Israel, as the Lord commanded Moses. (27:10-11)

Exegesis and Exposition

Property in the Promised Land was the gift of God to families, family groups, and tribes, who thus became His tenants (Lev. 25:23). In more specific terms it was the real property of its tenant-owners, and if it was sold it had to be returned to its original owners in the jubilee year (25:8-24).[63] The main purpose of this legislation was to prevent debtors from falling into complete ruin. It also ensured the inalienable right of property holders to their land, which among other benefits safeguarded the legal owner against being deprived of his or her holdings by corrupt means (cf. 1 Kings 21:1-16).

The order of inheritance is prescribed stage by stage, so as to cover all possible contingencies. In a family and tribal configuration such as was found in ancient Israel, there would be little difficulty in locating a relative, however distant, to inherit the property. The judicial pronouncement by God is described as a "legal requirement" (MT חֻקַּת מִשְׁפָּט, *huqqat mišpāṭ*), a fixed statutory enactment that determined rights and was established by divine authority. Some writers have regarded the procedure as a possible alternative to levirate marriage.[64]

The issue raises some interesting concerns involving the inheritance of property in the ancient Near East. When a man died, his holdings were normally distributed among his sons, with the eldest receiving the double portion that was the firstborn's privilege (cf. Deut. 21:15-17). Once this had occurred, the recipient was recognized formally as the head of the family. Daughters do not usually appear to have shared in their deceased father's estate, apparently because they would be expected to be married and have their own husbands to provide for them. Hebrew fathers usually made a testamentary deposition before death, and this safeguarded the interests of the beneficiaries. Where a man's offspring consisted solely of wom-

---

63. On the jubilee year see J. Morgenstern, *IDB*, 2:1001-2; J. Lilley, *ZPEB*, 3:715-16; J. B. Payne, *ISBE*, 2:1142-43; R. H. Alexander, *TWOT*, 1:358-59 and bibliographies; W. Eichrodt, *The Theology of the Old Testament* (London: SCM, 1961), p. 96.
64. On this see O. J. Baab, *IDB*, 3:282-83; P. Trutza, *ZPEB*, 4:99; R. K. Bower and G. L. Knapp, *ISBE*, 3:261-66 and bibliographies.

en, they were expected to marry men of their father's tribe so as to be entitled to receive their father's inheritance and also to prevent loss of title to his land.

In the ancient Near East the concept of "title" was not based upon noble birth so much as on the possession of land. Thus the aristocracy of any nation was one of landed wealth rather than of high breeding or cultural attainment. The concerns of Zelophehad's daughters are not the result of retrojection of later material into the preconquest period. Instead, they expressed an understandable social concern by forward-looking women for their own survival, particularly because they were aware that the division of Canaan, and with it their own destiny, was to occur in the near future.[65] God's decision showed that He was not willing to see the daughters of His people exploited or deprived of their legitimate holdings.

2. MOSES SET ASIDE (27:12-14)

Translation

Now the LORD said to Moses: Climb up this mountain of Abarim and inspect the land which I have given to the Israelites. When you have seen it, you too shall be gathered to your people, as Aaron your brother was gathered. For at the time when the community was rebelling against Me in the wilderness of Zin, both of you disobeyed My command to maintain My holiness before them at the waters. These were the waters of Meribah at Kadesh, in the wilderness of Zin. (27:12-14)

Exegesis and Exposition

As the aged Hebrew leader approached the end of a long and eventful life, God kept His promise by allowing Moses to view the promised land of Canaan. He was instructed to ascend a nearby mountain (MT הַר הָעֲבָרִים, *har hā'ăbārîm*) for this purpose. Abarim was a name for the northwest mountains of Moab, but the site was identified more closely in Deut. 34:1 as Mount Nebo. Once Moses had seen the land that his disobedience had prevented him from entering, he would die shortly thereafter and go to be with his brother Aaron. The expression "gathered to your people" is of a general nature, expressing the thought of reunion with previously deceased relatives. Wherever the phrase occurs it carries with it an intimation of immortality (cf. Gen. 15:15; 25:8), but it should not be understood in a purely literal sense. This hint at the possibility of an afterlife is the

---

65. See P. J. Budd, *Numbers*, pp. 299, 387-90.

closest that the Pentateuch comes to making a statement about existence after death.

The Scriptures make no attempt to suppress or ignore the faults of great personages but endeavor to assess individuals honestly and impartially. Moses is linked with his brother, Aaron, in failing to maintain God's holiness by being disobedient at the waters of Meribah at Kadesh (Num. 20:1-13). This act was recorded for the instruction and profit of future generations as a reminder that obedience to God is mandatory for all of the Lord's servants.

3. APPOINTMENT OF JOSHUA (27:15-23)

Translation

Then Moses addressed the LORD, saying: May the LORD, who is God of the spirits of all humanity, appoint a man over this community who will go out and come in before them, who will lead them out and bring them in, so that the LORD's community may not be as sheep without a shepherd. (27:15-17)

Exegesis and Exposition

In addressing his request to God for a successor, Moses described the Lord in terminology used at the time of the rebellion of Korah (Num. 16:22). The MT רוּחֹת לְכָל־בָּשָׂר (*rûḥōt lĕkol-bāśār,* "spirits of all flesh") describes the distinction between necessary and contingent existence. Humanity owes its frail state of being to the activity of God, who placed something of Himself in His creatures to which He could appeal and because of which He could expect them to worship Him. The concerns that Moses exhibited for a worthy successor are remarkably disinterested.

Translation

So the LORD said to Moses: Take along Joshua son of Nun, a man possessed of the spirit, and lay your hand upon him. Set him before Eleazar the priest and the entire assembly. Commission him in their presence, and delegate to him some of your authority, so that the entire Israelite community will follow his orders. He must stand before Eleazar the priest, who will obtain decisions for him from the LORD by consulting the Urim. At his instructions he and the entire Israelite community shall go out, and at his command they shall come in. (27:18-21)

Exegesis and Exposition

When the leadership of a given individual has been outstanding, the choice of a successor is crucial if previous traditions and accomplishments are to be maintained and exceeded. Joshua, who had been the commander of the Israelites in their fight with the Amalekites (Ex. 17:8-16), who was in charge of the Tabernacle after the incident involving Israel's pagan calf worship (33:11), and who was one of the twelve leaders sent out on the reconnaissance mission to Canaan (Num. 13:8, 16), was deemed the most suitable individual to become Moses' successor.

In all his years of service he had obeyed God, and indeed he had endeavored to protect God's holiness when prophesying occurred in the camp (Num. 11:27-29). The same spirit that actuated the prophesying had also come upon him (27:18), but there is no record of how or when this occurred. Moses was therefore instructed to take his Spirit-filled military leader and consecrate him formally as his successor. The commissioning ceremony would be held in front of the high priest and the entire Israelite people and would be marked by the symbolic imposition of Moses' hand, indicating transfer of office and doubtless his own blessing upon his successor.

Once Moses had delegated some of his powers to Joshua, the nation would accept him as their supreme military commander. But the new leader would not have the total prerogatives of the aged Moses, and the MT indicates a difference in function. He would not have direct approach to God, as Moses had, but when he needed to know the will of God on any given matter he would have to approach the high priest Eleazar, who would ascertain God's will by the use of the sacred lots. These articles, elsewhere called Urim and Thummim (MT הָאוּרִים וְהַתֻּמִּים, *hā'ûrîm wĕhattummîm*), were kept in the high priest's breastplate and were the means by which the Lord's will was ascertained. Since the culture of Israel had by now been established in terms of a body of law and the formation of a pattern of worship, fewer divine interventions of an ad hoc nature could be expected, and for the normal purposes of the religious community the decision of God through the use of lots would suffice. Precisely what these lots were and how they were shaped is unknown.[66] The two words in the Hebrew begin with the first (*'alep*) and last (*taw*) letters of the alphabet respectively. If this is the *merismus* motif, in which opposites are paired to denote totality (cf. Rev. 1:8; 21:6; 22:13), it could be interpreted to mean "complete truth in revelation."

Translation

Moses therefore did as the Lord had commanded him. He took Joshua and stationed him before Eleazar the priest and the entire

---

66. The most comprehensive discussion of these objects is by C. Van Dam, "The Urim and Thummim," doctoral diss. 2 vols. (Kampen, 1986).

community and laid his hands upon him and inaugurated him, precisely as the LORD had given instructions through Moses. (27:22-23)

Exegesis and Exposition

The ceremony of dedication and commissioning as prescribed by God was carried out to the letter, but with one small exception. God had instructed Moses to lay a hand upon Joshua. Instead, he placed both hands on his successor, as though to bless to the uttermost the man to whom he had given his new name, "the Lord is salvation." Joshua received some of the eminence and authority of Moses (MT מֵהוֹדְךָ, *mēhôdkā*, "[a portion] from your renown") and was placed under the authority of the high priest in matters of appeal to God once Moses had died. At that point Joshua would be the sole military leader of the nation.

Additional Notes

27:1 בֶּן־מְנַשֶּׁה: This part of the genealogy was omitted by the LXX.
לְמִשְׁפֹּחֹת מְנַשֶּׁה: This phrase was omitted by the Vulgate.

27:7 לָהֶם: לְ here has a masculine plural form where technically a feminine form, לָהֶן, is required. The retention of the masculine may have been deliberate, however, to demonstrate that, in this sensitive area, women were being treated on the same footing as male heirs. If this interpretation is correct, textual emendations to remedy the supposed discrepancy, as in the Samaritan Pentateuch and a few MT MSS, are unnecessary.

27:12 עֲבָרִים: The LXX reads τοῦτο τὸ ὄρος Ναβαύ, perhaps influenced by Deut. 32:48.
אֶת־הָאָרֶץ: The LXX adds χαναάν as an explanatory gloss.
יִשְׂרָאֵל: After this word the LXX adds a further gloss, ἐν κατασχέσει, "for a possession."

27:13 אָחִיךָ: Probably following Deut. 32:50, the LXX adds ἐν τῷ Ὡρ τῷ ὄρει.

27:14 כַּאֲשֶׁר: When כְּ occurs in clauses introduced by the relative particle אֲשֶׁר it often has a causal force, implying "because of the fact that." In 1 Sam. 28:18 the negative is explicit, whereas here the negative sense is conveyed sufficiently by the verb מָרָה without need for further specification.

27:20 מֵהוֹדְךָ: For "authority" the LXX, Syriac, and Vulgate versions read "glory." This is the only occurrence of the term in the Pentateuch. The "authority" to be transferred is at once civil and spiritual.

27:23 אֶת־יָדָיו: The Samaritan Pentateuch and Syriac versions have the singular form here.
בְּיַד־מֹשֶׁה: The Vulgate omits this phrase.

F. REGULATIONS FOR OFFERINGS (28:1-31)

Chapter 28 introduces a series of instructions dealing with ritual matters. The material can be analyzed as follows: (1) daily offerings (vv. 1-8); (2) weekly offerings (vv. 9-10); (3) monthly offerings (vv. 11-15); (4) Passover and Unleavened Bread (vv. 16-25); (5) Firstfruits (vv. 26-31).

1. DAILY OFFERINGS (28:1-8)

Translation

Now the LORD spoke to Moses, saying: Issue this command to the Israelites and tell them: With regard to My offering, be sure to present the food for My fire offerings, as a pleasing aroma to the LORD, at the specified time. And you shall tell them: This is the offering made by fire which you shall present to the LORD—namely, two unblemished yearling lambs each day as a regular offering. (28:1-3)

Exegesis and Exposition

The materials in this chapter have much in common with Lev. 23, which in one sense they supplement. They exemplify the pattern seen previously in the compilation of Numbers—namely, that of interspersing historical narratives with matters of priestly concern. It is this latter fact that furnishes the key to the question as to why there should be repetition of cultic material at this stage in Israel's wilderness experience, when virtually everything that concerned the worship of the community had been promulgated in great detail. Whereas all the enactments proclaimed previously had to do with the worship procedures of the community and by individuals, this chapter and the next are similar to pagan ritual calendars preserved in ancient Near Eastern temple archives to remind the priests of the occasions when specific cultic procedures were to be observed.[67]

The contrast between Lev. 23 and the present material has been stated aptly by Wenham. In Leviticus, the obligations of the lay worshiper are the predominant concern. In Num. 28-29, the priestly sacrificial duties are of paramount interest.[68] If Fisher is correct in paralleling these priestly materials in Numbers with a ritual calendar recovered from fourteenth-century B.C. Ugarit, he is presenting excellent Near Eastern evidence for an early date for Num. 28-29.

It was appropriate and necessary for the priests to know the mini-

---

67. Cf. L. R. Fisher, "New Ritual Calendar from Ugarit," *HTR* 63 (1970): 485-501.
68. G. J. Wenham, *Numbers*, p. 196.

mum sacrifices that could be offered each year, and since these prescriptions came just prior to the occupation of Canaan, they were of great significance for the Israelites. No matter what the nature of the day-to-day situation might be, God's worship must be followed regularly on a daily, weekly, and monthly basis, as well as during special seasons. This objective was fostered by the calendar drawn up in chapters 28-29, which integrated the sacrificial and festival regulations of Ex. 23:14-17; 29:38-42; 31:12-17; Lev. 23; and Num. 25:1-2.[69]

The sacrifices are arranged in order of descending frequency, commencing with the daily offering. God had to be satisfied as to the quality of the offering and the motivation of the worshiper before atonement could be accorded. The ritual formula of acceptance ("a pleasant aroma to the LORD") was first expressed in Ex. 29:18 and repeated frequently in Leviticus. Because it was a regular (MT תָּמִיד, *tāmîd*) procedure, the offering came to be known in later Judaism as "the Tamid."

Translation

You shall offer one lamb in the morning and the other between dusk and dark, with one-tenth of an ephah of finely ground flour as a grain offering mixed with one-quarter of a hin of pressed olive oil. This is the regular burnt offering that was instituted at Mount Sinai as a pleasing aroma, an offering made by fire to the LORD. (28:4-6)

Exegesis and Exposition

The daily sacrifice required one yearling male lamb to be offered in the morning and another in the evening (MT בֵּין הָעַרְבָּיִם, *bên hā 'arbāyim*, "between the two evenings"). Nightfall was the time prescribed for the offering of the Passover sacrifice (Lev. 23:5). Unlike some of the burnt offerings in Leviticus, the daily sacrifice was accompanied by a cereal offering. It was similar to that legislated for in Ex. 29:38-42, after Aaron and his sons had been consecrated to the priestly office. The grain offering amounted to about two quarts, and the olive oil with which it was mixed would be about one quart.

Translation

Its drink offering shall be one-quarter of a hin for each lamb. You shall pour out the drink to the LORD at the sanctuary as an offering. The other lamb you shall offer between dusk and nightfall, along with the same kind of grain and drink offering that you prepared in

---

69. *KD*, 3:216.

the morning. You shall present it as a fire offering, a pleasing aroma
to the LORD. (28:7-8)

Exegesis and Exposition

In addition to the cereal offering, a drink offering or libation of
about one quart was to be provided, and this constituted a departure
from some of the sacrificial practices in Leviticus. For "drink" the
NEB and *NASB* read "strong drink" (MT שֵׁכָר, *šēkār*), and the *NIV* has
"fermented drink," but other versions generally read "wine." The
common word for "beer" in Akkadian is *šikāru*, which is cognate with
Hebrew *šēkār*.

2. WEEKLY OFFERINGS (28:9-10)

Translation

On the *Sabbath, offer two unblemished yearling male lambs and
two-tenths of an ephah of finely ground flour as a grain offering
mixed with oil, together with the drink offering. This is the burnt
offering for every Sabbath day and is in addition to the regular burnt
offering and its drink offering. (28:9-10)

Exegesis and Exposition

The daily burnt offering furnished a regular opportunity for the
congregation to consecrate its total life to the Lord, who had bestowed upon Israel its life as a nation. The daily sacrifice was thus
basic to all other forms of worship, which were escalated according to
their importance. Thus the weekly Sabbath was observed by doub-
ling the sacrificial offerings of the other weekdays. Male yearling
lambs were sacrificed, accompanied by cereal and drink offerings as
prescribed. The amount of the grain offering was doubled for each
lamb on the Sabbath, but nothing is said about an increase in the
amount of olive oil. The ceremonies would doubtless occur at midday
or early afternoon.

3. MONTHLY OFFERINGS (28:11-15)

Translation

On the first day of each month you shall present as a burnt offering to the LORD two young bulls, one ram, and seven unblemished
yearling lambs, along with three-tenths of an ephah of finely ground
flour mixed with oil as a grain offering for each bull, and two-tenths
of an ephah of finely ground flour mixed with oil as a grain offering
for the one ram, and one-tenth of an ephah of finely ground flour

mixed with oil as a grain offering for each lamb, as a burnt offering of a pleasant aroma, a fire offering presented to the LORD. (28:11-13)

Exegesis and Exposition

In the Hebrew calendar,[70] which like all others in antiquity was an ecclesiastical almanac, the months commenced with the new moon. In preexilic times the new moon was celebrated as a minor festival (cf. 1 Sam. 20:5; 2 Kings 4:23).[71] Whereas pagan nations would indulge in the veneration of astral deities in their new moon festivities, the Hebrews were not permitted to worship anyone but their Lord (Ex. 20:3-5). For them, therefore, the new moon was not an object of superstitious adoration but a calendrical marker indicating that yet another month in their lives had commenced.

Because the occasion was deemed to be somewhat more elevated than the daily or weekly sacrifices, its observance was more elaborate than that of the Sabbath. Additional animals were sacrificed, and the grain offering for the bull was increased to approximately six quarts of fine flour. The ram was allotted the same amount of grain offering as that prescribed for each lamb in the Sabbath sacrifice, and the unblemished lambs were governed by the amounts set for the daily sacrifices.

Translation

With each bull you must have a drink offering of half a hin of wine, one-third of a hin for a ram, and one-quarter of a hin for a lamb. This is the burnt offering for each month throughout the calendar year. In addition to the regular burnt offering with its drink offering, one male goat is to be presented to the LORD as a sin offering. (28:14-15)

Exegesis and Exposition

The prescribed libations were about two quarts of wine for a bull, about one-and-a-quarter quarts for a ram, and approximately one quart for each lamb. The weekly offerings were augmented by the addition of a male goat as a sin offering. The Torah contains no directions as to the way in which the drink offering was to be presented or how the priest disposed of it, whether by pouring it on the sacrifice or on the ground beside the altar, or by some other means. What is clear, however, is that all the offerings presented to mark the commence-

---

70. The term comes from the Latin *calere*, "to call," because the priests proclaimed that the new moon had begun to rise.
71. J. H. Hertz, ed., *The Pentateuch and Haftorahs*, p. 695.

ment of a new month were to be sacrificed in accordance with prescribed Levitical rituals. This was in marked contrast to the un-
bridled, licentious behavior characteristic of the celebrations of lunar
occasions in pagan cultures.

4. PASSOVER AND UNLEAVENED BREAD (28:16-25)

Translation

On the fourteenth day of the first month the LORD's Passover is to
be observed, and on the fifteenth day of that month there shall be a
festival. For seven days you shall eat unleavened bread. On the first
day you shall convene a sacred assembly. You shall not perform your
ordinary tasks. (28:16-18)

Exegesis and Exposition

This section deals with the most important religious celebration
in the life of the Hebrews and recapitulates the original regulations of
Ex. 12. It reminds the Israelites that, although the Passover celebrations have been held in abeyance during the wilderness sojourn, once
the Israelites were in the Promised Land the Passover would be resumed. The third Passover ceremony was finally observed in the days
of Joshua (Josh. 5:10), four eventful decades after the second one had
been celebrated (Num. 9:2-5). The present legislation marks the distinction between the Passover as a sacrifice and the feast of Unleavened Bread as a festival. During this latter occasion, bread without yeast was eaten for an entire week. On the first and seventh days
of this festival no work was permitted, the two days being treated as
Sabbaths. Whereas Ex. 12 described the procedures to be followed,
the present passage is concerned with the numbers of animals and
their accompanying offerings.

Translation

You shall present to the LORD an offering made by fire, a burnt
offering of two young bulls, one ram, and seven yearling lambs, all of
them unblemished. Their grain offerings shall be of finely ground
flour mixed with oil. For a bull you shall offer three-tenths of an
ephah, and for a ram two-tenths. For each of the seven lambs you
shall offer one-tenth of an ephah as well as one male goat as a sin
offering, to make atonement for you. (28:19-22)

Exegesis and Exposition

The animals presented for sacrifice were the same numerically as
those for the monthly offering, and their cereal and drink offerings

365

were identical also. The requirement for a sin offering in both the monthly and Unleavened Bread celebrations served as a reminder to the Israelites that they must be ceremonially clean at all times.

There is an emphasis upon sin in the theology of the Hebrew rituals and a corresponding stress upon the precise mechanics to be observed before atonement for sin can be effected. Even though the believer in Christ claims cleansing from sin through the blood of the cross, he must maintain vigilance against the assaults of the devil, so that sin will not reign in his mortal body (Rom. 6:10). For the Christian, ceremonial cleanness is a shallow form of spirituality. The holiness that Christ demands must penetrate any veneer of religious propriety to produce a sanctified personality guided by moral, ethical, and spiritual considerations.

Translation

You shall present these in addition to the burnt offering sacrificed regularly in the morning. In this manner you must prepare the food for the offering made by fire each day for seven days, as an aroma pleasing to the Lord. It is to be presented in addition to the regular burnt offering and its drink offering. On the seventh day you must hold a sacred assembly. You must not perform your ordinary tasks. (28:23-25)

Exegesis and Exposition

All these offerings were to be presented in addition to the regular morning sacrifices and were to be accompanied by the prescribed grain and wine offerings. No shortages or imperfections of any kind would be tolerated. The final day of the festival was to be treated as a regular Sabbath, and an assembly of the people was convened for the purpose of worshiping their Lord. Such convocation days were "holidays" in the literal sense, because normal work was prohibited.

5. FIRSTFRUITS (28:26-31)

Translation

You must also hold a sacred assembly on the day of Firstfruits, when you present to the Lord an offering of new grain during the feast of Weeks. You must not perform your ordinary tasks. You shall present a burnt offering as an aroma pleasing to the Lord, consisting of two young bulls, one ram, and seven yearling lambs with their grain offerings of finely ground flour mixed with oil: three-tenths of an ephah for each bull, and two-tenths for the one ram, with one-tenth for each of the seven lambs, as well as one male goat to make atonement for you. Be sure that they are unblemished. You must

present them with their drink offerings in addition to the regular burnt offering with its grain offering. (28:26-31)

Exegesis and Exposition

The "day of Firstfruits" (MT יוֹם הַבִּכּוּרִים, *yôm habbikkûrîm*) was the beginning of the feast of Weeks (Ex. 34:22), when the wheat harvest commenced. Since this festival began fifty days after the feast of Unleavened Bread, it came to be known in NT times as Pentecost, from Greek πεντηκοστός (*pentēkostos*, "fiftieth"). It was thus the second most important festival in the Hebrew calendar. Elsewhere it was also called the feast of Harvest (Ex. 23:16), but the emphasis here is on the "day of Firstfruits," which was to be treated as a Sabbath because the loaves made from the new grain were offered on the altar (Lev. 23:17).

The animal sacrifices and their associated grain and wine offerings were identical with those prescribed for the feast of Unleavened Bread. As always, the animals were scrutinized by the priests to ensure that they were in perfect physical condition, and the offerings precise and exact in amount. All of these, as with the offerings for the feast of Unleavened Bread, were additional to the normal daily requirements. These enactments concerning Firstfruits are not connected with any specific historic event but must be viewed as a seasonal celebration of God's bounty and as an opportunity to recognize His provision by dedicating its firstfruits to Him. Harvest festivals were common in the ancient world and provided occasions of drunkenness, gluttony, and moral degeneracy. With the Israelites, on the other hand, the festival was to be one of worship and atonement for sin.

Additional Notes

28:2 לַחְמִי: The suffixal form of לֶחֶם, "food," makes the offerings specifically the Lord's. To accept the BHS suggestion of לֶחֶם, "food(s) of," would weaken the sense of the MT and is therefore unacceptable.

28:5 כָּתִית: This adjective was omitted by the Samaritan Pentateuch and the LXX.

28:9 הַשַּׁבָּת: After this word the LXX, Vulgate, and Targum Neofiti I add "you shall offer" as an explanatory gloss.

28:10 עַל־עֹלַת: The preposition עַל is used here to express addition, as in Gen. 28:9; 1 Sam. 12:19.

28:14 יָיִן: The Samaritan Pentateuch and some other versions insert "wine" after MT חֲצִי הַהִין as an explanatory gloss, but since the term occurs distributively later in the verse, the gloss would seem unnecessary.

לַפָּר: The sense here is again distributive, "for each bull," as glossed by the Samaritan Pentateuch and the LXX.

28:17 חַג: i.e., of Unleavened Bread (Lev. 23:6).

יֵאָכֵל: The niphal future is acting in its normal sense as the simple passive of the qal. The Samaritan Pentateuch and the LXX, however, render the verb by the active voice, which is unnecessary but perhaps read in conformity with the implied future active sense of the following verse.

28:27 עוֹלָה: Here the Samaritan Pentateuch adds an explanatory gloss, "an offering by fire," perhaps in an attempt to harmonize the text with the אִשֶּׁה of v. 24.

שָׁנָה: The Samaritan Pentateuch glosses this by adding "they shall be to you unblemished," apparently following the pattern of vv. 19, 31.

28:31 עֹלַת הַתָּמִיד: This is an appositional genitive form where an adjective occurs (cf. 2 Kings 17:6) instead of a noun (cf. Gen. 15:18; 2 Kings 19:21).

G. LEGISLATION FOR OTHER FESTIVALS (29:1-40)

Chapter 29 continues the priestly concerns of its predecessor and can be divided into three components: (1) blowing trumpets (vv. 1-6); (2) Day of Atonement (vv. 7-11); (3) feast of Tabernacles (vv. 12-40).

1. BLOWING TRUMPETS (29:1-6)

Translation

On the first day of the seventh month you must hold a sacred assembly. You must not perform your ordinary duties, for it is a day for sounding the trumpets. You shall offer a burnt sacrifice as a pleasing aroma to the LORD, comprising a young bull, one ram, and seven yearling lambs, all without blemishes. (29:1-2)

Exegesis and Exposition

The cycle of seven, which is prominent in Hebrew life and worship,[72] gained particular emphasis in the seventh month of the religious calendar. This month, corresponding to the last half of September plus the first half of October, was known as Ethanim or Teshritu (Tishri) at different times and marked the commencement of the civil year. Its position was enhanced by the fact that during the month three important religious celebrations took place. Since the

---

72. For the way in which the festivals were arranged according to the number seven see *KD*, 3:218-19.

Hebrew calendar was established on the pattern of the religious festivals, the significance of the seventh month for Israelite life and worship can hardly be overestimated.[73]

Because harvest would have ended by this time, the Israelites would be able to rest and worship for a month once they had occupied Canaan. The legislation of this chapter presupposes a Transjordanian standpoint and looks forward to a time when the Israelites would be settled agriculturalists. The concern of the chapter is statistical, dealing with the three great festivals in terms of the extra offerings required for the various occasions.

The sanctity of the first day of the seventh month required sacrificial offerings in addition to those of the daily and monthly sacrifices. The Israelites were prohibited from working and were ordered to assemble for divine worship and to participate in the ceremony of sounding the trumpets. The latter may have been intended originally to herald the presence of the new civil year, but in any event it called attention to the special character of the day as well as of the month that followed. This ancient tradition is still observed in the ritual of synagogue worship on this day. In Num. 10:10 God commanded the trumpets to be sounded at all appointed festivals and new moon celebrations, but this particular day was to be known for this special form of activity.

Translation

Their grain offering shall be finely ground flour mixed with oil: three-tenths of an ephah for the bull, two-tenths for the ram, and one-tenth for each of the seven lambs. Add to these one male goat as a sin offering for your atonement. These are in addition to the monthly and regular burnt offerings with their grain and drink offerings, as have been specified, and comprise a fire offering, a pleasing aroma to the Lord. (29:3-6)

Exegesis and Exposition

Only one bull would be required for this occasion, as opposed to the two bulls for the monthly offering and the feast of Unleavened Bread. The animals were to be accompanied by the prescribed amounts of grain and wine offerings, and, as with the monthly sacrifices and those for the feast of Unleavened Bread, a male goat would be required to secure atonement for the community.

Thus four sacrifices were to be offered on this day: (1) the yearling

---

73. For the extensive literature on the Hebrew calendar see S. J. De Vries, *IDB*, 1:483-88; J. Lilley, *ZPEB*, 1:687-92; D. F. Morgan, *ISBE*, 1:574-78 and bibliographies.

lamb in the morning, with its grain and drink offering; (2) the ordinary sacrifice for the commencement of a new month, comprising two bulls, one ram, and seven yearling lambs, with their accompanying offerings, and a goat as a sin offering; (3) the special sacrifices marking the nature of the day, comprising one bull, one ram, and seven year-old lambs, with their accompanying offerings, and a male goat for a sin offering; and (4) the normal daily evening sacrifice, comprising a yearling lamb with its accompanying offerings. These prescriptions furnish the detailed cultic and statistical undergirding of the legislation proclaimed in Lev. 23:23-25.

2. DAY OF ATONEMENT (29:7-11)

Translation

On the tenth day of the seventh month you must convene a sacred assembly. You must practice self-denial and refrain from working. You shall present a burnt offering as a pleasing aroma to the LORD, comprising one young bull, one ram, and seven yearling lambs, all of them without defects. Their grain offering shall be of finely ground flour mixed with oil: three-tenths of an ephah for the bull, two-tenths for the ram, and one-tenth for each of the seven lambs. Add to these one male goat as a sin offering over and above the sin offering for atonement and the regular burnt offering with its grain and wine offerings. (29:7-11)

Exegesis and Exposition

This section provides for the priests the detailed background to the enactments in Lev. 23:26, establishing the Day of Atonement as a solemn Sabbath. The sacrifices were similar to those presented at the monthly celebrations except that only one bull would be required, as with the special sacrifice marking the feast of Trumpets. The cereal and wine offerings followed the normal prescriptions, but the ceremony differed in that an extra goat was required for atonement.

Although the Day of Atonement is frequently included in the calendar of Hebrew festivals, it was the most solemn day in the year and should therefore be regarded more properly as a fast. In Lev. 16:29 the Israelites were commanded to "afflict themselves" on that day. The MT form of the verb עָנָה (*ānâ*, "to be bowed down," "be oppressed") seems to mean "humbling oneself," but without further explanation. By the time of Isaiah (58:35) the idea of fasting seems to have been part of the observance, with the possible symbolic addition of the wearing of ashes. Only the native Israelite was to indulge in self-abnegation on the Day of Atonement, the resident alien being excused from participating.

The ritual was to be observed six months after the celebration of the Passover, and the central feature was the effecting of atonement for the nation's sins of inadvertence. On that day alone in the entire year did the high priest enter the Most Holy Place to expiate transgressions and impurities that had not already been covered by the normal sacrificial rituals.

This solemn day, with its atoning activity, carries great significance for the Christian also. Its events make evident the intense hatred that God has for human sin. If such iniquity was allowed to go unreprimanded, the nation would follow a path leading to death (cf. Rom. 6:23). Since all have sinned and fall short of God's glory (3:23), an atonement efficacious for all forms of sin was required, since the Old Covenant sacrificial system did not provide it (Num. 15:30).

Thus the ceremonies of this most sacred day point forward to a time when the Lamb of God would be slain for the sins of the world (Isa. 53:6). The blood of bulls and goats could not cleanse from sin (Heb. 10:4), whereas the shed blood of Jesus the Messiah was able to reconcile to a gracious and loving God a world alienated by sin (2 Cor. 5:19). Jesus thus becomes the great High Priest (Heb. 7:24), whose atoning blood redeems (1 Pet. 1:18-19), cleanses (1 John 1:7), pardons (Eph. 1:7), justifies (Rom. 5:9), sanctifies (Heb. 13:12), and brings peace with God (Col. 1:20).

3. FEAST OF TABERNACLES (29:12-40)

Translation

On the fifteenth day of the *seventh month you must convene a sacred assembly and refrain from doing your regular work. Celebrate a festival to the LORD for seven days. You shall present a fire offering as an aroma pleasing to the LORD, a burnt sacrifice comprising thirteen young bulls, two rams, and fourteen yearling lambs, all of them unblemished. Their grain offering shall be of finely ground flour mixed with oil: three-tenths of an ephah for each of the thirteen bulls, two-tenths for both rams, and one-tenth for each of the fourteen lambs. Add to these one male goat as a sin offering, over and above the regular burnt sacrifice, with its grain and wine offering. (29:12-16)

Exegesis and Exposition

This section furnishes information for the priests about the large numbers of animals and offerings that would be an essential part of the feast of Tabernacles. The enactments for the festival occur in Lev. 23:34-43, where the reason for the occasion is given.

The festival began about halfway through the month and continued for seven days, with an extra day attached to serve as a closing feast. Judging from the number of bulls sacrificed (seventy in all), the occasion must have been one of great exultation. Tabernacles was also known by names such as the "feast of ingathering" (Ex. 23:16), the "festival of the Lord" (Lev. 23:39), or simply "the festival" (1 Kings 8:2). The feast of Tabernacles (MT סֻכֹּת, sukkôt, "booths") was rooted in the wilderness experience of the Israelites. The name sukkot(h) supposedly commemorated the final encampment site before the Hebrews left Egypt (Ex. 12:37–13:20), a site frequently identified with Tell el-Maskhutah in the Wadi Tumilat. It could also refer to a site in Gad near the Jordan (Josh. 13:27), which scholars have identified tentatively with Tell Deir 'Alla, located about two miles north of the Jabbok River.

The purpose of sukkot(h) ("tabernacles," "booths") was to remind future occupants of Canaan that their ancestors had once been desert nomads living in tents and that only by God's gracious provision did they enjoy the benefits of settled life in their own land.

The feast was scheduled to begin five days after the Day of Atonement, opening with a solemn assembly for worship that was treated as a Sabbath day. In addition to the regular burnt offering, thirteen bulls, two rams, and fourteen yearling lambs, along with their standard cereal and wine offerings, were brought for sacrifice. To protect the ceremonies against the penalty for inadvertent iniquity or ritual uncleanness a male goat was sacrificed as a sin offering. The first day's activities would set a pattern for the events of succeeding days, although the number of bulls sacrificed diminished steadily as the festival progressed.

Translation

On the second day you must offer twelve young bulls, two rams, and fourteen yearling lambs, all of them unblemished, and their grain and drink offerings for the bulls, rams, and lambs, as specified according to their numbers. Add one male goat as a sin offering over and above the regular burnt sacrifice, with its grain offering, and their wine offerings. On the third day you must offer eleven bulls, two rams, and fourteen yearling lambs, all of them unblemished, and their grain and drink offerings for the bulls, rams, and lambs, as specified according to their numbers. Add one male goat as a sin offering over and above the regular burnt sacrifice, with its grain and wine offerings. (29:17-22)

Exegesis and Exposition

On the second day of the post-harvest celebration the worshipers would see a reduction of one bull in the number of animals to be sacrificed, but apart from that the tariff was maintained unchanged. These offerings were in addition to the prescribed daily sacrifices. On the third day the number of bulls offered up was reduced to eleven, but apart from that modification the festival proceeded as prescribed.

Translation

On the fourth day you must offer ten bulls, two rams, and fourteen yearling lambs, all of them unblemished, and their grain and drink offerings for the bulls, rams, and lambs, as specified according to their numbers. Add one male goat as a sin offering besides the regular burnt sacrifice, with its grain and wine offerings. On the fifth day you must offer nine bulls, two rams, and fourteen yearling lambs, all of them unblemished, and their grain and drink offerings for the bulls, rams, and lambs, as specified according to their numbers. Add one male goat as a sin offering besides the regular burnt sacrifice, with its grain and wine offerings. (29:23-28)

Exegesis and Exposition

The stereotyped nature of the cultic formulation would make it easy for the harried priests to remember. Although each day's sacrifice is different to a small extent, the constant factor is the male goat as a sin offering.

Harvest or post-harvest festivities in the ancient Near East were boisterous occasions often marred by drunken excesses. Nothing of that kind was to characterize the honoring of the covenant Lord, however. Even in times of high exultation, everything that takes place in God's presence must be done in a decent and orderly manner. The apostle Paul rebuked the believers at Corinth for abuses in connection with the Lord's Supper and reminded them of the perils of partaking unworthily in holy activities (1 Cor. 11:17-34).

Translation

On the sixth day you must offer eight bulls, two rams, and fourteen yearling lambs, all of them unblemished, and their grain and drink offerings for the bulls, rams, and lambs, as specified according to their numbers. Add one male goat as a sin offering besides the regular burnt sacrifice, with its grain and wine offerings. On the seventh day you must offer seven bulls, two rams, and fourteen yearling lambs, all of them unblemished, and their grain and drink offerings for the bulls, rams, and lambs, as specified according to their numbers. Add one male goat as a sin offering besides the regular burnt sacrifice, with its grain and wine offerings. On the eighth day you shall convene a sacred assembly. You shall not engage in your customary work. You shall present a fire offering as an aroma pleasing to the LORD, a burnt sacrifice comprising one bull, one ram, and seven yearling lambs, all of them unblemished, and their grain and drink offerings for the bull, ram, and lambs, as specified according to their numbers. Add one male goat as a sin offering besides the regular burnt sacrifice, with its grain and wine offerings. You shall present these to the LORD at the appointed seasons, in addition to offerings involving vows and freewill gifts, as your burnt offerings, your grain and drink offerings, and your peace offerings. (29:29-39)

Exegesis and Exposition

The feast of Tabernacles stretched into the eighth day, which was much like a Sabbath day in that customary work was suspended. The MT עֲצֶרֶת (ʿăṣeret, "solemn assembly") indicates that the festival period would close, as it had opened, in an atmosphere of communal worship. In essence the ʿăṣeret and the מִקְרָא־קֹדֶשׁ (miqrāʾ-qōdeš) of v. 12 were one and the same.

The sacrificial offerings at the close were comparatively modest, comprising a single bull, one ram, and seven yearling lambs, all with their prescribed offerings of grain and wine. The foregoing regulations for the festival were to be the pattern for future generations in the Promised Land. Presumably the Israelites would give the animals spontaneously to God out of hearts filled with gratitude for the prosperity of their new homeland. Perhaps one reason the statistics in chaps. 28-29 were recorded was to give the priests sufficient information to recruit donors of animals for the festival.[74]

Translation

So Moses informed the Israelites on all matters in accordance with the LORD's command. (29:40)

Exegesis and Exposition

All of God's requirements concerning the detailed procedures to be observed at the great Israelite festivals were duly communicated to the people, as recorded in the obedience formula with which this chapter closes. The occasions for celebration provided a much-needed respite from the unremitting tasks of agricultural life and furnished legitimate opportunities for genuine enjoyment within the

---

74. For the Hebrew festivals see J. C. Rylaarsdam, *IDB*, 2:260-64; J. P. Lewis, *ZPEB*, 2:521-26; E. D. Isaacs and J. B. Payne, *ISBE*, 2:292-96 and bibliographies.

context of a moral and spiritual environment. The "holidays" were thus true "holy days." In a similar way, Christians are encouraged to rejoice in the Lord (Phil. 4:4) and to give thanks to God continually (1 Thess. 5:18) for all His wonderful gifts.

Additional Notes

29:6 אִשֶּׁה: There is no equivalent for this term in the LXX.

29:7 כָּל־מְלָאכָה: This is a general statement prohibiting any kind of work, which is specified in greater detail in vv. 12, 35 (מְלֶאכֶת עֲבֹדָה).

29:12 הַשְּׁבִיעִי: The LXX emphasizes this by using the demonstrative pronoun, τοῦ ἑβδόμου τούτου. The Samaritan Pentateuch and the Syriac version also read a demonstrative, suggesting the influence of an independent MS tradition.

29:13 לַיהוה: As an explanatory clause to remedy a supposed deficiency in the MT, the LXX added τῇ ἡμέρᾳ τῇ πρώτῃ.

29:16 מִנְחָתָהּ וְנִסְכָּהּ: The collective singular forms are replaced in the LXX by the plural αὐτῶν. In v. 19 the first of these two terms is singular and the second plural. The LXX reads αὐτῶν for both terms.

H. REGULATIONS CONCERNING VOWS (30:1-16; MT 2-17)

Chapter 30 deals with matters concerning vows that are different from what is contained in either Lev. 27:28-29 or Num. 6. Although it was placed after a section dealing with supplies of animals at festivals, it need not be regarded as having emerged from the same occasion. This material could have been revealed to Moses at an earlier period, such as the time when the Nazirite vow was legislated (Num. 6:1–21), or it may have been prompted by the decision regarding Zelophehad's daughters. In any event, its present position is in harmony with the festal occasions provided for in the two preceding chapters, since a festival would furnish an excellent occasion for the discharging of a vow. The literary components of the chapter are: (1) vows made by men (vv. 1-2); (2) vows made by single women (vv. 3-5); (3) vows made by married women (vv. 6-8); (4) vows made by widows (vv. 9-15); (5) summary (v. 16).

1. VOWS MADE BY MEN (30:1-2)

Translation

Moses addressed the tribal leaders concerning the Israelites, saying: This is what the Lord has commanded. A man who makes a vow to the Lord, or takes an oath of a binding obligation, must not break his word but must do everything that he has promised. (30:1-2)

Exegesis and Exposition

At the time this revelation was given, Moses communicated it to the heads of the Israelite tribes because it brought a new ethical dimension to personal and family life. The enactments were in the form of a מִצְוָה (*miṣwâ*, "commandment") imposed by divine authority and demanding obedience if the recipients were to prosper (cf. Deut. 5:32-33).

The opening section concerned vows made by men,[75] who would probably form the bulk of Israel's votaries. In peacetime such vows could involve a wide range of circumstances and might follow the pattern of promising to do certain things for God if He first achieved a specified benefit on their behalf. This kind of practice has been employed by people in desperate circumstances. The only acceptable kind of vow, however, is the unconditional variety, where the votary promises to do something for God without expectation of reciprocal action. Bargaining with God is a form of tempting Him or questioning His credibility, which is forbidden in Scripture (Ex. 17:7; Deut. 6:16; Matt. 4:7; Luke 4:12; Heb. 11:6).

The נֶדֶר (*neder*) was a positive promise or vow to donate or sanctify any portion of one's property to the Lord. By contrast, the MT לֶאְסֹר אִסָּר עַל־נַפְשׁוֹ (*le'sōr 'issār 'al-napšô*) meant "to take a binding obligation on oneself," and this has generally been interpreted as a negative vow, in that the person undertakes to abstain from something that, in the absence of the vow, might otherwise be permissible.[76]

The vow might have involved a personal act of deprivation such as fasting, but more probably it had to do with promises to God that involved a specific goal, such as the preservation of life in time of war, or survival during economic hardship. Regardless of the nature of the vow, the votary was under obligation to fulfill its content in detail because the vow had been made to the Lord. The *neder* may have been concerned predominantly with religious matters, whereas the *'issār* was perhaps applied to social or secular concerns, but this distinction is at best uncertain.[77]

2. VOWS MADE BY SINGLE WOMEN (30:3-5)

Translation

When a young woman who is still living at her father's home makes a vow to the LORD, or places herself under an obligation, and

---

75. For different kinds of vows see the preface to chap. 6.
76. So *KD*, 3:223; J. H. Hertz, ed., *The Pentateuch and Haftorahs*, p. 702; et al.
77. J. A. Thompson, *The New Bible Commentary Revised*, p. 195.

her father learns about her vow or pledge but does not object to it, then all her vows and every promise in which she had involved herself shall stand. But if her father overrules her when he hears about it, then none of her vows or the obligations in which she has become involved shall be binding. The LORD will absolve her, because her father overruled her. (30:3-5)

In antiquity the patriarch had power of life or death over all who lived with him. Although there were times when this tradition would be modified in practice, there were others when it was not, as in the case of Jephthah (Judg. 11:30-39). The Hebrews professed great love for their children and were doubtless often indulgent toward them. Many proper names seem to be in diminutive form, which may be an indication of affection.

The unmarried female child was under the special care of her father, who would protect her interests until she had a husband to care and provide for her. A man's oversight of his daughter's activities included ensuring that she did not make rash promises or enter into agreements that she was unable to honor. As with a man, a woman's vow could be a positive or negative form of commitment. The present legislation enlarged the basic concept of the inviolable nature of an oath by introducing case-law qualifications for women under different kinds of authority, so as to decide the overall question of when a woman's vow could be considered valid.

These verses concern an unmarried woman in her father's household who was enabled to make an oath to the Lord and fulfill it, provided it was not rash (cf. Eccles. 5:2) or improper. But if her father, in his love for his daughter, decided to overrule it, the Lord would respect the decision and would pardon (MT סָלַח, *sālaḥ*, "forgive") the woman for failing to fulfill the undertaking. This case provides an interesting example of a situation where the Lord is governed by human decisions.

3. VOWS MADE BY MARRIED WOMEN (30:6-8)

Translation

But if the woman marries while under a vow or an impetuously uttered binding obligation, and her husband hears about it but raises no objection to it at the time, then her vows shall stand, as will the pledges by which she has bound herself. But if her husband overrules her at the time that he learns of it, he shall nullify the vow she has taken and the impetuous utterance by which she bound herself, and the LORD will absolve her. (30:6-8)

377

Exegesis and Exposition

This case is that of a vow made by a woman who was still under her father's authority but married before the vow was discharged. As a votary the woman could have been an adolescent or an adult, but the implication is that her father approved tacitly of the undertaking, if in fact he had heard about it. The "impetuous utterance" (MT מִבְטָא שְׂפָתֶיהָ, *mibṭā' śĕpātêhā*, "rash statement from her lips") need not have met with the disapproval of the man whom she married subsequently, but if it did it was treated as though the woman's father had disallowed it. In marriage the husband is considered to be *in loco parentis*, and in the ceremony of "giving" the bride to the bridegroom the parent hands his daughter over to the authority and care of her new husband. Since in patriarchal societies women were subject to their husbands, a tradition perpetuated in a spiritualized manner by NT teachings (Eph. 5:22; Titus 2:5), the husband had the power to countermand any undertakings that he considered improper on the part of his wife. In practice, however, the new husband would have proceeded cautiously in case the bride initiated reprisal measures. In the event that the husband did override his new wife's vow, the Lord would once more respect his decision.

4. VOWS MADE BY WIDOWS (30:9-15)

Translation

But any vow or obligation taken by a widow or a divorced woman shall remain valid. If she made the vow in her husband's home, or put herself under a binding agreement by an oath and her husband learned of it but said nothing to her and did not overrule her, then all her vows and every agreement that she made involving obligations shall remain valid. (30:9-11)

Exegesis and Exposition

The general principle of the legislation concerning vows is now accommodated to the case of a widow and, even more rarely, of a divorced woman. Vows undertaken by these two classes of formerly married women follow the previous pattern of being regarded as valid by God unless countermanded by the woman's husband in some way.

Marriage was a divine institution rooted in humanity's innocence, and in the elegant language of the Church of England's *Book of Common Prayer* "was ordained for the hallowing of the union betwixt man and woman; for the procreation of children to be brought up in the fear and nurture of the Lord; and for the mutual society, help, and comfort that the one ought to have of the other, in both prosperity and adversity."[78] The family that was initiated by matrimony represented the foundation of a stable society, and the power that was vested traditionally in the head of the family was designed to promote the strength of that social unit and not to brutalize or coerce servants, children, or wives. As the family was strong, so the entire nation would flourish.

Translation

But if her husband nullified them formally at the time that he heard about them, whatever she promised verbally in the way of vows of obligatory agreement shall become invalid. Her husband has nullified them, and the LORD will absolve her. Her husband can confirm or nullify any vow or sworn promise that might be to her detriment. But if her husband raises no objections to her day after day, he thus confirms all her vows or binding agreements by virtue of not having objected at the time when he heard about them. But if he should nullify them at a subsequent period, then he shall be responsible should she default. (30:12-15)

Exegesis and Exposition

The vows made by the widow or the divorced woman remained in force if no formal objection had been lodged by the husband. But if they were disallowed, the Lord would absolve the woman of any further responsibility. The basic concern, as indicated by v. 3, is that the husband should exercise his nullifying privileges only if the vow seemed to be to the detriment of his wife, for whose care and security he was responsible. The significant phrase in v. 13, "to her detriment" (MT אִסַּר נַפְשָׁהּ, *'issar napšāh*), is rendered variously as "to afflict the soul" (KJV), "to afflict her soul" (NKJV), "to mortify herself" (NAB), "binds herself to mortification" (NEB), "to deny herself" (NIV), and "that is binding" (NJB).

Should the husband experience a change of mind while the marriage was still in existence, any recrimination would be his responsibility (MT נָשָׂא אֶת-עֲוֺנָהּ, *nāśā' et-'ăwōnāh*, "he will bear her guilt"). To atone for his guilt he would need to follow the provisions of Lev. 5:4-13. If this was neglected or ignored, he could expect to suffer punishment from the Lord.

---

78. *The Book of Common Prayer* (1662): The Form of Solemnization of Matrimony.

5. SUMMARY (30:16)

Translation

These are the statutes that the LORD commanded Moses relating to a man and his wife, and a father and his young daughter who is still living at home. (30:16)

Exegesis and Exposition

This concluding formula summarizes the חֻקִּים (*ḥuqqîm*), or binding statutes, that defined the status of a woman as far as vows were concerned. Probably the most familiar example of a woman under a vow was Hannah, the mother of Samuel (1 Sam. 1:11), whose promises to God were evidently approved by her husband, Elkanah. Vows were continued in the early Christian period (Acts 18:18; 21:23) and have been a feature of life ever since.

A tradition grew up among the Jews whereby an irresponsible son could vow formally to God all his earnings that would normally have contributed to the support of his parents. Jesus criticized this form of vowing (Matt. 15:3-9; Mark 7:11-12) as fraudulent and therefore a dishonest way of avoiding responsibility for the welfare of parents. Such an undertaking nullified God's commandment (Ex. 20:12) and was therefore evil.

James reminded his readers that the tongue, though small, is a very dangerous organ of the body (James 3:5). Promises can be made with comparative ease, but if uttered irresponsibly or without due thought they can prove very damaging. God, who is true to His word in every sense, is not deceived by flattery or swayed by beguiling utterances. He demands absolute honesty in those who commune with Him. Any variation from a direct positive or negative affirmation opens the way to ambiguity and prevarication, the result of which may ultimately be divine judgment (cf. James 5:12).

Additional Notes

30:3 לֶאְסֹר אִסָּר: The cognate form of qal infinitive construct and proper noun (cognate accusative construction) is used here for emphasis.

דְּבָרוֹ: The collective singular is employed here and is followed by the LXX, whereas the Samaritan Pentateuch preferred the plural form.

30:5 אֶת-נְדָרֶהָ וֶאֱסָרֶהָ: The Samaritan Pentateuch, LXX, and Syriac versions read plural forms here.

30:9 אֶת-נְדָרֶהָ: The Samaritan Pentateuch, LXX, and Syriac versions read a plural here, presumably to harmonize the text with v. 8.

380

The MT fluctuations between singular and plural are purely stylistic and do not require emendation in the interests of textual conformity.

עַל־נַפְשָׁהּ: Here the LXX adds an explanatory clause: ὅτι ὁ ἀνὴρ ἀνένευσεν ἀπ᾽ αὐτῆς.

30:16 אֶת־עֲוֹנָהּ: The Samaritan Pentateuch, LXX, and Syriac versions altered the MT feminine suffix to a masculine form, implying that a change of mind carries its own kind of penalty for the offender.

I. DESTRUCTION OF MIDIAN (31:1-54)

Chapter 31 describes a short but decisive battle waged against an enemy whose destruction had already been commanded by God. The material can be analyzed as follows: (1) Israelites mobilized (vv. 1-5); (2) campaign (vv. 6-13); (3) death of captive women (vv. 14-18); (4) purification of nation (vv. 19-24); (5) distribution of spoils (vv. 25-54).

1. ISRAELITES MOBILIZED (31:1-5)

Translation

The LORD spoke to Moses, saying: Take your revenge upon the Midianites for the Israelites. After that, you will be taken to your ancestors. So Moses addressed the people, saying: *Mobilize some of your men for the war to attack the Midianites and execute the LORD's revenge upon Midian. Send a thousand men from each and every Israelite tribe into battle. From all the family groups of Israel they recruited a thousand from each tribe—12,000 men armed for war. (31:1-5)

Exegesis and Exposition

This battle was the last that the aged Moses directed as civil leader of Israel. The chapter is a genuine historical narrative, not a contrived incident to explain how the spoils of war had to be distributed. Although the latter was an important matter for future consideration when the Israelites occupied Canaan, there could have been no distribution of booty without a prior victory. God ordered Moses to attack the Midianites in order to secure revenge (MT נְקֹם נִקְמַת, *nĕqōm niqmat*, an emphatic statement expressing thorough vengeance). This holy war was to be fought in fulfillment of God's demand that the Midianites be harassed because they had seduced the Israelites at Peor (Num. 25:16-18). After that campaign Moses would die, being informed in a gentle euphemism that demonstrated God's love and care for him.

In the ancient Near East, battles were regarded as waged between national gods, whose people did the actual fighting. If a nation was defeated, it was because the national deity was angry with his people. Thus in line 5 of the Moabite Stone[79] the reason given for the Israelite oppression of Moab was that Chemosh, the god of the Moabites, was angry with his land. In Israel's battles the Lord was the supreme commander and thus became known as the "Lord of armies" (Josh. 5:15; 1 Sam. 1:3; etc.). As the civil leader, Moses was responsible for carrying out the Lord's orders in terms of drafting troops and sending them into combat under the command of generals such as Joshua and Phinehas.

In this instance a division made up of one thousand men from each tribe was mustered for the attack on the Midianites. Each Israelite tribe thus contributed equally to the success of the holy war. The Midianites were not alone in their sexual liaisons with the Israelites at Peor (Num. 25:1-2), for their numbers included Moabite women who apparently had come from an area west of Midian.

As will be apparent in v. 16, it was the Mesopotamian soothsayer Balaam who advised the Midianite allies of the Moabite king to lead the Israelites into apostasy, perceiving this approach as the least violent means of accomplishing their ruin. For this calculated attempt to destroy God's holy nation, the Midianites were to be punished, but the Moabites were to be left alone. Under Hebrew law the penalty for adultery was death (Lev. 20:12; Deut. 22:22), so the killing of the Midianites would form a suitable punishment as well as serve as a warning to other pagan nations.

2. CAMPAIGN (31:6-13)

Translation

Then Moses sent them into battle, one thousand from each tribe, with Phinehas son of Eleazar the priest, who was in charge of the holy vessels and carried the signal trumpets. They fought against the Midianites, as the LORD had commanded Moses, and killed all their males. In addition to those killed in the conflict they slew Evi, Rekem, Zur, Hur, and Reba, the five Midianite kings. They also put Balaam son of Beor to death. (31:6-8)

Exegesis and Exposition

Moses sent the troops into battle under the leadership of Phinehas, son of Eleazar the high priest. This redoubtable grandson of Aaron appeared first in Israel's history as the zealous warrior of the Lord whose actions in upholding God's purity in Israel brought about

79. For text and bibliography see P. D. Miller, Jr., *ISBE*, 3:396-98.

the end of the plague that was ravaging the nation because of immorality with the Moabite and Midianite women (Num. 25:7-11). It was therefore eminently fitting for him to be the priestly attaché when the Israelites conquered Midian in battle, and his participation makes it clear that this was indeed a holy war.

In Deut. 20:2-4 the high priest's duties prior to a battle were of a morale-building nature, urging an expression of faith in God that would lead to victory. By contrast, among pagan nations various omens had to be assessed by priestly seers before advice was given about fighting or not. But here the living God of Israel assured victory for His armies as long as the covenant stipulations were honored. The same conditions apply, *pari passu*, to the New Covenant. One prominent model of the Christian in the NT is that of a soldier who is equipped with armor (Eph. 6:13-18). Such a person is encouraged to live the "overcoming" life (Rom. 12:21) by means of the spiritual weapons that are part of the Christian soldier's armory. The blessings of eternal life will be the reward for obedience, fidelity, and firm Christian witness (Rev. 2:7, 17, 26; 3:5, 12, 21).

The text of v. 6 is somewhat ambiguous regarding the duties of Phinehas. The MT reading וּכְלֵי הַקֹּדֶשׁ וַחֲצֹצְרוֹת הַתְּרוּעָה בְּיָדוֹ (*ûkĕlê haqqōdeš wahăṣōṣĕrôt hattĕrûʿâ bĕyādô*, "and the sacred vessels and the trumpets for signaling in his hand") has often been interpreted to mean that Phinehas carried into battle the Ark of the Covenant and its contents, as was done later on, for example, in the time of Samuel's youth (1 Sam. 4:3-5). The word כְּלֵי (*kĕlê*, "vessels of") could not refer to the Urim and Thummim, as has been suggested, since any form of decision about the battle was not required. Although כְלִי (*kĕlî*) in Deut. 22:5 means "a garment," it does not refer to the robes of the high priest but is instead describing an article of common clothing. In addition, although Phinehas had charge of the sanctuary's vessels, he was not Israel's high priest, a position that was occupied by his father, Eleazar (Num. 20:25-26). Consequently he had no authority to parade the Ark at the head of Israel's army. The best interpretation seems to be that the conjunction preceding *hăṣōṣĕrôt* is *waw explicitum*, "specifically the signal trumpets in his hand." These instruments were intended to assemble the community in time of war and also to remind God that His people depended upon Him for aid and ultimate victory (10:9). The trumpets were only to be sounded by the priests of Israel.

All the male Midianites who opposed the Hebrew warriors were killed in the conflict, including five Midianite rulers. One of those chiefs was Zur, whose daughter Cozbi had been slain by Phinehas in the act of adultery (25:7-8, 15). The other leaders are unmentioned elsewhere, but in a later tradition they were spoken of as מַמְלְכוּת

(*mamlĕkût*, "vassals") of Sihon (Josh. 13:21). The Midianites were the offspring of Abraham and Keturah (Gen. 25:2), and their relationship with the Hebrews varied from friendship in the early days of Moses (Ex. 2:15-18) to enemies of the Israelites in Canaan. The history of the Midianites is obscure, and for a time they may even have been part of a larger Ishmaelite configuration. They seemed to have lived in southern Canaan and in Transjordan, where they were associated predominantly with the Amalekites and Moabites.[80]

The list of executed persons of prominence included Balaam, son of Beor, who had so recently been foretelling Israel's victories. It is probable that he had stayed in the area of Peor with the Midianites as a consultant and thus perished when they did.

Translation

The Israelites captured the Midianite women and their little children, and they took all their herds and all their flocks and all their wealth as plunder. In addition, they burned down all the towns that they had inhabited and all their encampments. They carried off all the plunder and booty, both people and animals, and brought the captives, the plunder, and spoils to Moses and Eleazar the priest and the Israelite community to their encampment on the plains of Moab, along the Jordan across from Jericho. Moses, Eleazar the priest, and all the community leaders went to meet them outside the camp. (31:9-13)

Exegesis and Exposition

Since the conflict was a holy war, all the spoil was under the ban and therefore dedicated to God. In the absence of divine instructions to the contrary, the Midianite women, who had been contributors to Israel's apostasy, were taken prisoner instead of being killed, as the men had been. The ban extended to the inhabited towns and their surrounding campsites (MT טִירֹתָם, *ṭîrōtām; NKJV* "their forts"). People and animals alike were brought to the Israelite encampment area (MT יַרְדֵּן יְרֵחוֹ, *yardēn yĕrēḥô*, "Jordan of Jericho," a topographical designation), and were presented as booty to Moses and Eleazar.

This chapter furnishes one of the most complete sources of information about the way in which the Hebrews waged holy war. Victory was accorded to the Israelite forces by God when His people were obedient and the armed men were in a state of ceremonial holiness. Cities were often placed under the ban before being attacked, al-

80. Cf. G. M. Landes, *IDB*, 3:375-76; R. L. Alden, *ZPEB*, 4:220-22; T. V. Brisco, *ISBE*, 3:344-51.

though this procedure is not mentioned here. But the attack upon the Midianites was launched in order to avenge the recent threat to God's holiness. Often the entire population of resisting cities was destroyed, and what was left was considered booty devoted completely to God. Thereafter it was disposed of as God directed, and with this in view Moses and Eleazar the high priest inspected the spoils of war that the returning Israelites had brought.

3. DEATH OF CAPTIVE WOMEN (31:14-18)

Translation

Moses became angry with the military officers, the commanders of thousands and the captains of hundreds, who had returned from the battle. Have you allowed all the women to stay alive? he demanded of them. Look, these people caused the Israelites to sin against the LORD in the Peor incident through Balaam's advice, so that a plague came upon the LORD's community. Now kill all the boys and every woman who has had carnal relations with a man, but keep for yourselves all the young girls who have not been intimate with a man. (31:14-18)

Exegesis and Exposition

When Moses observed that his officers had captured foreign women, after the tradition of ancient armies, he was indignant. Such women had been the cause of Israel's rebellion against God in the first instance and had brought grave defilement upon His people as a consequence of the "advice" of Balaam. For "advice" (MT דְּבָר, *dābār*) the *NEB* reads "departure," a contrived and arcane interpretation of a common Hebrew term. Balaam was regarded as the culprit who counseled the Moabites and Midianites to commit the offenses at Peor (Num. 25). As a seer he had perceived that the quickest way to obliterate the Israelites was to pollute them ceremonially to the point where their God would slay them. Because the captive women had already brought new defilement into the Israelite camp, they would now have to pay with their lives. The same fate overtook the male youths, who would have brought sin into the camp as they entered it had they been allowed to survive. The only ones allowed to live were young virgins. They could become ceremonially clean and thereafter could serve as slaves in the community.

The OT practice of executing women and children in holy war has disturbed many readers of Scripture, who profess outrage at God's supposedly callous attitude toward "innocent" people. This judgment totally misunderstands the ancient Near Eastern situation.

385

God's holiness cannot tolerate sin (cf. Hab. 1:13), so atonement had to be made if humanity was to be reconciled to a sinless God.[81]

The Hebrew sacrificial system went some distance toward achieving this goal, although it was not totally efficacious (Num. 15:30). The sinner could make atonement in the prescribed manner and, if sincere, could receive forgiveness. By contrast, the captured Midianite women were already cultic prostitutes who, if incorporated into the Israelite community, would have spread the infection of sin.

The death sentence would halt the destructive activities of the offenders, preserve the holiness of the community, and remind the Israelites that the way of the transgressor is hard (Prov. 13:15). By killing the young males the continuity of their line was halted, and in holy war the one who secured this objective was to be accorded blessing (Ps. 137:9). When the magi visited King Herod to ascertain the location of Jesus' birthplace (Matt. 2:1-8), the insecure, homicidal monarch evidently had the same intention of halting the threat to his kingdom when he ordered the slaughter of all male infants two years of age or younger in and around Bethlehem (2:16).

4. PURIFICATION OF NATION (31:19-24)

Translation

All those who have killed anyone and have touched any of the dead must remain outside the encampment for seven days. Purify yourselves and your captives on the third and seventh days. You must purify each garment as well as everything made of hide, everything woven of goat's hair, and everything made of wood. (31:19-20)

Exegesis and Exposition

No form of ritual impurity was to be introduced into the camp. The warriors who had been in contact with the dead were to remain unclean for a week and had to conduct purification ceremonies for themselves and the girls who were captives on two occasions during that period. All clothing had to be cleansed by washing in order to remove symbolically the infection of sin (cf. Num. 5:1-4; 12:14-15). The ritual to be followed is contained in 19:11-22, which covered peacetime contingencies as well as the circumstances of war. These verses are a reminder that human freedom is always blood-bought.

---

81. See the comments by E. J. Young, *My Servants the Prophets* (Grand Rapids: Eerdmans, 1961), p. 24.

Translation

Then Eleazar the priest said to the soldiers who had gone into battle: This is the requirement of the law that the Lord commanded Moses: Anything of gold, silver, bronze, iron, tin, and lead that can withstand fire shall be exposed to fire, and then it shall be clean. But it must be purified with the purifying water also. Anything that cannot withstand fire must be passed through that water. On the seventh day you shall wash your clothes and be clean. After that you may enter the encampment. (31:21-24)

Exegesis and Exposition

The ordinance for cleansing the unclean from contamination as the result of death (Num. 19:1-22), which involved isolation, washing of clothes, and ritual sprinkling with the water of purification, is now applied to the booty brought back by the fighting men (MT הַבָּאִים לַמִּלְחָמָה, *habbā'îm lammilḥāmâ,* "those who went into the battle"). Sound sanitary and hygienic principles were involved in the process, which stressed sterilization and washing. Metal objects were to be sterilized by being exposed to fire, which would kill any germs or bacteria that were present, and then they were to be sprinkled with the water containing the ashes of a red heifer. Whatever was combustible was to be put into the water of purification to soak.

Tin (MT בְּדִיל, *bĕdîl*) is only spoken of occasionally in the OT. Tin was normally imported into Canaan for alloying with copper to manufacture bronze (cf. Ezek. 22:18-20), but it may also have occurred in the extraction of silver as a by-product. No source is named in Scripture as the place where the Canaanites obtained their supplies of tin, but in the Mari Age large quantities of tin were sent to Hazor for the manufacture of bronze.

To be certain of complete ritual purity, all the clothes of the defiled persons had to be washed at the end of the segregation period. The *NEB* understands v. 23 to prescribe fire alone as a purifying agent for the metals, but if the MT אַךְ (*'ak*) is translated as "nevertheless," the apparent textual difficulty is removed.

5. DISTRIBUTION OF SPOILS (31:25-54)

The Lord spoke to Moses, saying: You and Eleazar the priest, and all the family heads in the community, must add up all the plunder that has been captured, people and animals, and divide the spoils into two parts: one for the warriors who participated in the fighting, and the other for the entire community. (31:25-27)

Exegesis and Exposition

Since the captured towns were dedicated to God, a divine decision was required concerning the distribution of the booty. Accordingly God commanded Moses, Eleazar, and the family heads of Israel to assess the spoil and divide it into two sections. One of these would be the property of the warriors, and the other would be for the entire nation to enjoy.

This procedure marked a departure from the traditions of the ancient Near East regarding spoil taken in battle. In the pagan nations anything a warrior acquired as spoil was his own, save for any allotment that he might have to make to his god or his local sanctuary as tribute. The Hebrews distinguished between spoil (MT שָׁלָל, *šālāl*) and booty (MT בַּז, בִּזָּה, *bāz, bizzâ*) by thinking of the former as goods that were subject to division among the conquerors (Gen. 49:27; Ex. 15:9) and regarding the latter as goods and persons taken by the individual warrior for his own use (Jer. 15:13; Ezek. 25:7).[82]

Translation

You shall exact a tribute for the LORD from the warriors who fought in the battle, comprising one out of every five hundred persons, cattle, donkeys, or sheep. Take it from their half-share and give it to Eleazar the priest as a raised offering to the LORD. From the Israelites' half you shall take one out of every fifty persons, cattle, donkeys, sheep, or other livestock and give them to the Levites who are in charge of the LORD's Tabernacle. So Moses and Eleazar the priest did as the LORD commanded Moses. (31:28-31)

Exegesis and Exposition

God demanded that a tribute (MT מֶכֶס, *mekes*) be exacted (MT הֲרֵמֹתָ, *hărēmōtā*, "you shall cause to be taken") for Himself from the Hebrew warriors on a proportionate basis. That amount, consisting of one-fifth of one percent, was to be given to God in the form of a raised offering, a portion of which would become the perquisite of the priest.

From the share that was assigned to the community, an amount equivalent to two percent became the property of the Levites. In v. 30 the verb אָחַז (*'āḥaz*, "to seize"; cf. Akkad. *aḥāzu*, "grasp") indicates that the selected persons and animals were to be removed during the counting process and not drawn by lot. The warriors who had borne the brunt of the fighting had to offer to the Lord only a very small portion of their booty, whereas those who had not been actively en-

---

82. J. W. Wevers, *IDB*, 4:437-38; L. L. Walker, *ZPEB*, 5:509-10.

gaged in the battle contributed considerably more.[83] Thus all shared in the spoils of battle according to an established scale. Consistent with the normal practice of implicit obedience, Moses and Eleazar obeyed the Lord's commandment fully. The statute (v. 21) was not an ad hoc decision by God but an authoritative guideline for similar occasions in the future (cf. Josh. 22:8; 1 Sam. 30:24).

Translation

The booty that remained from the plunder taken by the warriors was 675,000 sheep, 72,000 cattle, 61,000 donkeys, and 32,000 women who had never been intimate with a man. The half-portion of those who fought in the battle totaled 337,500 sheep, of which the Lord's tribute was 675; 36,000 cattle, of which the Lord's tribute was 72; 30,500 donkeys, of which the Lord's tribute was 61; and 16,000 people, of which the Lord's tribute was 32. So Moses gave the tribute—which was the Lord's raised offering—to Eleazar the priest, as the Lord had commanded Moses. (31:32-41).

Exegesis and Exposition

The *šōṭĕrîm* dutifully reported the statistics involving captured prisoners and animals. The large numbers may appear rather surprising, especially since this foray by no means exterminated the Midianites. But as has been observed previously, vast herds and flocks were common in the second millennium b.c. and later, so that there is no reason to suspect the numbers. Although they seem to be rounded off, as was common in Near Eastern antiquity, they are consistent with all the other numbers in the book. Moses concluded the selection of the Lord's portion from the warriors' spoil, as he had been commanded. What happened to the virgins whose lives had been spared is unknown, but the thirty-two persons who had been devoted to the Lord would probably be made to help the priests' families as slaves. The remainder would become the property of the warriors.

Translation

From the Israelites' share that Moses kept separate from the soldiers, namely the portion belonging to the community, the amount was 337,500 sheep, 36,000 cattle, 30,500 donkeys, and 16,000 people. From the Israelites' share Moses took out one of every fifty persons and animals and gave them to the Levites who cared for the Lord's Tabernacle, as the Lord had commanded Moses. (31:42-47)

---

83. *KD*, 3:288.

Exegesis and Exposition

From the people and animals Moses selected the prescribed number, and these became the property of the Levites. As the assent formula indicates, all the procedures connected with the allocation of spoils were carried out by Moses strictly as prescribed, and nobody in the community was forgotten.

Translation

Then the officers in charge of the military divisions, namely the commanders of thousands and the captains of hundreds, approached Moses, and they said to him: Your servants have taken a count of the soldiers under our command, and not one of them is missing. So we have brought as an offering for the Lord the gold ornaments, the armlets, bracelets, signet rings, earrings, and necklaces, to make atonement for ourselves before the Lord. (31:48-50)

Exegesis and Exposition

As is the custom with all responsible field commanders, the Israelite officers had taken a headcount after the engagement and had discovered to their delight that not one of them was missing in action. This was indeed a divine act of magnificent proportions, a miraculous victory, considering the strength of the opposing forces.

The commanders (MT שָׂרִים, *śārîm*) of the various units all carried the same title in Hebrew, but the present translation has differentiated them to accommodate differences in responsibility and ranking. The basic military unit was one hundred men, and several units were doubtless under the command of one captain. The commanders were in charge of units of a minimum of one thousand men. The Midianites of Joshua's day were usually mounted on camels and did considerable damage to the Israelites in the period of the judges (Judg. 6-7), but there is no hint that anything other than infantry forces were engaged in the battle described here.

The victory served as a powerful stimulus to national morale, for it indicated to the Israelites that their God could save by many or by few (cf. 1 Sam. 14:6) and portended great success for the days ahead when the Promised Land was to be occupied. Out of gratitude the field commanders brought to the Lord as a sacrificial gift the gold ornaments captured in battle. These included gold objects (MT כְּלִי־זָהָב, *kĕlî-zāhāb*), little chains worn on arms (MT אֶצְעָדָה, *'eṣ'ādâ*), bracelets (MT צָמִיד, *ṣāmîd*), signet rings (MT טַבַּעַת, *ṭabba'at*), earrings (MT עָגִיל, *'āgîl*), and ornamental necklaces (MT כּוּמָז, *kûmāz*). Befitting the nature of the occasion the commanders presented to the Lord the most costly part of the spoils as a form of personal ransom (cf. Ex.

390

30:15) or atonement (כִּפֶּר, *kipper*). Possibly they were experiencing guilt feelings at the slaughter of the Midianites, whereas their own company had escaped unscathed.

Translation

So Moses and Eleazar the priest took the gold from them, all of it fashioned into ornaments. All the gold of the offering that they presented to the LORD from the commanders of thousands and the captains of hundreds weighed 16,750 shekels. Each soldier had taken his own plunder. (31:51-53)

Exegesis and Exposition

Gold ornaments were worn widely in the ancient Near East[84] by both men and women for personal adornment (Ex. 33:4; Jer. 2:32; etc.), as well as for official (Dan. 5:7) or cultic (Isa. 30:22) use. At this period the Midianites adorned their camels' necks with crescent-shaped ornaments (Judg. 8:21), but whether these were made of gold is unknown. It is probable, however, that Midianite chiefs would have decked out their favorite camels with expensive ornaments. Moses and Eleazar accepted these offerings from the soldiers through their commanding officers, since each soldier had his individual store of such spoil. The total was in accordance with all the other numbers in this campaign, amounting to 16,750 shekels, or about 420 pounds in imperial measure. The statistics resulting from the attack upon the Midianites give a good idea of the opulence of even a small kingdom in the ancient Near East, and not least when wealth (*pecunia*) is reckoned in terms of vast herds of animals (*pecus*).

Translation

So Moses and Eleazar the priest received the gold from the commanders of thousands and the captains of hundreds and brought it into the Tent of Meeting as a memorial for the Israelites before the LORD. (31:54)

Exegesis and Exposition

Just as the atonement money of the Israelites had been appointed for the service of the Tent of Meeting (Ex. 30:16), so also the offering of the commanders and captains was deposited within the sacred shrine. Indeed, it was dedicated to the same purpose as the atone-

---

84. J. M. Myers, *IDB*, 1:869-71; W. H. Mare, *ZPEB*, 2:164-70; R. K. Harrison, *ISBE*, 1:295; J. T. Dennison, Jr., *ISBE*, 1:539; K. R. Maxwell-Hyslop, *Western Asiatic Jewelry c. 3000-612 B.C.* (London: Methuen, 1979).

ment money—namely, as a memorial (MT זִכָּרוֹן, *zikkārôn*) or means of remembering the elect nation continually in the Lord's presence.

Additional Notes

31:3 הֵחָלְצוּ: This niphal imperative was replaced in the Samaritan Pentateuch, LXX, Syriac, and Vulgate versions by the hiphil form, but the reflexive sense of the MT is appropriate (cf. KJV "Arm some of yourselves").

וְיִהְיוּ: The BHS suggestion that this word should read יהוה would disrupt the normal flow of the verse. The LXX παρατάξασθαι ἔναντι Κυρίου is an explanatory gloss indicating that the foray was to be regarded as a "holy war."

31:6 לַמַּטֶּה: Here the LXX adds σὺν δυνάμει αὐτῶν.

אֶלְעָזָר: Here the LXX adds υἱοῦ ᾿Ααρὼν but does not mention the purpose of the activity, as does the MT (לַצָּבָא), presumably because of the previous gloss.

הַקֹּדֶשׁ: To the list of sanctuary equipment the Targum Pseudo-Jonathan adds the Urim and Thummim, which would doubtless be used in a "holy war."

31:8 עַל־חַלְלֵיהֶם: The preposition עַל is used here in the sense of "in addition to." Cf. 28:10.

31:13 וַיֵּצְאוּ: The Samaritan Pentateuch and the LXX read a collective singular here.

31:15 הַחִיִּיתֶם: The Samaritan Pentateuch, LXX, and Vulgate versions prefix this clause with the interrogative pronoun "Why?" This sense is implicit in the MT, however.

31:16 מַעַל: The LXX adds καὶ ὑπεριδεῖν, apparently for emphasis here, but the MT, though terse, is quite clear.

31:23 תַּעֲבִירוּ בָאֵשׁ: This clause is omitted by the LXX.

31:28 מִן־הָאָדָם: After this clause the LXX inserts καὶ ἀπὸ τῶν κητῶν, presumably to make the text conform to v. 30.

וּמִן־הַצֹּאן: The Samaritan Pentateuch here adds "and cattle," apparently in an endeavor to harmonize the text with v. 30. The addition seems unnecessary, however, since צֹאן also carries the meaning of "cattle."

31:29 תִּקָּחוּ: The Samaritan Pentateuch seems to be using a collective singular here.

31:37 שֵׁשׁ מֵאוֹת: For some unknown reason the Syriac version in this and subsequent figures to v. 40 increases the totals tenfold. Perhaps the translators thought that the amount allocated to the Lord was too small.

31:50 אִישׁ is here used distributively, "each man," evidently applying to all the individuals in the fighting force.

J. THE TRANSJORDANIAN TRIBES (32:1-42)

Chapter 32 deals with the settlement of two-and-a-half Israelite tribes in Transjordan, the territory so recently acquired by conquest. The area involved has been estimated at 150 miles in length and from 30 to 80 miles in width.[85] The chapter belongs to a period just prior to the invasion of Canaan by the Israelites. It can be subdivided into five sections: (1) petition presented (vv. 1-5); (2) reaction of Moses (vv. 6-15); (3) compromise proposed (vv. 16-27); (4) proposal ratified (vv. 28-32); (5) assignment of land (vv. 33-42).

1. PETITION PRESENTED (32:1-5)

Translation

Now the Reubenites and Gadites possessed a very large amount of livestock, and when they observed that the lands of Jazer and Gilead were a location that suited their herds, the Gadites and Reubenites came and addressed Moses, Eleazar the priest, and the leaders of the assembly, saying: Ataroth, Dibon, Jazer, Nimrah, Heshbon, Elealeh, Sebam, Nebo, and Beon, the land that the LORD subdued before the assembly of Israel, is good grazing country, and your servants possess livestock. So they said, If we have made a favorable impression upon you, let this territory be given to us as our heritage. Do not compel us to cross the Jordan. (32:1-5)

Exegesis and Exposition

Based on the numbers of captured Midianite animals listed as spoil in chap. 31, it is not surprising that the Reubenites and Gadites would have large flocks. Pasturage is always a pressing problem in mountainous areas unless there are upland plains or steppe land, and under the circumstances the two Hebrew tribes believed they had an admirable solution to the difficulty. The lands east of the Jordan between the Sea of Galilee and the Dead Sea consist of flat uplands, more than 2,000 feet above sea level. In antiquity much of this area was covered by forests, wadis, and valleys. The fertile soil, aided by a temperate climate, produced large crops of grain and fruit as well as providing grazing for large flocks. The southern area was broken by the Yarmuk and Jabbok rivers until it reached Mount Nebo. Although Gilead was located approximately in the center of this region, the name was sometimes applied comprehensively to the entire area. After the parched environment of the wilderness and the craggy up-

---

85. J. H. Hertz, ed., *The Pentateuch and Haftorahs*, p. 707.

lands of Edom and Moab, the elevated plains of Gilead must have appeared to the two tribes as the Promised Land itself, even though it lay outside the boundaries of Canaan. Jazer had been a fortified Amorite town north of Heshbon and close to Amman. It is perhaps the modern Khirbet Jazzir near es-Salt in Jordan.

The Gadites and Reubenites proceeded to lay their case before Moses, Eleazar the high priest, and the community leaders. Having surveyed the former holdings of Sihon and Og, they had been impressed by the land's suitability for farming and raising livestock. They therefore requested to be allowed to claim it as their possession instead of territory west of the Jordan when Canaan had been conquered.

Ataroth (probably the modern Khirbet ʿAṭṭarus), Dibon (modern Dhiban, where the Moabite Stone was discovered in 1868), Jazer, Nimrah (Tell Bleibil, north of the wadi Shuʿeib), Heshbon (perhaps Tell Hesban, about twelve miles southwest of Amman), Elealeh (identified with the ruins of el-ʿAl, two miles northeast of Heshbon), Sebam (perhaps the modern Qurn el-Kibsh, between Heshbon and Mount Nebo), the area of Nebo itself in the Abarim range of Moab, and Beon (possibly the later Baal-Meon, identified with Maʿin, southwest of Medeba) were doubtless choice locations in the Middle Bronze Age.

2. REACTION OF MOSES (32:6-15)

Translation

Moses replied to the Gadites and Reubenites: Are your countrymen to fight battles while you stay here? Why do you frustrate the intent of the Israelites to cross over into the land which the LORD has given to them? (32:6-7)

Exegesis and Exposition

Sensing a secessionist movement among the tribes and the prospect of their repudiating God's promise of a home in Canaan, Moses accused them of trying to thwart God's plans for the nation. Accordingly he asked them if they intended to pursue a pacifist role while their fellow Israelites were battling with the Canaanites. Being as close to death as he was, Moses was anxious not to entertain activity of the kind that had prevented the previous generation of Israelites from occupying Canaan shortly after leaving Mount Sinai.

Translation

This is the very thing that your fathers did when I dispatched them from Kadesh-barnea to reconnoiter the land. For after they had gone up to the valley of Eshcol and viewed the countryside, they

394

frustrated the intent of the Israelites to the point that they did not enter the land the LORD had given them. As a result the LORD's anger was stirred up that day, and He swore an oath, saying: Not one of the men twenty years of age or older who came from Egypt shall see the land that I swore to give to Abraham, Isaac, and Jacob, because they have not followed Me with complete dedication. Only Caleb son of Jephunneh and Joshua son of Nun have followed the LORD wholeheartedly. So the LORD's anger was stirred up against the Israelites, and He made them wander in the wilderness for forty years, until all that generation that had done wickedly before the LORD was extinct. (32:8-13)

Exegesis and Exposition

Moses surveyed briefly the situation that had caused that reversal of plans and accused the two tribes of doing the same thing a generation later. Though there was a different motivation on the second occasion, the trepidation of the aged Hebrew leader was not without warrant. Moses was afraid of a similar punishment befalling those poised to enter the land, despite all the evidences that God was with them. In the light of his own tragic experiences during the wilderness wanderings, Moses was anxious to forestall a similar eventuality that would have to be borne by Joshua, his successor. Were God to interpret this request as rebellion, Moses could envisage no certain future for the Israelites as the Lord stirred up His anger against them.

Translation

Now look! You are standing in your fathers' place, a brood of sinners, to increase still further the fierce wrath of the LORD against the Israelites. (32:14)

Exegesis and Exposition

Moses sternly accused the petitioners of being no better than their fathers and called them a "brood of sinful men" (MT תַּרְבּוּת אֲנָשִׁים, *tarbût 'ănāšîm*). The word *tarbût* means "increase," "offspring," and occurs here alone in the MT. The language used by Moses is echoed in John the Baptist's outburst (Greek γεννήματα ἐχιδνῶν, *gennēmata echidnōn*) against the Pharisees and Sadducees coming to him for baptism (Matt. 3:7). In both instances the speakers were thinking in terms of future divine anger being outpoured upon those addressed.

Translation

For if you turn away from following Him, He will once again abandon them in the wilderness, and you will be the reason for their destruction. (32:15)

Exegesis and Exposition

As Moses looked his own approaching death in the face, he voiced his worst fears for the future of the nation if God were to sense yet another act of rebellion. The people would again be abandoned in the wilderness. The causative form of the verb נוּחַ (*nûaḥ*, "cause them to rest"), shows that their fate would have been the result of God's direct intent as a punishment for apostasy. For this calamity, history would lay the blame upon the tribes of Reuben and Gad.

3. COMPROMISE PROPOSED (32:16-27)

Translation

Then they came very close to him and said: We will build sheep-folds here for our flocks, and cities for our families, but we will maintain ourselves in armed readiness and go as an advance unit of the Israelites until we have brought them to their destination. In the meantime our dependents will be living in fortified towns as a protection against the local inhabitants. We will not return to our homes until every Israelite has received his heritage. We will not be in receipt of any inheritance on the other side of the Jordan and beyond, because our patrimony will already have been allocated to us on this eastern side of the Jordan. (32:16-19)

Exegesis and Exposition

Convinced that their well-thought-out plan had nothing to do with either secession from the twelve tribes or rebellion against God's will, the petitioners approached Moses and reassured him of their integrity as member tribes of the nation. Their primary concern was to take advantage of the rich terrain as a source of food and to construct sheepfolds (MT גִּדְרֹת צֹאן, *gidrōt ṣō'n*) of stone as well as rebuild some of the ruined cities. This proposal could be of tactical importance for the nation, since it would afford protection for Israel's eastern flank once the other tribes had possessed Canaan.

The petitioners undertook further to muster as advance troops in the invasion of the Promised Land and to lend all necessary military support to the other tribes until the territory had been occupied and the land apportioned. By this means the tribes of Gad and Reuben made it clear that they would be full participants—indeed, leaders—in the invasion and occupation of the land, and that any thought of secession, revolt, or disobedience was the furthest thing from their minds.

Translation

Then Moses replied: If you do this thing and arm yourselves in the LORD's presence for battle, and if all of your armed men cross the Jordan before the LORD until He has expelled His enemies from His presence and the land capitulates before the LORD, then afterward you may return and be free of your obligation to the LORD and to Israel. This land shall then be your possession in the LORD's sight. (32:20-22)

Exegesis and Exposition

Satisfied with and relieved by this demonstration of loyalty to the Lord's purposes, Moses now stated the promise formally in conditional clauses, thus giving the propositions the nature of a contractual agreement. If the two tribes were fully mustered and served as advance divisions until the land was conquered, they would have discharged their responsibilities and would be free to return to Transjordan. The land of Gilead would be theirs as far as the Lord was concerned (MT לִפְנֵי יהוה, *lipnê YHWH*, "before the LORD").[86]

Translation

But if you fail to do all of this, then be warned that you will have sinned against the LORD. Have no doubt that your sin will bring its own punishment. So build cities for your dependents and pens for your sheep, but do what you have said you would. So the Gadites and the Reubenites replied to Moses, saying: Your servants will do as my lord commands. Our children, wives, flocks, and livestock will stay there in the cities of Gilead, but your servants will cross over, every man equipped for war, to do battle in the LORD's presence, just as my lord says. (32:23-27)

Exegesis and Exposition

Moses here shows the assembly that he regarded the undertaking given by Reuben and Gad as being in the nature of a covenant. He had outlined the conditions in the protasis ("if") section of his reply, and now comes a reminder of the curse that would befall the petitioners if they failed in their part of the agreement.

The Reubenites and Gadites agreed to abide by the conditions and gave Moses assurance of their support and active participation when the Israelites would begin to invade Canaan. Moses in his lifetime had seen enough of sin followed by retribution to speak with

---

86. Cf. R. J. Williams, *Hebrew Syntax*, p. 59, sect. 323.

authority on the matter. The KJV rendering of the latter part of v. 23, "Be sure your sin will find you out," has long passed into the realm of proverbial speech. The retributive effect of sin tends to have a cumulative force. Those who sow the wind will reap the whirlwind (Hos. 8:7). It is a fearful thing to fall into the hands of the living God (Heb. 10:13). Covenant fidelity is demanded of those living under the New Covenant as it was of the Old.

4. PROPOSAL RATIFIED (32:28-32)

Translation

So Moses gave orders about them to Eleazar the priest, to Joshua son of Nun, and to the family heads of the Israelite tribes. Moses said to them: If the Gadites and the Reubenites cross the Jordan with you, each one equipped for battle in the LORD's presence, and the land is conquered by you, then you shall allot them the territory of Gilead as their possession. But if they do not cross over with you armed, they shall receive heritages among you in Canaan. Then the Gadites and the Reubenites answered, saying, Your servants will do what the LORD has spoken. We will cross armed in the LORD's presence into Canaan, and then the property that we inherit will be ours on this side of the Jordan. (32:28-32)

Exegesis and Exposition

The proposal the Reubenites and Gadites made to Moses in v. 16 seems to have been for his ears only. The petitioners realized that a great deal depended upon their actions, which could have serious repercussions for the whole nation if they defaulted. But now that Moses was persuaded of their sincerity, the way was open for him to convey the content of the arrangement to the high priest and the heads of the nation's families. The result was an oral contract containing all the stipulations of the one negotiated privately with Moses and ratified by an oath sworn by the petitioners in public. As events turned out, these two tribes were as good as their word (Josh. 4:12-13; 22:1-6).

5. ASSIGNMENT OF LAND (32:33-42)

Translation

So Moses allocated to the Gadites, to the Reubenites, and to half the tribe of Manasseh son of Joseph the kingdom of Sihon, king of the Amorites, and the kingdom of Og, king of Bashan, the entire land with its cities and the territory surrounding them. The Gadites built Dibon, Ataroth, Aroer, *Atroth-shophan, Jazer, Jogbehah, Beth-nimrah, and Beth-haran as fortified cities and constructed pens for their flocks. The Reubenites built Heshbon, Elealeh, and Kiriathaim, as well as Nebo and Baal-meon (with a change of name) and Sibmah. They gave names to the cities they built. (32:33-38)

Exegesis and Exposition

The transaction was implemented by Moses, who allotted to the Gadites and Reubenites the agreed areas of Transjordan. For the first time, half the tribe of Manasseh is mentioned as participants in the Gilead inheritance. The Manassites were a fairly large tribe when their warriors numbered 32,200 at the first census (Num. 1:34), and by the time of the second census their fighting men had risen to a total of 52,700, making them a strong military element in the nation of Israel.

The tribe of Manasseh appears to have divided at this time into two sections for reasons that are not stated but that may have had to do with differences of habit and occupation.[87] Most of the fighting in Gilead seems to have been done by families from Manasseh, and under the leadership of Machir son of Manasseh they occupied the entire country (vv. 39-42). It is a mistake to interpret the term "half-tribe" in a strictly mathematical sense because it merely denotes a portion of the tribe. According to 26:29-32, there were eight sub-tribes of Manasseh, six of which were ultimately allotted territory on the west of the Jordan in the hill country of Samaria.[88]

Of the territory and places mentioned in the original proposal, the Gadites built or rebuilt Dibon, Ataroth, and Jazer as fortified towns and constructed sheep pens as they had promised. Unmentioned in the original proposal but built subsequently were Aroer (the modern 'Ara'ir), Atroth-shophan (read by KJV and some other versions as two places but only one in the LXX, NEB, NAB, and others), Jogbehah (identified with Ajbeihat, about seven miles northwest of Amman), and Beth-haran (modern Tell Iktanu, eight miles northeast of the Dead Sea).

Of the places listed in the original plan, the Reubenites built or rebuilt Heshbon, Elealeh, Nebo, and Beon (probably the same as Baal-meon). Unmentioned in the first proposal but constructed by the Reubenites was Kiriathaim, generally identified with modern el-Qereiyat, five miles northwest of Dibon. Sibmah is frequently regarded as an alternative name for Shebam in Num. 32:3. Names that suggested pagan affiliations such as Baal-meon were changed to re-

---

87. W. Haskell in *Unger's Bible Dictionary*, p. 690.
88. Hertz, p. 710.

flect the Israelite spiritual ethic, but these new names were not recorded. When a Moabite resurgence resulted in the reacquisition of traditional Moabite cities, the names would revert to their original forms.

Translation

The descendants of Machir son of Manasseh went to Gilead, captured it, and dispossessed the Amorites who occupied it. So Moses allotted Gilead to Machir son of Manasseh, and he settled there. Jair son of Manasseh went and captured its small towns and named them Havvoth Jair. Then Nobah went and captured Kenath and its villages and called it Nobah after his own name. (32:39-42)

As a reward, three family groups of Manassites—namely, Machir, Jair, and Nobah—occupied the general area formerly ruled over by Og, king of Bashan. Machir was allotted Gilead, while Jair settled in a conquered area of Bashan that he named Havvoth Jair ("Jair's tent villages"). The number of these settlements and their location present problems.[89] Nobah captured Kenath, perhaps modern Kerak-kanata, or alternatively Qanawat, a place some sixteen miles northeast of Bozrah,[90] and gave it his own name. This information explains how and why one section of Manasseh came to be living east of the Jordan while the rest of the tribe occupied land in former Canaanite territory.

Additional Notes

32:1 וְלִבְנֵי־גָד: After this clause the Samaritan Pentateuch adds "and the half-tribe of Manasseh," apparently to harmonize with v. 33. This addition is also inserted in vv. 2, 6, 25, 29, 31, but the LXX agrees with the MT.

32:2 וּבְנֵי־רְאוּבֵן: The LXX and Syriac versions reverse this order to harmonize with v. 1. The LXX maintains this pattern in vv. 25, 29, 31, whereas the Samaritan Pentateuch observes it throughout the chapter.

32:3 וּשְׂבָם: The Samaritan Pentateuch and the LXX read "Sibmah," perhaps in an attempt to concur with v. 38. The Syriac version reads "Sebah," whereas the Targum Onkelos strayed further from the MT by reading "Simah."

89. S. Cohen, *IDB*, 2:537-38; S. Barabas, *ZPEB*, 3:48; W. S. LaSor, *ISBE*, 2:634-35 and bibliographies.
90. Ibid., 3:6 and references.

32:4 הִכָּה: The LXX alters the force of this verb by reading πα-ραδέδωκεν, "handed over."

עֲדַת יִשְׂרָאֵל: The LXX, Syriac, and Vulgate versions modify this clause slightly by reading "people of Israel."

32:5 יֻתַּן: The verb in the apodosis of this conditional sentence is in the qal passive voice.

32:11 וַמַעְלָה: After this word the LXX adds οἱ ἐπιστάμενοι τὸ κα-κὸν καὶ τὸ ἀγαθόν, "those able to discriminate between good and evil," apparently to interpret the MT.

32:14 אֶל־יִשְׂרָאֵל: אֶל־ here is not necessarily a transcriptional error for עַל־, as read by the Samaritan Pentateuch. The LXX has ἐπὶ Ἰσραήλ, but the sense of the MT "toward Israel" is sufficiently sinister to allow אֶל־ to stand as an adversative preposition expressing disadvantage. Cf. Gen. 4:8; Jer. 21:13; etc. In effect it is equivalent to עַל־.

32:17 חֻשִׁים: For this word, "ready," BHS proposes to read חֲמֻשִׁים, "fifty," on the basis of חֲמֻשִׁים in Josh. 1:14; 4:12; Judg. 7:11. These passages, however, do not support such a precise division into groups, whether of fifty or otherwise, as BHS would imagine. The sense of the term is that of armed men fully prepared for battle and thus is general rather than specific.

אִם־הֲבִיאֲנֻם: אִם sometimes occurs with the relative particle אֲשֶׁר. Cf. Gen. 28:15.

32:19 מֵעֵבֶר לַיַּרְדֵּן: The preposition מִן is used here to express a relationship in terms of space. Cf. Gen. 12:8; Josh. 8:13.

32:22 מֵיהוה וּמִיִּשְׂרָאֵל: מִן here means "in the sight of," "from the standpoint of." Cf. Job 4:17.

32:30 אִתְּכֶם: After this word the LXX has a lengthy explanatory clause dealing with Reubenite and Gadite property.

32:33 בֶּן־יוֹסֵף: The LXX reads υἱῶν, "sons," but the MT phrase is appositional, and thus the singular is correct.

32:35 וְאֶת־עַטְרֹת שׁוֹפָן: The versions render this name in several ways. The Samaritan Pentateuch reads "Shaphim," the LXX has "S(h)ophar" and omits "Atroth," whereas the Vulgate reads "Etroth and Shophan."

וְיָגְבְּהָה: The Samaritan Pentateuch altered this word to read "Yagbohah."

32:38 נְבוֹ: The LXX omits this name, while for בַּעַל מְעוֹן the Samaritan Pentateuch and the Syriac version read a contracted form, "Baalmon."

32:39 וַיּוֹרֶשׁ: Strictly speaking this singular form should be plural, as with the Samaritan Pentateuch and the Syriac version, unless the intended sense is that of a unified body of troops.

32:42 נֹבַח: For this name the LXX reads Νάβαυ at the beginning and Νάβωθ at the end of the verse.

K. REVIEW OF WANDERINGS AND ORDERS FOR CONQUERING CANAAN (33:1-56)

In chap. 33 an itinerary of the wanderings from Rameses in Egypt to the final camp in Moab is followed by directions for conquering Canaan. The material can be analyzed into four units: (1) from Egypt to Sinai (vv. 1-15); (2) wilderness wanderings (vv. 16-36); (3) from Kadesh to Moab (vv. 37-49); (4) orders for conquering Canaan (vv. 50-56).

1. FROM EGYPT TO SINAI (33:1-15)

Translation

These are the wanderings of the Israelites who left the land of Egypt by their divisions under the leadership of Moses and Aaron. At the command of the LORD, Moses recorded the starting points of their wanderings. This is their itinerary, based upon the starting points. They set out from Rameses in the first month, on the fifteenth day of the first month, the day following the Passover. The Israelites started out confidently in full view of the Egyptians while the Egyptians were burying their firstborn, whom the LORD had struck down among them. The LORD had also executed judgment upon their gods. (33:1-4)

Exegesis and Exposition

The bulk of this chapter contains the names of places where the Israelites halted in their journey from Egypt to Moab. The period of time was forty years, the usual although not necessarily sociologically accurate designation of a human generation. Apart from their starting point and the end of their wanderings, forty places of encampment by the Israelites were listed. Of all the multiples of four, forty was the most significant in Scripture, and although it often signified completeness in terms of a generation (Judg. 3:11; 8:28) or divine favor in the case of David, Solomon, and Joash (2 Sam. 5:4; 1 Kings 2:11; 11:42; 2 Chron. 24:1), it was also used of camel loads (2 Kings 8:9), silver shekels (Neh. 5:15), and measurements (Ezek. 41:2; 46:22). In the NT it was the period of Christ's temptation in the wilderness (Matt. 4:2; Mark 1:13; Luke 4:2).

This itinerary was compiled by Moses and Aaron at the express command of God. It was meant to be in abbreviated form, listing the starting points and only rarely explaining matters of topography. Thus it was a concise travel diary that furnished names of stations in many cases known to the Israelites alone because of events that had occurred there. Shortly thereafter the winds and sands of Sinai

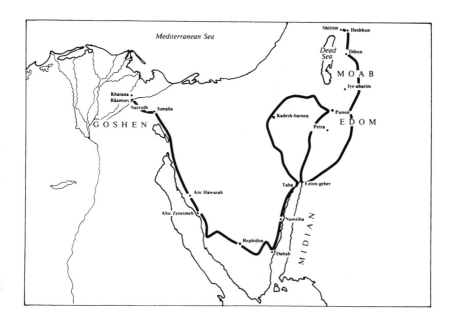

would blot out for all time the identification of the various locations, and all that would remain was the record compiled by Moses and Aaron. Only in large, well-known areas such as Kadesh-barnea would identification be reasonably possible, and even that presents some difficulties.

Many scholars have thus urged, with considerable justification, that the information in Numbers does not permit firm conclusions about the route taken.[91] Furthermore, differences between the itinerary of Num. 20-21 and that of 33:5-49 seem to suggest that two different routes were taken for at least part of the journey. To chronicle the wanderings of desert nomads over an extended period of time is a daunting task at best, but the information collected by Moses and Aaron and recorded by the šōṭĕrîm at least gives general guidance as to the direction taken, while leaving many questions of locale unanswered.

There is, however, a deeper issue to be considered. Many of the stopping places bore names that instructed, admonished, or encouraged the Israelites.[92] The locations were thus not so much areas on a

---

91. E.g., R. de Vaux, *The Early History of Israel* (Philadelphia: Westminster, 1978), pp. 551-64. For various views about the route of the Exodus see C. de Wit, *The Date and Route of the Exodus* (London: Tyndale, 1960); T. V. Brisco, *ISBE*, 2:238 and bibliography.
92. Hertz, p. 714.

map as memorials to God's power and humanity's weakness, as stages on a journey through life that were as much spiritual as physical, and above all else as a constant reminder of the justice and mercy of the Lord of the covenant, who had bound a self-willed, nomadic people to Himself in His great love for them.

The MT מַסַּע (*massaʿ*) can mean a "departure from camp" as well as a "station," but it is the former with which Moses was concerned predominantly. The journey began immediately after the first Passover, not with the grudging acquiescence of the Egyptians but with their urgent cooperation (Ex. 12:33), marching forth confidently (MT בְּיָד רָמָה, *běyād rāmâ*, "with a high hand"; cf. Ex. 14:8). Indeed, the Egyptians were far more concerned with the double catastrophe of the death of the firstborn and the demonstration of the Lord of Israel's superiority over the lifeless pagan deities of Egypt.

Translation

The Israelites left Rameses and camped at Succoth. They left Succoth and camped on the edge of the wilderness, at Etham. They left Etham, turned back to Pi-hahiroth east of Baal Zephon, and camped near Migdol. They left Pi-hahiroth and crossed through the middle of the sea into the wilderness. They journeyed for three days in the wilderness of Etham and camped at Marah. They left Marah and went to Elim, where there were twelve springs of water and seventy palm trees, and they camped there. (33:5-9)

Exegesis and Exposition

Camp was broken first at Rameses, most probably to be identified with Qantir[93] rather than Pelusium or Tanis, and went to Succoth, where they camped near Etham. The location of Succoth is debatable, having been identified by some scholars, following Naville's excavations in 1883, with Pithom (Tell el-Maskhutah) in the eastern area of the Wadi Tumilat.[94] But perhaps the neighboring site of Tell er-Retabah, which others think was the location of Pithom, may have been the Succoth of the Exodus narratives. At all events, Rameses and Succoth were not far from one another. The material

---

93. N. Bietak, *Tell el-Dabʿa*, 2 (Untersuchungen der Zweigstelle Kairo des Osterreichischen Archäologischen Instituts, Bd. 1, 3; 1975), pp. 179-221 and pls. 44-45.
94. E. Naville, *The Store City of Pithom and the Route of the Exodus*, Egypt Exploration Fund, Memoir No. 1 (London: 4th ed., 1903); idem, "Pithom DDDD Sukkoth," *JEA* 10 (1924): 32-36; A. H. Gardiner, "Pithom," *JEA* 10 (1924): 95-96; T. E. Peet, *Egypt and the Old Testament* (Liverpool: U. of Liverpool, 1924), pp. 86-88; K. A. Kitchen, *NIDBA*, p. 425.

recorded in verses 5-15 is in accord with that mentioned in Ex. 12:37; 13:20; 14:9; 15:22; 17:1; 19:1-2.

Of the stations mentioned, Etham (v. 6) is of uncertain location but was probably close to Succoth, while Pi-hahiroth was located near the Re(e)d Sea. If Baal Zephon can be identified correctly with Tahpanhes, it would have been close to the modern Tell Defneh. Marah, the place of brackish water, has been associated with 'Ain Hawara, about seven miles from the Re(e)d Sea. Elim may have been situated in some part of the Wadi Gharandel. It was remembered for having a plentiful supply of water and an imposing array of palm trees. The counting and listing of the trees on a piece of property is also found in Hittite records.

Translation

They left Elim and camped by the Re(e)d Sea. They left the Re(e)d Sea and camped in the wilderness of Sin. They left the wilderness of Sin and camped at Dophkah. They left Dophkah and camped at Alush. They left Alush and camped at Rephidim, where there was no water for the people to drink. They left Rephidim and camped in the wilderness of Sinai. (33:10-15)

Exegesis and Exposition

The station at the Re(e)d Sea (v. 10) was not mentioned in the Exodus narratives, but only because it may merely have been a marshaling station. Dophkah and Alush also do not appear in the accounts of this period in the book of Exodus. The former is an unidentified desert location, although Serabit el-Khadim has been suggested, and the latter may be the modern Wadi el-Eshsh. The location of Rephidim depends on that of Mount Sinai, and if the traditional site in the southern end of the Sinai peninsula is accepted, Rephidim would be identified with either Wadi Refayid or Wadi Feiran.[95]

2. WILDERNESS WANDERINGS (33:16-36)

Translation

They left the wilderness of Sinai and camped at Kibroth Hattaavah. They left Kibroth Hattaavah and camped at Hazeroth. They left Hazeroth and camped at Rithmah. They left Rithmah and camped at Rimmon Perez. They left Rimmon Perez and camped at Libnah. They left Libnah and camped at Rissah. They left Rissah and camped

---

95. E. G. Kraeling, *Bible Atlas* (New York: Rand McNally, 1956), pp. 107-9.

at Kehelathah. They left Kehelathah and camped at Mount Shepher. They left Mount Shepher and camped at Haradah. They left Haradah and camped at Makheloth. They left Makheloth and camped at Tahath. They left Tahath and camped at Terah. They left Terah and camped at Mithkah. They left Mithkah and camped at Hashmonah. They left Hashmonah and camped at Moseroth. They left Moseroth and camped at Bene Jaakan. They left Bene Jaakan and camped at Hor Haggidgad. They left Hor Haggidgad and camped at Jotbathah. They left Jotbathah and camped at Abronah. They left Abronah and camped at Ezion-geber. They left Ezion-geber and camped in the wilderness of Zin at Kadesh. (33:16-36)

Exegesis and Exposition

Many of these places are unidentifiable, and the late Arabic designations of sites in the Sinai peninsula are of little help. In most instances the Israelites left the wilderness stations without any sedentary population to carry on their names. Places such as Kibroth Hattaavah (Num. 11:34), "graves of craving," referred to incidents and not to specific locations. Hazeroth is generally identified with 'Ain Khodara, where there is a well and an oasis, while Bene Jaakan may be el-Beiran, about six miles south of el-'Auja. Jotbathah may have been a fortified place somewhere in the Arabah north of Ezion-geber, but its precise location is unknown. Abronah, on the other hand, has been associated with 'Ain Defiyeh, about seven miles north of Ezion-geber. The latter place was located at the head of the Gulf of Aqaba. All the other stations on the list are of unknown location. Some scholars have suggested on philological grounds that Kehelathah may be a variant of Makholeth (vv. 25-26), but even if this were the case, it does nothing to help identify either site.

3. FROM KADESH TO MOAB (33:37-49)

Translation

They left Kadesh and camped at Mount Hor, on the border of Edom. Then Aaron the priest ascended Mount Hor at the LORD's command and died there on the first day of the fifth month of the fortieth year after the Israelites came from Egypt. Aaron was 123 years old when he died on Mount Hor. The Canaanite king of Arad, who lived in the Canaanite Negev, learned that the Israelites were coming. They left Mount Hor and camped at Zalmonah. They left Zalmonah and camped at Punon. They left Punon and camped at Oboth. (33:37-43)

Exegesis and Exposition

The stay at Kadesh occupied the greater part of the wilderness period, extending over approximately thirty-eight years. This section of the itinerary describes the march to the Moabite border and the Jordan, which occurred in the fortieth year of the wanderings. The general area of 'Ain Qudeirat is well watered and fertile and would therefore have accommodated the bulk of the nation without undue strain. But it is possible that some tribes moved along the edges of the Paran and Zin wildernesses from time to time (cf. Num. 13:26; 20:1; Deut. 1:19, 46), perhaps in search of additional grazing lands. Verses 37-39 recapitulate the death of Aaron, while v. 40 mentions the Canaanite king of Arad without recounting his defeat by the Israelites (Num. 21:1-3). Oboth, mentioned in Num. 21:10-11, has been identified with 'Ain el-Weiba, close to Punon (modern Feinan), but this is not assured. Nearby Zalmonah has remained unidentified, but it may have been a wooded area. The chronological note about the time of Aaron's death is of interest if only to show that, during the entire period of the wanderings, a careful record was kept of times and seasons.

Translation

They left Oboth and camped at Iye Abarim, on the Moabite border. They left Iyim and camped at Dibon Gad. They left Dibon Gad and camped at Almon Diblathaim. They left Almon Diblathaim and camped in the mountains of Abarim, near Nebo. They left the mountains of Abarim and camped on the plains of Moab by the Jordan, opposite Jericho. There on the plains of Moab they camped along the Jordan from Beth Jeshimoth to the Abel Acacia Grove. (33:44-49)

Exegesis and Exposition

Iye Abarim (or Iyim in its contracted form) has been identified with the area of Mahay, near the brook Zered, but in any event it was on the southeast edge of Moab. Dibon Gad was the town of Dibon in Moab, modern Dhiban, about eleven miles east of the Dead Sea. Apart from the assumption that Almon Diblathaim was situated somewhere between Dibon Gad and the Abarim range, nothing is known about its location. In the Moabite plains the Israelite encampment extended from Beth Jeshimoth to the Abel Acacia Grove (MT אָבֵל הַשִּׁטִּים, 'ābēl haššiṭṭîm). Beth Jeshimoth has been identified with Tell el-'Azeimeh, close to the northeast shore of the Dead Sea.

4. ORDERS FOR CONQUERING CANAAN (33:50-56)

Now the LORD spoke to Moses on the plains of Moab by the Jordan, saying: Address the Israelites and tell them: When you have crossed the Jordan into the land of Canaan, you must expel all those who inhabit the land as you advance. Destroy all their carved images and their cast metal figures, and demolish all their high places. You must dispossess those who live in the land and occupy it, for I have given you the land to possess. (33:50-53)

Exegesis and Exposition

This material is a preface to God's final instructions to Moses about the treatment the Israelites were to mete out to the Canaanites. Because of their depraved religion the Canaanites were the enemies of all righteousness and thus a grave threat to the covenant faith of Israel. There could be no thought of fraternizing with such an enemy, who must be destroyed along with all that savored of pagan religion. Specifically mentioned cult objects were the מַשְׂכִּיֹּת (*maśkîyyôt*), which were apparently stone images of deities, and the צַלְמֵי מַסֵּכֹת (*ṣalmê-massēkōt*), or melted metal statues, probably of bronze.

Idol worship was strictly prohibited (Ex. 20:4-5), and for this reason it was impossible for Israel to contemplate peaceful coexistence with idolaters. They had to be dispossessed, because their land was God's gift to His people and must be occupied as such. Before He could rejoice in it, the territory would have to be sanctified by the presence of the kingdom of priests and holy nation that He had established by His covenant with Israel. The subsequent history of the nation shows tragically the extent to which they were unable or unwilling to fulfill these commands.

For the Christian there is always the tension involved in living in the world, yet not being of it. To follow a pattern of life that is unspotted by the world is a mark of "pure and undefiled religion" (James 1:27). Yet to this high ideal the believer has been called (1 Pet. 1:4) and has as his or her strength and example the great High Priest, who is "holy, harmless, undefiled, separate from sinners" (Heb. 7:26, NKJV). In a sterner vein, Paul admonished the believers in pagan Rome not to be conformed to this world but to be transformed by the renewing of their minds, so as to demonstrate the acceptable and perfect will of God (Rom. 12:2). Elsewhere the Jerusalem elders criticized idols as being pollutants (Acts 15:30), and Paul dismissed them as being "nothing" (1 Cor. 8:4) and "mute" (12:2).

Translation

Distribute the land by lot according to your family groups as a heritage. To a larger group you shall allot a larger inheritance, and to

408

a smaller group a lesser one. Everyone's heritage shall be whatever falls to him by lot. Your inheritance shall be according to your ancestral tribes. But if you do not expel the inhabitants of the territory as you advance, then any that you allow to remain there will become irritants in your eyes and thorns in your sides, for they will harass you in the land where you will be living. Then I will do to you what I intended to do to them. (33:54-56)

Exegesis and Exposition

Once occupied, the land must be distributed on a proportionate basis by the casting of lots, in which God could be expected to guide the outcome (Prov. 16:33). Failure to dispossess the native inhabitants would be disastrous. The MT שִׂכִּים בְּעֵינֵיכֶם (śikkîm bĕ'ênêkem, "thorns in your eyes") is balanced by צְנִינִם בְּצִדֵּיכֶם (ṣĕnînim bĕṣiddêkem, "thorns in your sides"), where two different Hebrew words for "thorn" are used. The expressions describe something that could disable and irritate the chosen people culturally and especially spiritually. The final admonition from God is that if His people disobey His instructions, He will reverse the planned course of events and impose upon Israel the devastation meant for the Canaanites. Israel cannot serve as God's light to the world if their eyes have been dulled and blinded by the god of this world (cf. 2 Cor. 4:4).

Additional Notes

33:7 וַיֵּשֶׁב: The emendation to a plural form by the Samaritan Pentateuch and Targum Pseudo-Jonathan is unnecessary if the collective noun "encampment" or "community" is understood as the subject.

33:9 שָׁם: To this word the LXX adds παρὰ τὸ ὕδωρ.

33:12 For דָּפְקָה the LXX has Ραφακὰ, and also in the following verse.

33:13 For אָלוּשׁ the Samaritan Pentateuch reads "Alish," and also in the next verse. The LXX has "Aileim" in both instances.

33:16 קִבְרֹת הַתַּאֲוָה: The LXX here has the interpretation of the MT, Μνήμασιν ἐπιθυμίας, "graves of craving."

33:20 לִבְנָה: Here the LXX reads "Lemona," whereas the Samaritan Pentateuch has "Lebonah" here and also in the following verse.

33:21 רִסָּה: For this place the LXX reads Δεσσά here and in v. 22.

33:23 הַר־שָׁפֵר: The LXX omits "Mount" and reads Σάφαρ here and in v. 24.

33:24 חֲרָדָה: The LXX has a more Hellenic form, Χαραδάθ, here and in v. 24.

33:26 תָחַת: The LXX renders this name by Κατάαθ here and in v. 27.

33:27 תָּרַח: For this station the LXX reads Τάραθ, as also in v. 28.

33:28 מִתְקָה: The Samaritan Pentateuch has a slightly different spelling, "Mithikah," here and in v. 29, while the LXX reads Ματεκκά in both instances.

33:29 חַשְׁמֹנָה: This location is named Σελμωνά in the LXX here and in v. 30.

33:31 בִּבְנֵי יַעֲקָן: The LXX preferred the more Hellenized form βαναία here and in v. 32.

33:32 הַגִּדְגָּד: Some MT MSS drop the article in front of the proper name and read "Gidgad," along with the LXX and Vulgate versions.

33:33 יָטְבָתָה: The LXX spells this name variously as Ἐτεβάθα (two hands of Codex Vaticanus, and Codex Ambrosianus), Ἰεταβάθαν (Codex Alexandrinus), and Σετεβάθα (Codex Sinaiticus), here and in v. 34.

33:36 בְּמִדְבַּר־צִן: Instead of the explanatory gloss הוא קָדֵשׁ, the LXX has a new sentence: καὶ ἀπῆραν ἐκ Γεσσιῶν Γάβερ καὶ παρενέβαλον ἐν τῇ ἐρήμῳ Σίν.

33:38 הֹר הָהָר: The LXX omits any mention of this location, merely saying that Aaron went up at the Lord's command and died there. Why the site was unmentioned is difficult to understand.

33:42 פּוּנֹן: The Samaritan Pentateuch reads "Phinon" here and in the following verse, and this was adopted by the Syriac version. The LXX reads "Pheino" here and in v. 43.

33:43 אֹבֹת: The LXX reads "Soboth" here and in v. 44.

33:44 בְּעִיֵּי הָעֲבָרִים: Greek seems to have been simply unable to cope with such a name, so the LXX translators rendered it by Γαί, here and in the following verse.

33:46 עַלְמֹן דִּבְלָתָיְמָה: The LXX translated this as Γελμὼν Δεβλαθάιμ.

33:49 מִבֵּית הַיְשִׁמֹת: Here the LXX reads ἀνὰ μέσον Αἰσιμῶθ.

אָבֵל הַשִּׁטִּים: For this place the LXX reads ἕως βελσὰ, the name being spelled variously as βελσαττὶμ (Codex Alexandrinus) and βελσαττεῖν (Codex Ambrosianus).

33:53 אֶת־הָאָרֶץ: The LXX begins the verse: καὶ ἀπολεῖτε πάντας τοὺς κατοικοῦντας τὴν γῆν.

33:54 לוֹ יִהְיֶה: The LXX adds a sentence to make ownership specific: εἰς ὃ ἐὰν ἐξέλθῃ τὸ ὄνομα αὐτοῦ ἐκεῖ, αὐτοῦ ἔσται.

7
Preparations for Settling in Canaan (34:1–36:13)

A. THE BORDERS OF THE PROMISED LAND (34:1-29)

Chapter 34 informs the Israelites about the extent of their boundaries when Canaan is occupied and tells of officers delegated for the task. It can be divided into five sections: (1) the south (vv. 1-5); (2) the west (v. 6); (3) the north (vv. 7-9); (4) the east (vv. 10-15); (5) appointed officials (vv. 16-29).

1. THE SOUTH (34:1-5)

Translation

Then the LORD spoke to Moses, saying: Give these orders to the Israelites, and tell them: When you enter Canaan, the land that has been assigned to you as a heritage will have the following borders. Your southern border shall extend from the wilderness of Zin along the Edomite border. Then your southern border shall run eastward to the extremity of the Dead Sea, then cross over south of the Ascent of Akrabbim, continue to Zin, and go south to Kadesh-barnea. Then it will go to Hazar Addar and over to Azmon. There the border will turn from Azmon to the Brook of Egypt, and it will terminate at the sea. (34:1-5)

Exegesis and Exposition

This chapter and the next look forward to the occupation of Canaan, which lay tantalizingly just across the River Jordan to the west of the Israelite encampment. Although God had promised victory to His people if they continued to obey His commands, nothing was left to chance in the organization of their new life in their own land. All necessary plans for a settled existence in Canaan must be formulated and communicated, so that when the time finally arrived the tribes would know what the limits of the land were.

The material in this chapter sets out the ideal limits of occupation, and it would be up to the Israelites to transform that ideal into reality. Since the entire book of Numbers has been occupied with thoughts of entering the land, it is appropriate for matters of topography to be considered at what is actually the climax of the book.

The annunciation formula places the divine imprimatur upon the formulations, which are to be transmitted by Moses to the people. Their new homeland is called by the explicative form the "land of Canaan"[1] and had been promised by God to the patriarchs for their offspring (Gen. 15:18) and subsequently to the Israelites themselves (Ex. 23:31). The prelude to the possessing of this land came with the victories in Transjordan over Sihon, the king of Heshbon, and Og, the king of Bashan. This eventually enabled the tribes of Reuben, Gad, and a section of Manasseh to enter upon their inheritance immediately. Now the Israelites looked forward eagerly to their promised inheritance as they stood poised on the east bank of the Jordan across from Jericho.

The southern extremity of Canaan[2] was to stretch from the wilderness of Zin and then follow the border of Edom (MT יְדֵי אֱדוֹם, *yĕdê ʾĕdôm*, "the edges of Edom"), and then go eastward to the Dead Sea (MT יָם-הַמֶּלַח, *yam-hammelaḥ*, "Salt Sea"). It would then proceed up the Scorpion Pass (MT מַעֲלֵה עַקְרַבִּים, *maʿălēh ʿaqrabbîm*, "ascent of Akrabbim") through the wilderness of Zin to the south of Kadesh. After proceeding through Hazar Addar and Azmon, two sites that cannot now be identified, it would turn northwest to the Wadi el-Arish and follow it to the Mediterranean Sea, some 45 miles south of Gaza. The "Edom" mentioned here is not the rugged mountainous terrain bordering on the Arabah but the area south of the wilderness of Zin, the latter comprising Kadesh and the associated oases. Prior to the infiltration of the Sinai peninsula by the Israelites, the Edomites may have laid nominal claim to the territory, particularly because it possessed ample supplies of water.

---

1. R. J. Williams, *Hebrew Syntax*, p. 17, sect. 20.
2. On the name see A. Haldar, *IDB*, 1:494-98; J. A. Thompson, *ISBE*, 1:701-8; C. G. Libolt, *ISBE*, 1:585-91 and bibliographies.

2. THE WEST (34:6)

Translation

Your western border will be the coastline of the Great Sea. This shall be your frontier to the west. (34:6)

Exegesis and Exposition

The Mediterranean Sea formed a natural barrier to the west of Canaan. This body of water was large when compared to the narrow rivers and small lakes of Egypt and Canaan. Maritime traders such as the Phoenicians and Greeks would readily acknowledge the magnitude of that large sea.

3. THE NORTH (34:7-9)

Translation

Your northern border shall be as follows: Draw a line from the Great Sea to Mount Hor, and from Mount Hor to Lebo Hamath. Then the boundary will go to Zedad. The border will continue *to Ziphron and terminate at Hazar Enan. This shall be your northern frontier. (34:7-9)

Exegesis and Exposition

The Mount Hor mentioned here is not the one on which Aaron died (20:22-27) but an elevation that was probably situated between Lebo Hamath (MT לְבֹא חֲמָת, *lĕbōʾ ḥămāt*) and the coast. A prominent peak of the Lebanon range, perhaps Mount Hermon, seems indicated. Zedad has been identified with modern Sadad, which lies north of the road linking Riblah with Palmyra.[3] Hazar Enan, on the frontier between Canaan and Hamath, is the modern Hadr at the base of Mount Hermon. Ziphron has not been identified.

4. THE EAST (34:10-15)

Translation

For your eastern boundary you shall draw a line from Hazar Enan *to Shepham. The border will go down from Shepham *to Riblah on the east of Ain and continue until it reaches the eastern side of the Sea of Chinnereth. Then the boundary will proceed down the Jordan and terminate at the Salt Sea. This shall constitute your

---

3. R. Dussaud, *Topographie historique de la Syrie* (Paris: Guenther, 1927), pp. 282-83.

land, with the boundaries that encompass it. Then Moses commanded the Israelites, saying: This is the land which you must assign by lot, which the LORD has ordered to be given to the nine and a half tribes because the ancestral tribes of the Reubenites and the Gadites have received their heritage, and so has the half-tribe of Manasseh. The two tribes and the half-tribe have received their heritage on this side of the Jordan, east of Jericho, toward the sunrise. (34:10-15)

Exegesis and Exposition

From modern Hadr the eastern boundary followed a route that is difficult to trace because Shepham, Riblah, and Ain have not been identified. The MT יָם־כִּנֶּרֶת (*yam-kinneret*) was so named because the lake supposedly resembled a harp when viewed from a high elevation. In Maccabean and later times it was known as Gennesar or Gennesaret (1 Macc. 11:67; Luke 5:1), and all were early names for the Sea of Galilee. Thereafter the border followed the Jordan and terminated at the Dead Sea.

God specified this terrain for the tribes to occupy—not the entire twelve tribes, however, but only nine-and-a-half of them, since Reuben, Gad, and a portion of Manasseh had already received their holdings in Transjordan. The perspective of the narrative is Transjordanian, as is made clear in v. 15. All parties were now in possession of the information relating to boundaries as well as to the arrangements for the Transjordanian settlers. This would obviate the possibility of intertribal jealousy and friction once the territory was assigned.

5. APPOINTED OFFICIALS (34:16-29)

Translation

The LORD said to Moses: These are the names of the men who are to allocate the land to you as a heritage: Eleazar the priest and Joshua son of Nun. You shall select one leader of every tribe to assist in allocating the territory as a heritage. These are the names of the men: Caleb son of Jephunneh, from the tribe of Judah; Shemuel son of Ammihud, from the tribe of Simeon; *Elidad son of Chislon, from the tribe of Benjamin; Bukki son of Jogli, *a leader from the tribe of Dan. (34:16-22)

Exegesis and Exposition

For equitable treatment to be apparent in apportioning the land, God ordered Moses to record the names of persons whom He had selected to work under the supervision of Eleazar the high priest and Joshua the civil leader. The tribe of Judah was represented by Caleb, who because of his consistent fidelity to the Lord was eminently worthy of such a responsibility. Shemuel, Elidad, and Bukki were doubtless equally trustworthy, but nothing further is known about them.

Translation

From the Josephites: Hanniel son of Ephod, a leader from the tribe of Manasseh; and Kemuel son of Shiphtan, a leader from the tribe of Ephraim; Elizaphan son of Parnach, a leader from the tribe of Zebulun; Paltiel son of Azzan, a leader from the tribe of Issachar; Ahihud son of Shelomi, a leader from the tribe of Asher; Pedahel son of Ammihud, a leader from the tribe of Naphtali. These are the ones whom the LORD commanded to divide up the inheritance among the Israelites in the land of Canaan. (34:23-29)

Exegesis and Exposition

None of the men listed here is mentioned again in the scriptural record. Fame and temporal success, however, are no substitute for obedience. The person who follows God's will from the heart (i.e., emotionally) and the mind (i.e., intellectually and volitionally) will reap the spiritual rewards given to those who are faithful to the point of death (Rev. 2:10). Though the leaders prove obscure as far as later history goes, the fact that they were chosen by God for their particular task guaranteed their survival during the period when Canaan was being conquered.

The brief moment in history that these selected leaders occupied was fundamentally important because they were laying the foundations of social and national life for centuries to come. Tribes would be known not only by their names but also by their territorial holdings. If God's plan for the allocation of the land was to be made effective and equitable, these representatives of the tribes would be fulfilling a vital function in the service of the nation.

The boundaries of the land represented God's ideal, but subsequent events proved that it was attained only in the early monarchy under the reigns of David and Solomon.

Additional Notes

34:4 חֲצַר־אַדָּר: For this site the LXX reads Ἀράδ.

34:6 וְהָיָה: The conjunction is adjunctive here, meaning "also," "even," as in the KJV "ye shall even have."

34:9 זִפְרֹנָה: The LXX here reads Δεφρῶνα, but two hands of Codex Vaticanus read Ἐφρῶνα, while Codex Alexandrinus reads Ζεφρῶνα.

חֲצַר עֵינָן: The LXX reads Ἀροσεναείμ, but perhaps two hands of Codex Vaticanus have Ἀροσερναείμ, while Codices Alexandrinus and Ambrosianus have Ἀσερναί.

34:10 שְׁפָמָה: The LXX reads Σεπφάμαϱ, with a variant, Σεπφάμα, occurring in Codex Ambrosianus.

34:11 הָרִבְלָה: The Samaritan Pentateuch and the LXX seem to have been influenced by a MS tradition that read "Arbela," involving a slight consonantal change from MT הרבלה to ארבלה.

34:20 בְּנֵי does not occur in the LXX, Syriac, and Vulgate versions.

שְׁמוּאֵל: For this name the LXX reads Σαλαμιήλ, based upon the MT form in 1:6.

34:21 אֱלִידָד: The Samaritan Pentateuch, LXX, and Syriac versions have "Eldad," presumably following the MT reading of 11:26.

34:22-28 נָשִׂיא: Most of the versions omit the designation "leader" in this section as follows: v. 22, omitted by one MT MS, the Syriac, and Vulgate; v. 23, omitted by two MT MSS, the Syriac, and Vulgate; v. 24, omitted by the Syriac and Vulgate; v. 25, omitted by the Syriac and Vulgate; v. 26, omitted by the Syriac only; v. 27, omitted by the Syriac and Vulgate; v. 28, omitted by two MT MSS, the Syriac and Vulgate.

34:23 אֵפֹד: For this name the LXX reads Οὐφί.

34:26 עַזָּן: For this name the LXX reads 'Οζά.

34:27 אֲחִיהוּד: The LXX reads 'Αχιώϱ here, but Codex Alexandrinus has a variant form, 'Αχιώβ.

34:28 פְּדַהְאֵל בֶּן־עַמִּיהוּד: Through an error the LXX has φαδαήλ υἱὸς βεναμιούδ, thus reading בֶּן twice.

B. LEVITICAL CITIES AND CITIES OF REFUGE (35:1-34)

Chapter 35 divides into two principal sections: (1) Levitical cities (vv. 1-8) and (2) cities of refuge (vv. 9-34). Both sections begin with the standard annunciatory formula "The LORD spoke to Moses."

1. LEVITICAL CITIES (35:1-8)

Translation

The LORD addressed Moses in the Moabite plains along the Jordan opposite Jericho, saying: Instruct the Israelites to allot to the Levites towns to reside in from the heritage that the Israelites will possess. You must also give the Levites *grazing land around the towns. Thus they will have towns in which to live and grazing land for their cattle, herds, and other livestock. The grazing lands around the towns that you will give to the Levites shall extend to a distance of one thousand cubits from the town wall. (35:1-4)

Exegesis and Exposition

This section does not constitute an assemblage of miscellaneous items in order to round out the book, as some commentators have supposed, but is specific legislation given to Moses shortly before his death and the subsequent entrance of the tribes into Canaan. It was directed at two specific matters, the first of which was of paramount importance in view of plans for the division of Canaan.

The Levites were God's special property (Num. 8:18), and as such they did not receive a territorial inheritance in Canaan as the other tribes of Israel did (Num. 18:24), because the Lord was their inheritance (18:20). God stipulated that four towns should be set aside out of every tribal heritage, with the accompanying grazing lands, for the benefit of the Levites. Those towns would become the inalienable property of the recipients. The extent of the grazing land was specified, so that there would be no disputes about easements, encroachments, or infringement of property rights.

Translation

Starting from the town wall on the east side you shall measure 2,000 cubits, on the south side 2,000 cubits, on the west side 2,000 cubits, and on the north side 2,000 cubits, with the town lying in the middle. This territory shall belong *to them as grazing land for the towns. Now out of those towns which you will give to the Levites you must select six refuge towns to which a person who has killed someone may flee. You shall give them forty-two other towns in addition.

So the total of the towns you will give to the Levites is forty-eight. You shall give these together with their grazing lands. The towns you will give shall be from the heritage of the Israelites. From the larger tribes you shall allot more, and fewer from the smaller tribes. Each shall contribute some of its towns to the Levites in proportion to the inheritance allocated to each. (35:5-8)

Exegesis and Exposition

The town would thus be in the center of a square of 2,000 cubits, i.e., about 1,000 yards on each side, which does not make for a particularly large town, to say nothing of a "city." In ancient Canaan, settlements tended to be small compared to some cities in Assyria, Babylonia, and Egypt. Although the term *city* is still used to describe refuge towns, the KJV tradition that many follow needs to be seen in proper perspective. The resultant Levitical towns would consist of a few families living together in close proximity and thus would be much like a modern Western hamlet or village. Rabbinical in-

417

terpretation sometimes derived the so-called Sabbath day's journey (see Acts 1:12) distance of 2,000 cubits from Num. 35:5.

From these towns six were to be segregated for the purpose of housing people guilty of manslaughter, but the remaining forty-two were to be retained strictly for accommodating the Levite population. The distribution of Levites among the various tribes would serve to remind the Israelites that the nation was intended to live as a kingdom of priests and a holy community (Ex. 19:6) and would thus inculcate ceremonial cleanness by example. The regulation proclaimed here was enacted in part in Josh. 21, where all forty-eight cities are listed, but it was never completed fully. Nevertheless, the ideal underlying the legislation was enshrined in Israel's laws.

2. CITIES OF REFUGE (35:9-34)

Translation

The LORD addressed Moses, saying: Speak to the Israelites and tell them: When you cross the Jordan into Canaanite territory, you shall then designate some towns to be refugee towns for you, to which a person who has killed someone unintentionally may flee. They shall stand as your refugee towns from the avenger in order that the killer may not die until he has stood trial before the community. These six towns which you allot shall constitute your refugee towns. (35:9-13)

Exegesis and Exposition

At an unspecified time in the future life of Israel in Canaan, the six towns mentioned in v. 6 are to be established as places of refuge (MT עָרֵי מִקְלָט, *‘ārê miqlāṭ*, "towns of asylum") for the one who has committed manslaughter.

In ancient Hebrew society, punishment in general was governed by the so-called *lex talionis* or law of retaliation (Ex. 21:24). This meant that the punishment meted out was to be of the same kind as the hurt or damage sustained.

This procedure is often taken by modern readers as a harsh and repressive measure, but it was very enlightened for its time in human history. The "eye for eye, tooth for tooth" concept imposed strict limits upon the amount of damages that could be exacted for any given offense. Thus in the case of capital crime only the murderer, when convicted by the eyewitness testimony of two or more witnesses, could be executed, and nobody else. By this means bitter recriminations against the murderer's family were avoided, and blood feuds stretching over several generations were prevented.[4] If the person who killed someone accidentally (MT בִּשְׁגָגָה, *bišĕgāgâ*) was able to reach a refuge city unscathed, he was deemed safe until he was tried in public. This, then, was the second concern (v. 6) of the legislation of the first section (vv. 1-8) of this chapter.

Translation

You shall choose three towns on this side of the Jordan and designate three towns in Canaanite territory to be refuge towns. These six towns will be places of refuge for the Israelites, for aliens, and for anyone else living with them, so that anyone who kills another person accidentally may flee there. If a man hits someone with an iron implement so that he dies, he is a murderer. The murderer must certainly be executed. If a man is carrying a stone capable of causing death and he hits someone with it so that he dies, he is a murderer. The murderer must certainly be executed. Or if a man has a wooden object in his hand capable of causing death and he hits someone with it so that he dies, he is a murderer. The murderer must certainly be executed. (35:14-18)

Exegesis and Exposition

Another section of case-law made the refuge cities available for aliens who had killed someone accidentally. It also makes a differentiation between manslaughter, where the death of the victim was not premeditated, and murder, where the victim died as the result of malice aforethought. It is thus the motive rather than a momentary surge of violent anger that distinguishes manslaughter from capital homicide or first-degree murder. The case-law material in this section assumes that murder was premeditated. Otherwise, the victim would only have been injured and not killed by one or other of the blunt objects described.

The reasons for committing offenses against the lives of others are many and varied, as Moses knew full well from his own experience as a young man (Ex. 2:11-13). Construction sites, then as now, could furnish potential murderers with both the means and the opportunity to inflict capital crime and under some circumstances to make the occurrence appear accidental. Accordingly, vv. 16-18 describe situations in which objects of various kinds have been used deliberately to cause death. Only evidence to the contrary produced at the offender's public trial would enable the charge of murder to be reduced

4. On murder see J. Greenberg, *IDB*, 1:738-39; G. L. Archer, *ZPEB*, 1:1032-33; D. G. Burke, *ISBE*, 3:241, 434-35 and bibliographies.

to manslaughter. Once a man had been proved to be a murderer, he was to be executed with no opportunity for appeal.

Translation

The one who avenges blood shall execute the murderer. When he encounters him, he shall put him to death. If anyone assaults a person because of hatred toward him, or throws something at him intentionally so that he dies, or out of hatred hits him with his fist, causing death, the person who struck him must certainly be executed, because he is a murderer. The one who avenges blood shall execute the murderer when he encounters him. (35:19-21)

Exegesis and Exposition

The execution had to be performed by "the avenger of blood" (MT גֹּאֵל הַדָּם, gō'ēl haddām). The gō'ēl, or "redeemer,"[5] in this context was a near relative who obtained revenge for the victim. The life of the victim was treated in the way that people or property might be redeemed, and only the life of the murderer was deemed an adequate equivalent for the victim's life. The officiant was a guiltless executioner discharging his duties according to the will of God as an official of the state (cf. Rom. 13:4) and was not to be murdered himself for taking life, since this was his appointed function. In this section, protection is afforded to the willful murderer only if he is able to escape to a refuge town before being charged with his crime. Otherwise the normal judicial procedures of trial and execution would apply (Deut. 19:11-12).

Translation

But if he assaults him suddenly without premeditation, or throws anything at him without intent to harm, or throws a stone at him that is big enough to kill, and although not aiming at him the man still dies, even though he was not his enemy or bent upon harming him, then the community must judge between the slayer and the avenger of blood according to these regulations. The community must protect the person accused of murder from the avenger of blood and must return him to the refuge city to which he was fleeing. He shall remain there until the death of the high priest who was anointed with the holy anointing oil. (35:22-25)

Exegesis and Exposition

The legislation concerning unpremeditated killing is amplified here (see also Deut. 19:4-5), so that there can be no doubt as to the

---

5. See, M. Greenberg, *IDB*, 1:321; H. Stob, *ZPEB*, 1:422; B. K. Waltke, *ISBE*, 1:372; R. L. Harris, *TWOT*, 1:144-45 and bibliographies.

nature of the crime and therefore its accompanying punishment. Emphasis is again placed on the concept of "intent" (v. 22: MT בְּלֹא צְדִיָּה, *bĕlō' ṣĕdiyyâ*, "without purpose"), so that an ostensibly aggressive act would be construed in terms of innocence, provided the assailant was not bent upon destruction of a personal enemy. Verses 24-25 describe the nature of community involvement in the crime, and from the MT it appears that a case was being considered and legislated for in which the killer had not been apprehended by the *gō'ēl* but also had not yet reached one of the refugee towns. Perhaps he had been detained by the authorities of his hometown or was endeavoring to escape and thus had not had the opportunity of fleeing to a refugee town.

Whatever the circumstances, the community authorities had three responsibilities to fulfill: (1) they were to make legally binding decisions about the killing and would thus be acting as judge and jurors; (2) they were responsible for protecting the accused from the *gō'ēl* until accidental death had been proclaimed as the verdict of the authorities; (3) once they were assured that the suspect was guilty of manslaughter and not murder, they were to provide safe conduct for the convicted person to the nearest refugee town that he was probably attempting to reach before being apprehended.Once there he was to remain free from any threat from the *gō'ēl* until the death of the current high priest. This provision should not be considered as constituting judicial banishment for a suspected criminal but a sentence of detention for manslaughter in a small town, where his security was guaranteed by the community under the law.[6]

Translation

But if the accused murderer ever ventures outside the limits of the refugee town to which he has fled, and the avenger of blood comes upon him outside the town, the avenger of blood may execute the accused person without being guilty of murder, because the accused should have stayed in the refugee town until the high priest had died. Once the high priest is dead, the accused person may return to his own property. (35:26-28)

Exegesis and Exposition

Loneliness, nostalgia, claustrophobia, or some other emotional or psychological factor could conceivably drive the detainee into the open, whereupon the *gō'ēl*, who may have been awaiting such an opportunity, had the authority to kill him (cf. Deut. 19:12) without recrimination. Thus the person guilty of manslaughter could consid-

---

6. See *KD*, 3:264-65.

er himself safe only so long as he stayed within the refugee town. In modern terminology the man could be considered to be confined in an "open prison," in which he was free to move around but not to leave.

The Scriptures do not record any patrolling or surveillance activity of a *gōʾēl* in the vicinity of a refugee town, but v. 27 lends credence to such a possibility. The only prospect the refugee had of permanent freedom consisted in the death of the high priest. If that occurred during the prisoner's lifetime, he was to be permitted to return to his hometown with a full pardon to resume a normal life there. The death of the high priest was interpreted as an atonement for the offense of manslaughter.[7] Thus great care was taken to establish the relative innocence or guilt of a person suspected of murder. It would be almost impossible under these regulations for an innocent man to be executed for a capital crime he had not committed.

Translation

These are to constitute legal precedents for you for all time wherever you are living. Anyone who kills an individual must be executed as a murderer when witnesses have testified. One witness shall be deemed insufficient testimony against a person for the death penalty. Furthermore, you must not accept a ransom payment for the life of a murderer guilty of a capital crime. He must certainly be executed. Similarly, you must not accept a ransom payment for the person who has fled to a refugee town, with the intent of permitting him to return home and live on his own property before the death of the high priest. You shall not pollute the land *where you live. Blood defiles the land, and no atonement can be made for the land on which the blood has been shed, except by the blood of the person who shed it. Do not therefore defile the land that you inhabit and wherein I also dwell, for I, the LORD, dwell among the Israelites. (35:29-34)

Exegesis and Exposition

The foregoing enactments are reinforced by being formally declared to be legal precedents (MT חֻקַּת מִשְׁפָּט, *ḥuqqat mišpāṭ*, "statute of judgment," KJV), as with the decision in 27:7-11 in the matter of Zelophehad's daughters' inheritance. They apply to the Israelites for all future ages, wherever the people may be living (MT לְדֹרֹתֵיכֶם בְּכֹל מוֹשְׁבֹתֵיכֶם, *lĕdōrōtêkem bĕkōl môšĕbōtêkem*, "throughout your generations in all your dwellings," KJV).

The enactments are clarified by an amplification of the law of

---

7. For other interpretations see J. H. Hertz, ed., *The Pentateuch and Haftorahs*, p. 722.

evidence. To secure a guilty verdict the offender's crime must have been seen by at least two witnesses. A dyadic adversarial relationship between the accused and a single witness was regarded as insufficient to convict a person suspected of murder. Personal grudges could thus not be settled in that manner.

An individual convicted of murder could not purchase his freedom, either by paying a fine or offering a bribe. This provision was intended to forestall an out-of-court settlement whereby the accused paid the injured family a sum of money as compensation. The rule for capital crimes remained fixed: The price of a victim's life was paid when the murderer's own blood had been shed. The number of witnesses is not specified here, but in Deut. 17:6 two or three were prescribed for murderers, whereas in 19:15 this rule was applied to all crimes. It did indeed become a permanent enactment in Hebrew life and was still in evidence in the NT period (John 8:17; 2 Cor. 13:1; Heb. 10:28).

The same rule applied to those who were convicted of manslaughter who were living in refugee towns. They were not permitted to purchase their freedom so as to evade serving their sentence of detention until the high priest died. The concept of time off for good behavior did not enter into the sentence, because the prescribed period must be served.

The Israelites were prohibited from polluting the land by manslaughter or murder. Spilled blood defiled the land because it had been shed outside the atoning context of the sacrificial system. A holy and just God could not dwell with His people in the land of promise if it was being defiled, because His holiness would be compromised as a result. God hates sin and defilement of all kinds and will punish the unrepentant offender. Forgiveness, however, can be obtained by true penitence and by bringing to the Lord the appropriate sacrificial offering.

The same principle also applies in the Christian dispensation. Anyone who resists divine grace throughout his or her lifetime will suffer the penal death awaiting the ungodly. But the sinner who is genuinely penitent and claims the cleansing efficacy of the blood shed by Christ for the forgiveness of sin will receive pardon and cleansing (Eph. 1:7; 1 John 1:7; etc.). The forgiven sinner must walk continually in faith and obedience, presenting his or her body as a living sacrifice, holy, acceptable to God, to constitute a model of spiritual worship (Rom. 12:1).

Additional Notes

35:2 תִּתְּנוּ: For this second plural form the LXX and Syriac versions read the third plural.

35:3 וּמִגְרְשֵׁיהֶם: Whereas this word ends in a masculine suffix (הֶם–), the Samaritan Pentateuch reads a feminine form (הֶן–). This simple modification changes the meaning from "the pastures of the Levites" to "the pastures of the cities." The LXX seems to support the Samaritan Pentateuch reading.

35:4 אֶלֶף: The LXX reads δισχιλίους so as to accord with v. 5.

35:5 לָהֶם: The Samaritan Pentateuch, LXX, Syriac, and Targum Pseudo-Jonathan read "to you." The MT seems preferable here.

35:6 The LXX commences this verse: καὶ τὰς πόλεις δώσετε τοῖς Λευείταις.

הָרֹצֵחַ: The Syriac version glosses this by explaining that the provision was for one who killed another accidentally.

35:10 כִּי אַתֶּם עֹבְרִים: כִּי here in a verbal clause has the temporal sense of "when." The LXX opened the verse with a future indicative active verb: Ὑμεῖς διαβαίνετε.

35:12 מִגְאָל: The LXX and Targums have the fuller form "avenger of blood" here to harmonize with vv. 19, 21, 24, 25, 27.

35:20 הִשְׁלִיךְ: The object is to be understood and is thus indeterminate in nature, hence the "something" of the translation. The LXX πᾶν σκεῦος is much more definite, probably influenced by v. 22.

35:23 בְּלֹא: לֹא with the inseparable preposition בְּ– is used in a privative sense, denoting absence: "without seeing."

35:24 עַל הַמִּשְׁפָּטִים הָאֵלֶּה: The preposition עַל here expresses the sense of normalcy in usage, "in accordance with."

35:32 הַכֹּהֵן: The Samaritan Pentateuch, LXX, and Syriac versions read the fuller form of the title, "the high priest."

35:33 אֲשֶׁר אַתֶּם בָּהּ: This relative clause does not have its own verb, but the Samaritan Pentateuch, the LXX, Syriac, and Vulgate versions, as well as the Targum Neofiti I, took steps to remedy the deficiency by adding "you live."

35:34 תְּטַמֵּא: This second person singular form was replaced by a plural in the Samaritan Pentateuch, the LXX, Syriac, and Targums.

C. RULES FOR INHERITANCE BY WOMEN (36:1-13)

Chapter 36 deals briefly with a situation that required a judicial decision from Moses as one of his final acts. It can be analyzed into two main sections: (1) problem of female inheritance (vv. 1-4); (2) decision by Moses (vv. 5-13).

1. PROBLEM OF FEMALE INHERITANCE (36:1-4)

Translation

Now the heads of the family groups of Gilead son of Machir, son of Manasseh, who were from the Josephite families, came and spoke

before Moses and the leaders who were the heads of the Israelite groups. They said: The Lᴏʀᴅ commanded my lord to give the land as a heritage by lot to the Israelites, and my lord was commanded by the Lᴏʀᴅ to give the inheritance of our brother Zelophehad to his daughters. Now if any of them shall be married to men from other Israelite tribes, their inheritance will be taken from our ancestral heritage and added to the inheritance of the tribe into which they marry. As a result, part of the inheritance allocated to us will be taken away.

And when the jubilee of the Israelites comes, their inheritance will be added to that of the tribe into which they marry. Consequently their heritage will be taken away from that of our ancestral tribe. (36:1-4)

Exegesis and Exposition

Machir was the eldest son of Manasseh by an Aramean concubine who established the family of the Machirites (Num. 26:29). According to 1 Chron. 7:16-17, Machir's wife was named Maachah, who bore two sons named Peresh and Sheresh. The latter had two sons and a grandson, and all these were described as "sons of Gilead, son of Machir, son of Manasseh." This statement, with the assertion in Num. 26:29 that Machir was the father of Gilead, from whom came the Gileadites, makes Gilead a real individual and not a collective designation for the inhabitants of the region, as some earlier scholars supposed.

The descendants of Machir settled in Transjordanian territory that had been captured from the Amorites (Num. 32:39-40). Machir's great-grandson Zelophehad had no sons to follow him, but instead had five daughters. A special dispensation from God had been required in order to ensure their inheritance rights (27:1-11), providing that in the absence of male heirs unmarried daughters living at home should receive their deceased father's estate (27:7). This decision had set a precedent, which in its full form (27:8-11) required the inheritance to pass to other family members if the man died childless.

But now another contingency had been foreseen, and in order to secure a further decision about female inheritance of property a formal approach was made to Moses, who had mediated God's earlier ruling. The leading members of the Gileadite families raised the question as to what would happen to territory belonging to Manasseh if any of their five female relatives married men belonging to other tribes. Their land would then become part of their husbands' family heritage, would therefore be lost to the holdings of Manasseh, and would consequently disrupt the amounts of land allocated under God's commandment.

425

Whereas at the time of the original decision the daughters of
Zelophehad had presented their petition to Moses (27:1), on this occasion it was the heads of the chief families of Gilead who sought the
counsel of Moses and the other Israelite leaders. For such senior tribal
members to make a formal petition of this kind indicated that matters of great importance were involved.

The intent of the first enactment was that the land should stay
within the family or, failing that, the family group, so that it would
not be lost to the tribe. But marriage outside the tribe of Manasseh
would mean that supposedly inalienable property could not even be
redeemed in the jubilee year (MT הַיֹּבֵל, *hayyōbēl*). This celebration
probably derived its name from the ram's horn that proclaimed its
beginning. Whatever its origin, the term was so ancient by the time of
Joshua that it needed the additional word שׁוֹפָר (*šôpār*, "ram's horn")
as an explanatory gloss (Josh. 6:5-6). The jubilee year followed seven
sabbatical years and was thus the fiftieth year in the Hebrew religious calendar. Its beginning was marked by trumpet blasts on the
Day of Atonement, and these proclaimed it as a sacred year. During
that period slaves were to be emancipated, and all holdings of land
had to be returned to their original owners (Lev. 25:8-38). By this act
the first division of the land among the tribes would be restored.[8]

2. DECISION BY MOSES (36:5-13)

Translation

**Then Moses gave a ruling to the Israelites at the LORD's instruc-
tion, saying: What the tribe of the Josephites asserts is correct. This is
what the LORD has commanded for Zelophehad's daughters: Let
them marry whom they think best so long as they wed within a
family of their father's tribe. In this way the inheritance of the Israelites shall not be transferred from tribe to tribe, but every Israelite
shall retain the ancestral heritage. (36:5-7)**

Exegesis and Exposition

Moses again sought the Lord's advice on this matter, and once
more the appropriateness of repetition was recognized (cf. 27:7). The
best interests of all would be served if Zelophehad's daughters married men within the tribe of Manasseh, and this accordingly constituted God's instructions through Moses to the tribal elders. In the
jubilee year the property would still be a part of the ancestral

---

8. G. J. Wenham, *Leviticus*, pp. 317-23; R. K. Harrison, *Leviticus*, pp. 223-30;
   J. Morgenstern, *IDB*, 2:1001-2; J. Lilley, *ZPEB*, 3:715-16; J. B. Payne, *ISBE*,
   2:1142-43 and bibliographies.

heritage, and there would have been no diminution of inalienable property rights because of holdings having passed from tribe to tribe. The women were given a choice to marry appropriately (MT לַטּוֹב בְּעֵינֵיהֶם, *laṭṭôb bĕʿênêhem*, "to the man good in their eyes"). The Hebrew expression "in the eyes of" refers to a person's cognitive faculties of assessment or to intuitive spiritual discernment.

Translation

Every daughter who possesses an inheritance in any Israelite tribe shall become the wife of a man from any family in her father's tribe, so that every Israelite may retain the ancestral heritage. Thus no inheritance may pass from tribe to tribe, but every Israelite tribe is to keep its own heritage. Moses therefore acted on behalf of Zelophehad's daughters precisely as the LORD had commanded him, for the daughters of Zelophehad, namely Mahlah, Tirzah, Hoglah, Milcah, and Noah, were married to the sons of their father's brothers. They married into the family groups of Manasseh son of Joseph, and their inheritance remained in their father's family group and tribe. These are the regulations and decrees that the LORD promulgated to the Israelites through Moses in the Moabite plains along the Jordan opposite Jericho. (36:8-13)

Exegesis and Exposition

The special enactment legislated for the five daughters of Zelophehad was to be given wider application by being made binding upon all the tribes. Every tribe was thus bound to preserve the integrity of its heritage, the long-promised gift of God to His people. Thus daughters would be required to marry within their own tribe, and this injunction was repeated with emphasis so that there could be no misunderstanding.

Moses obeyed God's commands, and Zelophehad's daughters were once again named, as befitted the memory of an important tribal head. The order of names is slightly different from that in 27:1, with Tirzah being placed second and Noah coming at the end of the list. Subsequently these redoubtable women married into the tribe of their father, and in this way their inheritance remained in the holdings of Manasseh. It is gratifying that when the women presented an urgent petition to Moses about their rights of inheritance, they were provided for fully by a God who is concerned for the plight of widows and orphans, and we are indebted to the *šōṭĕrîm* for recording a happy ending to the incident. The provision was an important element in Hebrew case-law, since in a patriarchal society the inheritance normally passed to the eldest son. Now it was possible for the first time to give inheritance rights a considerably wider scope.

427

The section ends with an obedience formula that covers all the material in the final chapters of the book of Numbers. It describes the enactments as commandments (MT מִצְוֹת, *miṣwōt*) and judgments (MT מִשְׁפָּטִים, *mišpāṭîm*), mediated through the agency of the aged Moses. The place of revelation is given, and the date is within Moses' lifetime. The narratives are thus grounded in history in the manner of the ancient Near Eastern annalists and point to the activities of the *šōṭĕrîm*, who continued to record events faithfully at the time the events took place or soon afterward, thus making for a written tradition of events in this formative period of the Hebrew nation.

As Wenham has pointed out,[9] there are reasons for thinking that the legislation concerning Zelophehad's daughters provides an appropriate conclusion to the book of Numbers. The entire composition has had as its aim the gradual movement to the land promised by God to Abraham and his descendants, and one of the last legal judgments that Moses gave at God's command contained the assertion that every Israelite tribe would keep its own God-given inheritance. The promises of God to Abraham (Gen. 17:8), so long in the fulfilling, are now on the point of becoming reality as the Israelite warriors stand opposite Jericho, poised and waiting to cross the Jordan under Joshua's leadership in order to occupy their heritage.

Additional Notes

36:1 מִמִּשְׁפְּחֹת: The LXX reads the singular, "family," ἐκ τῆς φυλῆς, and this was followed by the Syriac and Vulgate versions.

לִפְנֵי מֹשֶׁה: The LXX adds καὶ ἔναντι Ἐλεαζὰρ, evidently to ensure that Aaron's successor was not neglected in the proceedings.

36:2 צִוָּה בַיהוה: Some scholars have been puzzled by the third singular masculine pual perfect form here, and emendations have been suggested by BHS and by J. A. Paterson, *Numbers*, p. 66. There seems no good reason, however, for altering the MT narrative style by emending it to accommodate an active verb form. G. B. Gray, *Numbers*, pp. 477-78, held that the MT could well be retained here. The use of –בְּ as an agent before the tetragrammaton is rare (cf. Gen. 9:6), this function being normally exercised by לְ.

36:3 מִבְּנֵי: The LXX omits this word, merely reading ἑνὶ τῶν φυλῶν, and in this was followed by the Syriac version.

אֲבֹתֵינוּ: The Syriac version reads "of their father" here and also in the following verse.

36:6 אֲבִיהֶם: A feminine suffix (–הֶן) is obviously required here, and

---

9. G. J. Wenham, *Numbers*, p. 240.

the MT masculine reading was doubtless the result of a scribal error from force of habit.

36:12 מִמִּשְׁפְּחֹת: The LXX reads the singular ἐκ τοῦ δήμου here and is followed by the Syriac and Vulgate versions.

עַל־מַטֵּה: The preposition עַל here expresses a norm and means "in accordance with," "accordingly."

Epilogue

The present commentary has been written in the firm conviction that the book of Numbers can be placed reliably in its written form in the pre-Canaanite period of Israel's history. The precise date in the second millennium B.C. cannot be ascertained because of current ignorance of the date of the Exodus from Egypt. The internal evidence of Numbers indicates that there could be no possibility of historical error because the compiling and organizing of much of the narrative material was in the hands of specially chosen scribes and recorders, all of whose activities were monitored closely by Moses.

The book contains only the events of approximately the first two and the last two years of the wilderness wanderings, and it seems evident that this recording technique was intended to depict the entire period. Throughout this time there were no significant external influences to disturb the activities of the Israelite community and no opportunity for the scribes to do anything other than to record the various incidents as they occurred. Whatever may have been remembered subsequently about the events of the Sinai wilderness sojourn and handed on in oral form, there is no doubt that a written record of them was made concurrently or shortly afterward, frequently at God's express command. That standards of accuracy were observed scrupulously is indicated by the care with which the statistics were recorded and checked throughout the book. In short, the compilers were working under the authority of Moses, who in turn was directed by God, and they fulfilled their literary responsibilities in the best traditions of the ancient Near Eastern scribes.

These conclusions find interesting support in the sociological phenomena reflected in the post-exodus sections of the Pentateuch. The events of the wilderness period are compressed within the space of some forty-two years. This length of time has often been dismissed as being much too short a time to account for Israel's growth to nationhood as depicted by the books of Exodus, Leviticus, Numbers, and Deuteronomy.

Unfortunately such a rejection of the biblical evidence is based upon misguided notions fostered by the Graf-Wellhausen hypothesis of Pentateuchal origins, which in general terms postulated a prolonged, monolinear development of life and thought in Israel from rudimentary beginnings until it reached its cultural and spiritual height in the postexilic period. But what this theory, along with its advocates, does not seem to appreciate is that the internal dating supplied in the MT for the wilderness period is correct as it stands. The narratives are attempting to state that at this precise period the twelve tribes not only were being molded into a national unit, as a result of the covenant at Sinai, but also were being fashioned into a genuine high culture.

When the origins of ancient Near Eastern culture are examined, it becomes readily evident that they appear on the scene in the various nations in their fully developed form with little or no prodromal preparation and then begin to degenerate. How the various cultures originated is unknown. In general it can be said that there is seldom a recognizable prodromal period in evidence, and although the ancient Sumerians seem to have been aware of an earlier culture, presumably that of al-Ubaid, it does not seem to have played any significant part in their own development.

Similarly there is no demonstrated continuity between the predynastic (c. 4500-3100 B.C.) and protodynastic (c. 3100-2700 B.C.) periods of Egyptian life and the high culture that burst on the historical scene with the advent of the Old Kingdom period (c. 2700-2200 B.C.). This culture is experienced from its beginnings in its most developed form, but by the end of the Old Kingdom period it was already beginning to degenerate. It exhibited a brief, although modified, revival at the start of the New Kingdom period (c. 1570-1150 B.C.), thereafter to disappear slowly but inexorably into the dim recesses of history.

Human culture decays externally because of hostile attacks upon it and internally through the simplification of language and grammar, the use of stylized and conventional forms in building and art, and a general decline of the values that the culture enshrined originally. This pattern of change and decay is characteristic of the second

432

law of thermodynamics (entropy), and as a phenomenon that is a part of the world of nature it gives the lie to such unscientific nineteenth-century notions of progress as those entertained by Hegel, Darwin, and others. The Graf-Wellhausen hypothesis, erected on the basis of Hegelian lack of understanding of entropy, thus runs counter to fact when it envisages a rudimentary beginning to Israel's culture and sees it in its fullest development only in the postexilic period.

What we are privileged to witness during the interval of the wilderness wanderings is the establishing by God of Israel's total culture. It was mediated through Moses on the basis of a religious foundation known as the covenant. Within the short space of approximately four decades the Hebrews had been given a definitive culture and legal system that was to form the basis of their national life thereafter. Although it is true that there was a prodromal period that included the developing traditions of the patriarchs, the revelation at Sinai was new and distinctive and was made binding by agreement upon the twelve tribes, which thereafter constituted a unified nation. In Numbers we see something of the processes of revelation and can witness the biblical corpus of case-law taking shape.

As with all other ancient Near Eastern nations, the culture of Israel was safeguarded by a coterie of national priests, who were assisted in their functions by Levites. This hierarchy functioned within the environment of a portable shrine that God ordered to be built and that was the setting for an elaborate sacrificial program. The most sacred cultic object that the nation possessed was a gold-plated acacia box containing among other objects the tablets of the covenant stipulations given by God to Israel on Mount Sinai. A series of religious festivals, also of divine origin, served to strengthen the bond between God and His people and, within the context of worship, to afford them periods of relaxation and enjoyment.

But overshadowing everything else in Israelite life was its special sense of calling as a holy nation, which placed the people's existence in subservience to the high moral and spiritual demands of the covenant ethos. Thus when the Israelites were ready to emerge upon the historical scene as a nation that was realizing its destiny as God's witness to contemporary pagan society, they were actually taking their place in the history of the Near East as a typical high culture, not as a straggling band of seminomadic tribes who could not lay legitimate claim to such a status. But as with all others, their beliefs and general way of life could be expected to encounter the law of entropy, an eventuality already apparent within the lifetime of Joshua.

The effects of the law of entropy can be offset to a considerable extent by the infusion into the particular system of a force equal to, or greater than, the one that instigated the process of degeneration.

433

In the general theory of value it is axiomatic that values need to be augmented constantly if they are to be sustained at all. In the spiritual life the Word of God must be studied day by day if its intrinsic message is to break through the barriers of our intellectual and social veneer to promote growth in Christ. Similarly, periodic campaigns aimed at spiritual revival are necessary for the purpose of explaining what the basic values of the Christian faith really are and to exhort all to be quickened and nourished by them.

For the ancient Israelites, entropy could only be kept at bay by each member of the nation knowing and practicing the revealed will of God in complete obedience and trust. This is why the concept of the kingdom of priests and holy nation (Ex. 19:6) was so fundamentally important. A spiritually strong community that sustained the moral and ethical values of the Sinai covenant would be in a preeminent position to witness to the person and power of God in the world. As long as the nation clung tenaciously to the letter and spirit of its founding principles, its spiritual and temporal destiny was assured. But if those values failed to be augmented properly because of decay in the community of priests, degeneration was inevitable.

What applied to the old Israel is also true of its spiritual successor, the Christian church (cf. Gal. 6:16). If it is trusting and obedient to God's will as revealed in Jesus, it will grow in grace and in the power of the Holy Spirit. The process of entropy that had overtaken Israel in the postexilic era was halted dramatically by an infusion of a vast new power in the Person of the incarnate Christ. For the believer, the inner person grows daily by belief and fellowship with Christ the Savior, even though the individual's physical frame degenerates with increasing age, as long as the original spiritual values of Calvary are sustained. But if they are not, and the life of the person involved is depleted spiritually to the point where the original saving knowledge is no longer either evident or meaningful, total decay will be the dreadful prospect.

We do not know how all the other ancient Near Eastern nations acquired their "high" stage of cultural development. What is important for the present study is that the narratives of post-Exodus activities in the remainder of the Pentateuch have permitted us to observe the development of Hebrew "high" culture within a concentrated period of time and thus to discern something of the enormous energy required to formulate it. So potent was this divine force that it not merely enacted laws and rituals for the Hebrews themselves but made some of them valid for all people and all time, as with the Decalogue. The religious rites of Sumer, Egypt, Babylon, and other ancient Near Eastern peoples have long since disappeared into the dust of antiquity, but the Hebrew Passover lives on, being celebrated annually in commemoration of that distant time when God intervened in power to deliver His people from slavery in Egypt and to set them upon the path of nationhood.

In the commentary it was observed that there are very few tangible remains of Israelite life during the wilderness period, as is only to be expected from a nomadic existence against a desert environment. While it is commendable for archaeologists to look for traces of Hebrew remains or levels at places such as Pithom, Succoth, Rameses, or Kadesh-barnea, the enterprise will be frustrating, since the nature of Israelite life at that period was not conducive to the kind of relics that would have resulted from sedentary settlement. Indeed, any traces of nomadic occupation would have disappeared within a short period after the site had been vacated. But in any event, it should be remembered that the presence or absence of archaeological remains has no bearing upon the accuracy of the book of Numbers because of the special topographical circumstances surrounding its origin. It is only when the Israelites settled down in Canaan that discernible levels of their occupation become apparent, such as when they constructed inferior buildings upon Canaanite foundations.[1]

---

1. In a lecture at the University of Toronto on February 17, 1988, Professor Eliezer Oren of Ben Gurion University in Israel stated that his oversight of excavations at eighty sites in the Sinai peninsula between 1972 and 1982 led him to contradict the biblical account of the Israelite Exodus from Egypt. His researches indicated firm Egyptian control over the area during the period from 1300-1275 B.C., which for some scholars was the date of the Exodus, thus making escape virtually impossible. No sites supposedly occupied by the Israelites in the wilderness have been discovered, and even Kadesh-barnea exhibited no remains earlier than the tenth century B.C. Oren thus concluded that the Exodus was a myth, a conclusion supported by John Holladay of the University of Toronto, who had sought the remains of ancient Pithom at Tell el-Maskhuta, but found no structures earlier than the sixth century B.C.

Oren's view rests upon an improper understanding of the data. The biblical narratives indicate that, whatever the date of the Exodus, the Hebrews were ordered to leave the plague-stricken land by the Egyptian pharaoh himself (Ex. 12:31-33), and that when, after a change of mind, the latter tried to recapture his escaping slaves, the Re(e)d Sea engulfed the pursuing chariots with devastating effect (Ex. 14:25-28). Subsequently for four decades the Israelites pursued a nomadic existence in Sinai, and being tent dwellers they left no tangible remains.

This is even true of the sojourn at Kadesh-barnea and explains Oren's inability to recover Hebrew artifacts from the Mosaic era. Oren failed to note, however, that the area had been occupied from the Chalcolithic and Early Bronze periods (c. 4000-2000 B.C.). In Transjordan the situation was quite different, as noted in the commentary, but the locations involved were of course beyond Oren's scope of investigation. It would thus appear that, on any basis, to look for traces of earliest Israelite occupation anywhere in Sinai is a fruitless endeavor.

Holladay also appears to have been searching in the wrong place for

Because of the impossibility of identifying the remains of so distant a slave group as the Israelites at sites mentioned in the Pentateuchal descriptions of desert events, and puzzled by conflicting estimates of the nature and timing of the Israelite occupation of Canaan, some scholars have adopted a nihilistic approach to the problems of the Exodus and wilderness wanderings. Those who reject the MT account of Israel's desert origins generally follow the unscientific, flawed reasoning of Graf and Wellhausen in thinking that Israelite culture arose from obscure origins in Canaan, perhaps at some point between the time of Joshua and the end of the Judges period, when the Israelites were struggling to retain their hold upon Canaanite territory. Most of these scholars regard the book of Joshua as having very little historical credibility, whereas for them the book of Judges seems to reflect a view of a more peaceful occupation by Israel of the land of Canaan.[2] Difficulties continue to be experienced with regard to the size of the groups leaving Egypt and living in the wilderness, as has been noted already in the commentary. The most reductionist of these attempts to explain the MT אֶלֶף (*'elep*) entertains the notion that the Exodus involved a group numbering as few as 100 people or as many as 3,000, with their herds and flocks. These individuals are supposed to have trudged across the wilderness and to have settled ultimately in Canaan, where they "converted" the local people to the Israelite faith, the nature of which is not normally specified by exponents of these views.

This minimalist evaluation has nothing in common with the majesty of God's revelation at Sinai and is meaningless in the light of the divine establishing of the Israelite nation as a high culture. Furthermore it is untrue to the known character of the Hebrew people, who have rarely functioned as missionaries or evangelists. As far as numbers are concerned, whatever the significance of *'elep* in antiquity, the MT speaks consistently of large figures, whether of Egyptians, Moabites, or others, so that if minimalism is applied to the Hebrews it will also scale down other groups proportionately.

Israelite artifacts when he excavated Tell el-Maskhuta in the belief that it was ancient Pithom. A preferred location for that city would be at Tell er-Ratabah, some nine miles west of Tell el-Maskhuta, where Nineteenth Dynasty (Ramesside) remains have been unearthed, including a temple of Atum. Again, Pithom was not a Hebrew settlement, wherever it was located, and thus it is unreasonable to expect to recover any Israelite levels there.

2. For views on the supposed occupation of Canaan by the Israelites see G. E. Mendenhall, "The Hebrew Conquest of Palestine," *BA* 25 (1962): 66-87; J. M. Miller in J. H. Hayes and J. M. Miller, eds., *Israelite and Judean History* (London: SCM, 1977), pp. 254-78; V. Fritz, "Conquest or Settlement," *BA* 50 (1987): 84-100 and bibliographies.

Fortunately it is not necessary to be beguiled by such speculations, which in any case are devoid of objective evidence. To assess the situation properly we should look at what the Hebrews possessed as a high culture when they entered the Promised Land: (1) they exhibited a firm belief in the presence and power of their God; (2) they possessed a national consciousness and a sense of destiny, undergirded by recorded, objective spiritual standards that were actually engraved in stone, along with many other legal enactments relating to community life; (3) as a high culture they possessed a fully developed priesthood and a sophisticated system of worship in which sacrificial procedures played a prominent part. The operative center of their cultic activities was a portable shrine where Israel's God made His presence felt in a manner that earned the respect and fear of neighboring nations.

Despite all these evidences of high culture, which critical writers would accept without question were they posited of any of the Near Eastern pagan nations, some continue to suggest that the Exodus was nothing more than a "historical myth" and that there is no evidence that would support the traditions of Israelite origins as suggested in Numbers and elsewhere. To demonstrate the false nature of this contention, we shall look inductively at the historical situation, bypassing the book of Joshua for which archaeologists have little regard as a historical document and going beyond the book of Judges into the history of the early monarchy.

At that time the priesthood had been functioning to a greater or lesser degree in Canaan until David reorganized it, a benefit that Solomon inherited when his Temple was constructed. In that building, pride of place was given to the Ark of the Covenant. At some stage of the Ark's sojourn in Canaan the lid had been removed and the contents tampered with, so that when it was installed ceremonially in the Temple it contained only the two stone tablets "that Moses put there at Horeb" (1 Kings 8:9). If archaeologists are looking for genuine wilderness-period artifacts, here is a historical record of two of them, the Ark and the law tablets, coming from a period that even for liberal scholars begins to have chronological credibility.

As though this were not enough, the records of the later monarchy in Judah attest to the existence of yet another genuine wilderness-period artifact, and for this the historical record must surely be beyond reproach. In 2 Kings 18:4 reference is made to the bronze serpent that Moses had made to forestall the worst effects of a plague on Israel in the wilderness period (Num. 21:6-9). An unknown individual had taken pains to preserve the snake, and it may well have been kept in the Most Holy Place of the sanctuary. It was not in the Ark itself when Solomon's Temple was dedicated, but its traditional efficacy played an important part in Israelite life when the nation was relapsing into periods of idolatry. In the days of Hezekiah this relic of the wilderness period was being venerated under the name Nehushtan[3] to the point where incense was being burned as people worshiped it. Although Hezekiah may have had misgivings about destroying such a valuable national relic, attributed by tradition to the work of Moses himself, the nature of his religious reformation provided no alternative to breaking it in pieces.

But by far the most durable survival of the "Exodus event" is the Passover festival, which has continued among the Jewish people to the present day and will be for them an institution to be observed for all time. Its celebration is rooted deeply in the nation's history, and because of the nature of their religion it could never have survived if it had been based upon mythology. The Passover is honored by both Jews and Christians as the beginning of that series of events that led up to the establishing of the Israelite nation as a high culture.

The events at the Re(e)d Sea, Mount Sinai, and the recorded camping sites in the Sinai wilderness belong therefore to history, not mythology.

Moody Press, a ministry of the Moody Bible Institute, is designed for education, evangelization, and edification. If we may assist you in knowing more about Christ and The Christian life, please write us without obligation: Moody Press, c/o MLM, Chicago, IL 60610.

---

3. On Nehushtan see H. Van Broekhoven, Jr., *ISBE*, 3:516-17.

Selected Index of Subjects

Index of Authors

445

Selected Index of Scripture

15:3–9	380	**Romans**		
15:8–9	153	5:9	371
15:38	188	6:10	366
16:4	315	9:2–3	185
19:19	104	12:1	154
23:27	258	12:21	383
26:41	186	14:23	315
26:63–64	324		

1 Corinthians

Mark		1:25	210
1:12–13	33	6:10	123
1:13	402	9:13	106
5:23	153	10:8	338
7:11–12	380	10:9	278
8:29–30	324	10:11	28
14:38	186	11:17–34	373
14:61–62	324	12:12–26	93
		12:12–27	226

Luke

4:1	64	**2 Corinthians**	
4:2	402	5:21	279
4:12	183, 315, 376		
11:20	324	**Ephesians**	
11:24	33	4:15	27
22:67–70	324	4:11–12	246
		5:18	123

John

		6:13–18	59
1:20	324	6:13–17	383
1:32–33	64		
3:8	189	**Philippians**	
3:14–16	284	2:8	51
3:34	273		
7:31	324	**Colossians**	
8:4	107	1:20	371
9:25	317		
11:50	237	**2 Timothy**	
12:12–28	300	1:7	189
12:34	324		
19:29	256	**Hebrews**	

Acts

		1:2–3	30
2:1–4	317	3:7–4:11	28
7:22	14	7:24	371
8:15–18	153	9:7–15	273
9:4–7	301	9:24	273
18:18	380	10:4	371
20:35	59	10:13	398
21:3	380	10:28	423
23:3	258	10:38	315